MGA

The Revolutionary MG

TITLES IN THE CROWOOD AUTOCLASSICS SERIES

ALFA ROMEO 916 GTV AND SPIDER
ALFA ROMEO SPIDER
ASTON MARTIN DB4, DB5 & DB6
ASTON MARTIN DB7
ASTON MARTIN V8
AUDI QUATTRO
AUSTIN HEALEY 100 & 3000 SERIES
BMW CLASSIC COUPÉS 1965–1989
BMW M3
BMW M5
BMW Z3 AND Z4
CITROEN DS SERIES
CLASSIC JAGUAR XK: THE 6-CYLINDER CARS 1948–1970
CLASSIC MINI SPECIALS AND MOKE
FERRARI 308, 328 & 348
FORD CONSUL, ZEPHYR AND ZODIAC
FORD ESCORT RS
FORD TRANSIT: FIFTY YEARS
FROGEYE SPRITE
GINETTA ROAD AND TRACK CARS
JAGUAR E-TYPE
JAGUAR MKS 1 AND 2, S-TYPE AND 420
JAGUAR XJ-S
JAGUAR XK8
JENSEN V8
JOWETT JAVELIN AND JUPITER
LAMBORGHINI COUNTACH
LAND ROVER DEFENDER
LAND ROVER DISCOVERY: 25 YEARS OF THE FAMILY 4×4
LAND ROVER FREELANDER
LOTUS ELAN
MAZDA MX-5
MERCEDES SL & SLC 107 SERIES 1971–2013
MERCEDES SL SERIES
MERCEDES-BENZ 'FINTAIL' MODELS
MERCEDES-BENZ CARS OF THE 1990S
MERCEDES-BENZ S-CLASS
MERCEDES-BENZ W113
MERCEDES-BENZ W124
MERCEDES-BENZ W126 S-CLASS 1979–1991
MG T-SERIES
MGA
MGB
MGF AND TF
MORGAN 4/4: THE FIRST 75 YEARS
MORGAN THREE-WHEELER
PEUGEOT 205
PORSCHE 924/928/944/968
PORSCHE BOXSTER AND CAYMAN
PORSCHE CARRERA: THE AIR-COOLED ERA
PORSCHE CARRERA: THE WATER-COOLED ERA
RANGE ROVER: THE FIRST GENERATION
RANGE ROVER: THE SECOND GENERATION
RELIANT THREE-WHEELERS
RILEY: THE LEGENDARY RMS
ROVER 75 AND MG ZT
ROVER 800
ROVER P5 & P5B
ROVER SD1
SAAB 99 & 900
SHELBY AND AC COBRA
SUBARU IMPREZA WRX AND WRX STI
SUNBEAM ALPINE & TIGER
TOYOTA MR2
TRIUMPH SPITFIRE & GT6
TRIUMPH TR: FROM BEGINNING TO END
TRIUMPH TR6
TRIUMPH TR7
TVR 1946-1982
TVR: CARS OF THE PETER WHEELER ERA
VOLVO 1800
VOLVO AMAZON
VW KARMANN GHIAS AND CABRIOLETS

MGA

The Revolutionary MG

David Knowles

THE CROWOOD PRESS

First published in 2019 by
The Crowood Press Ltd
Ramsbury, Marlborough
Wiltshire SN8 2HR

www.crowood.com

British Library Cataloguing-in-Publication Data
A catalogue record for this book is available from the British Library.

ISBN 978 1 78500 567 1

Typeset and designed by D & N Publishing, Baydon, Wiltshire
Printed and bound in India by Parksons Graphics

CONTENTS

	Acknowledgements	6
	MGA Timeline 1950–1962	8
	Introduction	11
CHAPTER 1	THE MG LEGACY	13
CHAPTER 2	THE AERODYNAMIC SPORTS CAR	34
CHAPTER 3	CALL IT MGA	56
CHAPTER 4	THE MGA 1500	69
CHAPTER 5	THE MGA 1500 COUPÉ	101
CHAPTER 6	THE MGA TWIN CAM	113
CHAPTER 7	THE MGA 1600, 'DELUXE' AND 1600 MARK II	151
CHAPTER 8	ASSEMBLY OVERSEAS	179
CHAPTER 9	SUCCESSION PLANNING: FURTHER DEVELOPMENT OF THE MGA	202
CHAPTER 10	THE MGA IN MOTOR SPORTS	212
	Appendices	329
	Index	332

ACKNOWLEDGEMENTS

It is always right and proper for an author to acknowledge the assistance he or she receives in the course of researching a book of this kind. Any names which may have been inadvertently omitted from this list have been missed by accident rather than intent, and the help of all the contributors is genuinely appreciated. Some of their revelations were remarkable, but I will leave it to you, the reader, to find their gems. I am indebted to the following:

Michael Allison, MG historian and former MG Car Company employee; Mick Anderson, MGA Twin Cam specialist; Brian Aslett, MGCC South Africa; Lino Baggio, owner of the 'Canadian' 1957 Sebring MGA No. 49.

Robin Barker, owner of 1960 Sebring MGA, and seasoned MGA Twin Cam expert; Vernon Barker, Riley Register; John Barrett, MGA Deluxe enthusiast and expert; Geoff Barron, MGCC MGA Register Chairman; the family of Tony Birt, formerly of BMC Hambro; Mary Blaksley, widow of MGA racer John Blaksley, of the Fitzwilliam race team; Richard Blaksley, son of racer John Blaksley; Rutger Booy, Dutch MG historian; Ken Breslauer, Sebring historian; family of Phyllis Buckle, owners of Harry Herring MG models; Hugh Burruss, owner of 1962 Sebring MGA No. 52.

Ruth Cathir, Pathé; Sue, Bill and Bruce Chapman, Nancy Mitchell family; Pete Cosmides, Motorcar Garage LLC; James Cottingham, DK Engineering (owners of Sebring MGA); Tom Coulthard, MG enthusiast; 'Jim' (Sydney John) Cox, MG Car Company; Pat Coyne, MGCC South Africa.

Michael Dale, former BMC apprentice, leading ultimately to Jaguar Cars Inc. President; Lady Mary Barbara Damerell, daughter of Robin Carnegie; Roger Daniell, owner (for many years) of the ex-Dick Jacobs MGA Twin Cams 1 MTW and 2 MTW; Pedr Davis, celebrated Australian motoring journalist; Andreea DeMiere, Daniel Schmitt & Co. (Robert Redford MGA); Stefan Dierkes, Frua Register; Steve Dixon, custodian of MGA racers UPO 929 and SRX 210; Philippe Douchet, owner of MGA rally car MRX 42; Thomas Durham, DK Engineering; George Dutton, co-author of the book about the MGCC NW Centre, which supported the Le Mans MGA of Ted Lund.

Michael Eaton, NAMGAR historian and owner of 1957 and 1959 Sebring MGAs; Derek Edwards, Chairman of the MG Car Club South-East Centre; Gus Ehrman (and family), former Hambro, Inskip, BMC & BL Director and MG race driver and record breaker; Jill and Graham Eke, owners of the Glacier Blue MGA 1500 Roadster featured in this book; Ian Elliott, former Austin apprentice, BMC and BL publicity; Michael Ellman-Brown, who acquired the last MGA Twin Cam; Roger Enever, son of Syd Enever; Norman Ewing, MGCC South Africa.

Tanya Field, MGCC; the family of Richard 'Fitz' W-Fitzwilliam (Robin and Amanda); Roger Allan Foy, BMC Australia expert; Terry Frisch, owner of the fourth MGA Twin Cam; Carla Frua, niece of Pietro Frua.

Jennifer Galpern, research associate/Special Collections – Rhode Island Historical Society; Barney Gaylord, MGA enthusiast and 'The MGA with an Attitude' website owner; Julien Giambagli, 'Supercars.net' website; Bo Giersing, South African MGA enthusiast; Mervyn Gillespie, MGA and Dundrod fan; Simon Goldsworthy, editor, *MG Enthusiast* magazine; Adrian Goodenough, MG Car Company 1960–80; Paul Goodman, co-author (with George Dutton) of the book about the MGCC-supported Le Mans MGA of Ted Lund; Lynn Herson Grad, daughter of Joe Herson of Manhattan Autos; Frank Graham, owner of the 1961 Sebring MGA Coupé '43'; Malcolm Green, MG author; Michael Green, son of 'Dickie' Green (of BMC Comps); Joe and Cathy Gunderson, owners of the unique MG EX 186 prototype.

John & Sharen Halfpenny, owners of the 1962 MGA Coupé Deluxe '151 ABL', raced at events that year; Rupert Hambro, son of Major Jocelyn Hambro; Peter Hamilton, Riley Register; David Harrison, motoring enthusiast and writer; Don Hayter, MG Car Company design team; Bruce Henderson, Nigel Herring, grandson of MG's model maker Harry Herring; Mark Hester, MGCC MGA Twin Cam Group; Samuel and Pierre Heuer, driver (Samuel) of MGA EX 182 Twin Cam at Orton-Villars in 1958, and other Twin Cams at various events, and his son; Chris Higginbotham, MG enthusiast; Rob Higgins, former MGCC MGA registrar; Jane Hogan,

Bonhams (for KMO 326 photos); Brian Hogg, South African MGA owner and enthusiast; Robin Howard, owner (2018) of MJB 191; Piers Hubbard, MGCC MGA Register; Lisa Hudman, Archive Department, British Motor Industry Heritage Trust; John Hughes, MGA Twin Cam owner; David Humphreys, MGA Twin Cam owner with ex-Sebring 1960 engine.

Geoffrey Iley, MG Car Company and BMC Management, 1955–68.

Barrie and Maggie Jackson, MG Car Company Development Department; Stephen Michael Johnson, MG and Dick Jacobs enthusiast.

Gregory Keenan, Australian CKD MGA restoration expert; Rowland Keith Jnr, son of MG racer Rowland Keith; Jürg Keller, son of Swiss MG agent, Heinz Keller; Garry Kemm, MGCC Australia, MGA expert; Alistair Kennedy, *Marque News*, Australia; Bill Kirschner, TWA Retired Pilots Association – newsletter editor; Stephanie Knott, Providence Public Library, Reference Department.

David Lee, present owner (2018) of the ex-Peter Seymour MGA Coupé PBL 497.

Eddy Maher, son of Eddie Maher of Riley and Morris Engines; Adrian Malthouse, owner of the MGA Twin Cam and MGA 1600 Mark II featured in colour; Neil Manchester; Colin Manley, MGCC MGA Twin Cam Group; Roger Martin, MGCC MGA Register; Pam McCarthy, owner of first production MGA Twin Cam 'PMO 326'; John McLellan, MG author; Peter Millard Jnr, son of Peter Millard of BMC Canada; Theresa Mitchell, daughter of Terry Mitchell; Terry Mitchell, MG Car Company design team – Chief Chassis Engineer; Peter Morgan, MGCC MGA Register; Peter Morrell, Riley Register.

Peter Neal, MG Car Company design team, later MGCC archivist; Dave 'Kahuna' Nicholas, one of the 'BARC' boys, contemporary US MG racing enthusiasts; John Nikas, motoring author and historian; Doug Nye, motoring author and historian.

Bill Oesterle, owner of 1958 Paris Salon MGA Twin Cams; Jim O'Neill, MG Car Company design team – Chief Body Engineer; Terry and Sandi O'Neill, son and daughter of Jim O'Neill; Brian Osbourn, Dennis Ferranti Ltd.

Colin Panter, PA Images; Mike Peters, owner of MGA Coupé 'PRX 14'; Jim Plowden, owner of 1962 Sebring MGA No. 51; Alec Poole, son of Billy Poole of Booth Poole & Co. Ltd of Dublin; Jon Pressnell, MG, BMC, Morris (and many other marques) – author and expert; Ian Prior, owner of 1961 Sebring MGA No. '44'; Jon Proctor, TWA historian; Stephan Pröpsting, owner of 1960 Sebring MGA 'UMO 96' (Race No. 39).

Howard Quayle, MGA Register; Bruce Qvale, son of US importer Kjell Qvale.

Pablo Raybould; Peter Reason, owner of racing MGA Twin Cam 'VXT 280'; Tim Reid, son of MGA racer Mike Reid; Phil Richer, (late) MGCC Twin Cam Group; Roberto Rigoli, nephew of Pietro Frua; Hamish Riley-Smith, original owner of a Dublin-built MGA; Phil Robinson, owner of 'MJB 167'; Graham Robson, author and former industry 'insider'.

Jeremy and Jon Savage, owners of 'LBL 301'; Paul Scholes, Riley Register; Hermann Schwartz, Salzburg Rallye Club; Stuart Seager; Bob Seymour, formerly at Nuffield Exports; Peter Seymour, formerly at Nuffield and BMC; Roger Sharpe, website 'mgbsmadeinaustralia.org'; Steve Simmons, 'MG Nuts' website; June Simpson, daughter of Alec Hounslow (along with her sisters Jennifer and Lesley); Roger Skinner, owner of the Fitzwilliam Team MGA Twin Cam 'WGN 734'; Christopher Skomp, son of Fred Skomp, former owner of the 100,000th MGA; Donald Smith, former owner of MGA Twin Cam 'ORX 885'; Larry Smith, MG Vintage Racers (present-day racer of 1962 MGA Sebring car); Robert Smyth, Canadian MGA Sebring enthusiast; Bob Somerville, MGA Twin Cam website in Australia; Jonathan Stein, author and MGA Coupé expert; Koen Struijk, MGA Register (Holland); Cliff Summer, MGA Twin Cam owner.

Peter Thornley, son of John Thornley; John Thornley OBE, former Managing Director of the MG Car Company; Richard Trasler, relative of the Buckle family, owners of Harry Herring models of EX 181 and EX 172; Steve Tremulis, nephew of car designer and salesman Alex Tremulis; Stuart Turner, former BMC Competitions Manager.

Jerry van Kalleveen, MGA Register (Holland); Pim van der Veer, formerly BMC and BLMC Netherlands; Willem van der Veer, Dutch MG enthusiast; Marc van Zoest, owner of a Mexican CKD MGA Twin Cam; Edward Vandyk, MGA Twin Cam enthusiast, owner and MGCC 'Safety Fast' scribe; Robert Vitrikas, motoring author and historian.

Basil Wales, former Morris Engines apprentice and MG 'Comps'; Craig Watson, 'Autofan Media' (Australian writer on MG); Hilary Watts, niece of Syd Enever's secretary, Isla Watts and Doug Watts of 'Comps'; Mike Watts, son of Doug Watts; Bob West, leading MGA restorer and expert; Richard White, MG enthusiast; Parker Whiteway, who spotted a Cuban MGA whilst on vacation in Cuba; Bob Willcutts, TWA Retired Pilots Association – webmaster; Denis Williams, MG Car Company design team – body design technician; Maynard Mark Williams, owner of the first production LHD MGA, '100106'; Tom Wilson, MG enthusiast and historian; Steven Woodward, owner of 1960 Sebring MGA No. 38; Dickie (and Mrs Susan) Wright, MG Senior Engineer from 1956; John Wright, owner of 1962 Sebring MGA Coupé Deluxe; Tim Wright, son of Dickie Wright.

A brief note on terminology: This is a British book about a subject of great interest to an overseas audience. Spellings are, for the most part, inevitably anglicized, but where it has been felt important to stress a difference, the local terminology has sometimes been retained. The author has also used 'MG' – that is, without full stops ('periods' if you prefer) – even though he knows full well that this will not meet with the approval of some enthusiasts. Similarly, there is a perennial argument over whether or not the open MGA should be referred to as a 'Tourer' or a 'Roadster': the author has decided on the latter.

MGA TIMELINE 1950–1962

3 January 1951	The Morris Motors Board agrees a funding contribution of £850 that allows work to begin on 'EX 172' – a Le Mans car for George Phillips.
23–24 June 1951	1951 Le Mans 'Grand Prix d'Endurance' – 24 Hours: George Phillips (co-driver Alan Rippon) drives his special-bodied MG TD Midget (EX 172; 'UMG 400'; Car No. 43), reaching up to 116 mph on the Mulsanne Straight. Car retired following engine problems.
14 November 1951	Morris Motors Board authorizes £350,000 for a new MG Magnette for the 1952 Motor Show and a Wolseley for spring 1953 – one week before the merger is announced.
23 November 1951	Nuffield Group and Austin announce a merger, to be consummated the following spring.
28 November 1951	As a consequence of the merger, all future model plans are 'placed in abeyance' by the Morris Motors Board.
20 February 1952	As MG at Abingdon conceive a '1,500 streamlined Midget' – the basis of 'EX 175' – the first drawing is EX 175/1, dated 20 February.
21 October 1952	1951 Earls Court Motor Show; Donald Healey's 'Healey 100' becomes the 'Austin-Healey 100' overnight and an announcement is made at the Show on 23 October.
24 October 1952	MG's EX 175 proposal for a streamlined sports car with XPEG engine is shown to BMC management but is rejected for investment.
3 November 1952	John Thornley – assistant General Manager since 1948 – takes over from Jack Tatlow as General Manager at MG, Abingdon.
17 December 1952	The Morris Motors Board Minutes record that Lord Nuffield has resigned his role as Chairman (and becomes Honorary President); Leonard Lord takes over as Chairman of BMC.
12 February 1953	The Morris Motors Board sanctions the tooling cost for the 'Project No. 41 MG TF Midget' of £27,000.
11 June 1953	The Morris Motors Board considers and approves in principle 'DO 1049', which is Gerald Palmer's MG Midget proposal, with a provisional tooling cost of £250,000.
17 September 1953	The MG TF Midget enters series production (TF0501). On the same day, the Morris Motors Board authorise expenditure for a 'high performance version' of the BMC B-Series engine – which becomes the MG Twin Cam engine.
21 October 1953	1953 Earls Court Motor Show: MG 'Z' series Magnette and MG 'TF' Midget (1250) appear at the Motor Show. Triumph TR2 appears at same show.
1 June 1954	Drawing office established at Abingdon, with several key staff transferring from Cowley.
3 June 1954	First entry in MG at Abingdon's records against the Cowley Design Order Number, 'DO 1062 – New MG Midget' – for what would become the MG Series MGA.
29 June 1954	John Thornley writes one of his many memos – this one to R. F. Hanks – about his proposals for Le Mans 1955, in which MG would enter '*substantially standard DO 1062s, the object being to give a demonstration of high-speed reliability of the new model and qualify for the biennial cup. This is a thing one can only do once. In 1956 we must enter to win our class, and a pretty stiff class it now is.*'
8 September 1954	The Morris Motors Board formally approves 'DO 1062' (the future MGA) with a tooling estimate of £70,000. Abingdon had already been working on it for at least four months.
1 December 1954	The MG Competition Department is recreated, initially sharing the workshops of the Development Department, pending the completion of a new workshop next door.

4 April 1955	The final MG TF 1500 goes down the line at Abingdon (Chassis No. 10100 – after a production run of 9,602 cars).
16 May 1955	First production MGA starts down the line at the MG factory at Abingdon-on-Thames.
27 May 1955	The first production left-hand-drive MG MGA (an Orient Red car with black trim, Chassis No. HDC43/10106) begins assembly at Abingdon; build lasts until 8 July 1955 and the car is despatched on 13 July 1955.
11–12 June 1955	1955 Le Mans 'Grand Prix d'Endurance' – 24 Hours: a three-car team of 'EX 182' prototypes is entered. Two cars finish in 12th ('LBL 302' – Car No. 41; Ken Miles/Johnny Lockett) and 17th places ('LBL 303' – Car No. 64; Ted Lund/Hans Waeffler). Third MG ('LBL 301' – Car No. 42, Dick Jacobs/Joe Flynn) burst into flames after leaving the track in the sixth hour at Maison Blanche ('White House'), soon after the Mercedes tragedy. Fourth car – 'LBL 304' – was not raced.
13 July 1955	First US export specification MGA, an Orient Red LHD car HDC43/10106, is completed at Abingdon.
16 July 1955	First production RHD MGA leaves the factory, ahead of the September launch.
21 September 1955	One of the MGA show cars is airfreighted from London Airport to the Frankfurt Motor Show by TWA. The event is recorded in a short colour Pathé news film.
22 September 1955	Formal launch of the MGA, at the Frankfurt Motor Show (22 September–2 October 1955). An Orient Red car with wire wheels, flown in by air from London, is shown alongside another car.
7 October 1955	42nd Paris 'Salon de l'Automobile' (6 October–16 October 1955) opens to the public, who mainly flock to see the striking new Citröen DS19. The MGA is the only all-new British car on display.
19 October 1955	1955 Earls Court Motor Show ('40th International Motor Exhibition', 19–29 October): MGA makes its UK show debut at Earls Court; three cars are shown; red, white and blue specimens.
11 January 1956	The Minutes of the Morris Motors Board meeting approves tooling costs for the MGA Hard Top of a modest £5,000.
24 March 1956	1956 Sebring 12 Hours race: a three-car team of white MGAs driven by an all-American team of drivers wins the 'team prize'. Results were 4th in class and 19th overall (Kincheloe/Steve Spitler – Car No. 50), 5th in class and 19th overall (David Ash/Gus Ehrman – Car No. 49) and 22nd overall (Fred Allen/John Van Driel – Car No. 51). MGAs would compete at Sebring in 1957, 1959, 1960, 1961 and 1962.
7 May 1956	The Morris Motors Board formally authorises tooling costs of £8,000 for the MGA Coupé.
27 July 1956	The first CKD MGA kit leaves Cowley for Australia, to be assembled eventually at the Pressed Metal Corporation in Enfield, Sydney.
13 September 1956	Various BMC Executive changes are announced: George Harriman becomes deputy chairman and joint managing director with Sir Leonard Lord, J R Woodcock is deputy managing director of BMC (but retaining his post of deputy chairman of Morris Motors) and John Thornley, general manager of MG and Riley since 1952, becomes a director of BMC.
12 October 1956	Production version of Vanden Plas alloy hardtop for MGA announced (similar to version already seen on Alpine Rally in July). This had the MG project code of 'EX 196', dating from 7 February 1956. MG 'ZB' Magnette was also launched, with earlier version being known as 'ZA'. MG MGA Coupé, announced; this project received the MG code 'EX 197'.
17 October 1956	1956 Earls Court Motor Show (17–27 October): the MGA Coupé (an Old English White car with wire wheels – Car No. 20672) and 'ZB' Magnette make their public debuts. Display also includes a LHD MGA roadster with transparent bonnet on a rotating turntable.
22 April 1958	MG MGA Twin-Cam enters production. Car YD1-501 – mounted on the line 22 April, despatched 28 July 1958.
14 July 1958 (Monday)	MG MGA Twin-Cam launched. A 'demonstration day' is held at the Ministry of Supply Fighting Vehicles Research and Development Establishment at Chobham in Surrey, at which over 100 journalists are given the opportunity to try the new car.
31 July 1959	MG MGA 1600 (with 1,588 c.c. 'B' series engine) launched. Production started in May. The MGA 1500 had already earned some £21.5 million in US revenue for BMC.
6 April 1960	The final series-production MGA Twin Cam (YD1-2610, a Chariot Red roadster with red interior) starts its build at Abingdon. One more car, YD1-2611, would be specially built after formal end of production for Michael Ellman-Brown in May/June. Surplus chassis, with front and rear disc brakes, used for 'MGA De-Luxe'. Last MGA Twin Cam built May 1960 (*see* entry below).

18 May 1960	An MGA Twin Cam Roadster (YD1-2611; Engine No. 2245), specially finished in Woodland Green with Beige Interior for Michael Ellman-Brown, begins assembly at Abingdon, being finally marked as despatched on 14 June.
28 June 1961	MGA 1600 Mk. II launched, with 1,622 c.c. 'B' series engine.
12 March 1962	100,000th MGA produced at Abingdon (GHNL2-107989); the car is finished in metallic gold with cream leather interior trim and gold-painted spoked wire wheels. Exhibited at New York Motor Show, seemingly with chrome-plated wire wheels.
14 May 1962	The last MGA 1600 Mark II Roadster, Chassis No. 109070 starts assembly and leaves the production line on June 7th 1962, marking a total of 101,081 MGAs built.
22 May 1962	First production MGB – a left hand drive Iris Blue car, GHN3-102 – is built. A total of 12 production cars are built in May (including a single right hand drive car, GHN3-101) and production builds up for the September launch.
20 September 1962	ADO23 MG MGB launched. MGB features new 1,798 c.c. version of the 'B' series engine.

INTRODUCTION

In many walks of life, whenever dramatic change happens to something with a passionate following, there will be significant risk of a backlash from those loyal fans who resist the new in favour of what they already know and love. Such was the challenge faced by John Thornley and Syd Enever when they unveiled their new sports car in 1955. The aerodynamic form of the MGA owed little to the upright pre-war style of its predecessors, even if it drew on some of MG's record-breaking and racing exploits – with a clever Le Mans 24-Hour race angle.

It was a gamble because the stakes were high: MG was synonymous with sports-car culture, and such a bold deviation from the past could easily have upset the faithful – acolytes of the 'sacred octagon'. However, change was inevitable because the progress in automotive technology and evolving customer expectations meant that the spindly, square-rigger style of the old MG Midget, no matter how pretty, was outmoded and out of step with the rest of the market.

Even so, getting to the point of revolution was a protracted process: there were moves to reinvent MG, which began as the parent organization emerged from the end of World War II, exports in mind, just ten years before the launch of the MGA. It is therefore important to understand the forces at work over that crucial decade, and the context of how the 'new line' became possible, as well as the people who made it possible – or threatened to get in the way.

For this reason the first chapter of this book delves into the background in unprecedented detail to show what

This is where the MGA began its journey – on a sheet of paper laid on this dining table in Syd Enever's home in the Oxford suburbs. The scale model seen here is Enever's design for a further record breaker, EX 233, which was never developed.

ENEVER FAMILY

preceded – and precipitated – the genesis of the MGA. Of course the bulk of the book covers the whole story of a car that went on to sell in unprecedented numbers, with more than 101,000 examples emerging from the famous Abingdon-on-Thames factory by the time that the baton was passed to a worthy successor. Peter Thornley, John Thornley's son and author of an excellent biography *Mister MG*, credits his father with creative thinking so that projects such as the MGA moved forwards ahead of formal authority:

> Most of Pop's development projects were created ex-budget; if it had not been for a creative and amenable chief accountant Abingdon would not have survived as long as it did. And Pop would not have had half as much fun!

There should be no doubt that the MGA was an important car for many reasons: it broke with the past, won new friends, and provided a sound platform for an MG business and factory, which would go on to even greater heights during the subsequent eighteen-year production of the MGB. Remarkably it was conceived originally by MG's Chief Engineer when he sketched out his basic idea for a new aerodynamic MG on his dining-room table at his home in the Oxford suburbs.

It is also a fact that many modern designers cite the MGA, rather than its successor, as their favourite MG of all time, and some of them even feel that it could also form the basis of a pattern for the future of MG sports-car design. This then, is the story of 'the first of a new line', a truly revolutionary MG.

In March 1962, Syd Enever, MG Chief Engineer, made the following statement in the press release for the 100,000th MGA, Nuffield Organisation, with regard to the MGA and sports cars:

> We aim to give sports-car motoring to as many people as possible, and to give it to them at the right price. We do not wish to make a small quantity of high priced, specialized cars for the few. At the same time, we set out to provide the fastest possible car combined with the greatest possible degree of safety.

And in an interview in 1970 he said:

> A sports car, in appearance, performance and personality, should epitomise the character of the sport... the MGA started life on my dining-room table... nowadays, designers are part lawyers.

The following is a quote from John Thornley, MG General Manager, on clever production expansion at Abingdon:

> We made our assembly lines by building little low brick walls with pre-cast concrete channels on the top, that a motorcar would roll along: it was a channel one side, and a flat platform the other – so this would take varying tracks, and cars were propelled from one workstation to the next by the good old way of pushing! The benefit of this arrangement was that if, in looking at the factory layout, we decided that, if we shuffled those three lines up a little bit closer together, we could get a fourth line in here, you see, then all we had to worry about was the electrics and the compressed air; everything else was just standing on the floor. So five o'clock Friday, everybody stops, the maintenance boys move in, knock the whole bloody place to pieces, and by eight o'clock on the Monday morning, we're in operation with four lines instead of three, you know? Six months later, we had five lines instead of four – and this is how it went, by and large. And how, in this marvellous period that I could live over and over and over again, really... not easy though: we were designing over the other side; I was trying to produce more and more motor cars all time...
>
> .... taped interview, 1974, courtesy John McLellan

CHAPTER ONE

THE MG LEGACY

The story of the origin of MG has been told many times – how it began as an offshoot of the early Oxford-based garage enterprise of William Richard Morris, managed from 1922 by Cecil Kimber (he joined in 1921), who developed the business, with the benevolence of his patron, into a sports-car manufacturer of international renown.

From the earliest days there was something of a creative tension between the fairly mundane source material and the rakish, sporting creations drawn from them. From time to time, MG's exploits have perhaps veered too far towards the realms of the exotic and bespoke, and on nearly every such occasion the process has ended in tears: MG has been at its best when operating in the modestly priced section of the market, offering a hint of the exotic for a reasonable outlay.

Thus, for example, when Kimber gradually allowed enthusiasm and expenditure to burn through the budget, with a multiplicity of specialized models and much racing activity, the outcome in 1935 was to close the racing shop and abandon the prevailing model range. However, such is the appeal of a modest, everyman's sports car – typically in the guise of rugged giant-killer – that the MG badge lived to fight again, and has survived more than ninety years of history.

OXFORD TO ABINGDON

What became, almost by osmosis, the MG sports car, was created out of various Morris Garages premises before moving to a new £20,000 factory at Edmund Road, Oxford, in 1927 and then, just two years later, to a larger site in Abingdon-on-Thames, Berkshire, which evidently cost ten times as much. The site had formerly been occupied by part of the Pavlova Leather Works, demand for whose military leather coats had understandably dropped after 1918, but who nevertheless remained neighbours for many years in their reduced operation. So began the association of MG production with Abingdon, which would endure for fifty years.

For a long time prior to the story of the MGA, about which this book is, of course, mostly concerned, and especially before World War II when the range was at its most diverse, the Abingdon factory's overall output volume was seldom at the forefront of the parent organization's practical production considerations. However, the six years of war brought a great many changes throughout industry and society in general, not least the recognition, as the conflict drew to a close, of the importance of tapping into a growing demand overseas for the kind of sports car for which the MG name had become famous, as a way of earning much needed export currency.

During the war itself, the MG factory adapted to the changed circumstances with admirable efficiency, but an unfortunate consequence of Kimber's independent manner, which saw him and his management go out and seek gainful work contracts rather than gratefully accepting the sweepings from Cowley, was his effective dismissal in 1941, ostensibly for being too much of a free spirit in a corporate environment. Tragically he was to die in a train accident just four years later, and so never saw MG's post-war recovery – but also bear in mind the sobering thought that he died only ten years before the MGA appeared.

With the desire to build MG up again after the war came an almost inevitable series of tussles as various forces within the parent organization, some benign and some less so, sought to influence how the forecast increase in demand could be addressed. The decade before the MGA first arrived on the scene is consequently a very important period to understand: some of the key players in that period certainly shaped the MG Car Company in a way that made the first aerodynamic MG sports car a possibility, and its ultimate sales success so impressive.

MG MIDGET – THE GIANT KILLER

The concept of an MG Midget sports car is perhaps the idea most closely associated with the MG marque, but its early success was enhanced by the comparative misfortune of some of its larger and more expensive brethren. Cecil Kimber had presided over the evolution of the early 'Mark'

LORD NUFFIELD, CECIL KIMBER, MILES THOMAS AND HAROLD RYDER

William Morris, later Sir William and ultimately Lord Nuffield was the founder of Morris, Morris Garages and in consequence MG.
AUTHOR'S COLLECTION

Without William Richard Morris or Cecil Kimber there would never have been *any* MG cars, let alone an MGA, so their story bears brief reflection.

WILLIAM RICHARD MORRIS

William Morris (10 October 1877–22 August 1963) was born in a modest terraced house in Comer Gardens, Worcester, to Frederick and Emily Morris; when he was three, the Morris family moved to James Street in Oxford, and there began his lifelong association with the City.

Despite his mechanical aptitude and nascent business acumen, some of Morris's early business relationships faltered. Morris nevertheless bounced back – and thereafter built his enterprise through stealth and cunning.

According to Morris historian Peter Seymour, the fact that Morris had not only been a motor dealer, but had retained his own car retailing business, provided him with a level of insight into the business denied some of his rivals; Seymour maintains that 'all the dealers worshipped him because, fundamentally, he understood their business.'

CECIL KIMBER

Cecil Kimber in 'Old Number One' in 1925.
AUTHOR'S COLLECTION

Cecil Kimber (12 April 1888–4 February 1945) was born in the London suburb of Dulwich. The family moved to the North West, and Kimber attended Stockport Grammar School.

An increasing interest in the modern marvel of cars led him to get a job working for Sheffield-Simplex around the time that World War I began.

In 1921, Kimber had started work at Morris Garages. It was here that Kimber forged the basis of the 'Morris Garages Specials', which eventually evolved into the first true 'MG' cars – a dividing line that has long been hotly debated by historians. At Morris Garages, Kimber developed a range of special bodies for Morris cars, eventually leading in 1928 to the founding of MG as a separate marque specializing in sports cars. The new company moved from Oxford to Abingdon in 1929, and Kimber became Managing Director in July 1930.

Throughout the following decade the reputation of MG grew, and the factory spent quite heavily on racing and the creation of an increasingly complex model range – such that the range expanded again in the lead-up to World War II.

With war under way, car making at Abingdon ceased, and soon fed up with having to make do with the crumbs of war work passed down from Cowley, Kimber – aided by leading staff Propert and Cousins – began to seek out new contracts. This proved to be his undoing, as he was visited by Miles Thomas in November 1941 and forced to resign from the business he had come to love. Kimber soon found employment elsewhere, but he would never live to see MG's post-war reconnaissance, because he was one of two victims of a freak railway accident just outside King's Cross Station on the evening of Sunday 4 February 1945.

WILLIAM MILES WEBSTER THOMAS

William Thomas (2 March 1897–8 February 1980) was born at Cefn Mawr, Wrexham, in Wales. Thomas was educated at Bromsgrove and later Birmingham University. During World War I, he gained the DFC in 1918.

After the cessation of hostilities he found employment as a motoring journalist with *Motor*, and then became editor of *Light Car* in 1923, when he came to meet William Morris. Morris employed him to start a dedicated magazine, *The Morris Owner*, which began publication in 1924.

(William) Miles Webster Thomas, later Sir Miles Thomas, and, from 1971, Lord Thomas of Remenham.
AUTHOR'S COLLECTION

In the meantime, however, Thomas moved upwards through the ranks of Morris's organization, becoming General Manager and later Managing Director of Wolseley in 1933 and 1937 respectively. Eventually Thomas became Vice Chairman of the Nuffield Organisation in 1940. Thomas's relationship with Lord Nuffield became somewhat frayed. Morris historian Peter Seymour feels that the act that sealed Thomas's fate was becoming involved with the Colonial Development Corporation in October 1947, which Lord Nuffield probably viewed as a product of the Labour Government, and therefore anathema to His Lordship. The following month, Thomas left the Nuffield Organisation and pursued a career in other industries, including the BOAC Airline.

His legacy includes helping to identify the importance of the US market, and a modernizing shake-up of the old orders and designs, which led eventually, after he had gone, to the further changes that made the likes of the MGA possible.

HAROLD ALFRED RYDER

Harold Ryder (23 September 1888–10 October 1950) was born in Aston, Birmingham. During World War I he took charge of Doherty Motor Components, suppliers to William Morris; in due course he moved to Oxford and became a partner in Osberton Radiators at Osberton Road.

Morris bought the business in 1923 in order to expand it, and kept Ryder in charge, making him a director in 1926. Thereafter Ryder became one of Lord Nuffield's few truly trusted associates. When Nuffield's Vice Chairman Oliver Boden died in 1940, many expected Ryder to take his place; instead Miles Thomas was given the senior job, while Ryder was put in charge of Cowley and, by association, MG. It was Ryder who helped Abingdon get started again with car making post-war, and MG enthusiasts – including MGA owners – owe him a debt of gratitude if only for that. He was removed in 1947 after the management purge that followed Thomas's departure, and died just three years later at Yarnton, near Oxford.

H.A. (Harold) Ryder was a trusted associate of William Morris; when Kimber left, MG at Abingdon fell under Ryder's purview and he was instrumental in helping Cecil Cousins and Syd Enever to restart MG Midget manufacture at the end of the war.
AUTHOR'S COLLECTION

MGs which had evolved from Morris underpinnings, and if Kimber had had his way, they would have led to a kind of 'Junior Bentley' with a more thoroughbred countenance and far fewer mundane Cowley roots on show.

The ultimate incarnation of this attempt to claw the marque up-market came with the large and imposing MG 18/100, known as the 'Tigress', which was supposed to propel MG into a more exotic part of the market. Meanwhile, however, the MG Midget had been created on the basis of the contemporary Morris Minor, and was beginning to show its colours as a trusty and affordable means of entry into motor sports.

Kimber had great hopes for this grand sports car, the MG 18/100 'Tigress' – an exotic car with thoroughbred aspirations that was rather more in the mould of a Bentley than a Morris – but it was outshone by the smaller MG Midgets and was soon abandoned.

From modest beginnings as an offshoot of the Morris Minor, the early 1930s MG Midget evolved into a feisty light sports-car range, including this racing J4 Midget.
ENEVER ALBUM

SYD ENEVER

Syd Enever was the principal author of the MGA, but he cut his teeth at Morris Garages in 1920, and as well as MG's racing and record-breaking endeavours he became adept at successfully finding solutions where others failed.
ENEVER FAMILY

Hampshire-born Albert Sydney ('Syd') Enever (25 March 1906–9 February 1993) was absolutely crucial to the creation and development of the MGA, being Abingdon's celebrated chief engineer for a period that spanned both sides of the model's production story. Born in Colden Common, near Winchester, Syd was the last born of five children; his four sisters were Florence, Frances, Gertrude (who died young) and Leonore – so Syd was the only boy.

His parents separated in 1909, and his mother Maud set up home nearer her family's roots in Oxford. Syd was educated at South Oxford School, and while there he came to the attention of the headmaster, Mr Benson, who had the foresight to help secure a place for his promising young student at Morris Garages in Queen Street, Oxford, in the spring of 1920. This was before Cecil Kimber was employed there as manager.

After a year, Enever transferred to the Clarendon Yard premises in Cornmarket. Soon coming under the wing of Cecil Cousins, Enever became adept at servicing and repairing customer cars using all the equipment in the workshop. He also became well known in the garage for being an expert at diagnosing problems and fixing them in record time. At the age of twenty, Enever joined the MG Car Company's Experimental Department; when MG moved to Abingdon in October 1929, Enever was made head of the department – a meteoric rise for a twenty-three year old.

Over the following decade, Enever, along with the likes of 'Jacko' Jackson and Cecil Cousins (see profiles later), was right at the heart of the MG factory's racing and record-breaking exploits; this included a part in the design of Goldie Gardner's EX 135, and culminated in the last successful pre-war record-breaking attempt at the Autobahn in Dessau, Germany, in May 1939. Meanwhile in 1935, when the changes that led to the closure of the MG racing department took place, and principal design responsibility moved to Cowley, Enever stayed at Abingdon. With his aptitude and knowledge (much of the latter gleaned from visits to Oxford Reference Library), Enever was at the forefront of all the development work at Abingdon and an active participant in many of MG's endeavours, including, as we shall see, several factory-built specials.

When MG got its design office in 1954, Enever really came into his element, and as this coincided with the gestation of what would become the MGA, his story is absolutely fundamental to its development. As well as the MGA, Enever would go on to contribute to the MG Midget, the MGB and the MGC, as well as a number of one-off 'EX Register' concepts, although he retired just too soon to see the birth of the MGB GT V8.

After being precipitated into retirement in May 1971, Enever was invited to work as a consultant on Jensen and Jensen-Healey products, no doubt encouraged by Kjell Qvale. That venture did not last, however, and final retirement in October 1974 was not the happiest prospect for a man whose whole working life had been MG and who had no hobbies.

John Thornley often praised his friend and colleague, calling him a 'man of genius':

> *It is not correct to describe him as an untrained engineer because he trained himself; he had an insatiable curiosity about why things happened, a curiosity that went far beyond purely engineering and automotive matters, so he had knowledge of a wide variety of subjects, which would hold one spellbound – if only one could get him talking. By nature he is a quiet man – except when something stings him – and it is because of this taciturnity that he was not more widely recognized in his heyday.*

Syd's wife Ivy died in September 1992, and Syd himself passed away the following February. In an obituary written for *Safety Fast!* Enever's colleague Don Hayter wrote of his former boss and mentor:

> *Syd had the ability to transmit his ideas and enthusiasm to all he worked with, and his attention to even the tiniest detail was legendary. He always said that information on any aspect of engineering or materials was available somewhere in a book so that it could be taken and adapted to design use.*

The race debut of the 18/100 did not go well, however, and as a consequence the project went no further; by contrast the little MG Midgets became more numerous and successful and so cemented the basis of MG's future prosperity. Over the ensuing period of the early 1930s, MG went from success to success, and the model range expanded, the MG M-Type Midget giving way to the J2 and then the PA and PB Midgets, while there were 6 cylinder-engined Magnas and Magnettes sitting above the Midgets, with many parts in common.

The style of the J2 largely defined the 'form' of the MG Midget, even through into the Cowley-designed T Series, which, after the upset of MG racing activities being curtailed by Len Lord, replaced the P Types in 1936; with the intervention of World War II just three years later, the evolution of the pre-war style of the TA and the rare TB into the post-war TC would prove to be hardly noticeable to the untrained eye.

For many MG enthusiasts, the ultimate expression of the marque in the early 1930s was the K3 Magnette, seen here in 1933 Mille Miglia guise.
ENEVER FAMILY

ALEC HOUNSLOW

A formal portrait of Alec Hounslow, taken in the 1960s.
AUTHOR'S COLLECTION

Alec Leslie Hounslow (11 April 1911–17 October 1976) was born in Oxford. He joined MG in April 1925, aged just fourteen. However, his mechanical aptitude soon prompted his move to the racing department in 1931, where he remained until shortly after its closure in 1935. His major claim to fame in this period was that he acted as riding mechanic to Nuvolari, who won the 1933 TT. He left MG in 1935 after the closure of the racing shop, and moved to work for a short time at the short-lived Squire Cars at Remenham (near Henley-on-Thames); when that company folded in 1936, he worked for Billy Cotton and Arthur Dobson as a racing mechanic.

After World War II, Hounslow came back to Abingdon in 1946 as a service tester, and stayed there for the remainder of his career; after a brief spell in the Service Department in St Helens, he came back to the main Marcham Road factory, where, for example, he worked on the three MG TC Midgets that were raced by Ted Lund, Dick Jacobs and George Phillips. He also accompanied Captain George Eyston on his US MG record attempts (all qv).

Alec Hounslow worked hard and played hard, and expected the same level of dedication from his colleagues; he was seldom seen without a cigarette dangling from his lips ('apprentices used to bet on how long the ash on his fag would get' Henry Stone later wrote), and his capacity for liquid refreshment was legendary. Out of the factory he was an amazingly cheerful man and more than somewhat sociable.

When Marcus Chambers arrived at Abingdon at the end of 1954, Hounslow was somewhat sceptical as to the necessity for this new colleague, and it is fair to say that the two initially merely tolerated one another, rather than becoming firm friends. Eventually they forged a mutual respect for each other – but even so, the competition department was swiftly separated from Hounslow's development fiefdom, much of the actual work involved in doing this being undertaken while part of the team were away for the June 1955 Le Mans race. It was Hounslow's team that built the various running prototypes that contributed to the MGA story.

When it came to motor-sport endeavours – mostly the record-breaking attempts, once the competition department was split off from development – Hounslow's commitment to getting the job done was total and absolute, and he would lend his support to various extra-mural racing activities.

He retired in 1974, having come up with the novel carburettor installation on the MGB GT V8, an answer to a problem that had eluded everybody else – this was typical of his genius. Unlike some of his contemporaries, Alec Hounslow appears to have slipped fairly happily into retirement: his daughter says that he was always busy in his workshop and enjoyed fixing cars for friends. He died in Wallingford in October 1976, aged just sixty-five, from lung cancer.

JOHN THORNLEY

In the history of MG there have been a handful of people in control of the business who justify the epithet 'Mister MG'. Before the war it was unquestionably Cecil Kimber, but in the wake of his enforced departure in 1941, the mantle eventually passed to John William Yates Thornley (11 June 1909–16 July 1994). Even though Thornley was not initially the man in charge at Abingdon, nor the only man, by a long way, who deserves respect for his loyalty to MG, he was certainly its most prominent defender. Born in London in June 1909, Thornley was educated at Ardingley College and the University of London, before starting work as an articled clerk. After trading up from a motorcycle to an MG Midget at the age of twenty-one, Thornley wrote to Kimber and eventually persuaded the original 'Mister MG' to give him a job at Abingdon, where he started as service receptionist on 3 November 1931, moving up to the position of service manager two years later.

During the war, Thornley served in the RAOC and rose to the rank of lieutenant colonel, before rejoining MG in 1945. With the transfer of Riley production to Abingdon in 1949, Thornley was promoted again to 'Assistant General Manager, MG Car Co. Ltd and Riley Motors Ltd'. Thornley was not at heart a purely corporate man: he knew how to defend his corner in the context of the parent organization's machinations, but it was with MG at Abingdon where his heart and loyalties lay. He was a great ambassador for MG, particularly in his ability to forge alliances at all levels, because he managed to earn and exploit the respect and trust of the people both at the top of the parent organization and on the shop floor.

After he succeeded Jack Tatlow as head of MG's Abingdon operations at the end of 1952, Thornley forged a positive dialogue with the Cowley mandarins, in particular Vic Oak and Sidney Smith, starting a long-running series of internal memoranda that contained many of his well written 'thought pieces', in which he offered up advice, usually with a careful corporate bent but clearly promoting the 'Abingdon angle' as much as possible.

John Thornley, at the left of this 1954 photo of the record breaker EX 179 (which shared its chassis with EX 175, the forerunner of the MGA) assumes the position and role that Cecil Kimber might have taken in similar circumstances before the war. To Thornley's right are Syd Enever, Captain George Eyston, Alec Hounslow and Reg Jackson.
ENEVER FAMILY

After the departure of Cecil Kimber, life at Abingdon continued – there was a war on, after all – and supervisory management was ceded to Harold Alfred Ryder, an old associate of William Morris, who had been in charge of Morris Radiators at Cowley from 1919. Responsibilities during those years were very different to the pleasant peace-time task of turning out sports cars, but the men and women of the MG plant set to and contributed nobly to armament and other specialized operations.

However, with a likely end to war-time activities foreseen as early as the spring of 1943, the forward programme for Abingdon began to be a subject of debate. Despite his de facto role as Kimber's sucessor, Harold Ryder, who was no great enthusiast of sports cars, but nevertheless recognized the need for MG to get back into production. Miles Thomas contacted the heads of each of the Nuffield Organisation subsidiaries in March 1943 and Ryder responded by suggesting that the 1¼ litre MG saloon (a prototype of which – DO 811 – Thomas had been driving, and which would eventually emerge as the MG Y-Type) would be the best place to start.

By the autumn of the same year, tentative thoughts were already being formulated as to how MG would be organized after the war was over, perhaps with less of the independence of pre-war days. In October 1943 Harold Ryder wrote to Miles Thomas setting out his thoughts on the matter:

> Because MG is a small factory, it makes sense to put Nuffield Mechanisations at Cowley, and reinforce the policy of all MG design to happen at Cowley under Mr Oak and the Drawing Office and Experimental Department at Cowley. If MG is not allowed by government to make cars after the war, the factory can be used to make parts for other cars.

John Thornley's first introduction to MG came with his acquisition of an MG M-Type Midget, like this 1929 car.
AUTHOR'S COLLECTION

The upheaval of the BMC merger might have threatened to see MG and Thornley incur the wrath of the Corporation's new head, a man who could be as mercurial in his own way as Lord Nuffield himself. However, Thornley ensured he made an early positive impression on the new master – he once told the author:

> *Whenever I see the name of Len Lord – Sir Leonard Lord – Lord Lambury – in MG writings I always sit up a bit straight... by and large he has been much maligned in this context. Over the years he has been depicted as the big bad wolf, when in fact his overall attitude to us [MG] – and to me in particular – has scored above the line. Decisions that seemed to go against Abingdon's interests were naturally resented, but there was never anything discriminatory or spiteful about them. Most of his decisions, when viewed with hindsight, are seen to have been well justified.*

Thornley claimed that the Morris Motors takeover of MG in 1935 was an example of this: 'He wrote "finis" to all that we have come to know as "Triple M", and all hell broke loose. But by reverting to the old basis of quantity-produced units, sales took off.' At the same time, profitability also lifted – and with it the continued existence of the MG factory.

As we shall see, John Thornley and his principal ally Syd Enever did much to secure the future of Abingdon as a sports-car centre of excellence, and they ensured the success of both the MGA family and the products that followed. His book *Maintaining The Breed* was written in 1950, revised in 1956 and 1971, and reprinted in 1990, the later editions covering the MGA.

In other words, if the plans for the 1¼ litre and a handful of Midgets were not viable, the factory could simply become a satellite of Cowley.

POST-WAR REBUILDING

Whilst most of the important corporate activity in the Nuffield Organisation in the 1940s tended to focus on Cowley and Coventry, the fact remained that once the war was over, Abingdon was another factory looking to pick up where it had left off in 1939. Although there had been a fire at St Helens where some of the pre-war parts and equipment had been stored, the German bombers had paid little attention to the MG factory, and its facilities remained intact; sadly the Morris Bodies facility at Coventry had fared less well, and some body-making equipment associated with pre-war MGs had been destroyed by the Luftwaffe.

To some purists, the MG T-Type was an abomination, with its Cowley-designed body and chassis and Morris engine, but in truth it revitalized MG and formed a platform for increased sales and a head start after the interruption of the war years.
AUTHOR'S COLLECTION

REGINALD HANKS

Reginald Hanks became deputy to Lord Nuffield when his former boss, Miles Thomas, left the Nuffield Organisation. He was seen as a 'safe and steady' character but was instrumental in driving significant changes, recruiting key personnel; he might have stayed at the top had the merger with Austin never happened.
AUTHOR'S COLLECTION

Reginald Frederick Hanks M.I.Mech.E., MIPE (27 April 1896–15 December 1976) rose to become the effective head of the Nuffield Organisation, second only to Lord Nuffield (William Morris). He survived the union with Austin that created the British Motor Corporation (a merger he detested), only to return eventually to his first love, the railway industry. Born in Oxford, and redoubtably Edwardian, the young Hanks attended New College School (a private preparatory school dating back to 1379), and afterwards joined the Great Western Railway at the famous Swindon engineering works as an apprentice. This experience was enhanced in the usual manner with further education at the Oxford City and North Wiltshire technical schools.

After World War I, Hanks moved to Morris Motors, starting in the Service Technical Department in 1922. He progressively rose through the ranks: in 1933 he became assistant service manager, three years later he was chief inspector, and in 1937 production manager. Upon the outbreak of World War II he became general manager of the civilian repair organization, RAF, later fulfilling the same positions at Nuffield Mechanizations Ltd at Birmingham and Coventry. Next he was appointed to become general manager of Nuffield Metal Products, an important cog in the Nuffield empire.

The Commercial Motor of 23 November 1945 reported that Hanks had been appointed director and general manager of Nuffield Exports Ltd 'in succession to Mr S. G. K. Smallbone, who had resigned after thirty years' association with Nuffield companies'. Hanks had already assumed the role of general manager in May 1945, following a special export mission to India, in which he became staff captain, GHQ Mechanical Transport Inspection Directorate; in November he became a director for the first time. It was in this Nuffield Exports role in 1946 that Hanks and Nuffield Sales Director Donald Harrison began making exploratory trips to North America (Harrison would make several more). The Morris Motors records include an interesting letter of 29 October 1946, sent from Hanks to Sir Miles Thomas (at that time still Vice Chairman of Nuffield) during one of his trips to the USA. Hanks wrote:

As we have seen, Ryder initially approached Vic Oak at Cowley, but he also wisely sought counsel with Cecil Cousins and Syd Enever to establish what could be achieved. It is to their credit that they were able to dig out enough of the local jigs and production data for the pre-war TA and TB, and use them to lay out the basis of what would go back into production in September 1945 as the MG TC Midget. Sales of that model took off modestly but encour-

The MG TC Midget was the first post-war MG sports car, and its success has become a legend that has almost outgrown reality. Nevertheless, MG sports-car enthusiasts everywhere have much to celebrate; the TC was the first race car for such luminaries as Phil Hill and Carroll Shelby. It is easy to forget that the MGA arrived just ten years after the TC...
AUTHOR'S COLLECTION

As you know, we have not attempted to adopt the Austin and Standard policy, because there have not been enough cars available to exploit the American Market properly, except at the expense of many of our pre-war and loyal Distributors. My intention is to send Donald Harrison over to the USA and Canada just as soon as we have anything to offer in these new models, and we have several very useful contacts which are worthy of close investigation. Perhaps the best of them is under the auspices of Hambros Bank. This may sound rather queer, but Hambros have already taken the James Auto-Cycle in hand, and their sales figures are impressive. They set about organizing the job State by State, and build up good Sales-cum-Service depots before moving on to the next place. Incidentally, Hambros, too, support the notion that a small car like the Mosquito, and a unique production like the MG Midget, are the only lines worth pushing. Please do not take our present MG sales policy for the USA seriously. Collier Brothers are just enthusiastic amateurs, and we shall carry on with them only so long as we have such a few cars to offer. I see they have had ten to date.….

So it was Hanks who opened the door to the relationship with Hambros, which will form a recurring theme throughout the MGA story in later chapters, with particular relevance to American sales and motor sports endeavours. In 1947 he succeeded Sir Miles Thomas to become Lord Nuffield's deputy.

Like many of his colleagues, Hanks had a fairly jaundiced view of MG even at the end of the 1940s; in his eyes – and not without some justification, it must be admitted – Morris and Wolseley affairs were considered at that time to be more important, and he saw the Americans' affection for the MG, rather than the Nuffield Organisation's core products, to be something of an irritation.

During Hanks' reign, profits at the Organisation improved, and there were some short-lived overtures to Austin, but there were also various proposals to extricate MG from Abingdon, initially as part of a plan to consolidate all Nuffield Group car making at Cowley, and later as an idea to move MG production to join Riley at Coventry and to turn the Abingdon factory over to other uses. It was largely due to the efforts of MG's 'Pop' Propert and the connivance of John Thornley and Cecil Cousins that these plans were thwarted; unlike them, but in common with his predecessor, Hanks was certainly not sentimental over Abingdon, but at the same time he was not an opposing partisan.

In 1949 Hanks hired Gerald Palmer with a brief to reinvent MG and Riley, and this brought with it some exciting new products. When the BMC merger took place three years later, it was unwanted by Hanks; although Hanks survived until 1955, he found his authority increasingly marginalized, as the new man in overall charge ruled from his power base at Longbridge.

Hanks finally resigned his chairmanship of Morris Motors on 10 October 1955, just as Abingdon was in the throes of celebrating its all-new sports car, and refocused on his first love, GWR, as Chairman of the Western Region Board, later British Rail Western Region. He retired from this post in 1960. Notwithstanding his move back to GWR, Hanks retained a role at BMC and only finally resigned from that shortly after his sixty-fifth birthday on 5 May 1961.

agingly, with exports to Australia and South Africa being most important.

Interest in the USA began to build, but as we shall see shortly, the limitations of the import and distribution arrangements contributed to the fact that just six TCs went Stateside in 1947. Of course the TC would go on to become part of the great American love affair with MG sports cars, and the Collier Brothers who had the agency in New York were well placed to help foster the interest among well heeled sports-car fans, but it would be other factors (and new people, and a new investment model) that would drive the major MG successes to come, including of course the MGA. Even so, the path to MG sports-car enlightenment would, for the time being, involve a slightly challenging journey.

In his response of 2 May 1947 to an enquiry the previous month from a Mr Elbert of Clinton Missouri, F. E. James of Nuffield Exports explained, apologetically, that the company was only able to ship small numbers of MGs via Motor Sport Inc (the Collier Brothers' company at 745 Fifth Avenue, NYC). James explained that:

> …lack of adequate representation throughout the USA is mainly due to the fact that pre-war there was little or no demand for British cars in that territory. Now that there is some demand we are faced with a shortage of supplies, and our present production is insufficient to warrant the appointing of any new Distributors. I trust that at some future date it will be possible to quote for your requirements.

Just eight years later, the MGA would be on sale.

THE MOSQUITO INTERLUDE

During the war years, a prevailing view developed that the post-war customer would need compact, economical and modern motoring in the form of a kind of 'people's car' in the broad image, if not the precise reflection, of the 1938 Volkswagen, which history has dubbed the 'Beetle'.

At Morris Motors, Alec Issigonis was given a brief to create a post-war successor to the Morris 8, and his beetle-

The important post-war car project as far as Morris Motors was concerned was the so-called 'Mosquito', which eventually reached production as the Morris Minor. The design was led by Alec Issigonis. Much work was done on trying to forge the basis of a new generation of MG sports models on the same platform – all to no avail.
AUTHOR'S COLLECTION

THE ISSIGONIS FRONT SUSPENSION – AS SEEN ON THE MGA

Alexander Arnold Constantine Issigonis (8 November 1906–2 October 1988) had come to Morris Motors from Humber, and one of his notable early projects was the creation of a new independent front suspension system intended for the equally new 'Morris Ten' – Morris's first monocoque-bodied saloon car. In the event, the special front suspension was not used for the Morris, chiefly on cost grounds, but was due to be picked up on a related MG saloon, known as the 'MG 1¼ Litre' (or DO 802), had the war not intervened. The prototype of this MG saloon was used during the war years by Miles Thomas, and he became keen to see it in production when peace returned. When the production car did come to fruition, as the MG Y-Type, it was the first Nuffield Group project to utilize the Issigonis front suspension – which would subsequently see sterling service in the MG TD, TF, MGA, MGB and MGC.

shaped car became known as the 'Mosquito' – appropriate enough as the name of a 'buzz-box'. Eventually the Mosquito evolved into a three-tier family, with the 'two-plus-two'-seater bargain-basement Mosquito at the bottom (shades of the original pre-war Morris Minor or Austin Seven), above it a new 'Minor' four-seater, and at the head of the range, a four-/six-seater family sized 'Major'. From the latter, as we shall see, there were also thoughts of an 'MG Midget Major'.

With Morris as the high-volume marque, there would, logically enough, have been more luxurious Wolseley and nominally sporting MG offshoots. The latter could have included something ostensibly roadster-like but with little resemblance to anything that had hitherto emerged from the hallowed portals at Abingdon. In this context Cecil Kimber, out of MG affairs since 1941 and destined to die in a rail accident in 1945, was undoubtedly right to have been fearful of MG's post-war future as a sports-car maker.

Once the war was over, however, the need for a new product became more pressing, and in 1946 and 1947 the Mosquito project went through a series of fits and spurts as changes of direction led to it being revised as a more upmarket model. This was partly linked to Lord Nuffield's anathema

The proposed future Nuffield model range – with models in the MG, Morris, Riley and Wolseley marques – are seen here lined up in the main Cowley showroom, possibly ahead of an inspection by Lord Nuffield upon his return from overseas. Note the MG Midget Major (with soft top, and fake 'EXP 926' registration number, clearly derived from its DO926 project code) sitting between an MG YT (labelled here as an MG 1¼-litre Tourer) and a Morris Minor.

to the style of Issigonis's creation; his Lordship was often seen as meddling unhelpfully in Board matters, and he made it clear that he saw a clear post-war role for the more traditional pre-war styles of small Morris and Wolseley saloons. As the Mosquito evolved, the Wolseley became known as the 'Wasp' – cleverly reusing a model name from 1935/36; this alliterative use of insect names does not seem to have been separately extended to the MG variants, the only name seen in records being the 'MG 1100' (obviously not to be confused with the entirely unrelated production car of 1962). However, during this period there were some other curious ideas, such as the concept, put forward to S.V. Smith by Sir Miles Thomas, of driving largely finished cars down the road from Cowley to the former Pavlova Works, where, it was supposed, they could be subjected to road-testing and final inspection, and thereby imbued with the 'Abingdon touch'. Harold Ryder at Abingdon was resistant to the idea, but the direction came that it had to be explored: thankfully it was another hare-brained idea later abandoned.

The Mosquito programme would start to unravel when, as Jon Pressnell records in his comprehensive book *Morris: The Complete History*, it became apparent that while Issigonis was beavering away on a brand new range of flat-four engines for his revolutionary baby, Morris Engines were separately working on an entirely unrelated family of in-line single-overhead-cam power plants at Coventry.

In the midst of this upheaval came a full-size prototype for what was called the 'MG Midget Major', a two-seater sports car based upon Morris Mosquito underpinnings, which appeared in a display in the in-house Cowley studio showroom for Lord Nuffield on his return from one of his frequent trips to Australia. The 'Midget Major' bore the Cowley 'Design Order' Number of DO 926, which, helpfully for historians, was used on the mocked-up number plates fixed to the display car. The prototype may have been no classical beauty, but as seen in period photos, it came with a fairly neat removable metal hardtop, which would have provided quite a departure from the loose and leak-prone affairs on the contemporary MG TC Midget.

Here we see a proposed sporting member of the 'Mosquito' family – DO 926 was the so-called 'MG Midget Major' and would have had a 1.1-litre engine. The removable hardtop was a luxury not available to MG T-Type Midget owners.

In this last aspect at least, 'DO 926' was perhaps in line with the views of Sir Miles Thomas, who wrote in a letter to Ryder of 30 October 1947:

> I do want very careful consideration given to this question of new body models. I am perfectly sure that putting on models with cape cart hoods, or offering other types that might be described as 'open' would, with the exception of the case of the MG Midget, be a source of disappointment. The whole trend of motoring all over the world is for greater comfort, not less, and personally I think to go back to the old hood and sidescreens would be most frightfully retrograde.

However, perhaps mindful of plans brewing at Austin (the ill-fated Atlantic) and Triumph (the equally misguided TRX), he cautioned that 'anything in the nature of a modern convertible coupé with automatic actuation would be so expensive that it would take us right out of the price field.' The layout of DO 926 therefore offered, on the face of it, a neat compromise of either an open version or one with a hardtop – a concept that would come to fruition in the next decade with the MGA roadster and coupé. But aesthetically it was a long way removed from the style of the MG TC Midget, which was starting to earn overseas currency.

DO 926 had some other aspects in its favour: it could have used a new overhead cam 1100cc engine, which would most likely have been called the 'ZC11G', and there would have been economies of scale from the wider Morris and Wolseley variants. However, it was not to be: internal politics involving Lord Nuffield and Sir Miles Thomas, coupled with the concerns about government policy, meant that the 'Mosquito' became solely the basis of the 1948 Morris Minor, and all other peripheral marque variants of that car were dropped. It hardly helped that Lord Nuffield detested the styling of the Mosquito, without a traditional radiator grille; he described it scathingly as resembling a poached egg.

In the midst of all this turmoil, the surprise announcement on 19 November 1947 that Sir Miles Thomas had resigned from the Nuffield Group brought Reginald Hanks into the vice chairman role, reporting direct to Lord Nuffield. Hanks may not have seemed outwardly dynamic, but he could be determined and verging on ruthless where he felt a firm hand was needed; in December 1947 there was a drastic pruning of the Nuffield Board, with the removal of, among others, Harold Ryder and Victor Riley, promoting others in their places. It was Hanks, too, who really set the pattern for exports to the USA, which supported the future sales success for the MGA and beyond.

GEORGE PROPERT AND CECIL COUSINS

ABOVE **George Propert smiles for the camera in 1949.**

LEFT **George Propert (left) seated alongside Cecil Kimber for a staff photo in 1939.**
AUTHOR'S COLLECTION

Without the cunning and application of George Propert and Cecil Cousins, there would probably not have been any MG work at Abingdon by 1955, and certainly no sports car like the MGA.

GEORGE PROPERT

Northampton-born George Propert (21 June 1884–22 April 1976) had been apprenticed in the steam and gas engineering industry, but moved over to work on early cars in 1904. He joined Morris Garages as works manager in 1926. With the formation of the formal MG Car Company Ltd in 1930, Propert became general manager and lived in Abingdon from 1933. Henry Stone wrote of Propert that he was effectively Kimber's 'front man'.

Rationalization was very much in the minds of this reinvigorated Nuffield management, and there is a common view that if planning laws had allowed, Cowley would have been expanded to assimilate various outlying satellites such as Abingdon. It was an extension of this thinking that brought forward the idea of bringing MG assembly up to Durbar Avenue, Coventry, to sit alongside Riley production at the Foleshill works. There was a simple logic behind this idea: both MG and Riley cars used timber-framed bodywork sourced at Coventry's Morris Motors Ltd Bodies Branch, and both ranges were low volume and comparatively bespoke in nature.

With Riley's existing engine range out on a limb, there was an argument that fitting the sporting units to MG models made some sense, and Reginald Hanks felt there was enough of an

During World War II, Propert joined forces with Cecil Cousins (see below) and the two men toured various ministries looking for work. Eventually they secured a contract to overhaul some light armoured track vehicles, a precursor to major tank work and, in due course, the famous Albemarle aircraft contract which contributed to Kimber's dismissal from MG in 1941. After the war, Propert wrote a pamphlet about the collective wartime experience of the MG factory: this is a clear demonstration of his loyalty and affection for the Abingdon factory and its workforce. This passion, as the main text explains, saved MG from an alternative fate which would never have involved the MGA. He retired on 30 July 1949, and lived in Abingdon until his death in 1976.

CECIL COUSINS

Cecil Cousins (standing) with his old friend and colleague Alec Hounslow, during a trip they took together to the USA in 1975.
HOUNSLOW FAMILY

Reporting to Propert, Oxford-born Henry Edward Cecil 'Cuz' Cousins (14 April 1902–28 April 1976) joined Morris Garages in January 1920 as a fitter in the cycle shop in Clarendon Yard; as such he was an 'MG employee' even before Cecil Kimber's arrival the following year.

Working with fellow early colleagues Frank Stevens and Frank Lowndes, Cousins built the famous 'Old Number One', and would go on to be team manager for the MG 'Double Twelve' races at Brooklands in 1930 and 1931, which saw the MG Midget cement its reputation as a remarkable small sports car. A tall, gangling figure of six foot three, Cousins lived and breathed MG. He was responsible for car production at the company at the same time that H. N. (Hubert Noel) Charles was the chief designer. Whilst Charles was the qualified engineer with a good knowledge of theory, Cousins was the practically minded technician-engineer and the two often clashed, albeit with mutual respect.

After the war, Cousins helped with the creation of the first Abingdon-built mock-up for what became the TD Midget. In 1949, he worked in tandem with Propert to help save MG from being shifted to Coventry. By the time the MGA arrived, he was responsible for overseeing production at Abingdon, reporting to Jack Tatlow when Propert retired and then to Geoffrey Iley in the early Thornley years.

Cecil Cousins retired in May 1967.

ABOVE AND LEFT **Part of a short-lived proposal to marry MG and Riley techniques (and powertrains), the MG 'DO963/965/967' family, dating from June to October 1948, would have used traditional Morris Bodies coachbuilding techniques and the Riley 1.5-litre engines. DO 963 would have been a new MG Midget, DO 965 a saloon, and DO 967 a 'cabriolet' convertible. The lower part of the body has some similarities with the later EX172, EX175 and MGA. When the author interviewed Gerald Palmer in 1985 he remembered this car, which was still at Cowley when he arrived back there in 1949. The saloon (DO 965) had been built as a running prototype (Palmer recalls driving it) and it featured a grained, leathercloth finish roof, rather like the RM-series Rileys. This car was a serious attempt to replace the Y-Type, but unfortunately was too much of a unique coachbuilt exercise to succeed, and was probably caught up in the internecine battle between Abingdon and Coventry.**
ENEVER FAMILY

argument to sanction further studies of both new models and the production arrangements. For the car designs, a family of MG concepts was conceived over the summer of 1948 under the code sequence DO 963, 965 and 967: these were, respectively, an MG Midget two-seater (both soft-top and coupé), an MG 1½ litre saloon, and an MG 1½ litre convertible.

Those who remembered seeing the DO 963/5/7 proposals at first hand told the author that they used Riley engines and traditional body construction principles – ideal for the labour-intensive production techniques in use at Foleshill. The matter of possible MG production relocation to Foleshill (even as Abingdon started building the rather lacklustre MG YT Tourer for export) came to a head in November 1948. One day that month, Cecil Cousins – second-in-command to 'Pop' Propert – was called into his boss's office and told to provide a guided tour of the works to Tom Richardson, the Chief Planning Engineer from Morris Motors. The background to this is recorded in a confidential paper considered by the Morris Motors Board at their meeting of 11 December 1948.

Cousins would later recount how he kept emphasizing the cleverness and simple efficiencies at Abingdon, in the process perhaps helping to convince his visitor that the factory had more going for it than the mandarins at Cowley would have anyone believe. Cousins conceded to author John McLellan that Propert was the key player in this: 'I give Propert full credit. He was due to retire in July 1949, but he argued that Riley had no real production methods.' Cousins called Propert 'the Last of the Mohicans' – meaning that he was the last of the dyed-in-the-wool senior management MG sympathizers.

In the event, Propert's suggestion won through, and the tentative Nuffield plan was more or less reversed. As ratified at another Morris Motors Board meeting of 19 January 1949, Riley production would move from Coventry to Abingdon (and engineering responsibility to Cowley), and the Foleshill factory would became a subsidiary of Morris Motors Ltd Engines Branch; this took effect from 1 May 1949. When Propert retired at the end of July, he was replaced by Jack Tatlow from Riley (see Chapter 2), and Riley's Chief Engineer Harry Rush moved from Coventry to Cowley. So MG at Abingdon lived to fight another day.

Harry Rush was a long-serving Riley man – he is credited with the design of the distinctive blue diamond Riley badge in 1918 – but in 1949 he was the 'Chief Designer, MG and Riley Cars'.

ALL CHANGE AT COWLEY

As we have seen, for many years – and especially in the wake of Cecil Kimber's departure – the affairs of MG were ruled from Cowley, but seemingly with almost casual, indifferent control. Leonard Lord (knighted in 1954), Miles Thomas (knighted in 1943) and Reginald Hanks had all seen Abingdon as a curiosity in the Nuffield cupboard, and the production of small numbers of essentially old-fashioned sports and saloon models had hitherto, in their eyes, warranted only modest attention. With the changes in the post-war environment, however, the pace of change in the industry and the increased focus on exports, meant that MG, with its slightly premium connotations, would move up the corporate ladder.

The upsets of the Mosquito and the Foleshill-Abingdon interludes brought the role of MG and indeed Riley to a head: there was suddenly a case to bring in some new management blood. Into this atmosphere arrived Gerald Palmer, who was effectively head hunted back from Jowett, returning to Cowley in 1949. Palmer had retained his home in Oxford when he moved up to Bradford to work for Jowett, and he had heard on the grapevine that Nuffield was looking for a new design overlord.

After an interview with Reggie Hanks, Palmer was back at Nuffield, with what seemed an incredibly free brief. 'All I had to do was produce new cars for Riley and MG,' he told Graham Robson in 1977. 'There was no product planning, nothing: all I had to do was to come up with new ideas, which I hoped would be accepted. Luckily they were!' Not long after Palmer's arrival, the Morris Motors Board put a halt (at their meeting of 23 February 1950) to the 'proposed MG Magnette 1½ litre with Riley engine' – the DO 965 – which shows that the idea of using the famous 1930s MG model name considerably pre-dates the familiar Palmer-designed MG Z-Type saloon.

Meanwhile the Mosquito had been transformed into the new Morris Minor 'MM', launched to some acclaim at the 1948 Earls Court Motor Show – but it was clear that the MG Y-Type Saloon, and even the sports cars related to it, were becoming antiquated. At the same time, although there were plans for larger Wolseleys such as the 6/80, Palmer would swiftly dip more than a toe into Wolseley affairs as well as MG and Riley.

EXPORT OR DIE – POLITICIANS AND BANKERS

World War II was a costly episode in so many ways: alongside the terrible human and social costs, the expense of waging war had a crippling impact on national economies, irrespective of whether you were the victor or the loser.

GERALD PALMER

Gerald Palmer was a multi-talented engineer: not only did he design his own sports car, which helped secure him a job at Cowley, he went on effectively to revitalize the Jowett company, and came back, at the invitation of Reginald Hanks, to reconfigure MG and Riley. In the meantime he even designed his own beautiful home at Iffley, Oxford. A consummate gentleman, able to share the glory with his team, unlike the comparatively narcissistic Issigonis, Palmer deserves more credit than he is often given for his role at Cowley; he was ultimately undone by the travails of the unloved Riley Pathfinder.
AUTHOR'S COLLECTION

Born in Northwood, Middlesex, the young Gerald Marley Palmer (30 January 1911–23 June 1999) wanted to design sports cars, an interest fostered through the building of a special based on a Model T Ford.

He started work at the Scammell commercial vehicle factory at Watford. After his apprenticeship, Palmer sought to assuage his sports-car itch through the creation of a fetching and quite advanced prototype, which he called the Deroy.

Sadly, the financial reality of setting up a car company meant that the Deroy remained a one-off – but it did help him to knock on doors:

I was introduced to Cecil Kimber through Brian Robbins, the Secretary of the Institution of Automobile Engineers. I brought my Deroy down to Abingdon for him to see, and he seemed quite interested, sending me over to Cowley to meet the Technical Director, Vic Oak.

Before long he was working at Cowley, running the MG drawing office there. Amongst the projects he oversaw before war broke out was a redesign of the front suspension for the Morris Eight. By 1939 his job was listed as 'Automobile Engineer and Draughtsman'.

In the latter stages of the war, Palmer – still in his thirties – began to give thought to car making again, and seeing an advertisement from Bradford-based Jowett, he went to see the company's managing director, Calcott Reilly.

While at Jowett, Palmer was responsible for conceiving the Javelin, which went into production as war ended. But when an opportunity opened up at Cowley, Palmer jumped at it: 'I was naturally keen to be nearer home, and I was fascinated by the brief. I was to take over the MG and Riley work, and I had a free rein to come up with my own ideas.'

Palmer soon extended his influence to the Wolseley marque, too: 'Vic Oak also wanted a new small and large Wolseley, and so it seemed to me that they needed two pairs of bodies – what would become the MG Magnette and Wolseley 4/44, and the bigger, full six-seater Wolseley 6/90 and Riley Pathfinder.'

When Victor Oak resigned at the end of December 1953, Palmer was promoted: on 8 January 1954 *The Commercial Motor* reported that 'Mr G. M. Palmer, Chief Engineer of Morris Motors Ltd, has become group body and chassis designer responsible for both Morris and Austin designs. He is to be made a local director.'

Alongside the saloons there were other projects with an indirect bearing on the MGA story, such as Palmer's ideas for new MG sports cars, and a twin-cam engine – the stories of which are told in the following chapters. Palmer appeared in a special new directors' supplement in the May 1955 issue of *Nuffield Teamwork*, and he was described as 'Technical Manager for the British Motor Corporation'. Amongst the fascinating projects under his wing was a front-wheel-drive small Morris with an all-new V4 engine – and this was before Alec Issigonis came back to BMC from Alvis.

Gerald Palmer created this one-off highly sophisticated sports car, which he named the 'Deroy'; he took it to show Cecil Kimber, and on the back of that meeting was invited to Cowley by Vic Oak.
AUTHOR'S COLLECTION

continued overleaf

GERALD PALMER *continued*

However, the Austin-dominated BMC merger of 1952, and problems with the Pathfinder and its sister Wolseley, all contributed to an eventual parting of the ways for Gerald Palmer and BMC in the autumn of 1955. Officially he resigned on 4 October 1955, but in reality he had been told by George Harriman that his services were no longer required, ostensibly because Leonard Lord was unhappy about a review of the new Wolseley 6/90 in the 16 September 1955 issue of *Autocar*. As Alec Issigonis came back to BMC, Palmer went to Vauxhall courtesy of that company's Maurice Platt; he worked in Luton for the remainder of his full-time career, retiring in 1972. He died in June 1999.

GEORGE EDWARD DONO

George Edward Dono (15 July 1903–10 November 1972) deserves a footnote here. He joined Morris Motors as the director of its 'Sheet Metal Division' ('Morris Motors Ltd Pressings Branch' since 1939) in 1947, and began to build a modern body-making enterprise within the Nuffield Organisation known as 'Nuffield Metal Products', initially as an internal counterpart to Morris Motors Bodies Branch, but championing monocoque construction as opposed to the Bodies Branch's more traditional focus of timber-framed construction. In this he found a ready ally in Gerald Palmer, and as well as the body for the Riley Pathfinder, Dono assisted Palmer's plans for a new MG sports car.

In due course, the merger with Austin brought a different complexion to the body equation: Nuffield's body-making interests were rationalized and Austin led on the acquisition of Fisher & Ludlow. During the 1950s the tendency would become for Longbridge to take bodies from Fisher & Ludlow, and for Cowley to buy them in from the neighbouring Pressed Steel business, although NMP continued to supply Morris Minor bodies and was eventually reabsorbed into Bodies Branch, which supplied MGA and early MGB bodies but using 'Pressed Steel' pressings. Dono lived through that period of transition and into retirement in Woodstock.

ALBERT VICTOR OAK

Albert Victor Oak (4 November 1892–March 1969) was born in Burton-upon-Trent, Staffordshire, and grew up in the Small Heath area of Birmingham. In 1911 he described himself as an 'engineer draughtsman' in the motor industry. He rose through the ranks at Wolseley in the 1930s and became Chief Engineer at Morris Motors in 1937. He played a crucial role in the development of what became the Morris Minor.

On 31 December 1953 he formally tendered his resignation. In the run-up to the BMC merger Oak had been taking an important role in the development of a new Nuffield Group ohv small engine, which was swept away in favour of Austin-led designs. He had overseen the appointment of Gerald Palmer, given authority to the EX 172 Le Mans special (qv), as well as early work on what became the MGA twin cam engine.

Winston Churchill may have inspired the Allies to victory, but he was not to lead British Government for long after the German surrender in May 1945; at the General Election two months later, it was Clement Attlee who would lead a new Labour administration and begin to shape the pattern of the post-war British economy.

In 1946, an influential trade magazine, *The Ambassador – British Export Magazine*, soon became a conduit for Britain's push for exports in search of foreign currency, and the magazine's publisher and editor, Hans Peter Juda, coined the magazine motto 'Export or Die', which proved to be a rallying cry that was swiftly embraced by the government of the day.

In August 1946, the rather Orwellian-sounding Ministry of Information produced a short animated film using *Export or Die* as its title: the cartoon aimed to lecture Britons keen to acquire luxury goods denied them for many years as to why it was important to allow these goods to be exported to provide income for the national economy; exports, the narrator explained, generated money to buy food and raw materials such as timber. Far better, it was implied, that shiny new MGs be shipped abroad while those back home made do with a car laid up during the war years: 'We must sell the things we like to buy the things we need,' the narrator implored.

The motto would prove to be a recurring theme in the coming years (lasting until 1953), and focused the minds of big businesses with the potential to become major dollar earners. At the same time, the shift of ideology with a Socialist government meant that those voices calling for national ownership of big businesses received a more favourable ear, and such thinking made the main people within such enterprises increasingly nervous.

It is this industrial turmoil that provides some of the crucial context for the strange games and powerplay at Austin and

Nuffield around the same time that the various experiments with new model development referred to above played out. Government made frequent noises intended to encourage British car makers to rationalize their car ranges, with the suggestion that there should be less overlap or complexity in order to give exports a better chance of success.

It was hardly the first attempted intervention by politicians in the car business, and would certainly not be the last, but one of the effects was the pruning of product plans; this appears to have helped kill off the 'MG 1100' Mosquito proposals described earlier, as well as contributing to the stresses and strains that precipitated the departure of Sir Miles Thomas from the Nuffield Organisation in November 1947.

Matters of production came to a head in February 1948, when the government's Minister for Supply, George Strauss, announced that henceforth steel would only be allocated to car manufacturers who exported over 75 per cent of their output; this would prove to be a major challenge for many, and was one of the factors behind the creation of the aluminium alloy-bodied Land Rover later that year. Minutes of the contemporary Morris Motors Board meetings are littered with references to this constraint, and until the policy of rationing steel was eventually abandoned, it meant that car makers were coerced even more into the field of exports.

Against this backdrop, the car makers jostled for position, and Leonard Lord's Austin of Longbridge seemed to gain the upper hand over his Oxford rivals when the new Austin A40 Devon – with a new powertrain that would form the basis of the MGA engine just seven years later – was launched with much fanfare in New York in September 1948, just a month before the first post-war Earls Court Motor Show at which the Morris Minor made its debut. Also in London that October was the MG YT Tourer, Nuffield's somewhat lame attempt to chase after export currency.

Initially, Britain's 'Empire' markets of Australia and South Africa were the destination for MG exports; indeed the MG TC Midget was sold in much larger numbers in Australia than in the USA. However, exporters and politicians alike wanted to see efforts focused on the American dollar, and it was this as much as anything else that had fostered those exploratory visits to North America by Reginald Hanks and his colleagues, and the alliance which they soon forged with Jocelyn Hambro, who was also looking for ways to build the world of UK exports.

Of course the process of exporting actual goods is a whole industry in itself, especially when the goods themselves are such bulky and costly items as cars; getting an MG from the end of the production line in Abingdon and on to the driveway of its enthusiastic purchaser in, say, Los Angeles or New York, involved many stages, each laden with its own costs and logistical challenges. The sheer size of the USA also meant investment in supply lines and distributors as well as dealers, for spare parts and service information as well as the cars themselves.

Other factors such as import taxes, shipping handling charges and even external factors such as currency movements when the goods were in transit (the UK government devalued the pound sterling from $4.03 to $2.80 on 18 September 1949, for example) all contributed to making car exports to the USA a major draw on resources for the company making the product. Some companies – such as Austin – bit the bullet and established their own distributor network in the USA, but the arrival of Hambro Bank at Nuffield Exports Limited's door set the scene for how MGs would be sold in the USA right through the period when the MGA was in production.

The benefits that a middle-man such as Hambro offered were many: being in the money business they were naturally financially astute and able to combine efforts with different

The MG YT four-seater tourer, launched at the same time as the much more modern Morris Minor, was a Cowley idea, intended to respond to US market aspirations for a sportier offshoot of the MG Y saloon. It was not a particular success as Americans still wanted proper MG sports cars.
AUTHOR'S COLLECTION

portfolios and set up lines of credit, taking a percentage of all transactions to earn a profit. As Peter Thornley explains in his book *Mister MG*:

> If you wanted cars or parts shipped over, the dealer placed an order to the distributor who, in turn, placed an order with Hambro. They then ordered straight from the factory and the goods would be shipped straight to the distributor, at Hambro's instructions. For the bank, this meant no inventory, no warehousing; the paperwork would be shuffled and a profitable percentage earned.

Peter Thornley adds that throughout most of the 1950s, Hambro Bank's principal overheads were their New York office and six employees.

BUILDING THE AMERICAN MARKET

The challenge of getting MGs to markets across the USA due to that nation's vast size has already been mentioned; coupled to this was the fact that the company – or more precisely, its partner Hambro – had to vet and recruit a nation-wide series of distributors and dealerships, starting as we have seen from modest beginnings.

We saw earlier how Reginald Hanks had spent some time criss-crossing the USA, on the basis of which he pushed for a increase in MG TC numbers for that market, and in late 1947 Donald Harrison and Jock Forsyth of Nuffield Exports followed in Hanks's wake. Amongst other people who would

NUFFIELD EXPORTS LIMITED

In 1933, William Morris established a dedicated export arm to Morris Motors, based alongside the rail sidings at Cowley; it was said to be capable of handling up to 450 vehicles a week – probably appropriate in the context of the time. In due course the importance of the division mushroomed, and, as explained in the main text, it soon operated as a distinct business with its own Board, with the post-war export drive boosting its importance to the Nuffield Organisation as a whole. Even with the merger of BMC, the export organizations remained essentially separate, and Austin's own export division was for a long time outside the umbrella of the Hambro Organisation, an integral part of the US MG sales system. Thus, for example, MG and Austin-Healey affairs were only fully rationalized in 1963.

Although there were many problems with complexities of inter-company accounts that bedevilled Nuffield and eventually BMC accounts, the Nuffield Export personnel were considered to be a breed apart from the remainder of the business. By the time the post-war export drive was in full swing and the MGA was on the way, Nuffield Exports was expanding and a massive export handling facility was built at Cowley, from where Morris, MG, Riley, Wolseley and Morris Commercial products started their journey out into the wider export world.

Although he only came to the party in 1958, French MG distributor Jean-Pierre Richard told motoring writer and historian Jon Pressnell that he had the utmost respect for his contacts within Nuffield Exports.

> *They were extraordinary people, whom you could really respect, and who inspired a really fabulous loyalty. It was BMC, but Nuffield had kept its character. The name 'Austin' was never spoken. It was 'the others'... The Nuffield Exports people were men who'd been officers in the Army, the Navy or the RAF, who'd all fought the war. Export director Mike Trodd, for example, came from a command in the Gurkhas. Perhaps they didn't know much about cars, but they had extraordinary organizational ability and strong personnel and discipline skills. They were very correct people, and very strict with the question of payments. Distributors in Europe could do what they wanted, so long as the basic disciplines were respected – and they were easy to respect. If you had a problem, you'd ring Mike Trodd and say 'Mike, I've got a problem.' And he'd say 'Go and do it. I'll be behind you.' If there was a problem, they never wrote: they were on the telephone straightaway. And if there was a risk of something coming unravelled, they hopped on a plane. They'd arrive in the morning, and see the car. By midday it was 'Problem solved! Hup! Time for a drink!'...*

The name 'Mike Trodd' features in the story of the first MGA Frankfurt Motor Show car, covered in Chapter 4. Even after the end of the MGA, Nuffield Exports continued to thrive into the 1960s, until first BMC began to restructure its European operations, and then the merger with British Leyland. One of the challenges with the duality of Nuffield Exports and Hambro would be the complexities and financial overheads, as each part of the journey from Abingdon to the US customer's driveway involved somebody taking a percentage. In good times this was manageable; in times of slower sales, the entire chain could suffer. Nuffield Exports came to the end of the road in 1968.

go on to form part of the MG story in that country, they met Kjell Qvale (of San Francisco), Phillip Gough (of Gough Industries, Southern California) and Edward F. Furlow of S. H. Lynch (in Dallas, Texas). In Texas it was felt that there was particular potential to double sales from 50 to 100 per week in the spring of 1948.

HAMBRO

Jocelyn Hambro, the genius merchant banker who helped create the post-war climate of MG success in the United States, without which the MGA might never have been conceived.
RUPERT HAMBRO

In 1778 a thirty-four-year-old merchant named Calmer Joachim Levy, born in Denmark but who had lived in Hamburg for most of his early life, formally emigrated back to Denmark. Levy wanted to include the name of the place where he grew up as part of his name, but poor recording by officials meant that his name was written down as 'Hembroe' or 'Hambro' – and so began the story of a great banking dynasty. Before the end of the eighteenth century, Calmer Hambro was a banker to the King of Denmark; by two years into Queen Victoria's reign his grandson, Carl Joachim Hambro, had moved to London and founded the Hambro Bank there in 1839.

Just over a century later, in the immediate post-war climate, the merchant banks were encouraged to boost income from exports, particularly if it entailed earning dollars. Jocelyn Olaf Hambro (7 March 1919–19 June 1994), the grandson of Carl, launched himself into this enterprise with gusto.

Taking the unusual step (for a merchant banker) of actively seeking businesses to help, Hambro visited Louisiana and, with the benefit of $10,000 from the Bank of England and the support of the Hambro Bank, established the Hambro Trading Corporation of America, Inc. in New Orleans.

The principle was that Hambro would buy the commodities – initially as disparate as 98cc James two-stroke motorcycles and English pottery – at source, and then sell them on credit terms to the local distributors. One of the early challenges was establishing such a network in a country – let alone in mid-West states – where nobody had heard of Hambro. The motorcycle distribution initially took off, and more than 50,000 were sold, but as the Detroit car industry got into gear at the end of the 1940s, so customers turned away from eccentric British motorcycles.

Hambro's next good fortune was to link up with Nuffield Exports just as R. F. Hanks was trying to find a way to outflank his company's Austin rivals, who had recently launched their A40 Devon in the USA and were stealing the headlines and political credibility back home. Hambro, by now a director of the bank itself, bought six TC Midgets in 1948 and promptly sold them in the American mid-West. Over on the west coast, Hambro and an advertising associate Patrick Dolan launched a local MG car club in California, and got extra publicity by coverage in *Life* magazine.

Finding suitable distributors was another hurdle; for understandable commercial reasons that bound domestic car dealers, none of Hambro's new associates were linked to any of the established American car makers, and so Hambro fell into arrangements with a long-established coin-operated machine business in Dallas (Silas – S. H. – Lynch, who sold 'Seberg' jukeboxes), the Schlitz beer distributor in Chicago, and the local Philco radio distributor in Southern California (Gough Industries). It was evidently quite an adventure and an experience, not least for Hambro's wife Silvia, as he told Andrew St George: 'Our car distributors, based on beer, radios and bootlegging, didn't really understand how to treat my wife, and she was constantly pinched on the bottom by all of them.' From these modest beginnings, Hambro and Nuffield earned some £61,000 in the first year, and later with Nuffield and then BMC, built the business such that ten years after selling those first six MGs, BMC/Hambro reported sales of 33,000 vehicles in 1958.

In 1956 the arrival of the MGA in BMC/Hambro's swanky New York showroom at 27–29 West 57th Street, New York – once the American Piano Building – signalled that British sports car sales were on the up. Meanwhile Hambro Trading Company of America Inc., which also had the Rolls-Royce and Bentley concessions, was based down the road at 17 East 54th Street, and there was a west coast office in Los Angeles at 6399 Wilshire Boulevard. When BMC decided to fold its Nuffield and Austin distributor businesses into one, it was Hambro who benefited most, and by the end of the decade, the BMC/Hambro logo was all over US sales and marketing material, although largely for tax reasons there was a separate entity called BMC (USA) Ltd.

A more closely integrated business, British Motor Corporation/Hambro Inc. was formed in January 1963, several months after the end of MGA production, and moved its administration out of New York City to less grand premises at Ridgefield, New Jersey; the Hambro association was finally dissolved when BMC and Leyland Motors merged in 1968.

Qvale's introduction to MG is particularly noteworthy, as he would go on to forge a major distribution business, based in northern California, which contributed in no small way to MG's successful sales in the Pacific Northwest. The Norwegian-born businessman already had a Jeep dealership in Alameda, just south of Oakland, California, when he made a trip to New Orleans to meet with an importer (probably Hambro) to discuss expanding his line by adding James motorcycles.

Whilst there, Qvale was waiting on the street when, as he told an interviewer in 2008, '...this goofy-looking car pulls up to the curb in front of me!' Qvale asked the driver (who also happened to be the importer) where it was made; it turned out it was a British MG TC Midget. As the importer was also looking for someone to sell MGs in Northern California, Qvale returned to Alameda, sold the Jeep franchise and became an MG distributor. In 2005, *Automotive News* credited Qvale with a pivotal role in MG's post-war popularity in the United States, saying he was '...the most imaginative and probably the hardest working importer'.

Clearly dynamic businessmen such as Kjell Qvale would be vitally important to the task of Hanks and Hambro. Meanwhile, finding no significant interest in small Morris saloons (in direct contrast to Hanks' avowed hope that British small saloon cars would do well), it was immediately apparent where the business potential lay. Hanks wrote:

> It does seem so silly that, in travelling all these miles, the only thing I am able to talk about in any seriousness is the TC Midget, which was virtually obsolete many, many years ago ...and yet there is a certain class of people who like it! Put the same type of body on the 1¼ litre chassis and we have got something. But the price must be reduced... If we really want to come into the market, let us offer something the American factories do not offer to the public – and, I suggest, never can.

Further exploratory trips followed; on 6 May 1948 S.V. Smith and Donald Harrison crossed the Atlantic 'to assess the MG situation there', as the Morris Motors Board heard shortly before their departure. At this point it is worth remembering that many aspects of MG's future remained fluid; the strings were pulled from Cowley rather than Abingdon, and there was a lot of work being done on the proposed MG Midget Major, a very different style of MG sports car to the one that Americans had grown to love.

By the end of 1948, the Nuffield Exports sales volume had risen to 1,400, though not all of them MGs – yet hardly enough to worry the likes of Chrysler, Ford or General Motors. It would take a switch to a new model of MG Midget to lift the numbers even higher, and the answer was the TD Midget, which would see the number climb to 4,000.

In the process, Hambro signed up more early distributors, and inevitably these changed as new ones arrived and less successful ones (or ones for whom MGs were marginal business) fell away; for example, before long Silas Lynch backed out of MG sales and the Dallas distributorship moved to 'Clarence Talley Auto Company'. Newcomers to the MG line included S. H. Arnolt in Chicago (*see* Chapter 2), 'Waco', and later 'Ship and Shore' in Florida, not to mention a presence in Detroit, New York, New England, New Orleans, Philadelphia, St Louis and the Great Lakes. Meanwhile, as described earlier, the short-lived proposal to shift MG to Coventry came and went, and Riley production instead came south to Abingdon.

As World War II ended, Reginald Hanks and his deputy Donald Harrison, seen here, began to undertake trips to North America to see what opportunities there might be for Nuffield Group products – including Morris, Riley and Wolseley as well as MG. They soon found that all the Americans really wanted from them were MG sports cars. Harrison survived well into the BMC era and only retired in May 1962, by which time he was BMC's Director of Home Sales.
AUTHOR'S COLLECTION

When Nuffield and the much more heavily indebted Austin interests were more closely integrated, Hambro was involved in buying out the former direct Austin distributorships. Meanwhile across the USA's northern borders, BMC retained full ownership of the Canadian business arm, with no input from Hambro or any other intermediary. Of course, whilst sales of the MG TC Midget were the first step, there needed to be more new product, better focused to North American demands. This meant a combination of traditional style with more modern parts.

THE MG TD MIDGET

As we have already seen, the idea of a new Midget derived from the components that made up the MG 1¼ litre or Y-Type was not a new one in 1945 or even 1946: the thought had been circulating from at least the New Year of 1944, if not earlier. There is a letter in the Morris Motors files from Harold Ryder to Sir Miles Thomas, dated 2 February 1944, which reported on a prior meeting that Ryder had held with what he styled the 'Executives' at MG.

> I must say, they made a very good case for the introduction of a Midget. I think you will appreciate that this company was built up on a Midget car, and I feel that provided we run a 'bread and butter' line, which is an improvement on the standard, we could economically produce a Midget car – at least for a few years after the war in order not to give the public the impression we were falling out of the market which had given us such a good name. I have therefore contacted Mr Oak, and he informs me that the chassis of the 1¼ litre can be readily used for a Midget, and he is investigating the possibility of body styles and types, using as much as possible the standard panels.

Thus the idea was formulated of creating an open-topped sports car based on the floorpan and running gear of the saloon, which would be launched first, in May 1947. As described earlier, the fact-finding missions undertaken during 1946 and 1947 simply reinforced the attractiveness of this idea. Accordingly the instruction came down via Vic Oak and Harold Ryder to Syd Enever and Cecil Cousins to create a kind of Frankenstein combination of TC Midget and Y-Type underpinnings. In the process, Alec Hounslow, Henry Stone and Billy Wilkins in the MG Experimental Shop at Abingdon proceeded to chop a foot (300mm) out of the wheelbase of a Y-Type chassis, and mounted a TC body on it. After an initial review by Oak, some amendments were made, but the basic concept was approved.

The next step was to develop the concept into a buildable production car, and here the task fell to Jim O'Neill, who, as we shall see, would go on to become crucial to the MGA story. O'Neill worked at Cowley at the time, in the MG office there, reporting to assistant chief draughtsman Tom Ramsay: accordingly, what would become the MG TD Midget was ascribed the Cowley Design Order Number DO 968 (the MG YT having been DO 928).

The story of how the project evolved and became the successful car that was launched on 18 January 1950 (having been deferred from a 1949 Earls Court Motorshow launch) need not really concern us here, other than to note that in the absence of a great deal of corporate interest in his work on the drawing board, O'Neill found that the one person who did make an effort was John Thornley, who came over from Abingdon and made some modest suggestions to improve the lines of the new Midget.

The new TD came at an auspicious time, ready to meet the export drive in the wake of a massive devaluation of the pound against the dollar: sales got off to a good start, with well over 90 per cent of the 4,767 TDs built in 1950 being exported, with more than half of these going to the USA. As production at Abingdon began to ratchet up, the plant celebrated the completion of its 10,000th car in February 1951 – the car itself (perhaps in part for quasi-political reasons) being a Riley 2½ litre rather than an MG.

Meanwhile, competition activity in the new model brought forward worthwhile changes, and a 'Mark II' version; John Thornley sanctioned a team of TDs that were raced by Ted Lund, George Phillips and Dick Jacobs. Success – in the UK as well as the USA – led to further development and some bold ideas, which in due course would lead MG on a path away from the traditional square-shaped Midget and towards, ultimately, the MGA.

The MG TD Midget was the first post-war MG sports car that was a genuinely new confection, rather than a warmed-over 1939 model, but nevertheless its style was unquestionably 'old school' with fairly poor aerodynamic qualities.

AUTHOR'S COLLECTION

CHAPTER TWO

THE AERODYNAMIC SPORTS CAR

The TD might have been, technically, a new MG in 1950, with such modern features as independent wishbone front suspension, a wider track than the older models, and the availability of left-hand-drive steering for the first time in an MG Midget, and that steering being responsive rack-and-pinion. The underpinnings of the new MG Midget were therefore much more contemporary than the outgoing TC – but even so, it was still essentially evolved from the pre-war MG 'square-rigger' narrow-built aesthetic, and the archaic method of construction.

The perpendicular style might have served the marque well in the 1930s, but the appearance was now seen as 'old hat' – apart from amongst the die-hard traditionalists – in a modern world where schoolboys of all ages admired sleek contemporary sports cars such as the low-slung Jaguar XK120, the exciting modern full-bodied automotive styling coming out of Italy, not to mention the sleek, smooth looks inspired by new-fangled jet aircraft. By this time, of course, the short-lived Miles Thomas-supported MGs based on the Morris Minor structure had been abandoned, just as their sponsor had left the organization.

BREAKING THE MOULD: NEW SPORTS-CAR STYLES

In this period, a number of individuals as well as entrepreneurs identified a role for re-bodied MG chassis, and thus appeared some racing specials such as the Motto-MG, coach-built specials such as the Ghia-Aigle MG TD (six of these elegant cars were built by this Swiss company in 1953, of which at least two are known to have survived), and the low-volume run of Bertone-styled Arnolt MGs (*see* box).

Quite apart from the changing aesthetic sensibilities, there were other, more fundamental considerations, chiefly to do with the terrible aerodynamic qualities of the older shape, and the way the driver often sat quite high up in the vehicle, often perched behind a relentlessly flat windscreen (which admittedly could sometimes be folded flat) and a bluff, square-fronted radiator grille.

The beautiful proportions of the MG TC may have endeared it to its fans as the embodiment of classic English Roadster (and in 1951 earned it display in the New York

One of the dramatic show stars at the 1948 Earls Court Motor Show is the stunning, sleekly styled Jaguar XK120; its low, svelte lines were a marked contrast to the more perpendicular pre-war shape of the models with which it shared showroom space.
JAGUAR CARS

THE ARNOLT MG TD

Stanley Harold Arnolt II (1906–1963) had the mid-west distributorship for MG, and recognized a market for sports cars that married Italian styling to British underpinnings and credibility – rather like Italian tailoring with English cloth.

Meanwhile, over in Europe, the somewhat cash-strapped Bertone coach-building concern in Turin was trying to rebuild its fortunes in the difficult climate of post-war Italy, and father Giovanni and son Giuseppe (better known as 'Nuccio') decided to build a brace of smoothly styled sports cars on second-hand MG TD chassis, which they planned to exhibit at the 1952 Turin Motor Show.

Working with Franco Scaglioni, the Bertone business created a slim, modern shape that flowed creatively back from a modified TD grille shape, and the cars were displayed on the stand of local MG distributor Fattori & Montani. Arnolt expressed interest in buying cars, namely a hundred of each, roadster and coupé.

A deal was soon struck for what would be Bertone's first series production venture. Arnolt would arrange to buy new MG TD chassis from MG, they would then be shipped to Genoa, taken overland to Turin where they would be built up as 'Arnolt MGs', shipped back to Genoa again, and then taken by sea to Chicago. The car had its North American première at the second Annual International Motor Sports Show at New York's Grand Central Palace in April 1953, just under a year after Arnolt's trip to Turin.

Of the planned two hundred to be built, 103 are recorded as having been completed (sixty-seven coupés and thirty-six convertibles). Production continued for a while after the MG TF replaced the TD, but before long the supply of chassis dried up, and Arnolt moved on to his next project with another marque.

The small Swiss-based coachbuilder Ghia-Aigle, a former subsidiary of the well-known Italian carrozzerie, took an MG TD and created, with the direction of Giovanni Michelotti, a smoothly styled modern MG sports car, which it exhibited at the Geneva Salon of March 1953. Just three years hence, the MGA would make its first Swiss show appearance.
JULIEN GIAMBAGLI

The Arnolt MG TD was available either as an open-topped roadster, or as this rather elegant close-coupled coupé.
AUTHOR'S COLLECTION

MG took great interest in this special coachbuilt MG created by Bill Shipside (seen here with his creation) of T Shipside Ltd, a Nuffield Distributor in Nottingham.
AUTHOR'S COLLECTION

Museum of Modern Art), but the times were changing, and popular fashion in the 1950s was evolving; the modern trend was to embrace the next best thing and discard the tropes of the past. It was therefore against this background that in late 1950, MG chief engineer Syd Enever, encouraged by John Thornley and with feedback from North America, began to give thoughts to a new, radically different style for the MG Midget chassis.

Of course, his thought processes were unquestionably reinforced by the fact that from 1949, just down the road at Cowley, MG and Riley design chief Gerald Palmer had arrived and swiftly began designing a new, modern MG saloon car line, and within recent memory there had been those real possibilities of other, sleekly styled modern MG tourers, based on other Nuffield models, none of which had anything remotely sporting about them, nor had they received any direct Abingdon involvement.

Last but not least, despite the fact that MG and Riley production had been consolidated at Abingdon, there remained some perhaps malign forces on the Morris Motors Board who not only had a jaundiced view of sports cars, but who seemingly still fostered ambitions of further rationalization: the minutes of 28 February 1951 record that Donald Harrison 'would consider the possibility of merging the Riley and MG franchises'. However, at the Board meeting of 14 March 1951, at which Nuffield's future car production policy was also discussed, it was minuted that 'Mr Oak reported that it would be possible to commonise the projected MG Saloon and Wolseley 10 to a large extent', and furthermore that 'resulting from representations made by Mr Harrison, it was decided to abandon the prospect of merging the Riley and MG franchises'. The new MG saloon and Wolseley 10 would become the MG Z Magnette and Wolseley 4/44.

GEORGE PHILLIPS AND EX 172

The successes that George Phillips had racing his home-brewed TC Special, and in particular his exploits at Le Mans (*see* box), did not go unnoticed at Abingdon. John Thornley, still the MG service manager at the time, supported Phillips and his contemporaries Dick Jacobs and Ted Lund with seats in a trio of factory-prepared MG TD Midgets, which did well at various events in 1951. All three would in due course play important parts in the MGA story, but it was Phillips who had the first act.

During the winter of 1950–51, George Phillips visited Abingdon to discuss ideas for his 1951 Le Mans entry; as he later wrote:

> Having finished in 1950, I was automatically accepted for the 1951 race, driving any car I wished. I still wanted it to be an MG, so it was decided that the works would build, albeit unofficially, a special-bodied lightweight version of the TD. Work was started in the winter of 1951 in the development department.

Here, many have tended to accept the idea that the project which ensued was an entirely 'unofficial' one, totally under the radar, largely on the basis of Phillips' testimony. The author has found, however, that there was an official sanction by the Morris Motors Board of a sum of £850, which was agreed on 28 December 1950, for the 'Le Mans TD Midget Mark II for G. E. Phillips and E. Winterbottom.' At the same meeting, a sum of £1,500 was also approved to support the planned costs associated with Lt Col A. T. ('Goldie') Gardner's efforts with the EX 135 record breaker, fitted with a TD engine.

Whether or not the Board ever suspected the full extent of what was being planned by Syd Enever may be unclear, because the minutes record that the money was simply

This is Harry Herring's model of a version of EX 172 with a full-height windscreen, which he gifted to a friend and neighbour, whose family still treasure it more than sixty-seven years after it was made.
BUCKLE FAMILY

intended to cover the weight reduction of the car, and transport and insurance costs (which Phillips ended up paying himself!) – but the fact remains that the project started off with the benefit of official finance, even if the money was then used rather creatively. A sum of £850 in 1950 would be roughly equivalent to more than £23,000 in 2018 – useful, but hardly a king's ransom.

For Syd Enever, the opportunity to create a running prototype – swiftly assigned the Abingdon project code of 'EX 172' – was a godsend, because he had been tinkering with the idea of a road-going aerodynamic MG, building on his experience with the stream-lined EX 135 record breaker. A starting point was inevitably a small-scale model which Enever could take to his friends at Armstrong-Whitworth in

MODEL MAN: HARRY HERRING

For Henry Thomas ('Harry') Herring (24 June 1883–1 September 1974), like many who started as apprentices in the coach-building trade, the tools he used were mostly bespoke and had been personally handmade (in an interview for the *Oxford Mail* in March 1957, Herring said that 'no price can be put on my tools; many of them are not produced by manufacturers'). Herring, born in Abingdon and one of three generations to work at 'the Gees', joined the factory in 1933; by then he was already an experienced coach-builder, but his skills at pattern model making and the decline in ash-framed cars led in due course to his becoming Syd Enever's personal model maker. As it happens, Harry was not the first Herring at MG – that distinction went to his son John ('Jack'), who had joined in 1930 and managed to get Harry a job.

Harry's obvious forté was model making, a very special skill; as well as styling and wind-tunnel test models of production prototypes, Herring worked on similar models for Syd Enever's new-generation record breakers, as well as prototype patterns of new parts where a three-dimensional model was required. Nowadays, automotive designers rely largely on computer-aided design to the extent that some cars go almost all the way from keyboard to showroom, although viewing and test models are still needed at some point in most cases. However, no longer is there room for the skilled creation of masterpieces in wood: instead, some skilled modellers apply clay to wooden skeletons, whilst others mill their models from blocks of foam using a computer-controlled milling machine.

Jim O'Neill told the author that Harry Herring – who formally retired on 30 March 1961 at the grand age of seventy-eight – had wanted his son to inherit his mantle, but sadly it was not to be: 'Harry was very disappointed when the Works Manager said "Well, he's not in the same class", and Syd said "Well, that's it, then", and didn't bother to pursue it. I know that Harry was very upset about that and, who knows, his son might have turned out to be all right – I don't know how good he was.' Meanwhile the occasion of Harry Herring's retirement was marked with the presentation to him of his model of EX 181.

The third member of the Herring family to work at MG was Harry's grandson, also named John, who began work at Abingdon in 1950, working on the MG TD and TF; in 1955 he moved on to the MGA, where he was involved in welding chassis frames together using the parts supplied to the factory from John Thompson Pressings.

Meanwhile Harry continued making models in his spare time, and was even doing 'unofficial' work in his shed at home right up until he died at the age of ninety-one. It is a testament to his superb craftsmanship that none of his surviving models, some of them well over sixty years old, exhibit signs of age-related cracks, splits, paint flaking or distortion.

Whitley, not far from Coventry, where the aerodynamicist, George Beech, generously provided Enever with wind-tunnel services free of charge.

Enever's ideas, then as for many years afterwards, were translated into three-dimensional model form by Harry Herring, the factory's highly skilled model maker, who fashioned beautiful scale models out of wood. Many of these models ended up hidden away in a room at the factory where, thankfully, many of them survive.

George Phillips once said that he had originally suggested Enever should consider, for inspiration, the style of the contemporary Sunbeam-Talbot 90 drop-head (the later, more familiar 'Grace Kelly' Alpine was not launched until 1953); other loose inspiration could perhaps have come from the Jaguar XK120 or the Aston-Martin DB2, but the shape that eventually emerged, honed in the wind-tunnel at Whitley, was ultimately Enever's own.

The running prototype was a team effort by a small handful of craftsmen in the Development Department at Abingdon, all working under the direction of Alec Hounslow. In his autobiography, published about thirty years later, Henry Stone claimed that the creation of EX 172 had been almost entirely an Abingdon affair:

> Alec and I built all of the framework for UMG400 (EX 172)... the body was built in our shop by a panel beater named Wally Kimpsey; Alec and I made all the formers from 16-gauge, square, 5/8in tube. We drilled holes every half-inch to lighten the framework as much as possible. On the skin side, we left a few 1/8in holes for flush-fitting rivets. The internal hole on the square tubing had ¼in clearance to allow us to get a turned-down dolly against the skin rivet shank in order to head it; this took a great deal of time and work. The whole body was rubber-mounted and came off easily.

In the Cowley Design Order – or 'DO' – list there is an entry against 'DO 1017' described simply as 'aluminium panels for MG TD Midget'; as the earlier 'DO 1010' code (dating from 1950) was for the future MG Magnette, it seems entirely feasible that 'DO 1017' may have been the Cowley project code counterpart to Abingdon's EX 172. With typical Abingdon subterfuge, it seems that actual progress of the build, despite the Morris Motors budget and official nature of its MG project code, was initially concealed from the Nuffield Group Technical Director, Sidney Smith, who used to visit the factory every Tuesday. On these occasions, the car was wheeled surreptitiously out of sight into a nearby field.

Taken from Syd Enever's own photo album, the snapshots here and opposite above show EX172 in the process of being built at Abingdon in the winter of 1950/1951.

ENEVER ALBUM

ABOVE AND RIGHT: **Alec Hounslow in EX172 at Abingdon.**
ENEVER ALBUM

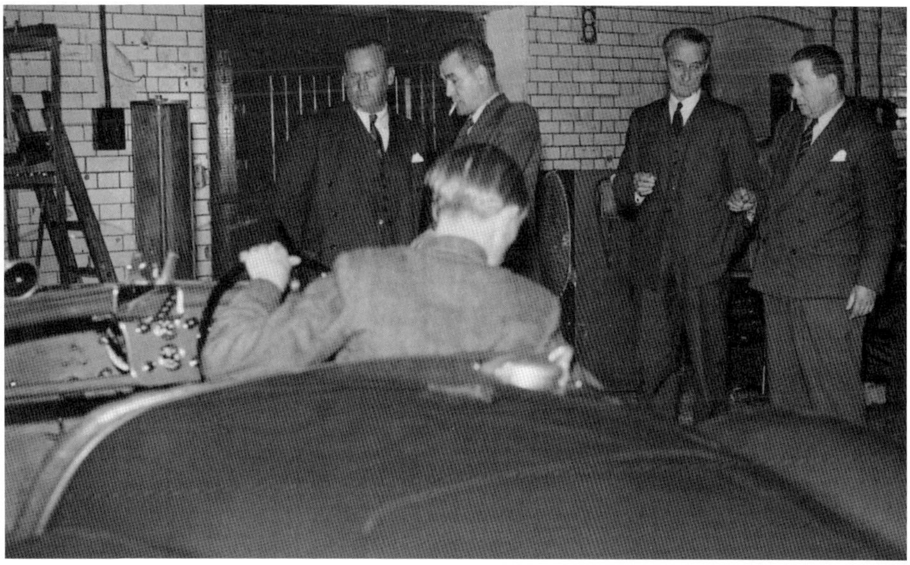

MG and Nuffield management look over EX 172 in the workshop at Abingdon; Syd Enever is talking to Vic Oak, whilst behind him, S.V. Smith (second from right) chats to MG and Riley Manager, Jack Tatlow (far right).
ENEVER FAMILY

Perhaps Smith was only expecting to see something that looked broadly similar to the donor TD?

Phillips records that when the inevitable day finally came that the car was completed, Smith would obviously have to see it: 'There was some apprehension in the works as to how he would react; fortunately he liked it, so everybody from John Thornley down breathed a sigh of relief.' Amongst the photos that record the car for posterity is one with Syd Enever in the cockpit and Nuffield management, in the form of Sidney Smith and A.V. 'Vic' Oak, standing behind, and also one from Syd Enever's own albums, which shows Oak, Smith, Enever and Jack Tatlow all admiring the car in the Experimental Shop at Abingdon.

SIDNEY VICTOR SMITH

In 1947, Harold Ryder was pensioned off, and his role as Morris director with a role to oversee MG was passed to Sidney Victor Smith (27 March 1896–September 1968) – a slim, somewhat saturnine figure, occasionally sporting a bristle-like moustache. John Thornley's deputy Geoffrey Iley told the author: 'Smith looked a bit like an older Errol Flynn, with his little moustache. The foremen at Cowley used to hide from him when he was on the way; he was an absolute tyrant!' Iles came to know Smith rather better, later in his career, and claims the man's bark was worse than his bite. In 1947, Smith ('Technical Director of Morris Motors') and his Nuffield Exports Sales Director colleague Donald Harrison, undertook a fact-finding visit to North America; one consequence of this was the creation of the underwhelming MG YT four-seater tourer, launched a year later as an open version of the YA saloon with the benefit of left-hand-drive for relevant export markets. It was Smith, too, who would be important in sanctioning the subsequent TD Midget.

Before long, Smith became Nuffield Group's Technical Director – a very important role with a direct line to the top; he was then given the same oversight of the BMC engineering functions following the merger, a testament to the respect in which he was held by everyone at the top, Sir Leonard Lord included.

It was Smith, as we shall see, who first received the message from the BMC Joint Board that MG had the go-ahead to create the MGA. In 1959, *Who's Who in the Motor Industry* listed Smith as Engineering Co-ordinator, BMC and he was still in that role the following year, when he was captured in a photo standing alongside Issigonis, Charles and John Cooper, and Charles Griffin. They were at the start of the process that would create the Mini Cooper, a car which would soon go into production as Sidney Victor Smith approached retirement a year later as he reached the age of sixty-five. His letter of resignation, on Morris Motors headed notepaper, is dated 28 October 1961.

TOP: **Sidney Victor Smith was known by some of his colleagues as 'Hitler Smith' on account of his small, bristly moustache.**

EX 172, with Syd Enever in the cockpit, and in the background, S.V. Smith (left) and A.V. 'Vic' Oak looking on.
GRAHAM ROBSON

The end result of MG's endeavours, parked up outside the Development Workshop prior to management inspection.
AUTHOR'S COLLECTION

Enever and Hounslow were justifiably proud of their British Racing Green creation, which combined some of the lessons learned through record breaking with the best contemporary MG practice – after all, the TD Midget, still a new car only recently into production, used steering and front suspension that was more modern than any MG sports car since the R Type. So EX 172, by now road-registered as 'UMG 400', made a series of forays on to the local roads of Berkshire and Oxfordshire, including a trip to the Enever household alongside the South Oxford bypass, where it was much admired by Enever's family and their neighbours. Although, of course, nobody could yet know it, this low, sleek shape was the first step towards what would become the MGA.

However, UMG 400 had obviously been built primarily with a particular short-term objective, which was to have the proposed shot at Le Mans in the capable hands of George Phillips. Phillips later wrote:

> When I went to collect the car from the factory I felt very proud, and very pleased with the look of the car ... the body was, for that time, a very pretty and workmanlike looking job, with its long low flying lines that looked really efficient. There had never been a road-going MG that looked anything like it before. Although in some aspects, one could detect its ancestry in the Gardner record-breaking car that Syd Enever had designed. The only snag was that the driver sat on it, instead of in it.

The problem of the driver sitting somewhat high in the cockpit was as much a consequence of its low build and cutaway door line as the uncompromising TD chassis, which, because it was narrow, meant that the seats were consequently perched above, rather than between the main chassis members. This would be a matter that Enever would look at further in the future – but for the time being, the task was to get UMG 400 to Le Mans and ensure it qualified for the race.

Barry Jackson (son of Reg) stands alongside UMG400, parked outside the Enever family home at Westminster Way, on the outskirts of Oxford.

ENEVER ALBUM

Family and neighbours of the Enever household admire UMG400 during a visit to Westminster Way. Syd stands to the right, while a smiling Alec Hounslow can also be seen in the centre.

ENEVER ALBUM

The businesslike cockpit of the unique EX 172.

GRAHAM ROBSON

Syd's daughter Susan sits in the cockpit of UMG400, parked on the drive at the family home. She is certainly a better 'fit' than George Phillips would prove to be when driving it at Le Mans.

ENEVER ALBUM

GEORGE PHILLIPS, MG AND LE MANS

When he became the chief photographer for *Autosport* magazine, former Fleet Street dispatch rider George Phillips (1914–1993) gained a special status in the world of UK motor sports, with a virtual access-all-areas automotive passport that took him to the circuits of Great Britain, Northern Ireland and mainland Europe with regularity. There was seldom a weekend without a motor race going on somewhere, and so Phillips could be found either clutching a camera or occasionally, if commitments allowed, behind the wheel of his own race car.

In 1947, Phillips had swiftly found that his brand-new MG TC Midget was a major disappointment in the performance stakes. Phillips became determined to modify the TC in order to improve its performance.

An engine re-build yielded some useful gains. Over the winter of 1947, a more drastic overhaul involved the replacement of the traditional steel and timber TC bodyshell with a lightweight Lester body, which reportedly shaved a useful 400lb off the kerb weight, so that, as Phillips later recalled, 'the difference in performance was absolutely phenomenal...' Thus enhanced, the Phillips TC Special began a distinguished racing career, which culminated in an entry for the first post-war Le Mans 24-Hours race in June 1949.

George Phillips, in his white overalls, at Le Mans in 1950. Others from left to right are his wife Barbara, Denis Jones (the team mechanic) and Eric Winterbottom. Success at Le Mans this year helped secure factory help for 1951.
GEORGE PHILLIPS

For this enterprise, the Special received a new alloy body and lightweight frame. By now, Phillips had attracted the interest of the MG factory, and John Thornley provided support to Phillips in terms of practical advice and a useful discount on parts. It would prove to be an important alliance.

The car went reasonably well until an intermittent ignition failure led to an incident that precipitated disqualification.

After a number of minor races in the remainder of 1949, Phillips built a new engine in readiness for Le Mans in 1950. The car ran flawlessly for the entire twenty-four hours. The original Phillips Le Mans MG achieved further success, but for 1951, there would be something rather more impressive with a direct bearing on the MGA story.

When it came to making arrangements to ship UMG 400 to Le Mans, Phillips – who christened the car 'The Streamliner' – had to rely on his own wits and enterprise, for, as he told an MG Car Club audience: 'Although the company had been good enough to build the car and gave me £150 towards my expenses, their help finished there. They never sent a mechanic or anyone from the works, and I was entirely on my own.' In fairness to MG, their motor-sport efforts were still being run on a shoestring, as we have seen under the somewhat baleful gaze of management at Cowley; Enever had also craftily used up most of the 'expenses' on building the car. There was an offer to Phillips that he could have the car afterwards for £700, arguably something of a bargain given everything that had been involved in creating it.

Some of Phillips' costs and resources were to be shared by his co-driver for 1951, thirty-nine year old Alan Charles Rippon, who had taken up racing two years beforehand in his eponymous 'Rippon Special': 'He was the ideal co-driver,' Phillips said; 'a very pleasant and affable character, who listened to what you said and never lost his cool. He paid the same as my previous partners, which was £100 towards the many expenses incurred in a venture of this nature.' After arrival at Le Mans, EX 172 sailed through scrutineering, thanks in part to the careful adherence to the ACO Le Mans construction rules, but not surprisingly there was a lot of interest in this very different-looking MG.

Phillips took the car out for practice, which was its first serious try-out since Syd Enever, Alec Hounslow and Henry Stone's impromptu blasts up and down the South Oxford bypass. Phillips said he was unsure about the front suspension, and more importantly was worried about pre-ignition or 'pinking', which after rechecking the timing and the fuel mixture, was eventually put down to the quality of the race fuel, other entrants having similar issues. Adopting a 'belt and braces' approach, Phillips took the head off the 1,250cc XPAG engine and refitted it with two gaskets: the

The MG factory team stand proudly behind UMG400. They are, left to right: Gerald Wiffen, Henry Stone, Syd Enever, Wally Kimpsey (who did the body), Reg Avenall, Jack Crooke and an unknown. Alec Hounslow is behind the wheel.
ENEVER ALBUM

George Phillips sits on (rather than in) his new MG special at the 1951 Le Mans 24 Hour race. Sadly EX 172 did not cross the finish line.
AUTHOR'S COLLECTION

consequence appeared to be a reduction in pinking, and so the car was deemed ready for the main event.

With the race under way, Phillips began with the tried and tested 'hare and tortoise' approach, settling for a steady early pace whilst some of the less experienced drivers injudiciously zoomed off at a more rapid speed and headed inevitably for early retirement. Even so, Phillips had to keep up a reasonable rate, and eventually found that he had managed to achieve a lap of the circuit in six minutes, his maximum on the Mulsanne Straight being a remarkable 116mph (186.6km/h), the kind of speed that anyone driving a conventional TD could hardly have contemplated.

Later he told his MG club audience: 'This really was exciting news!' – though it was soon clear that this excitement was a little premature:

> Whether I got carried away, or the engine had suffered damage due to the bad fuel, I will never know, but I was just about to overtake May's Bentley when there was a clatter and the engine went on three cylinders, so I limped around to the pits. As I had done more than twenty-five laps, I was able to remove the valve cover and discovered the worst: I had dropped a valve and it had punched its way clean through the piston. We refuelled, and I said to Alan to take it out and see what it could do on three cylinders.

The damage was done, and although EX 172 limped on, fuel was leaking copiously into the guts of the engine and so inevitably the end came when the big-end bearings failed. It was the end of an exciting but frustrating adventure, and also, as it would transpire, more or less the end of George Phillips' serious motor-racing endeavours, because his job as *Autosport*'s chief photographer meant that his employers understandably wanted him to focus on photographing racing cars rather than driving them. As a pertinent example, straight after his Le Mans stint, Phillips was obliged to head straight off to report on the French Grand Prix, whilst a friend returned the MG to Abingdon.

Phillips was straight talking, and says that he had a somewhat difficult conversation when he eventually managed to get to Abingdon:

> There were recriminations on both sides. I said, 'If I can build an engine in my kitchen that lasts for twenty-four hours and is used daily doing other events without any trouble, I would have thought that you could have done the same.' They in turn blamed me for being lead-footed, so nothing really came of that. When all the dust of that settled, they asked me how I felt about the car. I agreed the shape was good, but it was a pity the driver had to sit on it, instead of in it. If this problem could be solved, I said I thought perhaps it had the makings of a good car – and so from that exercise, I like to think the MGA was born.

Phillips also spoke to Doug Nye about his EX 172 experience, for an article in the short-lived magazine *Collectors' Cars*, which appeared in that publication's November 1979 issue:

> The previous year poor old Eric Winterbottom [who would be killed in the 1951 Dundrod TT race] had asked me what the rev limit was on my car, and I told him straight: 'When you get vapour coming out of the carburettors, change gear!' I reckoned that if the engine I'd built on my kitchen table would run for twenty-four hours like that, then a works-prepared engine ought to be absolutely unburstable – but it wasn't!

This certainly echoes what John Thornley told author Bob Vitrikas for the latter's MGA book:

> I was afraid that (engine failure) was going to happen because in talking to George beforehand, he was so utterly convinced of the indestructibility of the power unit that I knew in my bones that with the improved aerodynamics, he was going to overcook it.

Its work at Le Mans finished, Thornley reiterated his offer to sell the car, but Phillips declined – not solely out of pique, but doubtless because he probably could no longer see himself having the time to use it to its full potential.

There being little sentiment in automotive development departments, the dismantled EX 172 was cut up, too late for Phillips' co-driver Rippon, who apparently expressed some belated interest in having it. But Syd Enever had not given up on the idea of a streamlined successor to the T-Type.

THE AERODYNAMIC SPORTS CAR IN CONCEPT: THE STORY OF EX 175

The positive reaction to EX 172 was sufficient encouragement for Syd Enever to re-examine the concept but with the benefit of a bespoke chassis instead of the compromise of TD Midget underpinnings. George Phillips had suggested a return to the pre-war R-Type backbone chassis with its all-round independent suspension, but Enever knew that such sophistication was unlikely to provide a practical way forward. However, the idea of shifting the longitudinal chassis members out of the way was a fairly obvious means to provide an opportunity to lower the driver and passenger seats, and thereby not only to drop them 'out of the wind' but to lower the centre of gravity into the bargain.

Some have suggested that the emerging contemporary practice of American 'perimeter frame' chassis may have been a source of inspiration to Enever's fertile mind, but in fact there was also an example closer to home, for Gerald Palmer had adopted this philosophy for his new Riley Pathfinder. The DO 999 Pathfinder was initially intended to have a traditional coach-built body (hence the use of a separate chassis), and was deliberately designed with lower seating levels in mind; it was headed for a launch (with, in the event, a more modern steel body) and assembly at Abingdon from the tail end of 1953, under the corporate 'MG and Riley' production arrangements.

Whatever the origins of the idea, in the New Year of 1952 Enever took a new project code – EX 175 – and started

The second iteration of Syd Enever's vision for a new, more aerodynamic sports car came with this prototype, EX 175, which was made roadworthy with an XPAG engine (which necessitated a small bonnet bulge). The registration number 'HMO 6' led to someone, in those less politically correct days, to dub the car as the 'homosex'. John Thornley said it was a 'gorgeous motorcar'.
AUTHOR'S COLLECTION

TOP: **EX 175 came with a top that was fitted with a 'skylight', a feature denied the later MGA.**
AUTHOR'S COLLECTION

BOTTOM: **The rear three-quarter view of EX175 shows the greater differences to the later MGA: note the slightly more curvaceous rear wings, the bulkier bumper over-riders, the plinth on which the rear number plate is mounted, and the smaller 'D'-shaped boot-lid.**
AUTHOR'S COLLECTION

scheming its layout on his dining-room table at Westminster Way, Oxford. He delegated the task of drawing up the chassis to young draughtsman Roy Brocklehurst, the master drawing being EX 175/2 and the subsidiary drawings for the left- and right-hand chassis members being EX 175/3 and EX 175/4 respectively. By the end of the active work on the project there had been forty-four entries against the EX 175 code.

Perhaps also at the back of Enever's mind may have been the recent news that MG's parent Nuffield Group had agreed a deal to link up with Morris's deadly Austin rival; what the future held for the minor satellite of Abingdon was still unclear, but it was obviously better to be ready with new ideas when the time came: after all, from his experiences in 1935 with the closure of the Abingdon MG design office, coupled with the cancellation of factory racing, Enever knew what happened when new brooms swept in. And in this case, too, it would seem to be the same man behind the broom.

CORPORATE MARRIAGE: THE CREATION OF BMC

The project to move MG sports-car design into a new era was overshadowed by upheavals at the most senior Board table, as Austin and Nuffield came together to form the British Motor Corporation.
AUTHOR'S COLLECTION

Leonard Lord and Lord Nuffield parted company in 1938, and although 'Len' took on some roles in connection with Nuffield's charitable trusts, he was famously quoted by Miles Thomas as promising to one day take Cowley apart 'brick by brick'.

By the time war was ending in 1945, Lord Nuffield had become ever more remote from his business – despite a desire to be the decision maker and final arbiter on many aspects, for which he was either ill-qualified or where it seemed that his interference provided little more than a petty reminder of who was the boss. Meanwhile Leonard Lord had successfully presided over the expansion of the rival Austin organization, Lord Austin having died in 1941 and his successor Ernest Payton following suit in 1946.

With the race for British car makers to chase US dollars and comply with the constraints of government controls and threats of nationalization, the Austin and Nuffield organizations brokered an uneasy alliance in October 1948, just as the Morris Minor was launched at the Earls Court Motor Show. The joint statement spoke of a 'constant interchange of information' and a 'pooling of all factory resources'.

This arrangement seems to have been received with little enthusiasm by the middle management of both companies, and in July 1949 it was announced that the dialogue had been terminated: it looked as though there would be no marriage. In the background, however, political pressure to come together evidently continued, and culminated in a surprise announcement on the evening of Friday 23 November 1951 that the two organizations were planning a union of sorts, under the umbrella of an as yet unnamed holding company (although an internal working name was 'British Motors Limited').

In their joint statement at a packed press conference, tellingly held at Longbridge, Reginald Arthur Bishop (Nuffield's Head of the Central Publicity Department) and Alan Hess (Austin Public Relations Officer, and therefore Bishop's Longbridge counterpart) announced that unified control would lead not only to more efficient and economic production, but would also further the export drive and be particularly beneficial to manufacturing and assembly abroad. The statement noted that:

> *...amalgamation will be in both the national interest and to the advantage of the shareholders of both companies. Accordingly they propose a merger of interests on the basis that a Holding Company will be formed with an authorized capital of £5 million, divided into 20 million ordinary shares of five shillings each.*

The first four named directors were Lord Nuffield, Leonard Lord, Reginald Hanks (of Nuffield) and George Harriman (of Austin). The union was broadly welcomed by the media, who noted that the combined organization would make it the world's fourth largest vehicle manufacturer, although it was still some way below the American 'big three' of General Motors, Ford and Chrysler.

HMO 6 in full road-going trim; the similarities to the later DO 1062 'MGA' are obvious – but so are the differences, such as the bonnet bulge and the heavier bumper over-riders.

ENEVER FAMILY

When it came to the shape for EX 175, Enever could obviously look back critically on EX 172, because as well as a lower seating compartment, he was determined to smooth out the lines to create a more harmonious overall shape with doors on both sides. Using Enever's sketches as a basis, Jim O'Neill (at this stage still based at Cowley) oversaw a quarter-scale drawing by Dennis Drury, which Jim then sent to the Cowley Experimental Shop (run by George Smith), who scaled down the quarter-scale drawings in order to allow the creation of an eighth-scale model.

Here there is a slight degree of uncertainty, for O'Neill was adamant that the EX 175 model was made at Cowley in George Smith's shop, whereas an alternative version of events has it that the model was made in the usual way by Harry Herring at Abingdon. In 2018, whilst the model survives in the British Motor Museum collection at Gaydon, it is no longer clear who was responsible (Herring certainly made many other models, including ones of EX 172, the MGA and various variants), but the EX 175 model, tested in the Armstrong-Whitworth wind tunnel, looks remarkably close to the eventual MGA.

Finished in the same metallic maroon as was later chosen for the full-size prototype, the model (as well as Dennis Drury's drawing, EX 175/1, dated 20 February 1952) differs mainly in having trapezoidal air extraction vents on the sides of the front wings, an idea that was abandoned in favour of the small elliptical holes on the tops of the wings. In a 1979 article for *Automobile Quarterly*, Doug Nye quotes Enever as saying: 'I doubt if we seriously tested the effect of those side ducts at Armstrong-Whitworth's. As far as I can recall, we just didn't like the look of them and so we drew the ones on top... if they were tested at all, they were tested after the event.'

To build the full-size prototype, Enever next called on Eric Carter, his friend and ally at Morris Motors' Bodies Branch at Quinton Road in Coventry. It is important to appreciate that Pressed Steel, which would go on to play an important part in both the MGA and MGB stories, was then an entirely separate company, for whom Bodies Branch was often the client. Carter ran an experimental shop at Quinton Road, and it was here that the full-size pattern and panels of EX 175 were forged.

Speaking to journalist Doug Nye in 1979, Carter recalled Enever's visit of twenty-seven years earlier:

> Syd visited us with a sketch of a proposed style for the outside shape, plus some proposed details for a chassis. We made a start the following day with a full-size drawing, and on the third day details were issued to our experimental department in the form of tracings or slip sheets to start work on preliminary wooden formers to produce the panels. Within three months that prototype was finished, Bodies Branch being a small company with a maximum of 1,200 employees and cooperation between its various departments being first class, so no time was wasted.

Doubtless picking up on Jim O'Neill's bitter experience with the prototype TD Midget, Enever incorporated a 'goal post' into his very strong chassis frame; this was further braced to make a very strong rigid structure, which simplified Eric Carter's task of making a largely unstressed body. Enever passed the task of the detail design work to Roy Brocklehurst, who had come to Abingdon at the age of fifteen in 1947.

MG then went to fabricate the chassis – in fact they made two, the second of which would fulfil a separate purpose as the basis of the new record breaker EX 179 – of which more later. Meanwhile at Quinton Road, '...we had no trouble with mounting the body,' Carter recalled.

Jack Tatlow, still MG Managing Director at the time, called at Quinton Road to see the prototype on the eve of its despatch to Abingdon and, Carter told Doug Nye, '[Tatlow] was highly delighted'. The new metallic maroon car with beige leather interior trim was duly completed and trimmed for road use, fitted with TD 'XPAG' running gear at Abingdon (which necessitated a small bulge in the centre of the bonnet), and was eventually registered (in November 1952) with the Berkshire code 'HMO 6'.

Tatlow and his team were understandably impressed by the striking and revolutionary looks of Enever's and Carter's handiwork, glistening under the studio lights, and they planned to show it to the corporate decision makers. But unfortunately for the Abingdon team, they were just days too late: Leonard Lord had just made his highly public decision to sponsor Donald Healey's striking new sports car, and this commitment meant that, understandably, neither the BMC Chairman nor his generally compliant Board were prepared to sanction a second, totally unrelated sports car, inside a week.

JACK TATLOW

Jack Tatlow came to MG from Riley when the two operations were brought under joint production management in 1949. He was at Abingdon when both EX 172 and EX 175 were created, but had moved to another role in BMC by the time the MGA was launched.
AUTHOR'S COLLECTION

Coventry-born John (Jack) Tatlow (18 January 1902–28 May 1965) came to MG from Riley, following the corporate union of the two companies in 1949. He became MG's General Manager, taking over from George 'Pop' Propert.

Tatlow joined Rover at the tail end of World War I, but moved to Riley's Road Test Department in 1924, becoming the company's outside sales representative in 1926 and assistant sales manager two years after that. Over the following decade, he rose to become Service Manager and eventually General Manager in 1940. The reinvention of the Riley Motor Company after World War II owed a fair amount to the talents of Chief Designer Harry Rush and Jack Tatlow; Tatlow is listed in the 20 August 1948 Silverstone International as the 'entrant' of three Rileys, the same event that John Thornley had entered the MG TD Midgets of Dick Jacobs, George Phillips and Ted Lund (*see* competition Chapter 10).

When Riley production shifted to Abingdon the following year, Tatlow's job followed suit; he was appointed over Cecil Cousins. However, with the changes in the wake of the BMC merger, Tatlow swiftly moved to Morris Commercial Cars in November 1952, taking over from the incumbent, W. Gordon Graham, who was retiring. Meanwhile the vacancy that opened up at Abingdon allowed John Thornley to slip into the General Manager role, whilst in the process Tatlow's work moved closer to his home at 96 Baginton Road, Coventry – but not before he got to see and appreciate both EX 172 and EX 175 in their full-size forms. He died, aged sixty-three, in 1965.

John Thornley recollected that in November 1952:

> When he [Lord] put his foot down on the MGA prototype it was a perfectly rational thing for him to do; he had just 'bought' the Healey 100, and to his eyes, it and the EX 175 were clearly aimed at the same market, and it didn't make sense to him to have to tool two cars. It wasn't until I had pestered the life out of him, supported strongly by screams from the USA, that he saw the point.

That story is covered in the next chapter...

The birth of the 'Austin-Healey' just as MG were trying to secure support for EX 175 was a classic case of bad timing, it seems there was an early attempt at a consolation prize for Syd Enever, as recalled by Jim Cox, part of the Abingdon Development team:

> One day a bloke called Cordin brought a wagon down to Abingdon with sets of Austin-Healey 100 body panels. The lorry arrived and Syd was told to use as many panels as he could in a new MG – a sort of early 'badge engineering' exercise. Syd never looked at any of them; he just went ahead and decided to build his own car.

– but in the event, Abingdon would eventually have the last laugh, because rationalization at BMC led to Austin-Healey production being transferred to Abingdon in 1957, as Riley assembly ended at the MG works, and pressure on space at Longbridge conspired to squeeze the Healey out. But from the perspective of 1952, the situation at MG seemed far from rosy, and something else clearly had to be done, because although the TD Midget had been doing well, sales were unlikely to keep up their momentum.

In the meantime, however, another development at Cowley, in the official MG design office there (under the direction of Gerald Palmer), was an exciting and impressive concept for a new MG sports car aimed at satisfying both the contemporary American and European tastes. It would be fair to say that John Thornley – now in charge at Abingdon – and his close on-site ally Syd Enever – were alarmed at these developments (*see* box).

As part of his frequent flow of memoranda to senior management, John Thornley cleverly engaged in what was obviously a political campaign which subtly briefed against the Palmer sports car designs. In one of his memos to S.V. Smith, dated 5 January 1953, Thornley noted that:

AUSTIN-HEALEY

Leonard Lord and Donald Healey sit in the prototype 'Healey Hundred' at the 1952 Earls Court Motor Show; the deal which created the first Austin-Healey temporarily closed the door on a new aerodynamic MG.
AUTHOR'S COLLECTION

Much has been written about Leonard Lord's desire to create an Austin sports car to challenge the established rivals from MG, Morgan and Standard-Triumph. The alliance that Lord formed with Truro-born Donald Mitchell Healey (3 July 1898–15 January 1988) to transform the latter's 'Healey Hundred' into a larger volume product, the 'Austin-Healey 100', is the stuff of legend. Its arrival when Austin and Nuffield were early into their awkward marriage means that the Austin-Healey story has a bearing on the gestation of MG's replacement for the old T-Series Midget.

To start with the Healey story, the company's eponymous leader had made a name for himself as an engineer for Triumph before the war, afterwards becoming a manufacturer of low-volume and high-priced sports cars in the unusual location of Warwick; he was throughout a keen and shrewd entrepreneurial operator, and it is obvious why he and the equally sharp Leonard Lord found much in common.

At the end of the 1940s, Healey was reliant in part on a supply of Riley engines, now within the Nuffield Group. There was a meeting between Healey and R. F. Hanks in the spring of 1949, reported to the Morris Motors Board meeting of 18 May, at which Hanks reported that Healey's proposals 'would not be pursued'. There is insufficient space here to cover this fascinating story in greater detail, but suffice to say that perhaps, had matters gone a different way, there might have been a new 'Riley-Healey', although MG would doubtless have been unimpressed. Meanwhile, in November 1949, there would be a similarly abortive dialogue between Hanks and George Mason of the Nash Kelvinator Corporation who wanted a partner to design and build a small car – and so Mason, who also called in at Longbridge, concluded a separate deal with Donald Healey for the Nash-Healey sports car, which was introduced in 1951, and found a receptive audience in Leonard Lord.

Healey soon found out that Austin were supposedly keen to sponsor a sporting car that would use Austin components. Several small manufacturers, including Jensen and Lea Francis, were motivated to experiment with the idea and to build prototypes of their

A new series of small MGs has been designed by Mr Palmer. From the fact that these are at the present moment not beyond the drawing-board and rough mock-up stage, one

Gerald Palmer is generally credited with the clever sports-car concept that could have been made with alternative body styles, but his proposal was not the first. Denis Williams photographed this scale model at Cowley; Palmer told the author that it was not his work, and it is understood that it dates from before his arrival in 1949.
DENIS WILLIAMS

own, but there is little evidence to suggest that there was ever anything more than the rumour of Austin's interest – a rumour that Lord may well have been happy to foster.

Meanwhile, the future of the Riley engine, forged in the marque's heady pre-war, pre-bankruptcy days, was uncertain because the Nuffield Organisation was developing new power units which seemed likely to lead to the end of the Riley unit. Whilst Healey was understandably wary of upsetting Nuffield as engine supplier, after his rebuff from Hanks he made contact with Austin and arranged to get hold of an Austin A90 drive-train. In order to keep the project under wraps, Donald Healey masterminded the design work on his A90-engined sports car at home, rather than doing it at the factory. A deal between Austin and Healey for the supply of key components for the new Healey sports car was signed on 27 November 1951 – a little over eighteen months after the Reggie Hanks rebuff, and almost a year before the end result of Healey's endeavours would first be seen in public at Earls Court.

Around the same time that what would become the 'Healey Hundred' was being designed in the attic at the Healey household, over at Jensen there were also thoughts about creating a small Austin-based sports car. Jensen was, at the time, building the quite pretty but lacklustre Austin A40 Sports around the A40 Devon/Dorset saloon's 1,200 cc engine and drive-train, as well as the larger four-litre Jensen Interceptor (also with an Austin engine). Jensen was clearly keen to expand their relationship with Len Lord and so they worked on a prototype two-seat open tourer which was supposedly due to be shown to the public at the same 1952 Earls Court Motor Show as Donald Healey showed his 'Hundred'.

Jensen's car was not completed in time and the sole prototype became another one of those might-have-been dead ends. In later years, the car received a BMC B-Series engine and, following a crash, the front end was rebuilt with cut-down MG panels which gave it a vague resemblance to the MGA from some angles, which has occasionally prompted inaccurate speculation that it was some kind of 'missing link' in the MGA story. Also looking at the potential of an Austin powertrain was Frazer-Nash, who created a prototype sports car with the A90 engine that appeared at Earls Court in 1952 but, like the Jensen, went no further.

The 'Healey Hundred' duly appeared at the 1952 Earls Court Motor Show, and Leonard Lord and Donald Healey generated great fanfare and publicity in signing a deal that would lead to the sports car being rebranded as the 'Austin-Healey 100', and built in larger numbers at Longbridge. At the same time, Nash announced that they had finally selected Austin and its Fisher & Ludlow subsidiary to develop and build their 'Metropolitan' small car for US sales. Lord Nuffield was certainly there at the show, as no doubt was R. F. Hanks; one can easily imagine their private thoughts about those Nash and Healey deals, having met and rejected the relevant earlier overtures, and one can equally imagine the delight that Leonard Lord would no doubt have felt in having outflanked them. This may have been just another of several contemporaneous events which helped Lord Nuffield decide to resign as BMC Chairman on 17 December 1952.

In the end, MG and Abingdon would effectively have the last laugh, as responsibility for Austin-Healey production was transferred from Longbridge to Abingdon in November 1957. The marque itself lived on until 1970.

> would be entitled to draw the conclusion that they could not be in production before September 1954. A statement has been made, however, that they could be ready by March 1954.

Earlier in the same memo Thornley had suggested caution before abandoning the tried-and-tested XPAG engine in favour of the new B-Series in the crucial US market, an idea which evidently hit home with the short-term replacement for the TD Midget, as we will see below. Meanwhile, however, Thornley continued his warning about the Palmer sports cars:

> Undoubtedly these motor cars, or something like them, provide a very suitable long-term development from the TD, but bearing in mind what was said about the need for sending to the USA only well-tried designs, we must be extremely careful not to place ourselves in the position where we are utterly dependent for a continuation of the market upon the premature introduction of an untried motor car. Without wishing to be unkind, one must, based on one's recollections of the introduction of the 4/44 Wolseley, express grave doubts as to whether (a) this new motor-car could be ready by March 1954, and (b) if it were, whether it would be, from its inception, a thoroughly reliable and satisfactory vehicle – one must bear in mind that the design is to a very large extent unorthodox, and is a complete departure in many respects from existing small MG practice.
>
> If credence is given to the suggestion that this car could be ready in March 1954, it might well be decided that the existing TD, or the existing TD with the 1½ litre engine in it, could run on until that date. If then the new model proved to need more extended development, we should be forced into a position where either we were sending an unsatisfactory vehicle for sale in the USA, or we were leaving a big gap in the continuity of our supplies to that market, either of which would be disastrous.

We will see in the next section what Thornley offered as the short-term answer to the dilemma he described.

THE MIDGETS OF GERALD PALMER

This lovely contemporary colour photo from the BMIHT archives shows the Gerald Palmer 'MG Magna' with the folding windscreen lowered and stowed in the racing position.
© BRITISH MOTOR INDUSTRY HERITAGE TRUST

Gerald Palmer had never forgotten his proud creation, the one-off Deroy sports car, and with MG under his control from 1949, he briefly turned his focus to the creation of a new sports car to replace the old Midget line. Using the monocoque principle, and encouraged by his counterparts at Nuffield Metal Products (NMP), Palmer cleverly conceived a 'three-in-one' design which could have covered the divergent tastes of European and American customers. The first variant could have come in two separate subsidiary variants, with a fairly traditional MG Midget style with either swept back or cycle-type wings (the latter aimed at 'traditional' motor-sports activities). The alternative style was a more modern full-width body style.

The designer recalled:

I wanted to do an all-steel monocoque two-seater sports car. I had to get Vic Oak's agreement to start off development of the twin cam engine, although he was on the point of retirement, and it was really as a corollary of that that I did the monocoque sports car... I had much encouragement by getting the drafting of the monocoque done at NMP [Nuffield Metal Products] – their director George Dono was very supportive.

A full-size wooden model of Gerald Palmer's 'DO1049' proposal for a new MG Midget, with monocoque body and 'traditional style' wings.
AUTHOR'S COLLECTION

Gerald Palmer authored this beguiling monocoque sports car, with styling that could have swept-back separate wings in 'traditional' style. This is the running prototype (note the door handles missing from the wooden model).
AUTHOR'S COLLECTION

The first reference in the Morris Motors Board meeting to the idea of a new MG Midget from the creative mind of Gerald Palmer came on 21 June 1950; work on the proposal continued at Cowley and lasted at least three years. Created under the guise of the Cowley Design Office, Palmer's new creations were given the 'Design Order' (not 'Drawing Office') codes of 'DO 1048' for the streamlined car, dubbed the 'Magna', and 'DO 1049' for the more traditional-looking variant, referred to as 'New MG Midget for 1954'.

Palmer thought that his two-line (or more accurately perhaps 'two and a half' variant) approach was justified: 'Whereas the American market appeared to show a preference for the "traditional" styling, exemplified by the T-Series Midget, the European market would prefer a more modern style resembling the best of the Italian efforts, such as the Alfa Romeo.' In fairness Palmer was not the first person at Cowley to think of this, as evidenced by photographs taken by Denis Williams of a model that was in existence at Cowley prior to Palmer's 1949 return.

At least two prototypes to Palmer's design were built, one of which (representing the 'traditional Midget' style) was a runner (complete with early B-Series engine), together with a hardtop (at Palmer's particular insistence), and it was planned that if the car had gone into production, the bodies would have been built at Nuffield Metal Products at Birmingham, with final assembly at Abingdon.

It is worth noting that whilst Abingdon saw the MG TF Midget as 'EX 177', in Cowley parlance the TD facelift was initially referred to as 'DO1047' (although it was later known as 'DO1060') – in other words, the number immediately preceding those for

Palmer's new proposals. By this time, of course, Abingdon's own prototype, EX 175, was similarly also in existence (but, tellingly, had no DO number), and it was no surprise that Thornley and Enever had invested much personal energy in their own creation.

The windscreen of Palmer's MG Midget was designed to be of a folding type, not unlike that of the Austin-Healey 100/4 – although Palmer told the author that he was unaware of the Healey's windscreen arrangements when he thought of the idea for his MG.
AUTHOR'S COLLECTION

The Palmer Midgets were much admired within some quarters, even somewhat grudgingly at Abingdon; Jim O'Neill (then still at Cowley) and Roy Brocklehurst both felt it could have offered a life-line to MG had Syd Enever's EX 175 not offered a compelling home-brewed Abingdon alternative. O'Neill told the author: 'I do know that Abingdon were not at all impressed. Why, I will never know, because at the time I was absolutely sure that they were winners. Many years later, when I was working with Syd Enever, I asked him why Abingdon had rejected Palmer's Midget. He had no answer.'

Clues to why it failed to make the transition to production are not too hard to find. Apart from the inevitable 'not invented here' stigma of DO 1048/9, which Palmer said weighed as little as 1,350lb (612kg), was the fact that the idea of using monocoque construction was a very modern and expensive concept for a small British open sports car, and both Thornley and Enever firmly believed – at that time, at least – that a proper sports car still needed a separate chassis, like EX 175.

Even so, the project was costed up with the help of George Dono of 'NMP', and approved in principle by the Morris Motors Board on 11 June 1953 as 'Project 44 – The MG Car Company Limited – New Streamlined Midget (DO 1049)' with an estimated tooling requirement of £250,000. By this stage DO1048 and D1049 had become one. However, 'Mr Dono stated that this estimate of tooling cost had perforce to be regarded as entirely provisional.' This sum was greater than that for the Abingdon car (see later), but it is noteworthy that it was not far short of the £350,000 body tooling budget agreed in November 1951 for Palmer's monocoque MG Z Magnette and Wolseley 4/44.

Added to this major budget requirement was the vexed question of how and, equally importantly, where it would have been built; the MG factory was still immersed in the tradition of coach-built cars of the 1930s, with steel bodies over ash frames, and chassis frames made up in a section of the factory using brought-in components. Thornley and his colleagues had only just won the battle to keep MG at Abingdon, and so they would have been nervous at embracing a very different kind of motor car, which might also have been viewed corporately as being better suited to assembly at Cowley. The arrival at Abingdon at the end of 1953 of the Magnette – replacing the old-fashioned Y-Type – would eventually help allay these fears, but for Thornley and Enever, the sports cars were always at the heart of MG's soul and they wanted to be as much in control of their own destiny as possible.

The final piece of the jigsaw was the situation in which Palmer found himself at this time: the sports car ideas, whilst dear to his own heart, were not the most important part of his portfolio, and at the same time as his Magna was being built, there was a battle royal ensuing between the factions at Cowley and Longbridge, with Leonard Lord generally having the upper hand, such that Palmer, from the Nuffield part of the BMC family, regularly found his efforts and position undermined. Although Palmer was appointed as a 'Local Director' of the BMC Board in January 1954, he would not find the position a comfortable one.

When Palmer fell out with Lord over the Riley Pathfinder and Wolseley 6/90, he soon departed from BMC and so his sports-car ideas were largely confined to the dustbin of history, with the honourable exception of his idea for a more sporting engine (see Chapter Six).

Palmer cleverly contemplated the alternative of DO1048, known as the 'MG Magna', with a more modern body shape with smooth 'European' styling on the same basic body structure as DO1049.
AUTHOR'S COLLECTION

THE LAST T-SERIES MIDGET: EX 177 – THE MG TF

The MG TD had proved to be a noble replacement for the essentially pre-war TC: many decried its dumpier looks and lack of spindly wire wheels, but it was mechanically more modern where it needed to be, and was considered generally superior in many ways. However, the changes under way at that time in the automotive world – not just at home and the Commonwealth markets, but in Europe and North America too – meant that the appeal of the 'old-fashioned perpendicular' sports car was on the wane, other than perhaps in the eyes of the die-hard traditionalists for whom any change was anathema.

Whilst the TD had introduced such niceties as left-hand-drive and adopted the suspension improvements heralded by the MG Y-Type family, the TD was still essentially a narrow-gutted roadster with the aerodynamic performance of a house brick. The emergence of striking modern rivals from the likes of Triumph and, cruelly closer to home, from Austin, would only reinforce the old-fashioned image.

Modern cars were also getting faster and more comfortable, and whilst the appeal of the traditional MG sports car had seldom been centred on top speed, it was expected by most people that 'sporting' equated in some way to 'fast' – and, after all, the famous MG motto was supposedly 'Safety Fast'! Thornley and Enever were concerned, accordingly, that whilst TD sales had hitherto held up well, they were on a plateau and likely to be headed downwards.

With hopes for EX 175 scuppered – for the time being – the MG team looked at what they could do to 'improve' the TD on a modest budget, without departing too far from its classic nature. At the back of Thornley's mind would have been finding a way to bridge the gap between the old and the new – echoing the thinking behind Gerald Palmer's 'Midget/Magna' concept. As a consequence of this, EX 177 was born – in effect a mildly restyled TD Midget that was mocked up more or less on an experimental basis at Abingdon, and then taken to Cowley for formal adoption and production development (as 'DO 1060').

Thornley wrote about the situation in his memo to management on 5 January 1953 as follows:

> The sensible answer to these potential problems would appear to be to introduce the re-designed TD – the blue MG which has been tentatively called the TF – in September 1954, or even earlier if possible, and allow it to run on for at least a twelve-month, or perhaps even eighteen months, during which time Mr Palmer's new motor cars can be fully developed and tried, and all the bugs taken out of them.

In another memo, Thornley added that 'an attempt has been made to improve the shape of the TD without destroying its essentially characteristic appearance, and the blue car which is to be submitted for scrutiny by the joint Boards on the 8 January is an example.'

The MG TF Midget involved a new nose, with more swept-out wings and raked-back radiator grille. Inside the cockpit there was a somewhat baroque facia design, presumably a Cowley idea.

Whilst Thornley again acknowledged Gerald Palmer's sports-car designs – albeit slightly dismissively as 'ideas for

An MG TF Midget at the Abingdon factory (possibly the prototype), showing the markedly inferior engine compartment access compared to its predecessors. Having said that, the MGA would hardly be noted for the ease of access to its engine bay.

AUTHOR'S COLLECTION

The MG TF prototype, probably at Cowley. Note the Cadillac in the background; this car had been imported by Morris Motors for assessment.

AUTHOR'S COLLECTION

the future' – he also cannily brought in a fresh reference to EX 175, which he described as being 'tentatively called the Series UA'. On 12 February 1953, the Morris Motors Board duly reviewed the EX 177 project proposal and gave it the nod, formally authorizing the necessary tooling budget of £27,000.

Alongside the debate about body styling, Thornley argued that the 1,250cc XPAG was at the limit of performance development for road-going use, and hinted at ongoing testing of an enlarged 1.5-litre version, which would in due course become the 'XPEG' 1,466cc unit for the later 'TF 1500'. At the time, the B-Series engine as eventual successor to the old Nuffield units of similar capacity was seen as inevitable, but Thornley gallantly went to the defence of the XPAG, suggesting, in the context of the new unit, that 'if there is any doubt about it by the date of its due introduction – that is, September 1953 – then it would be preferable to consider the continuation of the XPAG engine for a few months...or provide the increased power [with] an over-bored version of the XPAG...'

The surviving parts of the DO Register record an experiment number DO 1041, 'TD Midget with Austin engine', as well as DO 1042, which is described as 'Midget with 1½-litre Riley engine' – so one way or another, it seemed it was considered that the TD Midget – or a successor – should see a change of powertrain of some kind. The fact that in the wake of the BMC merger it had been decided that the new DO 1010 Magnette, due in September 1953, would have the

THE B-SERIES ENGINE

MGA engines were finished in red; they were supplied from BMC's Longbridge engine plant. The car is an early MGA, HDD23-10452, owned by Jill and Graham Eke (*see also* Chapter 4).
BEAULIEU

Even before the BMC merger, Austin at Longbridge had been working on a new family of engines, including an 803cc unit (which became the A-Series) and a 1,250cc one (which spawned the B-Series). Design, logically enough, was by Austin Engines at Longbridge, under Johnny Rix and Eric Bareham. The debut of this Austin-designed engine in the Z-Series Magnette – the first 'Nuffield'-branded car to use the unit, by now in 1,498cc guise – was viewed with hardly any enthusiasm by the good folk at Abingdon.

The B-Series was widely felt to have been derived indirectly from pre-war Bedford design philosophy (Austin had already copied a Bedford truck engine); it was also viewed as a less than sporting unit, with its inlet and exhaust all lumped on one side. However, it was subjected to an impressive degree of testing during development, with eight extensive development trips through France and into Spain, including climbing the Algeciras mountains. The B-Series may not have been greatly admired at its introduction, but it would prove to be a tough engine, a reputation that served it well throughout the life of the MGA and MGB.

The fact that it did not hail from MG's old friends at Morris Engines, but came from 'the other lot', did not help its arrival at Abingdon. Jim Cox, who was part of the in-house MG engine team, remembers the change from the Nuffield to the Austin engine very well:

> *The XPEG engine was really at its limits, and so we decided to look at the Austin engine. We put a full-flow filter on it – for which we drilled through the block – and we developed the camshaft for more lift. Then we worked with Harry Weslake on the combustion chambers, and before long we found ourselves working on what would become the 'Le Mans' engine specification for EX 182.*

The definitive B-Series would go on to power a whole range of cars: firstly, as we shall see, the MG Z Magnette in late 1953, and a year later the Nash Metropolitan Series II, the Austin A40 and A50 Cambridge and Morris Oxford and Cowley in 1954, followed by the re-engined Palmer Wolseley 15/50 in 1956, the Wolseley 1500/Riley One-Point-Five in 1957, the Austin A55 and Morris Oxford Series V, MG Magnette Mk III, Wolseley 15/60 and Riley 4/68 in 1958/9 (and their later revisions), a number of commercial vehicles and third-party sales, and not forgetting, of course, the MGA and, in due course, its successor the MGB.

new corporate unit meant that the choice for the sports car seemed almost a foregone conclusion.

John Thornley was determined to keep the flame alive for Enever's EX 175 despite its evident rejection by the BMC Joint Board. Writing in January 1953, Thornley suggested a low-volume route for production, with a competition bias:

> There arises from the USA a demand for what, for want of a better term, may be styled a competition vehicle. There undoubtedly exists a very fruitful market between those of the TD and XK120 Jaguar. To fill this market the fully streamlined car that has been tentatively called the Series UA, is submitted.
>
> Produced in limited quantities, its price need be of no great concern, and if produced at or about the time of the Series TF would not lead the market to believe that it represented the ultimate shape of the quantity-produced MGs of the future. It would, however, have wide acceptance for competitive purposes, in the course of which it would undoubtedly acquit itself well, and would, in addition, have a wider appeal to those who require a really fast British car for use in long-distance travel.

In those cleverly framed thoughts, Thornley not only offered a way back for EX 175, but sowed the seeds for what eventually became EX 182, the competition cars that heralded the arrival of the MGA. By the time of the March 1953 Geneva Salon, Thornley's terminology for the TF's eventual successor had evolved from the 'Series UA' of January 1953 to one of the first recorded references to an 'MGA'.

ABOVE LEFT: **From the press launch of the MG TF Midget on 16 October 1953, this photo shows the stylized dashboard and yet retention of the 'classic' double cowl shape at the top of the facia.**
AUTHOR'S COLLECTION

LEFT: **This composite of three side elevations shows the transition from EX 175 (at top – taken from a drawing 'EX 175/1' by Denis Drury, dated 20 February 1952) via EX 182 (centre – taken from a drawing 'A7033R', dated 15 April 1955, by Denis Williams) and finally, at the bottom, the DO 1062/MGA (this elevation is of an MGA 1600, but the original drawing from which it was adapted was for an MGA 1500, drawing 'A7032R', dated 2 May 1955, again by Denis Williams). The stories of EX 182, DO 1062 and moreover the MGA 1600 are told in the following chapters.**
IMAGES VIA BOB VITRIKAS

In his post show report for S. V. Smith (dated 16 March 1953) on his findings, Thornley reported:

> The MG TD: no very great business is currently being done with this model. One is forced to the conclusion that in its present form it has more or less outworn its welcome, and is due for a change. It is questionable, too, whether the TF will give very much of a fillip to the market here, as the sporting fraternity who are the main buyers of the TD in Switzerland want more power and more performance than the TF is likely to offer. On the other hand, the MGA type is, in my view, likely to have a big future.

We shall see how that situation evolved in Chapter 3.

In the event, Thornley – the man in Abingdon's hot seat since the end of the previous year – eventually got more or less what he wanted: he got to drive the prototype of the MG TF on 12 May 1953, and everything proceeded towards a launch at the October 1953 Earls Court Motor Show, alongside the MG Z-Series Magnette. The export-focused sports car retained the tried-and-tested Nuffield power plant, whilst the sleek new Palmer-designed four-door had the new B-Series unit. It was an odd contrast on the same motor-show stand, and drew many quizzical comments.

Perhaps of even greater significance at the 1953 Earls Court show was that just across the hall, Standard-Triumph had on display a production version of their Triumph TR2 sports car, a special version of which had reached a speed of 124.889mph (200.946km/h) at the Jabbeke Highway in Belgium in May 1953. Thus the gauntlet had been thrown down by Standard's Sir John Black, and Leonard Lord was not one to lightly back away from such challenges.

In due course the TF would get the bigger engine that had been hinted at, but it would still be derived from the old Nuffield powertrain family rather than the new Austin one. Anyone who wanted to see an MG to rival the Austin-Healey 100/4 and Triumph TR2 would have to await something very different to the old T-Series...

THE NEW, AIR-SMOOTHED 1½-LITRE MG MAGNETTE

The MG Z Magnette was a radical departure for MG, and marked several firsts for the marque, including its 'BMC' powertrain and chassis-less construction. This is a studio mock-up of 'DO 1010'.
AUTHOR'S COLLECTION

Before the BMC merger, the Morris Motors Board had, following much prior deliberation, considered – on 15 August 1951 and again on 14 November 1951 – an MG Magnette for the 1952 Motor Show, and a Wolseley for March 1953, both with the old XPAG/XPAW engine; however, the coming together of Austin and Nuffield threw this out of sequence such that the Wolseley 4/44 took the 1952 Earls Court slot (with the old Nuffield engine) and the Magnette came a year after, but with the new powertrain.

Thus the first material effect of Gerald Palmer's tenure at Cowley was the launch at the 1952 Earls Court Motor Show of the Wolseley 4/44, with its 1,250cc Wolseley engine (the 'XPAW' equivalent of the MG 'XPAG') in an elegantly styled, all-new monocoque four-door saloon. Palmer's first all-new MG, the Z Magnette, saw broadly the same structure allied to the new 1,498cc B-Series engine, used for the first time in any of the newly merged BMC's marques.

The arrival of the new saloon was welcomed at Abingdon: it replaced the old-fashioned YB Saloon on the production lines, and as a brand new design, with the first use in the Corporation of the new powertrain, meant there had been investment in the factory by the new management. The Z Magnette was also generally well received by the press and the public, even if, almost inevitably, there were a few letters from irate traditionalists in some of the enthusiast publications, bemoaning the fact that the name of the new BMC model was shared with that of the great K3 which had won its class in the 1933 Mille Miglia.

During its time in production, the Z Magnette evolved into the improved ZB and Varitone (so in retrospect the original model became the ZA), and there were thoughts of different trim, bodystyles and even powertrain; in the meantime, when the MGA joined it in the factory, and with the growth of motor-sports activities, the position of Abingdon seemed to be in the ascendant as the BMC's sporting centre of excellence.

CHAPTER THREE

CALL IT MGA

In the midst of all the machinations about new sports cars came fresh activity on the record-breaking front. Goldie Gardner, who had run EX 135 with distinction for many years, had to retire from active record breaking, and the car became in effect a museum piece. Its roots were clearly in the original pre-war offset chassis derived from the increasingly ancient MG K3, and if MG was to continue to uphold record-breaking honours, it was clear that a new vehicle would be needed.

RETURN TO RECORD BREAKING: EX 179

By this time, George Eyston, an old friend of MG who had been involved in the marque's earliest record-breaking endeavours back in the Kimber days, had come back on the scene and serendipitously had a lot of business in the USA through his directorship of Castrol. Eyston approached the Nuffield management and convinced them that a fresh record-breaking attempt should be made, with an eye to lifting sales of the TF in the USA and no doubt aiding the cause of those at Abingdon who wished to see their EX 175 proposal yield fruit.

EX 179 posed at Abingdon in 1956. The colour scheme was metallic green over brown. The powertrain was now an experimental twin overhead camshaft 'B' series engine – the old XPAG having been confined to history.
ENEVER FAMILY

The MG team at Abingdon behind EX 179 in 1954. The chassis was basically the same as that of EX 175 – the effective prototype for the later 'DO 1062' MGA. They are, left to right, Harold Wiggins, Terry Mitchell (who designed the chassis), Syd Enever, Alec Hounslow, Harry Riddell, Cliff Bray, Henry Stone and, last but not least, John Law from the Experimental Department of Morris Engines at Coventry.
ENEVER FAMILY

The first move was for EX 175 to be fitted with fared-in wheel spats and a Perspex bubble-type cockpit cover, in which guise it was submitted in early 1954 for wind-tunnel testing. Tests soon showed, however, that it was not the suitable basis of a true record-breaker, and so it was agreed to clothe the second spare EX 175 chassis with an all-new body. The chassis was lightened in the traditional way, MG Development's Henry Stone and Harold Wiggins laboriously drilling hundreds of strategically positioned holes.

Terry Mitchell explained the rationale behind EX 179 in 1997: 'Syd had said he wanted it to be "the same as EX 135, but different" – about one inch thicker at the scuttle.'

The bodywork was made by Midland Sheet Metal using traditional wheel- and hand-forming techniques.

For 1957, EX 179 was fitted with a BMC 'A' Series engine and was re-liveried in cream and metallic brown, badged as a 'BMC Experimental Vehicle' (early PR ideas to call it a 'Morris Minor' were swiftly dropped; the Austin-Healey Sprite was still months from launch).
ENEVER FAMILY

In August 1959, David Ash towed EX 179 (now EX 219) to Bonneville behind his Ford Station Wagon, posed here in front of the local publicity billboard, together with an MGA roadster.
DAVID ASH

In its final outing in 1959, the by now 'veteran' EX 179 record breaker was given a new name – EX 219 – and a silver-blue 'Austin-Healey' identity and livery.
DAVID ASH

Under its long sleek nose, EX 179 used a larger-bored (72mm instead of 66.5mm) 1,466cc version of the XPAG engine, which had been developed by Morris Motors and denoted by them as the 'XPEG'. With the recent BMC merger, this engine had been made virtually redundant, and it doesn't appear to have been given serious consideration for any of the abortive MG exercises covered earlier. EX 179 achieved nearly 154mph at the Utah salt flats in the hands of George Eyston and Ken Miles in August 1954; in the meantime, BMC had agreed to sanction a production version of the XPEG engine for an improved version of the TF, which slipped quietly into production in July 1954 as the 'TF 1500' (the 'Midget' name having been dropped), gradually displacing the TF 1250, which continued in production until September. The new TF 1500 was known officially at Cowley as 'DO 1060'.

SALES IN DECLINE: THE END OF THE T-SERIES

The MG TF helped stem the fall in sales of the MG sports cars to a degree, but it was increasingly obvious that the old style had had its day – the modernity of the MG Magnette alongside the 'traditional' TF only served to emphasize the fact. The enlarged engine of the TF 1500, in the wake of EX 179, helped stem the tide to a small extent, but as the BMC merger took hold, the XPEG unit was part of a Nuffield line destined for oblivion.

In a letter to Syd Enever dated 12 October 1954, British ex-pat Ken Miles wrote '…we have had the 1500cc TF road-tested by all the magazines ready for the December issues, and the reports are most encouraging.'

History has been kind to the MG TF; it is frequently thought of as one of the prettiest T-Series MG models (facia excepted, perhaps), but when it arrived in 1953 it was regarded with disdain by many sports-car enthusiasts. It was clearly a reflection of MG's past glory rather than a step towards a future already hinted at by the EX172 seen in Chapter 2.
AUTHOR'S COLLECTION

Not only was there a road test of the TF 1500 and the ZA Magnette in *Road & Track*'s December 1954 issue, the cover featured both cars. Miles concluded that '…my own reaction to the car is that if we had had this engine when we first had the TF we would never have lost our position as the best selling sports car in the US. The increase in low speed torque is nothing short of fantastic, considering the small increase in engine size.' All this was positive, but it was nowhere near enough.

The fanfare associated with EX 179 was arguably a bit late to maximize publicity benefits, perhaps helping lift sales of the last of the traditional Midgets; but even so, only 3,400 examples of the TF 1500 were built before something far more radical took its place.

The transition from the TF to its replacement was not a smooth one, and this caused a great deal of trouble for the overseas distributors and dealer. Jon Pressnell spent some time looking through the extensive correspondence records left behind by John Dugdale, the English-born member of the sales and marketing team in New York. Dugdale, perhaps better known as a 'Jaguar' man, had worked at *Autocar* and in the post-war world was respected in New York as a link to the local representatives of Britain's Society of Motor Manufacturers and Traders ('SMMT'). As such, he was often the funnel for dealer disquiet.

Whilst the total number of TFs built may seem modest, as Pressnell pointed out in an article for *Enjoying MG*, whilst the TD total build was higher (at 29,664), that car was in production longer; more informative is the fact that the average build rate of the TD works out at 645 per month, and the TF was 480. The problem for MG dealers was that the end of production of the TF came in April 1955, and yet the car supposedly destined to replace it in June had slipped, as we shall see, to October. This meant that the MG sports-car supply line would be running dry just as the summer months were in full swing.

In a letter of 22 April 1955 to the SMMT's man in Washington, Donald Morren, Andy Regalia, general manager of Kjell Qvale's British Motor Car Distributors ('BMCD') of San Francisco, refers to the situation with obvious frustration.

> We were told that production had been set up on the new car to give us stocks in this country for an announcement of immediate delivery of the new MG by the middle of June. It has now leaked out and been confirmed that there has been a foul-up, although how this could be possible we do not know, and that the first cars will probably reach this country in a trickle only in October.

In fact BMCD were not alone: J. S. Inskip, the major East Coast distributor, had already cabled BMC boss Sir Leonard Lord, pointing out that he would be losing a large amount of business and also a lot of dealers in connection with 'this

LEONARD LORD AND GEORGE HARRIMAN

Leonard Lord, a complex personality and captain of industry, who eventually saw the need for a new MG sports car and duly authorized the creation of the MGA.
AUTHOR'S COLLECTION

LEONARD LORD

Leonard Percy Lord (15 November 1896–13 September 1967) was born in Coventry and after attending Bablake School, secured employment as a 'jig draughtsman' at Courtaulds in August 1913. From 1915 to 1918 he pursued an apprenticeship at Coventry Ordnance, and in 1920 became Chief Engineer of Holbrook & Sons in London, a firm that made machine tools. His next move was to Hotchkiss in April 1922, a year before the company was bought by William Morris. Lord then took responsibility for purchasing and commissioning updated mass-production equipment; he was moved to the Wolseley factory after its acquisition by Morris in 1927. Within another five years, Lord was General Manager, and soon after became Managing Director of Morris Motors Ltd, answerable only to Lord Nuffield.

There have been many theories expounded as to why Leonard Lord parted company with Lord Nuffield, including the most popular that they fell out over money or business control. Historian and former Morris Commercial Apprentice Peter Seymour is of the opinion that much of the cause lay in an alleged indiscretion at Cowley, when it was said that Lord Nuffield came into the office and chanced upon Len Lord and a young lady *in flagrante delicto*. Lord and Lady Nuffield held firm views on sexual morals – verging on the prudish – and in such circumstances it may have been that Len Lord had to go, in August 1936.

But as Lord was given a generous parting gift of £50,000 by Nuffield, and appointed to oversee a £2M 'Special Areas' Nuffield Trust in January 1937 (which he continued to manage for eleven months thereafter), their parting could not have been completely acrimonious.

Admittedly relations may have soured a little further when Len Lord moved to Longbridge, going there because Neville Chamberlain's Secretary of State for Air, Viscount Swinton, persuaded Lord Austin to employ him – and to add insult to injury, Swinton and Nuffield were already not on the best of terms.

After the war, Austin was quick to restart civilian car production, and was in a good position to launch new models such as the Austin A40, which was designed with export in mind. Overtures to Nuffield began in 1948 and were rekindled in 1951, culminating in the BMC merger. Famous for his mercurial temperament and frequent short temper, 'Len' Lord was also said to be capable of striking kindness and generosity. He was fond of promoting rival projects within BMC, typically setting Longbridge against Cowley – often wastefully – to see which would come out on top. In a similar manner, occasionally he would try to set Donald Healey's team against Syd Enever's, but in due course those two gained sufficient mutual respect to avoid being caught out by this.

In 1954 Lord was awarded a KBE; eight years later, on 26 March 1962, he was raised to the peerage as 'Baron Lambury, of Northfield in the County of Warwick'. By that stage, he had handed over his formal role at BMC to his protégée George Harriman (see below); his letter of resignation dated 2 November 1961 is on file in the Morris Motors papers, states simply 'Gentlemen – I write formally to resign my position as Director of your company. Such resignation to take effect on the 7th November, 1961.' Lord still took a strong paternal interest in the company and contributed to the dialogue behind the eventual BMH-Leyland merger; but his health was declining, and he died in September 1967.

GEORGE HARRIMAN

George William Harriman (3 March 1908–29 May 1973) began his career at the Hotchkiss et Cie Works of Morris Engines Ltd in Coventry in 1923 and became a trusted associate of Leonard Lord, following him to Austin (initially as Machine Shop Superintendent at Longbridge in 1940 – responsible for engine output).

By the end of the war 'Young George' (his father, employed at Morris Engines, was 'Old George') had risen to become General Works Manager. He gained an OBE in 1943, and was

Sir Leonard Lord's deputy was George Harriman; it was Harriman who took over from his mentor in 1961 and presided over the uncomfortable merger with Leyland seven years later.
AUTHOR'S COLLECTION

continued overleaf

LEONARD LORD AND GEORGE HARRIMAN *continued*

awarded the CBE in 1951. A year later, upon the BMC merger, Harriman became Lord's deputy; in September 1956 he became Deputy Chairman and Joint Managing Director of The British Motor Corporation, Ltd, and eventually succeeded his boss on 21 November 1961 as 'Chairman and Managing Director of the British Motor Corporation' when Lord – by then Lord Lambury – retired.

In a statement issued at that time it was suggested that Harriman had been 'reared in the Leonard Lord tradition'; it also said that:

> *Mr Harriman has not always too much patience with people who need to look things up. On tours of the works he gives subordinates the frightening impression of knowing everything about every piece of equipment there. At press conferences he can reel off lists of statistics in answer to spontaneous questions. He knows exactly what is what at BMC. The problems facing Mr Harriman in the future will nevertheless be far more complex even than the assembly lines here, but he has been groomed to deal with them.*

The statement concluded that he was 'an optimist about the expanding world market for cars'.

One of Harriman's known peccadilloes was his lack of faith in any form of market research – a principle he shared with Alec Issigonis.

Harriman was knighted in 1965. He was at the head of British Motor Holdings (effectively a union between BMC, Pressed Steel and Jaguar) when the fumbled merger with Leyland took place three years later. He resigned on 31 October 1968. In his latter years he suffered continuing ill health, and died less than five years later.

unfortunate affair'. It seems that he had also written direct to Reggie Hanks, suggesting that TF production be extended – but Hanks had written back stating that '...it would be impossible to set up production for 2,000 units as the jigs have already been dismantled, and the dealers should sell the world-famous Morris Minor and the MG Magnette sedan until the new model comes out.'

Of course this was cold comfort as neither the Minor nor the Magnette were what US dealers or their customers wanted – but as we have seen earlier, Hanks had always been frustrated that the cars he saw as core Nuffield products were so poorly received Stateside.

The story of the MGA's arrival is covered later; for now, we need to briefly turn the clock back to the period in 1953/54 when the new model came to fruition.

BACK TO ABINGDON: THE NEW DESIGN OFFICE

Jim O'Neill was one of the small team based at Cowley who transferred to Abingdon in 1954, and so he saw the creation of a new design function from outside. The previous year Gerald Palmer had taken over most of the car side at Cowley as Vic Oak headed towards retirement. According to O'Neill, this meant that the separate offices that he and his colleagues had at Cowley were demolished, and they went back into the main office.

Chief draughtsman Les Hall told O'Neill that he would henceforth be working under Ron French, but O'Neill wasn't prepared to work under those conditions: 'We'd been carrying on outside with Palmer doing MG stuff, and that was the way I wanted to continue. He said that wasn't on, so I planned to leave.'

However, Palmer immediately affirmed that the situation should go on as it had before, and that O'Neill would take charge of the body side of MG.

In the meantime, John Thornley and Syd Enever were pushing for greater design autonomy for MG, and for a proper design office to be established at Abingdon. As we shall see, this important step would prove crucial to the creation of the MGA. At this time, O'Neill was unaware of MG's plans:

> I think the move to Abingdon was helped by the decision that all BMC design would eventually go to Longbridge. I thought that although we were doing the design for MG at Cowley at that stage, that work seemed likely to go, and so I thought, why not take it to Abingdon instead? I had a word with Syd [Enever], and he said that they were in the process of trying to set something up. In fact Terry Mitchell had already gone over to Abingdon a few weeks earlier to do the record car – EX 179 – and had then come back again.

And so it was that Syd Enever's design department absorbed part of the old Cowley equivalent: 'I just transferred straight from Cowley to Abingdon, as did Denis Williams and Terry Mitchell,' said O'Neill.

THE DESIGN TEAM: NEW RECRUITS AND ALLIES

TERENCE MITCHELL

Terry Mitchell was highly regarded in his role as Chassis Engineer; by the time of this 1960s photo his title was 'Chief Chassis Designer', reporting direct to Syd Enever.
AUTHOR'S COLLECTION

Terence Henry ('Terry') Mitchell (9 September 1921–22 October 2003) joined the MG and Riley drawing office at Cowley in June 1950.

Inventive and always restless, Mitchell was seldom content unless he was tinkering with something mechanical and preferably new. During his career he built no fewer than ten remarkable specials. A keen proponent of De Dion rear suspension, several experimental MGs featured this hallmark of Mitchell thinking.

Mitchell went over to Abingdon in June 1954; he was one of the first to go there, ahead of Jim O'Neill and Denis Williams. Roy Brocklehurst was doing National Service. Roy Miles came over from Service doing specs, and we were about to start on the MGA. Initially reporting to Harry White, Mitchell took over as chief chassis draughtsman when White left to go to Rootes in 1958. As well as the MGA, Terry Mitchell played crucial roles in all the other subsequent Abingdon MGs, before working on what would become the Triumph Acclaim.

JAMES O'NEILL

By the time of this formal photo, Jim O'Neill was MG's 'Chief Body Designer'. As such, he was responsible for laying out the initial body lines for the future MGA, working from the basis of EX 175 and Syd Enever's direction

James Edward ('Jim') O'Neill (13 March 1922–12 December 2015) began his motor industry career at Pressed Steel in Cowley in 1936. Whilst there he learned the rudiments of body engineering; after eighteen months in the die machine shop, he moved to the drawing office, where his first task was to draw up some minor brackets for an MG. When Pressed Steel laid off eighty draughtsmen in 1939, O'Neill was one of them. He was lucky to find a job across the road at Morris Motors.

O'Neill was eventually one of the small team who helped turn Alec Issigonis's Morris 'Mosquito' concept into the Morris Minor reality. It was Jim O'Neill and colleague Jim Stimpson who between them detailed most of the body panels for the Minor.

Frustrated at a lack of obvious promotion prospects, O'Neill then moved to Austin at Longbridge – but after a few months the appeal of working far from home paled, and he managed to get another job back at Morris Motors in Cowley, where he soon found himself working on the detailed design of what would become the MG TD.

During 1949, Jim O'Neill found himself working on MG projects such as DO 999, the Riley Pathfinder and DO

Terry Mitchell was a skilled, practical and innovative engineer, never happier than when he was experimenting with his own projects, such as the series of specials he built – this one is seen with its proud creator at Abingdon.
MITCHELL FAMILY

1010, the future MG Magnette. The big change, however, was joining Syd Enever at Abingdon in 1954, when MG design responsibility came under Enever's wing. This was just at the right time for O'Neill to become one of the key members of the MGA design team. As well as the MGA Roadster, O'Neill oversaw the Coupé of 1956 and, in due course, the later MG Midget (including the pretty Jacobs Midgets) and MGB – from conception right through to the so-called 'rubber bumper' facelift of 1974. He remained at MG as chief body draughtsman until the factory closed, then became one of the team working on the Triumph Acclaim and after that the Rover 213. He finally retired in 1985.

HARRY WHITE

Harry White (born 1926) is one of the lesser-known members of the MG design team in the mid-1950s. The somewhat nervous young engineer was twenty-eight when he arrived at MG.

White was relevant to the MGA because amongst other work on the car, he was responsible for the front suspension layout. White went to Henry Stone, who recalled making up a dummy steering rack with a ball joint in the position it would be on the production rack: 'He wanted to move the suspension unit up and down on all locks to duplicate any angle variation that might happen on the road.' Stone recalled that White took all the data away and designed the definitive set-up for the MGA front end.

When Syd Enever wanted staff to work over a weekend to deal with a production problem on the first Austin-Healey Sprites in the spring of 1958, White apparently refused. He left MG soon afterwards and moved to Rootes Group, although according to former Rootes personnel, he did not stay there very long. Meanwhile, when White left Abingdon, his position was taken by Terry Mitchell.

DENIS WILLIAMS

Denis George Williams (born 7 August 1925) studied at the Oxford School of Technology, after which in July 1941, he secured an apprenticeship at Pressed Steel.

During the war he moved to Morris Motors, and by the end of the decade was working in the MG and Riley design office with Jim O'Neill, amongst others. In October 1953 he took up a position with Morris Motors Radiators, Oxford.

Here, Williams was responsible for drawing up the new MGA radiator grille and an MG saloon, which he admitted 'was not over interesting to me'; so when he was offered a job with MG's chief engineer, Syd Enever, he gladly accepted. This was in March 1955, just as the MGA was moving towards production.

Denis Williams in 1996. Williams drew the MGA radiator grille, and his name appears in the title blocks of a great many Abingdon drawings.
AUTHOR'S COLLECTION

At that time the Body Section was in a small office with just Jim O'Neill and Williams:

> We had one full size layout table and two drawing boards for detail work, though we soon moved into a new, larger office for all the design team. My first jobs were on the MGA that was due for release, and was mainly on a check layout for the body shell and some minor trim items, and later with detail items on the MGA Twin Cam. Another project was the EX 202 Magnette with the C-series engine, for which I laid out the front-end body lines incorporating a new wider radiator grille.

Williams was also largely responsible for the body shape of the twin cam-engined EX 186 prototype (*see* later), and in due course the MG Midget of 1961 and various projects thereafter.

DONALD BUTLER

Donald 'Don' William Butler (June 1930–14 January 2012) was born in Headington, Oxford, and started his career just down the road at Morris Motors. This was followed by time spent in the Cowley Specification Department. He next moved to Cowley's Experimental Pattern Shop, and before long entered into an apprenticeship in 1946. In 1951 he secured a place in the Morris Motors Drawing Office under chief body draughtsman Les Hall; here he worked on what would become the Wolseley 4/44, while Jim O'Neill was responsible for the contemporary MG Magnette.

Don Butler in 1996. Butler worked at Coventry on the body drawings for DO 1062 – the future MGA – alongside Eric Carter of Morris Bodies Branch.
AUTHOR'S COLLECTION

In 1954, Butler was recruited to work with Jim O'Neill on the DO 1062 (MGA). In all, Don spent twelve months at Coventry working on the MGA – primarily the inner structural body panels – at the end of which Syd Enever asked Leslie Hall to release Butler to work at Abingdon – but Leslie said no as he wanted Butler to work on the Farina ADO 9, including the MG Magnette Mk III.

When most of the Cowley design work moved to Longbridge at the tail end of the 1950s, Butler managed to secure a permanent place at Abingdon, in the spring of 1959. There, along with MG's Denis Williams, he worked on the MG Midget. In due course Butler moved to Longbridge where he worked on the Metro and Maestro projects.

ROY BROCKLEHURST

Roy Brocklehurst in the late 1960s, at which point he was Assistant Chief Engineer, Chassis Design.
AUTHOR'S COLLECTION

Roy Brocklehurst (18 June 1932–29 April 1988) was born in Didcot, then in Berkshire; when he left school in 1947 he looked for a local apprenticeship, and simply cycled down the road to Abingdon to ask if there were any vacancies at MG. He started there in June, and was soon under Syd Enever's wing.

Prior to his time in National Service in 1952–54, Brocklehurst benefited from training at the Oxford College of Technology, and is generally credited with drawing up the chassis of EX 175, the precursor of the MGA. He returned to Abingdon just in time to join the new design office, working with Jim O'Neill and Terry Mitchell. In September 1956 he became chief draughtsman; by December 1964 he was assistant chief engineer; and when Syd Enever retired in May 1971, he took over as MG's chief engineer.

Thereafter he moved onwards and upwards, and was soon working at Longbridge, for Charles Griffin; he eventually retired early from the Rover Group at Gaydon in 1987.

THE AERODYNAMIC SPORTS CAR: DO 1062

Although the TF had been a brave try by MG to pour new life into the old T-Type formula, and despite the fact that its cancellation without the replacement being ready caused great anxiety to US dealers and distributors, the old MG sports-car type was faced by a tide of new rivals and changing customer expectations. John Thornley sums up part of the problem, in his classic book *Maintaining the Breed*:

> At 85mph or so, the TF finds the atmosphere almost as impenetrable as a brick wall. One can go on piling on horsepower, pouring petrol in the tank and money down the drain and getting practically nothing in return except improved acceleration... clearly in this age of increasing speeds and expensive petrol, the Old Faithful shape had had its day.
>
> In considering the replacement of a body such as that on the TF by an all-enveloping style, serious problems of cost arise. If the wings, fuel tank and bonnet are removed from any of the T-Types, there isn't much left, and that … is made of 'two sheets of tin and a bundle of firewood' – an

Many British schoolboys of the 1950s were keen readers of the weekly high quality and justly popular part-colour comic *The Eagle*, most famous for its 'Dan Dare' science-fiction strip. The comic also featured brilliant cutaways, such as this one by Hubert Redmill (1916–1998) from the issue of 9 September 1955, just a fortnight before the debut of the real car that this 'road-going EX182' was supposed to depict. Many MG enthusiasts have understandably confused the EX182 and DO1062 project codes – but it was the latter which properly applied to the road-going car, which became better known as the MGA.
AUTHOR'S COLLECTION

over-simplification that stresses the point very well. Not only is the all-enveloping body inevitably more complex, but the cost of the tools necessary for the production of every square inch of the outer skin and much of the internal structure as well, can be very high. It was considerations such as these that caused HMO 6 to be shelved in 1953.

In June 1954, Thornley and Enever, back in charge of their own design facility at Abingdon, began to design, for production, the TF's replacement, following more or less the principle of EX 175. Thornley wrote:

> The fact that HMO 6 existed meant that the back of the design work was already broken, and the performance and behaviour of the car known with reasonable accuracy. The car, however, looked large by comparison with the TF, and in any event, had been built with lavish detail and equipment and with no very keen eye on cost.

The first entry in the surviving Abingdon register for 'DO 1062 – New MG Midget' was dated 3 June 1954, the first Thursday in June, and about three months before the Board meeting referred to later in this section.

However, this entry, DO 1062/1 is not a general arrangement, but the first of a great many detail drawings, described as 'scheme showing modifications to TF Suspension and Steering'; the probable reason for this is that much of the drawing work was being done by Morris Bodies rather than at Abingdon. There would be 313 entries by the end of 1954 alone, such as DO 1062/177 (dated 18 October 1954), described simply as 'MG badge' – presumably for the boot-lid, as DO 1062/242 of 12 November 1954 is for 'MG badge – radiator grille'. Some of the later entries would cover the Le Mans adventures (for example, DO 1062/316, 329 and 330); others were for racing equipment (DO 1062/343, dated 13 May 1955, is 'scheme for competition wind shield') and still later items are relevant to the models in later chapters – DO 1062/435 dated 4 April 1957 is 'name plate – twin cam'. We do know from his own testimony that Denis Williams was responsible for drawing up the distinctive MGA radiator grille.

Thornley spoke about the transition from EX 175 to DO 1062 in an unpublished interview of October 1974. Speaking of EX 175, he said that:

> The original prototype MGA was a very lush vehicle. As it moved into production we had a cost-conscious designer – and I don't think the management board of Morris Motors or British Motor Corporation had ever met such a being; all the people who had the 'yay or nay' over the design were inclined to exercise their cost consciousness, and so where the original MGA design as done by Syd had taken into account the cost, the big boys – who really ought to have known better – they cut it to ribbons. Rather unnecessarily. And it turned out jolly good, but it could have been absolutely superlative – the original prototype was a beautiful motor car...

The minutes of the Morris Motors Board meeting of Wednesday 8 September 1954 record approval of a tooling sanction for 'New project No. 56 The MG Car Company Limited. Open two-seater, Series MGA (DO 1062)' of £70,000 (equivalent to about £1.5M in 2018) – rather more than twice the comparatively modest sum of £27,000 which

The MGA – Nuffield Project Code 'DO 1062' – was subjected to aerodynamic testing in the Austin wind tunnel at Longbridge, the idea of securing a smooth aerodynamically efficient shape being quite a contrast to the design of previous MG production car bodies.

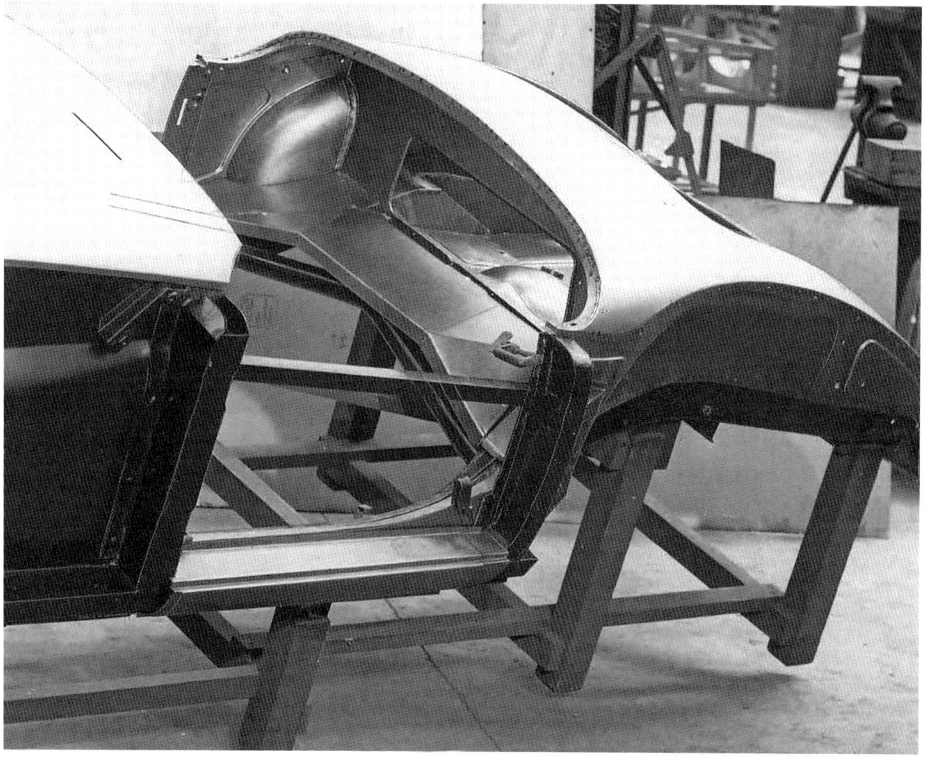

In this photograph arranged by Morris Motors Bodies' Branch, we can see the inner wings, door-posts and other structural bodyshell elements as well as the larger body panel pressings to the rear and front upper surfaces. Much of the design work on these 'inner parts' was undertaken by Don Butler working under the direction of MG's Chief Body Engineer, Jim O'Neill.
AUTHOR'S COLLECTION

BELOW RIGHT: **The MGA bodyshell is beautifully proportioned, with gracious curves in both plan and elevation, as this photo of the partially assembled bodyshell shows.**
AUTHOR'S COLLECTION

the Board had approved for the MG TF Midget – of course just a facelift, whereas 'DO 1062' was all new. Present at that crucial September 1954 Board Meeting were Sir Leonard Lord, Reggie Hanks, George Dono, Donald Harrison, Wilfred Hobbs, Sidney Smith and Gerald Palmer. As we saw earlier, the sum that had been tentatively approved for the Palmer Midget (as DO 1049) just a year earlier had been considerably more (£250,000, equating to circa £5.5M in 2018). Tellingly, the Board would later be called upon to approve a further sum of £100,000 to support 'Project No. B56' (i.e. DO 1062 – MGA) on 11 January 1956.

WHAT'S IN A NAME? 'LET'S CALL IT MGA'...

Until the advent of the new Abingdon-designed DO 1062, most production MG cars had used a single or twin character model 'code', famous examples being the K3, PA, PB, TA, TB, TC, TF, TF, Y and Z, occasionally with an appended name such as Midget, Magna or Magnette. However, by the time the new model was on the horizon, the alphabet had, in effect, been used up. The new car was clearly not related to the TF, and so 'TG' would not have made sense nor had much impact; the idea of 'UA' was played with very briefly, but did not look attractive. It was John Thornley who claimed credit for the brilliant idea of going back to the beginning – and the new car was, in a way, a 'new beginning' – and adding in the marque name as a composite, creating 'MGA' and allowing for a subsequent line of 'MGB', 'MGC', and so forth. There was another reason for this, too: as Thornley noted, by incorporating the marque name in this way, the likelihood of commentators leaving out the maker – as they could if talking about, say, a 'Cambridge', 'Oxford', or indeed 'Magnette' – was reduced. It was an inspired idea.

Chassis frames for the MGA were welded at Abingdon using pressings supplied by John Thompson Motor Pressings of Wolverhampton, with the parts collected in MG's own lorry. With the exception of the much later and very different MG XPower SV, the MGA was the last factory-built MG to feature a separate chassis.
CHRIS HARVEY

The news that MG's new sports car had received the green light was conveyed to Abingdon by Sidney Smith, who – as a director both of Morris Motors and of Bodies Branch – was told to convey the decision to go ahead by Leonard Lord. Eric Carter claimed to be the first to be told by Smith, who visited Quinton Road before going on to Abingdon. Smith duly told Carter to get started urgently, and added that he would send Enever up. Probably on Friday 10 September 1954 (as told to Doug Nye), Carter recalled:

> A new full-size sheet of paper was put up on the Friday and was squared up with 10in squares. Syd dropped by and told me of the changes from prototype. They weren't much at all, only larger bonnet and trunk lids, the deletion of the rear number-plate mounting, and slightly slimmer front wings – though this change was hardly noticeable. He said: 'We have been allocated £80,000 for tooling, and I want £50,000 for the chassis.'

Evidently the £70,000 referred to earlier had either grown slightly in the meantime, or someone was playing games with budgets, but either way this was still a paltry sum for a brand new motor car, even in the mid-1950s. 'We had been sitting on the thing for two years,' Enever told Doug Nye, 'and suddenly it was all panic and scurry! Huh! Management ...' Meanwhile, with his sheet on the board and marked up in readiness, Carter wasted no time: 'On the next day, the Saturday, we started the skin lines, and on the following Tuesday tracings and prints were being issued to the experimental shop to start work on wooden formers, metal-edged, to produce the first few production bodies.'

On the Wednesday (15 September 1954 perhaps?), a delegation from Pressed Steel at Cowley arrived, headed by that company's Director of Engineering, Bob Robertson:

> They had come up to discuss details and to quote on the job, and since they were then interested in plastic tools, and wanted the work, they offered to produce the tools – for the skin panels – free of charge. They said if they didn't stand up to production requirements they would then produce metal tools at an agreed price. This they subsequently had to do because the plastic tools just didn't stand up!

The men from Pressed Steel collected copies from Carter's drawings:

> They took back with them tracings of what skin lines were available to start their production drawings. Due to the expected sales of what they described as 'a few thousand' and the amount of cash allocated for tooling, the work to be done by Bodies Branch was by modern standards a knife and fork effort, but as production got under way and sales soared it was then possible to get some pressings and rolled sections made outside – things such as the A and B post pressings.

Two weeks into the project, Carter found that the workload was mounting, and as he told Doug Nye:

> Pressure from Pressed Steel for information was kept up, and we had to keep the experimental shop busy, and we had all the usual queries from the production departments on current models, which included things like the Morris Taxi, Travellers, vans, Riley saloons and the MG TF ... Everything was compressed into a very short time span to get the MGA into production. Just one example ... the seats were designed and drawn up in one day, using a totally new method of construction at that time, and no modification was made to them during the whole production of the

> model, except to suit the Coupé version when the squab was raised and narrowed at the top.

By this stage, Syd Enever had co-opted Jim O'Neill and Don Butler, both with extensive experience at Cowley where they had been working in the body design office under Gerald Palmer's overall control. By this stage (since summer 1954) O'Neill had, as we have seen, moved over to Abingdon's new drawing office, but his former workmate was still based at Cowley. Forty years after the events in question, O'Neill told the author (in 1994) that:

> On completing the quarter scale – based upon HMO 6 – I joined Eric Carter at Morris Motors Bodies Branch in Coventry to work on the full-scale layout. This meant staying at a local hostelry for a few months and working long hours to get the car into production. We were fortunate to have on loan from Morris Motors a young draughtsman who did all the detail drawings required by the Coventry plant – a magnificent effort by Don Butler.

According to Jim O'Neill, whilst he and Butler stayed in a small hotel in Coventry, O'Neill supervised his colleague, whom he credits with most of the detail work on DO 1062: 'I didn't do much of it at all while we were up there, because we'd already done the lines,' adding that his reporting line was direct to John Thornley.

When the author asked O'Neill why he thought Thornley had insisted on this arrangement, he had no answer: 'I don't really know why Thornley did that – he just said not to go to Syd but to go direct to him. He'd sign all my expenses sheets and ask me how things were going, and I'd tell him that it was progressing pretty well – which was largely down to Don Butler.'

Butler also described his involvement in DO 1062: 'Due to the pressure of work they needed some additional help, and so I was drafted in. Pressed Steel [under Charles Linder] was getting involved in the skin design and so I became involved, allowing Jim to get back to Abingdon to work on other projects.' So-called 'soft tools', most probably rubber and Kirksite dies used for low volume production, were already in use in the fringes of the industry – such as for Jensen bodywork panels, as used for the Austin-Healey 100/4, and Pressed Steel was interested in the potential of entering this sector.

Butler recalled later viewing the so-called 'model stack' for the DO 1062 body tools at Cowley: 'We could see there were certain areas – such as around the rear wheel-arch – that would have been difficult to form. Hence there were modifications to aid the manufacturing process prior to the production of the soft body tools.' Jim O'Neill also told the author that simpler lines were an important consideration in tooling terms: 'We tried to reduce costs by using some straighter sections with simpler pressing requirements.'

Comparing EX 175 with DO 1062, most of the changes appear subtle, but upon closer comparison they are certainly evident (see elevations on p. 54). The wheelbase was shortened by an inch, the front track made wider and the rear reduced slightly, and the shapes of the wings were made a little less curvaceous and 'fulsome' on the later car. At the rear, the small D-shaped boot-lid of EX 175 was dropped in favour of a slightly more practical shape (although luggage capacity was never a strong point), the raised plinth for the rear number plate was dispensed with, and the bumper over-riders were made less heavy in both look and mass. The fuel filler was swapped from one side to the other, the windscreen made less shallow, and various lamp types and their positions were all slightly altered. Naturally the bonnet bulge, needed for the XPAG engine, was dispensed with.

There were many other challenges, too, which arose and had to be quickly overcome, as Eric Carter explained to Doug Nye:

> The folding hood caused some headaches due to the long rear deck. The idea of a double fold to tuck under the deck occurred at about 8pm one evening, and an hour later the scheme was roughed out on paper. It turned out to be a neat and acceptable solution, with the side curtains stowed in front of it.

Having given the directive to move the project without delay, it seems that the senior management at Cowley and Longbridge took little direct involvement: 'They were not interested until there was something to see, consequently if snap decisions were made, they remained for the life of the vehicle.'

Eventually Morris Bodies' work was done: 'The prototype was delivered to Abingdon by lorry, was made roadworthy, and taken out on test by Alec Hounslow; when he returned he said 'We'll sell a hundred thousand of these!' showing some impressive foresight, as we shall see.

The quarter-scale model of EX182 alongside the eighth-scale one of EX175.

AUTHOR'S COLLECTION

Meanwhile, the first chassis were built in time-honoured fashion at Abingdon. In the Development Shop, Doug Watts, Henry Stone and Harold Wiggins made the first two by hand; as Stone recalled in *MG: The Insomnia Crew*:

> We had two wooden formers which gave us the shape of each side member. Doug and I cut out fourteen-gauge sheet steel with hand shears. We shaped the steel to the inside and outside of the wooden formers, and Harold Wiggins welded them all together. We then set up the side members on the marking-off table. All the holes for the necessary cross-tubes were drilled.

The two frames built in this way were one each, with a left-hand drive and a right-hand drive layout to prove the design. Changes from Roy Brocklehurst's design for EX 175 were modest, and mostly to suit the new BMC powertrain.

Pressed Steel swiftly discovered that their much-vaunted soft tools were not sufficiently durable for volume production, and so they had to meet the cost of fabricating proper steel-die tools. As Jim O'Neill concluded: 'I had never been convinced, but they had seemed certain: in the end only about three sets of panels were produced before the tools broke! So they lost out initially – but it worked out a very good deal for us. Of course they later went to do the MGB very successfully.'

However, some time had elapsed in what was a tight programme, which meant that the original intention to begin production of the new model, to overlap with the outgoing MG TF, could not be met by April; this would have a bearing on the debut of the new car, as we shall see.

Although DO 1062 was the future, the aborted XPEG-engined EX 175 was still around in 1954, and it was subjected to road testing that year as part of the development process. In the end, however, the 'old' prototype was used and abused as a test vehicle for a brake supplier, and once it had outlived its usefulness, it was unceremoniously cut up. It was time to hand over to the first true prototypes of what would become the MGA. En route would be some hand-built race cars, under the codename of EX 182 – but the story of those alloy-bodied specials belongs in Chapter 10.

MORRIS MOTORS BODIES BRANCH

Crucial to the development and manufacture of the bodies of the MGA, in both roadster and coupé form, was a subsidiary of BMC in Coventry. The division had started out as Hollick & Pratt, an independent coachbuilder who had supplied bodies to William Morris for his Cowley models, but it was bought out by Morris in 1923. When Morris consolidated many of his businesses three years later for tax reasons, the factory became 'Morris No. 2 Body Plant'.

Over the years, the operation expanded its interest to embrace not only traditional ash-framed steel bodies as used for the MG T-Series, Riley RM and Morris Travellers, but also more modern all-steel bodies, using major panel-work pressings brought in from elsewhere, typically the still independent Pressed Steel company in the outskirts of Oxford.

Situated between Quinton Road and Mile Lane, barely half a mile south of Coventry Cathedral, and also next door to the Armstrong-Siddeley works, the factory was effectively divided in two by a road, and space was always at a premium, especially when volumes grew with the MGA and subsequent MGB build, paint and partial trimming processes. Within the plant was the Bodies Branch Experimental Shop, where prototypes were hand-made to suit the 'client' designs; the key man here was Eric Carter (4 February 1907–8 April 1980), the body draughtsman, a 'can do' man typical of his generation.

Don Butler told the author that the work he did on the MGA, working alongside Eric Carter, served as a good education for him: 'Eric had worked at Riley and Daimler and could turn his hand to almost anything, working everything out from the basic rolled sections through to the finished pressings'. Carter and his team had a vested interest on behalf of their plant; once the designs had been translated into real panel work, the panels would be shipped in bulk from Pressed Steel Cowley to the main shop in Coventry for mass production of those completed bodyshells intended for assembly. These were then painted and part trimmed (including the installation of windscreens and hoods), and despatched south by lorry, six shells at a time, back to the Oxford area.

The completed shells were built up into complete cars at Abingdon, whilst other sets of body panels were crated up, either as shells or batches of constituent parts, and sent via Abingdon to Nuffield Exports to be shipped overseas for CKD assembly (see Chapter 8).

Morris Bodies continued to play an important role in the subsequent MGB story, but by 1970 the end for the plant was nigh, a consequence of rationalization after the BLMC merger. The last car bodies to be built at the plant were Morris Minor Travellers. The premises then passed to Coventry Climax, but were later closed, and the site redeveloped.

CHAPTER FOUR

THE MGA 1500

THE PRE-PRODUCTION PROTOTYPE

Nowadays the pre-production phase of almost any new car involves the production of whole series of specimens, progressively using more parts from suppliers and 'off tools', each undergoing various test regimes before being stripped or crushed – usually – to prevent them slipping out into the market place. Things were very different at MG in 1954, however: as far as is known, there was only one true pre-production MGA, registered 'KMO 326' in Berkshire (still Abingdon's county). The registration number dates from 15 December 1954, nine months before the model's eventual launch; history is often littered with uncertainty, however, and it is possible that 'KMO 326' originally belonged to an MG TF.

The pre-production MGA KMO 326 – chassis no. MGA/EX/1 – at Montlhéry in October 1955. Alec Hounslow (with beret and 'MG' dufflecoat) offers advice to Doug Watts during the record-breaking session at the French circuit (see later in this chapter), just as visitors to the Earls Court Motor Show were getting their first glimpse of the new MGA.

AUTHOR'S COLLECTION

There has been some debate in the past about the chassis number it was assigned, some saying it was 'MGA/EX/1' and others that it was 'EX 197/1'. This quandary is easily explained by the fact that 'EX 197' was the EX Register project code for the MGA Coupé, and as we shall see later, 'KMO 326' would eventually play an important part in the development of the hardtop variant. The style of the number with 'EX/1' as part of it accords with the established practice at Morris Motors, Cowley; indeed, there had been many other prototypes with 'EX' in their chassis numbers, which could easily be confused with MG's own in-house EX Register. Roger Enever, whose role in 'KMO 326' becomes apparent later, certainly remembers that 'the original chassis number was something like number 1'.

It seems logical, therefore, to assume that 'KMO 326' started off as MGA/EX/1, but was assigned another number two years later. Once built, 'KMO 326' was put to good use, including an outing to Montlhéry (see later in this chapter), and trials of disc brakes and experimental exhaust and cooling arrangements. In due course, 'KMO 326' was converted to a coupé – and consequently the continuation of its story belongs in Chapter 5.

Mark Maynard Williams owns the earliest surviving left-hand-drive MGA 1500 production car – chassis no. HDC43/10106 – mounted on the line at Abingdon on 27 May 1955 and despatched on 13 July.

MARK MAYNARD WILLIAMS

Meanwhile, with the design philosophy pinned down for the new 'MG Series MGA', the production engineering and factory changes were swiftly put into play. An obvious task was to clear the decks of the last of the square-rigger Midgets: the final TF 1500 went down the line on 4 April 1955, the last of 9,602 TFs: nobody could have known at the time that the car that was about to succeed it would go on be built in more than ten times that number.

As we saw earlier, the original plan was said to have been to launch the new car just prior to the Le Mans race in June, but with the delays to production caused by factors outside Abingdon's control, the plan changed to a traditional autumn launch at the British and European motor shows and a North American debut the following spring, with the related opportunities of the Sebring event in March. Meanwhile, the first production MGA started down the line on 16 May 1955.

It is instructive to compare some key specification and performance statistics of the TF 1,250 and the new MGA 1500:

	MG TF Midget (1250)	MGA 1500
Engine capacity	1,250	1,489
Maximum power (both at 5,500rpm)	57bhp	72bhp
Mean maximum speed	76/80mph	98/100mph
0–50mph in seconds	14.0	10.5
30–50mph in seconds, in top gear	14.8	11.1
Top gear ratio	4.875:1	4.3:1

FIRST SHOWING: PRESS RECEPTION IN LONDON

Although the first time that most people would see a production MGA would be either at the Frankfurt or Earls Court Motor Shows (see below), there was nevertheless an invitation-only reception at the University Motors' Hertford Street London W1 showroom. This event allowed some of the dealers and the motoring press to see the car before the overseas launch, and to provide coverage in their imminent publications.

The first press photo of the new model (see opposite page) was released with the following caption:

> **CONFIDENTIAL – Not for publication before Thursday 22nd September 1955**
>
> **THE NEW MGA SPORTS CAR**
>
> O.P.S. The new streamlined MGA 2-seater, developed from the EX 182 prototypes which ran with success at Le Mans this year. Exhaustively tested in a high speed aircraft wind tunnel, the body shape ensures greatly reduced wind resistance and the 1,489cc twin carburettor engine gives the car a sparkling performance. Apart from the new shape, this is the first MG open 2-seater provided with a luggage boot.

EARLY PRODUCTION MGA ROADSTERS

Chassis no.	Body Colour	Trim Colour	Steering	Initial UK Registration	Notes
HDE13/10101	Tyrolite Green	Grey	RHD	**LJB 205**	Home-market car; because of the duplication of the '10101' number, the chassis number of this car was changed to EX 182/42. Build began 16 May 1955.
HDC43/10101	Orient Red	Black	LHD	**LJB 439**	US Specification car. Provided with a mirror on the forward part of the right-hand front wing. Used as a 'shop car' and utilized for testing disc brakes amongst other development work (see Chapter 6). Listed as scrapped in December 1963.
HDE13/10102	Tyrolite Green	Grey	RHD	**LJB 370**	Used for extensive road testing (see Chapter 10); after a crash involving Roy Brocklehurst it was rebuilt as a black coupé and used for factory development work. The chassis number 10102 was later assigned to the final iteration of 'LBL 304' (see later).
HDE13/10103	Tyrolite Green	Grey	RHD	**LRX 238**	Factory demonstrator; sold off into private ownership in 1957. In recent years, acquired by Bob West.
HDE13/10104	Tyrolite Green	Grey	RHD	**Unknown**	Once thought to have been the original 'KMO 326' as taken to Montlhéry in October 1955, but subsequent research by the MGA Register suggests this car is unknown.
HDE13/10105	Tyrolite Green	Grey	RHD	**MBL 867**	Built between 25 May and 8 July 1955. Body No. 20006. Despatched from Production to Competitions Department, 18 October 1955. First registered (to MG Car Company Limited) on 1 February 1956. Made into a rally car, known affectionately at Abingdon as 'MaBeL' (see main text).
HDC43/10106	Orient Red	Black	LHD	**N/A**	The first production left-hand-drive MGA; exported to the USA. Build dates 27 May–8 July 1955 and despatch 13 July 1955. Body No. 2007 and engine No. BP15-GB-119.

Footnotes:
As noted in the main text, there was also KMO326 – but this was a pre-production car, first registered in December 1954. For an explanation of chassis number prefixes, see table at the end of this chapter.

Price (Home Ex Works) £595.0.0. Plus £249.0.10. Purchase Tax = £844.0.10.

With the compliments of the Nuffield Organization, Central Publicity Department, Cowley, Oxford.

[on later photos, the price was changed to (Home ex works) £595 plus £298 17s 0d P.T. = £893 17s 0d]

In the run-up to the launch, the early cars listed above were followed by others built largely for distributors and dealers, an example being University Motors, MG's Central London Agency.

FAR LEFT: **This is a factory pre-production prototype MGA 1500...**

LEFT: **...which, as can be seen from zooming in, has a prototype 'MG 1500' legend for the oval scuttle badge (compare with the colour photograph on page 78 of a production car).**
AUTHOR'S COLLECTION

JOURNEY TOWARDS THE LAUNCH: BY AEROPLANE TO GERMANY

For the introduction of their new streamlined MG sports car, BMC decided that the event needed an international stage, with some dramatic theatrics involved, attracting coverage by Pathé Newsreel in the process.

A left-hand-drive Orient Red wire-wheel-equipped car was taken to London Airport (nowadays Heathrow) and readied for its imminent journey by simply removing, at the terminal, the windscreen, and replacing the wire wheels with equivalent bare wheels without tyres; this allowed the car to be securely tied down inside a hollow Lockheed 'SpeedPak' container, a lightweight boat-like carrier that was then fixed with four clamps to the underbelly of a propeller-driven TWA Lockheed Model 1049 Super Constellation. This device was intended as an additional external luggage hold or freight carrier on what was primarily a passenger service, looking for all the world like a silver drop-tank.

The SpeedPak container itself was a little over 33ft long, 7ft wide and 3ft deep (10 x 2.1 x 0.9m) and weighed 1,836lb (832kg) empty. The payload was 395cu ft (112cu m), and up to 8,200lb (3,720kg) of cargo could be accommodated at any one time. A built-in electric hoist raised or lowered the SpeedPak to the ground for loading or unloading, and for ease of movement on the ground, two semi-recessed wheels were mounted underneath each end of the SpeedPak, which were useful when moving the unit up to the underside of the Constellation with its precious sports-car cargo on board.

The MGA was evidently quite a tight fit but clearly a fairly light load; once all the clamps were secure, the slightly bizarre ensemble duly rumbled down the runway at Heathrow before Captain G. W. (Gordon) Lambert took off for Frankfurt Rhein, Main Airport in what was then still known as West Germany.

The main Frankfurt Show car was transported from London Airport (nowadays Heathrow) to Germany under the belly of an aircraft; here it is being craned into the TWA SpeedPak...
AUTHOR'S COLLECTION

...and here it is safely on the tarmac in Frankfurt. In front of the Constellation is the MGA, being driven by TWA air hostess Carol Joyce, with local German MG agent J. A. Woodhouse sitting alongside her. Looking on are Herr Odendahl, Herr Eber (son of the Nuffield dealer in Krauznach) and Herr Weber, Technical Manager of Messrs J. A. Woodhouse.
AUTHOR'S COLLECTION

German customs officers make their checks of the unusually imported MG, while interested bystanders look on. On this occasion, Nuffield Exports' interests were taken care of by Mike Trodd, who went along as chaperone to the MGA.
AUTHOR'S COLLECTION

Six hundred miles and two and a half hours later, the Constellation landed on Frankfurt's quite short runway, and within just ten minutes of landing, the SpeedPak had been released and unpacked, the normal road wheels and tyres refitted, and the once more roadworthy MGA was driven away from the aircraft and off the runway by the TWA hostess, Carol Joyce. Alongside her in the passenger seat was the long-established Köln MG distributor, Jack Woodhouse of 'J. A. Woodhouse' in Stolberger Straße, Köln – Braunsfeld; just a few years earlier Woodhouse had commissioned a small number of German-built MG TD Midgets for sale to locally based US servicemen.

The photo opportunity over, the car was handed back to its official chaperone for the journey, Nuffield Exports' representative Michael J. Trodd (25 March 1925–September 2003), whose task now was to get the red MG safely to a press reception ahead of the Frankfurt Motor Show's official opening, a short distance of around five miles from the airport, on Thursday 22 September. According to a report in a subsequent issue of the Nuffield Exports magazine *News Exchange*, the first individual customer order occurred at this point: an American onlooker who had witnessed the car being unpacked from the belly of the plane duly followed the party to the press reception in Frankfurt, and asked to be placed on the list of orders.

WILKOMMEN MGA: THE FRANKFURT MOTOR SHOW DEBUT

Although the annual Earls Court Motor Show was the obvious place to stage a launch of a new British car on to the world stage, that world was a changing place by the mid-1950s, barely a decade on from the major global conflict of World War II. Western Europe was being rebuilt, in terms of infrastructure as well as the underlying economies. The continuing British quest to earn export currency meant that a presence on the continent was clearly an essential need for a company such as BMC, MG's parent.

The recovery of the West German economy was particularly impressive in the context of national defeat only a few years earlier, and the consequent division of the nation into two distinct countries, one aligned to the West and the other

The world motor-show debut of the new MG Series MGA was at Frankfurt in September 1955. Surely very few visitors to the show would have appreciated how it had got there.
MALCOLM GREEN

The first German market brochure for the MGA was essentially a blank version of the British one (see later in this chapter) but with German text over-printed.
ROBIN BARKER

under the yoke of Communism. With growing prosperity came an appetite for luxury goods such as motor cars, and whilst the domestic car makers were justifiably a cause of national pride, there was room for more exotic foreign car makers. In the case of British sports cars, there was also a ready market among the many American servicemen based in and around Berlin.

The bi-annual Frankfurt Motor Show, staged within a massive multiple-hall arena hard by the autobahn on the outskirts of the city of Frankfurt am Main, was a major shop window for automotive hedonism. Then as nowadays, the event was dominated by the major domestic players, and in 1955 the likes of Auto-Union, Daimler-Benz, Ford and Volkswagen all had their own discreet halls. These companies had much to celebrate: for example, in 1955 Volkswagen was shouting about their millionth motor car, inevitably one of Wolfsburg's ubiquitous Beetles. Meanwhile, however, there was room in the two smallest halls for the many overseas visitors, and it was in one of these that Great Britain displayed her wares, including sports cars to tempt the more adventurous European motorist.

Nuffield Exports made a feature of the new MGA, one of which as we have seen arrived by air on the eve of the show. The MG stand featured two MGAs, flanking the famous EX 179 MG record breaker; the second MGA was an Old English White specimen, and it is possible that this was chassis number 10180. Alongside the nearby British sports car displays featuring the Triumph TR2, Austin-Healey 100/4 and Jaguar XK140, MG no longer looked like an ageing laughing stock: the sleek, new, smoothly styled MGA was unquestionably the new kid on the block.

Five days after the Frankfurt Show closed, it was the turn of the 42nd Paris 'Salon de l'Automobile': here the MGA was the only all-new British car on show, though its presence was considerably overshadowed by the excitement of the debut of a local French marvel, the new Citröen ID19, with its space-age styling and futuristic oleo-pneumatic suspension system. In their subsequent report, *Motorsport* noted that 'the MGA was no longer new since the German show, and the model exhibited was actually fitted with very second-hand-looking wheels showing rust marks through the paint.' French sales of the MGA seldom reached very high numbers, typically perhaps 150 cars per annum due to the Anglo-French Trade Agreement in place at the time, although tax-free sales to US servicemen posted in France were a means to boost this.

A single MGA appeared at the 42nd Salon de l'Automobile in Paris, just prior to Earls Court. *Motorsport* were not overly impressed with its presentation, claiming it had scruffy wire wheels!
C/O STEVE SIMMONS

THE FRENCH CONNECTION

MGA sales in France were always modest, but nevertheless the model managed to appear in a lot of supposedly unrelated PR shots like this one – what we would nowadays call 'product placement'. Although there was almost no marketing budget for MG in France, Jean-Pierre Richard, importer of MGs into France in the 1958–70 period, latched on to Marcel Bleustein-Blanchet (21 August 1906–11 April 1996) who ran top French advertising agency Publicis. As Richard told Jon Pressnell: '*a friend of mine worked for Shell, who had their advertising account with Publicis. He said I had to meet Bleustein-Blanchet – which I duly did. He asked me what I wanted to distribute in France. I said MG sports cars. "My dream, my dream," he exclaimed. "The most beautiful car in the world! And the advertising contract is available?"*' The net result was that alongside the modest MG marketing, Bleustein-Blanchet used MGs in many other PR campaigns – much of it at no direct cost to MG! This explains why there are a number of photographs that appeared in French magazines in the period that just happened to feature an MGA…

The MGA was frequently photographed in the French media with fashionable young female fashion models – helped to a considerable degree by the contacts of Marcel Bleustein-Bianchet, principal of the famous Paris-based publicity agency, Publicis.
AUTHOR'S COLLECTION

ON HOME GROUND: THE EARLS COURT MOTOR SHOW, OCTOBER 1955

Whilst the importance of a European Motor Show debut should not be understated (and as we have seen, there were still annual shows in Paris as well as Frankfurt at that time; nowadays those two alternate), the obvious place for a patriotic 'big splash' was at London's Earls Court Motor Show, an event which had been running every year at the venue since the first post-war show in 1948. Seven years on, the political and financial climate in Britain had moved on from post-war austerity, and while export earning potential was still very important, materials were no longer rationed in accordance with output. Instead, however, government interfered in other ways, including setting and changing with annoying frequency the rates of purchase tax.

As we saw earlier, the 1953 MG stand had seen the slightly odd mismatch of the obviously new MG Z-Series Magnette (to some less kind observers a Wolseley in drag) alongside the inescapably 'classic' MG TF. The appearance of the Triumph TR3 and BMC's own Austin-Healey 100/4 now

The first opportunity for MG's home-market followers to see the new MGA was at Earls Court in October 1955, with a distinctive rotating display part at the heart of the MG display.
MALCOLM GREEN

Sir Leonard Lord and Lord Nuffield look pleased at the 1955 Earls Court Motor Show.

made the arrival of MG's all-new sports car line all the more important, and so naturally for the 1955 London show BMC made a big fuss of their new model, defined in the accompanying advertising material as 'the first of a New Line – to meet the challenge of tomorrow on road and track.'

The display on Stand 153 on the ground floor at Earls Court featured three MGAs; there was an Old English White right-hand-drive roadster with optional wire wheels and a one-off white interior, rotating on a turntable, another right-hand-drive car in Orient Red with black trim and equipped with a number of optional extras (radio, windscreen washer, heater, adjustable steering column) and lastly a left hand drive chassis, finished in white and chrome, and also mounted on a turntable. Also on the stand were a brace of MG Magnettes in Royal Tan and Steel Blue.

The MGA display at Earls Court featured a car rotating on the stand to show off its new aerodynamic shape to good effect.
AUTHOR'S COLLECTION

ROUND THE CIRCUIT: TESTING AT MONTLHÉRY

While the MGA display was drawing the crowds at Earls Court in October 1955, BMC staged a publicity excursion to the famous 'L'autodrome de Linas-Montlhéry' race track, about thirty kilometres south of Paris. On Saturday 22 October, two of the still fairly new 'Silver City' air ferries (whose name was taken from the Australian mining city of Broken Hill; the service had been running since 1948) set off from Ferryfield Airport (nowadays Lydd Airport) in Kent with a number of representative BMC cars on board, along with a party of mechanics, drivers and friends.

The Abingdon contingent included Alec Hounslow, George Burrell, Henry Stone, Douggie Watts and Tommy Wellman, whilst those driving included Ron Flockhart, Ken Wharton (who flew straight to the circuit, and back to London the

KMO 326 at the control tower of L'autodrome de Linas-Montlhéry in October 1955. Quoted in the December 1955 issue of Nuffield Organisation's in-house magazine *Teamwork*, Ken Wharton said that the conditions were the worst he had ever seen at Montlhéry; he flew out to France and back to London the same night.
AUTHOR'S COLLECTION

TOP: **The Glacier Blue 1955 MGA looks perfectly at home at Bucklers Hard, not far from Beaulieu, Hampshire.**

ABOVE: **Known to her owners as 'Diva', the Eke's Glacier Blue MGA 1500 was a right-hand-drive export model, and only returned to the UK on 4 July 1961.**
BEAULIEU

same night), Bob Porter (described as a 'car agent from Barnes, South London', there with his wife Mollie) and BMC team captain, Chief Superintendent John Gott of Hertfordshire Police (*see also* Chapter 10).

The group included an MGA, a road-going model bearing the registration KMO 326 (a number that we saw earlier and will see again). The planes flew into Le Touquet Airfield, just to the south of Boulogne, from where the party had a 168-mile (270km) drive to their destination. Along with the MGA, the party comprised a Riley Pathfinder (KRX 820), an Austin-Healey 100/4 (ROB 423) and, on the later flight, an Austin A90 (ROH 744) and a Wolseley 6/90 (XFC 213), the last two with BMC's still fairly new C-Series six. The idea was to subject models close to ones that could be driven straight from a BMC showroom to testing under the scrutiny of the Automobile Club de France's official timekeeper, with Marcus Chambers acting as BMC's official representative.

Jill and Graham Eke of Barkham, Berkshire, are the lucky owners of this beautiful early MGA 1500 Roadster, photographed especially for this book. HDD23-10452 was built in November 1955 and is in the eye-catching combination of Glacier Blue with grey trim and black hood.
BEAULIEU

HDD23-10452, being an early car, has a slightly different speedometer (with 20mph increments) and tachometer (rev-counter) graphics to those of later models (the change came in April 1956, at chassis no. 14090). The wood-rim steering wheel is a later addition by one of its owners.
BEAULIEU

The MGA 1500 (and early Twin Cams) had simple single-unit all-red tail-lamps with combined tail, stop and indicator functions – at a time when many cars still had trafficators. The flashing indicators work by means of a relay.
BEAULIEU

The distinctive oval vent with MGA logo; there was one either side of the scuttle. Compare this with the pre-production type on page 71.
BEAULIEU

There had inevitably been a round of prior testing by Dougie Watts and Tommy Wellman at MIRA, at which a Morris Isis, also planned for part of the trip, had been barely able to get up to 98mph (158km/h) and so was dropped from the French trip. The weather in France was not kind on this occasion; strong wind and rain throughout their trip were not the most conducive to the high speed runs that were planned, but nevertheless Ken Wharton achieved an impressive 102.54mph (164.98km/h) for an hour (higher than the advertised top speed of the production MGA), whilst John Gott achieved an even more impressive 112.36mph (180.78km/h) in the car in stripped-down racing guise, despite experiencing a burst tyre, which meant he had to restart. The trip features in a contemporary Pathé news-reel film *Against the Clock*, and was covered in the in-house *Nuffield Teamwork* issue of December 1955.

IN THE PRESS: MAGAZINE REPORTS AND ROAD TESTS

Inevitably the main British weekly motoring rivals, *Autocar* and *Motor*, along with popular motor sports weekly *Auto–sport*, were first behind the wheel of the new MGA and first

LEFT: **Note that unlike the contemporary MG Z Magnette, production MGAs never had MG 'medallions' in the centre of their hub caps (or 'knave plates', if you prefer). The only exception seems to have been a handful of pre-production cars, as some press photos do show cars with hub-cap medallions – possibly as a result of show shop preparations.**
BEAULIEU

September 28, 1955 299 THE MOTOR

—The M.G. Series-M.G.A. Two-seater

An Uncommonly Roadworthy 1½-litre Sports Car of High Performance

Individual modern styling marks the new M.G.—and more than that. At 60 m.p.h. the M.G.A. requires 27% less power to maintain its speed than the TF Midget. Hood and sidescreens continue the smooth shape as far as is possible.

CARS, like people, are in their varying degrees martyrs to fashion, and whether the current dictates of fashion are a good or a bad thing sometimes makes little difference. Some are brought up to date almost year by year to embody the very latest in everything, others hold out until the very last before falling into line with the majority, and a few, after a period of resistance, change their fashion only for a new one entirely their own.

It is to the last group, oddly enough, that the M.G. "A" two-seater (described on on pages 308-310) belongs. The new car has, to be sure, a smooth and good-looking body whose lines follow contemporary style, and a performance which puts it at least on a competitive footing with the smaller fast sports cars to which we have become accustomed. There, however, the resemblance virtually ends, for alongside the small machines with moderately stressed engines of 2 or more litres there is now a car of comparable size with an engine capacity of 1,489 c.c. The fact is, of course, of primary importance to the competitions driver as putting the car in the 1½-litre class; aside from competition, there are virtues in a small (and therefore light), engine which will be mentioned again later.

In its essence the M.G.A., although not in title a "Midget," is still small; it is compact, manoeuvrable and lively, regards the carriage of luggage as secondary to the sport of motoring, and responds to its driver's wishes in a way the larger car can seldom hope to do except at much greater expense.

However good its intangible qualities, it is by performance that a sports car will inevitably be judged in the first instance, and the figures recorded on the opposite page, which were established as usual on the Belgian motor road, provide all the assurance that may be needed that the car can hold its own in good company. On the noisy side mechanically in comparison with present-day touring designs, the M.G. engine was prone to run-on if switched off quickly after a fast drive, but was otherwise tolerant of all premium-grade fuels. The exhaust note will obviously please many buyers, its loudness increasing progressively with engine speed and throttle opening.

The special significance of a return to 1½ litres for a sports car lies in re-teaching an old lesson that the smaller the proportion of weight, and within limits the less the actual weight on the front wheels of a car, the more responsive will be its "handling"—a comprehensive term which needs no elucidation to the enthusiast. It will be seen that the M.G., without driver but ready for the road and with a small quantity of fuel in the tank, has some 53% of its weight carried by the front wheels, or only a few pounds more on the front than the back, while the position of seats and fuel tank ensures that the greater part of any additional load will bear on the back wheels. The total weight of the pre-production model supplied for test, which in contrast to subsequent production models had aluminium panelled doors and bonnet and boot lids, may raise a few eyebrows in a theoretical appraisal of power-weight ratios, but the majority verdict amongst

In Brief

Price: £595 plus purchase tax £249 0s. 10d. equals £844 0s. 10d.

Capacity	1,489 c.c.
Unladen kerb weight ...	18¼ cwt.
Fuel consumption	26.7 m.p.g.
Maximum speed	97.8 m.p.h.
Maximum speed on 1 in 20 gradient	80 m.p.h.
Maximum top gear gradient	1 in 13.7
Acceleration:	
10-30 m.p.h. in top ...	11.0 sec.
0-50 m.p.h. through gears	10.8 sec.

Gearing: 17.0 m.p.h. in top at 1,000 r.p.m.; 72.8 m.p.h. at 2,500 ft. per min. piston speed.

Inevitably the British motoring weeklies were first with reports and road tests of the new MGA; this is from the 28 September 1955 issue of *Motor*, from which we can deduce that the magazine took LJB 439' (as we saw earlier in this chapter, an Orient Red car, chassis no. HDC43/10101) to the continent as part of their test.
MOTOR

to print with full road-test reports. *Motor* said in its 'Road Test No. 23/55' of 28 September 1955 that the new car had a smooth and good-looking body 'whose lines follow contemporary style, and a performance which puts it at least on a competitive footing with the smaller fast sports cars to which we have become accustomed'. Notwithstanding this, the magazine observed that it would be by its performance that the MGA, as a sports car, would inevitably be judged in the first instance, but went on to say that its test figures – recorded on the Autobahn, as the magazine often did in Belgium – provided, it said, 'all the assurance that may be needed that the car can hold its own in good company'.

The magazine felt that the drive-train was a little noisy, and the engine was prone to run on if switched off quickly after a fast drive, but was otherwise tolerant of all premium grade fuels. Commenting on a familiar MG hallmark, the testers noted that 'the exhaust note will obviously please many buyers, its loudness increasing progressively with engine speed and throttle opening'.

John Christy, the editor of *Sports Car Graphic* magazine (perhaps better remembered for his later role at sister publication, *Motor Trend*) drove an early Orient Red LHD MGA Roadster on a visit to England at the launch.

The testers were clearly enthused by the authentic sports-car credentials of the little MG:

> To drive the MGA on a winding open road is sheer enthusiast's delight. Rack-and-pinion steering and small cars have always gone well together, and the lightness of the steering with a small, four-spoked wheel is matched by a quickness and precision which might not be expected from the lock-to-lock figure (for a very compact lock) of 2¾ turns. In this case the secret lies in an admirable example of useful and controllable over-steer.

There were a few raised eyebrows at what amounted to minor issues (for example, the magazine suggested that the instrument dials had 'markings which have suffered a little at the stylist's hands' – they would be revised in 1956 – see later) but in conclusion, *Motor* said:

> Lest there be any risk, however, of a number of small notes of criticism leaving a false impression, the newest MG must be summed up as enthusiastically as it was everywhere received. That the modern styling is generally approved there can be no doubt, but far more important is the introduction of a small car with a degree of roadworthiness high by any standards. The famous slogan of the factory has indeed never been better applied.

Autocar was similarly complimentary, reporting in its issue of 23 September 1955:

> There is immediate response to sudden pressure on the accelerator and the get-away from rest is very good, 70mph [113km/h] being reached in just over 21 seconds. On Continental roads it was possible to cruise for mile after mile with the speedometer needle between 90 and 100mph

[144 and 160km/h]. The MGA is, in fact, one of those cars whose cruising speed is determined by road conditions, and this became very evident after driving fast over the French and Belgian roads; but there is no feeling at the end of a hard day that the driver has been doing most of the work.

Long, winding hill-side roads are a joy to traverse; the car rockets to the top in third gear, and this gear is also extremely useful for overtaking other traffic and for town use. Fuel consumption benefits from the body shape; driving at 50mph [80km/h], with short periods at 70mph [113km/h], resulted in a figure of 30.8mpg [9.2ltr/100km], which was achieved on a give-and-take main road in Great Britain where, to maintain the predetermined average speed, the available acceleration had to be used. The road-holding and steering are of a high order. Even with the tyre pressures set for fast driving, there was no feeling of discomfort or pattering when on pavé and other poor surfaces. Fast cornering was a joy.

Autosport was unsurprisingly also very enthusiastic, reporting:

On driving off, one is at once impressed with the gearbox. It is as nearly crash proof as anything I have driven outside the automatic class. The changes go through beautifully, and third gear is high enough for frequent use on the open road. The makers suggest 80mph [130km/h] as cruising speed, which seems to suit the car admirably. I had the speedometer on the 100 [160] mark a score of times, under favourable conditions on the road. One tends to drive fast because the riding comfort is so good.

In North America, the MGA was in effect a new model for the 1956 model year, and in terms of a major motor show, it would not be until the spring of 1956 itself that the car would be widely seen at New York. In the meantime, on the other side of the country, BMC/Hambro and their local agents provided an opportunity to show off the MGA to local media at a gymkhana time-trials event, organized at the Santa Anita horse track, near the San Gabriel Mountains in Arcadia, Los Angeles County, by Gough Industries, the Southern California distributor.

This event drew in guests from the local media and dealer representatives alike, and more than a dozen of the new cars were made available for some timed trials through two small circuits, laid out in the horse track's vast car-parking area. This was supplemented later by more extensive hillclimb and road impressions.

The MGA was the cover star of the *Road & Track* issue of November 1955...

ROAD & TRACK

... and inside the magazine there was a report from the Abingdon factory, where Syd Enever and John Thornley showed off one of the prototypes.

ROAD & TRACK

One of the publications to report on the new car as a result of this event was *Motor Life*, which carried a report in its December 1955 issue. After admiring the new car's styling, the magazine felt that the interior was equally impressive: 'As a matter of fact, it is like a car from some other manufacturer. The MG enthusiast, however, will find that all the characteristics have been improved, nothing has been sacrificed in moving from the old to the new. Handling is better than ever.' The 'port of entry' price was quoted as $2,195, *Motor Life* concluding that 'For a car of so many good qualities, it is worth the money.'

Road & Track covered the new model's introduction in its November 1955 magazine, but the all-important road test was carried in the next issue. Under the headline 'A Classic Sports Car Goes Modern', the road-test editors enthused over the break with the old T-Type body styling: 'Now, with the 1956 MG "A", the break with tradition is complete. The car is indeed "all new", and we feel that early enthusiasm for its appearance can now be augmented by the knowledge of its very surprising performance.'

The magazine had been one of the few to road-test the MG TF 1500 (in its December 1954 issue) and so was able to make some informed comparisons between the last of the old generation and the first of the new, noting that they were very close in terms of power output and overall weight. The marked difference in performance was clearly identified as being down to the significant aerodynamic improvement, with the reduction in drag said to be 21 per cent. Just about every aspect of the new car was better in performance terms: acceleration benefited the faster the speed, and fuel

For certain export markets – especially the USA – white-wall tyres were still seen as *de rigueur* by many customers; they were also sometimes seen in other markets, such as Switzerland. This is a BMC-Hambro press photo of an early black MGA 1500 Roadster.
AUTHOR'S COLLECTION

consumption around the 65–75mph (104–120km/h) range was more than 20 per cent improved with the MGA.

Like their British contemporaries, *Road & Track* felt that the MGA was perfect for the less experienced sports-car driver:

> It handles faultlessly, and can be cornered and drifted by a beginner almost immediately. Compared to a car with independent rear suspension, the MG rear end drifts out rather more easily than expected, but there is neither understeer

Some of the guests in the lavishly decorated ballroom. In the group to the right of the car is Miss Kathleen Graham, Deputy-Consul of the British Consulate in New York, with members of the British Information Service, listening to Mr. H. Perren of Los Angeles.

(Below) Mr. J. S. Inskip, the New York Distributor.

NEW YORK PREMIÈRE

In the crystal ballroom of the Park Lane Hotel, New York City, the Hambro Automotive Corporation introduced the MGA to a large gathering of publishers, editors, motoring correspondents and Nuffield Dealers and Distributors

The MGA was feted in New York with a major party hosted by J. S. Inskip, the local distributor.

SAN FRANCISCO PREMIÈRE

At a special preview luncheon at the Palace Hotel in San Francisco, California, Mr. Kjell Qvale, President of British Motor Car Distributors Ltd., introduced the new MGA to Dealers and members of the Press. Mr. Qvale is shown here with Mr. R. L. Gibson (seated in the car), Vice-President and Executive Officer of the Automotive Financing Section of the Bank of America. Looking on are Mr. Nick Marsten (left) and Mr. Bill Joseph, two of the approximately 40 Dealers who attended the announcement.

On the west coast, it was Kjell Qvale who hosted a public launch for the MGA.

> nor oversteer. If you look over the MGA with a critical eye, drive it and note the price tag, you will probably ask the same question that we do: how are they going to supply enough cars to meet the demand?

In BMC/Hambro's own internal staff newsletter, *USA News*, it was reported in the New Year that:

> The buying public seem to be very pleased indeed that we have the new body styling. The MGA was announced as, has been advertised as, and is being sold as, a stock production model. We are most appreciative of the many fine editorials already in print where a fair and factual story of the MGA as a stock sports car is given. Also, when the new MGA raced for the first time at Maryland in the United States it was named the 'Car of the Day'. It also performed beautifully, taking first in its Class.

THE NEW YORK COLISEUM

Whilst J. S. Inskip hired the ballroom of The Park Lane Hotel in New York to introduce the MGA to the East Coast of the USA (invitations being sent out to key press and regional dealers), the public would also get to see the new streamlined sports car at an exciting venue. The premier brand new exhibition outlet for New York was the $35 million Coliseum, built at the City's Columbus Circle in 1955; the first New York International Motor Show opened there at the end of April 1956, and naturally one of the US car-market debutantes shown in its large halls was the MGA, which had gone on sale at the end of the previous year but without the benefit of a major automotive show presence. The MGA was far from the only newcomer at New York, however: other cars making their debut included the SAAB 93 and Citroën ID19.

The Coliseum itself was a windowless exhibition building combined with a twenty-three-storey office tower, and such was the fanfare that greeted its completion that it appeared on a 1956 postage stamp, being heralded by the New York mayor as 'one of the wonders of the modern world'. Contemporary architects were less enamoured of it than the mayor, but the fact remained that it would become a major venue, and the motor show was a good way to start a forty-year history. John Thornley was on hand to support BMC Hambro and represent MG factory interests, and by the end of the show he was able to report a fattening order book, with some 36,000 orders across the dealer network.

Meanwhile, across the country on the West Coast, Kjell Qvale of British Motor Car Distributors hosted an equivalent press and dealer event to the J. S. Inskip affair, this time held at the stunning Palace Hotel at the corner of Market and New Montgomery streets in San Francisco. In a similar vein, BMC Canada called on Ensign Motors of Toronto to welcome the MGA to the Canadian market. Meanwhile other international dealer and show debuts followed, such as Copenhagen and Montevideo: so by the spring of 1956, the MGA was truly a global sports car – even if getting enough cars to meet demand would prove to be a problem.

PRODUCTION AND ROAD TESTING

The factory on the Marcham Road in Abingdon-on-Thames was unquestionably at the heart of the MG universe, but the manufacture of the cars that left its premises was a process that depended upon a number of other factories and external component suppliers.

Running gear came from BMC plants in the Midlands, while trim and other ancillary parts came from either BMC subsidiaries or third party suppliers. The rear axles came from BMC 'Tractor and Transmissions Branch', the former Wolseley factory at Drews Lane in Birmingham, whilst SU carburettors were sourced at the Adderley Park East Works in Arden Road, Birmingham – another former Wolseley plant. Dunlop wheels were delivered to Abingdon, and tyres (typically Dunlop or Michelin) were fitted in a separate shop. Some other parts, such as the tail-lamp plinths fitted to later models, were also painted at Abingdon.

Right from the earliest days of Morris Garages, bodies had been brought in from outside; the MGA was no exception to this rule, and as explained earlier, bodyshells for this model were built up at Morris Bodies Branch in Coventry, using panels from Pressed Steel, Cowley, and some smaller suppliers. The parts and sub-assemblies were taken through the Bodies Branch paint and trim shops, and were finally shipped south by road transporter to Abingdon, where they were received and taken through to the assembly lines.

The route from Coventry to Abingdon in those days – long before the construction of the M40 motorway or modern bypasses – was mainly via the A34, and so each of the transporters, typically carrying loads of six painted, glazed and partially trimmed bodyshells, would wend their way southwards from Coventry via Banbury and the centre of Oxford (the latter step almost impossible to contemplate nowadays) before heading out of Oxford for Abingdon via the Botley Road and Cumnor Hill. To avoid production problems caused by external factors, typically three-quarters of a day's output of MGA body shells would be held in reserve at Abingdon.

En route to Abingdon, consignments of six painted and partially trimmed bodyshells pass through the centre of Oxford in 1959.
PIM VAN DER VEER

Pim van der Veer visited the MG factory in 1959 and took this photo of a recently delivered consignment of MGA bodies (actually 1600s), just delivered from Coventry.
PIM VAN DER VEER

Meanwhile the main longitudinal chassis frame pressings were the responsibility of John Thompson Motor Pressings of Ettingshall, Wolverhampton, although some of the smaller chassis parts were pressed at Abingdon on some of the factory's old equipment. The main chassis sections were collected from Wolverhampton in the MG Car Company's own lorry and delivered to Abingdon's welding shop, where complete chassis were assembled by a small skilled team at a nominal rate of six a day. The substantial side members were fixed in jigs to allow the various transverse tubes to be placed in position, along with the substantial 'goal-post' scuttle frame.

Tack welds of these jig-mounted chassis frame assemblies were followed by full welds, and each completed chassis, once inspected and approved, would be stamped with a unique number (on the left-hand cross member by the gearbox), and then went off to be coated in paint, being carried to the dipping tank on a conveyor which had been salvaged from Cowley and adapted for its new role. The painted chassis was then passed through an infra-red gas-agitated drying oven, and stacked and stored (full hardening took up to two days) ahead of use. At one point, according to former MG employee Adrian Goodenough, 'the MGA chassis were dipped at the end of the press shop, and the two operatives were Buzzer Morris and Bert Ellaway'.

Meanwhile, the painted and part-trimmed bodies from Morris Bodies were received into the upper level of the substantial two-storey entrance into the main assembly building which faced the Marcham Road entrance. Once inside the building, they were lifted on to trolleys and moved along the track, still on this 'first floor' level, various parts such as lighting and other electrical equipment being installed. Eventually the body would reach a stage where it would be ready to be lowered and carefully united with its chassis – at a point called 'the drop'. This was undertaken using 'Felco' electric cranes (sourced from Sheffield), and the bodies were made ready to be married up to the running chassis.

In the meantime, the chassis frame (generally chosen from stock: beyond the obvious need to ensure the right variant was being used, it seems that there was no predetermined relationship between body and chassis numbers) would have begun moving along the line underneath on the ground floor. The first items fitted were, logically enough, front and rear suspension and wheels, allowing the frame and body to be moved more easily along the main line.

The engines were partially built up at Longbridge, where they were tested (with the sump removed) by an electric machine; they were then delivered to Abingdon, often at night, ready for the next day's shift. The engines were then taken and 'dressed' with manifolds, carburettors, engine-mounting rubbers and the special cast gearbox extension, and the resulting assemblies were carted to the main assembly line in trolleys, from where they were lifted on to 'Ardegar' hoists on travelling gantries and, at the appropriate juncture, fitted to the chassis and mated up to the exhausts, which were supplied by Thompsons; various parts came from other specialists, as noted earlier.

A pair of left-hand-drive MGA 1500 Roadsters on the MGA line run parallel to a rather busier MG ZA Magnette line at Abingdon.

AUTHOR'S COLLECTION

Through the period when the MGA was being built, Abingdon was also home to whatever other models were current at the time – initially Z Magnette and some Rileys, including the Pathfinder, later Austin-Healeys, MGA Twin Cams and, in due course, the Sprite and Midget, and on occasion even Morris Minor Travellers. All these ran down manual lines where, after each work stage had been completed, the cry would come out to 'push 'em up'. In a time before 'measured day work', the men on the line largely drove production in order to meet their quotas, and team loyalty was all important because of the shared benefit in achieving their daily allocations. The main lines themselves comprised simple concrete-bedded steel channels on one side and, at regular intervals, timber trestles to allow the operatives to climb alongside the cars as they moved along the line.

By this stage there would be several unique identification numbers marked in various manners on the nascent MGA; as noted above, a chassis frame number, body number (from Bodies Branch), the main 'chassis number' (which we would nowadays call the 'vehicle identification number' or 'VIN'), and of course the engine number and numbers for various other key units, such as the gearbox. To help the operatives, a note in code on the windscreen was used to advise the precise specification – the type of wheels, lamps, speedometer (mph or km/h), left- or right-hand steering, and other aspects such as the lighting requirements for the intended market. Ultimately much of this information would form part of the important 'build card' or log book.

Although there are some patterns in the numbering sequences, some of which are explored later, and enthusiasts such as the MG Car Club's various registers keenly seek details from present-day owners, few formal records of the chassis frame and body numbers are known to survive.

In this view of the assembly lines there are rather more MGAs to admire, with Magnettes again on the next line across. Eventually Abingdon's focus would become entirely sports-car focused – other than the occasional Morris Minor Traveller during lean times.

AUTHOR'S COLLECTION

CUSTOMER SUPPLY ORDER, BODY AND OTHER UNIQUE NUMBERS

Along with the primary chassis numbers for each MGA (see table at the end of this chapter) there are other particular numbers which relate to each individual car. Alongside the basic chassis number, there is a second five or six digit number which it is believed served as a 'CSO' or Customer Supply Order Number, which related to the original reference that defined the specification of the car at the point of order, whether it was a home market order or one from overseas (in which case, it would have come through Nuffield Exports, the division which handled international MG sales at the time).

Canadian MG enthusiast Robin Barker believes that the number defined how the car would be built:

> *On a regular basis these CSO forms would have been sent off to the various assembly plants (obviously MG got all the CSOs for MGA, AH Sprite, Riley and so on). This then gave the MG factory the required details for cars that had previously been approved to be built on speculation, but until then were lacking in details. So this firmed up the production schedule that MG was to follow, and allowed them to create the necessary purchase orders to ensure that they had all the necessary parts on hand, on time for the assembly line to run smoothly. These MG purchase orders would definitely have included an order to Morris Bodies Branch to get the required body built to the correct colours and to the necessary delivery schedule.*

The CSOs for UK market cars had a 'Y' prefix but those for overseas had just numerals, up to six digits. Having studied them, Barker has noted a pattern to them: 'Often these numbers were sequential, indicating MGA CSOs were handled in small batches, but then there were large gaps in the sequential numbers indicating that the same numbering system was probably being used for batches of other models of BMC cars that probably were not even made in Abingdon.' Some cars appeared to be exempt, having no CSO number, but in the main these were special cases – such as cars for competition use by the factory, in which case the 'customer' was an internal one within BMC.

In a similar vein each MGA has a unique 'body number' which formed part of a sequential list. As the bodies (for fully assembled cars) were built up at Morris Bodies Branch in Quinton Road, Coventry, each car, as it started its journey down the body line, had to be defined against a schedule of work for any given day. For cars that were fully built up, the Body Numbers (or parts of them) appear to have been marked with a grease pencil on the inside face of both door shuts. These numbers also have a relevance to CKD cars (see Chapter 8), although it is not believed that the numbers were marked on the door shuts, as the bodies were, of course, only built up at their destination factories. As explained later, CKD MGAs also benefited from their own unique body reference codes.

Finally, each chassis, the engine and many other components unsurprisingly benefited from their own reference numbers. Sadly, as noted in the main text, any master documentation which presumably existed somewhere in the Cowley and Longbridge complexes does not appear to have survived, or if it has, it has yet to be discovered.

At the MG factory, here the Dispatch Supervisor Foreman, Jack Sparrow, attends to an MGA 1500 Coupé (see Chapter 5), immediately behind an MGA 1500 Roadster, with disc wheels. Both cars, right-hand-drive, may be fairly assumed to be destined for home-market sale.
AUTHOR'S COLLECTION

PAID TO BE CRITICAL

Two MGAs go out on test, heading for the Marcham Road gate. The drivers are Olly Pierce in the first car and Nobby Hall in the MGA behind him. Pierce had been part of MG's pre-war racing team, and Hall had been involved in testing the tanks made at the factory during the war.
AUTHOR'S COLLECTION

An image from the article in Nuffield *Teamwork* magazine of August 1958 entitled 'Paid to be Critical'.
AUTHOR'S COLLECTION

At our Abingdon factory, where every vehicle is subject to a stringent road test before it is passed for dispatch, a team of expert critics takes the last responsibility for preserving the high reputation of the MG Car Company.

To the men who work at Abingdon 'Safety Fast!' is more than a selling slogan. It is a well earned reputation and a standard of excellence diligently preserved which extends not only to the MG range, but to every car produced at the works. Subjected to sharp-eyed scrutiny of inspectors in all stages of its construction, each completed vehicle is put through a thorough test on the roads near Abingdon.

Not until its performance has satisfied an experienced tester is it allowed to leave the factory. The task of the road tester is an extremely responsible one, for so much depends on his own individual judgement. Naturally he must be an expert mechanic, and it is for this reason that most of the seventeen testers at MG are drawn from the Company's own workshops. And his job would also seem to be a popular one, for there is no lack of applications from young mechanics who, naturally enough, like the idea of driving about the local countryside all day in shiny new sports cars.

Only a few of them, however, measure up to the Company's high standard. Before a prospective tester is accepted he must undergo a thorough medical examination by the Works doctor. If pronounced fit he is 'adopted' by one of his seniors, and the pair will work together until the trainee has proved his ability. And since a tester is required to be more critical of a car's performance than the customer himself, he soon discovers that the job is not so straightforward as it first appeared. It begins when the completed car is driven off the assembly line into a vacant bay in the Testing Shop.

Here, after the routine safety check of oil and water, the engine is warmed up and the car is made ready for the open road. There are various routes that may be taken. The normal one is 11 miles (17.5km) long, winding past the golf course at Frilford Heath and

For a short period of production the engine number was stamped on to the bulkhead plate, but on later 1,500cc cars 'See Engine' was stated instead. Cars sent overseas had their own peculiarities: *see* Chapter 8.

At the end of the main assembly line, the headlamp beams would be set and the steering carefully tracked. The MGA was one of the few cars in the BMC family where there was extensive road testing at the factory before the cars were passed to the despatch department for onward distribution. The sight and sound of sports cars going out of the Marcham Road gate of the factory and burbling up the road on that twelve-mile test route is one of the fond memories that the author treasures from his youth; seeing MGs and Austin-Healeys in this way was one of the factors which through Tubney Woods, where the high hedges and overhanging trees help to magnify any of the sounds that are clues to certain defects.

For extended tests there is a 14-mile (22.5km) course, while a 7-mile (11km) circuit is also often used, particularly for checking rectifications. There is also a special town traffic route designed to put automatic and manumatic gearboxes to the test. The testers are usually confined to these routes, but if a particularly bumpy or straight section of road is required, Mr Sam Nash, the chief tester, knows of one or two good spots where he will test the car personally. En route the driver will first check his steering and brakes.

Satisfied as to their efficiency, he accelerates slightly, occasionally relaxing the pressure of his right foot to listen for the all-important telltale noises. For it is with his ears that a tester learns to detect any fault in the axles or engine. After months of intensive listening his hearing becomes almost supersensitive, and he soon discovers faults that even the keenest motorist would never notice. Half-way around the course the tester parks the car for a further static examination, while he also checks the body finish.

On the way back he may speed up a little, for a car that is silent at 30mph (48km/h) may produce all sorts of noises when driven faster. But it must be emphasized that higher speeds are only maintained for brief periods that, in the hands of these experts, can do no harm to the engine. In fact the nature of the course makes any speeding impossible, as anyone who knows the roads near Tubney Woods will agree.

There are also several self-imposed speed limits near villages or busy farms, for good relations with the public are of prime consideration to Mr R. Jackson, the chief inspector. Any complaints – and there are very few – are dealt with as sympathetically as possible, and where the test routes are found to be inconveniencing the public they are modified. Another feature of the courses is that all are circular, so that the car is driven in all directions of the wind, a further factor which can influence the sound of the vehicle.

Back at the factory the car is examined for oil leaks. This test is left until last to give the oil a chance to get thoroughly warm, when it will flow more freely. Should any defects be discovered, the mechanics in the Tuning Shop will rectify them for further testing. But most of the vehicles pass the stringent tests first time, when they are sent to the Finishing Shop for the carpets, which were removed before testing, to be replaced. The last touch to perfection is the final polish. There are no time limits imposed on the testers. Theirs alone is the responsibility for the roadworthiness of each vehicle, and history cards recording their verdicts are retained long after the cars are sold.

Bob Morris critically examines an MGA he has just taken out on test for a tyre rubbing on the wheel arch. Masking tape has been applied to the face of the bumper to protect it from flying stones.
AUTHOR'S COLLECTION

Consequently they do not work to any fixed schedule, and if production increases they may have to work longer hours to keep pace. Neither is bad weather allowed to interrupt their work, for even when conditions are icy or foggy, Messrs Sam Nash and Tom Viner, the Deputy Chief Inspector, investigate the state of the roads several times a day so that as little time as possible is lost. Yet in spite of the fact that approximately a quarter of a million miles were covered by these men last year, there was only one minor accident. And in this, let us add, the other driver admitted full responsibility. In the hands of such experts the future of the MG reputation for safety is assured.

fostered an early interest in cars in general, and these models in particular.

In later years, the sheer volume of production of the MGB meant that it was not possible to test every car (although the low volume MGB GT V8 was so treated) but in the gentler times of the MGA, the trips around the dedicated factory test route would have been familiar to local residents.

Once back from testing, the MGA would be passed back to the factory's Rectification Department if improvements were still needed; for example, in the spring of 1957, when *Motorsport* visited Abingdon to see the build process, it was said that around fifteen MGAs and Magnettes passed through Rectification every hour. The magazine observed that blemishes that needed to be retouched and polished out were indicated by chalk rings where necessary, and any other defects remedied; it further noted that 'the inspectors and testers responsible for locating defects play no part in the subsequent rectification, and consequently they are encouraged to be extremely thorough, knowing that their observations will not load them with additional work which could blunt their perception.' Before leaving the department, each car was passed under a series of neon strip lights to check that everything was visually in order.

At the end of this process, each car had its log book completed and signed off, the document comprising a chassis and a body card stapled together, carrying 'details of any defects the factory has put right, and which serves as a valuable check on the vehicle throughout its life in the hands of the owner'. Once all was deemed satisfactory, the completed car would be sent to dispatch. Cars destined for export might be driven to the docks or passed to the export section at Cowley, the latter involving teams of drivers (often female) with buses ferrying them back the thirteen miles from Nuffield Exports to Abingdon.

SALES AND MARKETING: MGA 1500 ROADSTER ADVERTS AND BROCHURES

The arrival of the MGA in September 1955 was heralded by an advertising theme which stressed how the new model marked a break with the past – full page advertisements in either full colour or black and white included the strap line 'First of a new line' and the sub-text 'to meet the challenge of tomorrow on road and track'. Along with these slogans, a graphic theme emerged which would recur in advertising and brochures alike, in the form of a series of triangular 'pennants' which typically carried the MG badge or MGA name. A typical narrative included a paragraph reiterating the changes:

> This potential trophy winner breaks clean away from traditional MG styling, yet inherits all the qualities and fine craftsmanship that have for over a quarter of a century distinguished its famous predecessors. Many of its features are identical to those embodied and tested in George Eyston's record-smashing MG Special. Faster... sturdier... safer, it holds the road like a limpet and its 1500cc ohv engine puts up a performance that is quite exceptional.

In the *Autocar* issue of 28 September 1955, various suppliers placed their own dedicated advertisements to share in the celebration of the MGA's arrival; typical adverts included ones from Castrol, Shell, BP and Dunlopillo, whilst some smaller suppliers and the occasional dealer or distributor added their own advertising.

In the USA, although *Road & Track* carried a Hambro advert for the MGA in the same issue that covered the launch (*see* earlier), using the twin slogans 'Designed to steal your heart!' and 'High in style, high in spirit' (*see* page 95), US advertising really began in earnest in the New Year of 1956; picking up on the neat triangular pennant theme also seen in UK advertising, a typical spot-colour advert referred to 'The entirely new MGA', with the sub-text 'the safest, fastest MG ever engineered!'.

Under a three-quarter black and white MGA image, the advertising prose was characteristically over-enthusiastic:

> You'll gasp with admiration when you see the sleek new lines and brilliant new colors of the entirely new MGA. And your appreciation of nimble performance and solid roadability will hit a new high when you take the wheel. Yes, in every design and engineering detail, this superb new model is the smartest, safest, fastest MG ever made.

When it came to showroom sales material, car makers typically pitch the customer literature slightly differently depending on whether the recipient is seen as a browser with casual interest, or a serious sales prospect. The former category could either be the person who popped in on the off chance, or a visitor to a sales event or motor show (such as Earls Court), and the likelihood was that he or she would be sent on their way with a fold-out leaflet, typically a largish sheet folded into four or six and by virtue of being printed on both sides, offering eight or twelve sides of information.

The 'serious sales prospect' would often be sent away with a full brochure in the form of a stapled booklet, with upwards of twelve sides and sometimes with an insert either bound in position or as a loose piece. Often the design of the leaflet and the brochure would be similar – hardly surprising as they would both be linked to a contemporary marketing campaign – but the brochures are rarer nowadays and so command a little more in the collectors' market.

For the MGA, the original brochures printed by in-house publisher The Nuffield Press (such as sixteen-page publication number E5557, where 'E' is Nuffield marketing code for 'export', and '55' indicates 1955) followed this style (other typical abbreviations were 'H' or 'H&E' indicating 'home' and 'home & export'), and used the same yellow backdrop as some of the first UK-market advertisements, with artwork of a speeding pale blue MGA 1500 Roadster and the launch slogan 'First of a new line'. The folded leaflets, sometimes known as 'brochure savers', followed a similar design pattern.

Initial UK marketing used the slogan 'First of a New Line', such as in this advertisement, which appeared as the car was announced in the UK.
AUTHOR'S COLLECTION

Sales literature included broadly similar brochures and fold-out leaflets with the same strap line, yellow background, blue MGA artwork and triangular pennant theme.
AUTHOR'S COLLECTION

In the mid-1950s, BMC car advertising generally relied on artwork instead of photography. This is a typical image from an early sales brochure.
AUTHOR'S COLLECTION

Monochrome advertisements were used where colour print was not available – or was deemed too much of an extravagance by Central Publicity.
AUTHOR'S COLLECTION

For several export markets the basic leaflet was overprinted in a different language with special locally defined slogans; thus, for example, the original German market version featured the slogans '*Das haben sie sich schon lange gewünscht – den MG in neuen kleid*' (which can be approximately translated as: 'You've been wanting this for a long time – the MG in a new dress'), and '*Hier ist er – der neue MG serie MGA*' (literally 'Here it is – the new MG series MGA'). A Dutch equivalent had the heading '*Eeerste van een nieuwe serie*'.

Similarly, the Nuffield importer in Italy, Fattori & Montani srl, with offices in Rome and Milan, had a version overprinted in Italian which read: '*La prima di una nuova serie – la nuovissima MG MGA*', while the French version read: '*Première d'une nouvelle série – la sensationnelle MG série MGA*', which probably needs no translation. Other variants are likely.

The date is 16 May 1956, and the occasion is the production of the 100,000th MG (that is, an MG of any kind). No more than 22,500 MGs in total had been built until the end of 1939, and hardly any more until 1945, so this total of 100,000 just eleven years after the end of World War II is a remarkable achievement in its own right. Standing proudly next to the car in their work-coats are the body-line charge-hand Fred Wake (left) and Bert Wirdnam (an electrician and racer pre-war, but by this time Superintendent in charge of the body and chassis line); on the other side of this MGA 1500 Roadster is Cecil Cousins, next to him a bespectacled Reg Jackson, and at far right, John Thornley's youthful Deputy General Manager, Geoffrey Iley. In less than four years time, the factory would be celebrating the 100,000th MGA in that model's own right (see Chapter 7) – another truly remarkable achievement.
AUTHOR'S COLLECTION

1956 AND 1957: MORE OF THE SAME

Although the world debut of the MGA took place in the autumn of 1955, it was not until the following spring – and its exposure to the North American press and customer base – that sales really took off. We saw earlier the flurry of correspondence that Jon Pressnell discovered, surrounding US dealers' anxiety at the fact that the TF had been 'killed off' before the MGA arrived; further anxiety accompanied hiccups in the supply chain of the new car.

In February 1956, Donald Morren (New York SMMT representative) made reference to adverse press reactions to some of the wider problems of BMC in the UK (and their impact on MG's image). Morren makes reference in his letter to a dealer in Arizona who was up in arms:

> He says that so far he has gotten only one MGA and he has spent some $3,000 announcing its arrival, cocktails, press reviews, etc, on the assumption that deliveries would be forthcoming. He managed, by demonstrations, to secure over thirty cash deposits on orders, but he has had to refund all this money, as he is unable to even guess when he will get cars.

The letter went on to report that the Arizona dealer's customers were buying Porsches:

> In some cases, however, he has managed to switch them to Austin-Healeys or Jaguars, but deliveries on these have been tight also. He went on to say that in order to operate his business he had to have a regular monthly supply of MGs, and he is thinking seriously of selling out unless I can give him some definite news. This dealer is one of many all over the country in this perilous predicament, and I would appreciate if you could get me some facts which would help me explain to them why there are so few cars being shipped to the States. One explanation put forward is that there is a great shortage of shipping space.

The last point has a ring of truth about it, as getting adequate shipping space was often a challenge faced by Nuffield Exports (their story in the context of the MGA is covered later in this chapter). Meanwhile, as well as the launch in New York, the MGA made an appearance at the Geneva Salon in March 1956 (the car, HDD43-10151, also appeared in Turin and was a Glacier Blue specimen – similar to the first MGA prototype driven to Switzerland, and the car photographed for this book).

The consequence of this late flowering was that beyond the usual round of minor changes that any car experiences during production, the MGA Roadsters built in 1956 changed little. The instruments that drew criticism from *Motor*, referred to earlier, were revised in April 1956 at Car No. 14090;

In the USA – the MGA's prime market – Hambro Automotive introduced the new MG using this spot-colour and monochrome 'heart-themed' artwork. AUTHOR'S COLLECTION

Another early Hambro advertisement proclaims 'The safest, fastest MG ever engineered!' adding that, 'You'll gasp with admiration when you see the sleek new lines and brilliant new colors of the entirely new MG A'. AUTHOR'S COLLECTION

The first MGAs delivered to Geneva were shipped by a Bristol Freighter of Silver City...

...and upon arrival in Switzerland were arrayed in patriotic red, white and blue formation.

AMERICA *DEMANDS* MORE B.M.C. CARS

An order for £1,000,000 worth of B.M.C. cars was placed on the second day of the Show by Mr. A. Woodfield, Vice-President of The Hambro Automotive Corporation, the B.M.C. Concessionaires for the United States of America. The largest to be placed at the Show, this order, which included the MGA and the Minor 1000, was the result of a 26-day tour of Nuffield Distributors made earlier by Mr. Woodfield when the potential demand for the cars was discussed. One Distributor alone required 470 MGA Coupés.

The first 120 MGAs left within the week for San Francisco on a ship specially chartered by the B.M.C. in co-operation with another large Motor Manufacturer.

The Distributor in San Francisco has expressed his intention to charter a former American naval craft and have fitted a flat deck on which British cars can be quickly transported to the United States.

At the Show, Mr. A. Woodfield, Vice-President of the Hambro Automotive Corporation of America, hands the £1,000,000 order to Mr. J. F. Bramley, B.M.C. Director of Export Sales.

At the 1956 Earls Court Motor Show, the Hambro Vice President was on hand to deliver an order for £1,000,000 worth of orders to BMC.

the speedometer now had 10mph (16km/h) increments marked on its face rather than the previous 20mph (32km/h) gaps. The big news during 1956, however, for the 1957 model year, was the addition of a Coupé variant – the story of which is told in the next chapter. From a wider BMC perspective, the Austin-Healey range was also evolving and so corporate sports-car efforts were not confined to MG affairs.

Meanwhile, a series of changes to the engine in 1956 meant that power went up from the original 68bhp at 5,200rpm to 72bhp at 6,000rpm.

The motor industry headlines during the summer of 1956 were dominated by a major strike across BMC, precipitated by the sudden firing of around 6,000 workers from the Corporation. The story appeared in Pathé newsreels at the cinemas, and on the television news. Within BMC, although MG was obviously interdependent on other factories for many of its fundamental components, the sense of familial loyalty and dedication to the company meant that the politics were less fierce than at Cowley or Longbridge.

Geoffrey Iley, John Thornley's deputy since January 1955 (*see* box in Chapter 6) recalls the special relationship with the unions at Abingdon:

> It seemed that the whole of BMC went on strike – except Abingdon. The local union officials came to see me, and they said 'Oh, we don't know what to do'... and the chap from the NUVB was very apologetic: he said 'Look, I've got to be on strike, and I'm on the local Oxford area committee, but I don't feel like calling my members out!'

Just prior to the big BMC strike, MG had celebrated the construction of its 100,000th MG car on 16 May 1956 (*see* photo on page 90; not to be confused with the 100,000th MGA of 1961 – *see* Chapter 7).

So the loyal workforce kept on working at Abingdon, building MGAs and other cars, most of them of course destined for export; Iley recalls:

> The chap from the GMB was a super fellow; he'd been a Mayor of Abingdon and was a dyed-in-the-wool traditionalist; he said 'I've been told and instructed to ballot my members, and I keep balloting them – and then I keep losing the ballot papers!' So the whole thing, as far as Abingdon was concerned, just fizzled out.

Consequently the Abingdon factory kept working away, using up the stock of power units, body shells and so on; Lucas and similar suppliers were not on strike, and so they were quite

Switzerland was a good market for MG cars for many years. In this photo, customers of J. H. Keller in Zürich take a look at one of the earliest MGA 1500 Roadsters to reach the Swiss market. The licence plate ZH-569 is a Swiss trade plate.

KELLER FAMILY

The showroom of J. H. Keller, with a K3 Magnette taking pride of place in the foreground, and a new MGA 1500 Roadster behind. The placard behind the K3 explains that the company was celebrating (in 1955) twenty-five years of representation of the MG marque in Switzerland.

KELLER FAMILY

pleased to supply the things for which Iley would normally have been chasing.

The strike, called just prior to the normal car-industry summer factory shut-down, lasted until August; threatened pickets never made it as far as Abingdon. Meanwhile in production terms, some more minor changes in September 1956 included the addition of sill finishers intended to neaten the appearance of the sill's lower edges (Chassis no. 19949), the addition of rear three-quarter windows to the folding hood (Chassis no. 20162) and other minor, mostly mechanical and therefore largely unseen changes.

A young Jürg Keller, son of Heinz Keller, poses for the camera in the early MGA Roadster LJB 370 during its trip to Switzerland (see Chapter 10, The MGA in Motor Sport). The location is outside the J. H. Keller AG Showroom at Bahnhofstrasse 1 Zürich, nowadays the site of a Swiss bank.

KELLER FAMILY

MG Press Car MJB 994 at the Uffington White Horse near Wantage. This same car appeared in a contemporary 1958 brochure...

PETER SEYMOUR

...and here is the colour image of MJB 994 as used in brochure E.5812. The registration number was later attached to a BMW 5-Series.

AUTHOR'S COLLECTION

The period of August 1957 to April 1958 saw a recession in the MGA's principal US market, and on 12 March 1958 the Morris Motors Board heard a report that due to the shortage of a sports-car market there, some 6,000 MGAs were in stock and sales had fallen to 750 a month; fortunately the market picked up in time for the summer market.

For 1958 the big story would be the introduction of the MGA Twin Cam in both Roadster and Coupé forms (see Chapter 6). Meanwhile, therefore, the MGA Roadster continued into 1957 and 1958 largely unaltered. Bigger changes would be seen in 1959, but in the meantime, BMC/Hambro, perhaps worried about the rather large stock levels, felt it necessary to remind customers of the MGA, and issued the following press release:

> The rugged little MG, three-time winner of the team trophy at Sebring, is America's favourite sports car by better than three to one. Extremely fine workmanship in every detail

is matched by features normally found only in much more expensive sports cars: anti-sway suspension... very low center of gravity... rack and pinion steering... oversize brakes... excellent power-to-weight ratio... adjustable, leather-upholstered bucket seats and enclosed luggage compartment. Its 1,489cc power plant develops 72bhp and 5,500rpm. This, plus a four forward-speed gearbox with synchromesh in top three gears, delivers 70mph in third gear and 100mph in top... 30 miles per gallon... priced from $2,462 at New York port of entry... made by the British Motor Corporation, the world's fourth largest maker of automobiles... sold and serviced by nearly 600 authorized dealers from coast to coast. For further information: T. R. Birt, Hambro Automotive Corp., 27 W. 57th Street, New York E 9-3150.

JOHN THORNLEY ON EXPANSION AT ABINGDON, 1953–1958

Speaking in October 1974, John Thornley looked back fondly on the five years from 1953 to 1958 (with Austin-Healey added to MG from 1957), which embraced the shift from timber-framed T-Series sports cars to the high point of MGA production:

> *The original Austin-Healey was 1953 – and this was the point where real expansion began. Up to 1953, we had been producing 250 vehicles a week as certain; [BMC] then brought in Austin-Healey, and the Austin-Healey 100 was running at about eighty or ninety a week, on top of our then TF. Then the MGA came in – and from that moment, and from 1953 to 1958, we went from 250 vehicles to 1,250 a week – and we went to 1,380 in one very memorable week, which has become the sort of norm for today.*
>
> *But this was in the five years from 1953 to 1958 – it was absolutely fantastic. How did we do it? We made the maximum use of the floor-space that we'd got. We had a building that gave us just enough height to be able to put a deck in, and run the thing on two floors, and we increased the deck area very considerably during this period – we put up three new buildings of 12,000 square feet apiece, but otherwise we packed everything into the space that we'd got.*
>
> *We made our assembly lines by building low brick walls with precast concrete channels on the top, which a motorcar would roll along: it was a channel one side, and a flat platform the other – so this would take varying tracks, and cars were propelled from one workstation to the next by the good old way of pushing.*
>
> *The benefit of this arrangement was that if, in looking at the factory layout, we decided that if we shuffled those three lines up a little bit closer together, we could get a fourth line in, then all we had to worry about was the electrics and the compressed air; everything else was just standing on the floor. So five o'clock Friday, everybody stops, the maintenance boys move in, knock the whole place to pieces, and by eight o'clock on the Monday morning we're in operation with four lines instead of three. Six months later, we had five lines instead of four – and this is how it went, by and large.*

The MGA was back again as one of BMC's stars of the Frankfurt Motor Show stand in 1957, as this contemporary advertisement from the local MG importers shows. AUTHOR'S COLLECTION

The MGA at the 1958 Geneva Salon in Roadster, Hardtop and Coupé guises (*see* next chapter), alongside the MG ZB Magnette and contemporary Morris, Riley and Wolseley models. By this time, Austin-Healey production had started at Abingdon, with the new Austin-Healey Sprite due in May, and the MGA Twin Cam in July.

KELLER FAMILY

By July 1958 – with the arrival of the MGA Twin Cam providing an excuse to talk about the sales success of the MGA as a whole – Nuffield Exports proclaimed that more than 30,000 MGAs had been sold in the USA. With earnings since 1955 of more than 42 million dollars, the company suggested that it might be considered to be 'one of the greatest, if not *the* greatest, single dollar-earner produced in the United Kingdom'.

An MGA 1500 Roadster parked up at Nuffield Exports premises at Cowley in 1957. The related story of overseas 'CKD' assembly is told in Chapter 8. Note that the sign in the background advertises the Pressed Steel Social & Athletic Club – Bowls Section next door, which opened in April 1953 and finally closed in 2016.

© BRITISH MOTOR INDUSTRY HERITAGE TRUST

Obviously credit must be liberally shared with all the workforce at Abingdon and throughout the BMC organization who made this growth in volume, but the drive undoubtedly came from the top, such as John Thornley and Geoffrey Iley (*see* Chapter 6), the latter having been tasked to 'get the cars out of the door'.

Although a new larger engine was on the horizon for the summer of 1959 (*see* Chapter 7), in-service changes to the MGA 1500 included an updated engine block introduced just a few months earlier in January 1959, the new designation being '15GD' in place of '15GB', the obvious change being the positioning of the starter motor, now raised higher on the gearbox mounting plate. By the time the larger engine came into play, the MGA 1500 had been manufactured for four years and seen record levels MG sports-car production.

EXPORT DRIVE

Although a significant proportion of MGAs were exported in kit form (*see* Chapter 8) a significant volume went to the model's principal market – the USA – in largely built-up form, albeit processed through Nuffield Exports, with suitable protection for the journey, such as protective covers and liberal coatings of Cosmoline or other protective coatings (all of which had to be 'undone' at the far end of the journey). The photographs here provide a seldom seen insight to the process.

This 1957 BMC/Hambro for an MGA 1500 Roadster features white-wall tyres but plain disc wheels (correctly without an MG medallion) rather than the almost ubiquitous wires.

AUTHOR'S COLLECTION

From the outset, the real sales drive for the MGA, like its predecessors, was for export. Here a car is being craned from dockside at London, into the hold of a ship. See how the windscreen has been removed and stowed under the temporary transit tonneau (stencilled with 'Nuffield Exports').

© BRITISH MOTOR INDUSTRY HERITAGE TRUST

A consignment of MGAs destined for export wait at the dockside in London. Although destined for a sea journey, and therefore fitted with headlamp protectors, their windscreens removed, and temporary tonneau covers fitted, this particular consignemnt of cars is not fixed into timber shipping frames.

© BRITISH MOTOR INDUSTRY HERITAGE TRUST

Viewed from above, the MGAs from Nuffield Exports, fitted into timber frames. Also in the hold are some Nash Metropolitans and a few Ford Zephyrs.

© BRITISH MOTOR INDUSTRY HERITAGE TRUST

They came in two by two: a pair of MGA 1500 Roadsters in their timber crates are carefully hoisted on to the Los Angeles dockside from the ship.

© BRITISH MOTOR INDUSTRY HERITAGE TRUST

RIGHT: **A dockside loader does all the work, while a number of Gough Industries representatives look on.**

© BRITISH MOTOR INDUSTRY HERITAGE TRUST

A wonderfully evocative image, clearly posed for the camera, with a line of export-specification MGA Roadsters, all bearing trade plates and many already fitted with black headlamp protectors, lined up especially for the photographer in Clifton Hampden's quaint High Street, a turn towards Long Wittenham just off the main road between Abingdon and Oxford. The photo by PA/ Reuters dates from 8 October 1957, and was issued with the caption 'From the old world to the new'. The second MGA has a trade plate with the company name 'B. J. Henry Ltd', the Oxford-based company which ran car transporters to ferry many Nuffield Exports cars to the docks, minimizing the mileage recorded on each car's odometer.

© PA IMAGES

Note how the chassis numbers have been stencilled on the timber crate; these cars are chassis nos 19245 and 19626... where are they now?

© BRITISH MOTOR INDUSTRY HERITAGE TRUST

Remarkably, the setting is hardly changed, some sixty years later...

AUTHOR PHOTO

MGAs went to North America by a number of different routes, dependent both upon the ultimate destination as well as securing sufficient cargo space; MGs mostly went from London or Liverpool, and at the other end it could typically have been Hamilton (Ontario), New York, the Port of Mobile Alabama, and on the west coast, the Port of Los Angeles. A major challenge was securing enough shipping space for the MGA; export numbers of the T-Series sports cars had been impressive in their own right, but the production volume and supply chain pressures of the new model had rapidly outstripped its predecessors. The common thread throughout this process, however, remained Nuffield Exports and (for US sales), Hambro Automotive.

PAINT AND TRIM COMBINATIONS

EARLIER CARS: 1500 AND TWIN CAM

MG MGA 1500 Roadster and MG MGA Twin Cam Roadster (up to Car 2192)

Body Colour	BMC Code	Main Trim Colour	Hood & Side-Screen Colour
Black	BK1	Red	Black or Ice Blue
Black	BK1	Green	Black or Ice Blue
Orient Red	RD3	Red	Black
Orient Red	RD3	Black	Black
Tyrolite Green/Ash Green *	GN7/GN2	Grey	Black or Ice Blue
Tyrolite Green/Ash Green *	GN7/GN2	Black	Black or Ice Blue
Glacier Blue	BU4	Grey	Black or Ice Blue
Glacier Blue	BU4	Black	Black or Ice Blue
Old English White	WT3	Red	Black
Old English White	WT3	Black	Black

* The first production cars, 10101 to 10105 inclusive, were all finished in Tyrolite Green (roadsters up to chassis no. 48979). Ash Green was introduced in February 1958 at chassis no. 48980.

MGA 1500 ROADSTER PRODUCTION – 1955 TO 1959 INCLUSIVE

Year	Right- Hand Drive Home	Right- Hand Drive Export	Left- Hand Drive Export	Left-Hand Drive North American Export	Right- Hand Drive CKD	Left- Hand Drive CKD	Grand Totals
1955	210	93	106	594	0	0	*1,003*
1956	794	721	1,150	10,589	48	92	*13,394*
1957	368	379	1,019	13,869	672	160	*16,467*
1958	368	349	848	12,462	509	275	*14,811*
1959	119	68	314	6,149	142	11	*6,803*
Totals	***1,859***	***1,610***	***3,437***	***43,663***	***1,371***	**538**	***52,478***

Footnotes:
Production figures shown for MGA 1500 Roadster only; other models are covered in later chapters. The figures show that 83.2 per cent of these cars were exported specifically to North America, while just 3.5 per cent remained behind for home market consumption. A similar figure (3.6 per cent) went for CKD export and 9.6per cent were exported in fully built-up form to other export markets. For details of CKD ('completely knocked down') production, see Chapter 8.

MGA 1500 CHASSIS NUMBERS

The chassis number digits are recorded on an alloy plate, fixed to the bulkhead in the engine compartment. On Abingdon-assembled cars only, the numerals were also stamped on the top face of the chassis frame (occasionally helpful to a restorer if the alloy plate is missing).

Early MGAs used a chassis number prefix system which provided a fair amount of detail about the car specification.

The codes are as follows:

1st digit: 'H' = MGA
2nd digit: 'D' indicates a Roadster and 'M' indicates a Coupé (*see* Chapter 5)
3rd digit: 'A' = Black; 'C' = Red (Orient Red – early cars only); 'D' = Blue; 'E' = Green; 'K' = 'Light Red' (Orient Red – 1956 onwards); 'L' = 'Light Blue' (1956 onwards); 'R' = White; 'T' = 'Light Green' (Ash Green or Tyrolite Green – 1956 onwards); 'H' = Primer or CKD (*see also* Chapter 8)
4th digit: '1' = RHD home market; '2' = RHD export; '3' = LHD export; '4' = LHD export to USA; '5' = RHD CKD; '6' = LHD CKD (*see also* Chapter 8)
5th digit: '3' = Cellulose Lacquer; '5' – Primer or CKD (*see also* Chapter 8)
Numbers: From 10101 (May 1955; the last MG TF had been 10100) to 68850 (July 1959); thereafter the MGA 1600 took over (*see* Chapter 7)

JAMES WOODCOCK AND REG JACKSON

James Woodcock.
AUTHOR'S COLLECTION

JAMES WOODCOCK

Warwickshire-born James Reginald 'Jim' Woodcock OBE (31 July 1906–1 January 1991) was for many years 'number two' to Reggie Hanks, and a Morris Motors' managing director.

In 1922 at the age of sixteen, Woodcock secured a highly regarded Wolseley apprenticeship, and rose through the ranks there to become Tool Room Superintendent. In 1935 he moved over to Morris Motors Ltd at Cowley as Supplies Supervisor, and in 1938 became Assistant Works Manager at Cowley. When World War II ended, he became Works Manager, Cars Branch, then Production Manager in 1947, and assistant to R. F. Hanks from 1953. On 21 January 1954 he was appointed to the main BMC Board as Deputy Managing Director, Morris Motors Ltd and thus was a powerful second to Hanks, often deputising in the chairman's absence. As such, he took an interest in MG affairs from Cowley, and as S.V. Smith's boss, he was also frequently in direct contact with John Thornley.

When Hanks resigned the Morris Motors Chairmanship in 1955, Woodcock was thrust even further into the Longbridge maelstrom and found the BMC management style uncomfortable. In that context, presiding over the factory that generated the enormous export sales success of the MGA was surely a welcome positive.

By the summer of 1961, as the centre of power at Cowley was transferring even further to Longbridge, Woodcock found that rather than being the Deputy Director of Morris Motors, he was to become just one of three: his role would be to take responsibility for home and export sales, service and advertising (much of that based at Cowley).

In 1963, when Lord Nuffield died, he left Jim Woodcock the princely sum of £5,000 'in recognition of his loyalty to me and that company'; most were then equally surprised when on 14 May 1964, Woodock resigned from all his BMC directorships (twenty-eight of them). Geoffrey Iley (who would become a BMC Board member on 12 May 1965) told the author: 'Lord Nuffield's bequest shows a strong bond and respect for his capabilities. I believe that he was side-lined and belittled at Longbridge, hence his early retirement.'

Woodcock lived in contented retirement at his home in Solihull where he died, aged eighty-four, on New Years' Day 1991.

This advertisement from the *Autosport* issue of 4 April 1958 for the MGA is significant, in part because of the image used – a car in motion with a female passenger's hair blowing in the wind. If one imagines this image switched as a mirror image, and the wheels rather crudely retouched, then the result is the image used for the MGA Twin Cam brochure cover (*see* page 139) first released to the public a matter of weeks after this advertisement appeared.
AUTHOR'S COLLECTION

continued overleaf

JAMES WOODCOCK AND REG JACKSON *continued*

REG JACKSON

One of Syd Enever's cohorts was Reg 'Jacko' Jackson, who was also part of the famous 'Insomnia Crew' that supported MG racing at the height of its pre-war activity. By the time that the MGA came on the scene, Jackson was MG's Chief Inspector; it was his job to ensure that all MGAs (and of course Abingdon's other products) left the factory to the best possible quality levels.
ENEVER ALBUM

Reginald Cecil 'Jacko' Jackson (19 February 1906–29 September 1976) was, at the time that the MGA was being built, Abingdon's Chief Inspector, but like many of his peers, he also had motor-racing in his blood. He was born in Windsor, Berkshire. In his teenage years he served a full apprenticeship with a car maker called GWK, based near his family home in Maidenhead. Jackson then made his way to Kennington, Oxford, where he became a chauffeur-mechanic; eventually he came back to Oxford and employment in another garage.

The break-through came with a job at the MG Car Company, initially at Edmund Road in 1928 (where Cecil Cousins set him to work on development of the new MG 18/80), and thereafter at Abingdon; from 1930 to 1936 he was in charge of MG racing activities, working closely with colleagues such as Syd Enever, Cecil Cousins and Alec Hounslow.

After the racing activities were curtailed, Jackson – like Syd Enever – retained involvement with the record-breaking endeavours of Captain Goldie Gardner, but scaled back his extramural competition motoring exploits. This was around the same time that Abingdon's production volume exploded, with the MG Magnette and MGA, and the other models that swiftly followed. MGA owners and enthusiasts throughout the world should know that at least part of the reason that the Abingdon-built cars were so well put together and tested was down to Reg Jackson and his team: the role of 'chief inspector' roughly equates to what nowadays would be known as 'quality control'.

MGA 1500 ENGINE NUMBERS

The old Nuffield engines, like those of the MG T-Series, had four-letter prefixes such as XPAG or XPEG. With the BMC merger, changes began as engine ranges were rationalized. For the early MGA 1500, the engine prefixes were initially 'BP15GB':

1st digit: 'B' = B-Series
2nd digit: 'P' = pushrod (the MGA Twin Cam was 'C')
3rd and 4th digits: '15' = 1,489cc
5th digit: 'B' = MGA ('A' was Z Magnette; 'C' a later Magnette)

For early cars, this engine number was stamped on the chassis plate, but this was soon abandoned in favour of a reference on the chassis plate to 'See engine'.

In 1957, the prefix was changed to '15GB-U-H' (the 'U' stood for a central gear change, and 'H' meant high compression). Then in January 1959 the engine was modified at chassis no. 61504, with a high-mounted starter motor, and the prefix became '15GD-U-H' (the 'D' indicating the revision in sequence with the other letters indicated above). The MGA Twin Cam and MGA 1600 engines are covered later.

CHAPTER FIVE

THE MGA 1500 COUPÉ

EX 197 – A COUPÉ FOR MG

John Thornley could see that whilst the MGA Roadster would be responsible for the bulk of MG sports-car sales, there was a growing appetite – in Europe in particular – for closed 'Grand Tourismo' coupés, suitable for long-distance journeys where some of the privations of an open sports car could become wearing. He could also see that there was a growing appetite from some customers for greater sophistication and security.

'In the early 'fifties, when we were playing with George Phillips' TDs – which finally grew into the MGA – I saw, in a production car race at Silverstone, three DB2/4 Aston Martins running in line ahead, and I became obsessed with the thought that they were of a shape that we should pursue.' However, although he championed this with the new DO 1062, 'by then the MGA was too far down the road, and mainly because of the boot-lid, the MGA Coupé bore scant relationship to the DB2/4!'

Also on Thornley's mind was the fact that Porsche had developed a solid business model through selling both open and coupé versions of its 1300, 1500 and 1600 sports models, and coupled with the proposed twin cam engine (see Chapter 6), there could be scope to expand MG's sports-car offering. With the sanction of the Morris Motors Board, therefore, Eric Carter, Jim O'Neill and Don Butler rekindled their relationship forged with the original roadster. At a Morris Motors Board meeting on 7 May 1956, Project 'B11: MGA Coupé, addition of a fixed head to a standard body', with tooling, was approved, at a budget cost of £8,000.

Jim O'Neill recalled the sequence of events: 'I remember going to Coventry with John Thornley and Syd Enever to view the car; none of us had any idea of what we were likely to see. When I saw it I felt that it was too round and lumpy – and I told Eric so.' Inspired by the shape of the Alpine Rally hardtop, Carter had gone ahead with the production of wooden patterns – known as 'bucks' – without formal authorization.

The reverse of this early MGA Coupé press image carries the text: 'The beautifully streamlined MGA is now obtainable in a fixed hardtop version. Of pressed steel construction, the domed roof is welded to the body and incorporates a wrap-around rear windscreen and fully wind-down windows.'

AUTHOR'S COLLECTION

Undoubtedly photographed somewhere in the general vicinity of Abingdon-on-Thames, this publicity photo of an early MGA Coupé, YWL 15, is characteristic of the genteel promotional style of the mid-1950s.

AUTHOR'S COLLECTION

An MG Abingdon 'blueprint' for the MGA Coupé; this particular drawing has been amended as a running revision to show a later MGA 1600 Coupé, the tail-light details representing the model of 1959/60. The reference numbers are drawing number A7047, originally drawn by Peter Neal on 18 October 1956, but revised on 2 March 1959 to show the revised tail-lamps.
BOB VITRIKAS

Jim O'Neill said that Carter was genuinely worried: 'Eric informed me that production tooling was already under way, although the cost had not been cleared, and implored me not to "rock the boat"... on MG's tight budget, questions would have been asked if they had been scrapped – hence Eric's concern; in retrospect I am sure that the MGA Coupé is a classic shape.' Don Butler added: 'People said that the shape of the roof was designed by Eric so that he could wear his trilby inside!'

Don Butler also said that he had understood the new variant to be only a toe in the water: 'I was told that it was originally intended that there would only be about fifty MGA coupés, and so very low volume tooling was chosen, with a high degree of hand work.' Jim O'Neill agreed that the tooling for the unique coupé body panels was relatively simple: 'The roof of the coupé was hand-formed in three sections by rolling and beating over a reinforced former; likewise for the windscreen pillars.'

Carter's ingenuity also came to the fore when it came to finding a way to provide an external catch for the door – the coupé's wind-down windows and quarter lights meant that an owner no longer had the recourse of simply reaching in through a side-screen to grab a cable inside the door. The ingenious solution was a pair of neat and relatively inconspicuous, vertically aligned, chrome-plated levers that were bespoke for the MGA Coupé.

In the usual manner, the MGA Coupé was allocated a number in Abingdon's EX Register, but as most of the changes were to the body and fixings, the majority of drawing work was undertaken at Coventry, and so the register lists no drawings against EX 197; indeed the single relevant page in the EX-Register has just the simple undated entry, reading 'All prototype and production part numbers issued by Bodies Branch, Coventry, for new panels, glasses, trim and hardware.'

Much of the early publicity for the MGA Coupé utilized studio photographs of a black car, registration 'ULJ 426' (HDA13-13355). Curiously the rear window shape of this car differs subtly from that of production MGA Coupés, having a style similar to that of the Vanden Plas hardtop. Jim O'Neill told the author that the car he and John Thornley had first seen at Coventry was virtually identical to what went into production.

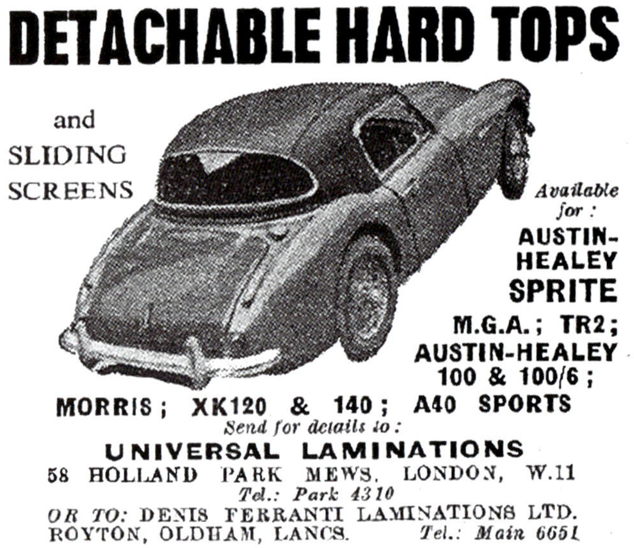

An advertisement from Universal Laminations/Denis Ferranti Ltd dating from July 1958, listing a hardtop for the MGA alongside ones for many other cars. There has long been some confusion about the true identity of the company responsible, not least because these GRP MGA hardtops bore a serial number tag that read 'Manufactured by Universal Laminations (Denis Ferranti Laminations Ltd)'. Brian Osbourn, long-time employee of Denis Ferranti, clarified this for the author: 'Universal Laminations was a trading name of Estaglass Ltd, and my records show that Denis Ferranti Ltd, based at Royton – where transformers were made – bought Estaglass Ltd, making it a subsidiary of the Denis Ferranti Group. Shortly after this, a new company was formed to take over the GRP manufacturing of Estaglass (trading as Universal Laminations) and becoming a subsidiary of Denis Ferranti Meter Ltd, based at Bangor, North Wales, which soon became the home of the group because Denis Ferranti himself had bought the Gorddinog estate at nearby Llanfairfechan.'
AUTHOR'S COLLECTION

THE VANDEN PLAS HARDTOP

The neat factory hardtop offered as an extra on the MGA from 1956 onwards was initially this alloy unit manufactured by BMC subsidiary Vanden Plas.
ENEVER FAMILY

What is believed to be a prototype Vanden Plas hardtop on an MGA at the factory in 1956. Note how, for reasons that are uncertain, the hub-caps on this car have MG medallions on them.
ENEVER FAMILY

From the outset it was intended that there would be a hardtop aimed both at competition use and for sale to those customers who desired the greater protection against inclement weather it could afford. In December 1955, two MGA 1500 Roadsters (Chassis Nos. 10869 and 10870) were dedicated for 'hardtop development', and one of them was duly despatched to Vanden Plas, the Kingsbury-based coach-building wing of BMC, for the development of a suitable removable hardtop in alloy. Meanwhile the Morris Motors Board sanctioned £5,000 to cover the estimated tooling cost of the hardtop at their meeting of 11 January 1956 (Project 'B3: MGA Hardtop').

The project code 'EX 196' was allocated less than a month later, on 7 February 1956, although as all the development and drawing work was done by Vanden Plas at their Kingsbury works, there is very little in the EX-Register beyond the initial allocation of the code number. By the summer, the first such hardtops were in use on competition MGAs, such as the Alpine Rally (see Chapter 10), and the customer announcement came in October. Research by Anders Ditlev Clausager in terms of Vanden Plas company records indicated that 1,450 were produced, up until June 1960, when the costly accessory was discontinued in favour of the cheaper GRP one.

Jim O'Neill confirmed that the alloy hardtops were very expensive:

> *Service Department felt there was no way they could market the Vanden Plas top with the normal service loading. Another hardtop was examined, made by Universal Laminations, constructed of wood and fibreglass and covered in vinyl. A fair amount of work would have been required to make this top suitable for production; however, before this could take place, the hardtop business of Universal Laminations was taken over by Denis Ferranti. They made a quality product in double-skinned fibreglass with steel reinforcements.*

Hardtops of both kinds came with different side screens – originally with rigid black-painted steel, later bare aluminium alloy frames (both with 'Plexiglass' (Perspex) windows) and later, from 1960, fabric-covered frames common to those for the MGA 1600 Roadster.

By 1960, when the MGA 1600 had replaced the 1500, BMC was offering a less expensive glass-reinforced plastic hardtop in lieu of the Vanden Plas alloy top. Initially made by Universal Laminations, manufacture was later taken on by Denis Ferranti Ltd. This appears to be an early prototype photographed in the studio.
ENEVER FAMILY

Although very practicable, durable and affordable, there is surely little doubt that the GRP hardtops introduced in 1960, as shown in this factory photo, lack something of the quality and sophistication of the more expensive alloy-panelled Vanden Plas equivalents.
ENEVER FAMILY

The black pre-production MGA Coupé prototype ULJ 426 (HDA13-13355). Originally an MGA 1500 Roadster built in March/April 1956, the build records indicate the despatch destination as Morris Bodies Branch, as a development vehicle. The studio photographs were taken on 3 May 1956: quick work by all concerned.
AUTHOR'S COLLECTION

The car in question was chassis no. 13355, and former BMIHT archivist Anders Ditlev Clausager told the author many years ago that it was built in March/April 1956, with an original despatch destination given as Morris Bodies Branch, and its purpose listed as a development vehicle. The studio photographs were taken on 3 May 1956, which of course was still several months before the production version first appeared. The car was later registered in March 1957, and after deteriorating badly it was rescued and restored, although according to current DVLA records in 2018, it seems to have been off the road for some forty years.

CABRIOLET THOUGHTS

Shortly before the MGA Coupé entered production, John Thornley spoke to Vanden Plas, the Kingsbury-based coach-building wing of BMC, about the possibility of a cabriolet version of the MGA.

This would have been quite attractive in theory, as for the first time it would have married the pleasures of open-top motoring with modern comfortable accoutrements such as quarter lights, winding door windows and lockable doors, whilst the more substantial hood might have been seen as being in the mould of the pre-war Tickford MG Midget and SA. However, what counted against it were costs (clearly it would have been even more expensive than the Coupé), and the fact that the extra weight would have further blunted performance. In the event, therefore, the idea was abandoned.

MOTOR SHOW

Mrs. Nancy Mitchell, who has had many sporting victories with M.G. cars, is one of the first to approve the new M.G. Series MGA Coupé.

ABOVE: **Nancy Mitchell poses alongside the new MGA Coupé at the 1956 Earls Court Motor show.**

LEFT: **An MGA Coupé body is inspected at Morris Bodies Branch. Note the different finishes on the wings and front valance, supplied as separate bolted-on pressings.**
AUTHOR'S COLLECTION

KMO 326 – THE DEVELOPMENT MGA

Pictured at Abingdon whilst still owned by MG, the special two-tone paint finish of KMO 326 is readily apparent.
AUTHOR'S COLLECTION

KMO 326 was often pressed into duty for high-speed testing, such as here at the MIRA high speed circuit.
AUTHOR'S COLLECTION

The very first road-going specification MGA, complete with bumpers and trim of a type commensurate with the subsequent volume-built cars, appears to have been KMO 326, which would go on to play an important role in the story not only of the MGA Roadster but also the subsequent MGA Coupé and even the early development of the MGB which followed afterwards. As well as the BMC publicity foray to Montlhéry, KMO 326 was pressed into use for development and as a kind of pool car; Don Hayter told a future owner of the car, Chris Longridge, that at one stage he used it almost daily for journeys to Coventry and MIRA, as well as borrowing it during his honeymoon.

After Longridge acquired the car he set out to research its early history, and successfully tracked down Don Hayter as well as John Sharpe, a former MG Development Department Technical Assistant. Hayter confirmed that KMO 326 'was indeed one of our development cars, specially ordered from the Bodies Branch as the first representative production standard-build car. It did many miles using development parts and comparative alternatives supplied by manufacturers.'

The next stage in the KMO 326 story was its conversion to a coupé; the EX Register code for the hardtop variant was EX 197, and it is instructive that at some stage, this car was given the chassis number EX 197/1. Over the fullness of time KMO 326 was used for ongoing development work on the Coupé, such as when the rear part of the passenger compartment was modified (for the original '1600') to fully separate the spare wheel from the area behind the seats, and at the same time a lowering of the parcel shelf, the dual aims being to better isolate the interior from noise from the back axle, and to try to gain a small amount of additional storage capacity in a touring coupé that was rather bereft of space.

Roger Enever's first race at Brands Hatch; note the buckled front nearside wing.
ROGER ENEVER

There is a popular story that the reason that this additional space was found in the rear of the passenger compartment was that Syd Enever did this to make room for his pet dog; however his son Roger doubts this had any basis in fact: 'we did have a Cairn Terrier, which was my sister's, Jane. I doubt if this was his consideration though!'

John Sharpe, who had started work at Abingdon in August 1959, had in fact driven KMO 326 to a meeting at the Swindon Pressed Steel plant on his first day at work. Subsequently he would drive the car extensively on development work, including when it had been converted to its penultimate 1600 Mark II guise.

continued overleaf

KMO 326 – THE DEVELOPMENT MGA *continued*

One of the later tests that Sharpe recalled was a comparison test between the maximum speed of the MGA and MGB with the same engine: 'The MGA proved to be 4mph faster than its replacement, the MGB' he would later recall. Whilst in Coupé guise, Syd Enever took KMO 326 on as his personal transport, and it was specially finished in metallic gold with a white roof – the latter a bespoke paint finish with ground-up mother-of-pearl. Inside the car was specially trimmed in magnolia leather.

Eventually the MGA was sold by the factory in 1964 to the Enever family, but there was a mild dilemma, as technically it was a hand-built prototype and not part of the MGA production sequence, and so did not have a recognizable chassis number. The answer was to give it an MGA chassis number – but of course the MGA had already been replaced by the new MGB – and so the cheeky solution was to add another number after the last true production MGA chassis number – and hence KMO 326 received the chassis number GHD109071. Bob West, who many years later restored the car, recalls that the chassis plate was of the MGB type.

Roger Enever behind the wheel of KMO 326 at Silverstone in 1964.
ROGER ENEVER

Copse Corner at Silverstone, with Roger Enever leading an MGB on 30 June 1964.
ROGER ENEVER

At this point, early in its racing career, KMO 326 still has its original full-sized MGA grille aperture – not necessarily the most aerodynamically efficient, and arguably likely to over-cool the engine bay.
ROGER ENEVER

Throughout its 'racing years' the MGA Coupé retained its ivory-painted roof.
ROGER ENEVER

KMO 326 in action, with Roger Enever at the wheel.
ROGER ENEVER

After a series of owners, KMO 326 was restored to a 'better than new' condition, resplendent in metallic gold, with a white roof and magnolia interior trim.
BONHAMS

Over the years, KMO 326 has had various engines fitted – 1498, 1588, 1622 and 1842cc.
BONHAMS

KMO 326 then passed into the hands of Syd Enever's son Roger, who soon took up racing in his new acquisition, during which its body became red in place of the gold. This initial racing period did not last long, however, and KMO 326 was later sold on Syd Enever's behalf, being bought by a K. R. Clark of Chipstead, Surrey, on 8 May 1965. Thereafter it went through a series of owners; more recently it was restored (by Bob West) to its gold and white guise, to represent the peak of its time as Syd Enever's personal car.

INTO PRODUCTION

As far as the general public was concerned, the MGA Coupé first came to their attention at the October 1956 Earls Court Motor Show. By then, of course, early production cars had been built, and indeed three were ready in time. Chassis no. 20671 was an Orient Red car with black upholstery, which was sent to University Motors, the London MG distributor and dealer. Chassis no. 20672 was an Old English White car, displayed on the stand at Earls Court; whilst a third, chassis no. 20673, a North-American specification car in Island Green with green trim, was put on display in the window of Nuffield House, the Piccadilly Showroom.

Within days of the conclusion of the Earls Court Show, an MGA 1500 Coupé press demonstrator (chassis no. 21210) was completed, and production began intermittently in anticipation of customer demand. Production then became more regular, and largely mirrored the development pattern of the corresponding Roadster, until both 1500 models gave way to the 1600 versions – the stories of which follow in Chapter 7. Probably the most useful improvement came at chassis no. 25110, in January 1957, when door locks were fitted to both sides.

SALES AND MARKETING: MGA COUPÉ ADVERTS AND BROCHURES

Much of the earliest press and publicity material for the MGA Coupé featured studio photos of the black prototype ULJ 426 referred to earlier, for the simple reason that at the time, that was the only running car in existence. As a new variant of the MGA 1500, the Coupé initially featured in UK sales literature in the form of revised versions of the original 1955 variant, but with some new coupé artwork substituted for some of the roadster images inside – an example being brochure H&E 5666 (the code signifying 'home and export' and the '56' indicating a 1956 print).

Just prior to the arrival of the MGA Twin Cam, BMC issued another brochure (E.5812 for export), the cover of which featured a partial side view of a Glacier Blue MGA Roadster, and standing alongside, an elegant lady in a belted black dress – and for once, no driver in view. Inside, images included a red Roadster (with registration number MJB 994) and a Coupé in what looks like Old English White (908 AWL).

The BMC/Hambro press release for 29 January 1958 was as follows:

For: Hambro Automotive Corporation
27 West 57th Street
New York 19, NY
Further Information: Josephson, Cuffari & Company
420 Lexington Avenue
New York 17, NY
(*Contact:* Bill Haworth-ORegon 9-6255)
FOR RELEASE 30 JAN AM AND THEREAFTER

British Made 1958 MG 'A' Coupé Offers Outstanding Performance

New York, 29 January: The 1958 British-built MG A-Type coupé offers true 100 miles per hour sports-car performance plus hardtop weather protection. MGs, long popular with American owners, are on display by more than 500 US distributors and dealers.

Selling in the $2,600 price bracket, the distinctively styled MG 'A' two-passenger coupé features an enclosed luggage compartment, wrap-around windshield and rear window, and mechanically is similar to the MG roadster. It has an economical 4-cylinder 1489 cc overhead-valve engine fitted with two British SU carburettors, and develops 72hp at 5,500rpm. In 1957 a streamlined experimental MG equipped with the 'A'-type engine captured five official Class F world records on the Bonneville Salt Flats, attaining a speed of 245.11mph [394.38km/h].

The fleet, low-slung 1958 MG 'A' coupé has an overall height of 50in [127cm], ground clearance of 6in [15cm], and a trim overall length of 156in [396cm]. The coupé has adjustable bucket-type seats, and its carpeted interior is richly trimmed in leather in various color combinations. Despite its small size, it offers comfortable seating, ample leg room, and is easy to enter. The new 1958 sports coupé has four forward speeds and reverse with synchromesh on second, third and fourth, and a three-quarter floating rear axle with hypoid final reduction gears.

Steering of the MG coupé is quick, featuring direct rack and pinion devoid of play, and providing instant response to the slightest turning. Its front wheels are self-centering and recover from turns fast and naturally. Front suspension has independent coil springs with hydraulic shock absorbers.

This home-market advertisement proclaims that with the roadster and coupé variants on offer, 'thrills come double'.
AUTHOR'S COLLECTION

Here, a Hambro advert aligns the MGA Coupé with the MG Z Magnette, saying that these MG models with their fixed roofs offered 'sports-car fun all year round'.
AUTHOR'S COLLECTION

A page taken from inside a brochure for the MGA, featuring the artist's impressions clearly based on the contemporary black-and-white press imagery.
AUTHOR'S COLLECTION

Hambro issued this photograph of an MGA Coupé with wire wheels (but, unusually, no white-wall tyres) for a press release in January 1958.
AUTHOR'S COLLECTION

Rear suspension is provided by semi-elliptic springs with hydraulic shock absorbers. The car's chassis has an exceptionally sturdy box frame, specially braced for torsional rigidity to offer superior handling on road or track.

Although 'MG' is perhaps the world's best known name in the sports-car field, many people do not know how the name originated – in fact the initials stand for the small Morris Garages, where the first MG was built in 1929. Today, the MG Car Company is an important part of the giant British Motor Corporation, fourth largest auto maker in the world. Many models have followed the first MG and have won world-wide design, road and track trophy honors too numerous to list.

The MG and other lines manufactured by the British Motor Corporation, the world's fourth largest auto maker, are imported by the Hambro Automotive Corporation, and sold and serviced by dealers throughout the United States.

PETER SEYMOUR'S MGA COUPÉ

An interesting MGA Coupé was a 1958 car first registered to the MG Car Company in February of that year as PBL 497. This Old English White car was, naturally, originally fitted with the normal 1498cc engine and all-round drum brakes, and it was retained by the factory for press and demonstration purposes, appearing for example at the special Chobham press event for the MGA Twin Cam on 14 July (see Chapter 6). Chassis number was HMR13-48248, and the original engine number (at the time of a factory Development Department Report of 20 March 1958 on the road-testing of PBL 497) was 15GB-UH.38237.

Evidently the car was subsequently retained by MG, but probably used for some development work, because by the time it was bought in the early 1960s by Bob Ehlers of Nuffield Export Technical Service, it was fitted with the MGA 1600 Mark II's 1622cc unit (*see also* Chapter 7). PBL 497 was subsequently bought by Ehlers' colleague Peter Seymour in 1965 or 1966, and the photograph reproduced on the next page shows Seymour alongside the car at his parents' home in Battle, East Sussex. Seymour got married in 1967 and although the MGA Coupé served duty on the couple's honeymoon, it was later sold.

The car was owned in the following decade by John Patrick, but as it deteriorated it was taken off the road. Thankfully it survives in 2018, in the ownership of David Lee, although it is now finished in red instead of the original white. Another interesting MGA Coupé registered PRX 14 was the first to be fitted with the new 1588cc '1600' engine; its story is also told in Chapter 7.

Peter Seymour stands alongside his MGA Coupé at his parents' home in Battle, East Sussex, in 1966. Originally finished in Old English White, it has more recently been restored in red. This car was present at the press launch of the MGA Twin Cam (see Chapter 6) because at that time, no MGA Twin Cam Coupés were available.
PETER SEYMOUR

THE MGA 1500 COUPÉ IN THE PRESS

The first of the UK weekly motoring magazines to test the MGA 1500 Coupé was *Autocar*, for the issue of 3 May 1957. The car tested by the magazine appears to have been NJB 381, an Old English White car with red interior (HMR13-23387), and the driving took place in England rather than the usual continental trip. The testers found the Coupé 'more sprightly', and that the model rapidly reached 90mph (145km/h), 'coupled with stability of a very high standard'. A 52-mile (84km) trip from Wilmslow in Buckinghamshire to Coventry via secondary roads was achieved inside an hour of fast driving and yet consumed fuel at the rate of 25mpg (11ltr/100km), though most of the test achieved closer to 30mpg (9.4ltr/100km). The magazine observed:

'From these examples, one can see that although the car is only a 1½ litre, it can cover the ground very quickly indeed, and in normal, fairly fast driving, about 28mpg [10ltr/100km] might be expected. When the car was driven with fuel economy in mind, 35mpg [8ltr/100km] could be exceeded' – certainly impressive for a sports coupé capable of 100mph (160km/h). The engine, gearbox, ride and handling all drew similar praise, as did the light and sensitive steering, but a few aspects of finish raised eyebrows, such as draughts and rattles for the wind-up door glasses (still a novelty for an MG sports car).

The layout of the instruments also drew criticism, as did the position of the rear-view mirror (which obscured the view forward of the nearside wing) – but the strongest concern was the difficulty of getting in and out of the car, a common issue for many other testers (MG responded about two years later by changing the door hinges, to allow the doors to open wider on chassis nos. 52916 on the Coupé in June 1958). In conclusion, the magazine summarized the MGA Coupé as being 'as pleasant to drive as it is to look at. It is an excellent successor to a famous line, with fine road holding and a performance which is worthy of the manufacturer.'

The monthly *Motor Sport* featured a road test of the MGA Coupé in their June 1957 issue, under the headline 'In the MG Tradition'. The actual testing of NJB 381 again took place in April, with some 1,200 miles (1,930km) being added to the clock. Generally the magazine was very complimentary, but

AUTOSPORT, AUGUST 16, 1957

TWO SHAPELY MODELS are posed together at the Battersea Pleasure Gardens in London—the one on the left being the M.G.A Coupé. "Proper" wind-up windows, outside door handles and full interior trim are amongst the amenities provided. The girl is Australian ballet-dancer Toni Reece.

JOHN BOLSTER TESTS

The M.G.A Coupe

Fixed-head Coupe version of a Popular Abingdon 1½-litre Sports Car provides Saloon-Car Weather Protection and a Top Speed of over 102 m.p.h.

ON the Continent, the sports car is normally a 2-seater coupé. In England, in spite of our atrocious weather, most sports models are open, and there is a scarcity of hardtops except among the larger makers. Now, M.G. have produced a proper little coupé, and it will sell like hot cakes. It is of modern appearance and compact size, and its wrap-around screen and rear window avoid that "shut-in" feeling. Above all, it is a genuine closed car with wind-up windows, and not an open 2-seater with a hardtop attached.

The M.G.A is a well-known car and has, of course, been tested by AUTOSPORT in open form. Only a brief description is, therefore, required. The basis of the machine is a very sturdy box-section frame. The engine is the 1½-litre B.M.C. unit, tuned in this case to develop 72 b.h.p. at 5,500 r.p.m. There are twin S.U. carburetters and the Lucas distributor has centrifugal and vacuum control.

The four-speed gearbox has the traditional central remote-control lever, and one is delighted to find that the fly-off handbrake has been retained. Wishbone independent front suspension, with helical springs and rack and pinion steering, is mated with a hypoid rear axle on semi-elliptic springs.

The appearance is attractive and the car is nicely finished. The instrument panel is well arranged, and the octagon motif of the past is mercifully forgotten. Entry and exit are not particularly easy because the doors are curiously restricted in their opening. Once one is in, the driving position is found to be excellent, and the seats are comfortable, though some drivers would prefer a little more support for the thighs.

The M.G.A is astonishingly fast for a 1½-litre production car. The coupé is better streamlined than the open car, and I obtained the excellent timed speed of 102.27 m.p.h. Third gear gives a useful 74 m.p.h., but what is entirely unexpected is the flexibility in top gear, the car coming down to a crawl on that ratio and accelerating cleanly away. As the weight is fairly substantial, one does not expect slashing acceleration, but this is quite a lively vehicle nevertheless.

On the road, 80 m.p.h. is a suitable cruising speed. The engine does not become distressed at high speeds until valve bounce begins at 102 m.p.h. When driven hard it is by no means quiet, however, though the noise is not unpleasant to many sports car enthusiasts.

The old M.G. trouble of clutch slip has been eliminated, and this component is smooth in action but grips at once after a quick change. The gearbox is very pleasant indeed and requires no special skill. Although the suspension is fairly firm, this is only noticed on particularly bad roads.

Naturally, good steering is expected on a car of this class, and the M.G. rack and pinion gains full marks. It is very accurate and not too heavy, nor does the driver feel that he must "hang on" at three-figure speeds. The coupé perhaps rolls fractionally more than the open car, but it handles well and has fairly high cornering power. The rear wheels tend to bounce during a violent getaway, but one is not normally conscious of the weight of the rear axle on its semi-elliptic springs.

The M.G.A can put up a useful average speed when driven in enterprising fashion. Third gear permits hills to be stormed at a pretty impressive velocity. It is above all a sporting type of car, and the closed body in no way modifies this characteristic. The fuel consumption of 26 m.p.g. that I obtained was during really hard driving. No doubt something in the region of 30 m.p.g. could be achieved during Continental touring, which is a good argument for buying this in preference to a more powerful sports car. It is, nevertheless, a pity that the spare wheel occupies so much of the luggage compartment, for the M.G.A

SLEEK coupé top offers less wind resistance than the normal hood, and results in a higher top speed than the sports car although the all-up weight is slightly greater. Luggage space is largely occupied by the spare wheel.

***Autosport*'s John Bolster tested the MGA Coupé for the magazine's issue of 16 August 1957. He achieved a top speed of 102mph (164km/h) and concluded that the car was ' an extremely attractive small closed sports car... with many of the attractions of the sporting Continentals'.**

AUTOSPORT

The MGA Coupé was simply slipped into contemporary MGA sales literature as a new variant; this image comes from inside the export brochure E.5812 of March 1958.

one or two niggles were noted, such as it wasn't possible to open the doors more than 45 degrees (a problem that would later be addressed in production – in June 1958, at chassis no. 52916, showing that BMC obviously read these road tests). The testers thought the driving position excellent, and gear-change was said to be a 'delight, being 100 per cent rigid, well placed, and ideal for really rapid cog-swapping'.

Motor waited a while and tested the MGA 1500 Coupé later, for its issue of 7 August 1957, with the headline 'An Economical 100mph Car with Exceptional Roadworthiness'. In the opening paragraph the magazine noted that whilst there were many cars capable of exceeding 100mph (160km/h), few were sufficiently economical to return fuel consumption better than 25 miles per (UK) gallon (11ltr/100km). However, they concluded that 'standing between these two extremes there is a choice of four cars, all of European origin, which will beat by a useful margin both the 100mph and the 25mpg mark, the latest recruit to this select company being the MGA model with the fixed-head coupé body.'

The cost-cutting implications of having just one external door lock bemused the testers, who felt that a nearside door lock might be acceptable for the bulk of cars sold with left-hand drive, 'but for the home market a lock on the driver's door would be more appropriate, and since in a closed car the driver would probably not wear headgear, the absence of a sun visor is hard to excuse'. The rather silly door-lock situation was addressed with production Coupés from chassis no. 25110 in January 1957; quite why the test car was not converted is a slight puzzle.

The car tested by *Motor* benefited from the optional heater and ventilator, which, according to the magazine, seemed 'more successful at supplying heated air, which was unwanted at this time of year than fresh air at ambient temperature – which was more to be regretted, as opening either the side windows or the ventilating panels permitted the entrance of rain water as well as raising the noise level'. These comments neatly encapsulate one of the well known problems of the Coupé: the compact, closed interior suffered from the same kind of heat transfer from the transmission and engine compartment as the open MGA, but with less chance for this warmth to dissipate when the weather itself was warmer.

Similarly, while the more slippery coupé shape helped the new model achieve a best top speed of 103.8mph (167km/h), there were downsides from the rather noisy running gear, clearly not possible to relieve by lowering the roof: 'The engine cannot be called mechanically quiet. There is a rattle from the pushrod valve gear which is an established characteristic of the type and does not denote mechanical defect – but the gearbox and rear axle are free from objectionable noise.' Summing up, the testers felt that the MGA Coupé was a welcome addition to the family:

> Moderately priced, economical to run and maintain, remarkably fast, exceptionally safe and above all a constant pleasure to drive and be driven in, it is not surprising that the MGA is beating all production records at Abingdon, and that it has established itself as the most popular sports car in the world.

Nine days later, John Bolster reported on the MGA 1500 Coupé for the 16 August 1957 issue of *Autosport*. Bolster drove the white Coupé NJB 381 previously tested by *Motor Sport* and offered broadly similar conclusions; he said that the MGA was, in his view, 'astonishingly quick for a 1½ litre production car', and, as with other testers, the better aerodynamics of the roof allowed him to achieve a higher top speed of 120.27mph (193.51km/h). Added to this, Bolster was impressed with how flexible he found the car to be in top gear, being able to accelerate in this gear from a crawl up to maximum speed. The test concluded that 'the MGA Coupé is an extremely attractive, small closed sports car. It forms a useful and reliable mode of everyday transport, but it also has a very real turn of speed. This is a British car with many of the attractions of the sporting Continentals.'

As the MGA 1500 evolved – with the Twin Cam, 1600 and 1600 Mark II variants – so the Coupé followed suit; for that reason, the Coupé variants of those models are included in the relevant chapters that follow.

MG MGA 1500 COUPÉ AND MG MGA TWIN CAM COUPÉ (UP TO CAR 2291)

Body Colour	BMC Code	Main Trim Colour	Facia Colour
Black	BK1	Red	Black
Black	BK1	Green	Black
Orient Red	RD3	Red	Red
Orient Red	RD3	Black	Red
Island Green/Ash Green *	GN6/GN2	Grey	Green
Island Green/Ash Green *	GN6/GN2	Black	Green
Mineral Blue	BU9	Grey	Grey
Mineral Blue	BU9	Black	Blue
Old English White	WT3	Red	White
Old English White	WT3	Black	White

* Ash Green was introduced in February 1958 at chassis no. 49000 (the last Island Green Coupé was chassis no. 48178)

MGA 1500 COUPÉ PRODUCTION – 1955 TO 1959 INCLUSIVE

Year	Right- Hand-Drive Home	Right- Hand-Drive Export	Left- Hand-Drive Export	Left-Hand- Drive North American Export	Right- Hand-Drive CKD	Left- Hand-Drive CKD	Grand Totals
1956	5	2	3	6	0	0	*16*
1957	398	182	198	3,326	0	0	*4,104*
1958	323	131	83	773	1	0	*1,311*
1959	102	28	48	663	0	0	*841*
Total	**828**	**343**	**332**	**4,768**	**1**	**0**	**6,272**

Footnotes:
Production figures are shown for the MGA 1500 Coupé only; other models are covered in later chapters. The MGA 1500 Coupé sold better proportionally at home (13.2 per cent) than the MGA 1500 Roadster, although one should be cautious as overall sales were significantly less (roughly eight times as many Roadsters were sold compared to their contemporary Coupés). Just over 76 per cent of these Coupés were sold in North America.

CHAPTER SIX

THE MGA TWIN CAM

We saw earlier in Chapter Two how Gerald Palmer had persuaded Vic Oak to sanction the development of a new twin cam engine for MG. Palmer's aim had not been just to create a potent sports car unit for his proposed T-Type replacement but to supply a superior power plant for his lovely Magnette saloon.

Palmer wanted his creation to stand comparison with the best of the new generation of post-war European sports saloons from the likes of Alfa Romeo and to snap at the heels of Jaguar who, as we shall see shortly, was known to have given thought to a four-cylinder to sit below its classic XK six. In this regard, Palmer would eventually find an ally in John Thornley, but sadly the Magnette Twin Cam (with the potential explored of a pillar-less body style) would never appear. As we have seen, Palmer's own 'Midget' and 'Magna' projects similarly went nowhere, but the engine he conceived went on to form part of both the MGA and the MG record-breaking stories.

MORE POWER NEEDED

To appreciate the context of how the idea for a twin cam B-Series got traction, it is necessary to briefly revisit the contemporary story of the recent events at MG and its parent company. Palmer's arrival in the summer of 1949 had been a breath of fresh air at Cowley – from where MG's affairs were still directed: within a year the Morris Motors Board were approving the costs for his new Magnette, which would sweep away the last vestiges of the upright pre-war styling of the Y-Type saloon.

The next step was the BMC merger and the subsequent move to dismantle much of the Nuffield power-train legacy; as a recent arrival (albeit one with pre-war experience at Morris Motors), Palmer had less personal interest vested in the outgoing engine family, and he was reasonably sanguine about the new Austin unit provided it could be made sufficiently refined, reliable and powerful (even if, at first, many at Morris Motors and MG initially detested its origins).

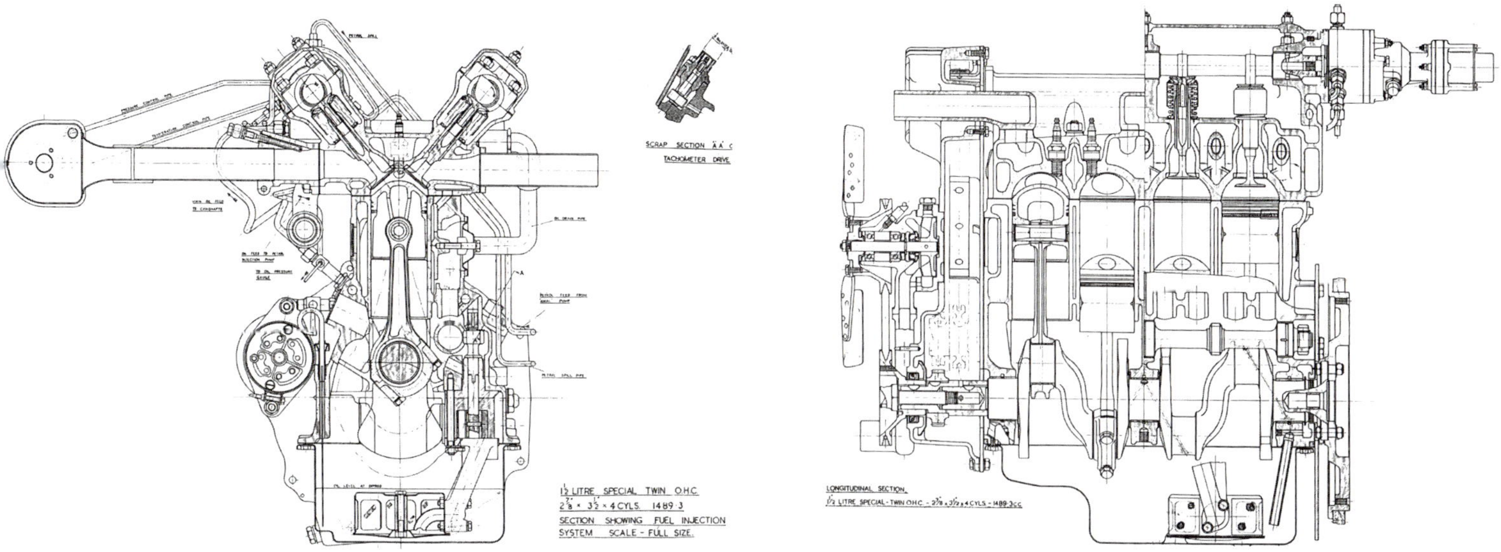

Gerald Palmer's cross-sections of his original MG Twin Cam B-Series concept, complete with take-off for an envisaged SU fuel-injection system that was never developed.

GERALD PALMER

Syd Enever (left) and Alec Hounslow (in fetching headgear) alongside the prototype MGA Twin Cam ORX 885 (note the peg-drive Dunlop wheels) and an MG Z Magnette, paused at the Flüela Pass, a high mountain pass in Graubünden, in the Swiss Alps, at an elevation of 2,383m (7,818ft) above sea level, which connects the cities of Davos and Susch.
ENEVER FAMILY

Alec Hounslow alongside ORX 885 in the Alps.
ENEVER FAMILY

Whilst the Abingdon team were undoubtedly crestfallen that the new management order had rejected their 'EX 175' sports car proposal, there had been some compensation with John Thornley's appointment as MG's new General Manager in November 1952. Just 45 days after Thornley was appointed, the old order was given a final nudge into oblivion when Lord Nuffield resigned his Chairmanship: Leonard Percy Lord was now truly ruler of all he surveyed, even though, as we have seen, Reginald Hanks still oversaw the remaining Nuffield interests – but in a subsidiary role: everyone knew who the real masters were.

It was at this time that Thornley stepped up his corporate charm offensive, in the form of his famous memoranda to management, offering a helpful steer to people who seldom had much of an idea about sporting motoring. The ink was barely dry on Lord Nuffield's signature of resignation when Thornley had begun penning a memo about engine power and the challenges of the ageing XPAG unit. Whilst as we saw earlier, there was at first little love at Abingdon for the new Austin engine, and Thornley's real objective was to seek support for his aerodynamic sports car, there is also little doubt that his cries about the inadequacy of the 'T Type' and 'Y Type' engines found a receptive ear with Gerald Palmer.

A process ensued which benefited from serendipity, because around the same time that John Thornley was expressing his concerns about engine performance, and Palmer was cogitating about a twin cam, the experiments began at Morris Engines in Coventry aimed at getting more power from the Austin-designed B-Series. Thus in the New Year of 1953, James Thompson and his Chief Experimental Engineer Eddie Maher began work to raise the power of the 1.5 litre four cylinder over and above the 60bhp and 4,600rpm which the proposed MG Magnette, with its Twin SU Carburettors, was promising to deliver at launch the following autumn.

The engineers soon found that there were some pretty fundamental problems because, as motoring correspondent Gordon Wilkins wrote in 'Sportscar Graphic': '*it was found that three minutes at 7,000rpm and full load would squeeze the Babbitt out of the bearing shells like toothpaste out of a tube*'. 'Babbitt' is the tin-based alloy commonly used to form the face of automotive engine bearings.

Taking on board the requirement for more power for MG applications (notwithstanding the short-term fix of the 1,466cc 'XPEG' Nuffield-family engine), the men at Morris Engines therefore built an experimental B-Series engine that could be set up to run for extended periods at 7,000rpm. At the same time, it seems that the bearing specialists at Vandervell were knocking at BMC's door, which would lead to them having the chance to use the new engine to help develop their tri-metal bearings.

Whilst as we saw in Chapter Two, Palmer had sports-car ideas of his own, he was mostly concerned with the performance of the forthcoming Magnette; having modelled its lines on the best that the contemporary Italian stylists could offer, it is hardly surprising that he was also interested in their engines, most notably the 1950 Alfa Romeo 1900, which featured an under-square four cylinder engine with cast-iron block, aluminium alloy cylinder head and double overhead cams, featuring a 90° included angle between the intake and exhaust valves.

Palmer was a regular visitor to the Thompson and Taylor premises at Brooklands, which had an Alfa Romeo agency,

TWIN-CAM ENGINES

Probably the best known British twin-cam engine was the Jaguar unit, first seen in the XK120 of 1948; although this was a 6-cylinder engine, a 4-cylinder XK100 variant was considered, but never put into production.
AUTHOR'S COLLECTION

The idea of improving the power output of an engine through multiple overhead valves and camshafts was not a new idea in the early 1950s, but it was nevertheless still an exotic concept normally reserved for the upper echelons of motor racing. The first celebrated production twin-cam 4-cylinder was the Alfa Romeo Twin Cam, which appeared in 1954 as an evolution of the Alfa Romeo 1900 mentioned in the main text.

Whereas the 1950 Italian engine had featured a 90-degree included angle between the camshafts, the 1954 version had an angle of 80 degrees and a smaller capacity of 1290cc; the MG twin-cam concept similarly graduated from Palmer's 90-degree original to Morris Engines' production specification 80-degree. The Alfa Romeo engine was advanced for its day, and would go on to have a long and distinguished life, remaining in use in a highly evolved form as late as 1994.

Meanwhile, however, BMC were not the only British car maker to contemplate a 4-cylinder twin cam, because Jaguar Cars developed a 4-cylinder version of their famous 6-cylinder 'XK' engine family, and even announced it in 1948 as a 2-litre variant of the XK120 sports car, a version to have been called the XK100, which according to contemporary factory literature accompanying the XK120 launch would have featured a 4-cylinder twin-cam engine of 1991cc and a projected power output of 103bhp and 5,000rpm.

Coventry-based Jaguar Cars – which grew out of SS Cars but changed its name after World War II, for obvious reasons – had been working on a family of new engines since 1943, the idea being to reduce the company's dependence on bought-in units from Standard. Various 4-cylinder engines were designed in the process, with the codes XF, XG and finally XK, and capacities around the 1790cc or 1970cc mark. Without doubt the rumour mill in Coventry would have made it known to Nuffield's engine designers that William Lyons was working on such an exotic powertrain for his post-war cars.

Although the 4-cylinder Jaguar unit never made it to production, there are a couple of tenuous MG links to it. Firstly, a key member of the design team behind the new XK engine was Claude Baily, an engineer who is sometimes thought of as the father of the Nuffield X-Series engines – including the MG XPAG units; after he left Morris Motors Engines Branch, he moved to Jaguar. Secondly, advice on the Jaguar's cylinder-head design came from the famous Harry Weslake – who was also an adviser for BMC on the B-Series and other engine families. Finally, the Jaguar 2-litre engine (as a 1970cc unit) had been fitted to Goldie Gardner's EX 135 record breaker in 1948 during a brief hiatus in cordial relations with Nuffield Organisation senior management (relations were back on an even keel by the time of the Morris Motors Board meeting of 15 November 1950).

Whilst the fitment of an 'alien' engine in the car meant that for a while it lost its MG badging, and was referred to formally as the Gardner Record Breaking Car, it is almost unimaginable that Syd Enever and his team would not have had a good look over this state-of-the-art power plant. Whilst, as already noted, the 4-cylinder XK engine never made it to production, the familiar 6-cylinder version would go on to win Le Mans and remain part of the Jaguar production story until 1992.

The other famous British twin-cam engine was the Lotus-Ford unit of 1962; however, the period of evolution of that power plant falls entirely outside the lifetime of the MGA, and shows, if nothing else, that the B-series twin cam was a good concept inadequately executed, a point eventually proved in 1986 when Rover Group created the M-Series. Two years after that, Roy Brocklehurst, recently retired from Rover, told Wilson McComb: 'It's ironic, really, that it's taken until now to produce a really successful dohc head on that B-series engine – that's the M-16. And it's still the same bottom end, with the 3½in stroke – 88.9mm.' In 1992 the M-Series begat the T-Series, which remained in production until 1999, still with B-Series heritage.

The MGA Twin Cam prototype ORX 885 in Switzerland, assumed to be in 1958.
ENEVER FAMILY

and it was not long before he was 'borrowing' both parts and ideas to formulate the early steps towards a twin-cam conversion for the B-Series unit, his intention being to create a 'Grand Tourismo' version of the new Magnette. Thus it was that at around the same period that Morris Engines were trying to extricate more power from the basic B-Series, that Gerald Palmer had successfully to persuade management to sanction work on his idea of a twin cam version.

'I actually laid out the basis of the Twin Cam B-Series on my drawing board at Cowley', Palmer told the author in 1996, confirming that it was then handed over to Jimmy Thompson and Eddie Maher at Morris Engines. One of Palmer's unfulfilled ideas was a version of the engine with a proposed new SU fuel injection system.

MORRIS ENGINES AND THE MG TWIN-CAM ENGINE

Within the labyrinthine structure of the early British Motor Corporation, the two broadly still separate entities that fell loosely under the 'Austin' and 'Morris' factions benefited from their own engine design teams; Austin's was based, logically enough, at Longbridge, and included Bill Appleby who, after he joined Austin in 1935, had created some stunning racing twin-cam Austin Seven engines for Murray Jamieson (1905–1938). From 1941, Appleby had been Austin's chief engine designer, and at the tail end of 1953, he was appointed 'Chief Designer, Engines and Gearboxes' for the whole BMC Group, and so had overall responsibility for both Austin and Morris engines.

W.V. 'Bill' Appleby was, from 1955, in overall charge of BMC's engines design operations; his background was Austin rather than Nuffield.
AUTHOR'S COLLECTION

As the team responsible for the A- and B-Series power plants, which rapidly usurped the old Nuffield engine ranges, it was clear that the Longbridge team was in a strong position. Meanwhile, however, the Morris organization still had its own engine division at Coventry, the evolution of which, as we have seen, benefited from the transfer of Riley car making to Abingdon, the result being the merger of Riley engine design into 'Morris Engines'. In charge at this division was James Thompson, as Chief Engineer, and under him sat Eddie Maher as Chief Experimental Engineer.

One of Thompson's early given tasks in the BMC era was the design and development of a new 6-cylinder engine that would be known as the C-Series, which appeared first in the Austin A90 Westminster at the 1954 Earls Court Motor Show, then a year later in the ultimately less successful Morris Isis; it also pepped up the Riley Pathfinder as the Riley 2.6, found a home in the Wolseley 6/90, and notably came into its own in the indomitable Austin-Healey 100/6 (and subsequent 3000), the car which, in due course, arguably for many would usurp the MGA Twin Cam as a British sports-car weapon of choice.

Few motoring histories record the crucial role played by Alnwick-born James 'Jimmy' Rochester Thompson (1903–1987), who at the time the MGA Twin Cam was being developed, was chief engineer of Morris Motors Engines Branch. Thompson had oversight for the early twin-cam unit that went into EX 181, even if much of the practical detail work was undertaken by the likes of Derek Frost, Bill Andrews and Basil Wales.

James Thompson.
ENEVER FAMILY

A crucial step towards a production version of the MG Twin-Cam engine came when the Morris Motors Board authorized, on 17 September 1953, expenditure of £25,000 by the

EDDIE MAHER, ENGINE MAESTRO

Eddie Maher at a family event in around 1961/62.
MAHER FAMILY

Edward Joseph ('Eddie') Maher (5 August 1910–27 September 1976), engine maestro, was born in Southern Ireland (now Eire) and as a boy was educated at the Cistercian College, a Catholic Boarding School in Roscrea, Tipperary. He initially continued his formal career studies at Thurles Technical School (also in Tipperary), trained as a civil engineer, but all that changed when Maher, still not twenty, saw Victor Gillow racing in the first Phoenix Park Grand Prix in Dublin of 12 July 1929 (Gillow would go on to win the second Saorstát Cup the following year, on 18 July 1930, in his Riley Nine Brooklands). Bitten by the motor-racing bug, Maher overcame parental disapproval and managed to secure a job at Riley in 1929, swiftly becoming the Coventry company's first premium apprentice, and trained further at Coventry Technical College.

Before long he moved into the company's experimental and racing department, taking charge of engine testing, engine production and in due course the entire engine design and manufacture side of Riley Motors. Maher was at the forefront of Riley's racing efforts throughout the 1930s heydays of the proudly independent sporting marque, often being at Brooklands and other leading circuits of the day when Rileys were racing. During the Second World War, Maher was seconded to Rolls-Royce, where he worked on carburettors for the famous Merlin engines, as used in the Supermarine Spitfire, before returning to Riley after the war ended.

It is worthy of note that the largely Maher-refined 4-cylinder 'DP25R' 2.5-litre engine in the last of the big Rileys, the Pathfinder, was in fact a 'twin cam' – although the camshafts were high mounted and driven from the crankshaft by duplex roller chains and short pushrods to Percy Riley's design philosophy rather than through direct operation from overhead camshafts in the modern manner. As Gerald Palmer took charge of the affairs of MG and Riley in 1949, it was clearly not only the sporting aspirations of MG that he was concerned about, but also the sophistication that customers expected from their Rileys. As we shall see later, there were thoughts of both 4- and 6-cylinder BMC twin-cam engines for a while.

In 1953, Maher contracted polio and suffered extensive paralysis in his legs, but managed to overcome this and continued to serve under what had become Morris Motors Engines Branch at Courthouse Green (see separate section on Morris Engines). Alec Poole, who as an apprentice and fellow Irishman came to know and respect Eddie Maher, describes how despite his need to walk with the aid of sticks, his friend maintained his cheery and positive disposition despite the challenges he faced as a consequence of his illness.

On one occasion later in Maher's career, Poole found his old friend, who he describes as 'a true gentleman and engineer', almost distraught: 'Donald Stokes Leyland had taken over BMC and some new bod had taken over control of Courthouse Green. The first thing New Bod did was to clear out of the drawing office all the old Riley drawings going back to year one and put them on the bonfire! The drawings that Eddie and his colleagues sweated blood over. The drawings that were torn up and they had to start on again if they got something wrong, before they were signed off. Such bigoted stupidity, for nothing.'

The story of the crucial role that Maher played in forging the competition versions of the A-Series engine, which underpinned the giant-killing prowess of the Mini Cooper in the 1960s, is worthy of telling but unfortunately is outside the scope of this book: suffice to say, without him BMC's (and privateers) successes with that engine would not have been so distinguished. Meanwhile Maher was proud to accept an invitation in April 1958 to become an honorary member of the Riley Register (and, a year later, its president), and many enthusiastic members of that august body subsequently had reason to be grateful for his many pearls of wisdom, freely given. A modest man, he was nevertheless well qualified, having earned the distinguished letters 'C Eng MIMechE' (Chartered Engineer and a Member of the Institution of Mechanical Engineers) and 'ARAeS' (Associate of the Royal Aeronautical Society).

Eddie Maher participating in a test convoy of a 'US Forces in Germany' registered MGA Twin Cam on the German Autobahn near Hanover in 1960.
MAHER FAMILY

Eddie Maher continued to work at BMC and latterly BLMC's engines division, retiring eventually from his final post as 'Chief Engineer, British Leyland Courthouse Green', to his home in Coventry; he told the *Coventry Evening Telegraph* for the issue of 17 September 1975, soon after retirement, that he had never regretted his diversion to the car industry: 'The friends I met while studying civil engineering built bridges and roads, but they never went out of the country – I went all over the world.' He died in the autumn of 1976, not long after his sixty-sixth birthday, his life no doubt shortened by the polio. His widow Maud celebrated her 102nd birthday in 2018.

Engines Branch on 'Project No. 45: high-performance version of BMC B-Series engine'. Meanwhile, however, in a classic case of backing two horses, Leonard Lord appears to have asked both the Austin and Morris engine teams to develop separate concepts for twin-cam engines to suit the projected brief. MG's deputy general manager at the time, Geoffrey Iley, says that this approach was commonplace at BMC:'Harriman and Leonard Lord, between them, had a reputation of always having two competitors in a project, because they felt that by doing that – by setting 'A' against 'B' – then the best idea would come through, no matter what the personal costs for the loser...'

The motor-sports story of the production MGA Twin Cam engine properly belongs in Chapter 10, but the emergence of two formative rivals for the role, and the unceremonious discarding of the losing contender, also warrants brief coverage here. Whilst as creators of the source unit the Austin team would seem to have held most of the favourable cards, this overlooks the fact that Morris Engines came from the same background as MG, and Syd Enever and Eddie Maher were good friends. In the 1930s, the record-breaking and racing Austin Twin Cams had been seen by Thornley and Enever as deadly rivals, and whilst obviously much had changed in twenty years, the old friendships and alliances still counted, and the BMC merger itself was still recent and, beyond powertrain considerations, barely begun.

Eddie Maher had Gerald Palmer's detailed drawings to use as a start point, but over at Austin, the engineers had no such luxury, and had to start more or less from scratch. Gerald Palmer remembered the beginnings of the Austin unit and told the author that he suspected that it may in part have been encouraged by Harry Weslake, who had a lucrative consultancy contract with Longbridge. It is generally believed that the Austin unit was almost entirely bespoke – created from scratch, with its 66-degree angle between its valve gear – but it seems likely that at least *some* of the donor parts may have come from the BMC store cupboard. Comparatively little is actually known of the Austin engine beyond a single overhead engine-bay photo, which, although taken in 1955, most likely only first appeared in print in 1958, and has been reproduced periodically ever since – the present volume included.

Into the middle of this was recently arrived Basil Wales, who in 1952 had started at Morris Engines in Coventry. Dropped in at the deep end, the following spring Wales found himself part of the team under the direction of Eddie Maher, the division's Chief Experimental Engineer, who had been tasked with developing the prototype Morris Engines twin-cam B-Series engine conversion. Wales is of the view that the Austin engine was B-Series based, just like its Morris rival.

It was evident that Gerald Palmer's concept was sound, and so several of his ideas survived the transition to formal design (although his ambitious plans for fuel injection did not). Under the advice of Harry Weslake, the included angle between the valves was reduced from 90 to 80 degrees (echoing the changes on the near-contemporary Alfa Romeo twin-cam design), ostensibly to improve the air flow slightly, but also to reduce the overall width of what was quite a bulky unit – which would prove something of a problem when it was eventually fitted to the MGA.

Basil Wales also credits research by his colleague, engineer Tony Jennings, who reviewed the range of previous head designs, concluding that the valve angle of 80 degrees was the optimum. Wilson McComb wrote that the design was undertaken by Derek Frost and Bill Andrews under Eddie Maher's direction. 'Debate has continued on the relative merits, but 80 degrees gives a very good volumetric efficiency,' Wales has said. Ironically it was the challenge of achieving satisfactory and consistent combustion that would overshadow the Twin-Cam engine throughout its life, and contribute royally to its eventual demise.

Needless to say, the twin cam was welcomed by John Thornley and his team at Abingdon, busily arguing their case for some degree of autonomy from central control, and buoyed up by their new design office. It wasn't long after this office had been established that John Thornley was crafting another of his memos to S. V. Smith; on 11 August 1954, Thornley wrote: 'DO 1062 is now so far advanced that, as a policy matter, it may be disregarded. However, as it is necessary that all future projects should be integrated, it is desirable that early approval should be obtained for our intentions.'

Thornley went on to explore the potential of a racing version of DO 1062 (the then still-unlaunched MGA), making reference to the plans for Le Mans in 1955 (*see* Chapter 10),

The definitive MG MGA Twin Cam engine.
AUTHOR'S COLLECTION

and an idea of a low-volume, twin-cam race version: 'A special series (50 or 100) competition version of DO 1062 incorporating the twin ohc B-Series engine with, possibly, fuel-injection, five-speed gearbox or overdrive, disc brakes, aluminium panelling, etcetera... price (guessing) of the order of £1,250.'

Thornley also speculated about a future four-seater Riley version of DO 1062, and of its eventual successor: 'Although DO 1062 may be expected to run for three years, its successor may have to be something quite different... my view is that we should start to build – in the manner in which Magna was produced – three or four different versions of our ideas...' The idea of successors to the MGA is discussed in Chapter 9; long before that, the MG Twin Cam powertrain had to be made real.

By the time of the June 1955 Le Mans event (*see* Chapter Ten), the rumours of a twin-camshaft version of the new MG were already rife; a French news item from the week prior to the event reported (in translation): '...in the light of the 1955 experience, they would prepare for the future boldly and confront the 1956 season with a new twin overhead cam engine.'

Eventually the first running prototypes of the rival engine designs were sent to MG for testing and trial fitment into EX 182 prototypes in readiness for a racing debut at the Dundrod TT race of 21 September 1955, four days after the MGA made its motor show debut in Germany. What ensued is told in Chapter 10; suffice to say here that the Austin engine disappeared before the event, never to be seen again. Similarly the racing debut of the Morris Engines Twin Cam was hardly auspicious, but the unit had won sufficient interest and support for development to continue over the autumn and into the New Year of 1956.

This is evidenced by another of John Thornley's memos, this time to S.V. Smith and dated 7 November 1955:

> We are already building a prototype of the MGB, which is the MGA fitted with the twin-camshaft B-Series engine, and with disc brakes on one or both axles as may be found necessary when more is known of the probable performance. The intention is that this model will be sold alongside the MGA, again with a substantial price differential, and will provide the prestige and competition vehicle for the USA and elsewhere.

By the turn of the year, discussion of production applications and likely volume requirements for the new engine was coming to a head, as evidenced by the fact that George Harriman asked John Thornley for his considered views about the unit at an 'Engine Development Panel Meeting' on 22 February. Thornley responded verbally at the next meeting of 6 April, but Harriman was soon the lucky recipient of another Thornley memo, dated 1 May 1956, in which the MG General Manager set out his thoughts in his typically erudite manner.

Referring again to the 'MGB' (obviously nothing to do with the later production car of that name), Thornley predicted that this car, in reality the twin-cam engine MGA, would serve to 'go out after the Porsche market'. He went on to stress that he was not seeking to build a highly specialized car like the Porsche: '...the only thing I covet about the Porsche is its market.' At the time, Porsche customers could

MORRIS, RILEY AND AUSTIN ENGINES

Any assessment of the history of Austin and Nuffield enterprises will swiftly identify the fact that Lord Austin and Lord Nuffield had very different approaches to building their empires: in simple terms, Herbert Austin preferred to do nearly everything in house (hence the focus on Longbridge for everything from foundries to assembly), while William Morris was adept at buying up and restructuring his suppliers, hence the Nuffield empire was wider spread. Morris acquired engine supplier Hotchkiss in 1923 to create Morris Engines, and later in the same decade operations were expanded into new premises at Courthouse Green, Coventry. Meanwhile the still independent Riley Motors was to make a name for itself throughout the 1930s, with a series of beautifully engineered sporting cars – but the company's finances became imperilled and the end result was acquisition by Nuffield. For a while, the Riley Engines branch retained much of its independence within the Nuffield empire, having created an all-new 'big four' only just prior to bankruptcy – but all pretence of pedigree came to an end after Victor Riley was dismissed from the Nuffield Board in 1947 as part of the Reginald Hanks purge (*see* Chapter 1). Therefore two years later, when Riley car making moved to Abingdon, the Riley Engines branch became a subsidiary of Morris Engines, the merger bringing with it Eddie Maher, who, at the age of thirty-nine, moved across to Courthouse Green to become Chief Experimental Engineer.

Over at Longbridge, the team led by Johnny Rix and designer Eric Bareham had created the A- and B-Series that underpinned first Austin and then BMC's corporate engine family, the effects of which would be felt long after the MGA – and the MG factory – had faded from existence. But for the MG Twin Cam engine, it would be Morris Engines, under Jimmy Thompson and Eddie Maher, who led the design and would assemble the units.

EX 181 – THE 'ROARING RAINDROP'

The supercharged Twin Cam engine as fitted to the MG EX 181 record car.
AUTHOR'S COLLECTION

Syd Enever (left) and Captain George Eyston stand either side of the then new EX 181 record car, resplendent in its original two-tone blue livery, at Wendover (Utah) in August 1957.
ENEVER FAMILY

Whilst Abingdon wrestled with the changes that accompanied the end of Riley assembly and the arrival of Austin-Healeys in 1957, Syd Enever had laid plans for a record breaker to form the next generation after EX 179. In order to achieve the objective of 240mph (386km/h) – or '4 miles (6.4km) a minute' – it was evident that a radically different design would be needed to work within the achievable power range of the experimental 1498cc Twin Cam engine, even with supercharging.

Syd Enever set to with various scale models, all made by Harry Herring and tested at Armstrong Whitworth, and rapidly formed the conclusion that a low tear-drop shape, with the engine mounted amidships, and with the driver prone at the front, would be the only way to achieve a low enough frontal area and the aerodynamic performance needed. Terry Mitchell got to work with the help of Roy Brocklehurst, and using sets of Sikorsky aerofoil profiles, the shape of the definitive new record breaker – formally EX 181, but popularly known as the 'Roaring Raindrop' – got under way.

The initial development of the supercharged Twin Cam engine was passed to Morris Engines, where Eddie Maher, Derek Frost and Basil Wales worked on creating a unit capable of the necessary sustained high performance. Meanwhile the body shape evolved and was turned into the traditional wooden 'egg crate', over which the unique 'Hiduminium 33' alloy body panels were formed at Midland Sheet Metal; the resulting panels were fixed to the underlying frame in a manner that made them removable for ease of service and modification.

Mechanically, the engine's cast-iron crankcase was bolstered with the addition of extra stiffening webs, and the crankshaft was given nitrided pins, running in lead-indium bearings. In addition, the connecting rods were made from steel forgings, with fully floating gudgeon pins. According to Basil Wales, no head gasket was used, the sealing relying on pressure rings in the tops of the bores, and the exhaust valves were sodium cooled.

choose from eleven variations on a theme, derived from combinations of five engines (1300 and 1600 pushrod, with single or twin carburettors; 1500 overhead cam) and three body options (open two-seater, coupé or cabriolet), covering a price range in the USA from $3,430 to $4,790.

As Thornley correctly observed, the cheapest of these German sports cars sold to some extent on the reputation of the more expensive models, helped by the fact that all the models looked very much alike. Postulating on the potential for three MGA body variants (*see* Chapter 5), Thornley said that '…the twin-cam engine would enable us to produce the prestige motor car, but if the engine can be produced at anything like a reasonable price, it can be assured of sale in reasonable quantities, not just short-run competition stuff.' Thornley went on to present some calculations, made reference to the idea of what he called a 'Grande Tourisme' version of the Magnette, and concluded that if the costs he presented were achievable, 'an estimated production of fifty cars per week incorporating this engine is not, I feel, unreasonable.'

On the salt flats in August 1957, a salt-encrusted EX 181 is seen with Stirling Moss at the centre.
ENEVER FAMILY

Alec Hounslow shows off the engine bay of EX181 at Abingdon in the autumn of 1959, outside a marquee set up in the MG Development Department car park. Note the new Triumph Herald in the background (presumably an STI press car on loan to a visiting journalist?) and, just visible, Terry Mitchell's home-made bubble car! Alec Hounslow looks at the engine with the access panels removed.
ENEVER FAMILY

By May 1957 the EX 181 was nearing its final form, and a handful of invited press were able to look over the unpainted record breaker, while Stirling Moss was on hand to check the cockpit arrangements. Two months later, the record breaker, resplendent in its beautiful metallic sky-blue livery, was crated up and loaded on to the *Queen Mary* for its journey from Southampton to New York. Unfortunately the load moved in transit, and as a result the large tail-fin was slightly damaged, necessitating repairs at the other end.

At Utah, the EX 181 was 'warmed up' by Phil Hill in readiness for the arrival of Moss on 20 August. Three days later he easily exceeded the original target of 4 miles (6.4km) a minute, achieving 245.64mph (395.31km/h) for the one kilometre record. Other records also fell: 243.08mph (391.12km/h) for the 3 miles (5km), 235.69mph (379.23km/h) for the 5 miles (8km), 224.70mph (361.54km/h) for the 10 miles (16km).

EX 181 was back in Utah again in 1959; this time the car had a metallic green livery, and the record-breaking honours fell to Phil Hill alone; the numbers, too, were even more impressive. The engine capacity had been increased to 1506cc, tipping it into the 1600cc category; it achieved more than 300bhp at 7,300rpm on a cocktail of methanol, nitrobenzene, acetone and sulphuric ether. A maximum speed of 254.91mph (410.23 km/h) made EX 181 the fastest ever factory-built MG. A combination of budget constraints and internecine BMC rivalries meant that, sadly, EX 181 proved to be the last of MG's record breakers.

However, Thornley also had a slight dig at the design, commenting that '...there is quite a lot of development work to be done on this engine before it is suitable for production. Generally speaking, its jointing is not carried out in a production manner, and oil leaks are legion, particularly once any part of the engine has been disturbed.' As we shall see later, the testers from *Autocar* who drove an MGA with one of the early production versions of the engines on the continent in the summer of 1958 would clearly have recognized this trait.

Before long, the engine – still in experimental guise – would make its second appearance in public when the EX 179 record breaker (*see also* Chapter 2) was fitted with a prototype twin-cam unit. Responsibility for developing this was a task that fell to Basil Wales. Writing for the MG Car Club magazine *Safety Fast!* in 2014, Wales said that Eddie Maher had given him the job of supercharging the engine, which would be run on an exotic benzene, methanol and petrol mixture.

By the summer, EX 179 had been modified, with the driver now seated in the right-hand-drive position, which suited the very different exhaust arrangements compared to the old Nuffield unit from 1954; in August 1956 the record breaker was back at Bonneville (accompanied by Alec Hounslow and Henry Stone from MG), and Ken Miles and Johnny Lockett secured sixteen records over the period of Wednesday 15 to Sunday 19 August, the highest being 170.15mph (273.77km/h) over 10 miles (16km). Three of the new engines had been shipped along with EX 179. For the following year, MG would develop an even more exciting record breaker, the 'Roaring Raindrop' (*see* box), and this time the twin-cam engine was right at the heart of the most ambitious yet of Syd Enever's creations.

Further development of the road-going twin-cam variant involved road testing on public roads and the Motor Industry Research Association test circuit near Lindley, because BMC had no test circuit of its own. Basil Wales drove a prototype for thousands of miles round Warwickshire as well as MIRA. He wrote that 'repeated runs with different settings eliminated flat spots, improved low speed pick-up, and generally made this potent engine drivable'. MG were concerned at the ability of the standard gearbox to cope with the higher performance, so Wales was obliged to drive the road circuit at MIRA with minimal use of brakes.

Photographs also show Syd Enever and Alec Hounslow in the Alps with ORX 885, accompanied by a Magnette; no doubt they called on their friends the Kellers in Zürich. Meanwhile Tom Haig, MG's chief road tester, also spent much time behind the wheel of the Twin Cam (in particular ORX 885), pounding it round the MIRA circuit. Memorably on one occasion, whilst out on the road near Banbury with Roy Brocklehurst, they experienced a loud bang, accompanied by a cloud of smoke behind the car, which was quickly followed by the discovery that one of the pistons had a hole in its crown – this was not necessarily the first time this had happened, but equally importantly it was not the last. It was something of an omen.

With the change in competition class rules to favour engines up to 1600cc, the launch of the Twin Cam was delayed from October 1957 to the summer of the following year. By increasing the bore size by 2.375mm, a larger displacement was created of 1588cc. In tandem with this, because the cylinder spacing had to change in order to allow machining of the block at Longbridge, there had to be changes to the cooling arrangements within the head; this meant the loss of the intermediary water jackets between cylinders one and two, and also between three and four. In turn, this also necessitated further changes to the pistons – an item that would prove to be one of the new unit's Achilles heels.

Writing in the MGA Twin Cam Group's *50th Anniversary Book*, Basil Wales, whose testing had mostly been on the original 1498cc twin-cam engine, explained the unintended consequence of the shift to a larger capacity for the production car:

> ...this enlarged engine obviously attracted more interest from the vital American market, with the result that the decision makers set up the manufacturing process to build all Twin Cam production engines as 1600cc units, but without delaying the introduction enough to do any of the prolonged testing that had been given to the 1500cc version.

From the start, John Thornley had only ever wanted the Twin Cam to be a low-volume specialized unit, allowing development with a more sympathetic type of owner, and building experience that perhaps could have provided dividends later. Production was therefore established as twenty-five units a week. In production, the MGA Twin Cam engine began life at Longbridge's engine plant, with basic machining in common with the standard B-Series overhead-valve units, and handling via the Birmingham plant's 'Transfer-matic' automated machinery; however, these special units – produced at a rate of up to fifty a week – were then shipped down the A45 to Morris Engines at Coventry (where, as we have seen, the design had been carried out).

HEADING FOR PRODUCTION

Aesthetically, and at first glance, the twin-cam version of the MGA differed only moderately from its humbler overhead-valve-engined progenitor. The most obvious difference came with the distinctive centre-lock peg-drive Dunlop wheels, similar to, but not the same as those fitted to the Jaguar D-Type. These wheels were favoured by John Thornley and Syd Enever, who often bemoaned the market's preference for wire wheels, but they were chosen for an additional equally pertinent reason: the necessity of clearing the bulky Dunlop

The engine bay of the pre-production MGA Twin Cam 499; the photo was taken by MG Draughtsman Denis Williams at the same time as he photographed the EX 186 prototype parked nearby.

DENIS WILLIAMS

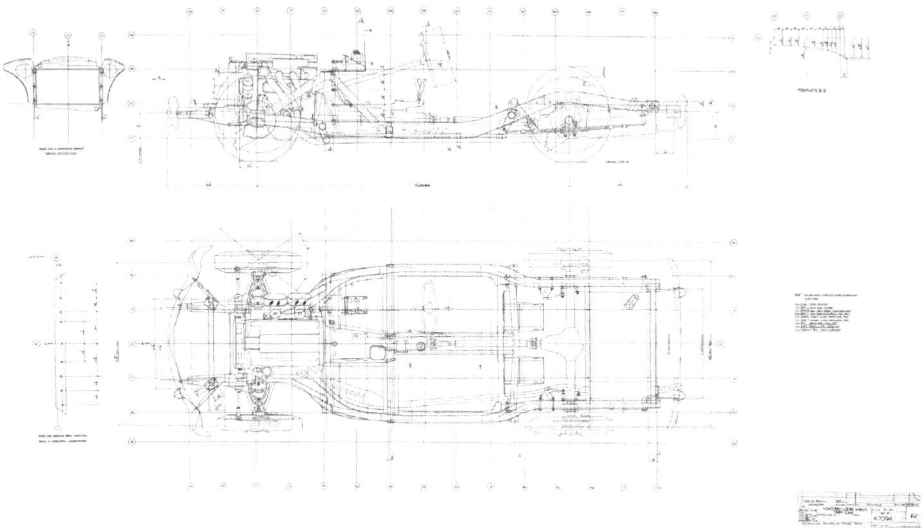

This sketch – more correctly 'Assembly Drawing A7094' – shows the EX187 MGA Twin Cam chassis, drawn on 21 February 1958.
BOB VITRIKAS

disc brakes. The latter were trialled on one of the shop MGAs, LJB 439 (HDC43-10101, the first production car), which became known as 'the Dunlop Disc Car'; references can be found in various MG Development Department Reports. For competition purposes, a rarely seen option was an alloy wheel using the same fixings and broadly the same appearance.

From early in production (chassis no. 592, in September 1958) access inside the engine bay was improved by the introduction of removable panels, designed by Don Hayter. Small script 'Twin Cam' badges were added by the oval scuttle vents and bootlid, and inside there were relatively minor trim and equipment changes. To suit engine-bay clearances, the steering rack was moved forwards by 1in (2.5cm), and the steering arms modified to suit.

The bonnet lid was slightly re-profiled to a greater curvature to provide improved clearance over the bulkier twin-cam engine, and there are several possible references of potential relevance to this – the earliest is in the EX Register against EX 187/34 ('Bonnet panel' dated 12 October 1955, long before production) and against EX 187/86R ('Scheme for bonnet panel' dated 25 March 1957). However, within the production period there is a 'Development Report' DDR No. 134 dated 12 December 1958, which reports (against DDW No. 578) that 'the [Twin Cam] bonnet has been fitted and is okay for clearance on the front dashpot'. This would appear to suggest that the change took place some way after MGA Twin Cam production had already begun, implying that early cars did not benefit from the change.

The author could find no references within the Abingdon factory's dedicated 'Assembly Number' and 'Sketch Number' registers (which often have entries corresponding to the other documentation, such as the EX Register and DDR reports), and so it may be fairly assumed that the bonnet-panel changes were all taken care of by Morris Motors Bodies Branch in Coventry, who, working with Pressed Steel as their supplier, had their own entirely independent document systems. The change being approved, the bonnet was then commonized on all MGA variants; curiously the change does not seem to appear in the normal chassis number change point records, perhaps because of the Bodies Branch factor mentioned; there is a similar vagueness in the later MGB production records where there were panel curvature changes.

Mark Hester owns this Twin Cam, chassis no. 499, UK registration number PJB 147. Several components, such as the unique bolt-on radiator support panels and a heater adaptor blanking panel, provide clues to the development carried out on this car. An MG Development Department Report (DDR No. 134, dated 23 May 1960) records experimenting fitting PJB 147 with special rings prior to testing at MIRA. After leaving Abingdon, it was sold by Mill Garage (Dick Jacobs – *see* Chapter 10) with a pushrod engine, but its history has been thoroughly researched and the car itself restored to its former glory under Hester's care.
AUTHOR

LATER ARRIVALS: NEW MEMBERS OF THE MG DESIGN TEAM

Upon his arrival at Abingdon in 1956, Dickie Wright initially worked under Harry White as a chassis draughtsman; when White left to go to Rootes, he reported to Terry Mitchell.
WRIGHT FAMILY PHOTO

DICKIE WRIGHT

Dickie Wright (11 April 1921–4 January 2012) began his career in April 1939 in Chiswick at 'Evershed & Vignoles', an electrical and mechanical engineering firm; he stayed there through to 1946. After the war, Wright began working for a series of motorcycle businesses dotted round the London area, during which period he worked with engineer Joe Ehrlich, for a while the owner of EMC Motorcycles. While Wright was working at Tandon Motorcycles in Watford, Ehrlich called in to see him: 'He said he'd like me to go and work with him at Longbridge, where he was working on a 3-cylinder two-stroke engine for the Austin A30 (which never made it to production), but I didn't want to work in Birmingham. He said I wasn't going anywhere where I was, and suggested MG.' Wright agreed it might be worth a try, and so Ehrlich said he would make enquiries. In due course, Syd Enever considered Wright to work under the then Chief Chassis Draughtsman, Harry White.

Upon arrival at MG in March 1956, Dickie Wright found himself pitched into working on the EX 186 prototype, and in due course would work on many MG and Austin-Healey projects, including the seat-belt installations on all models, and much of the adaptation of the current MG range to meet Federal legislation.

DON HAYTER

Don Hayter came to MG from Aston-Martin as a body draughtsman; he had also worked at Pressed Steel. Although he is probably better known for his important input on the later MGB, he arrived at Abingdon soon enough to work on the MGA Twin Cam.
AUTHOR'S COLLECTION

Don Hayter (born 24 January 1926) started at Abingdon on 1 February 1956. Although better known for his later work on the MGB, Hayter arrived at Abingdon early enough to contribute to the MGA story, with the Twin Cam being the first to benefit from his input. As he told the author in an interview in 1998:

The MGA 1500 was in production, and they were thinking about which engine to use for the twin cam. When I got there, the first Austin – Bill Appleby designed – engine was running around in one of the Tyrolite Green tourers. They hadn't got the first version of the Morris Engines twin cam – the Eddie Maher one –they had a mock-up but not a running engine. While I was there, the running engine came along, and one of the first jobs I ever did at Abingdon was connected with the installation of that Morris Engines twin cam. The access to the exhaust manifold was absolutely dreadful, because it was miles up from underneath, and you couldn't get down from the top with the narrow MGA bonnet aperture. So Syd asked me if we could get in from the side, and I said that we could trepan a hole in there, but of course you wouldn't want to leave a hole – you'd want a removable panel, otherwise all the muck would be flying straight through there, especially when the wheel was on lock.

So Syd gave me the go-ahead to do it, and Henry Stone and I marked up the hole just next to the 'goal post' scuttle support, as big as we could get, right opposite the exhaust manifold joint, and we made a panel to go over the hole. It wanted stiffening up, being a flat panel, so I suggested louvring.

That was the first time I did anything on an MG at Abingdon.

There is a reference to this work in one of the many MG Development Department Reports (DDR No. 148 of 18 March 1958), which reports (under reference DDW 275 and 283) that 'the bulkhead panels having now been assembled of which Mr Hayter has taken the right-hand one to Mr Carter of Morris Bodies Branch. A 1½ inch packing has been added to the Brake Master Cylinder.' It is not certain from the report whether or not these are the same 'bulkhead panels'. Meanwhile, Don Hayter would later be responsible for detailing the unique fastback coupé roof for Ted Lund's later Le Mans effort (see Chapter 10, The MGA in Motor Sports).

PMO 326 is in the foreground and PMO 946 behind, the cars having been reunited for the MGA Twin Cam Group's sixtieth anniversary re-enactment of the original launch.
AUTHOR

THE LAUNCH OF THE MGA TWIN CAM

The first time that the press had an opportunity to try the new MGA Twin Cam was at a special test day on Monday 14 July 1958, organized at the 'Fighting Vehicles Research and Development Establishment' at Chobham, Surrey – a site that still existed in 2018, albeit with the shadow of potential redevelopment hanging over it. Although there was much anticipation and excitement amongst the group of motoring correspondents gathered together for the event, not everything went as smoothly as had been hoped.

At the time that the Twin Cam was on its way, John and his first wife Joan Thornley (she preferred to be called 'Joanne', which confuses some historians, since John's second wife was called Ann) were approaching their silver wedding anniversary (they had been married in Abingdon's East St. Helens Church on 15 July 1933); this coincided with an extended business trip and vacation in the USA, where they toured the various MG Car Club centres (visiting thirteen in total, covering some 6,500 miles in the air and 3,000 on the road), culminating in a dinner at the Plaza Hotel in New York Centre; here John included an announcement of the forthcoming new model in his speech. The American distributors presented the Thornleys with an elegant silver fruit dish from Tiffany's, engraved with the initials 'JWT' and 'JET' (Joan Edwina Thornley) and the date 15 July 1958. We know from a brief item in *Road & Track* of October 1958 that Thornley told his audience that MG was about to introduce a new overhead cam engine, saying that when the pre-war overhead-cam engine cars had been discontinued, many of his contemporaries had thought that 'the end of the world had come' and had sworn one day to produce another racing overhead cam MG engine.

Meanwhile in John Thornley's absence, the task of readying the Twin Cam for launch at Chobham fell to his deputy, Assistant General Manager Geoffrey Iley, who soon discovered some of the challenges that would lie ahead for Abingdon's exciting new model. As Iley told the author:

Syd Enever is in the driving seat for this demonstration of the new MGA Twin Cam at Longbridge, with George Holmes of BMC Publicity enjoying the ride. At that time, Holmes was Exhibitions Manager for Nuffield, so he could well have been looking at ideas for the display of the Twin Cam at upcoming motor shows. Holmes later went on to have a corporate exhibitions brief for BMC and eventually British Leyland.
ENEVER FAMILY

One of the limitations of the MGA Twin Cam as a touring car – a problem shared with the standard model – was its limited luggage capacity; consequently, boot-mounted luggage racks were a popular accessory from the outset.
AUTHOR

Whilst the Twin Cam was being unveiled to the European press, John and Joan Thornley were guests of honour at a meal at the Plaza Hotel in New York, where John Thornley covered the new model in his dinner speech and he and his wife were presented with this elegant Tiffany fruit bowl by the local distributors. Their son Peter treasures it to this day.
PETER THORNLEY

> We started to get the cars ready, but when we ran them in, to our horror we found that about half of them developed terrible engine vibrations at higher speeds, with the cars running at around 100mph [160km/h] (the top speed was over 110mph [177km/h]). So we had a problem even before the launch! When we looked further into the cause, we discovered that Engines Branch at Coventry couldn't balance the engine crankshaft and clutch and flywheel as a unit, so they were balancing these components in isolation, then putting them together and hoping for the best!

lley found that the success rate of this balancing exercise was successful in about half of the cars.

The short-term solution was for him to rent an airfield at Grove (now the home of Williams F1): 'We had those cars being driven in shifts by mechanics around the clock, 24/7, to select the best cars for the actual launch.' No wonder that when the final call came for cars for the press to try, there appeared to be a shortage!

Meanwhile planning for the event itself began in May 1958, emboldened by a decision in the BMC hierarchy to make more of the Twin Cam launch by celebrating the motor-sports credentials of the rest of the Nuffield portfolio. The idea behind the venue was to use somewhere novel, modern and exciting, and the FVRDE's Deputy Director was soon persuaded, helped by the sight and sound (for noise appraisal reasons) of a drive-through at the site by a prototype. It seems most likely that this would have involved ORX 885, the usual test car.

The range of facilities on offer – a two-mile high-speed track, a so-called 'snake' course, and a series of sharply inclined test slopes – were perhaps not the optimum for testing a high-speed sports car, but had the benefit of novelty, and the potential to accommodate a large party of around a hundred invited journalists for what became a 'BMC Demonstration Day', and a further selection of thirteen MG, Morris and Riley cars (including two MGA 1500s – a Roadster and a Coupé – an MG Magnette ZB, a Morris Minor, a Riley One-Point-Five and a Riley Two-Point-Six). An appearance by EX 181 was planned as a special attraction.

In planning for the key Twin Cam element of the event, it had become apparent that only three suitable home-market specification MGA Twin Cams – that is, with adequate engine balance – could be made available for the guests to drive; however, a fourth demonstrator was identified through MG's London dealer and distributor, University Motors (whose Managing Director, Mike Bradstock, attended the event). Scrutiny of the registration numbers of the four key cars seen at the event supports the idea that three came direct from MG and the fourth from London (*see* side panel). The organizers decided to give the Twin Cams priority with the high-speed circuit, and allocate the other cars to the remaining sections of track.

In a subsequent write-up for the Nuffield magazine *Motoring*, Tony Lucas explained the way the event was to be managed:

> The guests were divided into three parties – Red, Yellow and White. Each party would try the Twin Cams on roster and the other cars in the meantime. As the snake circuit and high-speed track overlapped in part, safety precautions were essential and had to be watertight. Poster-size notices were printed to keep the slower cars out of the way of the very fast Twin Cams. In support of these notices, and to back up the course's traffic-light systems, personnel had to be recruited and rostered for duty.

From Syd Enever's personal photo album, showing a group of 'Nuffield' men from Abingdon and Cowley at the Twin Cam press launch. They are, left to right: Ernie Longshaw (MG Transport), Tommy Bownes (Riley Service), MG test driver Tom Haig, Syd and Alec Hounslow.
ENEVER FAMILY

GEOFFREY ILEY

Bill Appleby at left, and Geoffrey Iley (leaning on the windscreen frame) look on as an MGA Twin Cam gets the press preview treatment at Chobham in July 1958. Sitting in the driving seat is Mike Bradstock (boss of University Motors, MG distributors in London), and with his back to the camera is Percy Watson (of Nuffield Publicity at Cowley). Such was the success of the venue that it would be chosen a year later for some of the initial press outings for the new ADO15 Morris Mini Minor.
ENEVER FAMILY

Although he was not yet thirty years old, the man in charge of the MGA Twin Cam launch was a high flyer destined to become a Morris Motors Board Member before he was thirty-seven. Geoffrey Norman Iley (born in Sunderland on 24 September 1928) moved at an early age to Birmingham with his parents. His education was impacted by the onset of World War II, and he credits his subsequent move to Oakham School in Rutland as a turning point that shaped his early entry to, and rapid rise in, the car industry. He managed to secure an apprenticeship at Wolseley, and unusually, soon after he had completed his training, he had already obtained an engineering degree and a postgraduate commerce diploma. So he was well equipped for management stardom.

Iley came to the attention of both Reg Hanks and his deputy James Woodcock (see Chapter 4); after he left to pursue another opportunity in Birmingham, having been frustrated at a lack of progress, it seems that Woodcock was told by Hanks to get Iley back inside the Nuffield Organisation. 'One day I got a telephone call to suggest that I should go to the 1954 Motor Show, where I might discover something of interest to me. When I got there I met John Thornley and he offered me a job as his deputy! So I left Birmingham and went to Abingdon on 1 January 1955… which was just eight days before my first child was born!' Iley's first day in his new job started with a slightly bizarre introduction to his new colleagues: 'At Abingdon I was marched into John Thornley's office, and he had all the people like Cecil Cousins and Reg Jackson in there – and S.V. Smith said simply "This is Geoffrey Iley – he's John Thornley's new deputy" – and that was it!'

John Thornley told Iley: 'Your job is to get cars out of the door: I'll deal with design, development, competitions, the press and everything else'; thus Iley's task was to get cars out as quickly and in as much volume as possible, and from 250 cars a week, before Iley left Abingdon in August 1958, the factory was already producing up to 1,000 a week. Part of the secret was chasing parts from suppliers: 'We often suffered from a famine of components – every morning at nine I had a piece of paper on my desk reporting on what we were short of, and I would get on to the managing directors of the relevant suppliers.'

Geoffrey Iley was reunited with the press launch cars sixty years after the events shown in the photo above.
AUTHOR

Iley was destined to move onwards and upwards within the parent organization: 'I left Abingdon in August 1958; I went to Cowley to become Production Manager, and then to Longbridge where I became Deputy Director reporting to the Director of Supplies.' Iley eventually joined the Morris Motors Board as a director on 12 May 1965, but he left BMC shortly after the creation of BLMC.

In addition there were Nuffield staff (forty-two in total) allocated to three car depots, teams of mechanics (many inevitably from MG), refuelling teams, and for any guests who preferred to be driven, a driving team. With the planning completed, and all orders placed, the advance set-up team arrived at the Chobham site on Saturday 12 July 1958 and erected two main hospitality and marketing marquees, placed the various traffic signs and decorative red and yellow MG flags, while the caterer's contractors erected the main marquee, the latter a not inconsiderable size at 80 by 40 feet (24 by 12 metres).

Unfortunately for all concerned, Sunday 13 July 1958 brought a severe storm with gale-force winds, and the Chobham site was badly affected. Lucas wrote that '...it happened after lunch. The caterer appeared, shouting: "my kitchen has collapsed", and the twenty-four five-hundredweight bollards to which the marquee was anchored lifted in the wind. Over went the bollards, the canvas flapped inwards, and the Big Top came down with a rush!' By now it was five in the afternoon on the Sunday, and the event was due to start the following morning; the weather forecast predicted the winds were subsiding, but the challenge remained to rectify the devastation.

'Emergency calls went out, men arrived, the main marquee was prepared for possible re-erection on the following morning. Fortunately the day dawned warm and still. At 6.30am there were a dozen people putting their backs into the (almost) impossible task of getting back to where we were two days before. The main marquee was up by nine o'clock, as were all the other tents. All traffic signs and decorations were made fast once more, and the caterer went into action, producing a superb sit-down lunch at midday. The battle had been won.'

Syd Enever explains the virtues of EX 181 to John Bolster (Technical Editor of *Autosport*) who has shoe-horned himself into the record-breaking car's tight cockpit during the MGA Twin Cam press launch at Chobham in July 1958. A nonchalant Cliff Bray holds the cockpit nose open; behind Enever is Henry Stone, and standing off to the right is Tom Haig, all of them MG Abingdon stalwarts. Bolster wrote of the experience of driving EX 181 for the issue of *Autosport* of 18 July 1958.
ENEVER FAMILY

By 10am on Monday 14 July all the cars had been fuelled by a dedicated tender and were in position for the first guests, due to drive at 11.15am. '*Eleven o'clock came, the guests were welcomed, Morris Motors Band trumpeters played a smart fanfare, EX 181 rolled out three laps. The Show was on. Everyone had a smile on his face and the weather still smiled, too.*' Geoffrey Iley remembers that the band – a very highly regarded institution – who were described in the event programme as being present 'with the kind permission of Viscount Nuffield' – were playing Gilbert & Sullivan and Franz von Suppé's 'Poet and Peasant'. The whole event was programmed to last until four in the afternoon.

As noted, at least four early-production MGA Twin Cams were initially on hand; one of them retired due to a damaged dynamo bracket, and late in the day, another had a more ignominious fate, as we shall see. Despite the so-called 'high speed circuit', the site was arguably not best suited to sustained high speed driving, and whilst the guests could exploit the MG's typically excellent handling and road-holding, not to mention the powerful Dunlop four-wheel disc brakes, there was no real opportunity to fully explore the higher speeds of which the new model was definitely capable.

This certainly did not constrain the determination of many of those present to have a good try at testing the Twin Cam to the limit, fuelled by copious quantities of alcohol. As Geoffrey Iley explains: '*in the afternoon – after lunch – we arranged a driving test. John Bolster, Bill Boddy, Gregor Grant and all the others were there, and they all went out in turns to speed round the Chobham circuit – fuelled by gin & tonics – and this developed into an unofficial 'fastest of the day' contest. I remember that at the end, first place was taken by Paul Frère, in second position was John Bolster (who was best known for hill-climbing his special 'Bloody Mary'), in third place was me and Bill Boddy was a distant last. We all had a very good time – and lots of alcohol was consumed*'.

At the end of the day, it was time to sweep up; but there was a problem, according to Iley: '*when we came to count them up at the end, we found we were one short! So we went out around the circuit and we discovered that one of the cars was rammed into a concrete bollard. It turned out that a cornet player from the Morris Motors Band had persuaded a mechanic to take him out for a spin, and they had come a cropper. The passenger* [i.e. the cornet player] *had suffered a broken pelvis, and afterwards we had terrible trouble with the Musicians' Union*'.

In his report for the magazine's August 1958 issue, the writer for *Sports Car and Lotus Owner* had clearly enjoyed the new model at Chobham but complained that 'the only

THE TWIN CAMS AT CHOBHAM

While the crowd lean on the temporary barriers to watch a demonstration lap by EX181, the four main test cars (*see* list below) are parked in a sequence.
AUTHOR

Nuffield or MG mechanics attending to one of the MGA Twin Cam press cars at Chobham on 14 July 1958.
COURTESY MARK HESTER

It has long been understood (not least from the report by Tony Lucas referenced in the main text) that there were just *four* principal MGA Twin Cams on 'demonstration duty' at the press day at Chobham on 14 July 1958. This was also the number stated in another article in the in-house publication *Nuffield Teamwork*, (similarly entitled 'Debut by Demonstration'). We know that these cars were:

Chassis no.	Registration Number	Body/Trim/ Hood Colours
YD1-501	PMO 326	Ash Green/Black/Blue
YD1-502	PMO 325	Orient Red/Red/Black
YD1-503	VLP 500	Orient Red/Red/Black
YD1-530	PMO 946	Orient Red/Red/Black

It may be noted that three of these cars had typical Reading (Berkshire) 'MO' registration numbers (Abingdon-on-Thames still being in the County of Berkshire in those days), but the fourth car had a North-west London 'LP' registration number, which sits well with the contemporary report (*see* main text) that three cars came direct from Abingdon but a fourth had to be borrowed from University Motors, the major MG dealer in London.

One of the cars, PMO 946 (an Orient Red car), suffered from a broken generator bracket, and from studying contemporary black and white ITN film of the event, it seems that the car wearing this registration number became mysteriously lighter in colour; it has been postulated that after the bracket broke, the licence plates were simply swapped over to ORX 885 (a Glacier Blue car at the time). It seems likely that ORX 885 had been intended either as a static display or back-up car, and if this theory is correct, it was swiftly drummed into service to help 'keep the show on the road'.

In a not dissimilar vein, the pre-production car chassis no. 499 (a black car, registration no. PJB 147) was used for much of the factory's formal press-release photography, and it is possible that this black car was also at Chobham on static display. This brings the possible total number of MGA Twin Cams at Chobham to six; the presence of some standard MGA 1500 cars as well may explain why some of those who were there, such as Geoffrey Iley, thought there were more like ten cars present. Even further complication comes from the story that one of the cars was crashed in the afternoon: careful study of the ITN film shows a man who looks as though he might be a uniformed musician getting into the passenger seat of VLP 500, suggesting that it might be this one – the University Motors car – in which one of the Morris Motors bandsmen had his unfortunate excursion. If so, perhaps the damaged car was 'spirited away' to London after the event?

continued overleaf

THE TWIN CAMS AT CHOBHAM *continued*

There is frequent debate that there *were* six Twin Cams at Chobham: for example, in his write-up for the Australian magazine *Modern Motor* of September 1958, correspondent Harold Dvoretsky stated twice that this was the number of cars at Chobham, writing firstly that *'Six of the new jobs were waiting for us'* and, later in his article, when he was writing about the circuit, adding that *'... we belted those six Twin Cams around it with a will'* – though having said that, in shots showing the Twin Cams parked up while EX 181 does a few laps for the crowd, it appears that there were only four cars on duty at any one time.

PMO 946 at the Chobham event in July 1958.
COURTESY MARK HESTER

In addition to the MGAs, BMC had on hand examples of the standard MGA, MG Magnette, Riley Pathfinder, Morris Minor 1000 and Riley One-Point-Five, and as a bonus the EX 181 Roaring Raindrop. In terms of standard MGAs at Chobham, there was an MGA 1500 Roadster, and, chiefly because there were no MGA Twin Coupés available for the launch event, an Old English White MGA 1500 Coupé (registration no. PBL 497 – later owned by Peter Seymour of Nuffield Exports – which would subsequently be fitted with a 1622cc engine – *see* next chapter) and another Coupé, PRX 14 (Glacier Blue with grey trim; HMD13-53352), which would later go on to be the first MGA fitted with a 1588cc ohv engine (*see* Chapter 7).

VLP 500 sets off at Chobham in July 1958, with a uniformed passenger on board...
COURTESY MARK HESTER

snag was that time and demand meant that only three laps of the High-Speed Course could be completed in a Twin Cam. Thus the highlight of the day was over in less than five minutes, which is hardly time to form clear and determined impressions of the car.' Both Gregor Grant and John Bolster wrote positively about their Chobham experiences in the *Autosport* issue of 18 July 1958, although Grant said that he had to inflate the front tyres to 28 psi in order to get the best handling, having found a tendency to oversteer without this change; even so, he said that 'braking was so good as to be almost sensational, the Dunlop disc units giving the best stopping power that any MG has ever possessed.'

THE FIRST FIVE PRODUCTION MGA TWIN CAMS

Chassis Number	Start Build	Finish Build	Despatch Date	Body Colour	Trim Colour	Hood Colour	Type	Body Number	UK Registration No.	Notes
YD1-501	22 April 1958	4 June 1958	28 July 1958	Ash Green	Black	Blue	Home market Roadster	61007	PMO 326	Chobham launch car. Engine changed from 16GG-103 to 16G-U-165 and later AEH37R RH1009A
YD1-502	23 April 1958	29 May 1958	28 July 1958	Orient Red	Red	Black	Home market Roadster	61006	PMO 325	Chobham launch car. Original engine 16GU-110 later 16G-U-303
YD1-503	25 April 1958	12 June 1958	18 June 1958	Orient Red	Red	Black	Home market Roadster	61004	VLP 500	Chobham launch car. Engine 16GG-102. Restored by Bob West
YD3-504	1 May 1958	9 May 1958	9 May 1958	Orient Red	Black	Black	LHD Roadster	61003	N/A	Engine 16G-U-119. This may be the first MGA Twin Cam to be exported to the USA
YD3-505	1 May 1958	9 May 1958	9 May 1958	Old English White	Red	Black	LHD Roadster	61009	N/A	Exported to USA. As of 2018, under restoration in New Zealand. Engine 928

Footnotes:
Two known pre-production cars were a Black roadster with red trim, chassis YDL/14/499, registration number PJB 147 (built on an adapted MGA1500 chassis. It was registered 28 March 1958; restored by Mark Hester of the MGCC MGA Twin Cam Group; see also Chapter 10 for details of its excursion to Switzerland and Austria) and a Glacier Blue roadster NDL/13/500 – the latter with body no. B29604 and registration number ORX 885 (built in 1957, registered 22 January 1958; used extensively in testing). ORX 885 was initially retained by the factory and, for example, tested in February 1958 with a 1489cc twin-cam engine (no. XSP 572/3) with both SU and Solex carburettors, later at MIRA in April (Tom Haig driving; report date 28 April 1958 and again on 5 May, the latter attempting 130mph (209km/h) for two hours); it was later fitted with a 1622cc engine before being sold off in January 1962; thereafter it had a racing career, initially in the hands of MG's John Sharp, who fitted it with an MGB engine and modified the nose in a similar vein to that of Bob Olthoff's Twin Cam (*see* Chapter 10), with alloy wings which former owner Donald Smith notes are slightly flatter in profile than standard. After Sharp the car was owned by Ken Tugwell and Colin Pearcy. Recent owner Donald Smith told the author that amongst its changes: '[it has a] twin barrel SU fuel pump located in the boot, combined with a repositioned petrol filler cap, anti tramp rods, side exhaust and no interior trim'. The car survives in its much-modified racing form and is now (in new ownership as of 2017) finished in red, with a narrow nose aperture.
Meanwhile, the first production MGA Twin Cam Coupés were YM1-551, YM1-552, YM1-553 and YM2-554, built between 23 June and 23 September 1958; as noted above, none were at the Chobham launch event. The story of YM2-554, known as 'Black Mamba', which started as a Durban dealer demonstrator and had a brief racing career, is covered in the section on South African cars in Chapter 8.
YD1-501: Accessories: competition seats, heater, twin horns, windscreen washer. PMO 326 was the first production car off the line and appeared not only at Chobham in July 1958 but in several magazines, including *Autocar* of 18 July 1958. Records show that it was initially used by Wilson McComb (at the time press and publicity officer at Abingdon) and no fewer than three engines were fitted, AEH37R RH1009A being the last, which is still fitted. Damaged in an accident by a subsequent owner in 1966, the car was acquired by the late Roy McCarthy (an active motorsports racer) in 1980 and repaired in his body shop. Roy's widow Pamela still owns the car (in 2018) and recently told the author that the repairs required were not as extensive as might be supposed.
YD1-502: Accessories: competition seats, heater, twin horns, windscreen washer. After its use at Chobham and subsequently as a factory demonstrator had finished, PMO 325 was used for development work of the model as the anti rollbar, adjustable steering column, radiator blind, 1600 lamp assemblies and hood frame were all fitted at the factory. The initial engine, 16GU-110, was changed on 13 May 1959 (at Abingdon) for 16GU-303. It was eventually sold off to an unknown third party in 1960 and was acquired by someone in Ilford, Essex, on 17 October 1960. After being sold by the factory, the engine was changed again for E86859 on 2 August 1961 by its second owner. It then passed to a further owner in Hampstead on 23 March 1963. Present owner John Hughes of Sussex bought it from MG racer Norman Lefton, better known in MGA circles for racing the ex-John Gott Twin Cam 777 ENK (YD1-652), on 23 March 1964. In 1965, the engine sadly expired, and Hughes replaced it with an MGB unit but with the intention of reuniting it with a twin-cam engine.
YD1-503: Accessories: heater, windscreen washer. According to an advertisement when this former Chobham car and demonstrator was put up for sale in 2008, little was known about its first twenty years, but it was believed to have spent some of this period in the UK's West Country. The north-west London LP registration number means it is reasonable to speculate that this car had probably been allotted to University Motors (*see* section on press launch). As of 2018 it is owned by Cliff Summer.
YD3-504: Accessories: competition seats, heater. This car was originally shipped to Kjell Qvale in San Francisco, where it was soon prepared by Joe Huffaker for racing by Jack Dalton, and there is photographic evidence of the car with its engine bay on show at the Vaca Valley Road Race (Vacaville, California) of 5 July 1958, which was nine days before the MGA Twin Cam launch event in the UK. Huffaker told present owner Terry Frisch that the car was raced about three times before their focus shifted to Jaguar (in support of this, records show the car's second outing at the Nevada Grand Prix of 2 August 1958, and the third at Laguna Seca, Monterey, California, on 9 November 1958). The car was evidently sold and was later bought from a car lot in Woodward Avenue, Detroit in 1963 (a long way from California); that owner in turn sold it to Frisch in 2007. It should be noted that there is some debate as to whether or not this car was genuinely the first to reach American shores, as there is a claim that YD3-515, possibly a car featured in a promotional film at Lime Rock by David Ash, may have been 'the first in the USA'. That Old English White car started build on 9 June and finished build on 12 June 1958, and was despatched on the same day.
YD3-505: Accessories: heater. In 2018, this car was owned by Nick Langford in New Zealand.

As noted in the table, these first five cars have body numbers 61003, 61004, 61006, 61007, 61009. Body number 61001 was fitted to YD1-572.

The *fourth* Twin Cam at Chobham, chassis no. YD1-530 (PMO 946) had body no. 61012; it started build on 13 June, finished build on 24 June, and was despatched on 26 June 1958.

Behind the press announcement of the Twin Cam 'MGA' were two months of detailed organization

BY TONY LUCAS

DÉBUT BY DEMONSTRATION

The heading image of an article in Nuffield *Motoring* of October 1958, which describes the test day at Chobham the previous July. It is a little difficult to see, but there are four cars parked up in this view.

AUTHOR'S COLLECTION

Terry Frisch is the present owner of YD3-504, the first USA-specification production MGA Twin Cam and possibly the first to be exported to that country. The car is seen here with Frisch's grandson Joshua.

TERRY FRISCH

This photograph of the engine bay of PJB 147 dates from 23 August 1958, when the MGA Twin Cam was on show at an MG Car Club event…

MIKE MILWARD, COURTESY MARK HESTER

…and this photograph of the same engine bay was taken by the author at Silverstone nearly sixty years later (4 June 2018), also at an MG Car Club event ('MG Live').

AUTHOR

PMO 326 has chassis number YD1-501, and was thus the first production MGA Twin Cam. Its formal Abingdon despatch date was after the press launch.

MCCARTHY FAMILY

Mark Hester owns PJB 147, the pre-production MGA Twin Cam which may have been part of the launch event at Chobham.
AUTHOR

ORX 885 looks very different in 2018 – after being bought by John Sharp of MG, the nose was modified in similar manner to that of Bob Olthoff (*see* Chapter 10), and eventually a 1762cc engine was fitted.
H&H AUCTIONS

PMO 325, the second production MGA Twin Cam (YD1-502).
AUTHOR

PMO 946 was also at Chobham; it had chassis number YD1-530.
AUTHOR

VLP 500 – the University Motors Twin Cam. Interestingly, despite the fact that it had been registered in London, it was the third production car (YD1-503).
AUTHOR

Some of the observant guests at Chobham noted that the MG mechanics were carefully checking the oil levels of the cars every third lap – not necessarily a bad thing, especially if some of the less sympathetic testers were determined to exploit the hedonistic thrills of much higher rev limits – but nevertheless to some people an indication that perhaps there was more development work needed before serious customer deliveries could commence.

So successful was the Chobham event deemed to have been that the same venue was hired a little over a year later – on 18 and 19 August 1959 – for the press launch of BMC's all-important new 'baby car', the Austin 'Se7en' and Morris Mini Minor.

THE MGA TWIN CAM IN THE PRESS

Motor carried a road-test of a Twin Cam in their issue of 16 July 1958, under the promising sub-heading 'A Roadworthy Sports Car of Very High Performance', and began by noting that 'as the power (together with the disc brakes) is the feature of paramount importance in the latest MG, one may as well sum up the car to begin with by stating that it is relatively noisy, entirely tractable, quite untemperamental, and will probably appeal in the main to owners who wish to win races.'

As the general press preview was in the same week, it must be assumed that the magazine had taken their car away beforehand for their extended continental trip. For at least part of its time with them it was fed on a diet of 97 octane petrol rather than the recommended 100 octane, and the testers noted that the engine really needed the higher octane fuel to be at its best, observing that without it, the engine would 'pink' when pulling hard from low revs, and tended to run on after having been switched off.

Fuel consumption worked out at around 20mpg (14ltr/100km) overall, which the magazine felt rendered the modest 10gal (45ltr) tank something of a liability on longer journeys. The testers nevertheless loved the disc brakes and centre-lock wheels, noting that stopping from high speeds was consistently good, irrespective of the weather. They were rather less impressed with the state of the suspension, for after some 500 miles (800km) in the UK and 1,000 miles (1,600km) on the continent, the front shock absorbers appeared to have failed and there was quite severe scuttle shake in the range of 70–85mph (115–140km/h). In a time when many road testers tended to be reserved in their criticisms, this was quite a harsh assessment and doubtless raised some eyebrows at Cowley and Longbridge.

On a more positive vein, the magazine found that the steering was otherwise viceless, being 'neither especially light nor especially heavy, but absolutely positive and responsible in a manner which is rare. Just sufficient understeer is present to make the car straight running and insensitive to cross-winds, without requiring efforts of skill or strength on a winding road.' Also favourable was the opinion of the gearbox, thought to be excellent, with its easy and positive action, other than some criticism of the gear-ratio gap between second and third.

***Sports Cars Illustrated* was the name of monthly enthusiast publications in both the UK and USA. This is the cover of the September 1958 UK edition, which carried a report on the Chobham test day inside. The Chariot Red cover car, PMO 325 (chassis no. YD1-502) was actually one of the cars at Chobham.**
AUTHOR'S COLLECTION

Accessibility under the bonnet was noted as somewhat difficult, with, for example, the dipstick almost completely hidden from view, while the distributor could not be reached at all without first uncoupling the air duct to the interior heater. In light of the fact that *Motor* had evidently been told that the new model was not intended for very large-scale production, it commented that:

> ...such details as these may well be unimportant to the comparatively few people who, by their choice of the more costly model, indicate that performance is their first consideration. When one or two matters have been attended

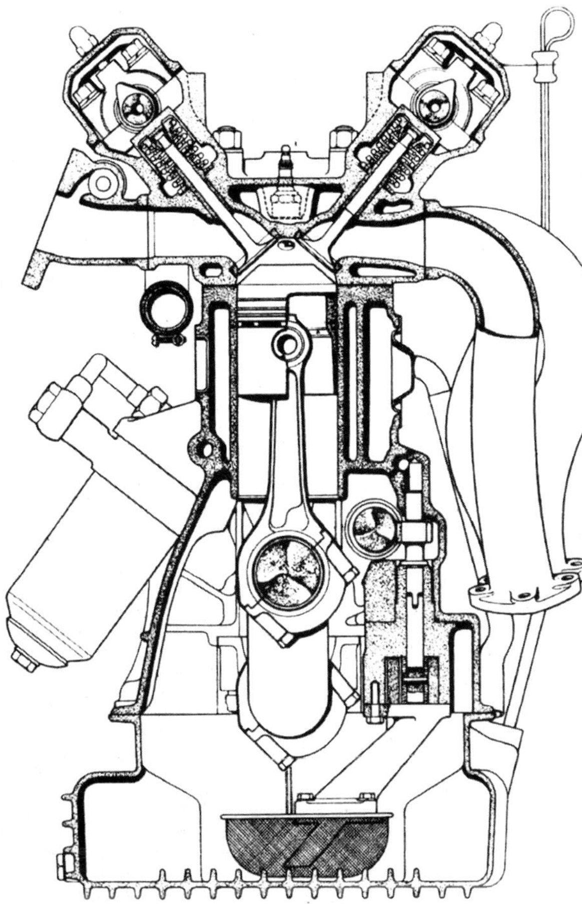

This cross-section shows the ninety-degree angle between the two banks of valves on top of what is otherwise still essentially a conventional 1,588cc B-Series engine
AUTHOR'S COLLECTION

to there is little doubt that numerous competition successes will come the way of the MG, the more so because of its favourable situation in the 1600cc category.

Autocar also reported on the MGA Twin Cam for their issue of 18 July 1958, which showed that, like their weekly rivals, they had been given the opportunity to subject the new model to the rigours of their road-testing procedure. As with the other magazine, *Autocar* took their charge on a trip to the continent, in their case the fast roads of Belgium. They observed that the engine started easily and quickly reached working temperature: 'It revs freely, and the limit marking on the tachometer is 7,000rpm; it was taken up to this limit repeatedly during the test.' It was also noted, however, that there was some engine vibration at 2,500 and 5,500rpm, but this aside, power built up noticeably after the engine topped 3,500rpm: 'By the time 4,000rpm is reached it really takes hold, and the little car begins to show its potential performance.'

The tester noted that:

There was a constant, rather obtrusive background of mechanical noise; most of this can be traced to the valve gear, particularly the tappets, which have a recommended clearance of 0.018in, but there is also a 'ring' associated with the first stage of the timing gears. Nor can it be said that the engine is smooth or silky. Exhaust-wise, the car is not objectionable, and it can be driven through city traffic without attracting undue attention.

The test car suffered from a loose silencer baffle, which must have been annoying on a long journey. High sustained speeds on the continental autobahns were found to be easily achievable, but the magazine noted that if this potential was utilized to the full, fuel consumption inevitably rose considerably.

The familiar complaints were made about under-bonnet accessibility, noting that the distributor was hard to get at (and became covered in oil during the test). All the testers' maximum speed and acceleration tests were carried out with the recommended 100 octane petrol. Even with this fuel, not to mention the Belgian 'premium' 89 octane petrol, it was found that, just as *Motor* had observed, the engine tended to 'run on' after being switched off. More alarmingly, the engine in the test car used a considerable amount of oil: 'Five pints [3ltr] were added to the sump during one journey of 800 miles [1,300km], and an overall oil consumption figure of 1,020mpg was recorded – approximately one quart [1ltr] of oil each time the petrol tank (capacity 10gal [45ltr]) was refilled.'

In common with most road testers, *Autocar* enjoyed the gearbox quality, although they were, like *Motor*, a little critical of the gaps between some of the gears, commenting that 'an owner using the car for circuit racing would, no doubt, prefer a gearbox with closer ratios. A 4.55 to 1 axle ratio can be fitted in place of the standard 4.3 to 1 ratio at an extra cost of £10 2s 6d.' Similarly the road-holding and cornering were both felt to be admirable, noting that 'the manufacturers' well known motto "Safety Fast" is particularly pertinent to this new model.'

A common complaint familiar to many MG sports-car owners was the vexed matter of cockpit temperatures; the testers noting on their car that 'the proximity of the engine and gearbox can bring about an uncomfortably high temperature around the legs and feet; it is probable that owners in hot climates will call for separate fresh air ventilators. On the other hand, the warmth would be appreciated in winter conditions.' Other gripes were minimal, and in summary *Autocar* assessed the MGA Twin Cam as having extra performance that was matched by its road-holding, steering and brakes, concluding that the new model maintained 'the MG tradition of good looks coupled with a very fine performance'.

Having included a news report on the new model in their September 1958 issue, *Road & Track* featured the MGA Twin Cam engine on the cover of the following month's magazine, but made it clear in their report that there had been some initial dalliances with under-par specimens:

The twin cam unit is a tight fit in the MGA engine compartment; this is Adrian Malthouse's car, which he purchased in 2003, and restoration work included much work on this engine: 'I was lucky to find an original unused "red" crank, sourced from the USA, probably one of the last in existence. I decided to use a new unmachined crank to ensure longevity of the engine. The engine was rebuilt by Peter Wood, a renowned MG specialist using some new parts and as many of the original parts as necessary'.
BEAULIEU

> In the fall of 1955, our Technical Editor inspected two experimental engines at the MG factory, but it wasn't until July this year that we were able to drive one. The first few samples were rushed over, and they just weren't quite right as delivered. We accordingly delayed our full-scale road test until this issue to give a fair and accurate test report.

Such candidness was seldom seen in most contemporary British motoring publications, used to more obsequious prose.

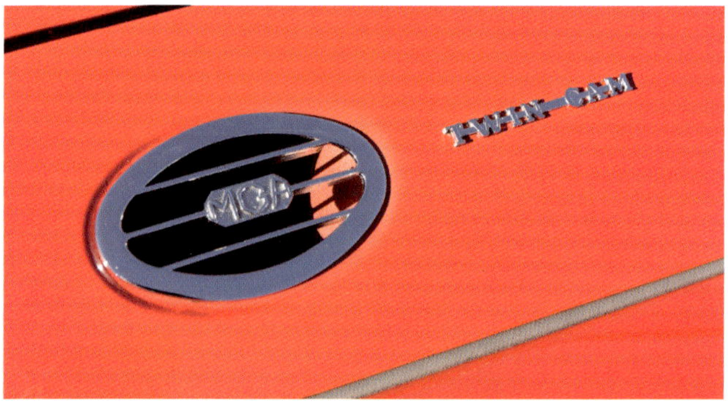

TOP: **Alongside each of the two familiar elliptical scuttle vents is a chrome-plated 'Twin Cam' script...**

BOTTOM: **...also seen below the MG badge on the boot-lid.**
BEAULIEU

ABOVE LEFT: **This Twin Cam was supplied new on 26 March 1959 to a Mr A. W. Wiggan of Worcester, through John Bryant & Sons (Birmingham). Adrian Malthouse is the latest of ten UK owners.**

LEFT: **Adrian Malthouse owns YD1-1446, a home-market Orient Red MGA Twin Cam Roadster; it was originally finished in black with green trim.**
BEAULIEU

The MGA Twin Cam came as standard with distinctive Dunlop steel wheels with peg drive and centre-lock nuts (with knock-off ears where allowed).
BEAULIEU

With the MGA Twin Cam came the introduction of a slightly more luxurious facia treatment, with leathercloth covering.
BEAULIEU

The MGA Twin Cam was offered as a Coupé, making a great touring car. This is Jonathan Stein's LHD example.
JONATHAN STEIN

The Coupé as a body type is covered in Chapter 5. This is the interior of Jonathan Stein's February 1959 US specification MGA Twin Cam Coupé (YM3-1147), which he owned between 1999 and 2012.
JONATHAN STEIN

The report in *Road & Track* is also interesting because the writers had the opportunity to try a second car which been modified, with a change to a 4.55 axle ratio and the close ratio Le Mans gearbox. As we have seen, *Road & Track* wasn't the only publication to experience early problems with the MGA Twin Cam; in the home market, *Autocar* and *Motor* both experienced problems with anything less than the best 100 octane petrol, and the oil thirst on *Autocar*'s test car was surely unforgivable. However, in their report of November 1958, the magazine was generally positive, commenting that the car was 'jolly good fun, even if it won't hit two miles a minute'.

THE MGA TWIN CAM AT MOTOR SHOWS

The first appearance of MG's exotic new sports car at the major motor shows took place in the autumn of 1958. The first of these was the Paris Salon of 2–12 October 1958, followed at the end of the month by MG's 'home show' at Earls Court, held between 22 and 31 October 1958. From surviving factory records and contemporary reports we can deduce that the Paris Show cars were YD3-564 and YM3-594, respectively an Old English White Roadster with red trim and black hood (with the accessories of heater and show tyres), and a Mineral Blue Coupé with black trim (the only factory accessory listed being a heater), both unsurprisingly left-hand drive; they were despatched on 16 and 17 September, a fortnight

At Earls Court in 1958, the MG stand featured a cutaway display version of an MGA Twin Cam Coupé in a special finish. The display car survived in this form and was used for a while for police training, before eventually joining the Heritage collection at Gaydon. Although it has a body number (61755) it does not appear to have been assigned a full chassis number.
GRAHAM ROBSON

For a number of years, the cut-away MGA Twin Cam served to support police training.
MARK HESTER

before the show opened. Alongside them was a standard MGA Roadster with the optional black hardtop fitted.

Both the Twin Cam show cars are now (2018) owned by the same man, Bill Oesterle, who is in the process of restoring them. Curiously YD3-564 was at one time owned in Marseille by someone called 'Fitzwilliam', but the author, intrigued at the potential connection (the surname is surely not common in Marseille), checked with the family of MGA race team principal Richard W. Fitzwilliam, but this Marseille resident was not related.

At October 1958's Earls Court show, the MG stand was dominated by a large rotating turntable, behind the glass outer wall of which pirouetted a sectioned MGA Twin Cam Coupé, finished in a bespoke metallic bronze finish ('Sandy Gold') with a 'Powder Blue' roof, and a 'Citrus Yellow' interior, not far from the personal colour choice that Syd Enever would select for his personal MGA Coupé KMO 326 (see Chapter 5). Also on the MG stand were a right-hand-drive MGA Roadster in Chariot Red with Red trim, wire wheels and whitewall tyres, and a left-hand-drive MGA Coupé to US specification, also with wire wheels and white-wall tyres, but finished in Old English White with black upholstery (although neither of these were Twin Cams).

Remarkably, the sectioned Twin Cam Coupé was later used for training purposes by the police, and consequently survives in the Heritage collection at Gaydon, having been completely restored between November 2012 and May 2013 by a group of twenty-five volunteers. Meanwhile, also on the stand in October 1958 were a brace of Magnette ZBs, one of them a Varitone.

After the expected debuts at Paris and London, MGA Twin Cams also popped up, fettled by the MG show shop, at other events such as Turin, in November (YD3-624, a Black Roadster with red trim and black hood, and YD3-625 – Ash Green with black trim and a blue hood) and Detroit's '46th Annual Show' later that month (YD3-620, a Black Roadster with red trim and black hood). Thereafter, the equally important spring shows saw YM2-1235, a Coupé finished in Old English White with red interior, at Geneva in March, and YM3-1037, a black Coupé with red trim, at New York's Third International Motor Show at the Coliseum in early April.

Other shows in 1959 where the Twin Cam appeared were Valencia, Spain (YD3-1726, an Old English White Roadster with red trim and black hood), Barcelona's 1959 Fair (YD3-1993, an Orient Red Roadster with black trim and hood), and inevitably, returns to Paris (YD3-2453, a Chariot Red Roadster with black trim and grey hood; and YD3-2462, a Dove Grey Coupé with red interior), Earls Court (YM1-2495, an Old English White Coupé with black interior), and the Scottish Show (YD1-2487, a Chariot Red Roadster with beige trim and hood).

SALES AND MARKETING: MGA TWIN CAM ADVERTS AND BROCHURES

The press pack for the new MGA Twin Cam appeared just ahead of the launch in July 1958 and followed the triangular pennant theme of earlier promotional material: the cover of the press pack was in black with six triangular pennants in red, amber and green. The Twin Cam was always envisaged as a low-volume sales prospect, and so much of the marketing

The MGA Twin Cam was launched with this simple 'spot colour' brochure in the form of a fold-out leaflet. This is the home-market version; similar leaflets are known in several languages.

AUTHOR'S COLLECTION

An advertisement for the MGA Twin Cam in the 18 July 1958 issue of *Autocar*, which covered the new model's announcement.

AUTHOR'S COLLECTION

was in the form of references to the model simply being added to existing advertising or marketing literature. Indeed in a letter dated 1 July 1958 – that is, nearly a fortnight before the Chobham event – from Nuffield Organisation Publicity Manager J. J. Field, addressed to 'all MG distributors, dealers, retail dealers and stocking traders', it was stated that:

THE AUTOCAR, 18 JULY 1958

Whenever a new car was launched in the 1950s and 1960s, it was common to see 'supportive' advertisements from key suppliers appearing in the relevant issue of *Autocar* or *Motor*. This advertisement from Smiths Instruments, featuring PMO 326, appeared in the 18 July 1958 issue of *Autocar*.

AUTHOR'S COLLECTION

> ...the Twin Camshaft MGA is an alternative version of the standard model, and is, therefore, not rated as a new car. Moreover, production will be on a limited scale and mainly for overseas markets. For these reasons, no advertisements will appear in the national newspapers, but the technical magazines will be included...

However, there was a dedicated orange spot-colour, largely black and white leaflet created for the Twin Cam, featuring some rather crudely retouched artwork (to try to make the wheels look like the special items used on production cars). This brochure was produced in a surprisingly large number of versions, including language variants, and consequently is not considered an especially rare item within the literature-collecting community. The UK market variant, including the one issued along with the press pack, had the slogan 'now... a special performance MGA' and proclaimed its disc brakes and twin overhead camshafts. Inside, the brochure declared:

An advertisement from Dunlop for their disc brakes fitted as standard to the new MGA Twin Cam.
AUTHOR'S COLLECTION

> For over three years this engine has been talked about in motor-sport circles – ever since, in fact, an MGA ran in the Tourist Trophy race in Northern Ireland in 1955 fitted with an early experimental version. Then again, on the Salt Flats at Bonneville, Utah, in August 1957 Stirling Moss achieved 246mph [395.8km/h] with the MG Special EX 181, and this time the twin-cam engine was highly supercharged. The MG engineers have held back the announcement of this long-awaited engine until they are quite satisfied with it.

Such advertising as there was for the MGA Twin Cam tended to take the form of references made within more general MGA advertisements, although at the time of its launch, BMC made a modest splash with an advertisement in the 18 July 1958 issue of *Autocar*, which featured the strap line 'One word for it – phenomenal!', and the supporting text 'The Twin-Cam MGA – a great British challenge to the world of motor sport', along with the proclamation that the new model offered the 'world's top performance-to-price ratio!' It was a promising beginning for arguably the most exciting post-war MG, but as we shall see shortly, the celebrations would prove to be short-lived.

FOR GERMANY: THE MGA „1600 SPEZIAL"

Although launched in Germany as the MGA Twin Cam (and most German-language sales literature referred to it as such), at least one early local brochure from April 1958 (with printing reference 14289) referred to the new car as the MGA „1600 Spezial" for reasons that are not entirely clear; this sales brochure, like many for European markets, was partially printed in the UK by the Nuffield Press, but with most of the text subsequently overprinted locally – in this case in Germany, through the offices of the importer (J. A. Woodhouse of Köln-Braunsfeld). According to Twin Cam expert Robin Barker: 'a later German Twin Cam brochure from August 1958 (16680) has the „1600 Spezial" reference changed to 'Twin Cam'.

SERVICE PROBLEMS

For customers who might not be used to the highly strung nature of the new model's engine, MG produced a small leaflet to provide some essential hints and tips, entitled 'Getting the best from your Twin Cam', with recommendations concerning the specialized maintenance required, and choice of fuel, sparking plugs and ignition settings, the latter as follows:

> The leaflet included sections on choice of fuel – 'octane ratings below 93 are not suitable...it is recommended that

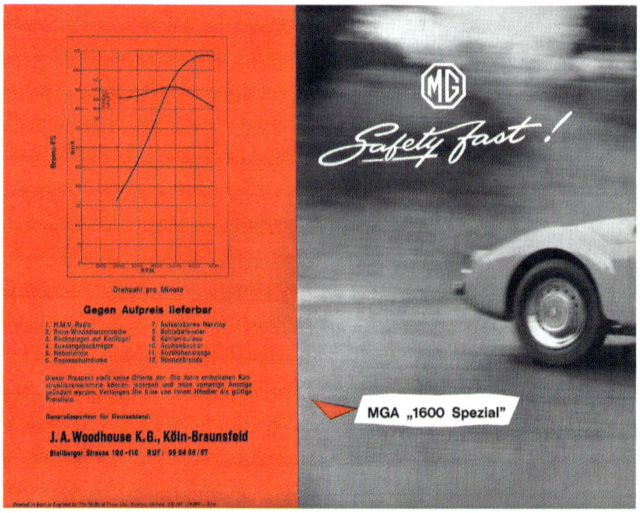

Rather than refer to the new model as something like the MGA 'Doppel-Nockenwellen', the German importer initially styled it as the MGA „1600 Spezial"; soon common sense returned, however, and the MGA 'Twin Cam' name was used.
AUTHOR'S COLLECTION

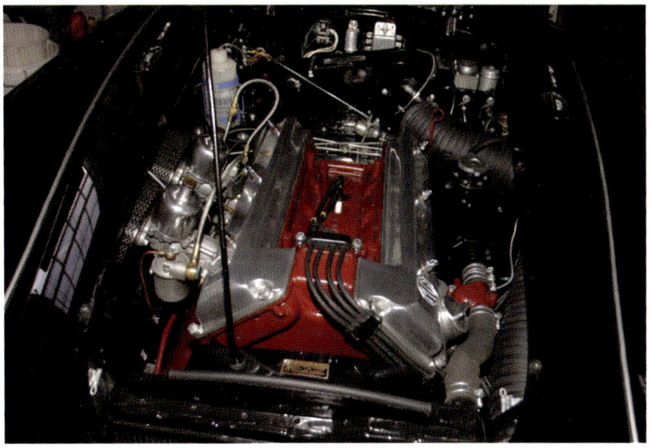

The elegant combination of 'MG red' and polished aluminium alloy on the twin-cam engine disguised a number of problems...

JONATHAN STEIN

fuel with an octane rating between 95 and 98 be used under normal touring conditions, but when optimum performance is required, the use of fuel rated between 99 and 101 octane will be found beneficial'; sparking plugs – 'the correct grade of sparking plug for normal driving conditions is the Champion N.3... for competition work or hard driving... the Champion N58R sparking plug should be used... new plugs should be fitted every 12,000 miles [19,200km]'; and lastly ignition settings – 'it is of the utmost importance that the correct ignition setting should always be maintained... under no circumstances should the ignition be advanced beyond TDC'.

The leaflet continued with sections on choice of fuel – 'octane ratings below 93 are not suitable...it is recommended that fuel with an octane rating between 95 and 98 be used under normal touring conditions, but when optimum performance is required, the use of fuel rated between 99 and 101 octane will be found beneficial'; sparking plugs – 'the correct grade of sparking plug for normal driving conditions is the Champion N.3... for competition work or hard driving... the Champion N58R sparking plug should be used... new plugs should be fitted every 12,000 miles [19,200km]'; and lastly ignition settings – 'it is of the utmost importance that the correct ignition setting should always be maintained... under no circumstances should the ignition be advanced beyond TDC'.

The very fact that MG felt it necessary to create and distribute such a leaflet surely speaks volumes about the nervousness felt at exposing what was a fairly highly strung sporting machine to the vagaries of less competent owners (and dealers), many of whom were more used to the philosophy of simply getting in the car, switching it on, and subjecting it to the general day-to-day abuse that a normal mass-produced motor car would be expected to handle without difficulty.

As we shall see in the remainder of this chapter, there was a great deal of anxiety and consequent effort associated with trying to address the service problems that transpired, but arguably what was probably the single most important remedy – which as we shall see was associated, to some extent, with the inconsistent engine balance that Geoffrey Iley had experienced in the run-up to the press launch – was only discovered when it was too late.

Meanwhile, however, over at Nuffield Exports, early deliveries of the first cars to overseas customers began to generate a few warranty horror stories, and it was clear that action was needed to avoid damage to the MG and BMC reputation. Bob Seymour was a Nuffield Exports Service Engineer at the time the Twin Cam came out, and benefited from specialist training in the new powertrain. The first place that he was able to put this to good use was in Eire, where the local agent, Booth Poole & Co. Limited – who built MGAs from 'completely knocked down' ('CKD') kits (see also Chapter 8) – had a number of customers who experienced significant problems with their Twin Cams.

Nowadays the average MGA Twin Cam owner can call upon many sources of help, but sixty years ago he or she was not so lucky. These cars are lined up at an MG Car Club event in the summer of 2018.

AUTHOR

Visiting Dublin, Seymour gained a good grounding in the problems being experienced in the field; accordingly towards the end of 1959 he made a major trip to North America to help tackle the problem, working out of Morris Motors (Canada) Ltd in Hamilton, Ontario (where MGAs were imported 'partially knocked down', having been crated up by Nuffield Exports in the UK) but also going out on various trips, not only in Canada itself (for example Halifax, Ottawa, Winnipeg, Calgary and Vancouver) but also across the border to visit various dealers in New York, Detroit and Washington. Seymour ran training sessions, and relayed his own testing technique for appraising the Twin Cam, which consisted of the following checks:

- Establish the operating conditions of the vehicle, and the owner's complaints
- Check that N3 spark plugs are fitted
- Road test the vehicle in the condition received, and make notes
- Check the engine number and modifications, and modify these where necessary
- Check and reset, if necessary, the ignition timing, the valve timing and the carburettors

A note added: 'Should it be necessary to fit expander rings to the pistons, check the performance of the vehicle before stripping the engine and after setting the timing.'

Seymour maintains that nearly every car he came across would 'run on' severely: 'I would spend hours tuning the carburettors trying to improve the tick-over, which was always lumpy, and after a while the engine would stall. It was often just not possible to get it right.' There were many other problems: if soft plugs were used in day-to-day use, a consequence would be burnt piston crowns when the car was opened up out of town.

Seymour also remembers 'spectacular engine blow-ups', when the tappet buckets tilted and locked solid in the cylinder head. In a manner familiar to any owner of a modern overhead cam engine that has suffered cam-belt failure, this would precipitate the camshaft shearing, the valves striking the pistons with devastating results. Seymour says that later engines had longer tappets, and later still the tappet bores were fitted with cast-iron liners. Throughout its production life, however, one of the persistent challenges was a consequence of the long timing chain which, by virtue of its tendency to whip, consequently risked the valve timing slipping from the optimum.

On at least one occasion, Bob Seymour experienced a failure of this chain on a car he took out on test, having undertaken a lot of work, only for a dramatic and explosive failure. Continual updates came from the factory, which appeared to be playing catch-up with the problems witnessed by Seymour and others out in the field. Further changes included swapping from a distributor with a vacuum advance (40510B) to one without a vacuum advance (40718A), the intention being to 'prevent "wandering" and an inaccurate spark position on each cycle'.

Near the end of production, the compression ratio was dropped significantly from 9.9:1 to 8.3:1, with a consequent drop in performance but less sensitivity to poor fuel. This brought the Twin Cam into line with much of the BMC range, where an 8.3:1 compression ratio had been standardized across most of the A and B series engines in the mid-1950s. As Seymour says:

> It is a pity this change was not introduced earlier as it may have prevented the engine from getting a poor reputation, and enabled the car to have a longer production run. Many cars that were already in service had these 'low' compression pistons fitted, without charge to the customer, even if the vehicle was outside its warranty period.

Other changes in the service situation included to the piston rings…

> …to try and reduce the oil consumption, and we had a great deal of correspondence from owners about this. In its day the Twin-Cam engine at 7,000rpm was high revving, and at this speed the sump oil was being thrown all over the place and especially up the cylinder bores! Oils have improved an enormous amount since then, but I think the real problem stemmed from the fact that there was insufficient development, especially road testing when the oil was hot (and it used to get very hot), before the engine was put into production.

Remarkably, Seymour found that most of the owners he came across were fairly forgiving of the Twin Cam's problems, although inevitably this was not always the case: 'In the end any owners who remained unhappy with their cars were given replacement pushrod 1600cc B-series engines, and this happened quite a lot in Germany.'

It was not just in Germany that Continental European MGA Twin Cams suffered problems. Jean-Pierre Richard, who had the MG franchise in France in the 1950s, spoke to author Jon Pressnell about the problems he had experienced with the Twin Cam. 'The Twin-Cams were forever holing their pistons. We tried everything, cold plugs, a lower compression ratio, but we could never find a way of getting them to work.'

Richard recalled receiving a phone call at three o'clock one morning: it was the president of the French MG club. 'He had holed a piston... By the time the Nuffield engineers arrived, about twenty to twenty-five Twin Cams had been sold in France – but '…fifteen of them were in the workshops, bonnet up and engine out. We realized we had to stop importing the cars, because if journalists got to hear of the problems

Until a change of approach in the early 1960s, the British weekly motoring magazines *Autocar* and *Motor* (seen here) carried manufacturer-funded advertisements on their front covers. Although the artwork depicts an MGA 1500 Roadster, the copy on this cover from 8 April 1959 makes reference to the option of the Twin Cam. Within a few weeks, however, the MGA 1500 would give way to the 1600.

MOTOR

we'd be roasted alive!' The eventual solution was to swap the engines for pushrod 1600cc engines, as in Germany.

SO WHAT REALLY WAS THE PROBLEM?

One of Alec Hounslow's team at Abingdon looking at the service issues with the engine was Jim Cox in Development, who told the author: 'We always had problems with that engine; I remember Laurie Hands – from Champion – came down and tried all sorts of different plugs, gaps, cores and so on, but without any luck. We had a customer in Cologne who kept burning holes in pistons, and for a while we couldn't replicate this. Then Tommy Haig burnt a hole in a piston on the way back from MIRA. Eventually we reduced the compression ratio to 8.3:1 by changing the pent-house top piston for a flatter, rounded piston...' Even so, whilst it helped, the lower compression ratio was not a cure-all. Many changes were identified in service, including piston type, piston rings and clearance, and various weaknesses in the timing-chain gear; even so, the tendency of pistons to 'hole' in their crowns was a common theme. During its brief production lifetime, there was a veritable phalanx of 'service notes' issued by MG to try to deal with problems experienced in the field.

The author is grateful to MGA Sebring owner and enthusiast Frank Graham (see Chapter 10) for sharing pearls of wisdom he gained first hand from Alec Hounslow and Cecil Cousins when he met them during their US tour (see Chapter 1) at the NEMGT-Register Gathering of the Faithful. At the time (1974) the Twin Cam was still regarded with great caution and suspicion by most MG enthusiasts; MGA Sebring owner Frank Graham was one of comparatively few Americans with a keen interest in the engine – at one time owning five of them. But the first MGA Twin Cam he owned had a hole in the top of piston number four, and the second had one in the top of number three – so there clearly could have been a theme.

Alec Hounslow (left) and his life-long colleague Cecil Cousins, photographed during a tour of the USA as guests of the NEMGTR in 1974, where they revealed to Frank Graham the problem of vibrating SU carburettors on the MGA Twin Cam.

HOUNSLOW FAMILY

Graham recalls that, characteristically, Alec Hounslow opened up over a few whiskies; he explained that naturally enough, once the stories of engine failures grew, it was initially felt that owners were probably mistreating their Twin Cams through over-revving, having the ignition timing too far advanced (a known weakness), or simply using fuel with the wrong octane rating. However, the many solutions adopted, such as centrifugal advance units or the low-compression pistons adopted near the end of production, never eradicated the piston failures entirely. John Thornley asked Hounslow and his team to find a fix, '...so they ran engines on the test bed, advancing the timing way beyond specification, and revving them until the bottom ends blew out, but they weren't experiencing holed pistons. Dick Jacobs had never holed pistons on his racing twin cams either but they were running Webers.'

What the team did note was that the balance of the production engines was well below the levels of precision that engineering had recommended (remember that Geoffrey Iley had found the engine balance problem when selecting cars for the launch event): 'The engine had two natural vibration periods at about 3,200 and 5,600rpm. With stock gearing the 3,200rpm period coincided with typical highway cruising speeds.' Knowing this, and the fact that racing engines with Webers – or indeed the supercharged record breakers – had never exhibited piston failures, Hounslow and his team ran their test units with the engine speed right where the vibration period occurred: 'They found that the float on the rear carburettor would hang on its spindle and not drop, which caused the rear carburettor to go full lean and hole either no. 3 or no. 4 piston.'

Graham notes that most Twin Cams where there had been a holed piston seem to have had it on either no. 3 or no. 4. The solution to this particular weakness was flexible mounting of the carburettors, along with better balance, but sadly it came too late to save the model. Nowadays nearly every MGA Twin Cam owner will probably have had his or her car suitably modified, and provided it is well treated, there is no reason why an MGA Twin Cam should be any less reliable than almost any other highly tuned classic sports car.

John Thornley made some candid observations to Kenneth Ullyett, writing in *The MG Companion*:

> Cynics have said that, for all the twin cam is a specialized version of the B-Series, the only things that are really interchangeable are the bore centres! As so frequently happens in redesigning of this sort, we could have saved ourselves a number of headaches if we had been able to start with a clean sheet of paper.
>
> In fact most designers experience troubles of this sort nowadays with engines having compression ratios approaching 10:1.

Thornley went on to suggest that even US manufacturers had faced similar issues with contemporary V8 engines of such compression ratios:

> I fancy some American designers were surprised to find that with units of certain types you do experience piston perforation as the result of high compression; also with other types you simply cannot allow any appreciable carbon formation to build up, or you run at once into fresh problems of detonation.
>
> As to excessive noise, one of the causes of the original charge of too much noise was simply that we had played for caution in piston clearances, and had given them nine thousandths [of an inch]. As a matter of fact even on our MG record-breaking engines, using forty pounds of boost, we never employed a greater piston clearance than seven thousandths. Now on the production twin cam we are down to about four thousandths, and this is proving entirely adequate.

These words were no doubt spoken when the Twin Cam was still in production, because although Ullyett's book was published on 14 November 1960, the model was referred to as being still current. By that time too, of course, there was also a conventional 1588cc overhead valve MGA on sale in place of the earlier 1498cc, and to follow that there would soon be the significantly revised 1622cc unit (see Chapter 7).

Some thirty years later Thornley spoke to author and historian Jon Pressnell, for an article in *Classic & Sportscar*. By this stage many of the key players in BMC were long gone, and Thornley had no hesitation in placing a significant chunk of the blame for the Twin Cam's problems with the incumbent Deputy Chairman of the day, George Harriman:

> I was eventually told by Harriman 'Oh, all right, go and build the Twin Cam – but you've got to use the standard block.' The thing hadn't got into production before there was a boss on the block special to the Twin-Cam, so we might as well have started off with a new set of bore centres and strokes and crankshaft and all the rest, and then done the whole job properly – because the bore centres limited the bore diameter, which postulated the stroke in order to get the capacity, we were hamstrung. It really wasn't on. There was no way you could make that engine bulletproof. We did wonders with it, but the engines really had to be under specialized control...

Perhaps, in hindsight, the bespoke Austin proposal might, with development, have been not so bad after all? So for MG at Abingdon, getting their unique sports car powertrain ultimately proved to be something of a pyrrhic victory, with rather too many challenges for the makers and the customers alike.

PRODUCTION HISTORY

At this point it is probably worth touching on the production history of the MGA Twin Cam itself. Accepting that the rate of engine production did not necessarily equate precisely to the car assembly, it is noteworthy that production of the new model started slowly and proceeded in fits and starts. Graham Robson undertook the task of analyzing car production, such as the data meticulously collated by the late Phil Richer of the MGCC MGA Twin Cam Group. This shows straightaway that the 2,111 MGA Twin Cams built over a period of twenty-six months average out overall at eighty-one per month, a rate of production that John Thornley believed was excessive.

In the wake of the launch in July, and because of increasing knowledge of, and interest in, the new model over the next few months, by the end of the year 508 cars had been built – roughly a quarter of the entire production run, as it happens. In the following year (1959) 1,550 were built in total – a modest 6.5 per cent of all MGA output that year; in 1960 the corresponding percentage was just 0.3 per cent. Running changes during production of the Twin Cam reflected developments across the remainder of the MGA family – most significantly in June 1959, at chassis no. 2193, the MGA Twin Cam Roadster saw the introduction of an MGA 1600 type of body, corresponding with MGA 1600 chassis no. 68851, while the corresponding MGA Twin Cam Coupé made a similar switch at chassis no. 2292.

It is said that when Marcus Chambers came back from Sebring in March 1960, his report of poor reliability was the news that killed the Twin Cam; however, the numbers above surely show that the writing was already on the wall long before this, because after an average peak output of around 220 a month over the first six months of 1959, the numbers dropped fairly drastically, such that over the three-month winter period of October to December just thirty-seven were produced in total.

Planning for Sebring would have begun the previous autumn – the cars were built in the period from December 1959 onwards, in readiness for the race in March 1960 – and perhaps there was still hope at that point that the future of the Twin Cam could be salvaged.

As we have seen, the final fix towards the end of Twin Cam production was to reduce the compression ratio to 8.3:1. This slightly blunted the overall performance, with the power output deficit some 8bhp. More than half the cars were being sold in North America, and by this stage, the damage to reputation – and the warranty costs – only served to accelerate the death sentence of the model.

John Thornley expounded his view that interference from above was part of the problem:

> We were just running into our troubles with burned pistons, which was the main difficulty, when the man who was production director of BMC going round the engine factory at Coventry lit upon the line where the Twin Cam engine was being built and said 'What's this? How many of these are you doing? Twenty-five a week? Well, you could easily do seventy-five, couldn't you?' That immediately meant that fifty Twin Cams a week went into the hands of ... fools. The piston trouble overtook us and Harriman said 'Cut the thing! There you have it. I told you, you ought not to have a twin cam engine anyway!'

The tragedy of the MGA Twin Cam is that, as we have seen in this chapter, by the time it went out of production, many of the problems that had plagued it from the beginning had been identified and solved – much of this, it has to be said, through the efforts of people involved in the field, such as Bob Seymour, and through diligent, almost forensic investigations by Alec Hounslow and Jim Cox. As Basil Wales later commented: 'The shame is that the benefit of the twin-cam engine was devalued by what can now be seen as poor quality control, but at the time tolerances for earlier "old-fashioned" designs were nowhere near as critical.' Tellingly, there would be no MGB Twin Cam.

AN MG MAGNETTE TWIN CAM AFTER ALL?

Neither Gerald Palmer nor John Thornley saw their aspiration for a series-production MG Magnette Twin Cam realized, but this did not prevent others from using the engine in another vehicle. Perhaps the most oddball was Terry Mitchell's home-brewed special, which comprised an Austin Westminster fitted with an MGA Twin Cam powerplant: evidently it was quite a revelation, though like most of Mitchell's creations, it ended up being sold to help fund the cost of the next project. The engine was a seized Sebring specification unit, and he fitted it into the Austin with a widened MGA front cross-member. It was last seen plying trade as a taxi in Oxford: hardly an ideal specification for such a vehicle.

Perhaps more promising, but no more realistic as a production car, were the Farina Magnettes built by Dick Jacobs, including a Mark III, built in 1959 and registered SHJ 855; in order to achieve this, Jacobs and his team had to re-model the back of the engine bay to accommodate the battery, the heater and the steering gear. 'Although the maximum speed is not startling, acceleration is very much improved,' a contemporary news item reported.

Bob Seymour told the author that in his view, the problems with the engine were complex but perhaps predictable:

> There were many modifications over the production period. A high performance engine in quantity production released into the hands of the general public didn't go smoothly! When the compression ratio was reduced from 9.9:1 to 8.3:1 (with a reduction of only 8bhp to 100), many problems went away – but as we know, it was too late and production ceased.

By the end, of course, the reputation had seemingly become irreparably damaged, and with little love for the powertrain at BMC Board level, the technical arguments for killing it off were almost inevitable. The arrival of the ordinary 1588cc overhead valve, and the announcement the following summer of the 1622cc Mark II version, with the potential for various performance-tuning stages, made it politically simpler to explain the decision to anyone who cared to ask.

Alongside the technical and reputational challenges that the MGA Twin Cam faced, there was another important factor: the market situation in North America and the cost. As explained in the next chapter, a recession in the USA in April 1960 put the MG factory on short-time working, and so in a time when the factory was under-utilized due to poor overall sports-car sales, the arguments in favour of sustaining a troublesome and expensive model were harder to justify.

Moreover, at a time when the MGA Twin Cam retailed for £1,266, a British sports-car enthusiast could buy an Austin-Healey 100/6 from the same stable for £1,227, or, from a rival dealership, a Triumph TR3A (with front disc brakes) for £1,050. Whilst the big Healey had a future, by the spring of 1960 the Twin Cam had sadly run its course.

END OF THE ROAD FOR THE TWIN CAM

The last series-production MGA Twin Cam, chassis no. 2610, was completed in April 1960 (see table below) and that should have been the end of the model's production story – but MG enthusiast and collector Michael Ellman-Brown had other ideas.

Ellman-Brown had started his life-long love affair with the marque when he acquired a 1949 MG TC Midget finished in Woodland Green – a colour that would become something of an Ellman-Brown hallmark.

Other cars followed, including a black MGA that was stripped down and repainted in order to follow the Woodland Green theme. Eventually the time came to replace the MGA, and Ellman-Brown decided upon a new MGA Twin Cam, placing his order in September 1959 with the expectation of delivery the following spring.

However, before long it became evident that perhaps all was not as well as it had seemed: Ellman-Brown heard that the last Twin Cams were going down the line the following week, and alarmed at the news, Ellman-Brown wrote to John

THE LAST FIVE PRODUCTION MGA TWIN CAMS

Chassis Number	Start Build	Finish Build	Despatch Date	Body Colour	Trim Colour	Hood Colour	Type	Engine No.	Notes
YM2-2607	6 April 1960	8 April 1960	8 April 1960	Dove Grey	Red	N/A	RHD Export Coupé	2264	9.9:1 compression ratio, unless modified
YD3-2608	6 April 1960	8 April 1960	8 April 1960	Dove Grey	Red	Grey	LHD Roadster	2270	The second engine number with the 8.3:1 compression ratio
YD1-2609	6 April 1960	11 April 1960	13 April 1960	Dove Grey	Red	Grey	Home Market Roadster	2269	The first engine number with the 8.3:1 compression ratio
YD1-2610	6 April 1960	13 April 1960	14 April 1960	Chariot Red	Red	Beige	Home Market Roadster	2249	9.9:1 compression ratio, unless modified. Last *series production* car. Registration no. '5617 VW'
YD1-2611	18 May 1960	3 June 1960	14 June 1960	Woodcote Green	Beige	Beige	Home Market Roadster	2245	Extra car built to special order for Mike Ellman-Brown. Body number B1937

Footnotes:
The first engine number with the 8.3:1 compression ratio, according to factory records, was engine number 2269, which as we can see from above was fitted to the second from last series production car. The previous engine in the sequence – and presumably the last 9.9:1 unit (2268) – was fitted to car YM1-2586, built between 11 February and 24 March 1960. Many twin cams were subsequently converted to 8.3:1 in service, but this table shows that production cars with an 8.3:1 engine from the outset are rare, even in MGA Twin Cam terms.
The later workshop manual advises that 'a domed-top piston giving a compression ratio of 8.3:1 has been introduced for standard use; the piston is available under part no. AEH690, and must be operated with a static ignition setting of 8 degrees BTDC. Pistons to part no. AEH681, giving a compression ratio of 9.9:1, are still available, but their use should be confined to competition work with 100-octane fuel only. The static ignition setting for 9.9:1 compression ratio pistons remains at TDC.

A TWIN CAM SIX?

The need for sophistication and power for the new generation of BMC Rileys was touched on earlier. An added factor was the emergence of smaller but still potent Jaguar saloons, such as the Mark I and later Mark II. In Gerald Palmer's mind was a family of new twin-cam powertrains to rival the Jaguar XK units. Morris Engines were given the task of designing an all-new conventional overhead-valve 6-cylinder unit, dubbed the C-Series, and this was intended to replace the existing larger saloon units such as the 4-cylinder Austin, the 2.2-litre Morris/Wolseley overhead-cam 6 and the big Riley 4.

Of these, the Austin unit had proved tough but unrefined, whereas the former Nuffield units had a reputation for refinement but fragility. The C-Series, in 2.6-litre guise, appeared in 1954 in the Austin A90 Westminster, and a year later in the Morris Isis; in due course the engine would feature in Wolseley, Riley and Austin-Healey models. However, the overhead-valve unit was intended to be just the start: the proposed twin overhead-cam version was principally intended for a more upmarket Riley Pathfinder, but no doubt could have found a home in MG and Austin-Healey sports cars had it gone ahead.

Palmer's rationale was: 'My twin-cam C-Series was modelled on the B-Series version. The whole idea was to take a standard crankcase, con-rods and so on, and to put the twin-cam head on top with hardly any changes to the bottom end.' The corporate intent was certainly there: the Morris Motors Board approved a new project on 10 March 1955 as 'No. 60 – Riley Motors Ltd: conversion of C-type 6-cylinder engine to ohc-type valve gear' with £40,000 for tooling. S.V. Smith asked John Thornley to investigate use of the twin-cam 6 in November 1955, and Abingdon embraced the concept: the EX Register includes a project entry for a 3-litre Riley saloon, under EX 206, and another, described as the 'Twin Cam Pathfinder (DO 1067)', against EX 207.

The plan was to show a prototype at the 1956 Earls Court Motor Show. In the event, the departure of Gerald Palmer in October 1955, coupled with the poor reception of the Riley Pathfinder, precipitated cancellation of the C-Series Twin Cam project in March 1956; the sole running prototype was then destroyed. Palmer confirmed to the author that he had never seen the twin-cam C-Series prototype, as his departure came before it was built. Instead of the big twin cam, in October 1957 the Riley Pathfinder was transformed into the short-lived Riley Two-Point-Six, but so poor were the sales of that model that it proved to be the last ever large Riley. A proposed Pininfarina-styled ADO 10R Riley (sister car to the ADO 10W, which became the Wolseley 6/99) was first approved on 10 July 1957, but was then cancelled just over a month later on 21 August in favour of a more modest 4-cylinder ADO 9R.

Instead of pursuing the twin-cam C-Series approach, capacity was later enlarged, mimicking the approach with the B-Series: the Austin-Healey 100/6 received an enlarged C-Series of 2.9 litres on 1 July 1959, to become the Austin-Healey 3000, alongside the Austin A99 Westminster and Wolseley 6/99 – and so BMC's dalliance with twin-cam engines withered with the end of the MGA Twin Cam.

Michael Ellman-Brown was fortunate enough to receive an album of photographs documenting the assembly of his MGA Twin Cam as it passed down the line at Abingdon. It was truly the last of the line as the factory was concerned.
MICHAEL ELLMAN-BROWN

CARS IN THE SHOP – 11 JUNE 1960

An interesting vignette of the cars – in particular MGA Twin Cams – that were sitting in the MG Development Shop at a particular time is provided by one of the pages in the department's DDR reports (DDR No. 134, dated 11 May 1960) [the author's supplementary notes are in square brackets]:

Reference DDW No. 938
Twin Cam Wiring: The following cars were checked to see if the wiring on the coil was correct:

Cars in Shop:
'**LBL 304**' – Chassis Number HDE13/10102 [see Chapter 10 for the multifaceted story of 'LBL 304']
'**PMO 326**' – Chassis Number YD1-501 [the first production MGA Twin Cam]
Unregistered – Chassis Number EX 191/417 [EX 191 was the EX Register code for MGA development work – *see also* Chapter 9: this may have been related to independent rear suspension development work]
'**MG 1**' – Chassis Number YD1-524 [this famous registration number later appeared briefly on an MG Midget and latterly on John Thornley's personal MGB GT Automatic]
Unregistered – Chassis Number EX 191/273 [*see above* comment on EX 191]

Cars in Service:
Chassis Numbers
YDH5-1041 [see Booth Poole & Co in Chapter 8: this was an Irish-assembled MGA Twin Cam]
YM1-847 [an Old English White MGA Twin Cam Coupé]
YD1-851 [an Orient Red MGA Twin Cam Roadster]

Press Car:
Chassis Number YD1-530 [PMO 946 – *see earlier* in this chapter]

Thornley with the details of the car he wanted. 'I particularly wanted Woodland Green paintwork, which was unofficially obtainable to special order as no green was listed at this time.'

No news came back from Abingdon, so after about two weeks of waiting, Ellman-Brown wrote again to John Thornley and asked to come and see him at the factory.

When the two of them met, Ellman-Brown recorded that his worst fears were confirmed: 'He told me he had hoped to adjust the specification on one of the last cars to suit my requirements, but hadn't realized how important the colour was to me. "I don't know what I can do about this, but get your dealer to put in an order and I'll see what I can do," he said.'

The next day, Ellman-Brown placed a fresh order through Parade Motors of Mitcham, and waited. A week later came a call to confirm that the order had been accepted.

Then came a suggestion from Mel Jones that Ellman-Brown ought to ask if his car's progress down the assembly line could be recorded for posterity in photographs, and via a call to Wilson McComb (then at Abingdon) the idea was agreed, and Stuart Seager agreed to photograph what was YD1-2611 (with body number B1937) as it moved from station to station on the Abingdon production line.

Finally, on 14 June 1960, Ellman-Brown went to Abingdon with John Smith of Parade Motors in order to collect the car: 'I could not have been more proud for there can be few people who have had a car specially made for them by a large manufacturer after production has ceased.'

And of course that was truly the end of the Abingdon factory's production story of the MGA Twin Cam: brought down by a heady brew of technical problems, a lack of understanding up and down the supply chain, and in many cases, unsympathetic owners. There would be cars that were actually assembled and finished later (in South Africa, *see* Chapter 8) but for Abingdon, the despatch of Ellman-Brown's Twin Cam was a poignant moment in MG history.

MGA TWIN-CAM CHASSIS NUMBERS

The chassis number details for the MGA Twin Cam followed a different form; the codes are as follows:

YD1 – Home Market RHD Roadster
YD2 – Export RHD Roadster
YD3 – LHD Roadster
YDH5 – RHD CKD (*see also* Chapter 8)
YDH6 – LHD CKD (sometimes marked incorrectly as YHH5; *see also* Chapter 8)
YM1 – Home Market RHD Coupé
YM2 – Export RHD Coupé
YM3 – LHD Coupé
YMH5 – RHD CKD Coupé (there were no LHD CKD Coupés; *see also* Chapter 8)

STEPHENSON'S ROCKET

D. N. Stephenson took a Twin Cam and used it as the basis of his own design concept, with fabrication by F.L.M. (Panelcraft) Ltd. The one-off was later wrecked in an accident with its creator at the wheel, possibly after an extended lunch...

AUTHOR'S COLLECTION

Undoubtedly the most unusual MGA Twin Cam was the one-off design by designer D. N. Stephenson, who took a Twin Cam (YM1-1701, supplied uniquely by MG as a chassis only in April 1959, and eventually registered '97 PPA') and spent £2,000 turning it into his own concept for a modern design, using alloy sheeting formed over a steel frame, the fabrication to his design being undertaken by F.L.M. (Panelcraft) Ltd. The style was perhaps, to be kind, something of an acquired taste, but in some ways it was arguably an improvement over the donor car, with larger interior space – the luggage compartment was accessed with the aid of a hinged Perspex back window, there were twin 15gal (69ltr) fuel tanks mounted inside each rear wing, and a vertically mounted spare wheel at the extreme rear inside the luggage compartment, thereby creating a far more generous boot space than the standard MGA Twin Cam. The seats were individually adjustable for reach, height and angle of recline – something unheard of in most sports cars at the time. The car was covered in the issue of *Autocar* dated 12 August 1960. It is believed to have been irreparably damaged in an accident some time later in the decade: the survival or otherwise of the remaining rolling chassis is unknown.

MGA TWIN CAM ENGINE NUMBERS

Following the format of the MGA 1500 (see Chapter 4) 'BC16GB' was the MGA Twin Cam, 'B'-series, 'C' camshaft, '16' 1,588cc. This changed, however, as the first two letters 'BC' and the final 'B' characters were dropped in favour of '16G-U', where the 'U' indicated a central gear-change.

Mark Hester, of the MGA Twin Cam Group, says:

> It is believed that this change coincided with the introduction of the pushrod MGA 1600, which was designated code 16GA [see Chapter 7], possibly to avoid confusion with warranty claims. The highest 16G engine number reported so far is 1055, and the lowest 16G engine number reported is 1020. There may not have been any overlap, probably just errors in reporting in more modern times as most people assume Twin Cam engines were all GB.

No externally visible changes to the engine other than the stamped aluminium plate on the back of the engine appear to have been made. Some cars, such as the 1960 Sebring Race Cars (see Chapter 10) have '16GB-DA' engine number prefixes; again Mark Hester explains: 'In March 1959, a close-ratio gearbox was introduced as an option. When fitted with this gearbox, the engine prefix should be 16GB-Da.' The only surviving 1959 Sebring Car also has a unique engine number, '18131-2'.

CONVERTING A TWIN CAM TO A '1600' IN SERVICE

The full story of what has become popularly known as the MGA 1600 Deluxe properly belongs in the next chapter, but as the production story of the Twin Cam drew towards a close, alongside the matter of using up components there was a near-parallel problem of dealing with any (perhaps irate) customers who wanted their twin-cam engines removed in service and replaced with one of the new 1600 ohv units.

Amongst the many documents that survive in the British Motor Museum archives is an eighteen-page document entitled 'Conversion – Twin Cam engine to MG 1600' (dated 3 March 1960), which sets out in detail all the service parts needed to undertake such a conversion, against 'Service Kit 48G.157'. The first page sets out the scope of the document as describing 'conversion equipment required, and parts superseded, to install an MG "1600" power unit into an MG Twin Cam car, Dunlop discs remaining.' What is also illuminating is that prior to scheduling the many changes needed, two donor cars are listed:

Twin Cam – car number 1523, engine number 1162
Twin Cam – car number 2135, engine number 1672

... with a note to say that 'BMC Service to record these cars having been so converted.'

From separate factory build records, we know that the first of those two cars, YD2-1523, was an Old English White car built between 3 and 5 March 1959, whilst YD2-2135 was another Old English White car, built between 22 and 29 May 1959, but supposedly shipped to Australia, and with engine 1749 rather than 1672 (perhaps its purpose as a test-bed 'guinea pig' had elapsed?)

Amongst the many changes to be undertaken as part of such a conversion, there is a brief note about radiator fixings (an important distinction of the Twin Cam), which states that 'radiator brackets are undrilled. If it is decided to use bolts and nuts for fixing, it is suggested seven bolts be used for the upright member of the bracket and three for the gusset. Otherwise these brackets may be spot-welded to the body – *see* Sketch SK.7234.Z.'

This sketch, dated 2 March 1960, is also recorded in the Abingdon 'Sketch and Arrangement Drawing Number Register' ('alteration to radiator support bracket to fit "1600" radiator to Twin Cam car'), is followed by another SK 7235Z, dated 4 March 1960 ('alteration to front bulkhead panel to fit "1600" engine to Twin Cam car') and both predate another sketch, SK 7242R of 8 April 1960, which is mentioned in the next chapter, complete with the description 'ADO 31 De-Luxe'. These have a bearing on the first MGA 'Deluxe', now owned by Mark Hester, the story of which follows in the next chapter...

CHAPTER SEVEN

THE MGA 1600, 'DELUXE' AND 1600 MARK II

THE MGA 1600

Even from the outset, there were pleas from a number of factions for a bigger engine in the MGA. However, it took time for these requests to filter through the system, and even then they did not always receive a warm reception from senior BMC management. Gus Ehrman told the author that he almost lost count of the requests that fell on deaf ears, not only in powertrain terms but also for practical things such as stronger bumpers and over-riders, which would be less vulnerable to the prevailing American high-street car-parking habits, and some of the creature comforts found in other cars. As Ehrman explained:

> When the MGA came out, we said 'Look, we have got to have a car with wind-up windows' – to which the response was that a sports car did not need wind-up windows. Similarly, we were not satisfied with the 1498cc engine – we could usefully have had a 1900cc engine or something like that. Finally, after three years of pleading, we got the 1600! The continual problem was that BMC management would not listen to what we asked for. They would say things like 'It's such a limited market, it's not worth the expense' – but at the time, British sports cars had the market sewn up.

As we shall see in Chapter 9, there were thoughts of both a 1.7-litre and even a 2.2-litre MGA – but neither came close to production.

By the time that the MGA 1600 was on sale, the detachable side screens used sliding panels for improved convenience of use and visibility – still not quite the sophistication that would later be seen on the MGB just three years later.
AUTHOR'S COLLECTION

BELOW: **MGA 1600 blueprint.**
BOB VITRIKAS

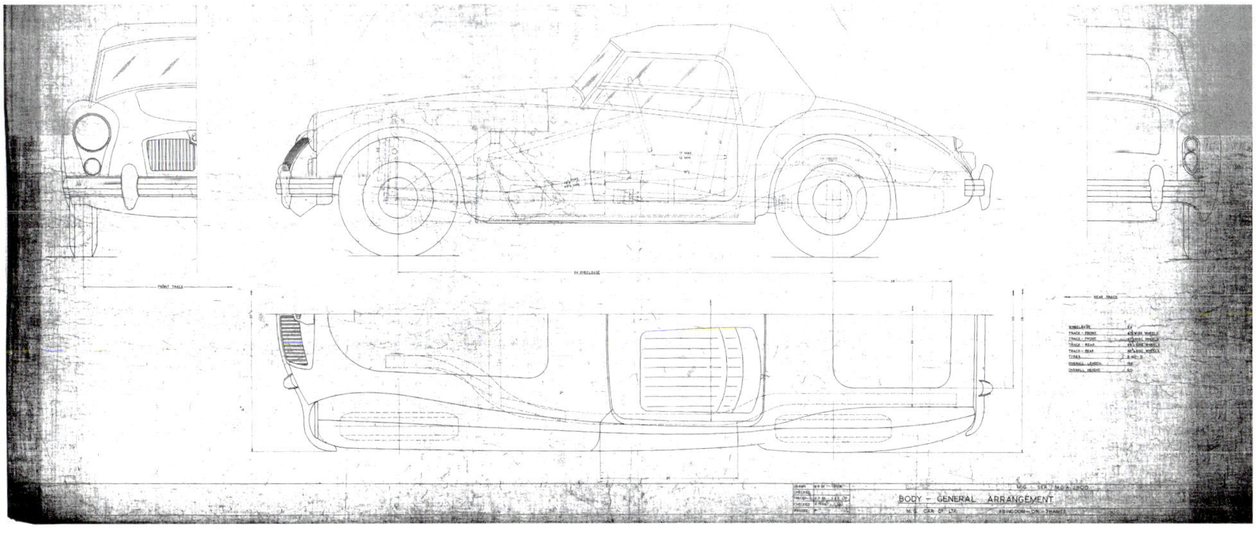

The facia of the MGA 1600.
AUTHOR'S COLLECTION

In the end, MG's success in getting the BMC Board to sanction the creation of the Twin Cam, enlarged at a late stage to meet the competition demands of a 1.6-litre racing class, helped facilitate the creation of a version of the B-Series engine that shared the Twin Cam's 1588cc capacity but with the conventional overhead valve train. The 1588cc B-Series engine capacity remained unique to the MGA; the Z-Magnette and mainstream BMC saloons generally retained the 1498cc capacity until the later change, coinciding with a major overhaul that brought in the larger capacity unit, covered later in this chapter (although BMC, being BMC, still kept the '1.5' engines for some models until well into the following decade).

PRX 14 – THE FIRST MGA 1600

Alec Rivers Fletcher and his wife Penny in PRX 14.
JEREMY RIVERS FLETCHER

Mike Peters is the present owner of PRX 14 – the first MGA fitted with a 1600 engine – which was later acquired by Alec (A.F.) Rivers Fletcher, and repainted in his favourite Bugatti Blue with white roundels.
MIKE PETERS

The first MGA to be fitted for testing purposes with the new 1600 engine was the 'show shop' Glacier Blue MGA Coupé 1500, registered PRX 14 on 30 June 1958 (MGA Coupé chassis no. HMD 13-53352; engine no. 15GB-U-H/43971). Originally a 1500, the car appeared in this guise at the press launch of the MGA Twin Cam (*see* Chapter 6). Having been used for assessment of the 1588cc ohv unit, and occasionally loaned to the likes of Nancy Mitchell and Jack Sears, PRX 14 would later be fitted with an over-bored 1844cc engine prior to the launch of the MGB, again for testing purposes.

A. F. Rivers-Fletcher later bought the car in 1979 and converted it for his own use, including having it repainted Bugatti Blue (a colour he used for all his race cars), using it at various hillclimbs and similar events during his period of ownership. He fitted it with an opening pop-up glass roof window, of a kind commonly fitted by aftermarket specialists (usually to family hatchbacks) in the 1980s, and had part of the rear parcel shelf cut away so that he could carry his film projection equipment that he often took with him to club events and lectures on his lifetime of motor-racing exploits.

More recently, PRX 14 was acquired by enthusiast Mike Peters, who entrusted it to James Horner to thoroughly but sensitively restore it; the work included removing the pop-up roof and making new microcell seats.

For the MGA 1600, BMC increased the capacity to 1588cc, matching that of the MGA Twin Cam, which remained in production. On the reverse of this image was a label with the words: 'Confidential – not to be released before 31 July 1959. MGA 1600: the neat engine installation is clearly visible, as also are the heater and windscreen-washing equipment. Despite the compactness of the engine compartment, access for routine maintenance is extraordinarily good.'
AUTHOR'S COLLECTION

The MGA 1600 brought in front disc brakes, although they were sourced from Lockheed, rather than Dunlop, who supplied the four-wheel disc units of the MGA Twin Cam.
AUTHOR'S COLLECTION

BIGGER ENGINE AND FRONT DISC BRAKES

Meanwhile the last MGA 1500 came at chassis no. 68850 (the last 15GD engine was 7816); the very next number in the sequence (68851) marked the first of the new MGA 1600 models, with the '16GA' 1588cc engine. This first car, destined for demonstration duties, happened to be a blue US-specification specimen, with a black interior and black hood, and was completed at the factory on 1 June 1959. Press cars with chassis numbers 69102 and 69103 followed the next day.

APPENDIX J

The 1958 FIA regulations, in particular 'Appendix J', Chapter 1, Article 253, defined the engine capacity ranges for each of the race classes. When this included a category of 1.3 to 1.6 litres, it was obvious that an engine near the limit – say, 1599cc – would have advantages over a smaller unit – which of course highlighted the effective handicap that was faced by the original 1498cc B-Series of the early MGA. It was this factor which influenced the move to 1588cc for first the Twin Cam (from its outset), and then the regular 'ohv' model, hence the original 'MGA 1600'. As we shall see in the motor-sport chapter, the change on the MGA 1600 Mark II to 1622cc would pose a fresh challenge, potentially pitching the MGA straight into the 2-litre class. The RAC handled the MGA 1600's certification ('FIA Recognition No. 29 – dated 17 September 1959') in readiness for the 1960 racing season – of which more later.

This North American (BMC Canada) PR image for the new MGA 1600 features the *de rigueur* wire wheels and white-wall tyres so often specified by customers.
AUTHOR'S COLLECTION

However, equally significantly, with the new model there was also a change of chassis number prefix system, with 'GHN' signifying a roadster (in place of the outgoing 'HD' code), and 'GHD' a coupé (instead of 'HM'), with a fourth prefix letter 'L' exclusively for left-hand-drive models whether roadster or coupé.

As well as the fitment of front disc brakes (Lockheed rather than the Dunlop units of the Twin Cam), the new model had larger front side lamps with integral indicators, tail-lamps made up of separate indicators and combined tail/stop lamps, mounted on body-coloured plinths in approximately the same position as before, and on the roadsters, improved removable sliding-window side-screens. To make the new engine size clearer to casual kerb-side by-standers, neat '1600' script badges were also added alongside the cowl vents and at the rear, all in the same location as the 'Twin-Cam' badges on that model.

Body numbers now came with a new 'B' prefix. Inside the Coupé cockpit, the spare wheel was moved back, so that it was now entirely contained within the boot compartment, and the rear window shelf became narrower. At the same time, the equivalent body and electrical changes were also introduced, as appropriate, on the MGA Twin Cam (chassis no. 2189 in May 1959 for the Twin Cam Coupé; no. 2193 for the Twin Cam Roadster in June).

The reverse of this photograph of 899 CFC makes reference to the MGA 1600 press date of 31 July 1959.
AUTHOR

New MGA '1600' features more go... more stop
In keeping with the traditional MG slogan 'Safety Fast!' the newest version of this popular sports car features a bigger capacity (1600cc) engine for vastly improved power and acceleration and a remarkably efficient brake system employing eleven inch discs at front and ten inch drum brakes at rear. Body styling is virtually unchanged except for slight modification at rear to accommodate an improved tail-light design. Sports Roadster and Coupé versions of this new model are available in a wide range of brilliant color finishes. Manufactured by the British Motor Corporation, the MGA 1600 is imported by Hambro Automotive Corporation of New York and sold throughout the United States by a network of over 600 dealers. Prices begin at $2,485 (POE West Coast).
FROM: HAMBRO AUTOMOTIVE CORPORATION, PUBLIC RELATIONS DEPARTMENT, 27 WEST 57TH STREET, NEW YORK 19, NY PL 9-3150

This side view of an MGA 1600 accompanied the Hambro press release. For some reason this particular car been fitted with MG Z Magnette hub-caps (with MG badge medallions).
AUTHOR

THE MGA 1600 IN THE PRESS

The MGA 1600 formally arrived in the market place on 31 July 1959; in June, as part of the run-up to this public announcement, BMC invited a small number of motoring correspondents to an entertaining drive in the Swiss Alps, the mountain driving intended to show off the benefits of the new disc brakes on the front wheels – Lockheed units instead of the all-round Dunlop disc brakes used for the MGA Twin Cam, which remained on sale. As BMC's sports-car interests also extended to the Austin-Healey, the same group of journalists was also able to drive examples of the recently announced 3000.

As reported in a subsequent issue of *Motorsport*, the party of journalists were flown out to Lyon by a specially chartered Viscount jet airliner, to find upon their arrival a dozen shiny new French-registered BMC sports cars lined up – six Austin-Healeys and the same number of the improved MGA. The task then posed by their hosts was to drive 300 miles to Cap d'Antibes in time for dinner. The suggested route avoided the N7 Autoroute and took in Grenoble, Gap, Dignon and Grasse, but Michael Twite of *Motorsport* (in a red MGA) teamed up with Gregor Grant of *Autosport* (in a Healey) and opted for the N7.

After an enjoyable drive and evening meal, the group retired in anticipation of a second day described by *Motorsport* as a 'gastronomic expedition'; two further days of fairly free motoring through towns and the open roads of Switzerland and France must have seemed like unbridled luxury to 1950s British journalists, but all good things come to an end, and in this case the cars were driven to Nice Airport, from where the various guests were to be flown back to England courtesy of Air France. Michael Twite concluded that despite having to tear themselves away from the joys of skiing and the Riviera, he and his colleagues had gained 'a healthy respect for the latest versions of the MG and Austin-Healey'.

Another motoring correspondent on the trip was W. A. (Bill) McKenzie of *The Daily Telegraph*, whose write-up appeared in the paper on 31 July 1959, just as the car was launched to the public. McKenzie wrote that:

> ...the extra power makes the car more flexible in slow traffic and raises the whole performance. I found on a test in the French Alps that it could climb the gradients of mountain passes on third gear. But if second were used for the hairpin bends and a change-up made soon afterwards, every mile of a long alpine climb could be covered in one and a half minutes, at an average speed of 45mph [70km/h]. The

An advertisement for the MGA 1600 from the 31 July 1959 issue of *Autosport*.
AUTHOR'S COLLECTION

Motor, 19 April 1961.
AUTHOR'S COLLECTION

> steering is light but as direct as the sports-car driver asks for. This makes for utmost control at high speed on the most tortuous course.

Obviously quoting from PR material, McKenzie added that the MGA had 'earned nearly £21,500,000 in North American markets alone. The new MGA1600 is expected to do even better.'

Motor subjected the new MGA 1600 to a road test for their issue of 2 September 1959; their photographs were of SMO 907, and the test headline summarized the benefits of 'extra acceleration and retardation for a popular sporting car'. The 1600 engine offered improved acceleration but not top speed, but at the same time the testers complemented MG on improved refinement: 'Complete docility characterizes the enlarged engine, as witness our recording of 10mph, and it runs happily on ordinary premium grades of petrol without demanding 100 octane, but it does not feel to pull its full weight below 2,500rpm.'

The magazine concluded that:

> With its share of the imperfections from which no car ever altogether escapes, this remains a very attractive and versatile sporting two-seater. Sturdy, well furnished and probably built with more thorough care than most of its contemporaries, it travels fast and is enjoyable to drive or ride in, yet can also serve as a reliable and weatherproof form of everyday transportation.

A week behind their rival, *Autocar* tested an Alamo Beige 1600 Roadster for their 9 October 1959 issue: slightly in contrast to their rivals, the testers commented that whilst the larger engine had improved performance, refinement had suffered (on their test car at least), noting that:

> There was a tendency for the engine of the test car to become rough and to vibrate at about 5,000rpm, but if the throttle pedal were held down, this disappeared as the engine speed continued to mount. Members of staff with experience of the previous MGA feel the more powerful engine to be rather more noisy and harsh.

Autocar noted that the new sidescreens were an improvement over the earlier versions (a point on which few MGA owners would disagree!), although as the testing took place during fine weather, the testers admitted that they had not really had a chance to test the new set-up for leakages in wet weather. Although the largely unchanged gearbox and cockpit layout were generally praised, the MG tradition of having the horn button on the facia rather than in the centre of the steering wheel was deemed an inconvenient anachronism.

The magazine concluded that the larger-engined MGA's 'powerful, responsive engine, combined with a moderately heavy but low-slung chassis, adequate steering and superlative brakes, and without any little vices or unpredictable traits in behaviour, maintains the traditional high standards of performance and safety of the marque.'

***Motor Trend*, October 1959.**
AUTHOR'S COLLECTION

Meanwhile the Nuffield Organisation's own internal publication, *Nuffield Teamwork*, declared that the MGA (in 1500 and Twin Cam guise) had already earned \$60 million sales in the USA alone; clearly the MGA 1600 was expected to build on this.

SALES AND MARKETING: MGA 1600 ADVERTS AND BROCHURES

For the home market, a new brochure H.6091 was produced, with a predominantly bright red cover and artwork of the 'MGA 1600' title above a left-hand-drive MGA Roadster and happy couple, the driver waving, and the 'Safety Fast!' logo off to one side. Inside, the brochure featured colour artwork of an MGA Coupé front on, which was clearly related to contemporary magazine advertising as well as another side-profile image clearly based on the US press image used for the MGA Coupé. The text suggested, of the MGA 1600, that:

...it looks fast. And that's how it goes. You would not expect less. Not from the new track-bred 'MGA 1600'. Not from this proud descendant of the world's most famous line of sports cars, embodying over thirty years' experience of racing and high speed, record-breaking achievements.

The home-market brochure for the MGA 1600 (publication number H6091).
AUTHOR'S COLLECTION

An advertisement for the MGA 1600 from a UK magazine, showing a Coupé
AUTHOR'S COLLECTION

A strap line used inside the brochure was the simple message 'the sports car today – is an MGA 1600', and a colourized image of the rear of a Roadster was accompanied by the observation that 'This is the view of the "MGA 1600" that other motorists see most often – the sleek, streamlined, sculptured tail that frequently disappears out of sight as swiftly as the car comes into view.' Also inside there was reference to the new features:

> To the world-famous sporting performance of the MGA the more powerful 1600cc engine now adds more vitality, more crispness, more get-up-and-go. And the new MGA 1600 offers you even more than improved performance, safer braking: it also features such additional advances as new rear-light styling, new flasher lamps, new sliding side-screens.

Home market adverts typically included the simple message 'more power for the MGA', and a paragraph listing features such as

> ...more driving power ... more braking power. Now ... more punch and more liveliness from a bigger capacity 1600cc engine. Power-packed for exhilarating performance. And increased safety from front-wheel disc brakes – smooth-acting and instantly responsive. Other new developments include a re-styled hood with full vision wrap-around rear window and sliding side-screens. Separate amber flasher lights are now fitted fore and aft.

In the USA, BMC/Hambro as usual went their own way with advertising, and a few themes drew on the superior performance and disc-braked stopping power. One advertisement, for example, featured some flowery copy, typeset inside as though within a virtual octagon, with front, side and profile views of a whitewall-tyred MGA Roadster and a rhetorical question:

> What is a true sports car? One born in competition – like the MG? Or one bred for the more tranquil joys of motoring just for the fun of it – like the MG? Two cars? No. One magnificent car. The new MGA 1600 – a safe, comfortable, go-anywhere kind of machine, submissive as a kitten, but cross-bred with tigers from the high-pressure lairs of racing.

It continued further in similar vein...

Another 1960 campaign featured the neat slogan 'Poetry in Motion', while a half-page advert used in California (shared between Gough Industries of Los Angeles and Kjell Qvale's British Motor Cars of San Francisco) featured an MG logo with a lit fuse on top, a simple line-art sketch depicting the MGA, and the slogan 'This little bomb – started the revolution' alongside.

A colour advert used in some larger circulation magazines featured an MGA 1600 driving off to the right of the photo, its driver sporting the *de rigeur* flat cap and, the copywriter having again been given free rein, with the text:

> Start of a perfect day – just set it in motion, throw out your cares, and fall in love with the road and all outdoors... because *you* drive the alert and responsive MGA 1600, it doesn't drive you. This is the fastest, safest pleasure machine ever to wear the Octagon, the most prideful in looks and actions. A big-hearted engine, sure-footed road ability, obedient controls and fade-free disc brakes make driving an affair of the heart. A test drive will reveal why this is the best known symbol of what a sports car should be. Your BMC dealer can arrange a perfect day for it. Is it a date?

Another full-page colour advert featured a courting couple, their MGA clearly parked in a movie drive-in theatre with a film showing, the text this time being:

> Best seats in the house... starring MGA 1600, the fastest, safest, smartest-looking sporting machine ever to wear the Octagon. Produced by BMC, the world's largest and most experienced manufacturer of sports cars. Scenario and direction by you, according to your mood for fun or competition. Special effects: a real barnstorming engine, road-hugging suspension, precise steering, fade-free disc brakes ... and an award-winning performance every time you hit the road. Ask your BMC dealer for an audition. You'll exit smiling.

In April 1961, a full-page advertisement appeared in the UK press with the slogan 'Pace, Price, Pedigree' and proclaiming that '...there's nothing in motoring to equal the MGA 1600 for the young sports-car enthusiast. With good looks, a genuine 100mph [160km/h], Lockheed brakes on the front wheels, and the MG 'Safety Fast' features of firm road holding and stable cornering – what more could you ask?' What more, indeed? Perhaps the all-round disc-brakes from the Twin Cam, or, in due course, an even better engine?

INDUSTRY HICCUPS: THE RECESSION OF 1960

Although 1959 proved a peak for MGA production, and indeed all Abingdon production to that point, in the ensuing period of April 1960 to February 1961 there was a second recession of relevance to the MGA (the first had been in 1958). As a consequence, in the autumn of 1960 there was a significant reduction in car sales, at a time when the US domestic car makers were also revising their attitude towards the inroads into their country that imported 'com-

December 1959 marked a milestone, when the 50,000th sports car built in a year at Abingdon was celebrated. In a news item in the in-house magazine *Nuffield Teamwork*, where this photo appeared, it was noted that at the time 'the rate of assembly is two cars every five minutes of the working day', and that with Abingdon having 1,100 staff, 'the production works out to one car per employee per week'. From the left are Phil Broad and Bill Singleton, and on the right, Ernie Boobier and behind him Jack Mathews, Jack Haywood and Fred Wake...

GRAHAM ROBSON; NAMES COURTESY ADRIAN GOODENOUGH

...but hang on a minute: isn't that a different MGA in this photo using the same sign, with Cecil Cousins, John Thornley and Syd Enever (looking towards the camera)? Between Thornley and Enever is Charlie Martin (Chief Rate Fixer), and between Enever and the sign is Jack Lowndes (Chief Factory Engineer). On the right are George Morris (Rectificati on Supervisor) and finally 'Ginger' Wirdnam (Production Manager). One might understand the desire for different groups of people for each photo, but why around a different car? By the very end of 1959, Abingdon had built a total of 55,398 cars that year.

AUTHOR'S COLLECTION; NAMES COURTESY ADRIAN GOODENOUGH

A lovely MGA Coupé 1600 with wire wheels and white-wall tyres appeared at the 1960 Paris Salon (6–16 October).
AUTHOR'S COLLECTION; PHOTO BY J. FONDINI

pact' cars were making, most of them from Europe. British sports-car sales – including those of MG, Austin-Healey, Jaguar, Sunbeam and Triumph – dipped dramatically, and the impact was typically felt at Abingdon and the various BMC plants that supplied the production lines there.

Contemporary reports indicated that MGA bodyshell production at Morris Bodies fell by as much as 60 per cent at this time, with up to 300 of the Coventry workforce directly affected, being reduced to a one-and-a-half-day week. One of the two lines of MGAs at Abingdon was temporarily turned over to Morris Minor van production, whilst one of the two Austin-Healey Sprite lines switched to building Morris Minor Travellers, both meeting a serendipitous increase in demand for such vehicles. Meanwhile the Austin-Healey 3000 line was still running, but at half its usual speed.

By the end of 1960, most of the Abingdon workforce was on a three-day week, and in January 1961 this fell even further, to two-and-a-half. However, in the spring the US market recovered as the recession came to an end, and meanwhile in BMC's home market, the UK government relaxed hire purchase restrictions, which in turn helped rekindle demand and in turn output. By April 1961, fresh orders for sports cars from the United States meant that all but seventy of the 800 employees at Abingdon were back up to a full five-day week, and confidence was improving ahead of the coming launch of important new variants of the MG and Austin-Healey ranges and, in the not-too-distant future, the new MGB.

THE MGA 'DELUXE' (1600 AND 1600 MARK II)

The decision to discontinue the Twin Cam (*see* Chapter 6) was not universally regretted across the BMC empire; its failure was mostly a disappointment to MG and Morris Engines (neither of whose reputations it had helped), as it had represented the noble concept of a semi-thoroughbred sports-car power plant of a kind that would surely have gladdened the heart of Cecil Kimber, had he still been around to have seen it. But with other changes on the way in BMC, not least important changes to the basic B-Series, which would be of relevance to the MGA Mark II and the subsequent MGB, Longbridge as well as the warranty departments affected across the organization would have been broadly relieved to see the Twin Cam go.

Mark Hester owns this car, the first MGA Deluxe, seen here at the MG Car Club annual 'MG Live' event in summer 2017.

WHAT'S IN A NAME: WHY 'DELUXE'?

There has never been any doubt about the existence of a low-volume variant of the MGA 1600 (in both original and Mark II guises) designed to 'use up' surplus sets of components made available by the cancellation of the MGA Twin Cam. What has been the subject of much debate, however, is what these cars should properly be called.

MGCC MGA historian Edward Vandyk and his MGA archivist colleague Howard Quayle have studied the variant in detail, and for a start, Vandyk is adamant that from the naming point of view, there is no such thing as a 'Mark I Deluxe': 'There is an MGA 1600 fitted with the optional Dunlop disc brakes all round and Dunlop Road Speed tyres. Indeed in period the name "Deluxe" was not used publicly by MG.' Of course MG never referred to the original MGA 1600 as a 'Mark I' – the term only came to be used retrospectively by enthusiasts to define the model which preceded the 'Mark II', just as there were never such models as an Austin-Healey 3000 Mark I, or an MG Midget Mark I.

It seems that the lack of a formal name for this variant led to the use of the 'De Luxe' (or 'Deluxe') as a convenient short-hand term. The term (however spelt) had long been used as a means of indicating a more highly specified variation on any given theme, and MG's parent BMC was no less guilty of applying the 'Deluxe' name to anything slightly special or better equipped. *When* this first came into use for the all-round disc brake MGA has long been a matter of conjecture: the author found reference to the use of the term 'De-Luxe' alongside 'ADO 31' in the Abingdon *Sketch and Arrangement Drawing Numbers Register*, where a sketch 'SK 7242.R', dated 8 April 1960, is described as covering 'De-Luxe ADO31: Sketch showing holes in dashboard for Dash fittings'. Not having seen the sketch in question, the author is not able to comment any further on what those holes might have been for.

This Chariot Red MGA 1600 Coupé Mark II 'Deluxe', with chassis number GHD2-107231, was built at Abingdon between 23 and 26 February 1962.
VALLEY CARS

The Coupé Deluxe version of the MGA 1600 Mark II was quite a rare car – just twenty-three were built between June 1961 and June 1962; indeed from the table shown here, we can see that this particular car was one of just six built in the same month.
VALLEY CARS

To avoid duplication, this section embraces both the 1600 and 1600 Mark II so-called 'Deluxes', but readers are also directed to the later section in this chapter specifically on the Mark II for more on the changes that model brought, in particular to the engine, the lighting equipment, and some of the trim and safety-related items. The departure of the Twin Cam left in its wake the thorny problem of what to do with the many sets of special components that were either already in stock, or somewhere in the pipeline and subject to supplier commitments that still needed to be honoured.

The solution was to create a new, semi-official model variant, which became popularly known as the 'Deluxe' (although, as noted in the panel above, the term does not seem to have been used in publicity material), which would combine, broadly, the chassis of the out-going Twin Cam, complete with four-wheel disc brakes, centre-lock disc wheels and various trim and other specific items hitherto reserved for the Twin Cam, with the conventional overhead-valve B-Series engine, which had in any case been expanded to 1588cc, and would soon become the much modified 1622cc units seen in the Mark II MGA.

This Chariot Red Coupé Mark II Deluxe has a neatly colour-coordinated red interior.
VALLEY CARS

Here, therefore, we have the use of 'ADO 31' (which is BMC code for the MGA 1600) and the use of the 'Deluxe' (strictly speaking 'De-Luxe') term in a factory document. It is worth noting that an earlier sketch in the series, 'SK 7234.Z' (dated 2 March 1960), relates to the adaptation of a Twin Cam body to take an MGA 1600 radiator – see Chapter 6 for the story of Twin Cams being converted in service – so clearly the crucial period when the MGA 1600 with all-round disc brakes came into being is around Easter of 1960. (The 'R' and 'Z' suffixes to these sketch numbers simply indicate the paper sheet size of the drawings involved).

Through their research, Vandyk and Quayle established an early external use of the term from the summer of 1960, but still not by the factory directly: 'The name 'Deluxe' was leaked into essentially one advert placed by a dealer, Parade Motors, for one of these cars when they were offered for sale in July 1960 by University Motors, the London area main dealer as, what we would now call, a limited edition.'

Moving on a year and into the 'Mark II' period, South African MGA owner and enthusiast Brian Hogg shared with the author details of a Nuffield Exports letter from S. B. King, Nuffield Sales Technical Executive, dated 1 June 1961 (Ref SBK/Sales/Tech/No.5: 'Confidential to all MG Distributors overseas – MGA 1600 Mark II Production Line Optional Extras'), which advised that the MGA 1600 Mark II was available ex-works with various options, including the Dunlop disc brakes all round, centre lock wheels and Road Speed tyres (all three together), along with other extras – but there was still no mention of any special name for these cars. (*See also* the side-bar on MGA 1600 Mark II optional extras later in this chapter.)

Somewhat after the event there was later reference to the 'Deluxe' variant in a brief retrospective in the MG Car Club magazine *Safety Fast!* in the July 1963 issue, which states:

> *When the Twin Cam ceased production in April 1960, the decision was taken to build an intermediate model to satisfy those who coveted the all-round disc brakes of that model, but not its rather temperamental engine. So some 1600s, known as the '1600 Deluxe', were built with pushrod engines in the Twin Cam chassis, and a very pleasant car this little known model proved to be.*

The author questioned Peter Neal, once part of the MG design team and more recently the MG Car Club's archivist, who felt it likely that the Deluxe name possibly came into use through the use of 'Deluxe seats' in the cockpit, but agrees that the MGA 1600 with all-round disc brakes and centre-lock wheels was never formally known as an 'MGA Deluxe' at the factory, notwithstanding that sketch register entry.

Just to add slightly to the confusion, the BMC/Hambro importers seem to have toyed with an alternative name: at least one US magazine road test of an MGA 1600 Mark II fitted with the 'Deluxe' accoutrements (plus a hard top) was referred to in the publication (*Sports Car Graphic* – the May 1962 issue; the car supplied for testing in Los Angeles by Hollywood Sports Cars, at an all-in listed price of $3,190) as a 'MGA 1600 Mark II Competition'.

The decision to do this appears to have been made in the spring of 1960, by which time the end of the Twin Cam was already anticipated. The first MGA recognizable as a Deluxe was chassis number 91240, which started down the line at Abingdon on 28 April 1960. In the meantime, the last true series-production MGA Twin Cam (chassis number 2610 – 2611 was, of course, a one-off) had been built between 6 and 14 April, the last of eight to be completed in April 1960.

This first 'MGA Deluxe' (for want of a better name) did not reach completion until 9 June 1960; it was registered as VJB 112 on 12 May 1960, and identified as a UK specification demonstrator, being retained by the factory until it was sold off on 17 January 1961. Despite about a dozen changes of ownership it has thankfully survived, and since 2013 it has been owned by Mark Hester, who as of 2018 is in the process of restoring it to its former glory. Hester has undertaken an audit of some of the surviving Lucas electrical equipment, such as the ignition switch and wiper switch, and found that they had been manufactured in March 1960, not long before the car was assembled.

In the meantime, a 'Confidential Service Memorandum' MG/327 was issued on 30 August 1960, which confirmed that disc brakes (front and rear) and centre-lock wheels were being made available as optional extras, with the steering assembly, front suspension and rear axle modified to suit. Despite this, there has been little evidence of any factory sales literature beyond a reference in the sections that refer to options, despite a handful of dealer advertisements coming to light over the years.

A *Driver's Supplement* (AKD1628 from May 1960) was entitled 'Supplement to be used with the *Driver's Handbook* AKD1172B when Road Speed tyres and disc brakes all rond [sic] are fitted as optional extras.'

The author is indebted to Graham Robson, who made a study of the MGA Deluxe when researching the subject for his excellent book *The Mighty MGs*, for the following production data, which shows a total of 395 overall, spread over a two-year period, more than 91 per cent of which were roadsters:

MGA 1600 'DELUXE' – PRODUCTION VOLUMES FOR BOTH SERIES

		Tourer (Roadster)	Coupé	*Totals*
1600				
1960	June	16	1	*17*
	July	7	-	*7*
	August	6	-	*6*
	September	2	1	*3*
	October	4	-	*4*
	November	15	1	*16*
	December	-	1	*1*
1961	January	3	3	*6*
	February	3	2	*5*
	March	12	3	*15*
	April	2	-	*2*
Sub-totals, '1600'		**70**	***12***	**82**
1600 Mark II				
	June	2	-	*2*
	July	33	1	*34*
	August	34	1	*35*
	September	16	-	*16*
	October	7	7	*14*
	November	18	2	*20*
	December	6	1	*7*
1962	January	7	3	*10*
	February	2	6	*8*
	March	1	2	*3*
	April	86	-	*86*
	May	66	-	*66*
	June	12	-	*12*
Sub-totals, '1600 Mark II'		***290***	***23***	***313***
Overall Totals		***360***	***35***	***395***

It is fair to say that two of those 395 are the 1961 Sebring cars, which were not coded in the records as 'Deluxes', and this would make the total 393. Either way, the addition of the totals of the MGA Deluxes and MGA Twin Cams therefore brings an overall total close to 2,500, which is likely to have been the agreed sanction originally determined for the MGA Twin Cam from the outset. The flurry of activity in the last three months of production, when 164 Deluxes were built (fully 42 per cent of the overall production number), shows how Abingdon was keen to 'clear the decks' in readiness for the new MGB.

SOME NOTABLE MGA DELUXES

91240: The first car which might be identified as an 'MGA Deluxe', as noted in the main text; built between April and June 1960. Registration number VJB 112. MGA 1600 Deluxe Roadster in Chariot Red with red trim and beige hood.

The early cars essentially featured MGA Twin Cam bodies, complete with the removable panels in the wheel arches, although the heater shelf was different for all cars with the standard overhead-valve engines.

97290: MGA Deluxe Roadster exhibited at The Paris Salon in October 1960. Chariot Red with black trim and grey hood.

98734: The second works demonstrator, registration number WJB 405. MGA 1600 Deluxe Roadster in Chariot Red with red trim and beige hood.

102042: June 1961 – MGA 1600 Coupé Deluxe in Old English White with a number of factory extras for J. W. Keller, the Swiss MG agents and good friends of the Thornley family (Heinz Keller was the godfather of Peter Thornley and his son is Jürg Keller).

104428: October 1961, registration number YRX 986; MGA 1600 Coupé Deluxe used as reconnoitre car for the 1962 Monte Carlo and Tulip Rallies. Raced at Oulton Park in 1962 by Christabel Carlisle.

104429: Registration number 151 ABL. 1962 Monte Carlo and Tulip Rallies (see Chapter 10).

107473: 1962 New York Coliseum Show. MGA 1600 Deluxe Mark II. Old English White with red trim and grey hood.

108651: June 1962. The last MGA 1600 Deluxe Mark II to go down the assembly line.

108652: June 1962. The highest chassis number for an MGA 1600 Deluxe Mark II.

ACCESSORIES FITTED TO MGA 'DELUXE'-TYPE CARS

Serial or CSO # Abbreviation	Serial or CSO # believed to represent ...	1600 Deluxe		1600 Mark II Deluxe	
		Number	%	Number	%
–	Home delivery – personal export scheme	1	1%	6	2%
–	HMV radio	19	23%	4	1%
1FL.	Single fog light	0	0%	3	1%
1FLBRG.	Fog lamp bracket		0%	1	0%
1WM.	Single wing mirror	0	0%	3	1%
2 H/MS	Probably '2 WMS' – two wing mirrors	0	0%	1	0%
2 SUN VISORS.	Two sun visors	0	0%	1	0%
2FLS.	Two fog lights	0	0%	1	0%
2WM. or 2W/MS.	Two wing mirrors	1	1%	2	1%
4.1 AX.	4.1 axle	1	1%	0	0%
4.55 AX.	4.55 axle	5	6%	60	19%
A.R.BAR.	Anti-rollbar	42	51%	77	25%
AT.	Ash tray	2	2%	8	3%
BAT.CVR.	Battery cover	3	4%	6	2%
BB.	Badge bar	0	0%	3	1%
CIG. LIGHT.	Cigar lighter	1	1%	2	1%
COMP. CLUTCH (C.O.P.).	Competition clutch	2	2%	1	0%
CENT.THERM.	Centigrade scale dual gauge	43	52%	24	8%
COMP. STS.	Competition seats	68	83%	52	17%
COMP.SCN.	Competition windscreen	0	0%	15	5%
CRG BOX.	Close ratio gearbox	15	18%	153	49%
DSC. or D.SCN.	De Luxe side screens	5	6%	6	2%
DURABAND TYRES	Tyres: Duraband	0	0%	1	0%
H.	Heater	78	95%	295	94%
H/D.	Home delivery [*see also* above]	0	0%	5	2%
H/L FLASH. SWITCH.	Headlamp flasher switch	1	1%	8	3%
HTDSC.	Hardtop and De Luxe side screens	24	29%	19	6%
INTERNAL WINDUP AERIAL.	Internal wind-up aerial	0	0%	1	0%
KILO. (Mark II only)	Speedometer: kilometres per hour	0	0%	25	8%
L.ST.COL.	Lockable steering column	0	0%	3	1%
L/C ENG.	Low compression engine	0	0%	38	12%
LA St WH. or L.A.ST.WH.	Light aluminium steering wheel	1	1%	4	1%
LC.	Luggage carrier	1	1%	3	1%
LC. INB	Luggage carrier in the boot	1	1%		0%
LTT. BATT	Supplied less tyre tube and battery	1	1%	0	0%
MPH. (Mark II only)	Speedometer: miles/hour	1	1%	284	91%
NUT	Nut instead of spinners	0	0%	26	8%
O. COOL.	Oil cooler	23	28%	31	10%
R.BLIND.	Radiator blind	1	1%	2	1%
RST.	Tyres: Dunlop Road Speed	71	87%	242	77%
SHOW TYRES.	Tyres: Show (white lettering)	0	0%	1	0%
SP. BODY.	Special body	0	0%	1	0%
SP. TRIM.	Special trim	0	0%	1	0%
SP.PET.PUMP	Special petrol pump	1	1%	0	0%
SP.SHOCK.ABS.	Special shock absorbers	1	1%	0	0%
TCBE.	Tonneau cover: beige	7	9%	15	5%
TCBU.	Tonneau cover: blue	7	9%	20	6%
TCGY.	Tonneau cover: grey	26	32%	180	58%
TH.	Twin horns	3	4%	7	2%
V	V numbers	23	28%	23	7%
WW.	Windscreen washers	56	68%	232	74%
WWT.	Whitewall tyres	0	0%	47	15%

Footnotes:
As this table shows, the record keepers at Abingdon varied their abbreviations slightly and so there is a likelihood of duplication where more than one code was used for broadly the same item. This information has been provided by MG Deluxe enthusiast John Barrett, to whom the author is grateful for his permission to reproduce it in this book; final confirmation of some elements only came in 2017 after some seventeen years of research.

This MGA 1600 at Abingdon has, uniquely, an unusual combination of tail-lamps, with the prevailing MGA 1600 plinth as well as the Austin Seven/Morris Mini Minor units seen on the MGA 1600 Mark II.

MGA DE-LUXE BODY NUMBERING

Body type	block start	block end	Number in block (Roadster)	Number in block (Coupé)
Roadster	B25818	B25818	1	
Roadster	B1938	B2000	63	
Coupé	*B1591*	*B1600*		*10*
Coupé	*B28667*	*B28668*		*2*
Roadster	B33000	B33040	41	
Coupé	*B33041*	*B33050*		*10*
Roadster	B35001	B35100	100	
Roadster	B37221	B37250	30	
Coupé	*B37251*	*B37263*		*13*
Roadster	B37311	B37435	125	
Totals			**360**	***35***

The last MGA Deluxe of all, a Mark II of course, was chassis number 108652, completed in June 1962, by which time Abingdon was well into the process of ramping up production of the MGB – which had neither a twin cam nor a four-wheel disc brake option. In North America there was reference in at least one publication (*Sports Car Graphic*) to a 'Competition' specification MGA, which appears to have been all but the same thing as an MGA 1600 Mark II Deluxe.

Detailed research into the story of the MGA Deluxe by the MG Car Club's Twin Cam Group has shown that Deluxes have very easily identifiable body numbers. Early on, they continue on from the Twin Cam range until they reach body number 'B1999/B2000', then they follow another format. The author is indebted to John Barrett and Mark Hester for their diligent research into the following analysis:

During a series of visits to Gaydon in 2000 and 2001, John Barrett extracted by hand all the records relating to the Deluxes from the main MGA chassis records: he copied everything on all the Deluxes, noting that: 'The Deluxe records were in crayon, not the fine tip pens we have today' (the code used was blue for a Roadster, red for a Coupé, green for a Deluxe Roadster, and brown for a Deluxe Coupé). Barrett found that the use of crayon by the original record keepers meant that it was often very difficult to read the specifications: 'There was too much information in too little space, written with a blunt crayon! To make matters worse, we didn't initially know what all these letters meant. The factory did not completely standardize its abbreviations, either...' *See* the table page 163.

THE MGA 1600 MARK II

By the time the next generation of MG sports car was on the horizon, the MGA was coasting towards retirement, but not without the honourable achievement of an unprecedented build total well in excess of six figures – a monumental feat for any sports car, let alone an MG built largely on the manual production lines at Abingdon. As we shall see in Chapter 9, attempts to update the MGA generally came to nothing, not only because of budgetary considerations but arguably because the basic material had been so right

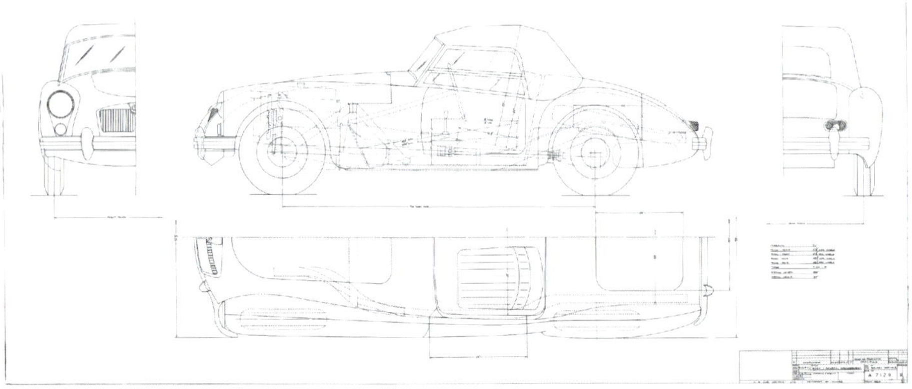

Blueprint for the MGA 1600 Mark II Roadster. The drawing number is A7128, dated 10 May 1961...

BOB VITRIKAS

from the outset that any alterations would have been seen as unnecessary.

Practical changes were driven by a combination of customer and distributor demand and legislative changes, especially to safety-related items such as lighting equipment. Furthermore development of some of the basic components by the parent company precipitated improvements or forced substations and specification alterations. An obvious change was under the bonnet, where evolution of the BMC B-Series engine led to the substation of the MGA 1600's largely unique 1588cc overhead valve unit by a much-improved engine with a slightly larger 1622cc capacity (98.981cu in). The first MGA 1600 Mark II was chassis no. 100352 (the last of the superseded 1600 was 100351, with engine 16GA 31660).

The MGA 1600 Mark II was released on 7 June 1961, with a series of press photos featuring a female member of staff from Cowley.
AUTHOR'S COLLECTION

MGA 1600 MARK II – UK PRESS RELEASE

Printed on a label on the reverse of a set of four photographs released in the UK to announce the introduction of a new version of the MGA was the following text:

Confidential – not to be released before 28 June 1961: MGA 1600 Mk II

Powered by a new 1622cc ohv engine developing 90bhp at 5,000rpm, with a compression ratio of 8.4 to 1 and a 4.1 to 1 rear axle ratio, the MGA 1600 Mk II has increased performance with safety at high speeds yet retains the reputation of its predecessor for good road-holding and stability. Distinguishable by the redesigned and repositioned rear light clusters, the new radiator grille and the Mk II boot and scuttle motifs, the car has built-in anchorages for BMC safety belts. It sells in the UK at the same price as the MGA 1600, namely £940.7.6 inclusive of purchase tax.

Copyright free: Press Office, The Nuffield Organisation, Cowley, Oxford

Unlike the Hambro press photos of the earlier MGA 1600 (see earlier) BMC got it right with the MGA 1600 Mark II, with the correct plain hub-caps for the standard disc wheels. Inevitably centre-lock wires remained an almost *de facto* choice for many customers.
AUTHOR'S COLLECTION

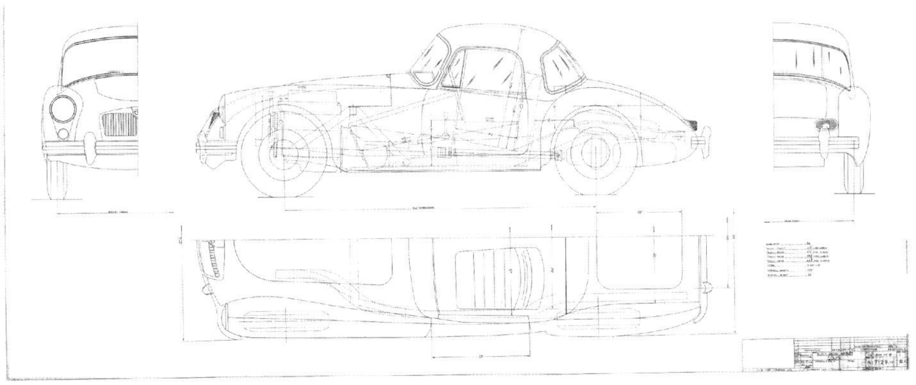

... and this is the equivalent blueprint for the MGA 1600 Mark II Coupé; this drawing is A7129, also dated 10 May 1961, like the Roadster drawing; there is an annotation 'issued for production' with Jim O'Neil's initials.
BOB VITRIKAS

The most immediately obvious change on the MGA 1600 Mark II was the recessed grille bars – which divided opinion amongst MG fans as much as almost any change ever does.
AUTHOR'S COLLECTION

The bigger capacity for the facelift arrived by virtue of a modest but worthwhile increase in bore from 75.4mm to 76.2mm (from 2.97 to 3.00in, a difference of $\frac{1}{32}$in), but this was just part of the story – the changes under the bonnet also extended to worthwhile improvements to the valve gear and combustion chambers, a modest increase in compression ratio (from 8.3 to 8.8:1 – although not in Australia) the net benefit being better power output (up 13 per cent to 90bhp for most markets; 84.6bhp in Australia) and this, coupled with a change to the standard rear-axle ratio (reduced from 4.3 to 4.1: 1), led to improved acceleration and maximum speeds in all gears.

Air-flow test rigs had been used to refine the profiles of the inlet and exhaust tracts, and higher compression ratio (where applied) was in part achieved by using flat-topped pistons in place of the previous slightly domed type. The engine was quite significantly altered in other more fundamental ways, with the block casting re-cored and the extent of the siamesing of the bores increased through the expedient of reducing the sizes of the water passages in the cast webs between the individual cylinder barrels. The crankshaft webs had also been beefed up, achieved through a slight reduction in the width of the main bearings (testing having shown there was capacity to safely permit this slightly counter-intuitive change), and there were stiffer con-rods and larger gudgeon pins. Other changes were the fitment of a new, slightly lighter flywheel and some strengthened gearbox casing webs.

From the rear, the other obvious exterior styling change was to the tail-lamps, which were in fact ADO 15 Mini units mounted horizontally on special plinths (the latter were painted at Abingdon).
AUTHOR'S COLLECTION

This press photo for the MGA 1600 Mark II was issued for the October 1961 Earls Court Motor Show, and is interesting for having a University Motors registration number, 4 UML. The statues symbolizing speed, seen on a plinth in the background, were erected in London's Hyde Park, and were called 'The Rush of Green' or 'The Bowater House Group'. The piece was created by famous sculptor Jacob Epstein (10 November 1880–19 August 1959), and had been unveiled earlier that year as one of the last pieces Epstein worked on before he died.
AUTHOR'S COLLECTION

Even if some motor-sports purists and die-hards might have frowned at a capacity increase that pushed the MGA into the 2-litre class, the significance of these changes (and a large part of the reason why the money was found to make them) was that they would apply to other BMC products using the B-Series engine. Whereas the MGA 1600's 1588cc unit had been largely bespoke for MG, at a time when most BMC saloons had stayed with 1498cc, the new unit addressed demand across the whole range, and the 1622 would feature in many BMC saloons such as the Austin Cambridge (which moved from A55 to A60), Morris Oxford (Series V to Series VI), Riley (from 4/68 to 4/72) and Wolseley

Nearing the end of the line, but not quite at the final inspection, the fitter underneath this Old English White MGA 1600 Mark II, photographed in 1961, is one of the Carter brothers (the MG workforce included many families). From here, the car would move on towards the last station, where it would be filled with fuel and receive another inspection before moving to the test department for road test. In the background to the left can be seen the Austin-Healey Sprite Mark II/MG Midget line.
STUART SEAGER, NAMES COURTESY ADRIAN GOODENOUGH

MGA 1600 MARK II – OPTIONAL EXTRAS

Original BMC accessory seatbelts are fitted to Adrian Malthouse's MGA 1600 Mark II.
BEAULIEU

The original Nuffield Organisation press release for the MGA 1600 Mark II was issued on 7 June 1961, with an embargo date of 28 June; the headline was 'New look and better performance for the MGA'. Meanwhile, as touched upon earlier, a memorandum was issued by S. B. King of Nuffield Exports on 1 June 1961, setting out the factory options available for the MGA 1600 Mark II:

Production Line Optional Extras: *With the introduction of the Mark II version of the MG 'A' 1600, distributors will no doubt wish to be reassured that the comprehensive list of optional extras offered on the MG 'A' 1600 will still be available. In the main this is so there are, however, a few minor alterations. The current list of production-line fitted optional extras is therefore as follows: Fresh Air Heater and Demister; Fresh Air Unit, Blower Assisted; Windscreen Washers; Wire Wheels; White Wall Tyres; Road Speed Tyres (5.90 × 15); Overall Tonneau Cover; HMV Radio; Alternative Axle Ratio – 4.55 to 1; Detachable Hard Top with de-luxe side-screens; Luggage Carrier; Dunlop Disc Brakes all round, including centre lock disc wheel and Road Speed Tyres (these three items are supplied together).*

Items not covered by this list and which are offered by BMC Service Limited, can be obtained by Distributors direct from BMC Service Limited, by means of normal Parts stock orders. In addition the following Competition extras can be ordered for initial factory fitment: Close Ratio Gear Box; Anti Roll Bar; Oil Cooler; Competition Windshield; Competition de-luxe seats.

The author found that close scrutiny of the equivalent 'home market' and 'export' variants of the sales brochures (H.6120 dated May 1961, and E.6121 dated June) was also instructive; whilst an adjustable steering column was listed as an extra on the home market, evidently it was listed as standard on export cars. Ace Mercury wheel trims seem to have been offered only in the export brochure, which also listed an oil cooler as a supplier option.

The side profile of the MGA 1600 Mark II was basically the same as that of the preceding variants, other than the changes to the lights and grille, hardly visible from this angle.
BEAULIEU

(15/60 to 16/60). Before long, the same basic unit would be stretched yet again to 1798cc for the BMC ADO 17 and the MGB, thereby directly handing on the baton between old and new MG sports cars.

Inside the cockpit, the most obvious change was that the facia (in most markets other than CKD ones) was covered with grained artificial 'leather cloth' with a non-reflective matt finish, by the name of 'Nuvon', rather than being left in body-colour paint, whilst externally the only really obvious changes were to the rear lamp clusters (which benefited from being up-to-date single units, compliant with new lighting regulations, even if they were an aesthetic compromise through being in effect BMC ADO 15 'Mini' units mounted horizontally) and at the front, a modified radiator grille with inset bars set back from the front of the grille aperture (*see* photos page 171).

The latter move was initially looked at rather disdainfully by some purists, even if there were practical benefits in terms of reduced vulnerability to accident damage; however, time has provided a more balanced view of the change to the grille, and some MGA enthusiasts actually prefer the style of the Mark II. As a sign of the advances of vehicle safety, seatbelt attachments (located on the propshaft tunnel, but bolted through to the chassis frame) were fitted as standard, even though the idea of compulsory fitment of seatbelts would only come many years after the MGA had ceased production.

A press photo for the MGA 1600 Mark II Coupé, issued at the time of the October 1961 Earls Court Motor Show; a year after this, MG would be celebrating the new MGB, also using aircraft in some of the press photography.
AUTHOR'S COLLECTION

THE MGA 1600 MARK II IN THE PRESS

Autocar briefly reported on the MGA 1600 Mark II in their issue of 30 June 1961, but subsequently subjected one (YJB 218) to their road-testing procedures, reporting on the outcome in the issue of 21 July 1961. The testers felt that the new version of the engine did not bring with it any significant improvement in refinement, but liked its sporting character and exhaust note. The magazine also thought that the 1622cc engine was a very flexible power unit, which pulled strongly from under 20mph (32km/h) in top. However, when pulling hard at low engine speeds, the common B-Series characteristic of occasional slight pinking was experienced when running on ordinary premium fuel, and 'this did not disappear when super grades were tried'.

For performance testing, *Autocar* wisely used higher octane fuels to meet the MG factory's recommendations in order to achieve maximum performance. However, whenever the engine was switched off, irrespective of the grade of fuel, the engine would run on 'for a second or two, shaking violently on its flexible mountings'. This will be a not unfamiliar experience for many owners of cars with twin-carburettor B-Series engines, both MGAs and MGBs.

Meanwhile, however, the road-holding was adjudged to be of a high order, it being noted that:

> All who drove the car agreed that it felt most stable when taken fast through a corner. A small amount of understeer is present, and the technique when cornering really hard

UK advertisements for the MGA 1600 Mark II proclaimed that the enlarged engine offered 'more power for your safety'.
AUTHOR'S COLLECTION

> is to use plenty of throttle to get the rear wheels to drift outwards a little. However, at no time at all did it show any unpredictable or awkward behaviour, and it must be judged a very safe car for the inexperienced and expert alike.

Despite the emergence of sporting rivals with better hoods and such conveniences as wind-up windows, the testers were very generous in their assessment of the MGA's hood and side-screens:

> One person can erect the hood, although it is easier if there is assistance. An over-centre catch at the centre of the windscreen top rail prevents the hood from lifting in the middle. It was free from flapping at high speed, although wind roar was so great that conversation was impossible above 70mph [113km/h]. There were no signs of leaks during heavy rain, and the hood stows in a remarkably small space behind the seats. Metal-framed side screens housed in an envelope in front of the stowed hood cannot be considered ideal but give reasonable protection from draughts. The sliding plastic window in each screen soon became scratched.

Perhaps the forthcoming MGB refinements could not come soon enough.

In their closing paragraph, the testers concluded that:

> In this latest MGA, which costs no more than the previous model, the engine modifications provide a little more performance, making this ample for most people's requirements but, more important, this is achieved in a more effortless manner. Basically, the MGA's traditional character, which has appealed to so many, is unchanged.

Road & Track tested the MGA 1600 Mark II for their September 1961 issue, sub-titling their report 'Made in Abingdon on Thames by Water Sprites'. The test car came with just 4 miles (6.4km) on the clock, and so was not run in – it was handed over in person by Gus Ehrman (qv) who was in charge of BMC's Los Angeles sales office. Notwithstanding a slightly 'tight' engine, *Road & Track* found that performance averaged out 5 per cent better than the MGA 1600 Mark I, which the magazine had tested for its October 1959 issue.

Jonathan Stein owned this MGA Coupé 1600 Mark II in the comparatively rare Dove Grey, nicely offset with a red leather interior.
JONATHAN STEIN

The interior of the MGA 1600 Mark II Coupé, a combination of red leather, red rexine and grey carpets.
JONATHAN STEIN

Top speed achieved was 105mph (169km/h), and 0–60mph took 12.8sec. Overall the testers formed an opinion that the Mark II was the best all-around sports car for the money, even if some of its virtues were at risk of being outclassed by younger opposition.

Less positively, the testers felt that the new engine was not as smooth as its predecessor:

> In piling up miles on the Mark II, we got an impression that the engine isn't quite as smooth or as quiet as before. Certainly a higher compression ratio often means rougher running, but we believe most of our impression was caused by a fairly loud exhaust note. The engine has no noticeable vibration period but, as with any four, there is a trace of rumble when decelerating. At low rpm the engine feels as though its being abused, yet it actually will lug in 4th gear at 1,000rpm, and full throttle gives smooth, reaction-free response.

BELOW LEFT: **Adrian Malthouse's Iris Blue MGA 1600 Mark II strictly speaking belongs in Chapter 8 as well as this one, because it was originally exported to South Africa. It has chassis number GHN2/102909, and the dispatch date was 31 October 1961.**

BELOW: **The 1622cc engine was a stepping stone to the 1798cc unit of the MGB.**
BEAULIEU

Iris Blue is one of the colours that was effectively a bridge between the MGA and MGB

BELOW: **The distinctive 1600 Mk II scuttle badges alongside the elliptical grilles seen on all MGA variants.**

BELOW RIGHT: **Notice the greater curvature of the bonnet on the later MGA body on the Mark II.**
BEAULIEU

The MGA 1600 Mark II tail-lamps are one of the distinctive hallmarks of this model. Owner Adrian Malthouse imported it from its previous Johannesburg owner in March 2000, after which it was thoroughly restored.
BEAULIEU

The interior of the Malthouse Mark II is black; note the matching facia treatment.
BEAULIEU

These misgivings aside, the conclusion was that the MGA in its 1600 Mark II guise remained 'truly the "universal" sports car' Nevertheless, by 1960 it was pretty much an open secret that an all-new MG sports car was in the works, even if the form it might take was still a closely guarded secret....

THE ONE HUNDRED-THOUSANDTH MGA

A rare production-line colour photograph taken by Stuart Seager of the unique gold 100,000th MGA, with its cream leather interior and – as built – gold-painted wheels. Watching from the left of the car, in his charge-hand's blue overcoat, is Bill Singleton. The surviving build card of this car records the body number as B39605, and there is a special note to the effect that during the build, 'chassis [is] to go to paint shop before body is mounted', which probably explains why Jack Privett from MG's Finishing/Paint Shop can be seen here behind the wheel; clearly he had been tasked with the special care of this uniquely finished show car. Also seen behind the car is Sid Himpson.

STUART SEAGER, NAMES COURTESY ADRIAN GOODENOUGH

Early in 1962, even as plans were inevitably advancing for the MGA's imminent replacement, the remarkable production tally of the model was already apparent and clearly worthy of celebration. On 12 March the 100,000th MGA went down the production line, and the event was recorded for posterity by Stuart Seager, whose colour photographs appear here. The car itself, GHNL2-107989, was uniquely finished in metallic gold with cream leather interior trim.

The corresponding Nuffield Organisation press release was issued on 29 March 1962, the same day that the car set sail for New York on the *Queen Mary* ocean liner; the release proclaimed that: 'It is particularly fitting that this historic car should be at the New York Show, as some 70,000 of the 100,000 MGAs so far made have been exported to the United States of America.'

At the factory, photos of the car show that its wire wheels were painted the same gold colour as the bodywork; however, by the time it had been shipped across the Atlantic and appeared in public again at the April 1962 New York International Motor Show, the painted wheels had been changed (not unwisely, surely) for rather better looking chrome-plated ones. Alongside the gold car was a white MGA 1600 Mark II Deluxe Roadster (GHNL2-107473), which had also crossed the Atlantic in style aboard the *Queen Mary*.

For a number of years it was thought that the gold car had either been lost altogether or, as author Wilson McComb suggested, the importer had resprayed it a standard colour and sold it off – but thankfully the unique specimen had survived. It transpired that it had been acquired by Tennessee businessman Russell Skomp from a dealer in Nashville (John Tune Import Motors), who had it on show and appears to have sold it to Skomp almost by accident: when the salesman (presumably unaware of the car's special status) shook hands with Skomp, the latter, determined to own it, resisted a subsequent appeal from the dealer principal to accept another car in lieu of the unique gold show car. In order to avoid a possible lawsuit, the dealer acquiesced and the gold MGA was handed over, its US tour prematurely abandoned.

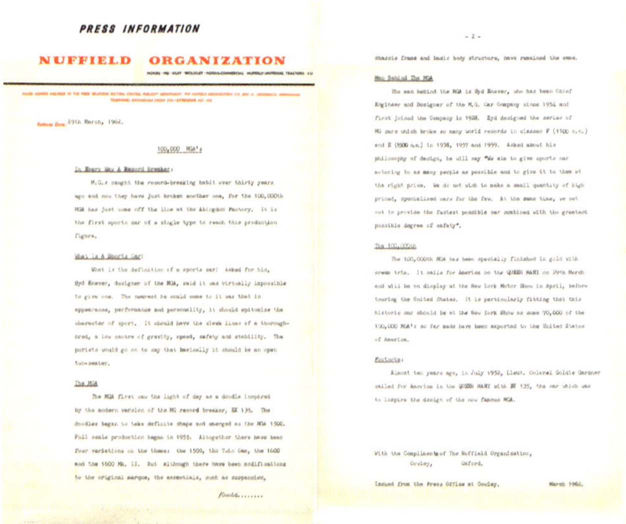

PRESS INFORMATION

NUFFIELD ORGANIZATION

Release Date: 29th March, 1962.

100,000 MGA's

In Every Way A Record Breaker:

M.G.s caught the record-breaking habit over thirty years ago and now they have just broken another one, for the 100,000th MGA has just come off the line at the Abingdon Factory. It is the first sports car of a single type to reach this production figure.

What is A Sports Car?

What is the definition of a sports car? Asked for his, Syd Enever, designer of the MGA, said it was virtually impossible to give one. The nearest he could come to it was that in appearance, performance and personality, it should epitomise the character of sport. It should have the sleek lines of a thoroughbred, a low centre of gravity, speed, safety and stability. The purists would go on to say that basically it should be an open two-seater.

The MGA

The MGA first saw the light of day as a doodle inspired by the modern version of the MG record breaker, EX 135. The doodles began to take definite shape and emerged as the MGA 1500. Full scale production began in 1955. Altogether there have been four variations on the theme: the 1500, the Twin Cam, the 1600 and the 1600 Mk. II. But although there have been modifications to the original marque, the essentials, such as suspension,

/Contd........

- 2 -

chassis frame and basic body structure, have remained the same.

Man Behind The MGA

The man behind the MGA is Syd Enever, who has been Chief Engineer and Designer of the M.G. Car Company since 1954 and first joined the Company in 1928. Syd designed the series of MG cars which broke so many world records in classes F (1100 c.c.) and E (1500 c.c.) in 1938, 1957 and 1959. Asked about his philosophy of design, he will say "We aim to give sports car motoring to as many people as possible and to give it to them at the right price. We do not wish to make a small quantity of high priced, specialised cars for the few. At the same time, we set out to provide the fastest possible car combined with the greatest possible degree of safety".

The 100,000th

The 100,000th MGA has been specially finished in gold with cream trim. It sails for America on the QUEEN MARY on 29th March and will be on display at the New York Motor Show in April, before touring the United States. It is particularly fitting that this historic car should be at the New York Show as some 70,000 of the 100,000 MGA's so far made have been exported to the United States of America.

Footnote:

Almost ten years ago, in July 1952, Lieut. Colonel Goldie Gardner sailed for America in the QUEEN MARY with EX 135, the car which was to inspire the design of the now famous MGA.

With the Compliments of The Nuffield Organization,
Cowley, Oxford.

Issued from the Press Office at Cowley. March 1962.

The official Nuffield Organisation press release for the 100,000th MGA, issued on 29 March 1962.

ENEVER FAMILY

The specially finished 100,000th MGA on the line at Abingdon in March 1962.

G. ROBSON

Publicity photo of the 100,000th MGA.

ENEVER FAMILY

The 100,000th MGA poses alongside 'Old Number One' at the MG factory in Abingdon. Those gold-painted wire wheels would be replaced with glistening chromed ones for the car's public appearance at the New York Motor Show in April 1962.

AUTHOR'S COLLECTION

The gold MGA with its special white interior had pride of place on the MG stand at the New York Motor Show. Note how, whilst the special paint, trim and whitewall tyres had survived the trip from Abingdon, the gold-painted wire wheels had been ditched in favour of plated ones. The interior also featured sheepskin carpets.

AUTHOR'S COLLECTION

When Russell Skomp took over the gold MGA, he used it for a short time until it was incapacitated by some minor fuel system malady, at which point Skomp simply parked it outside on his forty-acre ranch near Springfield, Tennessee, with just 8,000 miles on the odometer, and left it there. The special MGA sat in a field, largely untouched, for the best part of four decades until Russell Skomp passed away in 2000.

Soon after this, Russell Skomp's younger brother Fred acquired it, and so began a painstaking restoration.

In the end, Muncie Import Auto stepped in; they had successfully completed all the special interior work on the car and they agreed to help fix all the outstanding problems. Fred Skomp and his wife Cindy ended up with a superb, unique MGA, which they were both able to enjoy for a while.

582 AUTOSPORT, APRIL 27, 1962

A FINE TRIBUTE TO A GREAT SPORTS CAR

the 100,000th MGA

M.G.A. 1600 Mk II.

No wonder 100,000 happy owners chose M.G.A. Such success is earned by features which now include magnificent 1622 c.c. power unit with twin carburetters, front wheel disc brakes. Performance 0-50 m.p.h. 9·7 secs. Top speed 102·3 m.p.h. (*Autocar*) — in fact all the qualities of 'Safety-Fast' motoring.

THE M.G. CAR COMPANY LIMITED, SALES DIVISION, COWLEY, OXFORD

BMC proudly proclaimed the 100,000th production milestone in magazine advertising.

AUTHOR'S COLLECTION

The beautifully restored 100,000th MGA on display in the MOSS USA showroom.

MOSS

Now it sits in Moss Motors Museum in Petersburg Virginia – and even now has only 11,000 miles (17,700km) on it.

SALES AND MARKETING: MGA 1600 MARK II ADVERTS AND BROCHURES

Marketing of the new model in the UK played on the trad–itional 'Safety Fast!' slogan by declaring that the new MGA 1600 Mark II offered 'More Power to your Safety', a strapline seen not only in the home-market press release material, but also in the corresponding twelve-page fold-out home-market brochure H.6120 (with an equivalent numbered E.6121 for export) and contemporary magazine advertisements. Inevitably versions of the same basic literature appeared in various European markets; for example, the German MGA 1600 Mark II brochure proclaimed '*Mehr leistung... zu Ihrer Sicherheit*' which, obviously modelled on the UK slogan, simply means 'More power ... for your safety'. Clever UK marketing literature, aimed solely at distributors and dealers, made reference to 'More power to MGA 1600 sales'.

A special 100,000 badge was fitted on the cowl just beneath the normal 1600 Mk II badge.

MOSS

Meanwhile BMC/Hambro also issued a press release for the benefit of dealers and distributors to assist them with their own media advertising. Issued with a single three-quarter view of the new model, the BMC/Hambro text declared:

> The world's most famous family of sports cars has a new heir – the MGA 1600 Mark II. This 1962 version MG has a more powerful 1622cc engine capable of 90 brake horse-power – an increase of nearly 12 per cent over its forerunner, the MGA 1600. This added power is due to larger inlet and exhaust valves, a higher compression ratio of 9:1, and increasing the rear axle ratio to 4.1:1. The new Mark II MG will hit top speeds of over 100 miles an hour [160km/h] and will deliver from 25 to 30 miles per gallon [11 to 9.4ltr/100km]. Seatbelt anchorages are standard equipment on the Mark II. The classic styling of the MGA 1600 is virtually unchanged on this new model. An improved tail-light placement, setting the grille back to prevent parking dents, and more extensive use of leather upholstery in the cockpit are the only changes.

BMC/Hambro issued this photo of an MGA 1600 Mark II with their press release for the new model.

AUTHOR'S COLLECTION

Simple two-sided black and white brochures – more accurately leaflets – were popular at BMC/Hambro in the period 1960–66; this is the front face of the MGA Mark II leaflet issued in July 1961.
AUTHOR'S COLLECTION

A Hambro advert for the MGA 1600 Mark II: 'Back seat drivers, g'bye! This one is deliberately designed for a carefree twosome to slip into snug bucket seats, take the helm, give it the gun, flash through teeming traffic and head for their favourite open spaces.'
AUTHOR'S COLLECTION

For their magazine advertising in the USA, BMC/Hambro resorted to different tactics, for example, in one nationally run advertisement calling the Mark II 'the get-away car'; the copy included the exhortation:

> Back seat drivers, g'bye! This one is deliberately designed for a carefree twosome to slip into snug bucket seats, take the helm, give it the gun, flash through teeming traffic, and head for their favourite wide open spaces. Alone. This is the sports car for a guy and a gal who dare to get away with an MG, knowing that everyone's watching them. Enviously.

THE END OF THE ROAD

The last MGA 1600 Mark II Coupé was chassis no. 107031, but the Roadster finished at 109070: it was registered 326 ELO, built 14 to 19 May 1962, finished in Iris Blue, and with engine number 16GC 8851; it left the production line on 7 June 1962, marking a total of 101,081 MGAs built. By this stage the MGB was already entering early production: the first MGB, GHN3-102, a left-hand-drive car, was built on 22 May 1962 and finished, like the last MGA, in Iris Blue. There was little ceremony at BMC as the MGA came to the end of the line, as corporate focus had already shifted to this new model, with many creature comforts that the MGA lacked – such as wind-up door windows – and a larger (1798cc) engine. The Syd Enever MGA Coupé KMO 326 (see Chapter 5) was rather cheekily given chassis number 109071 after the event.

John Thornley, Syd Enever and their talented Abingdon team could be justly proud of the first production aerodynamic MG sports car; 101,081 cars had been built in a seven-year span, an unprecedented total for such a model, which had truly been a revolutionary MG, with 94 per cent exported in its seven-year production run. Surely none of them could have predicted the success of the car that followed in its wake: but that truly is a story for another book...

It is sometimes obvious that a product is nearing the end of its life when the marketing gimmicks become ever more preposterous. In the spring of 1962, the US arm of Beecham's popular 'Brylcreem' hair cream ran a competition with prizes of fifteen MGAs for the best answers to the question 'I feel like a tiger when I use Brycreem because...' and the author of the very best answer would also be given a real life Bengal tiger (or, if the winner was too nervous of being eaten or mauled to death, a substitute prize of $500). Imagine the understandable outcry were the idea of such a competition prize contemplated nowadays!
AUTHOR'S COLLECTION

This is the last MGA chassis to be welded up at Abingdon, truly marking the end of an era as the MGB would be of chassis-less monocoque construction. Left to right are Fred Baxter, Len Carter (foreman), John Herring and Dick Stevens (chargehand).

Sparks fly from the final MGA chassis at Abingdon in 1962.

MG MGA 1600 ROADSTER, MG MGA TWIN CAM ROADSTER (CAR 2193 ON) AND MG MGA 1600 MK II ROADSTER

Body Colour	BMC Code	Main Trim Colour	Hood & Side-Screen Colour
Black	BK1	Beige	Grey
Black	BK1	Red	Grey
Chariot Red	RD16	Red	Beige
Chariot Red	RD16	Beige	Beige
Chariot Red	RD16	Black	Grey
Iris Blue	BU12	Black	Grey
Alamo Beige	BG9	Red	Beige
Dove Grey	GR26	Red	Grey
Old English White	WT3	Red	Grey
Old English White	WT3	Black	Grey

MG MGA 1600 COUPÉ, MG MGA TWIN CAM COUPÉ (CAR 2292 ON) AND MG MGA 1600 MK II COUPÉ

Body Colour	BMC Code	Main Trim Colour	Scuttle Top
Black	BK1	Beige	Black
Black	BK1	Red	Black
Chariot Red	RD16	Red	Red
Chariot Red	RD16	Beige	Red
Chariot Red	RD16	Black	Black
Iris Blue	BU12	Black	Black
Alamo Beige	BG9	Red	Red
Dove Grey	GR26	Red	Red
Old English White	WT3	Red	Red
Old English White	WT3	Black	Black

MG MGA 1600 PRODUCTION TOTALS

Year	Right-Hand-Drive-Home	Right-Hand-Drive-Export	Left-Hand-Drive-Export	Left-Hand-Drive North American Export	Right-Hand-Drive-CKD	Left-Hand-Drive-CKD	Grand Totals
1600 ROADSTER *(INCLUDING DELUXE MODELS)*							
1959	520	137	543	11,378	248	112	12,938
1960	780	271	1330	12,253	764	80	15,478
1961	34	41	42	37	136	24	314
Totals	*1,334*	*449*	*1915*	*23,668*	*1,148*	*216*	*28,730*
1600 COUPÉ *(INCLUDING DELUXE MODELS)*							
1959	401	35	59	711	12	0	1,218
1960	400	66	96	826	52	12	1,452
1961	37	14	24	14	0	12	101
Totals	*838*	*115*	*179*	*1,551*	*64*	*24*	*2,771*
Grand Totals	***2,172***	***564***	***2,094***	***25,219***	***1,212***	***240***	***31,501***

Footnotes:
As with the earlier MGA 1500, production of the first series of MGA 1600 was dominated by export sales, with 80% going to North America. Figures for the Mark II are set out in a separate table alongside. For more about 'CKD' production, see Chapter Eight.

MG MGA 1600 MARK II PRODUCTION TOTALS

Year	Right-Hand-Drive-Home	Right-Hand-Drive-Export	Left-Hand-Drive-Export	Left-Hand-Drive North American Export	Right-Hand-Drive-CKD	Left-Hand-Drive-CKD	Grand Totals
1600 MARK II ROADSTER *(INCLUDING DELUXE MODELS)*							
1961	317	120	764	3,921	84	48	*5,254*
1962	60	39	392	2,365	88	0	*2,944*
Totals	*377*	*159*	*1,156*	*6,286*	*172*	*48*	*8,198*
1600 MARK II COUPÉ *(INCLUDING DELUXE MODELS)*							
1961	168	21	67	156	4	0	*416*
1962	51	10	18	26	0	0	*105*
Totals	219	31	85	182	4	0	*521*
Grand Totals	***596***	***190***	***1,241***	***6,468***	***176***	***48***	***8,719***

Footnotes:
These figures show the continuing dominance of roadster output and exports to North America as percentages of the total volumes, accounting for overall 94 per cent and 74.2 per cent respectively. Just 521 MGA 1600 Mark II Coupés were built, of which just 182 were destined for North America. It can also be seen that total CKD output as a percentage was down to 2.57 per cent of the grand total of 8,719 (*see also* Chapter 8).

MGA 1600 CHASSIS AND ENGINE NUMBERS

MGA 1600 CHASSIS NUMBERS

The chassis number details for the MGA 1600 record less detail than the earlier 1500. The codes are as follows:

1st digit: 'G' = MG
2nd digit: 'H' indicates a capacity range of 1400–1999cc
3rd digit: 'N' indicates an open two-seater Roadster; 'D' indicates a Coupé
4th digit *(where used)***:** '2' = MGA 1600 Mark II
4th or 5th digit *(where used)***:** 'L' = LHD
Numbers: MGA 1600 – 68851 to 100351; MGA 1600 Mark II – 100352 to 109070

MGA 1600 ENGINE NUMBERS

The first MGA 1600, with the 1588cc engine, had '16GA-U-H' prefix codes. The significance of these characters is '16' for 1588 cc; 'G' = MG; 'A' = a so-called 'Type' letter; 'U' = central gear-change (as opposed to a column change) and 'H' = high compression ratio (the engine prefixes were often just '16GA-U', as all had the same 8.3:1 compression ratio). For the Mark II, with the substantially revised 1622cc engine, the engine prefixes were '16GC-U-H' (compression ratio 8.8: 1) or '16GC-U-L' (8.3: 1), where the 'C' is a new 'Type' letter, and the 'H' or 'L' indicates high or low compression ratio respectively.

Elvis Presley so loved the MGA 1600 that he used when filming *Blue Hawaii* in 1960 that he acquired the car, and it remains part of the family collection to this day.
AUTHOR'S COLLECTION

Robert Redford is believed to have owned this Old English White MGA 1600 Mark II with red trim, having purchased it new in 1962.
DANIEL SCHMITT

Tommy Steele was in his heyday in 1959 when he starred in the now largely forgotten J. Arthur Rank Film *Tommy the Toreador*, which also featured Janet Munro, Sid James, Bernard Cribbins, Noell Purcell and Kenneth Williams – more familiar as stars of the '*Carry On*' film franchise. The MGA appears to be incidental, in this publicity still, issued by the film promoters.
AUTHOR'S COLLECTION

CHAPTER EIGHT

ASSEMBLY OVERSEAS

The design of the MGA, with its separate chassis and body made up of a number of fairly compact steel and alloy panels, meant that it was quite well suited to export in either partially built form or as a kit of constituent parts. The former would be termed 'Semi Knocked Down' (SKD) or 'Partially Knocked Down' (PKD), and typically involved a car that had been largely completed but then parts were temporarily unbolted – such as having the windscreen and wheels removed – to create a more compact prospect for shipping.

Dependent upon shipping arrangements, these cars would often be fixed into timber frames at Nuffield Exports; these frames could be easily stacked, and certain components such as the batteries would usually not be included in favour of fitment at the destination. This principle had been well used in the heady days of Nuffield Exports shipments of the MG TD and TF, and thus the concept continued with the MGA. 'Completely knocked down' (CKD) kits were more common in export markets, where local import duties meant that this approach was commercially more attractive, and MGAs would be supplied as kits that were either complete, or without certain components, such as tyres, batteries and trim, which could be sourced locally and therefore easily, so reducing tax liabilities further.

Bodies were sent direct to Cowley from Coventry as sets of primer-finished panels, and packed four cars to a crate, whilst similar crates were packed with chassis and essential components (the make-up of which varied slightly according to market, and in particular the choice of parts that could be sourced locally). It is for this reason that most of the chassis build numbers for CKD MGAs tend to appear in batches of four consecutive numbers at a time.

The MGA sold well in Canada, and was generally sent there 'partially knocked down'. Note the Ontario licence plate on this 1960 MGA 1600.
AUTHOR'S COLLECTION

These 1957 MGA 1500 Roadsters and Coupés (the latter in taller packaging) being prepared in the 100,000sq ft Nuffield Exports plant are clearly destined for Gough Industries in California, judging by the markings on the timber crates. Nuffield Exports had celebrated its twenty-first anniversary in July 1954, and the division claimed to export a car every one and three-quarter minutes. The timber crates seen here were all made at Cowley in a dedicated sawmill.
AUTHOR'S COLLECTION

Naturally the Abingdon build records for such CKD cars do not list a body colour; the final paint would be applied at the assembling factory, and often differed from contemporary home-market options, although much of the trim (unless locally sourced) could be listed as far as interior and hood colours were concerned. Once the kits arrived at their destination, the trim sets did not always end up being used in strict order – see the sections for each market later in this chapter.

Nuffield Exports was a veritable hive of activity, with a busy hub at Cowley's 'KD' Department, situated in 'T Block', which comprised a 120,000sq ft (1,115sq m) unit. Parts or complete cars were sent here and then packed and despatched. KD Engineering incorporated a design office and development workshop where assembly jigs were used to proof-build body shells, often having to adapt the build technique and associated jigs for far lower volumes and different local capabilities, sometimes using different welding and finishing techniques.

◄ Mr. F. Minns (right), of Minns Motors Ltd., Distributors in Edmonton, Canada, admires the MGA with Mr. A. J. S. Langford of Nuffield Exports Ltd.

In Canada, the MGA was shipped in largely fully assembled form; here an early car for the market is inspected by a Canadian dealer.

CKD AND SKD MARKETS

The countries where these export methods were used are as follows:

Completely Knocked Down (CKD):
Australia: Pressed Metal Corporation factory in Enfield (Sydney).
Cuba: Three known, two with pushrod engines and the other a Twin Cam. Uniquely the cars for Cuba, though shipped as 'CKD', had fully assembled and painted bodies because the local agent had no suitable facilities to build up and finish bodies. These limited exports, such as they were, ceased with the Cuban revolution in August 1959.
Holland (Netherlands): Molenaar Automobielen (J. J. Molenaar) in Amersfoort.

Canadian marketing in Toronto for the 1956 Model Year.

Parker Whiteway spotted this MGA at the Necropolis Cristobal in the spring of 2018 whilst visiting Cuba – evidently a sixty-year survivor from before the 1959 revolution! Note the black-painted chromework, five-stud wheels (which at first glance look quite like Twin Cam wheels), and even a home-made replacement for the elliptical scuttle grille. The hardtop appears to be missing its back window.

PARKER WHITEWAY

Ireland (Eire): Booth Poole & Co. Limited, Dublin.
Mexico: Automóviles Ingleses SA, Mexico City.
Philippines: Sixteen believed to have been assembled by 'Commercial Motors' of Manila from 'SKD' kits.
Republic of South Africa: Motor Assemblies Limited of Durban.

Semi Knocked Down (SKD):
Canada: Morris Motors (Canada) Ltd, Hamilton, Ontario.
New Zealand: Dominion Motors of Auckland (modest numbers; the first car was HDK 23-14652, an Orient Red MGA 1500 Roadster despatched on 11 May 1956 for the Invercargill Motor Show in New Zealand's South Island).

Why Not the USA?

Bearing in mind the size and importance of the United States as a major market for the MGA, one might fairly ask why, if local assembly arrangements worked elsewhere, it was not considered for the biggest sports-car market of all. There are several reasons for this: first, the complexity of the BMC/Hambro contractual arrangements, where Hambro took in effect a commission on sales of the imported goods, would not have sat easily with a local assembly operation. Second, the USA needs to be appreciated in terms of the vast continental spread across from coast to coast, and arguably splitting east and west coast sales would reduce the benefits of a US assembly plant in, presumably, one or other of those locations.

Finally the most obvious disincentive was the simple fact that import taxes on the MGs were nothing like as great in the USA as in many other countries; in the words of Michael Dale, who gradually took on roles of growing seniority in the BMC and later BLMC and Jaguar US business, 'import taxes into the US were negligible so it wasn't worth the candle'. In fact Dale had other thoughts on the whole CKD business: 'I was the factory representative for Latin America for a couple of years and we had a bunch of CKD factories operating. I doubt we ever had a single CKD pack with everything in it!'

Even though full CKD kit assembly in the United States was not pursued, cars were shipped with the windscreens removed to allow the cars to be stacked within the ship hold inside the simple timber frames fixed around them at the special Nuffield Exports facility at Cowley. Factory data on overall CKD totals for each MGA type is set out in the relevant preceding chapters; additional information, especially for the Twin Cam, is provided below where known.

CANADA

The need for dollars was a recurring factor in the period immediately after the war: as with the USA, this pressure also played out in the Canadian market, where the Austin Motor Company had made firm plans to build cars at Hamilton, at the western end of Lake Ontario, buying land and beginning to fit out the plant (where the MGA would later be assembled) in 1948, with ground-works and factory erection all swiftly in train. However, on 19 February 1949, the company announced – to obvious consternation from many Canadian politicians – that there had been a sudden about-face:

> The Austin Motor Company, which announced last autumn its intention to open an assembly plant at Hamilton, Ontario, to serve the Canadian and American markets, is to reconsider the scheme because of the continued need for dollar earnings. The company says that since the project was announced the necessity for exporting to Canada and America has become more vital than ever, and in the interests of dollar earning it is undesirable that Canadian or American material of any kind should be used in the manufacture of British cars.

It is known that a lot of preparatory work had already been undertaken by the time of this change of heart, which at least had the benefit of ensuring that the generously sized Hamilton facility was well equipped by the time that SKD work on the MGA did begin.

MGAs bound for Canada (where the BMC set-up was entirely separate from the Hambro arrangements south of the Canadian border) were processed via Nuffield Exports and shipped to their destination across the Atlantic and down the St Lawrence Seaway into Lake Ontario. Upon arrival at Morris Motors (Canada) Limited, the cars would be processed and reunited with their wheels, windscreen and any other missing items, prior to onward distribution across the country; those for the west of Canada generally went by train via Winnipeg.

BOOTH POOLE AND THE IRISH MGA

In the Irish Republic there were benefits in building MGs locally to meet the modest but regular demand and at the same time avoid the punitive import taxes on new cars, and by the time of the MGA there were three businesses with links to what had already become BMC, namely Brittains (Morris and Riley), Lincoln and Nolan (Austin and Austin-Healey cars and commercial vehicles) and Booth Poole (MG, Wolseley and Morris Commercial).

In the 1950s Booth Poole & Co. Ltd, of Liffey Bank, Islandbridge in Dublin, came about through a partnership between Lionel Booth and Billy Poole; the company took in CKD crates from Cowley and turned them into vehicles for sale across Ireland, from Dublin to Cork. The business also had a distributorship at

William Poole of Booth Poole was the charismatic man behind the Irish assembly of MGs including the MGA, MGA Twin Cam, and later, the MGB.
ALEC POOLE

Conyngham Road in Dublin. In this period, Booth Poole were the sole importers of MG and Wolseley cars, Morris Commercial vans and trucks, also Guy, Foden, Dennis trucks and Nuffield tractors throughout the Republic of Ireland.

Lionel O. Booth (12 June 1914–31 May 1997) was originally a solicitor in Dublin, but became both an Irish Fianna Fáil politician and a businessman. Having been educated at Wesley College in Ballinteer, Dublin, Booth first entered politics in the 1950s, serving on both Dublin County Council and Dún Laoghaire Corporation. He was unusual in Eire politics in being a Protestant. He became joint managing director of Booth Poole & Company Limited in 1956, and fourteen years later, became managing director of the Brittain Group of Portabello, Dublin (this company having in the meantime bought both Lincoln and Nolan and Booth & Poole).

Booth Poole was run by Booth's partner Billy Poole (1 September 1908–13 February 1988), who was responsible for manufacturing and sales, while Booth looked after service and his political duties. According to his son Alec, Billy Poole was 'one of those larger-than-life motor industry characters who had the freedom in those post World War II years to develop their businesses the way they wanted'.

An example Alec gives is his father's love of golf, and his ability to mix it with business:

> In Ireland golf has always been an everyman's game. Billy always had a young scratch golfer on the books as a salesman so the pair would turn up and play as complete bandits in the many motor trade golf outings. The same salesman would caddy for him in his golf forays to Sunningdale in the UK. He also made sure Booth Poole always had an MGA (and later an MGB) demonstrator on the books. Another salesman would be allocated the task of driving it in all Irish races and hillclimbs – back then there was no permanent race track in Ireland so they were all closed road events.

The first four MGAs rolled out of Booth Poole's premises in January 1956, an impressive feat for a car only four months on the market. The first chassis number in this sequence was 11571 and the last 11574; these were in fact the first MGA CKD chassis numbers. As Alec Poole explains:

> Assembly has connotations of getting a trimmed bodyshell and fitting the running gear. However, the whole process was much more comprehensive than that. In the earlier days of separate chassis construction the running gear would be assembled on to it to build up a rolling chassis, while the body would be built in parallel on a master jig, finished and painted before fitment, trimming, finishing and so on. The sports-car MG models such as TDs, TFs and MGAs were built in this way.

To assist pricing, Booth Poole were encouraged to use locally manufactured content where possible, such as tyres, glass, trim, batteries, and spark plugs on some models. The company was issued a batch of chassis number plates with each consignment of sets of car components in a container. Alec Poole says that Nuffield Exports did not specify which engine numbers should be paired with which chassis plate, but on build completion, Booth Poole recorded these combinations, together with body colours and any relevant data on their control ledger. 'This data was necessary for issuing build certificates for road registration. At the time these records were vital to the business, but nobody thought back then they would be of interest to anybody else with the passage of time!'

Alec Poole recalls the Booth Poole business had a very close working relationship with Nuffield Exports in Cowley and the MG Car Company in Abingdon:

> At that time brand loyalty was everything, and it is fair to say all parties treated each other like family. We liked to think with static build, quality wise we had more time to do it right, with details like increasing the number of spot welds and so forth. We built between fifty and sixty vehicles a week. Back then Dad thought he chose the colours but in reality it was Mum, without him realising it.

Whilst customers could probably specify more or less any colour scheme for their MGA, subject to Mrs Poole's approval, the upholstery remained leather, as in home-market cars.

Alec recalls times when people visited the assembly plant: 'They would ask Billy how many people worked there – Dad's standard answer was always – "About half of them".' Like many competent offspring of well-placed car businessmen, Poole's son Alec would later go on to pursue an apprenticeship at Morris Commercial (who generally took a dozen apprentices a year) and formed a firm friendship with his contemporary, Syd Enever's son Roger, the two of them also being passionate about car racing in the 1960s.

One of the customers who acquired an Irish-built MGA was Hamish Riley-Smith, whose father bought it for him. Riley-Smith says that the colour was originally 'Tartan Green', but within a year someone hit the back of the car when he was driving over to Dublin and so he had it resprayed gold. Trips across to Ireland in those days involved some excitement at

Hamish Riley-Smith was give this Dublin-built MGA for his twenty-first birthday; by the time of this photo, in 1964, it had been resprayed gold from its original green finish.
HAMISH RILEY-SMITH

Riley-Smith's Dublin-assembled MGA was used by its proud owner until family needs meant a sports car was no longer practical.
HAMISH RILEY-SMITH

the dockside too: 'In order to take a car on the Fishguard–Rosslaire overnight boat, the car was loaded on by net!'

The photographs seen here date from the early 1960s. Fortunately the car still survives and has been owned by Mr John Follet for many years. Equally remarkable is that Riley-Smith still has the original invoice.

Rarer still was the Booth Poole-assembled MGA Twin Cam, of which there were at least eight, and of course problems with customer cars brought Bob Seymour from Nuffield Exports to attend to them, as explained in Chapter 6.

Known chassis numbers are as follows:

THE MGA TWIN CAMS ASSEMBLED BY BOOTH POOLE & CO LTD

Chassis Number	Start Build (MG)	Finish Build/Despatch (MG)	Trim Colour	Hood Colour	Notes
YDH5-1039	1 January 1959	9 January 1959	Black	Black	Survives in South Africa
YDH5-1040	1 January 1959	9 January 1959	Black	Black	
YDH5-1041	1 January 1959	9 January 1959	Red	Black	Recorded in MG Development Department Records as being 'in the shop' at Abingdon on 6 June 1960
YDH5-1042	1 January 1959	9 January 1959	Red	Black	Recorded as scrapped
YDH5-1153	23 January 1959	30 January 1959	Black	Black	Recorded as scrapped
YDH5-1154	23 January 1959	30 January 1959	Black	Black	
YDH5-1155	23 January 1959	30 January 1959	Green	Black	
YDH5-1156	23 January 1959	30 January 1959	Green	Black	

Footnotes:
Body paint finishes were understandably not recorded at Nuffield Exports because they were applied at the assembling factory in Dublin. One of the cars listed as scrapped may be the one which became the basis of the 'Phoenix Special' (*see* main text). The four cars YDH5-1153 to 1156 immediately followed another group of four Twin Cams (YDH5-1149 to 1152) that were shipped to South Africa.

Alec Poole recalls that Robin Rennicks was his father's 'racing' salesman, and one day an MGA Twin Cam caught fire in the workshop (Alec wonders if this might be one of the Twin Cams listed in the table as being scrapped). Rennicks bought it from the insurance company; according to Alec Poole:

> As most of the damage was cosmetic, he re-clothed it in aluminium panelling as an open wheeler – a bit like a Lotus 7. Unlike some other references to it I have seen, I would not describe the Phoenix Special as crude: it was light and practical. Robin met Bob Olthoff, who raced what was the fastest of Twin Cams, because he worked at that time for Syd Enever in the Development Department at Abingdon. With Bob's help the Phoenix Special was a very quick and effective bit of kit.

There is more about Bob Olthoff in Chapter 10.

Marc van Zoest owns this rare Mexican-assembled MGA Twin Cam (YDH6-2535); the chassis plate in the engine bay has a YDH5 prefix that should really have been YDH6.
MARC VAN ZOEST

MEXICO CITY AND THE MGA

Automóviles Ingleses SA, Mexico City, was established in November 1946 and contracted to build small numbers of imported CKD cars over the following decade. The MGA was a good candidate because of its method of construction and sporting character, and so the first four CKD kits of MGA 1500 Roadsters were shipped from Cowley in January 1956 (chassis nos 11575 to 11578, following on directly after the Irish MGAs referred to above).

WHAT BECAME OF BOOTH POOLE?

The Booth Poole & Co. Ltd business thrived for years, even after the end of the MGA; they built a whole range of MGs, from Magnette saloons, MG 1100s and MG 1300s (both two- and four-door), TDs, TFs, MGAs, Midgets and MGBs (Tourer and GT). According to Alec Poole: 'Indeed, at a rough guess we must have made upwards of 2,000 MGs, with 200 of them MGBs.' As well as an interest in golf, the Pooles had a soft spot for fishing: 'Billy even had a fuelled-up loan car put aside for any BMC employees in the UK who wanted to go fishing in Ireland – a sport that was totally unspoilt back then.'

'With Billy's interest in motor sport, and his very close relationship with the MG factory, it was no surprise that Booth Poole built some early MGA Twin Cams. Later, to fly the flag, he bought the ex-Paddy Hopkirk/Andrew Hedges 1965 Le Mans 24-Hour class-winning MGB when the Comps Department had finished with it.' Alec Poole remembers driving a Booth Poole-built MGB in 1967 to the Targa Florio as a practice car for the Factory Team to help them learn the circuit, the car being driven there by Timo, Rauno, Paddy and Andy Hedges as well as Alec Poole himself. Alec Poole recollects:

> *We had a close relationship in the BMC family back then – indeed, even though Austin-Healey was not a Booth Poole agency, I had a really good rapport with Donald Healey, Geoff and Brian – and drove for them with Roger at Sebring and Le Mans. For Healey's part, they could have seen Roger as a thorn in their side because of his dad's position in MG as regards getting new prototype sports cars approved by Austin for production, but it was quite the opposite.*
>
> *But we knew the good times wouldn't last forever, and when British Leyland took control of BMC in the late Sixties companies like Booth Poole who were totally wedded to their brands had no independent future. They were taken over by the Brittain Group in the early Seventies, who had the Morris, Austin and Riley franchises, but they too suffered the same fate as BL faded. On the nostalgia front and pride in the product, many years later the Booth Poole MGB assembly jig found its way to British Motor Heritage Ltd and has been responsible for the manufacture of thousands of new bodyshells, including the MG RV8 to this day.*

Van Zoest's Twin cam was probably assembled in Mexico in 1960 (it left the UK in November 1959) and was one of twenty-four Twin Cams assembled by Automóviles Ingleses SA in Mexico City. The company later went on to become the basis of Mexico's VW business.
MARC VAN ZOEST

Records indicate that a total of 376 CKD sets were shipped to Mexico – although as the section on Australian CKD production below shows, at least two batches originally intended for Mexico were diverted to Australia. As the table here shows, the factory later took a number of Twin Cams, all of them with the normally optional 4.55:1 'competition' rear axle ratio.

The business was later bought by two prominent Mexican businessmen (Ernesto Krause and Rómulo o'Farril Snr) who were behind the first series manufacture of Volkswagens in Mexico in 1962, the business becoming, in 1964, 'Volkswagen de México SA de CV'. Unsurprisingly this would go on to become a major Mexican success story, whilst the local assembly of BMC-family products largely evaporated – an all-too-familiar story.

THE PHILIPPINES

In the Philippines, domestic taxes were imposed on luxury goods such as cars in the wake of World War II, and this encouraged a fledgling assembly business; amongst the early operators a local business, Commercial Motors Ltd (based in Manila), better known for the import and assembly of Mercedes-Benz. Although another company (Fabar) is known to have assembled some BMC models (mostly Austins) this arrangement did not begin until 1962, by which time, of course, the MGA was discontinued.

THE MGA TWIN CAMS ASSEMBLED IN MEXICO – Automóviles Ingleses SA, Mexico City

Chassis Number	Start Build (MG)	Finish Build/Despatch (MG)	Trim Colour	Hood Colour	Notes
YDH6-2524	23 October 1959	30 October 1959	Red	Grey	
YDH6-2525	23 October 1959	30 October 1959	Red	Grey	
YDH6-2526	23 October 1959	30 October 1959	Red	Grey	
YDH6-2527	23 October 1959	30 October 1959	Red	Grey	
YDH6-2528	23 October 1959	30 October 1959	Red	Grey	
YDH6-2529	23 October 1959	30 October 1959	Red	Grey	
YDH6-2530	23 October 1959	30 October 1959	Red	Grey	
YDH6-2531	23 October 1959	30 October 1959	Red	Grey	
YDH6-2532	2 November 1959	6 November 1959	Black	Blue	
YDH6-2533	2 November 1959	6 November 1959	Black	Blue	
YDH6-2534	2 November 1959	6 November 1959	Black	Blue	
YDH6-2535	2 November 1959	6 November 1959	Black	Blue	Owned (2018) by Marc van Zoest
YDH6-2567	11 January 1960	15 January 1960	Red	Beige	
YDH6-2568	11 January 1960	15 January 1960	Red	Beige	
YDH6-2569	11 January 1960	15 January 1960	Red	Beige	
YDH6-2570	11 January 1960	15 January 1960	Red	Beige	
YDH6-2587	25 January 1960	29 January 1960	Black	Blue	
YDH6-2588	25 January 1960	29 January 1960	Black	Blue	
YDH6-2589	25 January 1960	29 January 1960	Black	Blue	
YDH6-2590	25 January 1960	29 January 1960	Black	Blue	
YDH6-2591	24 February 1960	11 March 1960	Beige	Grey	
YDH6-2592	24 February 1960	11 March 1960	Beige	Grey	
YDH6-2593	24 February 1960	11 March 1960	Beige	Grey	
YDH6-2594	24 February 1960	11 March 1960	Beige	Grey	

Footnotes:
Body paint finishes were not recorded at the factory because these were applied at the assembling factory. Mexican cars were supplied with a 4.55:1 rear axle ratio. Many of these cars (for example Marc van Zoest's car, YDH6-2535) appear to have been assigned 'YDH5' chassis numbers, seemingly in error. 'Blue' hood colour is 'Ice Blue'.

It appears that Commercial Motors took in around sixteen CKD (more likely SKD) kits, the chassis numbers being 15596 to 15603, and either 24806 to 24813 or 24814 to 24821 (Garry Kemm, who has researched the subject, says that the records are not clear as to which the latter batch was). Little more is known about the assembly or the ultimate fate of these cars, although it seems feasible that some were acquired by overseas visitors, who may have subsequently exported some of them.

THE MGA DOWN UNDER: ASSEMBLY IN SYDNEY

Lord Nuffield had a great fondness for Australia, and for much of his career invested time, effort and money in trying to expand his influence and operations in the market. It is not necessarily hard to see why Australia had such appeal for him: the modern frontier spirit of a youthful country, less wedded to the prejudices and mannerisms of the 'old country', and yet imbued with fond nostalgia for the best aspects of 'home' meant that there were great opportunities to be grasped for the entrepreneurially minded businessman.

Craig Watson describes this photo, taken inside the main Car Assembly Building at Pressed Metal Corporation, Enfield, in about 1959: 'On the left are Morris JB vans, then comes the MGA line, and on the right are Austin A55 utilities (pick-ups), which were unique to PMC. The A55s and MGAs are mounted on "skuks", temporary chassis on trolleys for moving the vehicles along the line until painted. An MGA skuk is in the foreground of the photo. The toilets are on the far right, with the Paint Shop beyond. Final assembly was in the other end of the plant, behind the camera.'

CRAIG WATSON

Nuffield himself increasingly enjoyed long cruises to Australia, and whilst there set out to forge new alliances, often as far as possible without what he doubtless viewed as 'interference' from the Board back home, in an era long before the immediacy of the internet and emails. Exports from the UK to the 'old' so-called 'Empire' markets such as Australia were highly important in a time before local governments resorted to high import taxes as a way of encouraging indigenous car manufacture – but even as it became commercially expedient, the likes of Austin, Morris and Standard Triumph either built their own factories 'down under' or entered into productive arrangements with local companies.

By the time the MGA was ready to be introduced to the Australian market, BMC's local operation had a factory at Joynton Avenue in Zetland, a suburb of Sydney, where Austin, Morris and Wolseley cars were assembled using a mix of local and imported components. As a lower volume sports car, reliant significantly on crates of body components and some other items shipped out from Cowley, the MGA was sub-contracted out to the Pressed Metal Corporation in Cosgrove Road, Enfield (New South Wales), a facility part-owned by Larke Consolidated Industries.

Craig Watson, who researched their story, told the author that Larke Consolidated Industries had been originally set up, completed in 1952, as a joint venture between Larke Hoskins ('Larke Hoskins Consolidated Industries' was established in 1953) and Larke, Neave and Carter (LN&C, a related company that was the NSW agent for Chrysler), with a new company, Pressed Metal Corporation (PMC), set up to manage Enfield. PMC was 70 per cent owned by Larke Hoskins and 30 per cent by LN&C. Rover contracted PMC to assemble Land Rovers and Rover cars for all the Australian market from 1957, as they were not happy with the varying quality of vehicles assembled by distributors in different states.

An MGA body is united with its chassis on the final assembly line in the southern end of the Enfield factory.

CRAIG WATSON

After trial building and the creation of suitable jigs and fixtures, the PMC facility was ready to begin building MGAs from the crates of CKD components – but hardly in large numbers. A batch of just eight CKD MGA kits was shipped from Cowley on 27 July 1956, and it would be reasonable to assume that they were being unpacked and used for trial assembly by the end of the year. It is believed that these eight cars were shipped without engines, which would support the fact that when they were eventually sold in late 1957, their engine numbers were later than might have been expected for the summer of 1956 (*see* the table on page 190, 'The first eight Australian MGA CKD cars').

When production did get under way, it was initially at a rate of three a day, later peaking at around six to eight, but never in the kind of volume seen at Abingdon. Australian MGA historian Garry Kemm points out that when averaged out over the five years of Australian MGA production the rate comes out at no more than ten a week. The crates did not hold all the relevant parts for a single car; instead a crate might hold the chassis parts for four cars and four sets of other parts for those same cars, and another would have sets of tightly packed body panels. Suspension parts were also shipped in this way, as were engine blocks and heads for local assembly.

Locally sourced parts were used where feasible and cost effective; Australian MGAs naturally used local suppliers for tyres (typically Olympic, Dunlop and Goodyear), batteries, paint and some of the trim. Initially engines were built up at the BMC Zetland plant (using blocks and heads that had been machined in the UK but built up at Zetland, and then painted dark red), and were then married to their transmissions; the assemblies were sent by truck to PMC at Enfield. For the later MGA 1600 models, the engines were brought in fully assembled.

The contents of a single Nuffield Exports MGA crate; four MGA chassis and other components packed ready for boxing up and shipping to the overseas assembler. Other packs would contain body panels and mechanical components. Trim, tyres, batteries and other suitable parts were added locally.
CRAIG WATSON

Uniquely to some of the export market assembled MGAs, some gas welding was used, usually where conventional spot-welding guns could not reach, and evidence of this, along with some lead-loading of certain joints, can be a clue to the car's identity if all other evidence is missing.
CRAIG WATSON

Other changes came during production: Garry Kemm found from his extensive research that leather upholstery gave way to vinyl from March 1958, this logic being a combination of Australian government requirements, cost (savings made via government incentives for local content) and practicality: 'For the first MGA 1500s, trim and hoods were all of UK origin; trim was locally sourced after seventy-two cars (including pre-production), whilst hoods continued to be supplied from the UK for another 472 cars – in other words, for a total of 544 cars.' For simplicity, all Australian MGAs came as standard with wire wheels (an option on UK-built cars), and if a customer wanted a heater, this was usually installed by the dealer.

Whilst the Australian MGA production moved progressively from the 1500 to 1600 Mark I and finally Mark II, all the cars built were Roadsters, meaning that any Coupé sold would have been completely imported; similarly the Twin Cam was never built locally, meaning that the few Australian customers who ordered one of these new, would have borne the brunt of import taxes. Garry Kemm has established that MGA 1600 Mark II CKD crates were first shipped from Cowley for Australia on 5 April 1961, but with ample stock of Mark I parts at PMC, it seems that the first Australian Mark II was assembled in February 1962.

AUSTRALIAN MGA PRODUCTION

The first Australian CKD chassis numbers 18119 to 18126 were despatched from Cowley on 27 July 1956. These were for Pressed Metal Corporation to assemble and sort out the body jigs and any other issues prior to commencing full production twelve months later.

MGA 1500	928
MGA 1600 Mark I	964
MGA 1600 Mark II	148
Total:	2,040

AUSTRALIAN MGA CHASSIS NUMBER PREFIX FORMATS
For the first forty MGAs assembled in Australia, the 'HDH5' chassis number prefix was used; thereafter this was changed to a local prefix 'MGA/51'. The actual number was then in three parts:

The jig for the rear 'trunk floor assembly' (or the 'boot floor', if you prefer).
CRAIG WATSON

A bare MGA chassis on a timber trestle, as photographed for the assembly manual sent to CKD assemblers...
CRAIG WATSON

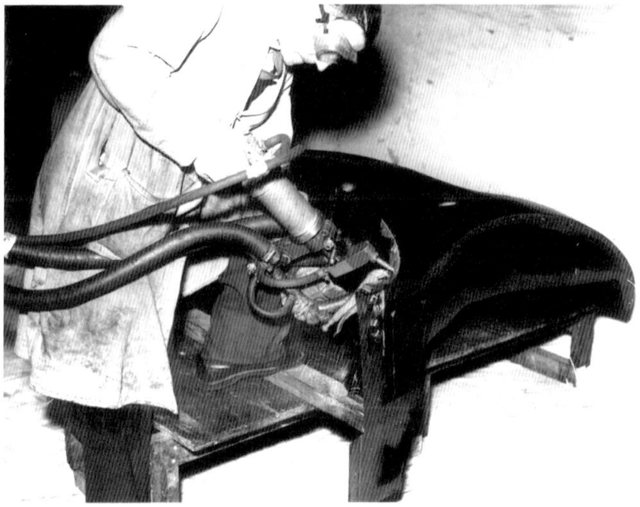

Spot welding, as here with the rear tonneau, was generally preferred where practicable.
CRAIG WATSON

...here with the body front and rear tonneau panels overlaid...
CRAIG WATSON

... and the doors and front valance fitted.
CRAIG WATSON

The **first part** was a single digit, '5', '6', '7', '8' or '9' as follows:
5 signifies December 1956 to November 1957
6 signifies December 1957 to November 1958
7 signifies December 1958 to November 1959
8 signifies December 1959 to November 1960
9 signifies December 1960 to November 1961

The **second part** was the UK-issued chassis number.

The **third part** was a locally issued number, starting at '1' for the MGA 1500 and at '501' for the MGA 1600, and also '501' for the MGA 1600 Mark II.

MGA 1500: Car type is represented by **MGA/51** ('5' indicates CKD RHD and '1' indicates enamel paint).
MGA 1600: Car type is represented by **YGHN 2**.
MGA 1600 Mark II: Car type is represented by **YGHN 3** (where **Y** = Australia; **G** = MG; **H** = 1400 to 1999cc; **N** = Two-seater tourer ('roadster'); **2** =1600; **3** = 1600 Mark II; Interestingly, the first series of MGB was also designated YGHN3 which confuses the issue).

An example of the chassis number plate that was first used on Australian CKD MGAs, in this case one of the pre-production batch of eight cars. Obviously it is of Abingdon origin and was sent with the CKD kits.
GARRY KEMM

AUSTRALIAN MGA ENGINE NUMBER FORMATS

To comply with Australian legislation, the engine blocks had to have the number stamped on them. As UK engines used alloy tags riveted to the block, these were removed from the engines on Australian cars, the numbers were stamped into the block, and then the tag would be wired on to the engine as a back-up of the actual number.

A 'Nuffield Australia' chassis plate, showing the MGA/51 model designation, the car and engine numbers, and the paint colour.
GARRY KEMM

B-series engines being mechanically bedded in. Every engine, whether imported whole or assembled locally, was mechanically bedded in. Every day sample engines were also hot-run tested to check for build quality or any problems.
CRAIG WATSON

MGA 1500: The engine number format broadly mirrors that of the UK-assembled cars, but with the addition of an extra 'A' signifying Australian engine assembly. However, when the UK-assembled cars changed to the **15GDUH** prefix (signifying the higher starter motor position – see Chapter 4), the Australian-assembled cars just continued with the **15GBUHA** prefix.
(**15** = 1.5 litres; **G** = MG; **B** = second variant of engine; **U** = central gear change; **H** = high compression; **A** = Australia)
MGA 1600: 16GA-U and 16GA-U-H prefix (as UK cars)
MGA 1600 Mark II: 16GC-U-L (as UK cars).

This plate records another exclusively Australian paint colour, Katoomba Grey, no doubt named in honour of the principal city of the Blue Mountains of New South Wales.

GREG KEENAN

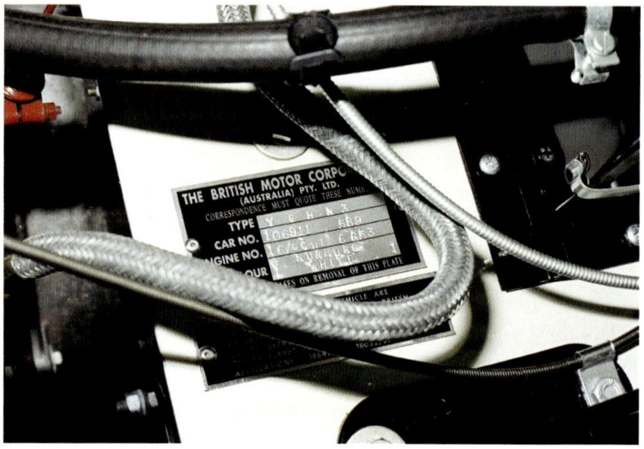

The YGHN3 model prefix used on the MGA 1600 Mark II was rather confusingly carried over to the early MGBs assembled in Australia.

GARRY KEMM

AUSTRALIAN MGA PAINT COLOURS

MGA 1500:

Bardiman Grey
Billeroy Blue
Carnation Red
Miran Green (later Guan Green)
Mamba Black

MGA 1600 *(pre mid-1960)***:** As MGA 1500 above

MGA 1600 *(mid-1960 onwards)***:**

Nurburg White
Monza Red (effectively a new name for Carnation Red)
Mamba Black
British Racing Green

MGA 1600 *(from late 1961)***:**

Nurburg White
Monza Red
Mamba Black
British Racing Green
Aintree Green
Katoomba Grey

MGA 1600 Mark II:

Nurburg White
Monza Red
Mamba Black
Aintree Green
Katoomba Grey

Paint was supplied by Balm (Dulux).

THE FIRST EIGHT AUSTRALIAN MGA 1500 'CKD' CARS

Chassis no. HDH5-	Body Colour if known	Trim Colour	Hood Colour	CSO No.	UK Body Number	Engine No.BP15GB-	CKD Code	Date Delivered	Original State
18119	White	Red	Black	833	Not known	13336	18A	4 October 1957	NSW
18120	White	Red	Black	834	Not known	13372	18A	31 October 1957	NSW
18121	Red	Red	Black	835	Not known	13378	18A	13 September 1957	NSW
18122	Red	Red	Black	836	28440	13353	18A	30 July 1957	QLD
18123	Green	Grey	Blue	837	Not known	13334	18B	18 July 1957	QLD
18124	Haze Blue	Grey	Blue	838	Not known	13306	18B	31 July 1957	NSW
18125	Not known	Grey	Blue	839	Not known	Not known	18B	Not known	Not known
18126	Haze Blue	Grey	Blue	840	28528	13285	18B	8 November 1957	NSW

Footnotes:

For these first eight cars (all Roadsters; Australia never received CKD Coupés), the chassis commencement date (from Cowley's CKD department) was 27 July 1956, and the dispatch date was the same day. The author is grateful to MG enthusiast Garry Kemm for this information; gaps in the table indicate information as yet unknown. The specification of these cars is described as 'CKD/2/EX R' – changed from 'CKD/2/M18A/18B', which is interesting as it shows that these cars had been diverted from Mexico, the clue being the codes, which can be translated as follows:

CKD/2/EX R – CKD; EX R = export, right-hand drive; CKD/2/M 18A/18B – CKD; M = Mexico; 18A = Pack 18A; 18B = Pack 18B. As Garry Kemm notes 'Each pack comprised components for four cars, so for reasons unknown the eighteenth delivery earmarked for Mexico was reassigned for delivery to Australia.' The body colour references such as 'Haze Blue', 'White', 'Red' and 'Green' are believed to be initial references that probably pre-date the formal assignment of names for the colours concerned; 'Haze Blue' was not used again as a colour name and is likely to have been what was later known as 'Billeroy Blue' (*see* paint colour information above). Routine CKD deliveries to Australia commenced almost a year after the first batches – that is, in July 1957 as described in the text.

The immaculate engine bay of Garry Kemm's Australian-built Nurburg White MGA 1600 Mark II.
GARRY KEMM

Garry Kemm's own Australian-assembled MGA 1600 Mark II is finished in the popular local colour, Nurburg White
GARRY KEMM

THE SECOND FIVE SHIPMENTS TO AUSTRALIA

After the initial batch of eight cars shown in the table, the next five shipments from the Cowley KD Department (each comprising sixteen cars per shipment) were as follows:

Date dispatched	Order of assembly
1 July 1957	fourth
9 July 1957	first
18 July 1957	third
24 July 1957	second
26 July 1957	fifth

Thus five batches, each comprising sixteen cars, were sent to Australia in less than four weeks. Garry Kemm speculates:

> There are probably a number of reasons why these batches were not assembled in order. Firstly the small cargo ships of that era would take varying amounts of time to complete the journey to Sydney due to weather, other ports of call en route, dock worker strikes, and so on. Also, once the crates were delivered to PMC, Enfield, they may not have been opened in order of receipt.

Note that on an Australian MGA 1600 Mark II, the facia was still left in body colour, unlike the contemporary home-market equivalent.
GARRY KEMM

THE SECOND FOUR BATCHES OF FOUR AUSTRALIAN MGA 1500 'CKD' CARS

Chassis no. HDH5-	Actual Body Colour if known	Trim Colour	Hood Colour	CSO No.	UK Body Number	Engine No.BP15GB-	CKD Code	Date Delivered	Original State
33806	Blue	Red	Black	23582	Not known	24537	3A	13 October 1957	VIC
33807	Blue	Red	Black	23583	Not known	24528	3A	23 October 1957	NSW
33808	Blue	Red	Black	23584	Not known	24530	3A	Not known	QLD
33809	Not known	Red	Black	23585	Not known	Not known	3A	Not known	Not known
33810	Black	Red	Black	23586	Not known	24378	3B	Not known	QLD
33811	Black	Red	Black	23587	Not known	24387	3B	25 October 1957	NSW
33812	Not known	Red	Black	23588	Not known	20853	3B	Not known	VIC
33813	Not known	Red	Black	23589	44384	24280	3B	Not known	Not known
33814	Black	Grey	Blue	23590	43895	Not known	3C	Not known	WA
33815	Red	Grey	Blue	23591	Not known	24379	3C	Not known	QLD
33816	Not known	Grey	Blue	23592	Not known	Not known	3C	Not known	Not known
33817	Black	Grey	Blue	23593	Not known	24395	3C	15 November 1957	NSW
33818	Black	Grey	Blue	23594	Not known	24323	3D	Not known	NSW
33819	Not known	Grey	Blue	23595	Not known	Not known	3D	Not known	Not known
33820	Not known	Grey	Blue	23596	Not known	24398	3D	30 October 1957	QLD
33821	Black	Grey	Blue	23597	Not known	24521	3D	Not known	NSW

Footnotes:

The chassis commencement date for all the above cars was 5 July 1957, and the despatch date was 9 July 1957.

The specification of these cars is described as CKD/2/A RHD, with the CKD Codes '3A', '3B', '3C' and '3D' for each batch of four cars (*see* table). The trim and hood colours in the third and fourth columns are as supplied and not necessarily as used; for example it is unlikely that a blue-painted car was built with red seats.

THE AUSTRALIAN MGA 'CKD' – THE FIRST BATCHES OF MGA 1600

Chassis no. YGHN2-	Actual Body Colour if known	Trim Colour	CSO No.	Car No.	UK Abingdon Body No.	Engine No. 16GAU	CKD Code	Date Delivered	Original State (Registration Number)
68904	Guan Green	Tan	30759	505	B21	114	71A	Not known	VIC (HCK 266)
68905	Mamba Black	Red	30760	506	B27	166	71A	4 December 1959	Not known
68906	Mamba Black	Red	30761	507	B26	201	71A	4 December 1959	WA
68907	Mamba Black	Red	30762	508	Not known	139	71A	2 December 1959	NSW
68908	Not known	Not known	30763	501	Not known	260	71B	Not known	VIC (HCA 242)
68909	Guan Green	Tan	30764	502	B23	174	71B	Not known	VIC (HCH 292)
68910	Not known	Not known	30765	503	Not known	250	71B	Not known	VIC (HCF 988)
68911	Guan Green	Tan	30766	504	B21	162	71B	Not known	VIC (HCA 849)

Footnotes:

The chassis commencement date for all the above cars was 21 May 1959, and the despatch date was 5 June 1959. The specification of these cars is described as CKD/2/A RHD, with the CKD Codes '71A' and '71B' for both batches of four cars (*see* table).

Occasionally the Australian-built MGAs, with their own local differences, were subjected to road tests by the local media, typically *Sports Car World*. Most memorably, Pedr Davis visited the Pressed Metal Corporation plant to see the MGA assembly operation for himself, and produced a comprehensive write-up for the *Sports Car World* issue of February 1958. At the time of his visit, Davis learned that PMC were building thirty-two other vehicles as well as the new MGA within the total plant area of 20 acres (8ha), which included what he was told was an 'ultramodern' £250,000 paint shop.

Davis described the Australian build process in some detail, and his article concluded by recording the end of the process, where:

> ...a group of inspectors give it a thorough workout, testing and checking that everything works. Once they are satisfied, the sparkling new MGA is handed over to the road

THE AUSTRALIAN MGA 'CKD' – FIRST BATCHES OF MGA 1600 MARK II

Chassis no. YGHN3-	Actual Body Colour if known	Trim Colour	CSO No.	Car No.	Engine No. 16GCUL	CKD Code	Date Delivered if known	Original State (Registration Number)
100403	Not known	Not known	65663	506	109	1	7 June 1962	VIC (HOO 648)
100404	Aintree Green	Tan	65664	502	108	1	Not known	Not known
100405	Nurburg White	Red	65665	Not known	111	1	2 May 1962	VIC (HNP 721)
100406	Nurburg White	Red	65666	504	114	1	28 May 1962	VIC (HNY 987)
100407	Nurburg White	Red	65667	507	112	1	Not known	NSW
100408	Not known	Not known	65668	514	101	1	4 May 1962	VIC (HNU 065)
100409	Not known	Not known	65669	508	Not known	1	Not known	VIC
100410	Not known	Not known	65670	Not known	Not known	1	Not known	Not known
100411	Not known	Not known	65671	503	105	1	25 September 1962	VIC (HOZ 641)
100412	Monza Red	Black	65672	512	107	1	Not known	SA
100413	Aintree Green	Tan	65673	501	106	1	Not known	NSW (BQZ 660)
100414	Not known	Not known	65674	Not known	Not known	1	Not known	Not known
100415	Not known	Not known	65675	Not known	Not known	2	Not known	Not known
100416	Not known	Not known	65676	Not known	Not known	2	Not known	Not known
100417	Not known	Not known	65677	Not known	Not known	2	Not known	Not known
100418	Not known	Not known	65678	516	122	2	4 May 1962	VIC (HNJ 223)
100419	Not known	Not known	65679	Not known	Not known	2	Not known	Not known
100420	Not known	Not known	65680	510	Not known	2	Not known	Not known
100421	Not known	Not known	65681	520	118	2	6 June 1962	VIC (HOC 409)
100422	Not known	Not known	65682	Not known	Not known	2	Not known	Not known
100423	Not known	Not known	65683	519	119	2	10 July 1962	VIC (HOO 697)
100424	Not known	Not known	65684	513	125	2	Not known	Not known
100425	Not known	Not known	65685	518	120	2	18 May 1962	VIC (HNW 997)
100426	Not known	Not known	65686	Not known	Not known	2	Not known	Not known

Footnotes:
Cars 100403 to 100414 inclusive were the first sequence, and chassis build commenced on 5 April 1961. Despatch date was 5 May 1961.
Cars 100415 to 100426 inclusive comprised the second sequence, and chassis build commenced on 11 April 1961. Despatch date was 5 May 1961, the same as the first sequence.

The specification for these cars was CKD/2/A RHD (see footnotes to previous table for explanation). Garry Kemm comments that 'There were twenty-four in total, and the UK factory must have been very keen to get some into Australia as Abingdon had only assembled fifty cars before the next twenty-four were assigned for Australia. Head office in the UK obviously did not know of the back-log of unsold 1600s ('Mark I'), or were unconcerned. There wasn't really any hurry to send these CKD Mark II kits to Australia, as the first one was not assembled until February 1962. Also there are some very early engine numbers including the very first 1622, 16GCUL 101.'

tester. Thus is born a new sports car. What we can describe in half an hour has taken a group of specialized enthusiasts a full Martian day and has absorbed to the full the vast resources of a huge organization.

Despite the imminent arrival on the market of the MGB, *Sports Car World* subjected an MGA 1600 Mark II to a road test for its August 1962 issue, and the write-up was generally favourable. Because of the retention of the lower 8.3:1 compression ratio for Australia, the power and torque were down slightly on equivalent models for other markets (for example, 84.6bhp at 5,650rpm and 98lb ft at 3,450rpm), and so too were top speed (102mph/164km/h) and acceleration (0–60mph took 14.5sec).

Comparison of these figures with those in the previous chapter shows a loss of 3mph on top speed and 1.7sec on the 0–60mph figure in comparison with those achieved by *Road & Track* in their Los Angeles test car. Photos accompanying the article clearly confirmed that the interior of the Australian MGA 1600 Mark II retained a painted facia without the vinyl covering adopted for cars fully assembled in the UK.

THE SOUTH AFRICAN MGA

South Africa, like Australia, has long been a good market for British cars, and the MGA formed part of the local assembly story. The first CKD kits were shipped out just before Christmas 1956, and having arrived at the Motor Assemblies Plant in Durban, were built up into the first locally assembled MGAs in February 1957.

Motor Assemblies had a history of contract building foreign cars, not only from the Nuffield Group but also Standard Triumph, Volvo and Chrysler products (including not only Chryslers but also the Dodge, DeSoto and Plymouth

Production of the MGA Twin Cam in South Africa began in February 1959; at this gathering in Durban, presumably some time afterwards, Sir Leonard Lord can be seen at the left. Also in the photo are Gordon Henderson and Clive Mitchell, the drivers of an MGA Twin Cam (Race No. 3 – YM2 554), and Barrie Thomas and Scotty Greig (who drove car No. 6 – YDH5 878) in the 1959 Roy Hesketh Six-Hour race of 28 March 1959. YM2 554, a black coupé, also served as a main dealer demonstrator, and a small portion of this car can just be seen on the right-hand edge of the photo.
BO GIERSING

brands), and later would add Fiat, Lancia, Nissan, Toyota and American Motors products to the portfolio. Prior to the MGA, Motor Assemblies built a total of 345 MG TD Midgets in 1950 and 1951, but the TF was not built in South Africa.

South African MG enthusiast Brian Hogg's MGA is chassis number HDH5 23914 and has engine number 'BP15GP 14425' and was also Motor Assemblies number MGA 11. Body colour is dark green, originally with a black chassis; many long-term owners of South African-built MGAs maintain that their cars originally had chassis painted in body colour rather than the usual black.

Brian Hogg told the author that on one occasion he went to visit Motor Assemblies and met an elderly gentleman who recalled the building of the MGA: 'He recalled that the first build took several days and was a silver-coloured car assembled for the "Boss's wife" – how true this was is open to conjecture!' Brian was told by this man that the colour of the car was, apparently, up to the customer: 'This is a peculiarity that still causes some dissension amongst owners of locally assembled MGAs.'

In addition to carrying a Motor Assemblies plaque (with a serial number), there is some debate amongst South African enthusiasts who believe that the chassis were painted body colour. However, 'My MGA has a black chassis,' Brian Hogg says, adding 'I am virtually the second owner, and it also has body-colour painted wheels and wheel trims, and the engine number is stamped on the plate in the engine compartment (all or most others have it under the plate "see engine").' Brian tried without success to contact the original owner of his early South African-built MGA. Bo Giersing is firmly of the view that although the chassis as received was painted the usual black, exposed parts ended up body colour because of painting on the chassis: 'This is confirmed on CKD car No. 3, originally Old English White, now Red, but the chassis within the engine compartment is still clearly Old English White on top of the factory Black. This car has never been restored and now belongs to William Kelly in South Africa,' he told the author.

There are several other clues to the South African build of an MGA: for example, all the welding used gas welds (a technique that could lead to distortion during assembly), and clearly the small rectangular plate referred to above is another clue – assuming it survives. Bo Giersing has become something of a sleuth in these matters:

SOUTH AFRICAN MGA ASSEMBLY

Model Type	Units	Production Period					
		1957	1958	1959	1960	1961	1962
MGA 1500 Roadster	404	March 1957 to June 1958					
MGA 1600 Roadster	184			August 1959 to October 1962			
MGA 1600 Coupé	64			November 1959 to May 1961			
MGA Twin Cam Roadster	64			February 1959 to August 1961			
MGA Twin Cam Coupé	24			August 1959 to March 1961			

Footnotes:
The total number of MGAs, of all types, built in South Africa, was 740, of which 404 were MGA 1500 Roadsters; 168 were MGA 1600 Roadsters; 60 were MGA 1600 Coupés; 16 were MGA 1600 Mark II Roadsters; 4 were MGA 1600 Mark II Coupés; 60 were 'early' MGA Twin Cam Roadsters; 4 were 'late' MGA Twin Cam Roadsters; and 24 were 'late' MGA Twin Cam Coupés.

There were eighty-eight Twin Cams in total.

THE FIRST SOUTH AFRICAN MGA 1500 CKD CARS

Chassis no. HDH5-	Body Type	Trim Colour listed	Hood Colour listed	CSO Number	Motor Assemblies Ltd Number	Date	Accessories
23629	Roadster	Red	Black	15338	MGA 1	14 December 1956	LTT&B
23630	Roadster	Red	Black	15339	MGA 2	14 December 1956	LTT&B
23631	Roadster	Red	Black	15340	MGA 3	14 December 1956	LTT&B
23632	Roadster	Red	Black	15341	MGA 4	14 December 1956	LTT&B
23633	Roadster	Green	Black	15342	MGA 5	14 December 1956	LTT&B
23634	Roadster	Green	Black	15343	MGA 6	14 December 1956	LTT&B
23635	Roadster	Green	Black	15344	MGA 7	14 December 1956	LTT&B
23636	Roadster	Green	Black	15345	MGA 8	14 December 1956	LTT&B
23912	Roadster	Red	Black	15346	MGA 9	21 December 1956	LTT&B
23913	Roadster	Red	Black	15347	MGA 10	21 December 1956	LTT&B
23914	Roadster	Red	Black	15348	MGA 11	21 December 1956	LTT&B
23915	Roadster	Red	Black	15349	MGA 12	21 December 1956	LTT&B

Footnotes:
The cars were assembled in Durban at Motor Assemblies Limited's Jacobs plant. The reference to 'LTT&B' in the production ledger means 'Less Tyres, Tubes and Batteries' (some later cars were 'LTT&B&GL', which means 'Less Tyres, Tubes, Batteries and Glass') as these components would be sourced locally. Note that the trim colour listed was not necessarily the colour used in the car actually built; for example, for Brian Hogg's MGA (chassis number HDH5 23914, engine number BP15GP 14425, and Motor Assemblies number MGA 11) the body colour is dark green, originally with green trim and a black chassis, but the list above indicates that the trim allocated against that chassis number was red. The stamping of the engine number on the VIN plate ceased when the switch was made from the BP15 GB engine to the later 15GB U H engine around car number 33000, engine 23000 (for more on MGA 1500 engine numbers, see Chapter 4).

The main body panel subassemblies from Abingdon were gas welded on a sub-frame, rather than spot welded as in the UK, and then mounted on the chassis to have the panel gaps set and for painting – lots of lead filling. Colours were not recorded, but often different from the UK. Most cars were fitted with windscreen washers, and the holes for the jets were made on the outside of the wipers, rather than between the wipers as on the UK cars.

Another potential clue comes from the fact that South African MGAs had their own local body number, the so-called 'Durban body number', which was stamped on a small, slim, rectangular plate which was then screwed directly alongside the original welded-on UK body-number plate. Clearly if this special second body-number plate is missing from a car, the tell-tale presence of a pair of small holes where the screws would once have been, could point to South African provenance.

South Africa uniquely received both roadsters and coupés, and also both the conventional ohv and twin cam engines (as we have seen, neither coupés nor twin cams were shipped in CKD form to Australia, for example). Bo Giersing maintains a register of all the Twin Cams built in South Africa (eighty-eight in total) and those imported (twenty-four), of which he advises that a total of ninety-two are recorded as survivors in one form or another, an impressive 80 per cent survivor rate. Giersing points out that initially, the numbering of the South African MGA Twin Cam CKD cars was fairly orderly, but it was not to last: 'Up to about MGA number 400, the cars were built strictly in order of receipt from Abingdon in batches of four, which makes it easier to identify cars which have lost their identity.'

'Black Mamba', one of the first MGA Twin Cam Coupés built at Abingdon, with chassis number YM2-554, seen here in the McCarthy Rodway Competition Shop in February 1959. McCarthy Rodway were the MG main agents in Durban, South Africa. From left to right are Mike Compton, Peter White, Ian Mantis, Bruce Adams, Willie Holland, Derrick Hall-Jones and Trevor Coleman; the occasion was preparation for the 1959 Roy Hesketh Six-Hour race. This car was also used as the main dealer demonstrator and personal transport of the managing director Noel Horsfield.

BO GIERSING

THE FIRST SOUTH AFRICAN MGA TWIN CAM 'CKD' CARS

Chassis no. YDH5-	Actual Body Colour if known	Trim Colour listed	Hood Colour listed	Durban Body No.	Motor Assemblies Ltd Number	UK Body Number	Abingdon Despatch Date	Durban Build Date (approx)
877	Old English White	Red	Black	64150	MGA 309	68629	5 December 1958	February 1959
878	Old English White	Red	Black	Not known	MGA 310	68630	5 December 1958	February 1959
879	Ash Green	Grey	Black	Not known	[MGA 311]	[68631]	5 December 1958	February 1959
880	Ash Green	Grey	Black	64591	MGA 312	68632	5 December 1958	February 1959
927	Not known	Black	Black	Not known	[MGA 313]	[68668]	12 December 1958	February 1959
928	Glacier Blue	Black	Black	64641	MGA 314	68669	12 December 1958	February 1959
929	Old English White	Black	Black	64656	MGA 315	68667	12 December 1958	February 1959
930	Old English White	Black	Black	Not known	MGA 316	68666	12 December 1958	March 1959
935	Orient Red	Green	Blue	Not known	MGA 317	68690	19 December 1958	March 1959
936	Not known	Green	Blue	64701	MGA 318	68691	19 December 1958	March 1959
937	Not known	Green	Blue	64716	MGA 319	69689	19 December 1958	March 1959
938	Not known	Green	Blue	64731	MGA 320	68688	19 December 1958	March 1959

Footnotes:
These early cars were all Roadsters, generally produced in batches of four in the usual CKD pattern. Numbers where indicated in square brackets are where the data is believed to be correct but unknown for certain. The first MGA Twin Cam Coupé built in South Africa was YHM5-2189, with a UK build despatch date of 12 June 1959, a UK body number of B1501, a Durban build date of August 1959, and a MAL number of MGA 408. This car was also the first MGA Twin Cam to be built with the later 1600-type bodyshell world wide; it is now owned by Edward Vandyk in the UK.

After the first batch of four Twin Cam Coupés, with body numbers 61751 to 61754, the Abingdon-built sectioned Twin Cam Coupé show car, now kept at Gaydon, was fitted with body number 61755. For the last four South African MGA Twin Cams (2597 to 2600) the chassis number prefixes were YD2.

The ID plates for Bo Giersing's MGA Twin Cam YDH5 1480, a 1961 nine-hour Kyalami ex-endurance racer currently (as of 2018) undergoing restoration in South Africa. Note the so-called 'Motor Assemblies Number' on a separate plate, No. MGA 401.

BO GIERSING

After that, it seems that the MGAs did not sell as well: 'It became a bit of a jumble, last in, first out. Twin Cam Roadster numbers 2009 to 2016 left Abingdon as CKD kits in 1959, but were only built in 1961, the last one in August 1961, long after production ceased at Abingdon. This also applies to the last Twin Cam Coupés, numbers 2378 to 2381, and 2410 to 2413, of which I have 2411.' After this, Giersing notes:

A contemporary colour photograph from the time of the South African launch of the MGA Twin Cam; the car is the imported Abingdon car YD2-958 (now back in the UK), and the location is the outskirts of Durban. The noticeboard proclaims the attributes of the new model.

BO GIERSING

Neil Murray (left) and Bo Giersing pose alongside their MGA Twin Cams, YM2-554 ('Black Mamba', one of the first batch of four UK-built Twin Cam Coupés built) and the South African-built YMH5-2330, one of a later batch (2328–2331).
BO GIERSING

YM2-554 (body number 61754) was returned to road-car use after its brief sojourn on South African race circuits and is now owned by MGA enthusiast Bo Giersing, who restored it in 2003. The name 'Black Mamba' was supposedly originally given to it by Bob Olthoff, and is said to be a combination of its appearance and its sound.
BO GIERSING

Between cars numbers 2524 and 2594, a total of twenty-four roadsters all with the same specifications and 4.55 rear axles, were sent to Mexico as CKD kits [see above]. One of the last batches of RHD export cars, YD2 2597 to YD2 2600, originally presumably intended for Australia or Rhodesia, were sent as CKD kits to South Africa in 1960, recorded as YDH5 cars in the factory records, but with YD2 on the VIN plates, and finally built at Motor Assemblies in Durban in 1961, together with eight earlier Coupés and eight earlier Roadsters.

Most of these cars survive, and YD2 2600 is back in the UK with Edward Vandyk.

Intriguingly a handful of the last South African MGA Twin Cams also benefited from 1762cc engines, created using kits shipped from the UK. Amongst the last cars built, YDH5-2015 and YDH5-2016 were destined for 'in-house' customers; 2015 went to John Sully, the Managing Director of Motor Assemblies Ltd, fitted with one of the larger engines, while 2016 was specially built for George Tuck, an ex-MG man who had risen up the BMC hierarchy and at this time was

THE FIRST SOUTH AFRICAN MGA 1600 'CKD' CARS

Chassis no. GHN- or GHD-	Body Type	Trim Colour listed	Hood Colour listed	CSO Number	Motor Assemblies Ltd Number	Date	Accessories
68944	Roadster	Red	Beige	30879	MGA 437	2 June 1959	LTT&B
68945	Roadster	Red	Beige	30880	MGA 439	2 June 1959	LTT&B
68946	Roadster	Red	Beige	30881	MGA 438	2 June 1959	LTT&B
68947	Roadster	Red	Beige	30882	MGA 440	2 June 1959	LTT&B
68948	Roadster	Beige	Grey	30883	MGA 442	2 June 1959	LTT&B
68949	Roadster	Beige	Grey	30884	MGA 443	2 June 1959	LTT&B
68950	Roadster	Beige	Grey	30885	MGA 444	2 June 1959	LTT&B
68951	Roadster	Beige	Grey	30886	MGA 441	2 June 1959	LTT&B
68952	Roadster	Black	Grey	30887	MGA 461	16 June 1959	LTT&B
68953	Roadster	Black	Grey	30888	MGA 462	16 June 1959	LTT&B
68954	Roadster	Black	Grey	30889	MGA 447	16 June 1959	LTT&B
68955	Roadster	Black	Grey	30890	MGA 464	16 June 1959	LTT&B

Footnotes:
The first South African MGA 1600 was chassis no. 68944; MAL 437. The last South African MGA 1600 was a Roadster, chassis no. 100343, dated 1 March 1961 (black trim, grey hood and CSO number 65762). The MGA 1600 Mark II is detailed separately in the table below. As with UK-built cars, the 'N' in the prefix indicates a Roadster, and a 'D' a Coupé.

Another of Bo Giersing's impressive collection of MGA Twin Cams: photographed in 2018, this is the Abingdon-built YD2 2136, now almost back on the road after more than thirty years off it.

BO GIERSING

the managing director of BMC South Africa; his car was also fitted with a 1762cc engine (engine number 2260).

These cars were not completed until August 1961, and so have the distinction of being the last MGA Twin Cams built – later than Michael Ellman-Brown's UK car described at the end of Chapter 6. The last MAL number recorded for a South African MGA was MGA 744.

THE DUTCH MGA STORY

The Dutch importer for Morris and MG, J. J. Molenaar's Automobielbedrijf N.V. in Amersfoort in the province of Utrecht, imported 736 MGAs to the Netherlands during the model's seven years in production (*see* side panel). The first MGA exported to the Netherlands was a 1500, chassis number HDA43-10168; it was received by Molenaar on 6 February 1956, and was registered on 14 February with the license number TP-25-69. It was sold to a customer on 6 April 1956, and as of 2018 it is still around in The Netherlands.

Because of prevailing import taxes in the country, J. J. Molenaar's Automobielbedrijf also imported CKD kits for assembly at a separate factory. Built up and painted at the factory, many of these cars were either sold locally or exported to Belgium. The reason for this lucrative assembly and local export market is explained by Dutch MG historian Rutger Booy: 'In 1953 the Belgian government decided to stop the import of complete automobiles, and to allow only the import of PKD or CKD kits to protect their own assembly factories. An exception was made for automobiles

THE TWENTY SOUTH AFRICAN MGA 1600 MARK II 'CKD' CARS

Chassis no. GHN2- or GHD2-	Body Type	Trim Colour listed	Hood Colour listed	CSO Number	Motor Assemblies Ltd Number	Date	Accessories
100905	Roadster	Black	Grey	65841	MGA 735	26 April 1961	LTT&B
100906	Roadster	Black	Grey	65842	MGA 736	26 April 1961	LTT&B
100907	Roadster	Black	Grey	65843	MGA 737	26 April 1961	LTT&B
100908	Roadster	Black	Grey	65844	MGA 738	26 April 1961	LTT&B
100909	Roadster	Red	Grey	65854	MGA 721	27 April 1961	LTT&B
100910	Roadster	Red	Grey	65855	MGA 722	27 April 1961	LTT&B
100911	Roadster	Red	Grey	65856	MGA 723	27 April 1961	LTT&B
100912	Roadster	Red	Grey	65857	MGA 724	27 April 1961	LTT&B
100913	Coupé	Red	N/A	65881	MGA 727	27 April 1961	LTT&B
100914	Coupé	Red	N/A	65882	MGA 725	27 April 1961	LTT&B
100915	Coupé	Black	N/A	65883	MGA 726	27 April 1961	LTT&B
100916	Coupé	Black	N/A	65884	MGA 728	27 April 1961	LTT&B
101075	Roadster	Red	Grey	65849	MGA 732	4 May 1961	LTT&B
101076	Roadster	Red	Grey	65850	MGA 733	4 May 1961	LTT&B
101077	Roadster	Red	Grey	65851	MGA 735	4 May 1961	LTT&B
101078	Roadster	Red	Grey	65852	MGA 736	4 May 1961	LTT&B
101079	Roadster	Black	Grey	65853	MGA 738	4 May 1961	LTT&B
101080	Roadster	Black	Grey	65854	MGA 734	4 May 1961	LTT&B
101081	Roadster	Black	Grey	65855	MGA 739	4 May 1961	LTT&B
101082	Roadster	Black	Grey	65856	MGA 740	4 May 1961	LTT&B

Footnotes:
There were just twenty (five batches of four) South African MGA 1600 Mark IIs – all of them listed here with the author's grateful acknowledgement to Bo Giersing.

ABOVE: **Shipside's showroom at Schipol Airport attracted custom from travellers passing through.**
LEFT: **On 29 January 1958, the freshly painted body of the first MGA to be assembled by Molenaar is inspected after being taken from the baking oven.**
CONAM VIA RUTGER BOOY

made in Holland, and these were even exempt of import duties.'

As there was a US air force base in Soesterberg (also in the Utrecht province), a number of these cars ended up going overseas again with their new military personnel owners. Many of these were sold via a dealer called Shipside (based at Schiphol airport), who provided tax-free shipping; many US servicemen would pick up their new MGA, use it for a European tour, and then ship it home afterwards.

Containers with CKD kits in sets of four were shipped from Abingdon to Delfzijl in the north of Holland, and were then brought the roughly 125-mile (200km) distance south to Amersfoort by barge. Starting in March 1958 with standard pushrod engine cars, Molenaar not only assembled the 1500, 1600 and 1600 Mk II models from CKD kits, but also three sets of four MGA Twin Cam cars (see table below). Rutger Booy notes that the assembly of the MGA 1500 and 1600 lasted until June 1961. The 1600 Mark II was then assembled from October 1961 to March 1962.

THE FIRST TWELVE DUTCH-ASSEMBLED MGA 1500 'CKD' CARS

Chassis no. HDH6-	Original Body Colour if known	Trim Colour	Engine No.BP15GB-	Date Received at Molenaar	Date Delivered to Dealer	Dealer	Final Destination	Dutch Licence Number
40400	Black	Green	30399	17 April 1958	4 August 1958	Shipside, Schiphol	USA	none
40401	Red	Black	30472	17 April 1958	7 May 1958	Transol Car Sales, The Hague	USA	none
40402	Red	Red	30514	19 June 1958	19 June 1958	Export to Belgium	Unknown	none
40403	Black	Red	30488	10 June 1958	12 June 1958	v.d. Mark, Amsterdam	Private, Amsterdam	ZG-32-07
40625	Blue	Grey	29737	20 March 1958	18 April 1958	Export to Belgium	Unknown	76-49-GH
40626	Red	Black	31071	20 March 1958	10 April 1958	Export to Belgium	Unknown	none
40627	Black	Red	31069	20 March 1958	17 April 1958	Export to Belgium	Unknown	16-VX-96
40628	Blue	Grey	29732	20 March 1958	10 April 1958	Export to Belgium	Unknown	none
40985	Old English White	Red	31637	20 March 1958	20 June 1958	v. Butselaar, Apeldoorn	Private, Vaessen	ZG-69.70
40986	Old English White	Red	31638	20 March 1958	27 June 1958	Kouwenberg, Tilburg	Private, Tilburg	ZG-74.20
40987	Old English White	Red	31755	20 March 1958	17 May 1958	Molenaar, Amersfoort	USA	n/a
40988	Blue	Black	31633	20 March 1958	12 July 1958	Transol Car Sales, The Hague	USA	n/a

Footnotes:
The author is grateful to Rutger Booy for this data. Although later chassis numbers 40625 and 40627 were the first CKD MGAs to be assembled by Molenaar, both were exported to Belgium, but came back to Holland at a later date, September 1969 and August 1960 respectively. CKD cars came in batches of four, but it is not known why chassis numbers 40400 to 40403 were received on different dates. None of the hood colours, CSO nos, UK body nos or similar codes are recorded. Of the cars listed in the table, those believed to be still 'active' are chassis nos. 40625, 40627 and 40985.

THE MGA TWIN CAMS ASSEMBLED BY J.J. MOLENAAR'S AUTOMOBIELBEDRIJF

Chassis Number	Start Build (MG)	Finish Build/Despatch (MG)	Trim Colour	Hood Colour	Notes
YDH6-1094	9 January 1959	16 January 1959	Red	Black	Equipment includes adjustable steering, Centigrade thermometer, heater and twin horns
YDH6-1095	9 January 1959	16 January 1959	Red	Black	
YDH6-1096	9 January 1959	16 January 1959	Red	Black	
YDH6-1097	9 January 1959	16 January 1959	Red	Black	
YDH6-1301	6 February 1959	13 February 1959	Black	Black	Equipment includes adjustable steering, heater and twin horns
YDH6-1302	6 February 1959	13 February 1959	Black	Black	
YDH6-1303	6 February 1959	13 February 1959	Grey	Blue	
YDH6-1304	6 February 1959	13 February 1959	Grey	Blue	
YDH6-1390	20 February 1959	27 February 1959	Black	Black	Equipment includes adjustable steering, heater and twin horns
YDH6-1391	20 February 1959	27 February 1959	Black	Black	
YDH6-1392	20 February 1959	27 February 1959	Red	Black	
YDH6-1393	20 February 1959	27 February 1959	Red	Black	

Footnotes:
The Twin Cams were in three batches of four: YDH6 1094 to 1097, YDH6 1301 to 1304, and YDH6 1390 to YDH6 1393, all assembled in the Netherlands in the period from April 1959 until December 1959. Of these twelve MGA Twin Cams assembled by Molenaar, six were registered locally in the Netherlands, three went to the USA (Michigan, California and Delaware), one to Caracas in Venezuela, one to Manila in The Philippines (where, as we have seen, MGAs were also assembled), and one to an unknown ultimate destination. Pim van de Veer (formerly associated with BMC in the Netherlands) recalls that of the six Dutch Twin Cams, one was acquired by Han Vetter (founder and chairman of the Dutch Centre of the MG Car Club), a second went to fellow enthusiast John Muys, and a third to Ad Bouwmeester (son of the founder of a major Dutch insurer, 'De Goudse', who later became its chairman; *see also* his participation in the 1958 Tulip Rally, covered in Chapter 10).

J. J. MOLENAAR

Johannes Jacobus Molenaar from Amersfoort had been importing MGs from early 1932, and on 1 January 1933 he was appointed official importer. In 1936 the Morris branch in Delft ceased deliveries, and because Mr Molenaar was a personal friend of Lord Nuffield, the import of Morris cars and trucks was transferred to his company. Pim van der Veer told the author that his late father had been involved in the Delft business, and says that the main reason it failed was due to management embezzlement.

Sales of both Morris and MG went well, but the start of World War II halted all trade with the UK and no more cars could be imported. During the war the company was placed under German control, although they never found the thirty-six brand new Morris passenger cars Molenaar had bricked up in the attic of his company building. As soon as the war ended and the Dutch government needed cars for the transport of food, Molenaar was able to meet demand through supplying these Morris cars.

After 1945, the import of cars started again. Morris Motors in the UK was able to deliver quickly, but because of scarce foreign exchange, car imports cost too much. The solution to this problem was to import CKD kits and start an assembly factory. In 1948 Molenaar started in a rented factory near Utrecht, and in January 1953 a larger factory was opened in Amersfoort. This was necessary because sales of Morris automobiles in the Netherlands increased rapidly.

The Morris Minor was a particular success. In 1947 only 1,500 Morris passenger cars were registered in Holland; ten years later this number had increased to nearly 15,000. Not only were passenger cars such as the Minor, the Oxford, the Six and the MG TD assembled, the range included commercial cars such as the J-Type vans and the larger 1½-ton, 3-ton and 6-ton trucks as well. From 1959 on even the Austin A40 and Austin Mini were assembled. At the height of its assembly period Molenaar employed some 300 people, of whom 250 worked in production. The output was almost 4,000 cars per annum, and these cars were fitted with as much local content as possible, for instance tyres, batteries, glass, radiators, trim and lots more.

Not all cars were destined for the Dutch market: Molenaar also produced for export to countries such as Belgium, Germany, France and Algeria.

Johannes Jacobus died suddenly in the spring of 1957, about a year before MGA assembly began at Amersfoort, and the management of the company was taken over by his son, Johannes Leonardus. Because of rising costs, assembly of CKD parts became less profitable in the early sixties; although the UK did not enter the European Union until 1973, the import of new motor cars became cheaper and the competition, especially from Japanese imports, increased. The last 180 Morris cars were assembled in 1966.

DUTCH MGAs SOLD OR ASSEMBLED BY MOLENAAR

	Imported fully built	CKD assembly	Totals
MGA 1500	140	164	*304*
MGA 1600	183	144	*327*
MGA 1600 Mk II	58	24	*82*
Twin Cam	11	12	*23*
Totals	*392*	*344*	*736*

Footnotes:
At the time of writing, the Dutch MGA Register knows of 167 of these MGAs, and is keen to hear from any owners of cars as yet unlisted by them. Licence plates for MGAs registered temporarily for export would start with the letters GN, which stands for 'Geen Nederlander', meaning 'Not Dutch'. These plates were issued to automobiles that were exempt from tax and were destined to go abroad. Local assembly of the MGA 1500 and 1600 by Molenaar lasted until June 1961; the Mark II was then assembled between November 1961 and March 1962. *See* the separate table for details of the twelve MGA Twin Cams assembled in the Netherlands.

J. J. Molenaar's impressive showroom, photographed in 1959, with an MGA in the foreground.
TEUS HOOGEVEST VIA JERRY VAN KALLEVEEN

ABOVE: **Koen Struijk's father Kees is the lucky owner of this MGA 1500, restored in 2018. Like many on the roads today, it is a US import, unsurprising as North America took by far the largest proportion of MGA production.**
KOEN STRUIJK

RIGHT: **The first MGA (HDK 23-14652; engine number 4783) for New Zealand, imported fully built up by Dominion Motors. Originally shown at the 1956 Invercargill Motor Show, it was first registered as 'CN 8161' in Christchurch on 20 December 1956 and much later bought in 2007 and restored by current owner Neil Manchester.**
NEIL MANCHESTER

CHAPTER NINE

SUCCESSION PLANNING: FURTHER DEVELOPMENT OF THE MGA

In any car company, by the time a new model is on sale, those responsible for the future direction of the marque in question will have turned their attention to the next project. The revolution that brought forward the MGA was a bold and significant step, but even before the first specimens were heading down the Abingdon production lines, John Thornley and Syd Enever were thinking of their next moves.

As we saw in Chapter 2, Thornley had given a lukewarm, politically astute nod towards the MG Midgets of Gerald Palmer, but by the time the MGA was in full swing, the Palmer era was over and his sports-car concepts had been abandoned. Even so, the idea of a monocoque future soon became seemingly inevitable, and so what would become the basis of the MGB began to take form. Beginning with a concept called 'EX 205' (MG Two Seater – ADO 23; eleven entries from 20 June 1957 to 2 February 1958, after which a note was added 'transferred into ADO23 book'), this project eventually evolved into the later EX 214 and ADO 23 – the true basis of the MGB, the stories of which deserve exploration in another book.

Talking to Kenneth Ullyett in 1960, John Thornley admitted that most efforts to improve the MGA were doomed to failure:

> We were thinking in terms of giving the MGA a facelift – after all, the car had been in production from 1955 to 1959, and there comes a time when the designer is called in to give a car extended currency, no matter how successful is the basic conception. As the MGA doesn't wear out, anyway it was necessary to consider a change even if only to interest the potential buyer going into the showroom.
>
> As nobody likes change merely for the sake of it, our design team was set the problem of ascertaining what really could be an improvement. We played about with alternative fronts, but, bearing in mind the MGA is an idealized design, conceived as an entity, it is hardly surprising that no matter what we did to the front, the result was less satisfactory, and usually less aerodynamic.
>
> We experienced the same not-unanticipated disappointment when we experimented with the back end. Each of the alterations seemed to have a stuck-on look, and it didn't

An eighth-scale model by Harry Herring with a clever removable tail section, intended to show how a more bulky boot could have been accommodated..

AUTHOR

One of Harry Herring's superb models, created at the behest of Syd Enever as a possible facelift for the MGA Twin Cam – sometimes referred to initially as the 'MGB'. The nose is blunter in shape, and the rear wings have been stretched with vestigial fins, all the rage at the time.

AUTHOR

take long to realize that worthwhile improvement was not to be had this way. So we analysed the mind of the MGA user and asked ourselves: 'What does he want?' And this produced a simple answer: 'Even better performance.' This meant a little more urge in acceleration, and an even better maximum, with the corollary that the car should be made to stop even better. As we already had the 1588cc engine in the Twin Cam, we decided to standardize that as the '1600'. And to produce stopping power in keeping with the improved performance, we fitted Lockheed discs to the front.

The idea of a bigger engine as well as more power was a common demand from the USA, as Gus Ehrman told the author (*see* Chapter 7, the MGA 1600). There were certainly thoughts of a brand new powertrain, in the form of a V4 engine, and whilst the project was really aimed more at the BMC mainstream as well as the MGA's eventual successor, there was an MGA-based project called 'EX 216' (entries were EX 216/1, dated 16 September 1958 to EX 216/13, dated 29 December 1958, mostly related to modifications needed to the front cross-member and other installation requirements). Roy Brocklehurst told the author: 'We were often used by Longbridge as a sort of experimental department – we fitted a V4 engine into an MGA, and subsequently tried it in the first MGB.'

Don Hayter said that Syd Enever disliked the uneven exhaust beat created by the V4 configuration, but denied to the author that the Abingdon works ever had an MGA with a V4 engine that could be driven: 'No – we never had a running engine. We did installations – we dropped one into a car – but we never had a running V4. I'm not sure what Longbridge did – they had one of our cars for years and years, first an MGA and then an MGB. Whether or not they ever put a V4 engine in it, I don't know.'

The grille on this quarter-scale Herring Twin Cam model is wider and more upright than that of the production MGA.
AUTHOR

This contrasts slightly with what Roy Brocklehurst told journalist Jon Pressnell in another interview: '[the V4] was quite a nice power unit... I'm sure if that engine had gone into production we could have made a reasonable motor car around it... It was extremely smooth...' Peter Neal has written that the MGA V4 was tested at MIRA in December 1958, but confirms that the idea never took off.

Before long, however, whether Syd Enever liked them or not, both the V4 and a related V6 unit were abandoned when BMC concluded that they would have been too costly to develop, necessitating ripping up and reorganizing much of Longbridge's engine production facilities at South

IDEAS OF A NEW ENGINE: LONGBRIDGE'S EXPERIMENTAL V4

As BMC laid plans for a technology-led future in the late 1950s, fired by forward-looking design and engineering trends at the time, Sir Leonard Lord sanctioned a special engine research 'cell' at Longbridge under the management of Dr Duncan Stuart. Their key task was to look at future powertrains for the corporation, and one of their projects that was given the green light for further development was a family of narrow-angled V4 and V6 engines, provisionally in 2- and 3-litre capacity respectively.

Although the BMC units were clearly inspired by Lancia engines used in the Appia and Aurelia, the concept would have echoes in the family of V4 and V6 engines that Ford's European arm would create a few years later; but whilst the Ford units would reach production, the BMC project was cut short. Graham Robson has described the engine as having a single cylinder head with a single overhead camshaft, and two SU carburettors required even for the 'base' versions, and two sets of exhaust pipes and downpipes – adding to complexity, transverse bulk and cost.

The costs of putting the new unit into production, and finding the space to build it without disrupting existing outputs of the 'A' and 'B' series engines, undoubtedly militated against Stuart's revolution, as undoubtedly did the fact that the older units were still highly successful and fit for purpose. The fact that Alec Issigonis was not in charge of the project probably didn't help, either. It would be another thirty years before Volkswagen would introduce their narrow-angle 'VR6' engine, which used a broadly similar concept of a very narrow angle between the cylinder banks.

Works. Also, despite the unusually narrow V formation of their cylinders, they would not have been ideally suited to the short-nosed transverse front-wheel drive configuration favoured by Alec Issigonis for his ADO 16 and 17 family saloon projects.

In the event, MG enthusiasts had to make do with the twin cam, the original 1600 and the final 1600 Mark II, the stories of which have, of course, been covered earlier. Anyone seeking a larger engine in an open MG roadster would have to wait for the MGB of 1962, with its 1798cc unit.

Meanwhile, throughout the MGA production period there was a running EX-Register code 'EX 191 – development work on production MGA', which eventually ran to 450 entries, from 19 May 1955 through to 7 February 1961. The old Cowley 'Design Order' code for the MGA, DO 1062, persisted in parallel, with hundreds of detail sketches and drawings for things from suspension to bumpers and carpets (twenty of them for carpets alone). The very last entry was DO 1062/448 of 11 August 1966 (a one-off late entry for 'steering geometry MGA Mk II'), although the last regular entry, DO 1062/447, was dated 9 November 1960.

Significantly this development work included a recurrent theme of independent or semi-independent rear suspension. Some of the interesting entries include the following:

EX 191/142–149 (dated 28 May 1957): relates to 'overdrive'.
EX 191/150–156 (dated 9 July to 19 August 1957): refers to rear disc brakes as well as 'adjustable independent rear suspension'.

Thereafter there are various intermittent 'IRS' entries, including EX 191/200 and 201 (dated 14 and 28 January 1958 respectively) for 'independent rear suspension – trailing arm with coil springs'.
EX 191/270 (dated 12 August 1958) is referred to as 'proposed air cleaner for 1700cc MGA'.
EX 191/320 (dated 1 January 1959) is for 'independent rear suspension – 15-degree arms', and similar themes continued through 1959.
EX 191/423 (dated 23 March 1960) refers to '25-degree arm – IRS Scheme', and EX 191/444 (dated 19 April 1960) describes 'assembly of 25-degree arm'.

During 1961, there was also a parallel code kept at Abingdon for the MGA 1600 as part of the EX-Register but under the BMC 'ADO 31' code sequence: it ran from ADO31/1, dated 21 February 1961, to ADO31/21, dated 28 October 1961.

EX 195 – A CHEAPER MGA

Before focus turned to what would become the MGB, however, MG had other diversions en route. The first of these was, of course, the twin-cam engine and the addition of disc brakes (see Chapter 6). Then there were the special projects, such as EX 183 and EX 186 (see Chapter 10). Next in line was a project to create a 'cheaper MGA' – the very idea of which was a source of some irritation for Thornley. The background to this exercise was a direction from BMC headquarters to develop a small sports car intended to adopt some of the running gear of the Austin A30 or Morris Minor 1000, which at Abingdon soon translated into a short-lived project called EX 188. However, desk-top exercises soon led Thornley to the conclusion that a sports car based on the Morris Minor platform was both unattractive and unaffordable.

Nevertheless, it was obvious that Abingdon was not the only player in this competition: Leonard Lord asked a similar question of Donald Healey, and it was fairly common knowledge inside BMC that Austin Engineering at Longbridge had been dabbling with ideas for a small sports car for several years. Underpinning all this thinking was the concept of the so-called 'buzz box' – in effect a modern interpretation of the original pre-war Austin Seven as a low-cost car for the masses.

With little evident enthusiasm, Abingdon entered into the fray with a project for a lower cost MGA under the code EX 195. Fitted with a single 1¾in SU carburettor, Morris Minor propshaft and Austin A30 steering box, the exercise began in November 1955. The following year, to keep up the pretence of enthusiasm under BMC management's gaze, EX 195 was reworked to take a 950cc 'A' series engine in place of the single carburettor 1498cc 'B' series engine. Cliff Bray, working in MG's Development shop, told the author that this car was built with a 9.41 rear-axle ratio, and that it achieved a totally underwhelming maximum speed of just 75mph (120km/h).

Nevertheless, work on EX 195 continued even after the imminent arrival of the Austin-Healey Sprite – which, it had been decided, should be built at Abingdon – was a foregone conclusion. In his notebook, Cliff Bray recorded that the MGA Utility Rebuild ('A' series EX 195) was built between 27 March and 24 April 1958. This version featured 8in front brakes, 7in rear brakes, an 11.41 Riley 1.5 differential, special propshaft and a Magnette gearbox. Entries were made in the register as late as 1959 for the 'cheap' MGA, which was even tried with smaller (13in diameter) wheels – but in the end the idea was never pursued.

With most MG sales being to North America, where the MGA was already regarded as a 'small car', there seemed little evidence that the USA had any desire for a tiny-engined MGA with less, rather than more performance than the standard car. Jim O'Neill once told the author that despite efforts to cheapen the components, the cost saving for EX 195 was something under £50. EX 195 stayed alive for as long as it did primarily because Abingdon were aware that the Healeys were working on what would become the Sprite, and as Thornley put it, '…we had no intention of being left out of the race.' However, once the Austin-Healey Sprite appeared in May 1958, the cases for EX 188 and EX 195 evaporated. They were not mourned at Abingdon.

MORE POWERFUL MGAs

At the other end of the spectrum to the 'cheapened' MGA were experiments with larger engines. Evidence of this comes from entries in the Abingdon Development Department work schedules, which include references to both a '1700cc' MGA and, even more intriguingly, a 2.2-litre version.

As noted above, the 1700 appears in the EX-Register against 'EX 191/270' (dated 12 August 1958) in the context of 'proposed air cleaner for 1700cc MGA', and just under a year later in Alec Hounslow's Development Department Report ('DDR') No. 134 of 13 June 1959 as 'Reference DDW No. 495 – MGA 1700 Engine – cancelled on Mr Enever's instruction'.

One of Syd Enever's efforts at creating a facelift for the MGA Coupé, with a squarer roof profile, an enlarged boot and a stepped two-tone colour scheme. This model by Harry Herring was to one-sixteenth scale.

ENEVER FAMILY

A similar fate befell another exercise to contemplate a 2.2-litre MGA; the author has been unable to find more information, beyond its cancellation (the reference is DDR No. 172, dated 14 July 1958: 'The 2.2 Litre engine has been installed in the Twin Cam Engine and checked by Mr Enever. The mock-up has now been stripped down, and the parts,

Richard Harvey acquired this very well built 'two-plus-two' MGA, which looks about as close to a factory-built prototype as possible. However, it is believed to be a very well executed private conversion.

RICHARD HARVEY

MGA POLICE CARS

Ever since before the war, MG had maintained a relationship with various British police forces, and so it was hardly a surprise when the MGA found favour with some of them. In order to adapt the car to the practical needs of a patrol car, the factory developed a series of sensible modifications, an obvious example being a beefed-up electrical system, including a larger dynamo. The changes were recorded under a dedicated code 'EX 194', which comprised some seventeen entries. Despite a two-seater sports car not being the most obvious candidate as a police car, forces known to have taken MGAs included Bristol Police District, Glamorganshire Constabulary in Cardiff, Lancashire Police District, Northumberland Police, Oxford City Police and Selkirk Police District.

A Ford Zephyr of the Lancashire Police Force dwarfs the contemporary MGA patrol car. 596 KTB, one of fifty-five MGAs used by this force, had chassis number 70931 and was supplied in Old English White with red trim and a grey hood (just ten were delivered in this colour scheme; most were black).

AUTHOR'S COLLECTION

with the exception of the engine and clutch, returned to their respective Stores), but there was a 2199cc Austin engine which had been used in the Austin A70 and was later adapted for the Austin Gipsy (BMC's answer to the Land Rover, and in production from 1958 to 1968), and it seems possible that this was the powertrain in question; certainly its final drive was of some interest to Syd Enever and his team when they were exploring options for independent rear suspension on first the MGA and later the MGB.

One of the obvious deficiencies of the MGA – especially as the basis of a touring car – was the lack of luggage capacity in the boot, and it was obvious that any larger MGA – such as EX 189 – would have needed a larger luggage-carrying capability. Models by Harry Herring were built showing a bulkier tail for the MGA – whether two-seater or two-plus-two – but aesthetically the effect was not an elegant one, and the rear end of the MGA remained largely untouched (other than the tail lighting) until the end of production in 1962.

FOUR-SEAT CONVERTIBLE

John Thornley pondered the idea of a slightly longer MGA chassis as the possible basis of a 'two-plus-two' open MGA – which as an alternative could, he suggested, become the basis of an open-topped Riley. The concept was given the EX-Register code of EX 189, and the front sheet of the register section also made reference to the car as the 'four-seater version of MGA – MGE'. Although a well-built four-seater MGA is known to exist (see photo previous page), there is no hard evidence to prove that this was related to EX 189.

FASHIONABLE TRENDS

Syd Enever had an eye for fashionable trends and no doubt his trips to the USA as part of the EX 179 and EX 181 record-breaking bids only served to heighten his awareness of contemporary design in the US domestic automotive industry. As well as the tendency towards larger bodies and ever more prominent tail fins, bulkier chrome-plated bumpers and other protuberances, an obvious feature that was assuming growing popularity by the second half of the 1950s were two- or even three-tone colour schemes.

MG draughtsman Peter Neal was tasked with producing these two-tone ideas for the MGA by Syd Enever; neither really worked.
PETER NEAL

Peter Neal was asked to take one of his sketches further, with this airbrushed sketch…
PETER NEAL

…and here is the end result, photographed at Abingdon. Thankfully the idea went no further.
ENEVER FAMILY

OTHER MG NAMES CONSIDERED IN THE WAKE OF THE MGA

Having started the ball rolling with 'MGA' (or, more correctly, 'MG Series MGA'), thoughts inevitably soon turned to the next projects in the sequence – the MGB, MGC and so on. History has recorded the production applications of these names (as well as MGF, of course), but back in the mid-1950s, the first ideas were as follows:

MGA: What began as DO 1062, EX 182 and EX 191.
MGB: The initial suggested name for EX 187, the MGA Twin Cam – rendered pointless when the production car ended up looking very similar to the standard MGA. Of course the 'MGB' name was eventually used on a production car (ADO 23) built between 1962 and 1980.
MGC: A Syd Enever idea for a larger, 6-cylinder MG sports car or sports coupé, which never progressed beyond a paper concept. From August 1957, EX 210 was, in this vein, a slightly later '2.6-litre MG (four-seater sports)'. The much later production MGC (ADO 52) was a 3-litre 6-cylinder offshoot of the MGB, built between 1967 and 1969.
MGD: EX 188, listed as a 'New Midget with A30 engine – the MGD'. This was in essence something that was known in and around Abingdon and Cowley as the 'Buzz Box', and formed MG's entry into the design process, which eventually resulted in the ADO 13 Austin-Healey Sprite.
MGE – EX 189, listed as a 'four-seater version of the MGA – MGE'.

The principle made its way across the Atlantic, too, and as well as the obviously American-influenced Fords and Vauxhalls, a growing number of models in the 'BMC' family soon sported two-tone colour schemes. Closer to home for Enever was the emergence of the 'Varitone' version of the MG ZB Magnette. This prompted him to look at ideas to add some similar excitement to the MGA, and as well as the sketches by Peter Neal and the Harry Herring models seen here, at least one full-size roadster was converted with a chrome trim splitting the upper and lower half of the MGA body into different colours.

In the end it was obvious that the curvaceous lines and petite nature of the MGA body styling did not lend itself to such treatment, and the concept was abandoned; however, when it came to the MGA's successor, a horizontal trim line was introduced, running on both flanks from head to tail lamps, and although no MGBs were ever offered in production with two-tone colour schemes, early concept sketches showed the possibility.

THE EX 205/2 – THE FRUA-BODIED MGA

The story of what eventually became the MGB began, naturally enough, within the orbit of its predecessor. Although the definitive MGB, ADO 23, had its roots in another monocoque concept, EX 214, the process of finding a successor to the MGA actually began with an assumption that MG would stick to a separate chassis frame; indeed John Thornley and Syd Enever even went on record as saying such in one of the former's internal memos. The project code for this concept was EX 205, and the first styling models – Harry Herring ones as well as full size – were developed by Jim O'Neill and apprentice draughtsman Peter Neal, working to a brief from Syd Enever.

The Frua MGA was photographed outside their premises by its makers, Carrozzeria Pietro Frua, before it was shipped from Italy to England; as built it had a neat and simple removable hardtop.
FRUA FAMILY/STEFAN DIERKES

In the midst of this process, Peter Neal's sketches were taken by Enever to show BMC Deputy Chairman George Harriman, who decided to send an MGA chassis to the Italian coach-building concern of Frua, with a commission to build a one-off prototype. According to Don Hayter, Harriman had been to one of the European motor shows

> ... in Switzerland, or Italy, probably – and he had a look at their cars, and said that what we wanted was something 'better and newer for the US market'. Of course the Yanks kept on screaming at us for something new, so we knew this anyway. So Harriman said to Frua 'Do me a car', and we got the message to send them a chassis. So we shipped an MGA chassis out in a crate, and the Frua-bodied car came back; nobody went out there with it.

The Frua MGA, door open, as photographed by the Frua company before shipment to their client.
FRUA FAMILY/STEFAN DIERKES

The interior of the Italian car featured generously upholstered seats and vast areas of red-piped cream leather; perhaps more Maserati than MG?
FRUA FAMILY/STEFAN DIERKES

The resultant car, resplendent in red with a white leather interior, was a striking creation with a larger, more modern (for 1957) shape than the MGA, but of a style more like an upmarket Maserati, or perhaps elements of the imminent Aston-Martin DB4. It was, to many eyes, a beautiful job, but perhaps not really an MG – and certainly rather 'over-bodied' for a car with a 1.5-litre 4-cylinder engine.

Contemporary photographs from the surviving Frua family archive dating from April 1957 show that as built, the Frua MGA came with either a white folding roof or a neat close-coupled white hardtop, although by the time it was photographed back in the UK it had also acquired a neat fastback coupé roof as an option. When MG weighed the prototype, they found that it was heavy – even allowing for the fact that hand-built prototypes with lots of lead-loading and excesses of luxurious trimmings often *are* rather portly – and this helped sway the design team's views towards the monocoque method of construction, cutting out some of the duplication between chassis and bodysill structures. Hayter says: 'It weighed about two tons – it was massive, completely unfeasible, and it wouldn't go – I think they drove it on the road only once or twice...'

The MG drawing office nevertheless drew up a general arrangement drawing of the Frua car – referred to in MG parlance as 'EX 205/2.R' – with the drawing dated 20 June 1957. The task was undertaken by Don Hayter, who told the author:

> I got to measure and draw that body so that we had got a record of it, as Frua didn't send any drawings with it. The

A photograph taken in the 1960s of Harry Herring's model of the Frua MGA.
ENEVER FAMILY

> drawing survives at Gaydon. I've still got the folder with all the dimensions in it that I recorded when I measured them off the Frua car. Harry Herring did some wood formers for me to use that fitted in places so I could produce a proper layout.

Harry Herring also made a model using the drawings.

The Nuffield Exports Board, meanwhile, considered at their meeting of 10 July 1957 the following bond: 'It was resolved that the seal of the Company be affixed to a Bond with the Commissioner of H. M. Customs and Excise in the sum of £13,000 with reference to the temporary importation of one MGA car chassis fitted with Italian prototype body.'

TOP AND ABOVE: **Pictured in April 1957 at 'Parco di Valentino' in Turin, not far from the Frua premises, prior to despatch.**
FRUA FAMILY/STEFAN DIERKES

This superb 1957 Kodachrome image of the Frua MGA comes from Syd Enever's own record of this impressive car, soon after delivery.
ENEVER FAMILY

Harry Herring's model of the Frua car – EX 205/2 – survives at Gaydon.
AUTHOR

Once the job of the Frua MGA had been done, BMC had no further use for the prototype; the bond had effectively granted the company a temporary import licence, without the payment of duty based on its purchase cost – which of course was considerable. There being little or no sentiment in the car business, and no point in re-exporting a one-off concept that had to remain secret, BMC decreed that the Frua prototype should be cut up with an acetylene torch whilst a local customs and excise officer, Mr Fishpool, looked on.

Jim O'Neill told the author that the hardtop survived, it being reasoned no doubt that the customs and excise man need not know of its existence, and it was used as inspiration for some of Abingdon's own efforts at EX 205. Now even that has gone, the only evidence of how it looked being the Harry Herring model, which survives in the British Motor Museum collection.

Peter Neal was tasked with sketching a version of the Frua car with a different nose, based on that of Jim O'Neill's original EX 205/1.R, called EX 205/3.R – but in the end EX 205 was abandoned in favour of another project – EX 214, of June 1958 – which led eventually to the MGB. But that is another story...

INDEPENDENT REAR SUSPENSION

According to Don Hayter, Syd Enever dallied with no fewer than three types of suspension in the MGA:

> There was the obviously conventional one, there was a trailing arm and coil spring – which is what the MGB was originally going to have – and we also did an inclined angle swinging arm with a fixed differential in the middle – rather like the Porsche, although before they used it (not that we were the first to consider this idea). That chassis was built, and I remember it lay on the bank outside the drawing office for years, rusting away.

One of the MG factory Development Department Reports (DDR No. 145, dated 18 February 1958) includes an update on progress with what had been given the DDW number of 225 ('MGA with coil spring rear suspension') to the extent

This very rounded coupé is a Harry Herring model of EX 205, a proposal for what would have been in effect a rebodied MGA. Note the slightly heavy grille and two-tone body-colour treatments – themes that evidently appealed to Syd Enever at the time.
AUTHOR

that 'the parts have been made and fitted to LJB 370 and will be put to test as soon as possible'.

Hayter recalls that Roy Brocklehurst had a nasty incident in the MGA with the trailing arm suspension: 'He took it out with Tony Felmingham and they flipped it coming down from Fox Hill. It flicked over in the air and laid upside down across the ditch, with roof untouched. They opened the doors and fell out into the ditch – no seat belts in those days of course! Then they hitched a lift back to the factory in a passing Royal Mail lorry!'

Peter Neal adds that this car was also the MG Development MGA 'LJB 370' and the incident took place in March 1959: 'Apparently one of the rear wheels got caught up in the rear wheel arch on full bump and sent the car cartwheeling into a ditch.' According to Neal, 'LJB 370' was rebuilt and back out on test at MIRA inside of two weeks...

The idea of a special rear end for the MGA – either fully independent or with a De Dion axle – eventually died a death, not least because of a lack of suitable components from the BMC cupboard – and although the concept was revived for the MGB, similar challenges led to the retention of a conventional leaf-sprung live axle in the MGA's successor. By the start of the 1960s, the development story of the MGA was drawing inevitably to a close, and the future of the MG sports-car story lay in a worthy successor...

This model represents **EX 214** – an early representation of the monocoque sports-car concept that would soon develop into the **ADO 23 MGB.**
AUTHOR

BELOW: **Fast forward to 2017, and this is the winning design in a competition organized by SAIC, the present owners of the MG brand, to design a new MG sports car for 2025. The young designer Li Qin, of China's Tsinghua University, chose the MGA as his inspiration...**
SAIC MOTOR

CHAPTER TEN

THE MGA IN MOTOR SPORTS

COMPETITION: THE EUROPEAN THEATRE

The 1950s was a golden era for the moderately well-heeled motor-sports fan, who could find reasonably easy entry into an exciting arena, provided he (or, occasionally, she) could scrape together enough disposable income, show reasonable skill behind the wheel, have a modicum of engineering empathy and, ideally, manage a smattering of self-discipline and organizational common sense – although many succeeded with some of these qualities in short supply.

In the United Kingdom, circuits and pit-lanes occasionally still bore witness to the fading post-war remnants of former European aristocracy or British nobility with grand titles in waiting. However, a slightly more egalitarian social order had nevertheless been forged in the fires of war; provided you had the necessary aptitude and acumen, and established the right connections, you could still go far. Mind you, it could help your progress greatly in terms of gaining race entries if you 'knew the right people' and could find your way into membership of the Steering Wheel Club, founded in 1947 at No. 2 Brick Street, in London's Mayfair.

To start with, the MGA was often entered in mixed-model MG club races, such as this Peterborough Motor Club meeting at Silverstone on 28 September 1957.
AUTHOR'S COLLECTION

Therefore the nascent racing driver could, with a little effort and the coveted invitation, turn up to race at one of the many circuits dotted around the country. If he (or she) had some driving skill and the necessary staying power, they could also find themselves climbing up the pecking order, earning championship points in the better organized event series, occasionally attracting the attention of the car makers and their competition team managers; the bolder participants might even venture on to the Continent to famous circuits such as Le Mans, Montlhéry or the Nürburgring, or the exciting if dangerous Italian road races.

What the actors in this theatre could seldom count upon was using this activity as the basis of any reliable form of income: participants had to make do with the modest prize money to defray their outgoings, and meanwhile do their best to placate their long-suffering family members and – where applicable – an understanding employer, the tolerance of these sometimes unwilling bystanders being especially tested when racing involved long weekends away from base.

Consequently few of this happy band made a living out of their hobby, but the distinctive sweet aroma of Castrol 'R' was a drug which, for the addicted, was hard to resist: they did it for the glory of the chase and saw no need to justify their desire. The decade, coming just after the six years of war, was one where grasping an opportunity for adventure, exploration and reinvention, through the glamour of motor sport, was an alluring antidote to the greyness of everyday lives for many born in the UK during the inter-war years. If asked why they raced cars, many would have happily echoed Mallory, climber of Everest, who when asked why he did it, supposedly replied 'because it is there'.

Of course many players came and went: fragile budgets, destructive crashes and major failures, coupled with changing domestic and career priorities and indifferent skill levels, eventually weeded out many. Whilst the decade began with an atmosphere of jolly amateurism, by the end of the period the professional motor-racing team and sponsored drivers had become the norm, even if we were yet to see simple colour schemes subsumed beneath the tedious blanket of garish corporate sponsorship liveries.

In the middle of the period, however – just around the time that the MGA arrived on the scene – some drivers and their associates – occasionally aristocratic heirs-in-waiting, or well-connected motor dealers – formed the basis of some adventurous motor racing équipes, and of course many of them cut their teeth on MGs. As we shall see, the use of an MG as a racing entrée was just as true in North America and Australia as it was in the home market.

As we saw in Chapter 2, one of the drivers who had formed a close friendship with the MG factory was George Phillips, who as well as being a fairly competent and adventurous driver, was also the chief photographer from the start for *Autosport*, first published in August 1950. This weekly publication was voraciously devoured by the motor-racing set, who lapped up the reports of activities across the motor-sports world with the enthusiasm of any seasoned sports fan. As Phillips increased his commitments towards covering races rather than driving in them, his active involvement in MG affairs reduced, but those of his associates blossomed.

THE COMPETITIONS DEPARTMENT

Under the pressure of the export imperative described in earlier chapters, MG was hardly the only sports-car maker in the 1950s with an eye on the US market; Standard Triumph was looking at boosting the prestige of its recently facelifted TR3 sports car, and Rootes was becoming active in the rally world, spending money to recruit Grand Prix drivers as rally drivers for the company's Sunbeam products. In this context, John Thornley worked his persuasive magic and convinced the BMC Board to sanction the creation of a new competition board and associated department.

In the wake of the abandonment of the plan for MG to transfer to Coventry (*see* Chapter 1), a 'Competitions

DICK JACOBS

Graham Warner at Snetterton, 6 August 1960. Dick Jacobs (white shirt and sunglasses) is delightedly admiring the winner's trophies.
STEVE JOHNSON

We have already seen how George Phillips had formed a firm bond with MG and the Abingdon factory, which would feed into the origins of the MGA. Phillips and two of his contemporaries were known as the 'Abingdon Angels', the second member of the trio being Richard William Jacobs (8 November 1916–2 November 1987), better known to all as Dick. Dick Jacobs was the proprietor of the family business, Mill Garage, in South Woodford in the Essex/north-east London fringes.

In December 1945, Jacobs wrote to MG and the following year secured an MG franchise, taking delivery of his first new TC Midget in October 1946. From 1948 onwards, Jacobs began racing MGs himself, and eventually joined George Phillips and Ted Lund in planning and executing MG team efforts, first in T-Types and later in other models. Whereas Phillips soon throttled back his time behind the wheel in favour of his photography job, Jacobs kept up the pace until the fateful events at Le Mans in June 1955 (*see* main text).

Those events in France precipitated his retirement from active racing, but he took on a new role as team manager, supporting drivers in MG Z Magnettes, MGAs and notably MGA Twin Cams, and later a pair of very pretty MG Midgets with special alloy coupé bodywork. Under Jacobs' wing were drivers who would go on to enjoy notable racing careers, such as Alan Foster, Tommy Bridger and Roy Bloxham.

The site of the Mill Garage was forced, through compulsory purchase, to 'make way for progress' in 1974 with the construction of the London end of the M11 motorway, and in the February 1974 issue of the MG Car Club magazine *Safety Fast*, John Thornley wrote, in the context of a piece about Dick Jacobs and George Phillips and their racing of TCs, TDs and Y-Types, that '…it was largely through the interest and enthusiasm engendered by these exploits that I was able to persuade the Board of BMC to authorise me to set up the Competitions Department.' Jacobs wrote a highly readable autobiography, *An MG Experience*, published two years later.

Committee of MG and Riley' came into being in October 1950, and at first its primary concern seems to have been consideration of whether or not to support Captain 'Goldie' Gardner in his continuing record-breaking exploits. The terms of the Nuffield Organisation's approach to motor sports was enshrined in a paragraph in the Morris Motors Board Minutes of 16 October 1950: 'After full discussion, it was decided to restrict activities to reasonable cooperation with owners of standard products who wished to compete in races for which such models were eligible.'

A month later, during a discussion about support for 'Goldie' Gardner on 15 November 1950, the Board went further, recording that 'it was explained to Mr Tatlow that the Company would not compete in any events under its own name, but that, subject to Board approval, it would give all reasonable support to owners of MG and Riley cars competing as private entrants.' Hardly a ringing endorsement of the philosophy that 'racing improves the breed'.

Thus by the time of the merger, there was already a Nuffield Competitions Committee, but apart from the obvious fact that this did not embrace the Austin part of BMC, it was, according to John Thornley, virtually moribund; he was not immune, however, to the benefits of convincing Leonard Lord and his lieutenant George Harriman of the case for an all-embracing 'BMC Motorsports Committee', with Abingdon its natural home. Thornley had been seeking the advice of Sammy Davis, and on his recommendation considered the possibility of engaging Marcus Chambers, recently returned from Africa, to run the operation from the MG factory.

Before this could happen, the formality of the creation of the BMC Motorsports Committee had to be concluded, and this was done on Monday 13 December 1954, alongside the dissolution of the old Nuffield equivalent. At this initial meeting it was agreed that, among other things, the new committee would take on board the plans already in train for MG (in particular, Le Mans), have oversight of the racing activities of the Donald Healey Motor Company, and work to a budget of £100,000 from BMC plus an additional float of £10,000 from Castrol – no doubt thanks to the influence of Sir George Eyston, a Castrol director. This was in itself quite a coup, because previous attempts in 1951 to elicit contributions from the oil industry to support motor-racing activities had drawn a blank.

The next step was the formal enrolment of Marcus Chambers to the committee, which took place on Tuesday 4 January 1955. Alongside Chambers were John Thornley, Reg Bishop (of BMC Central Publicity) and Bob Grice, the Chief Road Test Superintendent at Longbridge. It is interesting to note that there was nobody from Cowley. The BMC Competitions Committee first met for business a week later, on 13 January 1955, and amongst the decisions made, it was noted that 'the MGA 1500 already entered for Le Mans to replace the TF in June' – the clear reference here being to the name of the new model, rather than EX 182; there was a hope that the Twin Cam was 'supposed to be available in 1956', and an admission that the new Competitions Shop would not be ready until 1 April. Also tabled, more in optimistic hope than any certainty of reality, was 'an idea specification for the Magnette using twin-cam engine and disc brakes ... with close ratio gears and knock-off wheels, with 300-mile fuel tank'.

Three months later, on 8 March (and less than a month before the new shop was due to open) the committee considered that there might be approval of a limited number of Westminsters with high-performance engines; also a twin-cam 6-cylinder later; that there should be help with Lance Macklin's Austin-Healey for Le Mans; and lastly there was some discussion about the plans for record breaking, with the new twin-cam overhead-cam engine and wind-tunnel tests of 1/8 scale models at Armstrong Whitworth. It was noted that Stirling Moss had been approached with an indicative date of August 1957, noting not only the benefits of public relations value of the great driver, but also the virtue of his size which, it was suggested, could save as much as 20–30hp.

Denis Williams was responsible for this general arrangement (Drawing A.7033.R, dated 15 April 1955); he told the author: 'It was for EX182, the light alloy body. It was fitted in the rear with a very large fuel tank with a quick-release filler cap in the centre of the trunk lid for quick refuelling... the driving light in the radiator grill was originally going to be a Marchal unit, made in France, but was replaced by Lucas in order to maintain the Britishness of the vehicle. The small windscreen in front of the driver would be made from Perspex.' The title block is also interesting because it includes the DO 1062 Cowley code and the description 'MG Series MGA – Le Mans 1955'.

BOB VITRIKAS

MARCUS CHAMBERS AND STUART TURNER

Marcus Chambers in attentive pose with his trademark pipe, during the BMC test session at Montlhéry in October 1955 (see Chapter 4).
AUTHOR'S COLLECTION

MARCUS CHAMBERS

Marcus Mordaunt Bertram Chambers (8 August 1910–5 August 2009) had his first foray into the world of motoring with a job at a motor garage in London's Oxford Street in 1931. Within a year he was running his own garage in Wandsworth, south-west London, and became involved in managing the HRG sports-car team later in the decade.

After serving in the Royal Navy in World War II, he returned to HRG racing; then he was made aware of BMC's plans for motor sport and made contact at just the right time. Chambers arrived at Abingdon to find that various racing and rallying projects were already under way – most notably the plans for the 1955 Le Mans, the cars for which were being built in the MG Development Department by Alec Hounslow and his team. Chambers attended a meeting at Longbridge on 13 December 1954 to formally establish setting up a new BMC Competitions Department, and to agree to disband the existing Nuffield Competitions Committee: 'A general mood of improving confidence prevailed because post-war problems – such as steel shortage and rationing – were beginning to fade. An aura of hope pervaded a corporation that was coming to terms with welding together Austin and Nuffield's Morris, MG, Riley and Wolseley.'

Before long, the new team was fielding various marques (even if, initially, Austins had to be prepared for quasi-political reasons at Longbridge) and in due course Austin-Healey and the various Minis were added to the mix. It was a busy time, and Chambers found himself travelling all over Europe and North America. By 1961, however, Chambers was finding the heavy personal commitment of BMC's international motor-sports exploits too much and so he left, his place being taken by Stuart Turner. Chambers was not out of the motor-sports game for long, however: he joined Rootes within two years.

STUART TURNER

Stuart Turner (born in Stoke-on-Trent on 14 January 1933) began his motor-sports career in the 1950s and soon found his niche as an excellent navigator, in between practising as wages clerk (in a time of ledgers rather than spreadsheets). 'I was taking a correspondence course in the hope of becoming an accountant,' Turner told the author, adding that 'such a course didn't exactly fit with doing up to sixty rallies a year, so it was with much relief that I stopped it when I joined *Motoring News*.'

The job at *Motoring News* was as the magazine's sports editor, and it was whilst still in that role that Turner moved over to become Competitions Manager for BMC in 1961, aged just twenty-eight. Clearly the MGA was nearing the end of its career at BMC, but nevertheless Turner presided over its swansong in 1961 and 1962. He told the author that at the time the MGA was regarded 'as a good, sound car but the cars for UK rallying were the various TR models... in particular the TR3, and we'd often see fifty or more of the things on events, not least of course because cars were standard (and therefore affordable) back then.'

'My most memorable pre-BMC memory of the MGA is when Erik Carlsson and I hired a Morris 1000 for Erik to get the feel of Scottish roads before the RAC Rally he won. He drove off the road to avoid a head-on with a lorry. We clambered back up to the road where Pat Moss and Ann Wisdom were waiting for us with an MGA. I know you won't believe me, but all four of us got into the MGA to get back to the hotel... once I joined BMC the Austin-Healey 3000 and the Mini Cooper took 99.8 per cent of my time and nervous energy! Mind you I wasn't totally blinkered – Margaret and I bought and much enjoyed an MGB!'

Although the focus was therefore not quite as strongly on the MGA, MG Midget and other MG models as marque enthusiasts might have hoped, being at Abingdon was seen by Turner as a real privilege: 'Looking back, maybe we didn't realize at the time how valuable it was for BMC Comps to be based at MG. The spirit there was great, and I don't think we'd have done so well if based at, say, Longbridge with all the politics.'

The Competitions Department inherited some events from its predecessor, and whilst these commitments were honoured, Marcus Chambers was in many cases less than enthusiastic about them, with some of the drivers drawn from the MG Car Club and friends-of-friends. A known event was, of course, Le Mans, and work on this was embraced by the new team, even if at times Alec Hounslow perhaps implied that he felt he didn't need the advice of newcomers.

EX 182: RETURN TO LE MANS

We saw in Chapter 2 how the process of transition from EX 175 prototype, to DO 1062, and on to the showroom MGA was subject to pre-production delays; but irrespective of these the factory had a race to enter in the summer, and the spring was spent in preparing the cars for Le Mans.

By this time there were problems with getting the series-production version of what it was already known would be the MGA ready for launch. The body-tooling delays were pushing the start of full production later into the year, and so John Thornley faced the dilemma of a team of new production-related (if specialized) sports cars that were scheduled to race less than two months hence, but which were quite obviously not yet in production. Under the 'prototype' category, the cars could readily adopt hand-built chassis and light alloy bodywork.

The decision to defer the public launch of the car to the autumn meant that MG had to go back to the Automobile Club de l'Ouest (ACO Le Mans) to seek – successfully – a change of category from production to prototype, and as the company was not yet ready to share the new model name, the experimental EX 182 was made public. Whilst EX 181 was yet to be seen in public (and the entry for EX 180 related to some not-especially-exciting Morris Minor tuning), the EX 179 record breaker was, of course, already in the public consciousness, and had some connections – the basic chassis design – and so the use of the EX 182 code in this way added a certain frisson to the special nature of these exciting new MG race cars.

The bodywork of the racing cars looked very similar to the production specification, other than faired-in bodywork where the bumpers might otherwise have been, but in place of steel, the shell was built up from 18-gauge alloy panels, shaped by Morris Bodies on the wooden master buck at Coventry and then carefully worked and fixed to the frame at Abingdon using countersunk rivets. Alloy panels were in some cases made removable using Dzus fasteners, and alloy sheet replaced the timber flooring of the production specification. A neat fairing was formed to cover the unused passenger side of the cockpit, with the expectation that this could later be opened up for subsequent events. At least four complete sets of alloy panels were prepared, and these were used to build the first four cars – the ones destined for Le Mans, including the practice car.

The lovely Harry Herring model of EX 182.
ENEVER FAMILY

Meanwhile, for the EX 182 chassis, the side rails were built up from three pieces on each side: 'Harold Wiggins, Douggie Watts and Tommy Wellman used offcuts to make the chassis sides, with neat butt welds; this is one of the ways to tell a genuine Le Mans car,' Jim Cox maintains. The power-plant was, of course, something fairly new for Abingdon, where the XPAG and XPEG had ruled the roost for years before the Austin-developed B-Series arrived. We have already seen how the MG men were initially suspicious, but in the wake of the new unit's adoption in the MG Magnette, it was inevitable that the new Competitions Department would need to get to grips with this interloper from Longbridge.

Jim Cox was one of those in the Development Shop at Abingdon who worked on turning the B-Series into the basis of a Le Mans-ready engine. Cox explained:

> We put a full-flow filter on it – for which we drilled through the block – and we developed the camshaft for more lift. Then we worked with Harry Weslake on the combustion chambers, and before long we found ourselves working on what would become the definitive 'Le Mans' engine specification for EX 182.
>
> I started with the Weslake head and improved it; I tried sodium-cooled valves, but these proved too difficult. In the end we arrived at Stellite-tipped valves, and with all the other changes, we achieved 82.5bhp.

Special features of the race engines included blocked-off waterways and the lack of gaskets, the latter resulting, as Cox explained, in very boring work as the heads were lapped to the block: 'This was a very slow and tedious process, and we would take turns at it.'

Syd Enever's ever-inventive mind was always coming up with bright ideas, which Jim Cox would be asked to investigate:

> Syd wanted to use a cross-flow head – four or five were made – and he wanted to use two sets of carbs, one pair each side of the head. The idea was that there would be a normal pair on the conventional side, and two smaller ones – I think they were one inch SUs we tried – on the opposite side. The theory was that the smaller carbs would give improved low-end power, but this didn't work and so we finished up with a ⅝in balance pipe around the back of the engine.

Also subject to development was the exhaust: 'Much work was required on the manifold to avoid any unnecessary loss

ABOVE LEFT: **Installing the B-Series engine in one of the EX 182 Le Mans cars.**
AUTHOR'S COLLECTION

ABOVE RIGHT: **John Thornley discusses the performance of EX182 with driver Ken Wharton.**

RIGHT: **Pat Moss, alongside the car, discusses the EX182 with MG's Chief Designer Syd Enever.**

of power,' as well as fitment of a racing clutch 'with no take-up springs, unlike a road car', and inevitably a close-ratio gearbox. The initial specification more or less determined, Cox then set about ensuring that the engines themselves performed reliably: 'We tested them to about 7 per cent above the margin required in order to ensure that the engines would survive on the track.'

The final build of the four EX 182 cars for Le Mans began in earnest in March 1955; Dick Jacobs noted that they were well under way by the time he paid the factory a visit on Wednesday 23 March, when he also learned that the first shake-down testing at Silverstone was scheduled for just over a month thence, on Thursday 28 April. Alongside the MG regulars, other specialists came to Abingdon to work on the EX 182 race cars, such as Joseph Lucas Limited, who undertook the wiring (Clive Jenkins was part of the Lucas contingent named in a three-page article on the project in the *Nuffield Teamwork* issue of June 1955).

Once the Le Mans cars had been built they were initially subjected to testing by Tommy Wellman, Cliff Bray and Douggie Watts, and in due course were deemed ready for the invited drivers, logically including Dick Jacobs. When the initial test day at Silverstone arrived, the weather was showery and the track damp, and the first of the cars was warmed up for a few laps by Alec Hounslow, before Ken Wharton and Dick Jacobs had sessions behind the wheel. The guest drivers were impressed with the new car at its first serious test outing, but fed back some observations on the handling, also on what they thought was a poor seating position, and an unfortunate tendency for fumes to come into the cockpit; however, these were all minor issues that were duly addressed by the development mechanics.

A week on from that first session, Marcus Chambers invited Jacobs back to Silverstone (on Thursday 31 March) for a further test session. Jacobs wrote: 'When I arrived at the circuit I was introduced to Johnny Lockett, a well-respected motorcycle racer, who had been invited to try the cars, as he had been invited to join the team. Between us, we covered some eighty to ninety laps, doing well over 250 miles (400km) during the day.' Modified rear springs had addressed the rear wheel lift that Jacobs had complained of the previous week, and a trial modification on the front suspension was found to have cured an oversteer problem.

> It was now possible to drift the fast corners in the approved style and the car felt right, which gave the drivers more confidence... there was still some engine fume trouble but it wasn't as bad as the previous tests. The new positions for the seat, pedals and steering wheel made the car much more comfortable. We came away from that test day much happier at the progress that was being made.

In the session of 28 April both Dick Jacobs and Ken Wharton were brought in to drive the cars. In his book about the Competitions Department, Bill Price records that Alec Hounslow led the way with three warm-up laps, on what was a damp track surface, and then Jacobs and Wharton took turns, and with some adjustments, lap times came down even further. Price includes extracts from Marcus Chambers' notes of the day, which state that further work needed included addressing excess heat in the cockpit, bringing the pedals nearer to the driver, installing a driver's footrest, adjustment to the door pocket to prevent the driver's arm from catching it, a lower steering ratio, and some work to make the driver's door open wider (this would be a criticism levelled at the early production MGA, too). We also know from the writing of Brian Moylan (another member of the 'Comps' team) that others present at Silverstone on that day were Captain George Eyston, John Thornley, Doug Watts, Dickie Green and Ron Bettles.

The cockpit of the Le Mans specification EX182 was neatly tailored around the driver.

A contemporary Pathé newsreel film, *Famous car races again*, covers one of these sessions at a clearly very wet Silverstone circuit, with Ken Wharton behind the wheel, and John Thornley and Marcus Chambers on stopwatch duty, and there is also a short preview in this film showing mechanics fitting the engine into LBL 304.

After these test sessions, Marcus Chambers' report to management concluded that: 'Performance tests at Silverstone had shown that a sustained lap speed of 85mph [136.8km/h], with a max lap speed of 94mph [151km/h], was theoretically possible.'

With all the testing concluded, the necessary adjustments made (including swapping the original 3.7:1 rear axle ratio for 3.9:1), and the final cleaning and polishing completed, all four cars were ready by the first week of June to be taken across the Channel to meet their destiny at 'la Sarthe', popular shorthand for the famous Circuit de la Sarthe Le

Ken Wharton was one of the drivers invited to shake down the EX 182 prototypes at Silverstone as part of their development.
AUTHOR'S COLLECTION

EX182 in competition guise, with distinctive large driving lamp.

MG AT LE MANS

The world-famous 'Quatre-Vingt Heures', held in the French town of Le Mans since 1923, has long been regarded by motor-racing enthusiasts throughout the world as the pinnacle of motor-sports endeavour – the automotive equivalent, perhaps, of climbing Everest. Whilst its organization and setting have always been resolutely French, the annual summer spectacle has always drawn large numbers of British entries and spectators: for a single weekend every June (other than the war years) convoys of Britons have invaded France and enjoyed the sights and sounds of cars racing down the fabulous Mulsanne Straight in the pursuit of glory.

We have already seen how George Phillips, with encouragement from MG, had raised the profile of the marque in 1949, 1950 and 1951 with his TC- and TD-based specials, but the association of MG with Le Mans goes much further back. The marque first appeared at Le Mans in 1930 with a brace of MG M-Type Midget 'Double Twelve' Le Mans Sports cars, though neither finished. There were several other fairly unsuccessful entries over the years, although a Midget finished in sixth place in 1933, and a K3 Magnette finished in fourth the following year.

In 1935, MG entered three MG PA Midgets, and recruited six leading female racing drivers to drive them, under the direction of Captain George Edward Thomas Eyston (27 June 1897–11 June 1979). The team were known popularly as 'Eyston's Dancing Daughters', and they went on to take the top three places in their class. Although there was a race in 1939, understandably the following years were a gap in the sequence, and it was not until 1949 that the annual event resumed.

The attraction to John Thornley and Syd Enever of the Le Mans race as a means of launching their new MG sports car was obvious; Thornley could also see that with care, a successful finish could qualify the team for the Biennial Cup and so, all being well, secure a guaranteed entry at Le Mans 1956; in one of his memos to management, he declared that, in 1956, 'We must enter to win our class, and a pretty stiff class it is.' The fates would, however, interfere with this noble ambition.

Mans. Whilst the Le Mans party were away, Henry Stone and Tommy Wellman remained behind and oversaw the operation to shift the competitions shop out from Development.

En Route to Le Mans

The EX 182s were conducted in a line from Abingdon to the ferry, driven by Alec Hounslow, Douggie Watts, Cliff Bray and Jim Cox on Sunday 5 June 1955.

We drove the four cars [three in the race plus LBL 304 as a spare] and I was in the third car, Douggie Watts in the last one. We were all going down the road in convoy on the way to Dover and the next thing I knew the back end had gone. I was about two-thirds of the way round a left-hand bend and the car spun three times – I can remember Douggie shouting to me 'Hold on to it Jim!' and then the car suddenly swung the other way round and shot forwards. The car went up the bank as I put the anchors on, and to our amazement there was no damage other than a slightly bent

The four cars ready to start their expedition to Le Mans in June 1955, parked up in formation at the MG factory. Jimmy Cox is seated in LBL 302 (no. 41, to become no. 42 in the race), Alec Hounslow is in LBL 301 (no. 40, to become no. 41 in the race). LBL 303, car no. 64 (Cliff Bray driving) was the reserve, and furthest from the camera is the practice car, LBL 304 (Doug Watts driving here). In the background, Marcus Chambers and Henry Stone survey the scene.
CLIFF BRAY

front number plate. I don't know to this day whether or not Marcus Chambers ever got to hear about this!

En route there were a few rather more obviously planned stops, including for refuelling at Chas. Hayward & Sons Garage in Ashford, Kent.

Folkestone, on the Sunday evening, was the venue for an initial rendezvous of much of the party for the Le Mans adventure, who celebrated their imminent trip across the Channel with a party at the Burlington Hotel. Whilst some of the party would only be joining later in the week, the entourage from the outset was already quite substantial. In overall charge was John Thornley, supported by his wife Joan, whilst Russell and Meg Lowry were present as interpreters and, in Russell's case, also acting as the scribe who would helpfully record events for posterity. The author has been able to draw from a full copy of Lowry's account, which Lowry originally passed to John Thornley and from which the latter quoted in his own excellent book *Maintaining the Breed*.

Marcus Chambers was in control of the competition side, and Syd Enever was accompanied by some of his team. Sammy Davis – veteran of the Bentley victory at Le Mans in 1927 – was to take charge of the pit, while Babe Learoyd oversaw the transport logistics, and Freddie Crossley was on hand as a helper. Along with the aforementioned mechanics driving the cars (Jim Cox, Cliff Bray and Doug Watts, led by Alec Hounslow), others from the Abingdon workshops were

Key members of the team responsible for preparing the beautiful EX 182 Le Mans cars stand proudly behind two of them at Abingdon, with the BMC Competitions transporter (the 'camion', built by Appleyards of Leeds) behind. *From left to right:* Harold Wiggins (machinist), Dickie Green (recent recruit from Aston-Martin, who drove the transporter), Doug Watts (shop foreman), Alec Hounslow, Syd Enever, and technicians Jimmy Cox, Cliff Bray and Gerald Wiffen (who accompanied Green in the 'camion').

CLIFF BRAY

Dickie Green (driving the 'camion'), with Gerald Wiffen sitting alongside. Like the Chambers, the Thornleys travelled in slightly more comfortable fashion by Riley Pathfinder.

For the proposed driver contingent for the race itself, Dick Jacobs, Joe Flynn and Johnny Lockett were coming with their respective wives, Ted Lund was there, and Ken Miles joined the group, having flown over from the USA. Hans Waeffler (born 7 August 1914 in Basel, Switzerland) and his wife were to come separately from Zürich to meet the party in France. Altogether it was evidently quite a sizeable party that would be descending upon the Château Chêne de Cœur.

On the morning of Monday 6 June, the party drove the short distance to Dover, where they boarded the British Transport Commission's cross-channel ferry *Lord Warden*, a precursor of the later roll-on, roll-off ferries of later years. The ferry had a smooth crossing to Boulogne-sur-Mer, and the MG team were able to clear French customs soon after midday.

Pressing on southwards, the party encountered a severe storm, although the spare EX 182 race car, along with the necessary spares and tools, was safely stowed inside the smart new BMC Competitions transporter (driven by Dickie Green, with Gerald Wiffen also in the cab). At the head of the convoy was a Riley Pathfinder driven by Marcus Chambers, also carrying Mrs (Patricia) Chambers and Harold Wiggins. By late afternoon the party had arrived at their base for the next few days, the Château Chêne de Cœur, home of la Comtesse de Vautibault, a friend of Captain George Eyston. The château had ample garaging and plenty of accommodation for the thirty-six people who would be staying there.

After a good night's rest came the all-important attendance at the *pésage* on the Tuesday morning, where the cars would be checked over in scrutineering, all of this conducted

The EX 182 cars stopped at Chas. Hayward & Sons garage in Ashford, Kent, to refuel before their rendezvous with other members of the team at Folkestone.

MGCC

The convoy has arrived at the Château Chêne de Cœur, with Mrs Patricia Chambers standing alongside her husband's Riley Pathfinder and Cliff Bray leaning against the nearside rear wing.
CLIFF BRAY

The transporter doubled as a well-equipped mobile workshop, with a neat trestle arrangement that could be assembled at the rear. Here, car no. 64 is tended in the courtyard of the château.
CLIFF BRAY

in the main square at Le Mans. As Russell Lowry recalled: 'The MGs, immaculate in British Racing Green and shining like the morning sun itself, in perfect formation, dead on time, and attended by smart, green-overalled mechanics, made a terrific impression... everyone was most congratulatory about the new cars, as cars.'

About the only change required was that the tips of the exhaust pipes had to be cut square instead of diagonally, so they did not disturb any dust on the ground. Back at the château, a Pathé film crew arrived and began recording what would be the basis of a newsreel short about MG's mission. On Wednesday 8 June, others arrived; Stan Nicholls as timekeeper (laden with spares for the Riley Pathfinder, whose bearings had suffered during the trip from Boulogne to Le Mans) and the King brothers and their wives, who arrived in a pair of Triumph TR2s.

Practice took place in the evening, and as Dick Jacobs recorded in his autobiography, the cars lapped in excess of the qualifying speed of 80mph (129km/h), although Johnny Lockett evidently had problems when his fan belt snapped and he lost the coolant. Fortunately there was no damage, and his car was soon back on form, with the help of Dickie Green. On the Friday before the race, the news came through that other cars had dropped out of contention, and the consequence was that the third reserve car (No. 64) for Ted Lund and Hans Waeffler had been bumped up off the reserve or *suppléant* list and was to be allowed to compete. However, there would also be some chopping and changing of the other EX 182 race numbers, as explained in the table below.

Saturday 12 June dawned bright and clear, and the cars and the transporter posed with the party for photographs before making their way to the circuit. The previous Thursday the 1098cc Coventry Climax-engined Arnott race car had crashed out in practice, and a consequent benefit for MG was that the now vacant Arnott pit was next to theirs – so Stan Nicholls was able to expand his timekeeping activities into the spare space. The next stage was the arrival of the *commissaires*, whose role was to check off equipment and spares.

THE EX 182 LE MANS CARS RACE NUMBERING

Chassis no.	Engine No.	Le Mans 1955 Race No. Pre-Scrutineering	Le Mans 1955 Actual Race No.	First recorded Reg. No.	Mechanics driving to the race	Drivers at Le Mans in the race	Finish overall	Finish in class
EX 182/38	EX 182/43	40	41	LBL 301	Alec Hounslow	Lockett/Miles	12th	5th
EX 182/39	EX 182/42	41	42	LBL 302	Jim Cox	Jacobs/Flynn	DNF	DNF
EX 182/40	EX 182/44	64	64	LBL 303	Cliff Bray	Lund/Waeffler	17th	6th
EX 182/41	EX 182/45	Test car	Test car	LBL 304	Doug Watts	Practice car	N/A	N/A

Footnotes:
There were changes in the race numbering for Le Mans in 1955, but confusion has been caused by photographs during scrutineering and the race itself. Jim Cox said: 'When we first went out, LBL 301 was number 40, LBL 302 was 41, LBL 303 was 64, and LBL 304 was the spare car used for practice. After scrutineering, for some unknown reason, we had to change the numbers to 41 and 42 – so logically you would have thought, leave 41 alone and make 40 into 42 – but no, they didn't do that, they made 41 into 40, and 41 into 42.' The fact was that the number 40 had been allocated to an Osca, which necessitated the renumbering of the MG EX 182s: 40 became 41, and 41 becoming 42.

MG MECHANICS

Cliff Bray glances at the camera from the cockpit of one of the EX 182 cars.
CLIFF BRAY

Whilst Marcus Chambers and Alec Hounslow were the senior figures in the Le Mans venture, naturally they were supported in this endeavour by a team of mechanics chosen especially for the task: these were Cliff Bray, Jim Cox, Dickie Green, Doug Watts, Gerald Wiffen and Harold Wiggins. Henry Stone and Tommy Wellman stayed at Abingdon to reconfigure the Development Shop, to separate it out from 'Comps'.

Bristol-born **Victor Henry Clifford 'Cliff' Bray** (10 January 1923 –29 September 2007) grew up in Abingdon. After leaving school, he took up an apprenticeship at the MG factory in September 1938. With the war effort under way, Cliff moved to MG's busy press shop, where he remained until February 1942. After war service, Cliff joined the MG Rectification department under George Morris (no relation to Lord Nuffield). In late 1949, Cliff moving to the production line for a year. The following year he returned to Rectification, where he worked again until October 1954. In that month, he joined Syd Enever's Development Team and was soon heavily engaged in competition work. With Abingdon's Competitions Department up and running, Cliff Bray was part of the team working under Alec Hounslow which created racing TDs and the MG Magnette for the 1955 Monte Carlo rally, as well as the team of four alloy-bodied 'EX182' prototypes which he then helped escort to the Le Mans circuit in June 1955. He also accompanied his boss to Switzerland later with a brace of MGA Twin Cam prototypes. Historians, the author included, can be grateful for the fact that Cliff Bray was a meticulous record-keeper, writing up car builds and test sessions and maintaining a detailed diary.

Dickie Green (left) and Jimmy Cox smile for the camera at Le Mans, 1955.
MG CAR CLUB

Jim Cox is really **Sydney John Cox** (born in Abingdon in 1931), but when he joined the MG factory, as there was already an important 'Syd', he was henceforth known as 'Jim' or 'Jimmy'. In 1945, Cox Senior managed to secure his son a job at Abingdon as a junior office/messenger boy; the role meant that Cox got to access all areas of the factory, and as he was a bright lad and a willing learner, he achieved a kind of practical on-the-job apprenticeship, including helping out on the MG TC Midget assembly line. After returning from National Service, Cox's friend and mentor Bert Wirdnam helped secure him a role in the Development Shop, where he fell under the wing of Jack Crooke, who helped him learn the mysteries of engine building. Projects with which Jim Cox became involved included EX 172, EX 175, EX 182 (driving one of the cars to Le Mans), and the two post-war record cars.

Richard ('Dickie') F. Green (16 May 1918–20 December 2008) enjoyed working on cars and motorcycles. When 'de-mobbed', Green responded to an advertisement placed by Marcus Chambers, and started work at North Downs Engineering in March 1947. From there, he went to Wade Engineering (working on superchargers) and in 1952 to Aston Martin at Feltham. In 1955, Green heard about Marcus Chambers' move to Abingdon, and so he followed suit, where he became heavily involved in the development of EX 182 within the MG Development Department. His son Michael told the author: 'Dad did much of the testing, and he was now courting one Doreen Sherwood from Aston Martin and would show up in the EX 182 – which had no MG badges on it – while at other times he'd arrive in a TF1500.'

Dickie Green, photographed at Le Mans in 1955 by Marcus Chambers.
MICHAEL GREEN

The anxious MG mechanics look on as their charges go through scrutineering; note the race numbers were still 40, 41 and 64 at this stage. *Left to right* the mechanics are Gerald Wiffen, Alec Hounslow, Doug Watts and Jim Cox.

CLIFF BRAY

Although Dickie Green remained with MG for the rest of 1955, in February 1956 he emigrated to California, and began the next exciting chapter of his career.

Gerald P. S. Wiffen (born 1934) had also started as a tea-boy, like Jim Cox, but in the same way he swiftly proved so versatile and quick to learn that he became a fitter and a vital part of the 'Comps' family; in a 2009 interview with Simon Taylor for *Motor Sport*, rally legend Paddy Hopkirk said of Wiffen: 'Gerald usually prepared my cars, and he was a totally professional, hands-on engineer. Nothing was too much trouble, the smallest detail...'

Douglas Alec 'Douggie' Watts (16 July 1919–12 January 1993) lived all his life in Abingdon, and had a line to the top within MG as his sister Isla was Syd Enever's long-serving (thirty-five years) secretary. He became Competitions Department foreman, and remained in that role right through the heydays of the Mini Coopers. When he left school he took up employment with Abingdon brewery Morlands. During the war years he joined the Royal Engineers, serving in North Africa and Italy. After demob and with his engineering skills to hand, he joined the MG Car Company, working in the Rectification Department as the MG TC Midget started production, and soon progressing to MG TF road-test inspection work. It wasn't long before Watts was transferred from Development into the newly formed Competition Dept, as its inaugural shop foreman; he eventually became Shop Superintendent under Stuart Turner. By the time of the successful heydays of the Big Healey 3000 and Mini Cooper 'S', Watts had two foremen under him responsible for more than twenty mechanics.

After the Competitions Department closed in 1970, Watts continued to work at Abingdon as a supervisor until his eventual retirement.

Doug Watts, photographed around the time of the Le Mans EX 182 adventure.

HILARY WATTS

Harold Wiggins (14 October 1910–March 1970) was a skilled welder and fitter, and his expertise was often employed in the fabrication of special one-off parts, as was typically employed on the EX 182 and prototype MGA chassis. He worked in Development Department, and Henry Stone referred to his colleague as 'Wiggo the Wonder Welder'.

The 1955 Race

The race began, as usual, at four o'clock in the afternoon, with the usual dash across the track to clamber in the cars and start the engines, before heading out on to the circuit. Fangio caused something of a stir when he caught his foot in the steering wheel as he got into his Mercedes, meaning that he was slow starting, something for which he would soon more than compensate. Lowry recorded that the EX 182 lap times were initially 5min 45sec, which dropped to 5min 30sec; Sammy Davis issued a direction that the drivers should slow down, and they soon fell into a rhythm, with Lund leading in No. 64, followed by Lockett in No. 41 and Jacobs in No. 42.

Car No. 41 out on the Mulsanne Straight.

AUTHOR'S COLLECTION

Two of the EX182s, no. 41 followed by no. 42.
AUTHOR'S COLLECTION

Car no. 42 in fine fettle at Le Mans; sadly it would prove to be an unlucky race for its driver, Dick Jacobs, seen here running well prior to his accident.
AUTHOR'S COLLECTION

Then there was a sudden explosion out on the track, barely 150 yards from the MG pit: there had been a serious accident involving Pierre Levegh (Mercedes), Lance Macklin (Austin-Healey) and Mike Hawthorn (Jaguar D-Type). Levegh had collided with the rear of the Austin-Healey, which in turn had swerved to avoid the disc-braked Jaguar, slewing in towards its pit, and as a consequence the Mercedes had launched into the air, into the nearby earth embankment, showering the crowd with the shattered parts of the car and related debris. Levegh was killed instantly, eighty-three spectators were killed, and about 180 sustained injuries, many of them severe. It was without question the most terrible motor-circuit accident in history.

Jim Cox saw the accident clearly from his vantage point at the pit:

> In my opinion, Mike Hawthorn misjudged coming into the pits – he must have been doing about 120mph – because instead of coming in behind Macklin, he cut in front of the Healey. As a result, Macklin pulled to the left just as Levegh was coming up behind him. The Healey was full of fuel and therefore riding very low; it also had that tapered rear wing line, and so Levegh's Mercedes simply rode up the Healey's wing and shot into the air, dug into the bank, and all the stuff from the wreckage flew into the crowd. Many people were killed; it was a terrible thing to see.

In the midst of the panic surrounding the Levegh crash, there was also some confusion about what had happened to Dick Jacobs in his MG. Jim Cox was on the look-out for Jacobs, which was why he was in a position to be able to witness the Levegh crash so clearly. Many present thought that the race would surely be red-flagged and stopped, but the race officials decided to keep it running, reasoning that a huge exodus of the crowd would have caused traffic chaos, with the nightmare scenario of ambulances and emergency crews

A still undamaged car no. 64 on the Mulsanne Straight.
AUTHOR'S COLLECTION

The EX 182 of Lund/Waeffler leads the Dickson/Sanderson Triumph TR2 and the Porsche 550 Spyder of Olivier/Jeser under the famous Dunlop bridge.
AUTHOR'S COLLECTION

being prevented from trying to save the injured. Meanwhile, as Russell Lowry wrote: 'Even before the black drift of smoke from the Mercedes had faded I saw a much smaller, grey curl of vapour rising from an undeterminable point further away. Soon it was gone and attracted no further attention.'

The race ground on, with much of the excitement tempered by the growing news of what had happened; Lockett and Lund brought in cars 41 and 64, handing them over to their co-drivers Miles and Waeffler, but the team began to wonder what had become of Jacobs in No. 42, who was due another two laps before handing over to Joe Flynn. Then came some news over the tannoy that the little MG had crashed and caught fire at Maison Blanch (White House); the news was alarming for the MG pit, and not least for Janet Jacobs. At eight o'clock came the news that Dick Jacobs had been taken to hospital (at Coulaines, to the north of Le Mans). Whilst the information was thin and unclear, Ted Lund had seen his colleague out of the wreck and receiving assistance at the roadside.

In his post-race report, Marcus Chambers wrote, succinctly: 'The second car, no. 42 (Jacobs/Flynn), had an accident in the twenty-eighth lap at White House Corner. No other car was involved, so it could only have been an error on Jacobs' part. He had acknowledged a slow down signal on the completion of the previous lap.'

In a 1974 interview with Clive Richardson for *Motorsport*, Jacobs had spoken of problems with a softening of the Armstrong shock absorbers; whatever the cause, he was out of the race and had been seriously injured.

Fred Crossley managed to get through to Coulaines and brought back the news that Jacobs was indeed quite badly injured, but his only words of concern had been to apologise to John Thornley for crashing the car. Meanwhile communications with the outside world, in a time before modern telephony, were difficult, to put it mildly, and John Thornley prepared a note to be sent out to BMC HQ via the Castrol agents on site. The Mercedes team withdrew, but the race itself went on, the eventual Jaguar victory proving to be rather a hollow one. In the midst of all the confusion, a UK newspaper (the *Evening Standard* on the Monday immediately after the event) also carried an obituary for Dick Jacobs.

Jacobs had been comparatively lucky (if that is the right word for a near-fatal experience) in that the chart keeper for the MG team, Dr Michael King, also happened to be the Nuffield Organisation doctor.

Meanwhile back in the race, after seventy-one laps, the remaining pair of MGs had swapped pilots again; records show that Johnnie Lockett kept up a fairly consistent lap of 5.37 miles and Lund reached as fast as 5.22 and 5.23 respectively, and a very impressive top speed of 116.69mph (187.75km/h) was achieved flat out on the famous Mulsanne Straight. Rain swept in at dawn on the Sunday, described by Russell Lowry as coming 'at first absent-mindedly, and then with increasing, vicious intensity'. At five in the morning, Lockett (41) and Lund (64) took over again, going back out on to the wet circuit. In trying to bring the times down for No. 64, Lund then dropped his guard slightly and struck the back end of a Jaguar D-Type (car No. 8) which had been abandoned at Arnage by its driver, Don Beauman, the previous night, following an accident in the eleventh hour.

Dick Jacobs' EX 182 no. 42 on fire at 'Maison Blanche' (White House).
MG CAR CLUB ARCHIVES/ AUTHOR'S COLLECTION

A crowd of onlookers gaze at the wreckage of Dick Jacobs' MG EX 182. The presence of the chef seems particularly incongruous.
CLIFF BRAY

Marcus Chambers subsequently wrote simply that '...on lap 175 at 09:05 on Sunday, Lund rammed a ditched Jaguar, bent his frame, damaged the left front wing and headlamp, and put the wheels 1¼ inches out of track. This was rectified at the next pit stop, and the car qualified 40 minutes from the end of the race.'

Ted Lund relayed his own recollection of the incident in an interview with Jonathan Wood, published in *Thoroughbred & Classic Cars* in January 1975:

> During the night a D-Type Jaguar tried to pass me at Arnage and slid right into the sandbank, and remained there for the rest of the race. Then later, towards the morning, I did the very same trying to pass a Triumph TR2, at the same corner. Needless to say I shot into the back of the D-Type in the same sandbank. I could have cried on the spot ... to think through lack of concentration and probably tiredness after twelve to fourteen hours of racing I had done the very thing I should have been aware of.

Lund brought the car back in to the pits and, as Chambers' report referenced above, the damaged near-side front wing was bashed clear of the wheel, and Hans Waeffler took it back out again. The two MGs kept going, as reliable as clockwork, only their brakes needing adjustment. By eleven, car No. 41 had 200 laps to its credit; three hours on, Lund brought in the other car to report some steering problems: it was checked over, found to be okay and he was sent off again, with nine laps needed for the qualification. The requisite laps achieved, the message went out to keep going carefully, mindful of the heavy rain, to ensure they both finished.

At four o'clock, as the curtain came down on a stressful twenty-four hours, car No. 41 was the first MG past the chequered flag, having achieved 249 laps at 86.17mph (138.64km/h), and fifth in its class; after a short interval, Ted Lund in car No. 64 followed, with a tally of 234 laps at 81.97mph (131.89km/h) and sixth in class. After some muted celebrations on the Sunday night, when John Thornley was able to visit Dick Jacobs in hospital, the team began the winding-down process on Monday, including recovery of the remains of the burnt-out No. 42 as well as Macklin's damaged Healey.

Joe Flynn, who had been intended to be Dick Jacobs' co-driver, was said to have been sufficiently upset at his lack of an opportunity to drive that he walked the entire circuit on foot, an exercise which it is recorded took him about eight hours. Meanwhile, John Thornley's messages had got through to Sir Leonard Lord, and Dick Jacobs found that a medical team arrived to look after him, and flew him back to the Churchill Hospital in Oxford.

Breakfast started at six on the Tuesday (14 June), and the various parties then departed to their destinations, Russell Lowry recording that his final cup of tea, at the tail end of the trip, was enjoyed at Folkestone in the company of Ted Lund, Ken Miles and the Chambers.

Le Mans Aftermath

Dick Jacobs' recovery was a slow one, meaning that it was four months before he was able to walk, and another two before he returned to the Mill Garage full time; these events had decided that his racing future would be better served as manager rather than active participant, and so began a new era of the Jacobs MGs, some of which feature later in this chapter.

After Ted Lund struck a ditched Jaguar D-Type, Alec Hounslow (far side) and Dickie Green (with his back to the camera) did their best with hammer and crowbar to make the car fit to continue.

CLIFF BRAY

The broken headlamp and buckled wing dealt with, Hans Waeffler took car no. 64 back out.

CLIFF BRAY

MARCUS CHAMBERS REPORTS BACK AFTER THE 1955 LE MANS RACE…

Marcus Chambers' post-event report was intended for BMC management. Within it, he hoped optimistically for a reasoned outcome rather than the anticipated popular backlash.

As a result of the accident, the form of next year's race is most likely to be changed, and there is no reason why we should not take steps through the RAC and other channels, to see that the race is run on lines to suit us and other British manufacturers. If we look back at the early years of this race, it will be remembered that it was for standard production models to which minor modification was permitted. This category still remains in the race, but the introduction of the prototype has almost eliminated the Standard Production Sports Car and it is at present impossible to win the race or a class except with a prototype. In the opinion of the Competitions Manager, prototypes should be excluded, but bodies that conform to the FIA rules should be permitted, together with permitted modification to the chassis. I think the race would regain some of its past value, and one-off jobs such as the Nardi would make way for some serious entries and permit the return of the private entries, which have by now been almost eliminated. Concerning the accident itself, no doubt the competent authority will make a pronouncement in due course, but whilst it is to be deplored, it should be realized that it was brought about by a chain of circumstances which might never occur again in a lifetime. Morris racing will still go on, for the same reason that ships still cross the Atlantic, although the Titanic is no more.

In the wake of Le Mans, there was an inevitable public and political retrenchment, and there was an interim cessation of most motor-sports events in France, Germany, Spain and Switzerland; and in the USA, the American Automobile Association (AAA) turned its back on motor sport, leading to the creation of the United States Automobile Club (USAC) to fill the void left by the dissolution of the AAA's Contest Board. The most immediate impact on the Competitions Team was the cancellation of July's Alpine Rally, an event for which the EX 182 entry was at an advanced stage of preparation, not to mention transport and hotel accommodation that had been booked in advance.

A European Odyssey

Thus John Thornley sanctioned a group of five cars to be taken on a brief 'European odyssey', from 3 to 13 July. The group included one of the EX 182 cars (LBL 301, as already prepared for the cancelled Alpine event), one of the early production MGAs (LJB 370, a Tyrolite Green Car, chassis no. 10102), along with a Magnette and an Austin Cambridge (both these saloons fitted with MGA Le Mans-type engines) as well as an Austin A90 Westminster.

The objective was to visit the Alpine cols, the circuits at Nürburgring and Montlhéry, with Syd Enever in tow (supported by Marcus Chambers, Alec Hounslow and Douggie Watts) along with British drivers John Milne, Bill Shepherd, G. Gibson and John Williamson, and Swiss drivers Heinz Keller (the Zürich importer) and Hans (Harry) Zweifel. As Marcus Chambers recalled, the trip involved staying in some excellent hotels, during a journey of more than 2,300 miles (3,700km), and helped identify many improvements needed: 'The factory engineers were being educated by the rally drivers, who were prepared to give the cars a lot more "stick" than the factory testers.'

Some references have included Superintendent John Gott in the list of drivers, but his name was not on the original report from Marcus Chambers. In that same report, it was noted that for the EX 182:

> Excessive heat in the driving compartment would have necessitated the removal of the undertrays if these cars had run in the actual Alpine trial. The constriction of the hot air from the engine compartment, and the use of light

Syd Enever in crash helmet stands alongside LJB 370, a Tyrolite Green pre-production MGA at what looks like the Reims circuit. The opportunity for designers, mechanics and the BMC racing drivers to work together proved highly beneficial to the development of the production cars.

ENEVER FAMILY

MGA prototype 'LJB 370' in the Swiss Alps.

'LJB 370' at Montlhéry in 1955. MGA on the wall is a coincidence.

The small BMC Competitions convoy of July 1955, with an Austin A90 Westminster (POM 755, which became a team rally car, and would be driven by Joan Johns, Doreen Rich and Pat Moss in the 1956 Monte Carlo), the pre-production MGA LJB 370 (Syd Enever, in open neck shirt, stands alongside), and an Austin A50 Cambridge. The stop is at the French Alpine pass of Col de L'Iseran, near the border with Italy.

ENEVER FAMILY

alloy ramps, floorboards and gearbox cowling, scantily protected with rexine, is responsible for this. In common with the other cars fitted with the Le Mans-type engine, this one suffered from heavy oil consumption, mainly due to the use of three-ring pistons. Oil leaks from flexible pipes on this car were slight only. There were sharply divided opinions as to the gearbox ratios, one faction persisting that closer ratios would have improved overall performance in the mountains. In all other respects the car proved to be ideal for the purpose.

Meanwhile, as far as the production type MGA was concerned, it was recorded that:

> The salient lesson on this car was that the engine lost tune at the bottom end towards the end of the trip; this has not yet been accounted for, and is being investigated. The gear shift was found to stiffen to an uncomfortable degree when hot. Moreover, reverse and second gear were lost completely at Nürburg, and came back of their own accord later.

Heinz Keller, of the Swiss Nuffield Agents, in LJB 370 at the Col du Galibier, a mountain pass in the southern region of the French Dauphiné Alps near Grenoble.

KELLER FAMILY

A fuel stop – taking on Supershell petrol – during the Swiss adventures with LBL 301 in 1955.

KELLER FAMILY

Just after the fuel stop, the convoy – with an MG Magnette in tow – prepares to set off again.
KELLER FAMILY

Heinz Keller again with LJB 370, this time at the Col de L'Iseran, the highest paved pass in the Alps.
KELLER FAMILY

> Also, the gearbox lost oil. The gearbox has been removed and returned to Mr Appleby for investigation.

There was also comment on the DM.12 brake linings, and their perhaps unsurprising tendency to suffer from fade in the mountains, whilst the fact that various pieces of trim and fixtures fell off or became detached was referred back to Bodies Branch for their own investigations. As Chambers noted in an article for *Thoroughbred & Classic Cars* in February 1977, the intrepid crew finally called in at the Montlhéry circuit on their way home.

Autocar **staged a road test of LBL 303 for the magazine's issue of 29 July 1955. The car had been converted from its Le Mans form to one intended for the subsequently cancelled 1955 Alpine Rally.**
AUTHOR'S COLLECTION

LJB 370 at the Col de L'Iseran.
KELLER FAMILY

ENEVER FAMILY

Shortly after this European foray, MG invited Harold Hastings of *Autocar* to Abingdon in order to try out one of the EX 182 cars in Alpine Rally trim (photos show that it bears the registration number LBL 303). In their subsequent report of 29 July 1955, the writers conceded that 'it isn't often that the opportunity arises to put a prototype car through its paces, but *Autocar* was recently given such a chance when car No. 64 in the Le Mans programme was placed at its disposal by the MG company...' The car had clearly been converted in readiness for the cancelled Alpine Rally, and so had the fitted alloy passenger seat area tonneau removed, the associated door made openable, the aero screen replaced by a full-width production-type screen (with windscreen wipers), and the Lucas 'flame thrower' spotlight had been removed from the grille.

Unsurprisingly, the car had been thoroughly overhauled (it had, after all, been damaged at Le Mans) and so *Autocar* were duly impressed that when they collected it from Abingdon, it bore no trace of its twenty-four-hour ordeal, and 'one could again admire the graceful lines of the body'. In what amounts to a road test, the magazine drove the car for a few days and clearly put it through its paces. As such, they had some advice to offer MG:

> During a fast change the synchromesh could be beaten into top gear, and the change down from third to second was stiff, but this could have been owing to the fitting of the new gearbox. For optimum performance on a production version the gear ratios appear to be a little wide, particularly between second and third. With a three-quarter full tank and two people on board it is possible to spin the wheels in the getaway on a dry road.

Performance was, understandably, a bit better than the production MGA that the magazine would eventually get to

An EX 182 in Alpine Rally trim (with full height windscreen) and wearing the registration number LBL 304.
CHRIS HARVEY

LBL 301, complete with the special aerodynamic low headlamp nose. The headlamps were Riley Pathfinder secondary units. Note also the way that the side/ indicator lamps have been let into the front valance, directly below the headlamps.
AUTHOR'S COLLECTION

test, but was clearly a revelation in comparison with the old traditional T-Series.

> All performance figures taken were with a passenger aboard, the hood down and approximately 16gal (73ltr) of fuel in the tank. Under these far from ideal conditions a maximum speed of 103mph (165km/h) was recorded on the clock, which against calibration was extremely accurate above 40mph (64km/h); this corresponds to approximately 5,720 engine rpm on the 4.3 axle. Similarly the standing starts were 0-40mph in 6.2sec, 0-60mph in 13.8sec, and 0-80mph in 25.8sec.

All of these were impressive figures for a not especially exotic 1.5-litre car in the mid-1950s. In their enthusiastic summary, *Autocar* commented that:

> It seems quite evident that the production version is eagerly awaited. If the engine can be offered without too much detuning, and the weight kept down to around present level, this delightful car will be a serious contender in the small high performance class, and should have a ready sale in home and overseas markets.

THE GOLDEN JUBILEE TOURIST TROPHY RACE, DUNDROD

The story of the gestation of the Morris Engines twin-cam engine is told in detail in Chapter 6, but the saga of its

The only MG Twin Cam engine to appear at Dundrod in September 1955 was fitted to LBL 301, racing as car no. 34. Driven by Ron Flockhart and Johnny Lockett, it crashed out of the event.
AUTHOR'S COLLECTION

THE TOURIST TROPHY AND DUNDROD

The Tourist Trophy race, known more commonly by the familiar 'TT' initials, was first staged on the Isle of Man in 1905. The Isle of Man TT for cars (not to be confused with the motorcycle TT) lasted for seventeen years, and then, after a hiatus of five years, it was brought over to the Ards Circuit in Ulster, Northern Ireland. A quirk of local legislation meant that roads in Northern Ireland could be closed for the purposes of motor racing, unlike everywhere else in the United Kingdom.

In 1933 and 1934, MG won the TT in their magnificent giant-killing K3 Magnettes, and Rileys won in the following two years. However, the risks of road racing were firmly brought home in 1936 when a Riley crashed and collided with a row of spectators, eight of whom were killed. The consequence of this was that racing at Ards came to an end, and for the run-up to the war period it transferred to the Donington Circuit in England.

The accessible allure of road racing remained, however, and so in 1950 the TT eventually came back to Northern Ireland and Dundrod in Country Antrim, where the circular 7.4-mile (12km) road circuit comprised sections of what are now the B38, B101 and B154. In the 1950 race MG's Dick Jacobs, George Phillips and Ted Lund took the first three places in their class in their matching set of MG TD Mark II Midgets.

For the 1955 race, much was made of the fifty years since the first Isle of Man event in 1905, and hence it was publicized as the Golden Jubilee TT. Coming after Le Mans, and just prior to the MGA launch at Frankfurt, the MG factory entered their three cars as prototypes again; they also laid plans to test out the experimental work on the twin-cam engines. However, the events at Dundrod that year meant that the Golden Jubilee road race would be the last to be held there.

appearance at the Golden Jubilee Tourist Trophy at Dundrod in September 1955, and the prior demise of its unfortunate Austin Engines rival, merits coverage here because of the competition connection and above all the implications of the events at the Northern Ireland circuit for subsequent MG racing activities.

For Dundrod, MG started where they had left off after Le Mans, which meant adapting the three survivors, Jacobs' car having of course been destroyed. The Austin twin cam necessitated a bulge in the bonnet of LBL 303, whilst LBL 301, with the Morris Engines twin cam, was fitted with a modified nose with low-mounted Riley Pathfinder driving lamps. The third car retained the overhead-valve Le Mans engine type.

In his book *The Works MGs* (co-written with Mike Allison), Peter Browning states that MG was able to benefit from a generous gesture from Mercedes, who apparently invited Tommy Wellman and Henry Stone to Ireland with one of the cars, allowing them to share the course which the Germans had exclusively booked for their own testing of their SLRs. 'During these tests, the twin-cam cars had surge problems running with the twin-choke Solex carburettors.' This would lead to a switch to Webers.

The carburetion problems that had plagued both twin-cam prototypes in testing remained an issue. On the Sunday before the race the car was tried out at the MIRA high-speed test circuit, but the engine cut and spluttered on right-hand corners because of fuel surge away from the jets.

Eddie Maher worked frantically in order to fabricate a special intake manifold that would adapt twin Weber carburettors to the engine and thereby, it was hoped, deal with the handling-related fuel problem. At the last minute, on Thursday 15 September 1955, the completed manifold was sent by air from Coventry to Belfast. Prior to this, the cars had to get to Belfast too, and to achieve their goal, the Abingdon troupe had deployed in two directions: the transporter went via the A55 through Anglesey to Holyhead, while the EX 182s went by road to catch the rather decrepit ferry from Liverpool, with a brief stop en route in Preston with Ted Lund, one of the drivers for Dundrod. Jim Cox is keen to correct the story in Bill Price's book, which suggested he spun his charge on the wet journey to Liverpool; perhaps, Cox suggests, the story had been confused with his escapade on the way to Folkestone in June.

MGA No. 34 on the Dundrod circuit.
AUTHOR'S COLLECTION

Car no. 34 (LBL 301) is fuelled up at Dundrod in September 1955.
AUTHOR'S COLLECTION

Car no. 35 (LBL 303) was fitted with a more conventional overhead-valve B-Series engine. Note the bulge in the bonnet, originally intended to clear the bulkier Austin Twin Cam engine, which had been removed at Abingdon prior to the Dundrod race.
AUTHOR'S COLLECTION

THE THREE DUNDROD EX 182 CARS

Race Number	Registration Number	Chassis Number	Drivers at Dundrod	Notes
34	LBL 301	EX 182/38	Ron Flockhart/ Johnny Lockett	Fitted with the experimental Morris twin-cam engine (1498cc) and experimental Girling front disc brakes, and low headlamps. The car suffered from intermittent misfiring, and eventually crashed out of the race. In his report of 14 October 1955 after Dundrod, John Thornley wrote: 'In its cooler moments it showed a very good turn of speed and lapped at 79.46mph [127.85km/h].'
35	LBL 303	EX 182/40	Jack Fairman/Peter Wilson	Originally fitted, before shipment to Ulster, with an experimental Austin twin-cam engine, which was removed before the car was driven to the race and replaced with a Le Mans specification push-rod engine. The bonnet featured a bulge to accommodate the original Austin engine. Like LBL 301, this car was fitted with front disc brakes. In the race it finished in twentieth place. Thornley wrote: 'Reliable and fast, lapped at 77.39mph [124.5km/h], completed the race at 71.07mph [114.35km/h], finished fourth in its class behind three Porsches, and ahead of all the works TR2s.'
36	LBL 304	EX 182/41	Ted Lund/Dickie Stoop	Fitted with a Le Mans specification pushrod engine, this car retired early after eight laps, with a split alloy fuel tank. Thornley recorded: 'This tank had been extensively road-tested, but its failure in the race was undoubtedly attributable to the peculiar conditions. The car "took off" once per lap on "Deer's Leap", and the buffeting of 20 gallons [90ltr] of fuel proved too much for the tank's seams.'
P	LJB 205	EX 182/42	Practice car	Indicated with a 'P' inside the white roundels, this car was for practice prior to the race itself.

Footnotes:
Note that EX 182/39, the Dick Jacobs Le Mans car, is not included, having been destroyed and scavenged for parts.
See Chapter 4 for more on the origins of LJB 205, and later in this chapter in the section about the Fitzwilliam Racing Team; originally applied to a home market car, chassis number duplication prompted the number of this car to be changed to EX 182/42 – which was originally also the engine number of the Jacobs Le Mans car.

THE AUSTIN TWIN-CAM ENGINE

As an alternative to the Morris Engines design, the Austin design team came up with this Austin Twin Cam unit. Although tested by MG prior to its intended appearance at Dundrod, it was removed from the engine bay immediately prior to the cars being shipped to the event.
AUTHOR'S COLLECTION

Although the engine which featured in the record breakers and the production MGA Twin Cam was a development by Eddie Maher of Gerald Palmer's original proposal, an alternative one-off was designed and built from scratch by Austin's William G. ('Bill') Appleby, the Chief Engineer (Engines) at Longbridge. Like Maher, Appleby had competition engines in his blood, having been the senior draughtsman under Tom Murray Jamieson for the exotic twin-camshaft Austin 750cc racing engine which challenged the MG Midget 'Q' and 'R' type racers, and subsequently had been part of the design team behind the Austin A40 engine which evolved into the 'B' series BMC corporate engine which sat under the bonnet of the standard MGA.

Whereas, as we saw in Chapter 6, the Morris Engines unit was fairly obviously derived from production components, with a nod to production logistics, Appleby's engine was rather more specialized, adopting a 66-degree angle between the plane of the camshaft gaskets and the block. It should be pointed out that although it seems to have become accepted that the Austin engine was entirely bespoke, some people who were there at the time – such as Basil Wales – believed that the base of this unit was still the B-Series, or at least some of its basic components. Whatever the truth, it is clear that the Austin engine would have been even more costly to produce in quantity than its rival.

Both engines were to be tested in the MGA, and it was originally intended that they should both show their mettle by being entered in the Tourist Trophy race at Dundrod in September 1955, just prior to the launch of the MGA at Frankfurt. The Austin engine, brought in from Longbridge, was fitted into its MGA host by Tommy Wellman and thereafter despatched for testing sessions at MIRA. Both the twin-cam engines were fitted with Solex carburettors rather than the usual SUs. However, John Thornley's subsequent report (dated 14 October 1955) made the following observations:

> *The maximum rpm of the 66-degree engine restricted the performance to much the same as that of a standard Le Mans car. It was therefore decided, as there was little prospect of being able to correct both engines in the time available, to substitute a further Le Mans engine for the 66-degree engine, and to pursue correction of the carburetion difficulties on the 80-degree engine.*

Syd Enever called Alec Hounslow to do the job; the task was delegated to Tommy Wellman, at home, having had his supper and making plans for an early night before setting off at six for the long journey to the ferry and Belfast. At ten o'clock, the call came to go back to MG and, with Henry Stone, to extricate the Austin unit and substitute a Le Mans pushrod one. The job was completed by four in the morning, the Austin engine was placed in its crate, the lid nailed down, and the package was shipped out at the first opportunity, never to be seen again.

Jim Cox pointed out to the author that Syd Enever and Eddie Maher were good friends: 'It was hardly surprising that he tended to favour the Morris Engines unit.' Marcus Chambers mused that the Austin engine had been dropped 'for reasons which I never understood'. There were various rumours as to what subsequently became of the Austin unit, including one that it had been secreted at MIRA (although it has not been found in more than sixty years) – but it never featured in subsequent BMC history.

Meanwhile the hastily fabricated manifold duly arrived at Belfast Airport. Working all through the night in a hangar at the airport, the team fitted the new manifold and the Webers in time for the Friday practice session (16 September), where, as John Thornley later recorded in his post-race memo, it performed tolerably well, to everyone's relief. For the race on the Saturday, it would be Ron Flockhart and Johnny Lockett sharing the drive.

THE STORY OF LBL 301

Heinz Keller poses with LBL 301 during a test session in the Alpine region in 1955.
KELLER FAMILY

Bob West restored the later version of LBL 301 to its Fitzwilliam team colours.
BOB WEST

For owners and historians alike, delving into the sometimes murky history of a race or rally car which has been through a long and tortuous process of evolution over several decades, can be both fascinating and frustrating in equal measure. Many exotic cars have led comparatively well-documented and pampered existences, but the same is generally not the case for something that, whilst revered nowadays, was once viewed almost as dispensable. Such has been the challenge for anyone interested in the fate of the famous EX 182 Le Mans cars, the LBL 301-2-3-4 sequence.

The story begins with EX 182/38 (*see* tables earlier in this chapter), and along the way takes in the famous collection of the late Jerry Goguen, a leading light in the New England MG T Register and owner for a time of a fabulous private MG museum. It was on show in restored 'Le Mans' guise and incorrectly labelled as the 'Lund/Waeffler car' (*see* tables). After Le Mans (driven by Miles and Lockett to finish in twelfth place overall, and fifth in class), it was returned to the factory and kitted out in readiness for the 1955 Alpine Rally, which was cancelled in the wake of the Le Mans tragedy. Photographs show it in the Alps with Heinz Keller, MG's agent in Zürich, where it seems reasonable to assume that it still retained its alloy bodywork.

Next move was its appearance at Dundrod in September 1955, for which LBL 301 was fitted with experimental low-nose bodywork and the experimental Morris Motors twin-cam engine (qv). The car crashed in the event and it seems was rebuilt on a new chassis (shown to date from September 1956), but being allowed by the factory to retain its identity.

In 1957, we know that Richard W-Fitzwilliam brokered a deal to 'borrow' two alloy-bodied cars (LBL 301 and LBL 303), and a steel-bodied one with some alloy components (LJB 205) from the MG factory to race alongside his own car, UPO 929, in order to take part in major European races denied to Abingdon by BMC edict. Fitzwilliam's associate Robin Carnegie recorded that when they collected these cars from Abingdon, Marcus Chambers had pointed out that they had been fitted with experimental disc brakes, as part of the development process for what would become the MGA Twin Cam. The Fitzwilliam racing team used their cars extensively, and comprehensively wrecked at least one of them (LJB 205) and managed to damage another (LBL 303).

For many years there was a certain amount of mystery about what became of LBL 301 after it was handed back by the Fitzwilliam Team. Interest was fuelled when the car, up for sale from the Goguen collection, prompted debate about its provenance. Eventually it was acquired by enthusiast Jon Savage, who recruited leading MGA expert and restorer Bob West in 2006 to help uncover the story of its missing years. Race reports

The chassis plate in LBL 301.
BOB WEST

from 1959 appeared to indicate a further race history for the car, by someone by the name of Southam (a mention in the issue of *Motorsport* of April 1959, for example, in a report on the racing season opening event at Goodwood on 14 March 1959, says tellingly that 'Southam's Le Mans ex-Carnegie M.G., now rebodied, retired at Woodcote'. Similarly *Autosport* of 20 March 1959 reported that 'among the MGA contingent was W. Southam, in a red model which turned out to be extremely fast and which was, apparently, an ex-works Le Mans car, bearing the chassis number EX 182').

After extensive research, Jon Savage tracked down a Wilson Southam in Ontario, who confirmed he had raced LBL 301 at Goodwood in 1959, at a time when he was up at Oxford.

Bob West and Savage related the story to Tony Dron, who wrote up the story for *Octane Magazine*. It transpired that the young Southam, a member of a wealthy family with interests in the Canadian media, had visited Abingdon with his own damaged Austin-Healey in 1958, only to come away with an offer to borrow one of the Le Mans/Fitzwilliam cars – EX 182/38. A friend of Southam's who had helped out in the subsequent racing endeavours, Nicholas Ouroussoff, told Bob West that he had been visiting the MG works at the time that the car was being prepared; as Dron wrote: 'Ouroussoff remembered seeing an original, somewhat battered aluminium body hanging up in a sling, still in Fitzwilliam Racing Team colours.'

For Southam, MG had fitted a new red-painted steel body, and he went on to buy, rather than borrow it in February 1959, just in time for the above-mentioned race at Goodwood on 14 March. The Canadian later took the red car back to Ontario and sold it in Hamilton in the very early 1960s. After that, it moved in turn to Louis Gehring, next to Gordon Whatley (who restored it to represent the 1955 Le Mans car), and then it was sold to Jerry Goguen, who added it to his MG Museum collection, where it remained until Jon Savage acquired it. After careful, sensitive and painstaking detective work and restoration by Bob West, it was finished in the Fitzwilliam Team livery, broadly as raced with such distinction (first placed British car) at the Mille Miglia in 1957.

Information from the Kithead Trust: 'LBL301' was first registered in Berkshire on 21 April 1955 (as was LBL 303). It passed to an owner in West Sussex [the Fitzwilliam Team] in February 1957, back to Berkshire in June 1958 [MG again] and to Oxford in February 1959.

LBL 301 at Goodwood, with Bob West at left, the present owner Jon Savage in the hat, while the late Barry 'Sideways' Smith can be seen fourth from the left.
BOB WEST

Meanwhile *Motorsport* had been on hand to watch the second day of (wet) practice, and observed wryly (of the overall race contingent) that 'most of the time was spent watching the good drivers show how well they could drive, and the bad ones making it even more obvious that in the interest of human safety they should pack up and go home.'

However, Jim Cox recalls that at Dundrod, 'Ron Flockhart was driving, and after practice said that he wouldn't go out in the car as it was. We sat in the garage and tried to sort out what to do – we had the car in pieces with Syd Enever looking over it; we took the carburettor to pieces and everything.' It was eventually established that fuel starvation was being caused by a loose particle of metal which had obstructed the supply to one carburettor. But even after the particle problem was dealt with, there was a misfire at high speeds, which continued to affect performance. The problem became sufficiently bad that Flockhart's car (race number 34) would have been retired had it not crashed out of the race. Subsequent investigations found that there was a hairline crack in Eddie Maher's manifold, which had caused the mixture to weaken intermittently when hot, as the crack opened up.

Despite the disappointment at Dundrod, the twin-cam engine had certainly shown promise, and an exciting future was expected, even if the eventual wait of another three years for a production version would be regrettable.

Unfortunately there was a serious accident early in the race, which caused the death of two drivers, and a further accident later in the event caused the death of another. It is possible that the time lost while the problems with the MGA were being traced kept it out of this incident, in which several cars were destroyed. A ferocious battle at the front of the race between the Mercedes SLR of Stirling Moss/John Fitch and the Jaguar D-Type of Mike Hawthorn and Desmond Titterington ended with Hawthorn spinning off in the Jaguar and ceding the win to Moss – on what happened to be his own twenty-fifth birthday. Victory was, however, rather overshadowed by the tragic events earlier in the race.

Coming soon after the terrible tragedy at Le Mans, the furore in some of the British and Northern Irish press was perhaps understandable, and very quickly the BMC Competitions Committee, acting on a direction from George Harriman, decided to scale back motor-sports endeavours, eschewing 'racing' in favour of 'rallies'. Meanwhile the RAC also took the decision to end the Tourist Trophy road races in Northern Ireland, although the motor-cycle events endure to this day on the Isle of Man.

ROAD RACING AND RALLYING

Even if road racing was to be prohibited by order of the BMC Board, the edict did not affect rallying – or at least, John Thornley was careful to ensure the distinction was made. On the basis that rallies were seen as tests of road craft and endurance, and speed was not supposedly the prime objective, it could be argued that entry into rallies could be looked upon as a measured response to the popular public alarm about racing, particularly if road or part-road circuits were employed. The grey area would, of course, be some of those events, particularly the Italian ones, where the events were thinly disguised races which happened to take place on roads. As we shall see, Abingdon made a gamble in this regard for 1956, but would be more circumspect in 1957.

In the meantime, what is believed to be the first factory-supported rally event in a production type MGA was the exotic-sounding Thames Estuary Auto Club's National Cats-Eyes' Rally on the weekend of 4/5 February 1956, where Pat Moss and Ann Wisdom competed in MBL 867's first outing. It was not the most promising debut, for the MGA eventually retired due to lateness. A few weeks later the next rally event for the Works MGAs was the RAC Rally, which was held in March 1956. Stirling Moss's sister Pat had driven for MG previously in the TF, but this time she co-drove an MGA (MJB 167 this time, wearing race number 79) with Nancy Mitchell. They finished fifth in class, and were the third-placed ladies in the event.

Nancy Mitchell and MaBeL

Intrinsically linked (especially in MG circles) with the rallying story of the MGA is Nancy Edith Mitchell (8 January 1915–14 January 1996), who was often behind the wheel of MBL 867 – MaBeL – that fittingly is owned by her family in 2018. Soon after the war, Nancy took up competitive motor sports, driving her own HRG in the Eastbourne Rally in 1947 and more memorably the 1948 Rallye des Alpes. 'Mitch' as she was known to her friends, earned a reputation for superb driving skill on frozen road surfaces, earning her the nickname 'Ice Queen'.

The BMC relationship began with a ZA Magnette at the 1956 Monte Carlo. As well as the MGA, Nancy drove many other BMC rally cars with aplomb, including the works MG Z Magnette, Riley One-Point-Five and the hefty big Austin-Healeys. She retired from active motorsport in 1960 and became motoring correspondent for *Vogue* magazine.

The MGA that Nancy Mitchell drove extensively in 1956/7 was one of the first production cars, HDE13/10105, despatched to the Competitions Department on 18 October 1955, and first registered to the MG Car Company Ltd on 1 February 1956 as MBL 867 – from which the car earned the nickname 'MaBeL'. It is possible – but unproven – that this was also the car which, wearing KMO 326 licence plates – went to Montlhéry in October 1955.

After a short but successful race career out of the Abingdon stable, the car was sold in 1957 to Robert Butler of St Albans, and went on to have a racing life through the subsequent ownerships of Neil Dangerfield, Roy Mertens, Derek Sandle, John

Nancy Mitchell with her fantastic trophy collection, posed on top of OBL 311.
CHAPMAN FAMILY

Jenkins, Richard Cook and Pat Antill, before being acquired by renowned MGA restorer Bob West, who restored the car in 1992; there were poignant reunions with Nancy Mitchell and, later, with Pat Faichney. The car is now once more in the treasured ownership of Nancy Mitchell's family.

Nancy Mitchell with her MGA Coupé.
CHAPMAN FAMILY

THE 1956 MILLE MIGLIA ROAD RACE

Whilst rallies were generally seen as noble endeavours, there was always a certain combination of elegance and daring in the speed-focused discipline of road racing, and arguably nowhere was this more evident than in Italy, where Latin passion, romance and style mixed with the fragrance of racing oil in an unrivalled, exotic manner. The Mille Miglia – literally

Posed for the camera in 'road-going' trim (for example, with full-size windscreens), on the left is MJB 167 with Peter Scott Russell and Tom Haig (in the dark coat), and alongside at the right, MBL 867 with Pat Faichney and Nancy Mitchell (with sunglasses and the light-coloured coat).
BOB WEST

Another photo of the two red factory MGAs for the 1956 Mille Miglia, seen here before the event with Peter Scott Russell, Tom Haig, Pat Faichney and Nancy Mitchell.

'a thousand miles' – was unquestionably the most exotic of them all, and the spectacle of every kind of car, from tiny Fiats to pedigree Maseratis, drew an excited caravan of international press and hangers-on every year.

Naturally the Mille Miglia had been firmly cemented into the MG psyche with the stupendous success of the 1933 race, where the K3 Magnette had defied all the odds and won its class as well as many Italian hearts, and after the hiatus of the war years, the event was rekindled. Notwithstanding the race's popularity, however, the danger and the death toll were issues which could not be ignored, and in the wake of the tragic events at Le Mans in the summer of 1955, and the road race at Dundrod later the same year, there were inevitably question marks over the future of any race being held on public roads.

For 1956, the thirty-third Mille Miglia of 28/29 April 1956 began (and finished) in Brescia in the north of Italy. It was evident that the MG factory's entry was slightly under the radar as far as BMC 'top brass' were concerned, the directive having come down to stop racing activities but not rallies; nevertheless a pair of factory MGAs were entered. MBL 867 ('MaBeL') was set to be driven by Nancy Mitchell and Pat Faichney, with race number 227, whilst the other factory car, MJB 167, was driven by Peter Scott Russell and Tom Haig under race number 229.

Hitherto MG had traditionally painted their competition cars in the 'British Racing Green' livery, but for the outing to Italy, it was decided to paint the MGAs in red, the theory being that this would confuse the local patriotic race follow-

Nancy Mitchell and Pat Faichney during their remarkable race at the Mille Miglia of 1956.
BOB WEST

Nancy Mitchell and Pat Faichney in 'MaBel' during the 1956 Mille Miglia; the number 227 indicates the time they had been given to set off from the *Via Rubuffione* in Brescia – at nearly half past two in the morning of 28 April 1956.
BOB WEST

ers, understandably often anxious to favour their compatriots in Italian race cars: the locals were said to leave level crossing gates conveniently open for Italian cars, and closed for others. Over the years, several people (Peter Scott Russell being one) have claimed that painting the cars red was their idea; whatever the truth, for the 1956 Mille Miglia, both the factory MGAs were red.

The weather was atrocious, and it seems remarkable that the British MGAs were fitted with no more protection from the elements than miniscule half-moon aero screens, meaning that the drivers and their equally unfortunate navigators were exposed to the elements, soaked through by the unrelenting rain, which brought rivers to near flood level and temperatures below the Italian norm for May. Marcus Chambers, with Alec Hounslow and Douggie Watts, took a Morris Oxford Traveller and intercepted the race caravan at Rome and Florence, providing basic but essential petrol and oil top-ups for the cars, and drink replenishment for the crews.

Most MG histories have tended to ignore or overlook the other MG stories of this event, which was the MGA entry by a local crew, Mille Miglia veterans Emo Terragnoli and Alessandro Suppi, who also finished fourth in the same class and in ninety-first place overall. *Autosport*'s Gregor Grant brought in his MG Magnette (race number 301) to finish in 151st place, and wrote up the story of the race in the next issue of 11 May 1956.

Inevitably the race headlines were dominated by Ferraris (also red, of course) and the five drivers killed, but nevertheless the British MGs survived and were placed well in their 1500cc class, MJB 167 coming second and MBL 867 third, with Nancy Mitchell achieving the bonus of a special gift from the local MG dealer for being the highest placed female driver at the end; apparently he was so delighted that the day after the event he took Nancy to a local silversmith in Brescia and allowed her to choose an item (a flower bowl) to be specially engraved.

Motorsport was enthralled by Nancy Mitchell's performance, and in their June write-up called her the 'prima donna of the event', noting that she drove the entire race herself:

> ...taking Pat Faichney for company. The MGA was standard and fitted with two tiny aero-screens, so that both girls were soaked to the skin. Nancy had never been round the course, so that all the time new and interesting terrain opened up before her. Rally experience in mountain country where you must drive on reflexes made the journey possible.

Notice how exposed Nancy Mitchell (behind the wheel) and Pat Faichney were in their MGA during the 1956 Mille Miglia. Incredibly, Mitchell drove the whole way. Faichney later claimed that she spent most of the race peeling oranges and feeding them to Mitchell! Peter Scott Russell similarly drove his car the whole way, so that his poor partner Tom Haig also had no stint behind the wheel.
BOB WEST

THE 1956 MILLE MIGLIA

Race No.	Colour	UK Reg. No.	Drivers	Overall Placing	Class (*see* footnote)	Notes
227	Red	MBL 867	Nancy Mitchell/Pat Faichney	74th	3rd	BMC Competitions entry. Highest placed all-female crew.
228	Old English White	N/A	Emo Terragnoli/Alessandro Suppi	91st	4th	Private Italian entry.
229	Red	MJB 167	Peter Scott Russell/Tom Haig	70th	2nd	BMC Competitions entry.

Footnotes:
The event date was 28–29 April 1956; it was the thirty-third Mille Miglia. Sheila van Damm (in a Sunbeam Rapier) finished ahead of Nancy Mitchell, but her co-driver this year was Peter Harper.
The class was for 'under 1500c limited price open sportscars'.
MJB 167 was later fitted with a replacement body at Abingdon in 1957, after which it was then sold to Pat Moss, who used it as personal transport as well as for various national competitions.

MJB 167 at a recent MG Car Club event.
AUTHOR PHOTO

This was inevitably journalistic hyperbole, and did scant justice to the role played by Pat Faichney, exposed to the same lashing of the elements as her accomplice. Mitchell herself paid tribute to her colleague when she recalled the event some years later for Wilson McComb, in a retrospective article about her career: 'Pat Faichney sat beside me the whole of that race, and tried to feed me from time to time. I bit her, poor girl!' By the end the two of them had travelled 1,009 miles (1,624km) in 15 hours, 7 minutes and 28 seconds; they were so exhausted and damp that they had to be lifted bodily out of the cars.

After the event, and safely back in the UK, Peter Scott Russell telephoned John Thornley from the Steering Wheel Club, and, as he later told Peter Browning, 'I told him we had the two MGs there, all covered in Italian mud, racing numbers and a big trophy that Nancy had won... I asked him if he wanted us to put them in the big BMC showroom in Piccadilly, just round the corner...'

'God, no, don't do that!' an alarmed Thornley had replied to Scott Russell; 'Len Lord doesn't even know there were two MGs in the Mille Miglia. Bring them back to Abingdon and we'll put a cutting torch through them!' Thankfully the destruction did not happen, but it showed that once again Abingdon had sailed fairly close to the wind, but lived to tell the tale. Peter Thornley has said that his father generally subscribed to the theory that it was sometimes better to sin and later seek forgiveness: the 1956 Mille Miglia seems to fall neatly into that category.

THE 'FITZ' FITZWILLIAM AND ROBIN CARNEGIE TEAM

An early entry into the British post-war motor-racing limelight was Richard W-Fitzwilliam, known to the racing fraternity simply as 'Fitz' (but never, his son Robin insists, as 'Dick'). His emergence on British race circuits seems to have been with a glamorous blue Zagato-bodied Alfa Romeo and a Lago Talbot, but with the acquisition of a very early MGA in late 1955, Fitz formed the beginnings of his eponymous racing team.

Fitz's first MGA was special in many ways: UPO 929, acquired at the start of January 1956, would form the kernel of a successful team, some cars loaned by MG as a clever way to support opportunities for motor-sport publicity without the expense or political challenge of running the team. Whereas these other cars were drawn from the exclusive pool of Abingdon's own early MGA racing pioneers, UPO 929 was very much Fitz's own property. Chassis number was 10708, and the first engine was BP15-GB-655. (According to 1960 records held by the Hall family, this was one of six units originally built for MG's abortive 1956 Le Mans entry.)

With Fitz almost from the start was Robin Carnegie, who later wrote a personal memoir of his exploits within Fitz's entourage, some of which was serialized in the MG Car Club magazine *Safety Fast!* in the mid-1990s, and from which I have drawn, with grateful thanks to the club's MGA Register. Carnegie recorded that although he had seen Fitzwilliam race in his Alfa-Romeo and Lago-Talbot, it would be an MGA – initially just UPO 929 - that was the sports car which united the two friends in a racing relationship which endured for several exciting years, with - as we shall see - many remarkable adventures along the way.

The Fitzwilliam team began in a modest but clearly well funded way, with Fitz and Robin Carnegie sharing much of the driving. Whilst this alliance between Fitz and Carnegie would eventually form the kernel of the 'Fitzwilliam Racing Team', this was not formalized as a legal entity until February 1957; for the time being, the two friends shared expenses as well as time behind the wheel. Fitz had noticed that for 1956 there was to be an *Autosport* Race Championship, with a whole season racing leading to points and prizes.

The National Snetterton Race

The first formal outing for UPO 929 was on Sunday 25 March 1956 at Snetterton; there had been an unwritten agreement that Fitz would prepare the car over the preceding winter and spring period, but when Carnegie collected it, he found that nothing had been done other than the fitting of a cut-down competition windscreen; meanwhile he observed that the car 'had a lot of miles on the clock'.

The MGA would clearly have benefited from a close-ratio gearbox and stiffer suspension, but evidently these would have to follow the next trip to see Marcus Chambers at Abingdon. Even so, in the five-lap National Snetterton race, Carnegie brought UPO 929 (wearing race number 34) home in second place to another MGA, race number 42, driven by Robin Richards; there were just 5.4 seconds between them, and Carnegie was justifiably pleased at such a result from an ill-prepared car.

Goodwood: The *Autosport* Championship

Just over a week later, Fitz took the same car to Goodwood for the first round of the *Autosport* championship, finishing in third place in his class and starting the season off with his first four points. Also in the race was Carnegie, but driving a Jaguar XK120 under race number 99. According to Carnegie's memoirs, he and Fitz visited Abingdon again in April or May of 1956 and whilst there they acquired a close-ratio gearbox, some competition shock absorbers, and a custom-made front valance, which disguised the awkward panelwork otherwise exposed by the removal of the front bumper.

The 1,000km Nürburgring Race

Evidently Marcus Chambers was reasonably impressed by the news that Fitz and Carnegie had secured an entry to the 1,000km Nürburgring race of Sunday 27 May 1956; with the

Richard W-Fitzwilliam stands behind UPO 929 (race no. 46) ahead of the 27 May 1956 Nürburgring 1,000km – the first British entry at this event. Despite a noble effort, the MGA failed to finish.

CALL IT MGA

RICHARD 'FITZ' W-FITZWILLIAM

Robin Carnegie (left) and Richard W-Fitzwilliam, the latter with sleeves rolled up and hand resting on his personal MGA, UPO 929, at Oulton Park on 22 September 1956.
W-FITZWILLIAM FAMILY

Richard W-Fitzwilliam – 'Fitz' to his friends – behind the wheel of his MGA UPO 929 (wearing race no. 82) at the race at Goodwood on 31 August 1957.
W-FITZWILLIAM FAMILY

To some of his racing contemporaries, the six-foot-three, slim, dark-haired and bespectacled Richard John Godric Wentworth-Fitzwilliam (3 February 1916–3 October 1987) – better known to many as 'Fitz' ('he was never called Dick' his son Robin insists) – seemed to be something of an enigma; even his good friend and racing associate Robin Carnegie claimed not to know much about his friend's background or what he did for a living. Fitz himself spoke little of his background, and consequently some writers have attempted to fill the vacuum with speculation wide of the mark – but Fitz was not Scottish, never a heavy drinker, and even if he may have been the life and soul of the party, he was certainly not a philandering womanizer, as some have implied.

Fitz's approach to life sometimes seems to have given him an air of aristocratic insouciance, and friends and even his family could be both enthralled and bemused at his behaviour – some felt he could be at the same time careless and yet incredibly generous, often giving scant attention to anything he thought peripheral, such as making crucial accommodation arrangements for his team's overseas race trips. A clue comes from Fitz's full given name, Richard John Godric Wentworth-Fitzwilliam. A scion of the aristocratic Wentworth-Fitzwilliam family, Fitz was born in Daventry, into a line that could trace its origins back to Norman England, when Sir John Fitzwilliam of Sprotborough married into a family with massive landholdings in Yorkshire.

The following account of the history of the Fitzwilliam aristocratic lineage may seem incidental to a story about MG sports cars, but it is part of the background to an important and interesting MGA racer and team principal, and helps set the scene for his exploits in the 1950s, especially after his father Toby's death at Midhurst in 1955.

Over the centuries the Fitzwilliam empire grew to encompass significant estates in Britain and Ireland, perhaps most famously the largest private house in Europe, the enormous Wentworth-Woodhouse near Rotherham, South Yorkshire. By the middle of the nineteenth century, the formal family name was Wentworth-Fitzwilliam, but like all grand aristocratic lines, succession was governed by the arcane primogeniture rules which stated that the next Earl would be 'heirs male of the first earl's body lawfully begotten'. Such criteria unfortunately proved to be the downfall of Fitz's father's claim to the earldom. Fitz's grandfather, George Charles Fitzwilliam, had married his wife Evelyn Lyster (a former chorus girl) in Scotland whilst still under age, and so there were doubts about the legitimacy of George's first son – another George, known to his family as 'Toby' (Fitz's father).

UPO 929 racing as no. 91.
FITZ FROM HIS DAUGHTER AMANDA GRAVES

All of this might have been irrelevant to Fitz had not the Eighth Earl died in a plane crash in France in 1948, leaving a daughter but no male heirs. The Ninth Earl was in his sixties, unmarried and with no children, and this precipitated a court case in March 1951 to settle who should inherit the title and estate as the Tenth Earl – either Toby, or his younger brother Tom. In the event, Toby lost out, and so his son Richard – Fitz – missed out on the grand prize.

Fitz went to Stowe School, but was expelled and then sent to Montreux, Switzerland. He married Joan Ellery in 1940 but divorce followed in 1942; in 1943 he married Doreen Ann Scorror, whose family farmed in Southern Rhodesia. Doreen would be his long-suffering spouse, eventually taking charge of lap-time monitoring. In those early days, 'Fitz' enjoyed motoring around southern Africa in a series of Cadillacs and Rolls-Royces, according to his son Robin.

Whilst in Southern Rhodesia, Fitz – a great fan of still and moving film – secured an exclusive agency for Kodak equipment. In those days, Kodak film was banned in South Africa and yet Fitz took to smuggling the film across the border and was arrested. Meanwhile the W-Fitzwilliams (the family seldom use 'Wentworth-Fitzwilliam') were part of the Rhodesian 'set', Fitz partnering the future Queen Elizabeth and her sister Margaret during a royal visit. However, in light of the inheritance question, the family (with Sallianne, born 1946) returned to the UK ahead of the 1951 court case. Even though the title and succession eluded Fitz, there was a generous Fitzwilliam allowance, and this subsidized his racing exploits, eventually, his son suggests, burning his way through some £300,000 before the racing team was wound up in the early 1960s.

To the young Robin, all this racing and the associated circle of friends was enthralling and house parties regularly saw many famous visitors: 'In those days we lived at Bignor Park, which isn't far from Goodwood, and our house was always full of racing guests such as Stirling Moss.'

Before the money ran out, Fitz maintained the trappings of a high-cost lifestyle, including ownership of a V12 Ferrari, as Robin recalls:

I think it might have been a 275. I remember he was driving through the West End and it was misfiring, so he was revving it furiously by Marble Arch when a traffic policeman come over. Father explained what was happening and the policeman pointed out that it was only firing on six cylinders, and so he suggested to my father that he should floor it up and down Hyde Pork to clear the carburettors.

Doreen, Fitz's long-suffering wife, was often in the pits keeping the score as the team raced. But once Fitz had burned through most of his inheritance, relations were strained; Robin remembers that one morning, after breakfast, his father came in, simply said 'I'm leaving', and drove off. Robin didn't see his father again for several years. At Christmas 1968, Fitz married his third wife, Jacqueline Marie Cragg; next year Amanda Jane W-Fitzwilliam was born. Sadly, things went downhill for the schoolboy-who-never-grew-up:

Of course the money ran out eventually – and it was that, more than anything, which brought an end to the racing. The motto on the family crest reads 'Let your desires be ruled by reason' – well, he certainly never did that!

Late in his life, Fitz went to live in France, but when the money really had run out, it was Robin who, with family help, brought his father back in 1987 and set him up in a modest flat in Croydon. He died in October that year. But according to Amanda, even when he was ill ' ... he still loved adventurous things, such as flying model planes. He certainly loved his cars, and he lived life to the full.'

LBL 303 with some signs of battle scars to its front valance, with Fitz at the wheel at Goodwood on 10 June 1957. He finished in sixth place in the National Goodwood Marque Handicap race.
FITZ FROM HIS DAUGHTER AMANDA GRAVES

Taking to the grass at the edge of the circuit, Fitz nonchalantly throws up a small cloud of dirt.
FITZ FROM HIS DAUGHTER AMANDA

Fitz out on the circuit at Nürburgring during the 1956 1,000km. As present day owner of UPO 929, Steve Dixon points out, the performance of this plucky little car is all the more remarkable, in that the MGA was in a class dominated by six bespoke Porsche 550 racing sports cars.
FITZ FROM HIS DAUGHTER AMANDA GRAVES

BMC racing moratorium from on high, the factory had not made an entry of its own for the German circuit, but could see that these privateers could bring some continental prestige if their race was a good one.

Flying out from Lydd Airport in one of the new Silver City freighters (£14 return per car, according to Carnegie, who took a Ford Zephyr, while Fitz was in the MGA) the duo drove from Le Touquet Airport to Adenau, just over six miles (10km) north of the Nürburgring circuit. Fitz had booked the entourage into the Hotel zum Wilden Schwein in the centre of Adenau – which, according to Carnegie, showed unusual forethought on the part of his team mate, never known for his efficiency with regard to such peripheral organization.

Their arrival at Adenau was probably on either the Thursday or Friday before the actual race, on the basis that the race was on the Sunday but was preceded by two full days of practice. Fitz and Carnegie were pleased to be greeted by MG's local agent (Carnegie doesn't specify a name, other than calling them the 'agent from Bonn', but we can guess it was probably Jack Woodhouse of Cologne, who, as we saw earlier, had, only months beforehand, greeted the arrival of the MGA at the Frankfurt Motor Show; in any case Bonn is en route from Cologne to Adenau).

Having had a run around the daunting but exciting circuit, Carnegie and Fitz signed on and found their allotted garage in the *Fahrerlager* (literally 'paddock'), a large square of lock-ups, where cars were kept and worked on prior to going up on to the circuit through a tunnel. After meeting their local contacts, who had driven up to help them, Carnegie records how surprised and delighted they were at the welcome afforded them: 'Although we were the only private entry from England, and in fact the first ever in the 1,000 kilometre race, we were quite insignificant compared to the rest of the entry.'

Carnegie certainly had a point: even in their seven-entry 1.5-litre class, every other car was a Porsche 550. Fitz took UPO 929 out practising, and after a handful of laps at about 13min 30sec came in to see if everything was in order. Carnegie wrote:

Our German friends had a quick look round, and all seemed well until one of them spotted an ominous drip from the rear end, which turned out to be a split fuel tank. So the car was taken back to the working area adjacent to the Fahrerlager, and then followed what to me was an extremely scary episode. The eldest of our helpers insisted that if one drained the tank, stuck the bung back in and then filled the tank with carbon monoxide by piping some exhaust fumes into it, when one brazed the split, which luckily was accessible without removing the tank, it would not blow up. It didn't. However, we all stood well back, and I would not recommend it as a normal procedure.

Steve Dixon describes himself as custodian of UPO 929 – the remarkable MGA which served for many years as the kernel of the Fitzwilliam Racing Team, often raced by Richard W-Fitzwilliam or Robin Carnegie.
AUTHOR

The simple, business-like cockpit of UPO 929 seen here in 2018.
AUTHOR

As for the race itself, despite a brave effort, the exploit ended disappointingly in disqualification, as the subsequent report in *Autocar* related:

> The only private British entry, the Fitzwilliam/Carnegie MGA, dropped the exhaust valve of the rear cylinder during practice. All the valves were replaced while the drivers continued their practice in a car borrowed from a local agent. During the race the trouble recurred – same cylinder, same valve – on the straight which approaches the pits. Carnegie was driving at the time and the car was second in its class. Fitzwilliam hurried out to the scene with a mechanic and, between them, they removed the head and the broken bits of valve. Carnegie rejoined the race on three cylinders. Unfortunately, after only three laps of this unbalanced existence, the car was black flagged and disqualified as the regulations insist that only the driver may work on the car when it is out on the circuit.

The race over, Carnegie drove to Dunkirk to catch the midnight ferry to Dover.

Oulton Park

The next appearance for UPO 929 was at Oulton Park in Cheshire on 9 June 1956; Carnegie was to drive, and related that as far as he could tell, nothing had been done to the car since its ignominious return from Germany within the previous fortnight. Unfortunately the valve problem that had contributed to the problems at the Nürburgring returned to haunt the team, and four laps into the ten lap race, Carnegie was forced to retire. His journey home, on a short tow rope behind Alan Foster in his Dick Jacobs prepared MGA, was apparently an experience not to be repeated.

'Troisième 12-heures Internationales de Reims'

After Oulton Park, it was back across the Channel at the end of June, this time to the Reims Circuit, in north-eastern France, where there was to be a weekend of racing as a prelude to the main event, the French Grand Prix. Carnegie drove his Ford Zephyr with its triple SU-equipped Raymond Mays head, whilst his sister Mary came too as team helper and time keeper; meanwhile Fitz drove his MGA. Their race objective was the 'Troisième 12-heures Internationales de Reims', and in the programme Fitz was listed as 'R.-W. Fitrwilliam'.

On this occasion, preparation for the overseas trip left something to be desired, Carnegie recalled:

> Fitz was true to form and had made no arrangements at all. So when we arrived at Reims there was naturally not a bed to be had anywhere. We toured the town without any success at all, eventually resorting to the Gendarmerie to ask for advice. They were not a bit concerned and sent us off to an address in the red light district, where we were excellently looked after. The Madame gave us two perfectly acceptable rooms and breakfast in the morning, which consisted of strong black French coffee and a glass of Cognac.

The Twelve Hours of Reims of 29 June 1956, with the redoubtable UPO 929 (as car no. 27); Fitz Fitzwilliam/ Robin Carnegie were plagued by gearbox troubles (the team notes refer to a 'broken clutch in the fifth hour'), and they finally ended up being disqualified for assistance given in the eighth hour.
CALL IT MGA

The simple, clean lines of the MGA 1500 have surely seldom been bettered.
AUTHOR

The race was no less of an eye-opener than the accommodation (what Carnegie's sister and Fitz's wife Doreen thought of the latter is not recorded). Reims was a circuit set out as a triangle of three straights, and so the general philosophy was to go flat out between the three hairpins. This was the policy that Carnegie adopted for his stint, until a loud bang underneath caused him to come into the pits.

> Being a twelve-hour race, and because there was always a chance of a lot of the others dropping out, Fitz and our helpers decided it was worth taking the gearbox out, to see what the problem was. It turned out to be a broken withdrawal fork, which had been rattling around in the bell housing making such a noise – so they stitched it all back together again, and told me to go out and try to drive without a clutch.
>
> However, I could not get on with it at all, and so it came for Fitz to have a go. He managed wonderfully well, being able to change gear without any trouble, and he plodded on to finish. However, sadly and I think most unnecessarily, someone objected that we had too many people working on the car and of course we had to have a push start and so we were disqualified.

Thus the team were frustrated again and returned home without a prize, but with some interesting memories of their stay in northern France. 'It was good experience, and perhaps taught us to make sure we read the regulations properly,' Carnegie had to admit.

UPO 929 wears race no. 74.
FITZ FROM HIS DAUGHTER AMANDA GRAVES

Mallory Park: the BRSCC Production Car Race

A week after their French escapade, Carnegie was scheduled to race at Mallory Park, the twenty-four-lap BRSCC Production Car Race being part of the *Autosport* Championship. However, on checking with Fitz, Carnegie found that the car was not ready: 'In fact nothing had been done to it at all, so I had to get the gearbox out, and as the parts required were not the sort of thing that most agents kept in stock, I had to go to Abingdon to collect what was necessary...' The car was nevertheless made ready, and Carnegie took part, but could only manage fourth in his class, with other MGAs driven by Alan Foster and Peter Simpson ahead of him.

Nürburgring: Support Event to the German Grand Prix

Later in July, Carnegie records that Fitz took UPO 929 off to Germany, prior to taking part in a race at Nürburgring on 4 August. Carnegie claimed to know nothing of this adventure, other than noting that it left scant little time before he was due to drive the same car at the Bank Holiday meeting at Brands Hatch two days later. We can deduce, however, that the event in Germany was a support event to the German Grand Prix on 5 August, and Fitz finished eighth in his class behind the inevitable Porsches. There then followed a frantic dash back through Germany and France to catch the ferry to Dover.

Brands Hatch

Remarkably, Fitz arrived at Brands Hatch with the car in one piece, handing it straight to his friend, who noted: 'he disappeared, leaving me with the MGA, which was filthy both inside and out, and was still showing his Nürburgring numbers. It took me the best part of an hour to clean out all the fag ends, toffee wrappers and bits of paper. There wasn't time to do more than check that everything was tight, and have a quick look round.' Even so, Carnegie out-performed the rival MGAs of Peter Simpson and Alan Foster, whose 4.5:1 axle ratios should have been an advantage. Carnegie brought in the little green MGA second in his class, earning another six points in the *Autosport* championship.

ROBIN CARNEGIE

Occasionally confused with his contemporary Lieutenant-General Sir Robin Carnegie, 'Robin' Carnegie – one of Fitz's first faithful racing compatriots – was in reality Robert Andrew Carnegie (24 June 1926–26 January 1994), a descendent of the original Earl of Northesk, ennobled in 1662.

Robin Carnegie would not have been destined for a seat in the House of Lords had not his father's cousin David, the eleventh Earl, died childless; the title therefore jumped sideways to Robin's father John in 1963, and then, upon John's death in 1975, to Robin in turn. Racing in the period when the MGA came on the scene, these grand commitments of nobility would have seemed a long way in the future for a young man only just entering his thirties, even if the looming future responsibilities of title succession probably already seemed inevitable.

In his racing period, Carnegie lived in Midhurst, West Sussex, not far from Goodwood, where his parents farmed the family's English estate at Dumpford, Rogate. The Carnegies evidently knew the Wentworth-Fitzwilliams, even if Robin Carnegie did not know them well himself; meanwhile his motor-racing debut appears to have been in a Ford Special in a race at Silverstone on 2 August 1952, before graduating to a Jaguar XK120 the following year.

Carnegie later raced a Jaguar C-Type, owned and entered by Johnnie Keeling, between September 1954 and April 1955. Meanwhile in April 1954, he raced an Allard at the same Goodwood Easter Handicap race where Dick Fitzwilliam was due to drive his glorious Talbot-Lago T26, although on that occasion Fitz did not make the race. The approach from Fitz came at an opportune moment for Carnegie, who recorded later that 'I had sadly quite recently inverted Johnny Keeling's C Type at Ibsley and written it off, so I was without a car; so from misfortune stemmed opportunity.'

Robin Carnegie's 1957 Mille Miglia Trophy and his helmet posed on the bonnet of LBL 301 at Mary Damerell's home in 2012, during a reunion organized by Bob West and Roger Martin of the MGA Register.
ROGER MARTIN

Racing with the Fitzwilliam Team and their cohort of MGAs dominated Carnegie's attention from 1956 through to 1959, after which he dabbled with Lotus, and then Elva; finally, for the 1963 season, he gained a seat in Morgan race cars under the patronage of Chris Lawrence. The death of his uncle in November of that year seems to have drawn Carnegie's more serious racing efforts to a close. He succeeded to the family title, becoming the Thirteenth Earl of Northesk in 1975. He died in January 1994, but not before committing the story of his exploits with the Fitzwilliam Team to paper. I am grateful to Robin Carnegie's daughter Mary and the MGA Register, for their permission to draw from his entertaining narrative.

DICK JACOBS AND THE MGA

Dick Jacobs is seen here second from the left in a small group of five people. On the reverse side is written Alan Foster, Tommy Bridger, World Cup race, Snetterton, 6 August 1960.
STEVE JOHNSON

The Richard W-Fitzwilliam and Robin Carnegie team wasn't the only équipe racing MGAs. We saw earlier how Dick Jacobs had become a good friend to the Abingdon factory, and remained faithful to MG; as the proprietor of a business with an MG franchise, and his recent near-death experience at the wheel of a factory MG at Le Mans in 1955, Jacobs was able to call upon much goodwill.

A group of friends and employees gathered together and raced under Jacobs' patronage, using the MGA and MG Z Magnette as their weapons of choice. Alan Foster raced his own MGA, and rather like Fitz's UPO 929, Foster's car performed well throughout the 1956 *Autosport* championship; by the time the season was drawing to a close with the Oulton Park event described later, Foster was lying in second place in his 1500cc class on points.

Jacobs took Alan Foster and his MGA under his wing for late 1956 and 1957 – in fact Foster related that Jacobs had given him little choice: Foster had been leading a Goodwood marque race with his self-prepared MGA, but on the last lap had run out of petrol! A furious Jacobs had grabbed the MGA keys, given Foster the keys to his own road car, confiscated the MGA, and prepared it properly at Mill Garage!

At the October 1956 WECC Stapleford Aerodrome Hillclimb, Foster finished third in his class; the following May he won a handicap class at Goodwood; and then at the Whitsun Goodwood meeting he was second in class. On the August Bank Holiday event at Crystal Palace he was second, with the fastest lap. Then from 17 August 1957, at the 750MC Six-Hour relay race, Jacobs entered a hardtop-equipped MGA Roadster team which he dubbed 'Les Coupés Emgee'. However, the big break for Jacobs and the MGA would have to await the arrival of the MGA Twin Cam...

THE 1956 ALPINE RALLY

As we have seen, the 1955 Alpine Rally – which would have been held just a few weeks after Le Mans – had been cancelled to allow the world of motor sport to come to terms with the lessons to be learned from the tragedy in France. The Competitions Department at Abingdon clearly had to refocus their efforts, and thus it was, for example, that it was

Nancy Mitchell at the wheel of 'MaBeL' at the start of the 1956 Rallye des Alpes; Pat Faichney is in the passenger seat. They would go on to win both a Coupe des Dames and the equally coveted Coupe des Alpes.
AUTHOR'S COLLECTION

John Gott and Ray Brookes stand either side of MJB 191 at the 18th Rallye de Alpes – the Alpine Rally – in July 1956, a race which, despite many exciting moments, would not ultimately be as successful for them as it would for 'MaBeL'.
PABLO RAYBOULD

down to some of the privateers – such as Richard Fitzwilliam – to uphold octagonal honours. In North America, too, as will be covered later, the arrangements in 1956 would be largely independent of England.

By the summer of 1956, however, some of the dust had settled, and as we have seen, a factory MGA had successfully taken part in the RAC Rally in early March. Continental races such as the Nürburgring 1,000km and the 12 Hours of Reims were still out of contention for the MG factory (hence the gloriously serendipitous openings for privateers) but the next significant outing for Marcus Chambers and his Abingdon acolytes would be in France and Italy, with the 18th Rallye des Alpes.

The 1956 Alpine Rally started at Marseille on 6 July, after the usual drive in convoy for the BMC team through France in order to get there, with John Gott (at the time, Hertfordshire Constabulary Superintendent, based at St Albans) in the lead. As well as the five MGAs there were two service cars and a total of six mechanics; the total number of entries was seventy-nine, and this year, they were faced with 4,103 miles (6,602km) of challenging driving.

Also joining the troupe for the rally would be a pair of MG Magnettes, with a film crew to record the event for posterity – and publicity through the newsreels, then still a common feature at cinemas, where they would be shown as an adjunct to the main film. The group stopped off en route in Lapalisse, where inevitably Marcus Chambers had sniffed out decent accommodation and excellent dining, while the BMC Transporter was sent on ahead. At Abingdon, the cars had been fitted with Le Mans-type oil coolers, but leaks from the pipes during the drive to the start prompted the decision to abandon the coolers.

Marseille in July can be very hot, and in 1956 the weather was true to form. After scrutineering, the cars were all held in the customary *parc fermé* (literally 'closed park') ahead of the start. From Marseille, the route in France took in Aix-en-Provence, Gap, Embrun, Briançon (in the Hautes-Alpes) and the Col de Montgenèvre (near the Italian border); then in Italy, Ponte Gardena, Brescia and Lake Garda, with a stop at Moderno and then on to Riva and Trento.

At Monza there was a session at the circuit, where Jack Sears was the fastest MGA, lapping at 83.2mph (133.9km/h) and was now lying third in his class behind two Porsche Carreras. After this, the next service point for Marcus and his mechanics was on the road to the Passo di Gardena. Three of the cars remained penalty free – Nancy Mitchell, Jack Sears and Bill Shepherd – but the gearbox on Nancy Mitchell's car (MBL 867) had a serious oil leak.

During these sections, both John Milne (MRX 43) and John Gott (MJB 191) suffered damage to their cars; Milne nearly lost his car entirely when he overshot a bend when clouds of dust obscured his vision, while Gott struck a roadside stone marker with his nearside wheel, bending the axle and half-shaft, and wrecking the nearside leaf spring. Gott and his co-driver Ray Brookes managed to lash up the axle temporarily with the help of a block of wood, gaining a 22-minute penalty. The mechanics found a garage and soon had the spring replaced, but as the axle casing was bent, there was a struggle to locate the centre bolt; at this point poor Douggie Watts put his knee out with the effort and was forced to retire in agony, although help at hospital was soon found.

Despite these incidents, both cars were kept in the next stages, which took the rally from Cortina across to Zagreb in Yugoslavia and its terrible dusty roads, littered with all manner of dreadful detritus: many punctures were experienced, by the other competitors as well as the MGs. The other curse of mid-1950s Yugoslavia was the atrocious quality of the pump petrol, which inevitably led to detonation and consequent lack of power.

Towards the end of their mammoth journey, Jack Sears crashed his MGA (MRX 42) when coming down from the Col de la Croix-de-Fer, a high mountain pass in the French Alps linking Le Bourg-d'Oisans and Saint-Jean-de-Maurienne (nowadays a well known cycling venue), and so he was out.

Robin Howard is the current owner (2018) of MJB 191, restored to its best known Old English White and green hardtop guise.
ROBIN HOWARD

The car rolled on to its roof, destroying the windscreen and hardtop, but thankfully the crew (Jack Sears and Ken Best) were both unharmed. Meanwhile, John Gott's car broke its tortured half-shaft inside the differential at the Col de Aravis: at this point, a lesser man might have admitted defeat.

As Gott later wrote: 'Coasting to a stop we told Jack and Nancy, who were formatting on us, that our rally was run, fervently wished them "good luck" in their battle with the mountains ahead, and sadly watched their red tail-lights twisting and turning down the valley, until they finally vanished some thousands of feet below.' No sooner had their team mates disappeared into the gloom did Gott and his co-driver Ray Brookes realize that they were alone, in the dark, and miles from anywhere.

However, Gott was made of sterner stuff than most, and despite the trouble happening on a remote mountain top at night, he and his co-driver Ray Brookes pushed the car and, as Marcus Chambers recorded '...freewheeled down towards a light in the valley, where they hoped to get help. Arriving at the building from where the light came, John knocked at the door. This was cautiously opened on a chain by a forbidding-looking lady, who told him in no uncertain terms where he could go.' The building turned out to be a home for unmarried mothers-to-be! Gott wrote: 'The stern-faced matron apparently did not really believe that we were stranded rally drivers and suspected we were real "wolves"!'

Pushing the car again, the duo got as far as a hotel, where they borrowed some kitchen knives – with these, and the

THE 1956 ALPINE RALLY

Race No.	Colour	UK Reg. No.	Drivers	Overall Placing	1300–1600cc Class	Notes
308	Red	MJB 167	Bill Shepherd/John Williamson		5th	This duo lost marks by leaving the San Candido control five minutes early.
314	Red	MRX 43	John Milne/Douglas Johns		4th	Managed to finish despite nearly crashing out of the race when over-shooting a bend.
324	Old English White	MJB 191	John Gott/Ray Brookes	Retired	Unplaced	A remarkable tale of endurance, despite which they were penalized 220 points.
326	Red	MBL 867	Nancy Mitchell/Pat Faichney	15th	3rd	Also won both the coveted 'Coupe des Dames' Ladies' Prize and a 'Coupe des Alpes'.
330	Red	MRX 42	Jack Sears/Ken Best	DNF	DNF	Crashed at the Col de la Croix-de-Fer, when lying fifth in General Classification.

Footnotes:
The event date was 6 to 13 July 1956; it comprised a series of testing challenges over a course of 4,103 miles (6,602km) for 1956, from Marseilles to Zagreb and back to Marseilles. No overall prize is awarded, only 'Coupes des Alpes' for drivers who completed the series without penalties. Eighty-three cars departed Marseille from 19:00hr on 6 July, and thirty-four reached the finish. The event was recorded in a Pathé Film *BMC – Ladies First*.
All the MGAs were fitted with the new Vanden Plas-made hardtops (black on all but MJB 191, which had a dark green hardtop – a stipulation of John Gott). We saw MJB 167 and MBL 867 earlier in the description of the 1956 Mille Miglia; the Old English White MJB 191 had started life as a factory MGA demonstrator, with its motor-sport debut at Silverstone on 2 June 1956 at an 'Eight Clubs Race Meeting', with Pat Moss driving (race no. 46). MRX 42 (chassis no. HDK13-15995) and MRX 43 each made their debut on the Alpine.

MGA's boot-lid stay, they somehow worked the broken half-shaft piece out of the differential. These two bits they took into Annecy on a school bus, where they got them welded together; Ray refitted the halfshaft and they got the MG down to Marseilles under its own power.

Commendably, it was Nancy Mitchell and Pat Faichney who grabbed the headlines for BMC, finishing fifteenth overall out of the thirty-four finishing cars, ahead of the four other MGAs; furthermore they did so without a single penalty point, and won a highly coveted 'Coupe des Alpes' – this was only the third time that a female crew had achieved this impressive feat.

THE LIÈGE-ROME-LIÈGE RALLY

At the end of August was the Liège-Rome-Liège rally, in which four factory MGAs were entered. John Gott was effectively the team captain, his day job in the police force giving him the gravitas and organizational skills appropriate to the task. His co-driver was Chris Tooley, who would subsequently write about their experiences for *Autocar*. 'The Liège' – or aptly christened 'Marathon de la Route' – was an arduous ninety-three-hour test of both driver and machine, in 1956 embracing some 3,200 miles (5,150km), starting from the Spa race circuit in the middle of the night on Wednesday 29 August 1956, heading initially for the Black Forest.

The roads were of all kinds, including for the first time that year several rough Yugoslavian sections covered in the same thick talcum-powder-like dust seen by crews the previous month on the Alpine Rally. Crossing in and out of six countries, taking in forty-two passes, with sixty-five control points, and harsh penalty points for lateness, the event was well known for its high attrition rate, typically losing up to two-thirds of the entry by the finish. On this occasion, the four MGAs found themselves in the 2-litre class, with another forty competing.

From the Black Forest, on to Munich, the rally headed south into the Bavarian Mittenwald, then on into Italy via the Brenner Pass, on to Ortisei and towards the beautiful but highly testing Dolomites, full of sharp hairpin bends over 90 miles (145km) of arduous driving, often with nothing to prevent an errant driver launching off the edge of the road into thin air. As the evening set in, the cars crossed the Yugoslavian frontier, and soon headlamps were tunnelling their way through plumes of white dust.

For Tooley, his over-riding memories of Yugoslavia were:

> ...of dusty and winding narrow roads which occasionally became fast, smooth autostradas. These fine roads would then stop suddenly and we would be back into the dust again. The Adriatic at dawn looked beautiful, but we were too busy at the Riviera control at Rijeka checking the oil levels really to appreciate the scenery.

The next day saw re-entry into Italy, and by the evening, the testing Stelvio, Gavia and Vivione passes offered the next trial for the cars and their crews.

> Above us, and apparently reaching to the very sky, headlamps swept out into space as the cars ahead negotiated the hundred-odd hairpins. On the way down we overtook four cars that had set out much earlier. Only nine cars did the Stelvio without penalty, and out of the eighty-five that had left Spa, only fifty-five were still running.

Reaching the Gavia, the Gott/Tooley MGA was running well, frequently in the upper rev range around 5,800rpm: 'On some stages of up to ten miles at a stretch, only first and second gears were being used. We had survived a dive into a rock wall to avoid a bus, and had found that starting handles are useful for levering wings away from tyres...' After Vivione came a section of flat Italian plains, and a risk of falling asleep at the wheel, a problem only partially ameliorated by 'pep pills' (probably amphetamine).

During the fourth day, the cars passed through Izoard, Col de Vars and Col d'Allos with relatively few problems. Tooley said that navigation was not necessary, as spectators and frequent

MJB 191 lines up with 301 LBL (a very nicely made Le Mans replica) and MRX 42 alongside the replica of the BMC transporter at Le Touquet in 2016.

ROBIN HOWARD

THE 1956 LIÈGE-ROME-LIÈGE

Race No.	Colour	UK Reg. No.	Drivers	Overall Placing	1300–1600cc Class	Notes
15	Red with Black alloy hardtop	MRX 43	John Milne/Richard Bensted-Smith	14th	7th	
24	Red with Black alloy hardtop	MRX 42	Gerry Burgess/Sam Croft-Pearson	DNF	DNF	Retired with damaged sump.
38	Red with Black alloy hardtop	MBL 867	Nancy Mitchell/Anne Hall	26th		Second in Ladies' Class.
75	British Racing Green (body and alloy hardtop)	MJB 191	John Gott/Chris Tooley	13th	6th	

Footnotes:
The event took place from 29 August to 2nd September 1956. It is not known for certain why MBL 167 did not compete on this occasion, but suffice to say that by 1957, it had been fitted with a new body for that year's Lyons–Charbonnières.

road sign arrows indicated which direction to take; meanwhile 'the driver off duty dozed as well as he could. Horn blasts and the wailing of tyres do not, however, induce deep slumber.'

During the fourth night there was a further alpine stretch of fourteen cols, this time in France. There was heavy rain, and this hampered efforts for all the survivors:

> The Col de Lauteret was in cloud, with a thunderstorm thrown in for good measure; floodwater in the valleys kept pulling the car to one side, and our exhaust note at high revs was formidable and tiring. The last day across France was a medley of rain and sun, sleeping and driving, dreaming that you were driving and suddenly finding out that you were.

The event finished where it had begun, at Spa, and whilst it was a Mercedes 300SL in first place and a Porsche in second, Abingdon honour was upheld with three of the four MGAs finishing, out of just thirty-five of the original eighty-five to make it through. Just behind Gott and Tooley were John Milne and Richard Benstead-Smith in MRX 43, while Nancy Mitchell and Anne Hall took twenty-sixth place overall and second in the Ladies Class in MaBeL. Only one other British car finished, a Triumph TR3.

It was the end of a fine season for the BMC factory MGAs, which would be out again in the spring of 1957 at the Lyons-Charbonnières Rally of 21 March 1957, where the redoubtable Nancy Mitchell, accompanied by Doreen Reece, would bring 'MaBeL' home to win the Ladies Prize, a Coupe des Dames and thirty-second place overall. In the meantime, however, there was still MGA racing activity at the hands of the privateers, including, of course, the Fitzwilliam and Carnegie alliance.

THE SEASON FINALE – OULTON PARK 1956

In the mid-1950s *The Daily Herald* was a major British newspaper of its time, and it sponsored the *Autosport* Championship in 1956, whose final was on Saturday 22 September 1956. Of course as an unashamed 'race' event, the MG factory were notably absent, and so it was for the privateers to uphold MG's honour. In the 1,500 class were four MGAs, driven by Peter Simpson, Alan Foster and David Dixon, and the Fitzwilliam/Carnegie team. The race was run on a special handicap basis, with credit laps given, which could change the end result.

Simpson, who started with eight credit laps and drove with A. Asquith, was described by *Autosport* in their post-race report as having had, in their view, clear potential to have won, but he was thwarted by ignition problems which meant that he finished in third place. Meanwhile David Dixon's MGA was driven 'sedately' but nevertheless finished the race. Alan Foster, who also started with eight credit laps, crashed out of the race. Carnegie claimed that Foster was trying hard to catch him, ending up right on his tail, which proved to be his downfall: 'For several laps he tried to pass,

Robin Carnegie in dark overalls prepares to greet his victorious colleague Richard W-Fitzwilliam in the latter's own car, UPO 929 (race no. 21) at the end of the Autosport Three Hours at Oulton Park on 22 September 1956.

FITZ FROM HIS DAUGHTER AMANDA GRAVES

and then on lap fifteen he tried to take me going through Old Hall Comer, got it all wrong and ended up in the ditch.'

Foster's fate was similarly explained by *Autosport*:

> Running parallel with three other cars in the thrilling dash down from Old Hall to The Cascades, Alan Foster found his MGA a little too near the inside edge. The car slewed off course and skittered sideways along the grass, missing a substantial tree (behind which a marshal stepped just in time) by a foot or so. Striving desperately to regain the road, Foster unfortunately straightened up just in time to enter the protective ditch, finishing up with his car canted up the inside bank at some 60 degrees. Efforts to extract the MG merely resulted in fruitless wheel-spin and steaming grass, and lacking the help of a dozen strong men or so, he was obliged to abandon the race.

Meanwhile Fitz and Carnegie, in UPO 929 as usual, had been given a useful nine credit laps; beforehand, and evidently unknown to Carnegie, Fitz had taken the MGA to Bill 'Jonesie' Jones, who had been responsible for looking after Johnny Keeling's Jaguar C-Type. Carnegie discovered that his partner had got Jones to polish the ports and grind in the valve seats, and had fitted hollow push rods – fairly basic tuning practice. In addition, Jones had gone further, lightening the fly wheel and balancing the core engine components.

As winners of the 1956 *Autosport* Championship, the Fitzwilliam MGA (with Robin Carnegie driving) graced the cover of the magazine's issue of 28 September 1956.
AUTHOR'S COLLECTION

A loose seat caused problems during the race for both drivers, but despite the inconvenience they made good time, and with Foster gone, looked set for a good result. Meanwhile Fitz's wife Doreen was on timing duty; according to Carnegie, half an hour before the end of the race, she worked out that on handicap the duo were leading the race by two laps: 'Provided Fitz kept everything together, we were going to win. Doreen did not dare tell Fitz this, because she thought he would get so excited he would do something silly, so we just continued to hang out "steady as you go" signals, and hoped for the best.'

With their nine credit laps, the Fitzwilliam MGA, with eighty-two laps and an overall time of 2 hours 58 minutes and 31.4 seconds and an average speed of 67.29mph (108.27km/h), won by 76.2 seconds over Ken Rudd in his AC Bristol: so Fitz and Carnegie were able to celebrate not only the *Autosport* Trophy and a replica, but a prize of £100. As the principal sponsor of their eponymous championship, it was natural that *Autosport* would make something of a splash about the Fitzwilliam/Carnegie championship win, and accordingly the cover of the magazine's issue of Friday 28 September 1956 featured a photo of Carnegie in UPO 929, cornering at Oulton Park's 'Old Hall Corner' the previous weekend. Inside the same issue there were several relevant advertisements including a full-page MGA advertisement from the MG Car Company's Cowley Sales Division, heralding the result.

At the top of the same issue's 'Pit and Paddock' column, the magazine speculated that '*Autosport* Championship winner R.W. Fitzwilliam has acquired three Le Mans-type MGAs for 1957 long-distance sports car races. The team will probably include Peter Simpson, Tony Everard, Robin Carnegie and Fitz himself.' It was the first public clue as to what would become a proper team.

THE FITZWILLIAM RACING TEAM

By the close of the 1956 season, W-Fitzwilliam and Carnegie had expanded their 'band of brothers' to incorporate other owner/drivers with a common interest, and with this in mind, coupled with the knowledge on the Abingdon grapevine that MG's factory-built racing MGAs were likely to be underemployed in 1957 (and that the factory might be open to finding uses for them), plans were formulated to put the Fitzwilliam Racing Team into being and on a firm footing. In

Richard 'Fitz' W-Fitzwilliam and Robin Carnegie collect two of the cars loaned to them – LBL 303 and LBL 301 – from Abingdon. The famous BMC Competitions Department transporter LBL 405 is parked behind.

CALL IT MGA

this regard, Carnegie's friend Johnny Keeling, and John Blaksley (shortly to be married to Keeling's cousin Mary), were to be the financial brains behind the creation of a proper memorandum of agreement.

The grand plan began rather serendipitously with one of Fitz's visits to Abingdon, where he had seen the EX 182 cars covered with dust sheets and detritus. Fitz wrote to John Thornley to see if something could be done to bring these cars back into competitive action, and Thornley invited Fitz and Carnegie to go and see him. Carnegie would later recall:

> As far as we were concerned our meeting was an unwarranted success. Not only were the MG Car Company going to loan and prepare for us the two aluminium-bodied cars, they were also going to race-prepare a standard car, supply three spare engines, spare gear boxes, three each of 3.9 to 1 and 4.5 to 1 back axles, as well as all the spares which, from their experience, they thought we might need.

The Fitzwilliam Team cars all sported the distinctive white shield with red diamonds, taken from the Wentworth-Fitzwilliam family crest.

AUTHOR

The next consideration was to find someone suitable to tend to the four MGAs. Near the back of the *Autosport* issue of 23 November 1956, a small advertisement appeared under the 'Situations Vacant' section, inviting interested workshops with suitable experience to get in touch: 'A garage, or mechanic, required to maintain and possibly travel with three cars racing in England and abroad – Box 2287.'

Towards the end of the month, a letter came in response from a north-west London garage called Ecurie Oppidans; the name may have sounded pretentious but it came simply from the address, Oppidans Mews in Hampstead. The proprietors were Leslie Marr and Derrick Edwards, who had prepared and raced their own Aston Martins and Connaughts. In his letter to the anonymous 'Box 2287' of 26 November 1956, Derrick Edwards explained that:

> Leslie Marr has now decided to withdraw from racing, which will virtually leave our Work Shop in a position to take on work on Sports or Racing Cars. My assistant and I are both B.R.D.C. mechanics, and we are proud of our record that in three years of Formula 2 and Formula 1 racing, our cars have never retired with mechanical trouble, apart from accidents sustained during racing.

Edwards said that the team were self-sufficient and well travelled: 'I personally have experienced all travelling conditions in twenty-six different countries, and I feel that perhaps some arrangement could be made whereby we could get together for our own mutual benefit.' Evidently Fitz and his colleagues agreed, for an arrangement was duly concluded for Ecurie Oppidans to service and garage the team's four cars in Hampstead when they were not being raced. Carnegie commented that 'even though neither Derrick nor Ginger were very communicative, we all got on together very well.'

In the meantime, Fitz had already met with Marcus Chambers on 12 November 1956, and they agreed the friendly terms under which the factory would be prepared to loan out three of their special MGAs; the following day, Chambers set out the terms of the arrangement in writing as follows:

> 1. We expect you to insure the cars for £1,000 when being used at home or abroad except during races or practice periods.
>
> 2. In event of the car being severely damaged, and the resulting work being beyond the scope of your organisation, the car to be returned to the factory where we will effect repairs. If the special bodies are so damaged as to make repair uneconomic, then you must expect us to use standard components to repair them. Time taken to carry out repairs must be dependent on the commitments of the department, but every effort would be made to cooperate.
>
> 3. If any car should be a total loss in a race we would not expect you to make good the loss to us, neither would we be able to replace the lost car in your team.
>
> I feel your co-drivers will be happier now that they can see this arrangement in writing. It was nice seeing you yesterday. I think we should have regular meetings from now on, so as to keep matters moving and tidy up loose ends.

With the principle of a free loan of cars (and spares) agreed, and the terms of insurance defined, it was time for the team members to come together and form their association, to which end a meeting was held at John Blaksley's London flat on Wednesday 9 January 1957. (The author is grateful to John Blaksley's widow Mary and his son Richard for access to the surviving papers, from which some of the following detail is drawn.)

It was agreed in principle that Ecurie Oppidans would be engaged for a sum of £25 per week (roughly equivalent to £600 in 2018), which would also secure the services of their mechanic, referred to only as 'Ginger', as well as full-time garaging in Hampstead; a phone call the next day to Edwards finalized the terms. It was also agreed that Robin Carnegie would be technical adviser, and solely responsible for instructing Edwards on the maintenance of the cars.

At the same time, the future team began to formulate its plans for overseas events, and it was agreed that there would be an entry in the May 1957 Mille Miglia, at the team's own expense (*see* later in this chapter). Meanwhile, any cars that were not accepted would be entered for Spa for the same day, and it was reported that the MG factory's distinctive competition *camion* would be at Zürich that weekend.

These points and others were then all set out in a draft memorandum of 11 February 1957. In the memo, it was explained that the MG Car Company would 'prepare three MGAs (the cars), one of which will have a standard body and two will have aluminium bodies, to be ready for racing at the beginning of the 1957 season'. These three cars would be loaned 'free of charge to R. Fitzwilliam on the understanding that the cars will be raced primarily in certain long distance international races'. It was also made clear that MG had asked that the team did not make an entry at Le Mans. The six drivers were listed as R. Fitzwilliam, R. Carnegie, J. O. Blaksley, P. A. Everard, J. Hogg, P. Simpson and, as team manager (and reserve driver), J. A. Keeling.

The cost of maintaining the cars by Derrick Edwards would be inclusive of all overtime at home and abroad, although it was agreed that 'when mechanics travel abroad, their expenses will be paid by the team'. Alongside the three factory cars, it was agreed that Fitz would lend his own MGA (UPO 929) as 'a race and practice car when required, and will be reimbursed direct expenses in connection therewith'.

In a touch of light-hearted humour, the memo also set out a direction that 'the team will operate on a friendly and sportsmanlike basis. It will be the policy not to indulge in extravagances whilst on trips to, at and from meetings. Single rooms would be booked when possible. Personal luxuries (such as dumb blondes and ritzy hotels) will be the responsibility of the person concerned.' As a prelude to the new season's racing, it was declared that Fitz had arranged for the team to hire the Goodwood circuit on 1 and 2 March, and that all four cars and the entire team would be present.

To accompany this, Fitz and Carnegie were due to fund accommodation individually; and it was noted that on 2 March, 'the motor press have been invited to Goodwood and subsequently to RF's home in the evening.' There seems little doubt that several gentlemen of the press would look forward to enjoying the generous hospitality of Fitz and Doreen and the rest of the team. Before this could happen, the cars had to be collected from Abingdon, and Fitz, Carnegie and Blaksley drove them back.

MG had painted the noses of each of their cars using different colours around the grilles; of the two aluminium cars, LBL 301 was originally 'Yellow' and LBL 303 was 'Red', the standard-bodied car LJB 205 was 'White', and Fitz's car UPO 929, initially with a plain nose but a blue rectangular patch low on the driver's side front wing, was to become 'Blue'. All four cars were painted Tyrolite Green.

Carnegie wrote that:

> Red and Blue were fitted with full length screens, and the other two had black hardtops, which we soon decided to discard, for we all found them much too hot and noisy. They were all painted that rather nasty light pea green that was a standard MG colour. They all had knock-on wire wheels, larger tanks with a central filler, close-ratio gears and standard axles.

The contemporary colour photo overleaf of the cars lined up together at Goodwood shows them as Carnegie remembered them, they only ever raced with the team with cut-down competition screens.

FITZWILLIAM TEAM MEMBERS

Johnny Keeling – generally regarded as the organizational brains of the Fitzwilliam team – pours the champagne, whilst Fitz looks on appreciatively.
RICHARD BLAKSLEY

John and Mary Blaksley at their home in London with UPO 929, about to embark on the exciting trip to the Nürburgring 1,000km in 1957.
BLAKSLEY FAMILY

Johnny Keeling: When the idea of a Fitzwilliam Racing Team was proposed, clearly it would involve more than just Richard W-Fitzwilliam and Robin Carnegie. In addition to this, Carnegie was of the view that having got the cars, there was no way he was going to get involved in the Fitzwilliam Racing Team if it was going to be organized by Fitz, and in this regard, Fitz agreed. They immediately both thought that the person they should ask to take on this task was Johnny Keeling, who had owned the C-Type Jaguar that Carnegie drove before the MGA, but had written off. Carnegie later wrote: 'We thought that if we offered him a drive, his most efficient office could do some of the administration. He happily refused the drive but was thrilled at the idea of being chef d'équipe.'

Thus Keeling took on the important role of team manager and the organization of those critical but unexciting aspects where Fitz's enthusiasm and application fell short of what was needed.

John Owen Blaksley (6 July 1921–22 June 1982) was also in the mix at this time. He and Keeling had been at Christchurch, Oxford, together and were firm friends with a common motor-racing interest. Blaksley became part of the Fitzwilliam Team, and helped collect the MGAs from Abingdon in the spring of 1957. Highlights for John Blaksley were the May 1957 Mille Miglia (with Peter Simpson, finishing in sixty-fifthth place) and the Nürburgring 1,000km at the end of the same month, where, along with Ellis Cuff-Miller, Blaksley finished in forty-first place; then at Reims in mid-July he shared an impressive drive with John Hogg and Peter Simpson to finish in twenty-seventh place, both the highest placed MG and fourth in their Porsche-laden class.

John Goldsborough Hogg (21 January 1925–1 August 2003) was born in Middlesex. His motor-racing exploits began in 1953 with an Allard and then a Jaguar C-Type, but were largely concluded with the trips to the Mille Miglia, Nürburgring, Reims and with the Fitzwilliam Team in 1957; thereafter he focused on other outlets for his hobbies.

Patrick Anthony ('Tony') William Beresford Everard (28 November 1922–18 September 2011) raced in an Aston-Martin DB2 in 1953 and part of 1954, then graduated to a DB3 before he joined the Fitzwilliam Team for one season.

Peter Simpson had come to some prominence driving his Healey Silverstone in which he had achieved sixth place overall in the 1951 Isle of Man Manx Cup Race; Simpson still owned the Healey when he joined the Fitzwilliam Team, and indeed kept it until 1962, but it was with Fitz and his group that Simpson raced at the Mille Miglia, Reims and the Nürburgring.

John Blaksley in UPO 929 at the Nürburgring 1,000km in May 1957. They finished in 41st place.
RICHARD BLAKSLEY

The Fitzwilliam Team organized a test session at Goodwood on 2 March 1957 once their four MGAs had benefited from the attentions of 'Écurie Oppidans'. Here, Robin Carnegie gets into LBL 303 ('Red') nearest the camera, identified by the nose colouring. Behind 'Red' are 'Yellow' (LBL 301), Fitz's own car UPO 929 (later to become 'Blue', but not distinguished with a painted nose at the time of this photo) and 'White' (the original LJB 205).
CALL IT MGA

After the test session at Goodwood, LBL 301 and LBL 303 were taken back to Abingdon for some modifications, while the Ecurie Oppidans men administered to the needs of LJB 205 and UPO 929. It would soon be time for the new team's first big overseas adventure – to the heart of Italy. However, they were waiting to hear how the work was progressing on the two cars they had taken back: Chambers calmly announced that they had fitted the latest Dunlop disc brakes on all four wheels. The team would have no time to test the cars when they got them back, but would find the modifications beneficial.

ABOVE LEFT: **The business-like cockpit of LBL 301: what stories it could tell!**
BOB WEST

ABOVE RIGHT: **The engine bay of LBL 301 has been beautifully presented thanks to Bob West's sensitive restoration.**
BOB WEST

RIGHT: **LBL 301 was eventually restored to later Fitzwilliam Team Colours (Tyrolite Green and white nose) by MGA expert Bob West.**
BOB WEST

MAY 1957: THE LAST MILLE MIGLIA ROAD RACE

The 1957 Mille Miglia event would, in some ways, prove to be as fateful in the course of motor-racing history as the dreadful events of Le Mans had proved two years earlier. Italy's history of road racing, an idea no longer tolerated in most other countries, was about to reach a crisis point. In the various teams' planning for the event, of course, none of this could be known, but needless to say, everybody who was anybody in the field of road racing wanted to be on the start line at Brescia on 11 May.

This year, the factory team was absent: the entry in 1956 had doubtless prompted some sleepless nights at Abingdon in case the BMC Board had taken umbrage – but in any case, there was now a lot going on at Abingdon, and running a long-distance road event in Italy was not high on the priority list; besides, the new Austin-Healey 100/6 was proving promising, and a new engine for the MGA was still more than a year away. However, this obviously opened up the opportunity for the privateers, and at the forefront of these were the Fitzwilliam Racing Team, newly equipped and set up with the benefit of the three factory cars on loan to them.

All four of the Fitzwilliam team's MGAs made the trip to Brescia, and the pilots were as follows: for LBL 301, Robin Carnegie racing as car no. 357; for LBL 303, Peter Simpson/John Blaksley as car no. 347; for LJB 205, Fitz as car no. 358; and lastly, UPO 929, to be raced by John Hogg and Bill 'Jonesie' Jones as car no. 404. Planning for the Fitzwilliam effort had been overseen by Johnny Keeling, whose organizational skills clearly exceeded those of Fitz himself by a significant margin. Carnegie would note that 'Johnny, with the help of his office, had prepared a most complicated schedule to cope for all our different travelling arrangements, and provided tickets for ourselves, various travelling companions, Derek, Ginger and the van and of course the cars, which were to be driven to Brescia.'

Doreen W-Fitzwilliam, Bill 'Jonesie' Jones and Carnegie conducted two of the Fitzwilliam MGs, and Ginger the team's new van, and had an uneventful trip through France: they stopped overnight in Basel, then took the train through the St Gothard tunnel, continued by road through Switzerland and Italy, and arrived in Brescia on the Wednesday before the Mille Miglia's scheduled Saturday. The days were spent getting the cars ready, Derek and Ginger fitting the full-length competition screens because none of the team wanted to drive the cars with hardtops fitted.

Scrutineering took place in the Piazza Vittoria, the main square in Brescia, where each entry was given a fairly basic inspection, a seal was fitted to the steering column to deter cheating by switching cars, the race numbers were painted on the nose, tail and both sides, the entrants' international competition licences and medical certificates were checked, and a third party insurance payment of some £40 was taken, paid using copious quantities of Italian lira.

1957 Mille Miglia: John Hogg and Bill 'Jonesie' Jones in UPO 929 (race no. 404) entering Pescara just prior to the control.

FITZ FROM RICHARD BLAKSLEY

LBL 301 in the 1957 Mille Miglia. Remarkably this car would go on to be the highest-placed British car at the end of this arduous race.

BOB WEST

At shortly after a quarter to four in the morning of 11 May 1957, Peter Simpson and John Blaksley wait to be flagged off from the start ramp in Brescia's Via Rubuffione in that year's Mille Miglia. The car is LBL 303.
FITZ FROM RICHARD BLAKSLEY

Keeling's organizational skills evidently extended to mapping out and arranging fuelling stations for the Fitzwilliam team, which were at Ravenna, Rome and Bologna, whilst the team's own 'refuelling' needs were catered for by the resourceful Doreen, who sorted out easily managed chocolate, sandwiches and fruit, with liquid catered for using bicycle water bottles, which Derrick and Ginger secured in the doors.

The Fitzwilliam MGAs were not alone in aiming to uphold octagonal honours: also in the race were Britons Jeff Sparrowe and Mike Reid (in car no. 353) and Pietro Nava and Giuseppe Ribolla (in car no. 229), both Italian Mille Miglia 'veterans' who had previously successfully completed, respectively, the 1956 event in an MG Magnette and the 1953 event in a Fiat 500. Last but not least was car no. 355, to be driven by the Belgian husband and wife team of Jacques and Annie Spiers from Renaix. The Italians' car was fitted with a black Vanden Plas hardtop and a neat Perspex 'bug deflector' fitted transversely across the bonnet.

The race number of the cars in the Mille Miglia had a special significance, representing the start time for the car in question, with the smaller cars setting off earlier than the most powerful ones. Thus, for example, Fitz's car, number 358, was scheduled to start at 03:58 in the morning, just a minute after Carnegie set off in no. 357. In 1957 a remarkable 391 cars had been entered, spanning a no less impressive total of twenty-five classes based on engine sizes; of these, 310 cars started the event, and both Ferrari and Maserati entered works teams.

The Mille Miglia start involved seemingly endless lines of cars queuing for their allotted start, which involved climbing a ramp in the tree-lined Via Rubuffione, under the glare of spotlights, before being sent off into the night. Supervising the operation was the bowler-hatted figure of Renzo Castagneto, known as 'the father of the Mille Miglia'. The first leg from Brescia headed out towards Padua, and as the sun slowly rose in the sky, the drivers were able to benefit from the growing light. The way was made clear by the dozens of strategically placed red and white Mille Miglia direction arrows.

A lone spectator looks on from his vantage point within the sturdy barriers as Hogg/Jones (race no. 404) motor past during the 1957 Mille Miglia.
FITZ FROM RICHARD BLAKSLEY

1957 Mille Miglia with spectators watching as Hogg and Jones pass them by.
FITZ FROM RICHARD BLAKSLEY

Peter Simpson driving, with co-driver John Blaksley alongside him, in LBL 301 – race no. 347 – in the 1957 Mille Miglia.
BLAKSLEY FAMILY

Whilst the various MGA drivers were maintaining a decent pace down the field, many eyes were focused on London-born Spanish playboy, Alfonso Antonio Vicente Eduardo Angel Blas Francisco de Borja Cabeza de Vaca y Leighton, Marquis of Portago, who was driving one of the Ferraris; his beautiful actress girlfriend, Linda Christian, was on hand to lend her lover moral support. Meanwhile back in the more mundane MG world, Robin Carnegie had a fairly uneventful race, other than a few near misses on some damp and slippery roads in the four Italian mountain passes at Antrodoco, Radicofani, Futa and Raticosa, and a dramatic trip through the forecourt of a garage near Bologna: braking hard on a bend, he shot through a fortuitous gap behind the petrol pumps and got back on the road to rejoin the race.

Fitz, however, came to grief. Robin Carnegie wrote that his friend 'went off the road somewhere between Rome and Viterbo and hit an advertisement sign for Haig Whisky, which I suppose one could say was appropriate. He managed to get the car back on the road with the help of some local spectators, and despite the chassis being out of line, got back to Brescia, but sadly not within the time allowed.'

Writing in his comprehensive book *Mille Miglia 1957 – Le Classi Minori*, Carlo Dolcini tells a slightly different story:

> ...Fitzwilliam was seventh into Rome. Not long afterwards, he got his entry wrong going into a Via Cassia corner and hit a tree, which fell and broke his nose. Helped by spectators, Fitzwilliam was in pain but didn't want to stop. He restarted despite the accident and drove without a helmet or goggles for at least seven hours before stopping at Piacenza [about 90km from Brescia], where he was admitted to hospital.

The other cars in the Fitzwilliam Team all made it through to the end, as did the other MGAs.

Mike Reid had the idea of participating in the 1957 race, having been inspired by the write-up in *Motor Sport* by Denis 'Jenks' Jenkinson of the latter's epic drive with Stirling Moss in the 1955 event; Reid's own MGA (SRU 555, first registered in January 1956) had served him well in races, and he won the 1956 *Motor Sport* Trophy and a cheque for the princely sum of £50. This money certainly came in handy: 'Our entry was confirmed only ten days before we had to leave, and my hard-

A fairly substantial wall provides a comparatively well protected viewing facility for spectators during the 1957 Mille Miglia.
FITZ FROM RICHARD BLAKSLEY

THE 1957 MILLE MIGLIA

Race No.	Colour	UK Reg. No.	Drivers	Overall Placing	Class/Position	Notes
229	Red?	N/A	Pietro Nava/Giuseppe Ribolla	133rd	GT 1.6/8th	Time 15:00:02.0. Black hardtop
347	Tyrolite Green (Red nose)	LBL 303	Peter Simpson/John Blaksley	65th	Sports 1.5/6th	Time 13:34:05.0. Fitzwilliam Team member
353	Tyrolite Green	SRU 555	Jeff Sparrowe/Mike Reid	134th	Sports 1.5/9th	Time 15:00:24.0. Car first registered January 1956
355	Unknown	N/A	Jacques Spiers/Annie Spiers	153rd	Sports 1.5/10th	Time15:44:01.0
357	Tyrolite Green (Yellow nose)	LBL 301	Robin Carnegie	31st	Sports 1.5/4th	Time 12:55:21:0. Fitzwilliam Team member
358	Tyrolite Green (White nose)	LJB 205	Richard 'Fitz' W-Fitzwilliam	DNF	Sports 1.5/DNF	Crashed between Piacenza and Mantova ('did not finish' – in fact he limped home but was out of time). Fitzwilliam Team member
404	Tyrolite Green (Blue nose)	UPO 929	John G. Hogg/William P. (Bill) 'Jonesie' Jones	85th	Sports 1.5/8th	Time 13:51:27:0. Fitzwilliam Team member

Footnotes:
The event date was 11–12 May 1957; it was the 34th Mille Miglia, and also the last of these road races. There were no official MG factory entries – even if the Fitzwilliam Team were technically using cars which happened to be 'on loan' from Abingdon. Impressively, Carnegie in LBL 301 was the first British car to finish.

used MGA was in no fit state to go anywhere. I had run the bearings during a particularly hectic race at Goodwood the previous weekend, the clutch was burnt out, and 28,000 miles of rallies, racing and business use had worn out a lot more.'

Those ten days were spent overhauling the car, before leaving on the overnight ferry on the evening of Sunday 4 May. By 5am the following morning, Reid and Sparrowe were on their way from Dunkirk, and by the end of the day, they had reached Italy.

Reid and Sparrowe set off from Brescia at 03:53, their experience unsurprisingly closely echoing that recorded by Carnegie, who left four minutes after them. Their early experiences in the race were evidently also much like those of their rival, although their car developed a seemingly insatiable appetite for oil: 'Whenever we are forced to slow we stopped to put in more oil; better to have the rocker box awash than the oil pump starved'. Losing the dipstick didn't help much, either.

Alongside the British MGA entries at the 1957 Mille Miglia was this Italian pairing of Pietro Nava and Giuseppe Ribolla (both of whom had competed successfully in previous Mille Miglias), who went on to finish in 133rd place. Note the bug deflector mounted in front of the driver's line of sight.
AUTHOR'S COLLECTION

The plucky duo suffered various challenges apart from oil consumption and fuel problems: the brakes began to pull to one side prior to the Androco Pass, making progress even more difficult, but they kept up an impressive overall average of 70mph (113km/h) and fulfilled their objective of finishing the event, ending up in an entirely honourable 134th place.

Meanwhile, by the end of the 1957 Mille Miglia, Richard Fitzwilliam was the only MG driver not to finish: Carnegie was in 31st place, Simpson/Blaksley in 65th, Hogg/Jonesie were in 85th, the Italians (Nava/Ribolla) finished in 133rd, Reid/Sparrowe immediately behind them in 134th, and the Belgian Spiers couple were in 153rd. However, headlines were dominated by the Marquis of Portago's fatal accident, one of three drivers, a policeman and eleven spectators who died. As Mike Reid later wrote:

> This added sadly to the long list of fatalities throughout the history of this race. During the months that followed there was much bitter argument. Finally the Italian government banned the race because of the casualties. It was impossible to guarantee spectators protection over 1,000 miles. We were privileged to have been able to take part in the last of the real old road races, but shocked by the awful toll.

Thus ended another historical legacy of road racing, but perhaps not without reason.

THE TALE OF LJB 205

LJB 205 wearing race no. 25B out on the circuit at Silverstone, on 17 August 1957.

FITZ FROM RICHARD BLAKSLEY

Of the four cars that the Fitzwilliam Team raced, 'LJB 205' seems to have been the most unfortunate. Originally Tyrolite Green like the rest of the team (Robin Carnegie referred to it as a 'horrible pea green'), LJB 205 began life as the first production MGA; as we saw earlier, a mix-up in chassis numbers, when the first two cars were accidentally ascribed the same chassis number (10101), meant that the first one was changed to 'EX 182/42', creating a fifth EX 182 car, which was then road-registered as 'LJB 205'. From the start this was a steel-bodied roadster, but with some aluminium body components, and it was built up to racing and rally specification. Originally intended as part of MG's forward competitions programme, LJB 205 was used as the Dundrod practice car (*see* earlier), but evidently became slightly surplus to requirements at Abingdon, and so was an obvious candidate to be part of the loan of three cars to Fitz Fitzwilliam. LJB 205 was duly taken out to Italy to begin what it was hoped would be a promising racing career. Rare colour photographs from the 1957 Mille Miglia clearly show LJB 205 as still painted Tyrolite Green, with its white nose.

Then came the first major upset during the 1957 Mille Miglia on the road between Rome and Viterbo: 'Father hit a Haig Whisky sign sideways on, but nevertheless limped on to Brescia,' his son Robin says; 'then Mother drove it back to the UK and took it all the way to Abingdon – when none of the mechanics would drive it.' This is all the more remarkable when you consider that the petite five-foot-three and long-suffering Doreen Fitzwilliam had broken her back in a road accident three years earlier; she not only spoke no foreign languages but had never driven on the continent before. A subsequent contemporary report, lauding Mrs Fitzwilliam for her Herculean effort, recorded that 'she left Brescia at 9am on the Tuesday morning, got lost on the Autostrada, and crossed the Alps by the St Gothard, the car running appallingly badly. Reaching Reims during the Wednesday morning, she telegraphed the AA for a booking on the 3.20 Silver City Aircraft from Le Touquet – and just managed to catch the plane.'

After arriving in Kent, Doreen drove on to Henley to stay there overnight, and at eight o'clock the following morning (Thursday) she drove the remaining 22 miles to Abingdon: 'A new frame was ready by 9.30 and the body had by then been removed from the crashed car.' The report goes on to state that the car was ready by Sunday: 'By 5pm the engine had been installed... and the car went out on test. Within half an hour, and through no fault of the test driver, the car had been badly damaged again in an accident.' Although the connection to 'LJB 205' is not necessarily proven, the story of an incident very much like this is relayed in Brian Moylan's book *Works Rally Mechanic*. Moylan, part of the competition team, wrote that he had been working on an MGA with his colleague Doug Hamblin so that it could be made ready to go back out to Nürburgring for the Fitzwilliam team to pick up for their next race.

Moylan did not refer to the previous history of the car he was working on, but in fairness his assigned task was merely to rebuild it. This meant working on a Sunday – which fits with the story of LJB 205 but, as Moylan relates, 'Alec Hounslow didn't believe in days off, and Sunday was just another day.' The duly rebuilt car was taken out for a road test on the Oxford Southern Bypass, which often did double-duty as MG's informal test track. Normally all would be well, but on this occasion, Moylan – with Hamblin driving – proved to be unlucky. 'We would drive to the crest of a slight rise, from where we had a good view of the whole stretch of the road, then, when it was clear, we would start the run.' On this occasion, the only vehicle in sight was an Austin A70 parked by the side of the road in the distance. As Hamblin edged up to maximum revs, foot flat to the floor, the A70 driver indicated that he was

NÜRBURGRING 1957

Towards the end of May 1957 it was time for the Nürburgring 1,000km race again, and the Fitzwilliam Team decided to go in strength with four cars: the re-bodied LJB 205, now, as we have seen, painted red, albeit with a white nose; LBL 301, now seemingly 'White' rather than 'Yellow'; LBL 303, known as 'Red'; and of course UPO 929, known as 'Blue'.

Of the team, only Fitz and Carnegie had driven at a previous race. Carnegie recorded that 'Derrick and Ginger had going to move off. Moylan sounded the horn as a warning, but to his consternation the A70 driver proceeded to turn across the road and in order to come back towards the little MG. the MGA went broadside on, into the back offside corner of the Austin – and I went out over the windscreen.'

Despite rolling down the road, Moylan was remarkably uninjured, but his colleague had a broken wrist; meanwhile the occupants of the A70 'were unscathed – but were a very funny colour'. The MGA chassis was bent but the running gear undamaged, and so the car was somehow nursed back to Abingdon. Moylan recalls that an unsympathetic Alec Hounslow said to him: 'We've still got to get four cars ready for tomorrow morning, so you'd better start getting the engine and the rest of it into the ex-Le Mans car.' The timescale, of a rapid turnaround and the unfortunate write-off of the car on local test on a Sunday also fits with other testimony, for John Thornley mentioned such an incident in a letter to Robin Carnegie of 21 May 1957: 'You have doubtless heard by now that Fitz's car must have had a hoodoo on it, as having rebuilt it in about 72 hours flat, we pranged it on the opposite side from Fitz last Sunday afternoon. Still he should have a decent car for the Ring.'

The contemporary report on the incident picks up the tale by going on to record that 'By 12.30 pm on the Tuesday, another new car had been prepared, complete with racing engine and all the modifications, and it reached Germany in time for the first practice period on the Thursday.' Writing in his own memoires, Carnegie appears to corroborate this, when he noted that in the run-up to the Sunday 26 May 1957 Nürburgring 1,000km race, the Fitzwilliam Team's fourth car was no longer the green original: 'Apparently after Doreen got it back from Brescia to Abingdon, it was rebuilt by the Competitions Department, taken out to be tested, but crashed. So they hurriedly built up another one, which they re-registered LJB 205, and which Doreen nobly drove out to Nürburgring in time for practice. The new car was coloured red, and was assigned by Fitz, in his usual spontaneous manner, to Jean Bloxham and Patsy Burt.'

Afterwards, Fitz honoured his wife's impressive determination and commitment by presenting her with a beautiful octagonal silver powder compact, decorated with a miniature enamelled Fitzwilliam shield and engraved with the words 'Brescia to Abingdon, 13/5/57–16/5/57 from Fitzwilliam Racing Team.' Meanwhile, the 'reborn' LJB 205 lived to race another day. Once its exploits with the Fitzwilliam Team were behind it, LBL 205 was sold off by the factory; it was at one point owned by a Mr Sinclair, but is believed to have been scrapped sometime in the 1960s.

In appreciation of her monumental efforts in conveying LBL 205 back from Italy to Abingdon, Doreen W-Fitzwilliam was presented with this elegant octagonal compact complete with the Fitzwilliam crest...

ROBIN FITZWILLIAM

...on the reverse of which were the words: 'Brescia to Abingdon, 13/5/57–16/5/57 from Fitzwilliam Racing Team'.

ROBIN FITZWILLIAM

thoroughly checked the cars but had not changed an engine or lifted the heads,' adding that he had mistakenly thought that 'as they had all run so well in the Mille Miglia, and which had been considerably less of a strain on an engine than something like Nürburgring, it was as well to leave things as they were'. This proved to be false optimism, as Jean Bloxham's car (the red-bodied LJB 205, race no. 57) was out after six laps with oil pump failure, while LBL 301 (race no. 24), driven by Carnegie, suffered a valve failure on his twenty-eighth lap and so also went out.

Robin and Jean Margaret Carnegie driving LBL 301 on to the ferry for the crossing to France, en route to Nürburgring in May 1957. The nose now appears to be white rather than yellow.

FITZ FROM RICHARD BLAKSLEY

A Tyrolite Green MGA MCO 151 was also part of the Fitzwilliam convoy to Germany.

FITZ FROM RICHARD BLAKSLEY

Comparative fortune smiled on John Blaksley and Ellis Cuff-Miller, whose race in UPO 929 was fairly uneventful other than an intermittent starter motor fault, finishing in forty-first place, while Fitz and Peter Simpson in LBL 303 (race no. 23) also made it through to secure an impressive eighteenth place overall (the highest of the MGs). Alongside the British entry, Nürburgring 1957 also saw a Swedish/German entry (no. 65, driven by Bo Elmhorn/Bertil Nässil/Dieter von Reiswitz); however, it expired after just four laps.

Back in the UK, the next event of interest to the privateers was the 10 June Whitsun meeting at Goodwood, where all four of the Fitzwilliam cars were entered, and were up against the Alan Foster MGA of Dick Jacobs. In a typical spirit of chivalrous abandon, Fitz allowed Patsy Burt a drive when her own car, a Cooper Climax, had experienced difficulties in an earlier race; at the end of the race, it was Carnegie, Alan Foster, Fitz and Ken Mackenzie in third, fifth, sixth and eight positions in turn.

The Blaksley papers caption this photo of LBL 303 from the pits at the Nürburgring 1,000 km, on 26 May 1957, as 'Derrick [Edwards] warming up "Red"'. This MGA went on to finish in 18th place, driven by Fitz and Simpson.

CALL IT MGA

LBL 301 (by now known as 'White') at Nürburgring being 'warmed up by 'Ginger'). The car failed to finish, a dropped valve ending its race after twenty-eight laps.

BOB WEST

In the Fitzwilliam pits at Nürburgring we see Jean Bloxham sitting in '57' (the red, re-bodied LJB 205); in blue overalls behind is Patsy Burt, and the small figure with the headscarf behind the pit wall is Doreen W-Fitzwilliam.

FITZ FROM RICHARD BLAKSLEY

The cars line up at Nürburgring in May 1957; one of the Fitzwilliam Team cars can be seen second from the camera (this is 'Red') race no. 23), and in the background is the distinctive Nürburgring clock tower.

FITZ FROM RICHARD BLAKSLEY

Patsy Burt stands just behind LJB 205 (with the bonnet up), and the rear of one of the green Fitzwilliam MGAs (LBL 301) can be seen in the garage towards the left.

FITZ FROM RICHARD BLAKSLEY

Compare this recent photo of LBL 301 as restored by Bob West with the 1957 photo from Nürburgring with the back end of the same car visible inside the pit garage.

BOB WEST

THE 1957 NÜRBURGRING 1,000KM

Race No.	Colour	UK Reg. No.	Drivers	Overall Placing	Class	Notes
23	Tyrolite Green (Red nose)	LBL 303	Richard W-Fitzwilliam/Peter Simpson	18th	S 1.5	Thirty-seven laps
56	Tyrolite Green (Blue nose)	UPO 929	John Blaksley/Ellis Cuff-Miller	41st	GT 1.6	Thirty-eight laps
24	Tyrolite Green (White nose)	LBL 301	Robin Carnegie/John Hogg	DNF	S 1.5	Dropped valve after twenty-eight laps
57	Red (White nose)	LJB 205	Patsy Burt/Jean Bloxham	DNF	GT 1.6	Oil pump failure after four laps
65	Unknown	N/A	Bo Elmhorn (Sweden)/Bertil Nässil (Sweden)/Dieter von Reiswitz (Germany)	DNF	GT 1.6	Unknown failure after four laps

Footnotes:

The event date was 26 May 1957. As explained in the main text, there had been a slight 'realignment' of the colour schemes of the Fitzwilliam Team cars, due chiefly to the replacement of the original Tyrolite Green LBL 205 with a new, re-bodied replacement, finished in red. Contemporary colour photos of LBL 301 appear to indicate a change of nose colour from yellow to white – although a sixty-year-old photo is not necessarily reliable evidence.

Bo Elmhorn of BMC Sweden would later become involved in racing the Mini Marcos; Elmhorn, Nässil and fellow countryman Pehr Brolén each raced MGAs in the Swedish Grand Prix of 11 August 1957, finishing twelfth, thirteenth and fourteenth respectively.

At least one source also lists car no. 84 (driven by Germans Helmut Busch and K. H. Zimmerman) as an MGA, but in reality this was a Porsche 356A.

At the Goodwood Whitsun Meeting of 10 June 1957, Fitz Fitzwilliam (LBL 303', race no. 72) went on to finish in sixth place in the National Goodwood Marque Handicap race.

ABOVE: **Goodwood, 10 June 1957: Fitz at speed in LBL 303.**
FITZWILLIAM FAMILY (AMANDA GRAVES)

LEFT: **Richard W-Fitzwilliam received this BMC-sponsored plaque in recognition of his third place at Goodwood on Whit Monday, 1957 (10 June) in UPO 929, racing as car no. 74.**
W-FITZWILLIAM FAMILY

Sometime after the event at Goodwood it appears that LBL 303 was possibly involved in a road accident, but according to Carnegie, there was some mystery surrounding the circumstances:

> I heard the car had been returned to Abingdon, and was told they thought it was not worthwhile repairing, and I have no idea what subsequently happened to it. They were not prepared either to supply us with another standard car, which I am bound to say I thought was justified, partly because there was nothing further to be gained as far as they were concerned by loaning us another standard car, and also because apart from Reims, our plans were a bit unsure.

REIMS 1957

The Twelve Hours of Reims in 1957 started at midnight on Saturday 13 July; it continued through the night and dawn, and finished at midday on the Sunday. The Fitzwilliam Team had secured just two entries, and so with the jostling for a drive from all five team members, the task was split between LJB 205, with Peter Simpson, John Hogg and John Blaksley; and in the other car, LBL 301, it was Fitz and Carnegie sharing the drive.

The redoubtable Ginger and Curly had installed a new engine in the steel-bodied LJB 205, but it still proved slower than the alloy-bodied LBL 301, which also benefited from disc brakes. Both cars had 3.9:1 rear axles for this event.

For John Hogg in LJB 205, during the race a pit stop at two in the morning was needed to cure a misfire (due to a broken rocker), whilst Carnegie hung on until 07:30, when he heard a familiar bang, tinkle-tinkle '…and a valve had gone. I managed to get the car back into the pits, and as in any case it had to be repaired in order to drive it back to England, Derrick and Ginger, with Peter and John Blakesley's help, fitted a piston in just two hours for Fitz at least to finish the race, so that we were classified, albeit nearly last...' LJB 205 finished in twenty-seventh place, and LBL 301 was thirtieth.

After the race, the loaned factory cars went to Ecurie Oppidans' garage in order to prepare them for the Crystal Palace race meeting on 5 August; meanwhile Fitz took UPO 929 home to Bignor Park. At Crystal Palace, Carnegie drove LBL 301 and Fitz piloted LJB 205; amongst others they again found themselves up against the likes of Alan Foster and Ken Mackenzie, the former apparently using a 4.8:1 rear-axle ratio. Both the Fitzwilliam cars finished, but not with particular distinction. There would be other outings to Silverstone later the same month, but in the MGA motor-sports story, the next part of the tale to relate is the factory entry at the 1957 Liège-Rome-Liège.

In the meantime, the Fitzwilliam Team returned their two remaining loan cars to Abingdon.

Carnegie recalled:

> When Fitz and I returned LBL 301 and LJB 205 we were very kindly given lunch by John Thornley. His concern seemed to be far more that we had enjoyed our season with his cars, than that we had been successful, which of course had primarily been our intention in any case. Later on when I helped Ginger return all the spares in the van, very few of which had in fact been used, we were perhaps understandably not greeted by Marcus Chambers nearly so kindly, for we had wrecked one car in the Mille Miglia, and they had wrecked another trying to replace it, and LBL 303 had been badly damaged. So there was perhaps some reason for Marcus feeling slightly aggrieved...

There would be another outing to Snetterton on 12 October, where they brought UPO 929 home in seventeenth place. However, 1958 would see a new phase for the Fitzwilliam Team: Johnnie Keeling, John Hogg, John Blaksley and Ecurie Oppidans had moved on, their one-year adventure with the loaned works cars at an end. (The story continues later in this chapter.)

THE 1957 LIÈGE–ROME–LIÈGE

For Marcus Chambers and the Competitions Team, an important event for them in 1957 should have been the Alpine Rally, but this was cancelled in the wake of the Suez crisis, with the worries about fuel shortages. Accordingly efforts were put into readying a four-car team of MGAs for the Liège, scheduled for the end of August. The cars were all equipped with hardtops.

Team captain John Gott was paired with Chris Tooley in MJB 167 (chassis no. HDC13/12026; race no. 48), while Nancy Mitchell and Joan Johns were in OBL 311 (race no. 5). John Milne and Bill Shepherd were in MRX 43 (race no. 24), while George Harris and Georges Hacquin were in the fourth car MRX 42 (race no. 87). Whilst Gott/Tooley and the ladies made it through (to finish fourteenth and sixteenth respectively, with Mitchell/Johns winning the Ladies' prize), both the other cars retired.

THE 1957 LIÈGE–ROME–LIÈGE

Race No.	Colour	UK Reg. No.	Drivers	Overall Placing	1300–1600cc Class	Notes
5	Red with Black alloy hardtop	OBL 311	Nancy Mitchell/Joan Johns	16th	9th	1st in Ladies' Class
24	Red with Black alloy hardtop	MRX 43	John Milne/Bill Shepherd	DNF	DNF	Retired – accident
48	Red with Black alloy hardtop	MJB 167	John Gott/Chris Tooley	14th	8th	
87	Red with Black alloy hardtop	MRX 42	George Harris/Georges Hacquin	DNF	DNF	Retired – damaged suspension

Footnotes:
The event date was 28 August to 1 September 1957. Mitchell and Johns were the first Britons ever to win the *Coupe des Dames* at the Liège.

At the Tulip Rally in April 1958, MG was represented by a single MGA 1500 Roadster, race no. 49, driven by Nancy Mitchell and Gillian Wilton-Clarke, who finished the event thirty-fourth overall, fourth in class and fourth in the Ladies' Class. After that, it was up to the Midnight Sun Rally of 11 to 14 June, where Pat Moss and Ann Wisdom were partnered in an MGA 1500 (OBL 311, race no. 25), finishing fifth in class despite arguably having a far from ideal car for such an event.

THE MGA TWIN CAM IN COMPETITION

The arrival of the MGA Twin Cam in July 1958 could not have come a moment too soon; had it been launched earlier, there is a chance that it could have been entered in a summer event such as the 1958 Alpine Rally, staged a week before the Twin Cam's debut; as it was, BMC's focus for that year was mainly on those recent additions to the Abingdon family, the Austin-Healeys – both Sprite and 100/6. Indeed there were five of the latter at the Alpine, and there were no MGs – just as MG would prove to be a 'no show' at Sebring in 1958.

Shortly before launching into competition activity with the new model, two representatives of the Development Department at Abingdon took a pair of cars to Switzerland and Austria, linking up with Heinz Keller, who was MG's Swiss importer in Zürich, and was also a good friend of John Thornley. The cars were the black MGA Twin Cam PJB 147 (YDL/14/499) and an alloy-bodied EX 182 on a twin-cam chassis, with the registration number LBL 304 (painted red and with a low headlamp nose, as previously seen at Dundrod the previous September). The 'portability' of registration numbers at Abingdon makes it a challenge for historians to be certain of which car was which; as we have seen, registration numbers often seem to have jumped from one car to another.

Meanwhile the continental trip, between Saturday 9 August and Thursday 21 August 1958, would chiefly take in Gaisberg (one of the Salzkammergut Mountains near Salzburg, and, since September 1929, a home to Austrian hillclimbing and

The EX 182 LBL 304, now fitted with a twin-cam chassis and engine, is seen here at the Gaisberg Hill Climb in Salzburg, Austria, on 15 August 1958. Swiss driver Dr Harry Zweifel is at the wheel, but failed to secure a placing at the finish.

LEFT: HERMANN SCHWARZ, SALZBURG RALLYE CLUB RIGHT: CLIFF BRAY

Zweifel was back two days after the Gaisberg Hillclimb, this time at the Zeltweg Airfield, where he finished in seventh place, behind an unbroken line of six Porsches. He was fourth in his class, too – with, of course, Porsches above him in the top three places.
CLIFF BRAY

the Salzburg Rallye Club) and Zeltweg (an Austrian Air Force base, near Styria). The journey was undertaken by two of the MG Development Team, with Cliff Bray driving LBL 304 (described in Cliff Bray's contemporary notes as 'the EX 182' and, as noted, in low headlamp guise) and Alec Hounslow driving PJB 147, with a luggage rack on the boot to carry their travel bags.

The initial leg of the journey was the usual Silver City aerial ferry flight out from Lydd to Le Touquet, punctuated by a stopover at Abbeville (a commune of the Somme, in the north of France), followed by a twelve-hour drive to Zürich on their first Sunday, in order to meet up with the Keller family.

On the Monday they set off again for Salzburg via Munich (München), where they met up with Dr Harry Zweifel (25 April 1920–4 July 1991) and his wife. Keller had entered Zweifel, driving LBL 304 (as race no. 117) in the 1958 Gaisberg Hillclimb of Friday 15 August, the fifth round of the 1958 European Hillclimb Championship, the event being part of the 'Grosser Bergpreis von Österreich – Salzburg–Gaisberg' (literally the 'Grand Mountain Prize of Austria'). Zweifel was a popular Swiss driver of some renown, and as we saw earlier, had been involved in tests of the then still secret MGA in the Alps in July 1955. The MGA was sadly not placed at Gaisberg, and the event was fairly predictably won by a Porsche 550 RSK, driven by Wolfgang von Trips, whose time was 9 minutes and 21 seconds.

Two days later, the low-nosed LBL 304 (still wearing race no. 117) was at Zeltweg (later to become a short-lived home to the Austrian Grand Prix), at the 'Internationales Auto-und motorradrennen Flugplatz Zeltweg' (literally the 'Zeltweg Airfield International Car and Motorcycle Race'), where Zweifel finished in seventh place (behind a field of Porsches in all six top places); it was the German racing Count, Wolfgang von Trips, who took the honour of first place in a Porsche 718 RSK (race no. 114). The MG was, however, also fourth in its class, a category that was shared with von Trips' winning Porsche.

Occasional claims that the road-going car was entered in these events appear mistaken; the original programmes for both Gaisberg and Zeltweg clearly show what is erroneously listed as an 'MGA-EX/128 Sport', and the diary of Cliff Bray records that PJB 147 had not initially been taken to Zeltweg, as the road car had dutifully sacrificed its radiator after the one in LBL 304 was damaged during the first run at Gaisberg; the black car was duly repaired at Salzburg and then driven over on the Saturday to join the party (by now including a Swiss-registered MG Magnette) before the race the next day.

LBL 304 in Austria during its trip to meet up with the Keller family, with (*left to right*) Cliff Bray, Harry Zweifel (who drove at Gaisburg and Zeltweg) and Alec Hounslow.
CLIFF BRAY

Looking slightly the worse for wear, LBL 304 poses with (*left to right*) Heinz Keller, Alec Hounslow, Cliff Bray, and an unidentified lady friend. Note the Swiss ZB Magnette behind, with white-wall tyres.
CLIFF BRAY

There is speculation that despite the use of the LBL 304 number, the low-headlamp car was in reality LBL 303, if its basis was indeed that of EX 182/40 (see earlier in this chapter); there follows an argument that this same car – in effect as described above, a 'Twin Cam EX 182' – formed the basis of SRX 210, described later. Meanwhile a photo shows the alloy-bodied car evidently suffering from a buckled and torn nearside rear wing, and some moderate damage to the front nearside; whether this took place during the difficult drive through the Austrian Tyrol en route to Zeltweg, or in the race itself, is not clear.

Cliff Bray told several people that initially he and Hounslow returned to Abingdon without LBL 304, although evidently it presumably came back eventually, ostensibly in time to be ready to form the basis of SRX 210, the story of which is told later in this chapter. Meanwhile, having been left behind with the Keller family by Hounslow and Bray, LBL 304 took part in the sixth (and final) event in the 1958 European Hillclimb Championship on 31 August 1958, the Ollon-Villars Hill Climb near Lake Geneva ('Championnat D'Europe de la Montagne, Ollon-Villars Course International de Côte'), racing as number 137 and wearing Zürich trade plates over the top of its original UK number plates. The driver on this occasion was Samuel Heuer, but he was not successful; the event was almost inevitably won by a Porsche.

Samuel Heuer's son Pierre told the author: 'My father remembers that they changed the original Champion 18 spark plugs for a Platinum spark plug before the race. And the car was brought to Heinz Keller with English number plates, which were then replaced by Swiss garage number plates.' Jürg Keller, who was there (as Heinz Keller's twelve-year-old) also recalls Heuer's drive: 'I remember they had problems with the engine, which was probably the reason they changed the spark plugs,' Keller told the author, adding that: 'the mechanic was probably our Workshop Manager Mandi Ruf.' Interestingly Heuer does not recall any body damage on the car.

Heuer told the author that he also drove at the Mitholz-Kandersteg Hill Climb (13/14 September 1958), but the author has been unable to confirm with certainty that this was with LBL 304. The author is grateful to Hermann Schwarz from the Salzburg Rallye Club, Jürg Keller and both Samuel Heuer and his son Pierre for information about these hillclimb events.

As a final comment – for now – on LBL 304, the author also found an entry in the Abingdon Development Department files in the form of 'Development Department Report No. 134', dated 1 September 1958, which reads 'Twin Cam: Reference DDW No. 400 – rebuild aluminium-bodied car – this is now completed – Car No. LBL 304.' The report – which admittedly does not specify the precise nature of that rebuild – is signed off by Alec Hounslow.

After its MG chaperones had gone back to England, the Kellers entered LBL 304 in at least one more event, the Ollon-Villars Hillclimb near Lake Geneva on Sunday 31 August 1958, with its race no. altered to '137'. Note also the Zürich ZH-560 trade plate fixed on top of the UK licence plate.
MALCOLM GREEN

Samuel Heuer at the wheel of LBL 304 with a beautiful mountain setting.

This is an important image, inasmuch as it clearly shows the LBL 304 UK licence plate on the rear of the car, overlaid with a temporary Swiss plate. Samuel Heuer is driving.
PIERRE HEUER

THE 1958 LIÈGE–ROME–LIÈGE

Over the last five days of August 1958 (27th to 31st), BMC participated in that year's Liège–Rome–Liège with a team of six cars, just one of which was an MGA – an early Twin Cam (PRX 707, race no. 78; chassis no. YD1-528; engine 16G/U/159) finished in Orient Red with a glossy black-painted Vanden Plas alloy hardtop. Drivers were John Gott and Ray Brookes, and their charge was only lightly modified in readiness for the event, with the obvious exceptions of basic rally equipment and the essential 20 gallon (90ltr) fuel tank.

LBL 304 at a hillclimb event in Switzerland.
CLIFF BRAY

John Gott and Ray Brookes in their red MGA, PRX 707, during the 1958 Liège.

PABLO RAYBOULD

Factory options from new included a heater, black tonneau cover, oil cooler and competition ('deluxe') seats.

Writing in the December 1958 issue of the Nuffield Press in-house produced magazine *Motoring*, Gott stressed the toughness of this event:

> It is approximately four times as severe as the Monte, being over 1,000 miles longer, run at a higher average speed over more difficult country, yet taking ninety-six hours on the road as against the Monte's seventy-two. It is therefore the supreme test of the car and the BMC Competitions Department rightly regards it as a 'must', particularly valuable as a test-bed for a new design.

John Gott (left) and co-driver Ray Brookes at the end of the 1958 Liège.

PABLO RAYBOULD

Gott's brief from Marcus Chambers was 'to finish at all costs, and to find and report on any bugs'.

The usual gruelling challenge of the worst of the Yugoslavian roads, which made up roughly a third of the event total of 3,300 miles (5,310km), contributed to a loose distributor clamp – eventually diagnosed and fixed by the mechanics. Otherwise PRX 707 had a good race, at the end of which Gott wrote: 'We felt surprisingly fit as we triumphantly clocked in at Spa at 10.32pm, Sunday 31 August, having explored some of the worst roads in Belgium, Germany, Austria, Italy, Yugoslavia and France.' The car finished in ninth place at the end of the event, beating two of the Austin-Healey 100/6 entries, although Pat Moss and Ann Wisdom gained the most BMC headlines in their fourth-placed big Healey. Notwithstanding the obvious fact that BMC Comps were clearly focusing on the Healeys, it was an impressive rally debut for the Twin Cam MG.

What was especially interesting, bearing in mind the in-service weaknesses of the production Twin Cam, was the fact that Gott's car appeared to cope remarkably well with the atrocious Yugoslavian petrol; for, as Gott wrote:

> The Twin Cam engine, being meant for competition, is not so smooth or so quiet as the single-cam unit, but even with its 9·9:1 compression ratio it coped surprisingly well with the Yugoslavian 'paraffin', and returned over 20mpg [14ltr/100km] at 'touring' speeds. However, working on a rev. range of 6,500rpm on the timed tests, this naturally fell to around 12mpg [24ltr/100km].

Next in the autumn 1958 calendar for the still-new MGA Twin Cam was the Goodwood Tourist Trophy Race of 13 September, where of course the factory were absent owing to the corporate moratorium on racing; here, Dick Jacobs had Tommy Bridger and Alan Foster in car no. 28: their story is covered later in the section on the Jacobs Twin Cams.

MONTE CARLO RALLY, JANUARY 1959

The next factory MG outing was also the debut event for the second 'Comps' Twin Cam, RMO 101, a Coupé this time – arguably better suited to the venue, the Monte Carlo rally. No doubt preparing to eat his words after the previous autumn's Liège, the smart new red Coupé was driven by John Gott with Ray Brookes, the same partner he had had at the previous event. However, Gott skidded on an icy patch and as a result he was out of the event.

JOHN GOTT

John Gott stands beside a travel-weary PRX 707 during the 1958 Liège.
PABLO RAYBOULD

John Gott MBE (25 March 1913–3 September 1972), born in Cheshire, had driven in the HRG team before the war, and so was known to Marcus Chambers when the latter was looking for sound new allies capable of being both a competent driver and team 'captain'.

As well as his HRG experiences, Gott had tackled the RAC Rally in a Frazer Nash and, as Chambers later wrote: 'He came with well-rounded experience, and some firm ideas about how things should be done, particularly on the planning and preparation side of things.' Tempting Gott to join BMC had an added advantage of robbing Standard Triumph of one of their drivers. Gott went on to lead several rally entries with BMC. In 1960 he was appointed Chief Constable of Northamptonshire, when he retired from factory-backed rallying. He kept up his love of racing, however, and tragically died on the Lydden Hill circuit in his own car (an ex-BMC Comps Austin-Healey 3000, SMO 746) in September 1972.

1959 SEASON – FACTORY MGA TWIN CAMS

Chassis no.	Colour	Reg. No.	Despatch Date	Events (Drivers)	Race Number/Results
YM1-596	Orient Red	RMO 101	18 September 1958	Monte Carlo Rally (John Gott/Ray Brookes)	Race no. 106, retired (accident; skid on ice)
				Tulip Rally (John Sprinzel/Stuart Turner)	Race no. 29, 42nd place
				Acropolis Rally (John Sprinzel/Richard Bensted-Smith)	Race no. 12, retired (accident)
YD1-1626	Ash Green	SBL 707	7 April 1959	Tulip Rally (John Gott/Chris Tooley)	Race no. 28, 53rd (with penalties)
				Alpine Rally (John Milne/Stuart Turner)	Race no. 22, retired (accident)

Footnotes:
YM1-596 had engine no. 169/4/289; a Coupé, it would go on to race in later events, including the last factory Twin Cam entry (*see* later).
YD1-1626 is possibly a recipient of one of the 'spare' bodies left over from the last-minute decision to change the 1959 Sebring MGA Twin Cams from Roadsters to Coupés (*see* section on Sebring later in this chapter). After its participation in European events it was shipped to South Africa, initially for use by George Tuck, who used it and then sold it on. In the MGCC Twin Cam book of 1981 it was recorded as being owned by Denis Prophet in Canada. Perhaps unsurprisingly, SBL 707 is sometimes confused with PRX 707, but they were different cars, as can be seen. Additional confusion comes from the fact that a false licence plate PRX-707 was applied to one of the 1959 Sebring race cars. Meanwhile the 'real' PRX 707 (YD1-528, despatched 22 August 1958) had already taken part in the 1958 Liège–Rome–Liège, where, as related in the main text, it had finished ninth at the hands of John Gott and Ray Brookes. It was later owned by MGA Twin Cam historian Phil Richer.
The Monte Carlo Rally took place between 19 and 25 January 1959. RMO 101 started from Glasgow.
The Tulip Rally took place between 27 April and 1 May 1959. There were four MGA Twin Cam privateers in this event, including YD3-1167 (Dutch car ZX 35 60; race no. 33) and YD1-1580 (UK registration XWU 825). The six Twin Cams, factory and private, received race numbers in the sequence 28 to 33 inclusive.
The Acropolis Rally took place between 28 and 31 May 1959.
The Alpine Rally took place between 23 and 29 June 1959. There was only the one MG, but no fewer than four Austin-Healeys and two Austins.

THE TULIP RALLY

After the disappointment of the Monte, RMO 101 would be out again at the end of April at the Tulip Rally, the Acropolis, at the end of May. Also at the Tulip was a new MGA Twin Cam Roadster, registered SBL 707 (which occasionally leads to confusion with PRX 707, an entirely different car) as well as an impressive turnout of four more private MGA Twin Cams, including a Dutch-registered entry driven by Ad Bouwmeester and Jacques Zwart (a left-hand-drive Orient Red roadster, YD3-1167) and a British-registered one, XWU 825, driven by Harry Mainz and his co-driver Rex Vicat-Cole (YD1-1580; Glacier Blue, engine no. 1200).

RMO 101 finished in 42nd place, SBL 707 came in 53rd (with penalties), and the Dutch car an honourable 24th. Of the other three, Mainz did not finish, and it appears the remaining two failed to start. While RMO 101 was rested, SBL 707 was out again at the Alpine in the fourth week of

The MGA Twin Cam Coupé RMO 101 ready to go off to France for its January 1959 entry in the Monte Carlo Rally, where it would be driven by John Gott and Ray Brookes; sadly it was destined to crash and be forced to retire.

PABLO RAYBOULD

A youthful Ray Brookes (left) admires the twin cam engine of RMO 101 ahead of its foray to the 1959 Monte Carlo rally. They would set off from Glasgow this time.

PABLO RAYBOULD

Driven by John Gott and Chris Tooley, SBL 707 (MGA Twin Cam YD1-1626) finished 53rd in the Tulip Rally at the end of April 1959.

PHILLIPE DOUCHET

SBL 707 had a less successful outing at the 1959 Alpine Rally, John Milne and Stuart Turner being forced to retire after this accident.

PHILLIPE DOUCHET

June, with John Milne and Stuart Turner sharing the duties in the only MG in the event (over-shadowed by Abingdon's Austin-Healeys). Regrettably the car was forced to retire after a collision that broke the front offside suspension.

The last event of the 1959 season for RMO 101 was the Acropolis Rally, held over 2,000 miles (3,220km) of roads in Greece and Yugoslavia, from Trieste to Athens; being in June, this was at the height of the hot Mediterranean summer, with the inevitably dusty roads. Mount Parnis, familiar to any Athens tourist, with its 4,600ft (1,400m) elevation and numerous hairpin bends, provided an approximation of the Alpine equivalents, and a speed test at the Hellenic Air Force's Tatoi airfield, to the north of Athens. Sadly it was not to be a lucky outing for John Sprinzel and Richard Bensted-Smith, as their charge – race no. 12 – crashed out of the event.

THE FITZWILLIAM TWIN CAMS

On 1 June 1958 there was a lone Fitzwilliam entry at that year's Nürburgring 1,000km, with Robin Carnegie and David J. Hayles driving the team's only remaining MGA (the redoubtable UPO 929) as race no. 59; but after going all the way to Germany they failed to start, due to fuel leakage problems. Within three months, however, the team's efforts would move up a gear with the acquisition of a new car by Richard W-Fitzwilliam.

In September 1958, Fitz took delivery of an early MGA Twin Cam, finished in Orient Red, with the registration VUF 541 (chassis no. YD1-600; despatched from Abingdon on

Richard W-Fitzwilliam takes over the keys to his first MGA Twin Cam, VUF 541.
W-FITZWILLIAM FAMILY

Robin Carnegie driving Fitz's MGA Twin Cam VUF 541 (race no. 46) at Goodwood on 25 April 1959.
CALL IT MGA

23 September, and first registered on 25 September 1958). This was the first of three Twin Cams that he would manage through an arrangement made with Paul Fletcher and Chris Martyn, who agreed to enter their Twin Cams under the banner of the Fitzwilliam Racing Team.

The first significant appearance for two of the Fitzwilliam Twin Cams was at Goodwood on 25 April 1959. Paul Fletcher drove his black car (WGN 734) with its special alloy body (see box), and Carnegie was in Fitz's red car, VUF 541; however, both retired, Fletcher with a faulty valve, and Carnegie with a faulty water pump, which had caused his car to overheat.

At the next event, on 18 May at Goodwood, again for the Whitsun Trophy, Chris Martyn's TWN 900 was part of

THE FITZWILLIAM TEAM MGA TWIN CAMS

Chassis no.	Colour	Reg. No.	Original Owner	Factory Despatch Date	Notes
YD1-600	Orient Red	VUF 541	Richard W-Fitzwilliam	23 September 1958	First registered 25 September 1958; first event Goodwood on 25 April 1959 (driven by Robin Carnegie, race no. 46). At the Nürburgring 1,000km on 7 June 1959 it was race no. 20.
YD2-669	Black	WGN 734	Paul Fletcher	2 October 1958	Given a uniquely reshaped nose and painted black. First event Goodwood on 14 March 1959 (handicap race). *See also* separate table below.
YD1-1782	Old English White	TWN 900	Chris Martyn	17 April 1959	Original engine 1407. First event 2 May 1959 at Silverstone (race no. 33), then MGCC Silverstone on 16 May (also race no. 33), followed by Goodwood's Whit Monday meeting on 18 May (race no. 54) and the Nürburgring 1,000km on 7 June 1959 (race no. 19).

Footnotes:
With the return of the factory MGAs, the Fitzwilliam Team's initial constitution also came to an end. Although Richard W-Fitzwilliam had acquired his own MGA Twin Cam, he had also recruited the owners of two other cars to form part of a racing équipe, nominally under his control. VUF 541 is owned by Bob West and is in the process of being restored (2018). WGN 734 has been rebuilt as closely as possible to its original racing guise and is owned (in 2018) by Roger Skinner. Nowadays, TWN 900 is on a different chassis and has a pushrod engine.

the entry, while WGN 734 was driven by Fletcher. Carnegie again drove VUF 541, which he said appeared to have had almost nothing done to it since the last event.

> We were entered in the ten-lap Touring and Grand Touring Car race, in which we had to run with the roof up, and a ten-lap Marque race. Paul managed a fifth in the Marque race, a few seconds behind Alan Foster in Dick Jacobs' Twin Cam, and I didn't figure, finishing half way down the field in both races.

Carnegie noted that the Twin Cam was obviously faster than their earlier MGAs, but also that they were up against some stiff opposition.

Next up for the Fitzwilliam Équipe was the Nürburgring 1,000 Kilometre race on 7 June 1959 – although without the organizational skill of Johnnie Keeling, Carnegie expressed the view that 'it was more a matter of good luck than judgement that we all got there'. By the summer of 1959, most of the privateers, including the Fitzwilliam team – and, as we shall see, the Jacobs team – had realized that the factory had little interest in developing the twin-cam engine for serious motor-sport use, their focus instead being on the big Healey.

The Fitzwilliam team had entered the three MGA Twin Cams for the 1959 Nürburgring 1,000km race: VUF 541, racing as car no. 20 and driven by Robin Carnegie and Bill de Selincourt; TWN 900, racing as car no. 19 and driven by Christopher Martyn and Douglas Graham; and WGN 734, racing as car no. 66 and driven by Paul Fletcher and John Dashwood. However, in the meantime, Fitz had also entered a Lotus Elite (race no. 85, driven by Peter Lumsden and Peter Riley) and this finished in twenty-third place.

Sadly there was no such good fortune for the Twin Cams, as all three Fitzwilliam MGs were out of the race by the ninth lap (Paul Fletcher's car, with its Barwell-developed cylinder head, ignominiously retiring with a half shaft failure on the very first lap). The same month, Fitz acquired a pair of Elva front-engined Formula Juniors – and this was the beginning of a move away from MG for him and his team.

Thus it was after Nürburgring that Fitz decided to move away from the MGA Twin Cam, but with some regret because of the friendships forged at Abingdon and his continued faith in the basic car; the factory's own shift towards the big Healey was also a factor. At this point Robin Carnegie left the Fitzwilliam Team: although his friend asked him to continue, Carnegie declined because 'often I found it hard to put up with his delightful disorganization – and it was all getting too serious, and I only did it for the fun.'

DICK JACOBS AND THE TWIN CAM

Just as Fitzwilliam picked up on the Twin Cam, so Dick Jacobs swiftly recognized the potential of the new model, and having acquired an early car, he entered it in the *Autosport* Four-Hour event at Goodwood in September, with Alan Foster

Alan Foster in the Dick Jacobs MGA Twin Cam (race no. 26) at the Goodwood Tourist Trophy race of 20 August 1960, in which he finished in fourteenth place and third in the 2-litre GT class. Meanwhile Tommy Bridger in the other car, racing as no. 27, did not finish due to a burst tyre.
AUTHOR'S COLLECTION

THE JACOBS MGA TWIN CAMS

Chassis no.	Colour	Reg. No.	Original Owner	Despatch Date	Notes
YD1-573	Ash Green	1 MTW	Dick Jacobs	22 August 1958	Initially unregistered until 2 March 1959. Engine no. 185. First race with Alan Foster and Tommy Bridger in the *Autosport* Four Hours at Goodwood (13 September 1958).
YD1-1085	Ash Green	2 MTW	Roy Bloxham	January 16th 1959	First registered 2 March 1959. Engine no. 685. Acquired by Dick Jacobs from Bloxham at the end of the 1959 race season.

Footnotes:
Both cars were later purchased by Roger Daniell, who still owns them as of 2018. Events in 1959 included the *Daily Express* BRDC International Trophy Race at Silverstone on 2 May, and the BRSCC International Race at Brands Hatch on 29 August.

PAUL FLETCHER'S MGA TWIN CAM SPECIAL

Paul Fletcher in his special Fitzwilliam Team MGA Twin Cam WGN 734 (race no. 39) is hard on the tail of Mike Reid's car, MJB 778 (race no. 42), at Goodwood in July 1959. M. H. J. Flux is in the MGA Coupé bringing up the rear.
ROGER SKINNER

July 1959, Goodwood: Paul Fletcher went on to win the five-lap handicap race with an average of 76.84mph (123.64km/h); he also posted the fastest lap of the race at 78.98mph (127.08km/h).
ROGER SKINNER

Paul Fletcher was determined to stamp his authority on his MGA Twin Cam, which he ordered new from the factory as a right-hand-drive export car, with a number of competition extras from the outset. Having taken delivery of it in October 1958, a new twin-cam engine was sent to Barwell Engineering, where it was extensively re-built at a remarkable cost (in 1959) of £1,500. In the meantime, the car had been to Fred Peel at Peel Fabrications where it was given a new, all-alloy shell with a new front end design of Fletcher's own creation, which bore a passing resemblance to William Watson's Aston-Martin DB3S of 1953.

The car raced under the Fitzwilliam flag at Silverstone in April 1959 (see main text and table) and it really stood out from the crowd. The main upset during the season was when the car was rolled at Silverstone at the Six Hour relay race on 15 August 1959, though fortunately Fletcher was unhurt and unperturbed; judging by photographs from the event, the car was also only lightly damaged, and was repaired in time for its outing in September (see below).

The car competed at various BARC events, such as Goodwood (26 June, race no. 35 – fourth place behind Alan Foster in one of the Jacobs Twin Cams; 11 July, where he won his handicap race; and 26 September 1959, race no. 48, where he came in fifth). However, by the end of that year Fletcher's enthusiasm for the car was evidently waning, as he briefly raced an AC in the spring of 1960 but then moved across to single seaters. WGN 734 (the number having been first registered in London after July 1958 as a 'personal export delivery vehicle') was duly sold on, and after being owned by Simon Richardson for around eight years, it passed to Paul Briault, who subjected it to quite extensive alterations, with a flip-front and reshaped tail.

Then in 1978, MGA Twin Cam expert Peter Wood acquired it, with good intentions for eventual restoration, but the car was badly damaged when Wood suffered an arson attack in 1986. The interior and bodyshell were amongst the sad casualties of this incident, and the remains languished until 2008, when Roger Skinner persuaded Wood to part with it, and undertook a remarkable exercise to recreate the original Paul Fletcher car, with the assistance of Fletcher himself as a guide.

Chassis no: YD2-669; Original engine number: 16GB-U/282
Production start build: 29 September 1958
Production finish date: 1 October 1958
Despatch date: 2 October 1958 ('personal export delivery')
Paint: Black; Trim: Red; Hood: Black
Factory accessories: Competition 'de-luxe' seats; heater; sliding side screen; black tonneau cover; windscreen washer

The distinctive MGA Twin Cam raced originally by Paul Fletcher under the banner of the Fitzwilliam Team. WGN 734 is seen here at Silverstone in 2017; it is owned by Roger Skinner.
AUTHOR

Roy Bloxham in 2 MTW (race no. 30) and Alan Foster in 1 MTW (race no. 31) during the 2 May 1959 Silverstone race. Both cars were Ash Green with black hardtops; the dark band on the front valance of 2 MTW was red, and the equivalent on 1 MTW was painted yellow, helping their identification when out on the circuit.
AUTHOR'S COLLECTION

The two Jacobs cars – 1 MTW and 2 MTW – side by side at the MGA Twin Cam Group's sixtieth-anniversary re-enactment of the MGA Twin Cam launch (see Chapter Six).
AUTHOR

and Tommy Bridger sharing the driving: they were rewarded by finishing fourteenth overall and third place in the 2-litre class, with a pair of factory Porsches in the top two places. Soon after this was a second at Snetterton in a one-hour race.

With this early promise, Jacobs decided to manage two cars, eventually registered in March 1959 as 1 MTW and 2 MTW (the latter still owned at this stage by Roy Bloxham); over the winter of 1959/60 the cars were modified, with all the standard steel unstressed panels being replaced by alloy ones, the result being a reduction in weight of around two hundredweight. Although the factory was still under the BMC racing purdah, Jacobs was a trusted friend; also the memories of his experience at Le Mans in 1955 were still very fresh in Thornley's memory, and so some engine development assistance was forthcoming for the 1959 season.

Jacobs soon agreed to buy 2 MTW, and thereafter it would be driven by Les Leston and later Tommy Bridger. As recorded in an article in *Motorsport* in 1974, in Jacobs' first full season in 1960, during which fifty-six entries had been made, the outcome was 'six firsts, including a class win for Gil Baird, driving Foster's car in the *Autosport* Three-Hour Race; four seconds; three thirds; and a fair amount of teething troubles'.

Writing in the MG Car Club's *Twin Cam Fiftieth Anniversary* book, present-day owner of both the Jacobs Twin Cams, Roger Daniell, recorded that:

> Towards the end of the season, during the Goodwood Tourist Trophy race, Tommy [Bridger] rolled the car at Madgewick corner after a tyre burst. The body was badly damaged and it was replaced with 'a spare body taken out of the rafters' – and so 2 MTW was reunited with its original body and it was out racing again a week later.

Eventually, however, Jacobs realized – as did Richard Fitzwilliam – that the factory's interest in the Twin Cam was waning, and of course as we saw earlier, the model was cancelled in the spring soon after Sebring (of which more later in this chapter) – and so both the cars were put up for sale.

THE SOUTH AFRICAN BOB OLTHOFF AND HIS TWIN CAM YRX 310

Robert Jacob 'Bob' Olthoff (10 October 1937–18 April 2004) was born in Krugersdorp, to the north west of Johannesburg. In 1959 he acquired an MGA Twin Cam and proceeded to do well in South African races, including four first places, one second and six fourth places.

Thus he was already an enthusiastic driver and able mechanic by the time he decided to come to the UK in 1960; he got married at the same time, and upon arrival, set up home at Botley, Oxford.

After touting his services to various luminaries such as Colin Chapman of Lotus, he soon found himself working at Abingdon in the Show Shop under Tim Binnington. Prior to his arrival he had raced his own MGA Twin Cam (YDH5-929), and when he came to London with his new wife in March 1960 he had asked for money rather than wedding presents to help further his racing ambitions.

Olthoff soon arranged for his own Twin Cam (YDH5-929) to follow; he campaigned it over the following two years with enthusiastic but unofficial support from MG, including a complete rebuild of his car in the Competitions Department at Abingdon. It emerged from this in Olthoff's characteristic Springbok colours of green and gold, instead of the original

A contemporary colour photo of the Olthoff MGA Twin Cam that would become YRX 310, but still wearing its South African licence plate AD-188-B.
EDWARD VANDYK

The engine bay of the Olthoff Twin Cam.
EDWARD VANDYK

white with a maroon flash he had added in the spring of 1961 in preparation for that year's Nürburgring 1,000km race, in which he had competed with John Whitmore.

Olthoff competed in over forty events in his Twin Cam between 1959 and 1962 in South Africa, the UK, Eire and Germany, including eleven first places and over twenty podium finishes. He was third in the 1961 *Autosport* Championship. He was on hand as a reserve driver and mechanic at Sebring in 1961, and the following year, as we shall see later in this chapter, he was rewarded with a stint behind the wheel. Three months later he was co-driver at Le Mans to Ted Lund in the latter's special-bodied MGA, SRX 210 – the story of which is also covered below.

Of some interest is the fact that Olthoff's Twin Cam (UK registration number YRX 310) benefited from development of its engine, the capacity growing from 1588 to 1762cc, in which configuration he drove it in at least two races in Eire in 1961, and in the 1962 Nürburgring 1,000km – the only MG in the German event that year. Olthoff reported that the enlarged engine developed 142bhp, a considerable improvement over the standard engine, and this enabled him to achieve the record for the highest recorded speed of 137mph (220km/h) for an MGA at Phoenix Park in Dublin in July 1961.

Bob Olthoff in his special MGA Twin Cam at Brands Hatch on Boxing Day, 1961.
EDWARD VANDYK

As of 2018, YRX 311 is owned by Edward Vandyk.
AUTHOR

The car is now owned by Edward Vandyk, who has extensively researched the story of Bob Olthoff's MG racing exploits. He pointed out to the author the curious fact that the EX Register entry for the larger piston used in the 1762cc engine bore the number EX 187/310 (dated 26 June 1959, described as 'piston for 3⅛in bore – BC.16.GB'), which matches the registration that Olthoff later applied to his car (YRX 310). Coincidence?

AN EXOTIC MG FOR LE MANS

Buoyed up by the excitement of their 1955 Le Mans entry, and the hope that further glory awaited the following year, John Thornley and Syd Enever started scheming a specialized sports car, the objective being a special tool for racing, which drew on the basis of the production MGA but moved the game forwards – just as, for example, Jaguar's XK sports cars begat Coventry's stunning C and D-type racers.

Effectively MG had two attempts at this, using slightly different approaches but with a broadly common objective. EX 183 was listed in the register as 'Experimental 1956 Le Mans Car (Tubular Chassis)', with twenty-seven entries culminating in EX 183/27, a ¼in scale general arrangement drawing. This was in effect a space-frame 'silhouette' version of the MGA, complete with Dunlop disc brakes; however, it didn't go beyond one single car, which was soon to be broken up.

The designer of EX 183 was the irrepressible Terry Mitchell, who conceived a space frame on which to mount a light alloy EX 182-style body EX 182 bodies. Harold Wiggins and Brian 'Bunny' Hillier built it in the Development Shop, but it was clearly built 'on the quiet', and although driven sparingly on public roads, it was never subjected to performance testing. Peter Neal recalled that it was Spartan inside and had no passenger door, so getting into it to ride as a passenger was quite an exercise. He recalls going on a short ride in it with Denis Williams driving, but he can't be certain after more than sixty years whether the engine was a normal B-Series or a prototype twin cam. Speaking to the author in 2017, Denis Williams recalled the occasion: 'I remember taking Peter into Oxford in an MGA that may well have been EX 183 on one occasion. While we were waiting at traffic lights a bus touched the rear of the car. The driver denied touching us, but probably needed to explain the broken fog light glass when he returned to the depot at the end of his shift...'

EX 183 was eventually dismantled on the orders of John Thornley, who was nervous of the project's discovery by top management.

Notwithstanding the abandonment of EX 183, next up was EX 186, which was a project entitled 'Twin Overhead Camshaft "Le Mans" Type 1956 – MGA Type Chassis'. EX 186 would eventually materialize as a striking one-off, with bodywork drawn up, under the direction of Jim O'Neill, by MG body draughtsman Denis Williams, and which owed something to the style of the contemporary Mercedes-Benz SLR. Williams told the author of his work on EX 186:

> It was proposed to build and race a team of three or four special racing versions of the MGA at Le Mans. I was given the task of laying out the full size body lines and all the structural details required for the completed body. In the event only one car was built, the body being made by Midland Sheet Metal of Nuneaton, with whom I liaised closely during its construction.

Rear suspension was of the De Dion type (a favourite of chassis draughtsman Terry Mitchell), with much of the work from February 1956 onwards undertaken by new recruit Dickie Wright, who joined MG in March 1956. He told the author:

The model of EX 186 survives at Gaydon.
AUTHOR

Sitting in the Development Shop at Abingdon, the resemblance of EX 186 to the MGA can be appreciated, even if the styling was sufficiently different to make BMC unwilling to sanction its use in motor-sports endeavours.
DICKIE WRIGHT

> EX 186 was my first job; little had been done on it at that stage, only the odd drawing. Terry Mitchell and I set out the layout with ten-inch lines. It started as a 'hospital job', then suddenly it had to be finished. It was Syd's baby, and Ted Lund wanted to drive it. There was the intention of building more than just the one. Denis Williams was given a fairly free hand with the body design; it had hints of Mercedes SLR and Jaguar D-Type. There wasn't much testing done – Tom Haig did drive it once or twice. Then it just disappeared; it was often hidden in the yard under a cover when the high-ups visited!

Eventually, without any official sanction from above, EX 186 began to take shape, with, as already mentioned, the alloy bodywork the responsibility of Enever's friends at Midland Sheet Metal (who also created the panels for the EX 179 and EX 181 record breakers). Syd Enever's son Roger certainly remembers EX 186, not least the occasion when his father brought it home to Westminster Way, Oxford:

> I seem to remember him doing about 120mph [190km/h] with me in the passenger seat, as he gave it a good going up the bypass. You certainly couldn't do that there now! But I always remember it as such a beautiful car; he designed some flip-up lights for it, but they just went for the faired-in glazed headlamps. It was a lovely car, with that clever De Dion rear axle and the twin-cam engine.

Present owners of MG EX 186, Joe and Cathy Gunderson, were told by former MG Development Department employee Henry Stone: 'We didn't build the car to race at Le Mans, we built it to *win* at Le Mans!' However, to do this MG would have needed a team of cars, as it did in 1955 – if nothing else, a 'team prize' might have been achievable. In the event, however, EX 186 remained a one-off, and apart from some rudimentary testing by Tom Haig, the exercise was clearly hampered by BMC's racing ban and the 'under-the-radar' nature of the car.

When a group of enthusiasts from the MG Car Club's north-western centre approached John Thornley for support for their plans to enter an MG at Le Mans, he became enthusiastic about the idea of using EX 186 – not surprisingly, Ted Lund is said to have been equally enthusiastic – but to have gone along with this would have resulted in some awkward conversations with Longbridge, whose edict about racing activities was still firmly in place.

In the event, MG's ambitions for EX 186 were frustrated; for the 1959 Le Mans, all hopes would rest on SRX 210 (*see* later; owned by Ted Lund from June 1960), and EX 186 remained under the dust sheets. However, the situation remained a precarious one; Terry Mitchell told the author that around Christmas 1959 the order suddenly came from John Thornley to make EX 186 disappear: 'He told us that someone at Longbridge had got wind of it, so it was crated up and shipped off to San Francisco.' In fact EX 186 was dispatched in January 1960 to Kjell Qvale at British Motor Car Distributors Ltd, at 1200 Van Ness Avenue in San Francisco. Qvale stored EX 186 until 1966, at which point it was sold, licensed, and used as an exotic road car, though for less than a year.

When it needed intensive servicing or repair, the MG was taken off the road and stored in a barn on a walnut farm in Red Bluff, California. Joe and Cathy Gunderson and their friend Steve Willis purchased the remarkably complete car (albeit without its original engine, transmission and some other components) in 1982, and embarked upon a long-term research and restoration project. Tracking down missing original parts was a key challenge of this unique restoration, and Joe Gunderson recalls that the car was made to run only in 1989; the final restoration was completed in 2006 with the help of Worthy Cummings. Steve Willis passed away in 1998.

EX 186 in the workshop at Abingdon.

DENIS WILLIAM

The unique EX 186 was eventually spirited away to San Francisco, and the tender care of Kjell Qvale. The lettering on the glass door in the background welcomes visitors to the 'Skylight Salesroom'; this photo was taken in the old 'British Motors' building on 1200 Van Ness Avenue, San Francisco.

ENEVER FAMILY

As acquired by enthusiasts Joe and Cathy Gunderson and their friend Steve Willis, the EX 186 was in remarkably complete condition apart from the engine. It would prove to be a long-running and painstaking journey of discovery and restoration.
JOE AND CATHY GUNDERSON

BELOW LEFT: **The simple, purposeful cockpit of EX 186 as restored.**
CURTIS JACOBSON

Meanwhile, back at Abingdon, all other traces of EX 186 were eradicated – Jeff Clarke recalled being told by Alec Hounslow: 'There are two De Dion MGA axles in the shop: I want you to take them out and destroy them!' Clarke duly collected the spares and proceeded to cut them up with an oxy-acetylene torch: 'We said there'd be a bloke in San Francisco who would have given his eye teeth for them – but Alec wasn't going to have an argument about it.'

Joe Gunderson suggests that these were not necessarily whole axle units: 'As related by Henry Stone, these were two differential units that were destroyed; they contained different gear ratios from the 3.91:1 existing on the car.'

And so ended the exciting EX 186 project.

EX 186 remained a 'one-off' but fortunately survived; after shipping to the USA it eventually passed into the hands of Joe and Cathy Gunderson, who have undertaken a painstaking restoration over a number of years.
JOHN NIKAS

EX 186 IN THE EX REGISTER AND OTHER RECORDS

The engine in EX 186 is not the original unit, but has been carefully specified to match the factory specifications.
CURTIS JACOBSON

Under the code name 'EX 186', the project began with EX 186/1 in the summer of 1955 (the first entry in the register was EX 186/32, dated 10 August 1955). Work on the road-going MGA Twin Cam (EX 187 – 'Twin Overhead Camshaft Version of MGA with Disc Brakes') proceeded almost in tandem, starting with EX 187/1, dated 2 June 1955.

For his special Le Mans racer, Enever was interested in exploring the idea of retractable headlamps – a rare concept in 1955 – and indeed thirteen entries (EX 186/13 to EX 186/25) cover this idea, although a hand-written annotation says that these were 'no longer required' – the cost, complexity and perhaps the weight militated against the idea. From EX 186/32 to EX 186/87, there was a flurry of intense activity throughout August and September 1955, then a brief hiatus until the beginning of December, at which point work appears to have halted, no doubt as the decision by BMC to withdraw from motor racing took effect.

Then, after a gap of nearly two years, activity restarted in May 1957 (EX 186/94) but proceeded in fits and starts throughout the following period through December 1958 and on to the spring of 1959, the last in this sequence being EX 186/198 of 22 April 1959. The final entries were in August and September 1959 (the last entry, EX 186/202, was dated 3 September 1959), after which, as described in the main text, the car itself was spirited away.

Also useful as a source of information about EX 186 are the diaries of Cliff Bray (qv), which record:

EX186: Proposed Le Mans Car

Twin Cam engine and special alloy body; modified MGA frame with De Dion rear suspension. Engine number 16G/U/316; gearbox no. 1881 with close-ratio gears; differential ratio 11/43; tyres 5.50 × 15 front, 6.00 × 15 rear; 22mph (35.5km/h) per 1,000rpm.

DATE	DETAILS
19/03/1959	Build commenced
09/05/1959	Chassis to Midland Sheet Metal Company
20/05/1959	Returned to Development
26/05/1959	EX186 cancelled as a Le Mans entrant
31/01/1961	EX186 shipped to San Francisco, USA

The talents of Harry Herring were called on again for this wind tunnel and viewing model of EX 186. As originally conceived, it was to have had concealed 'pop-up' headlamps, an idea ahead of its time for a British sports car.
ENEVER FAMILY

MG EX 186 SPECIFICATION

Body: Unique hand-formed alloy bodyshell made by Midland Sheet Metal. Overall length 14ft 5in (4,394mm). Complete alloy belly pans; many panels removable with the aid of Dzus fasteners. Perspex windscreen and headlamp covers. Small 'luggage compartment' cover designed to contain the spare tyre mandated by ACO Le Mans
Chassis: Based on the familiar MGA unit, but with many changes: for example the MGA 'goal post' member was lowered and moved back. Aluminium floor boards riveted to the chassis rails. 94in (2,387mm) wheelbase and 49in (1,245mm) track
Engine: Originally a 1489cc twin cam B-Series; now a 1588cc. Specially fabricated steel oil pan
Carburettors: Originally Twin Weber 45DCOE (now fitted with 42DCOE)
Fuel system: Bespoke 26gal (118ltr) baffled tank with twin dual-ended Jaguar-style SU fuel pumps
Cooling: Bespoke aluminium radiator with thick core; no coolant thermostat or cooling fan utilized
Exhaust: Bespoke unit carefully replicated during restoration using factory drawings
Wheels and suspension: 15 × 4J Dunlop peg-drive knock-off steel wheels. Front suspension is broadly similar to the standard Twin Cam; different upper control arms, aluminium alloy steering rack housing and lightened spring pans. The rear suspension uses leaf springs and a De Dion cross beam with rigidly mounted differential
Brakes: Dunlop four-wheel disc brakes. Brake and clutch use separate Girling master cylinders
Headlights: Lucas 'Le Mans 24' 7in (17.8cm) round units, small position marker lights, tail lamps with brake lamps integrated and number-plate lamps, but no flashing indicators
Weight: 1,600lb (726kg)

The low, sleek lines of EX 186, seen here in all their restored glory, would have been a scene stealer at Le Mans, but it was never to be: BMC ruled that the project should be abandoned, and the single prototype was spirited away.
JOE AND CATHY GUNDERSON

PRIVATEERS AT LE MANS: TED LUND

Edward ('Ted') Walter Kingstone Lund (24 September 1917–14 July 1978) grew up in the Stockport area in Cheshire. His involvement in the world of motor racing began when he was thirty, with a supercharged MG PB Midget. Although he was by no means exclusively associated with MG, his octagonal leanings were undoubtedly helped by the fact that his father had gone to school with Cecil Kimber, and both had been active in the Manchester Motor Club.

Ted Lund's friendship with the MG factory, and his participation in various race events with a factory TD Midget from 1950, put him in good stead when it came to seeking help with his racing exploits. Having participated at Le Mans in 1955 where, as we have seen, he co-drove with Hans Waeffler, Lund was an enthusiastic supporter of John Thornley's bold plan to return to France in 1956 and 1957 – but when BMC management clamped down on MG's racing activities in the wake of the tragic accidents at Le Mans and Dundrod of 1955, the factory's plans for a stab at the 1956 season, possibly with a new, special MG, were cast aside.

Nevertheless the term 'privateers' in the heading above is perhaps inaccurate, because there is no doubt that the three appearances of SRX 210 at Le Mans in 1959, 1960 and 1961 were a thinly veiled factory effort, with the car largely conceived at Abingdon, built there and – especially when it came to the remodelling of its bodywork for the second and third years – designed by the MG design staff and assembled in the Development Shop. However, it is equally true that the driving force behind these exploits was Ted Lund, aided, abetted and partially financed by the MG Car Club's North West Centre, and the actual entries were not made as factory ones.

Ted Lund at Le Mans.

BOB WEST

When John Thornley and Syd Enever had schemed out first EX 183 and then EX 186, there can be little doubt that the involvement of Ted Lund formed part of their thought process; certainly Lund saw, and was greatly enthused by, EX 186, which he described to Jonathan Wood as 'a beautiful twin-cam sports racing car, looking like a smaller Mercedes 300SL', telling Wood that he thought the top speed would be in the region of 140–160mph (225–260km/h), '... and the cost of the project around £15,000'. Of course as we have seen, EX 186 fell foul of corporate politics and ended up being hastily spirited away to the USA; but Lund was a determined man, as indeed was John Thornley.

The consequence was the creation of a new Le Mans car, SRX 210, which used a new MGA Twin Cam chassis and bodywork which was based on surviving parts of LBL 303 (the paint sequence of BRG, Tyrolite Green and red are proof) in part a consequence of the lack of an official BMC-sanctioned budget. Of course this status makes the untangling of the true story of SRX 210 all the more difficult, as well as fascinating.

The first entry for the Lund car was the June 1959 Le Mans race, and in terms of appearance SRX 210 looked not too far removed from that of an MGA Twin Cam out of the showroom – and thereby would have received some tacit approval from BMC even if, in their eyes, it remained a private effort. Having said that, despite the standard look (other than the colour scheme) the complicated origins of the car meant that it was certainly not the same as a customer could have bought from his or her MG dealer.

Externally, SRX 210 in its initial guise was most obviously distinguished by its paintwork – Ash Green with a British Racing Green side flash on both sides – a colour scheme that could almost have graced a contemporary Austin-Healey 100/4. The livery had been applied previously to Lund's Ash Green road-going MGA Twin Cam, YD1-527; one can imagine that this additional subterfuge would have made it easier to refer casually to *either* car as 'Ted Lund's MGA' if a visitor happened to ask awkward questions.

Naturally the windscreen was reduced in height and there were no bumpers, the valances front and rear being smoothly fashioned with an infill piece at the front, which still revealed the top and bottom edges of the recess of the standard car,

SRX 210 in its original roadster guise at Le Mans in 1959 – the first of three trips to the circuit in successive years. The car was driven by Ted Lund and Colin Escott and started well enough...

BOB WEST

...but when the car struck an unfortunate Alsatian dog the consequences, despite these repairs, would be overheating and retirement just three hours from the end of the race.

BOB WEST

This photo of the engine bay of SRX 210 was signed by Ted Lund, with a dedication to MG's Jim Cox that reads 'To engine maestro Jimmy – thanks a lot'.
JIM COX

MG mechanic Henry Stone helps free up the damage caused by the impact with the unfortunate Alsatian.
AUTHOR'S COLLECTION

just as it had been on the 1955 Le Mans cars. Close study of the photos from 1959 shows that the front valance had a circular patch on each side where the sidelights had been fitted for the low headlamp wings used on the Dundrod car, but much more likely the red-painted 'Keller car' (LBL 304) of 1958, which we saw described earlier.

On the offside front face of the nose, roughly half way between the edge of the grille and the line of the headlamp, there was a neatly fashioned oval carburettor inlet duct, which fed through the engine bay to another oval exit hole on the back of the offside front wing – which was cleverly concealed by the positioning of the white number roundel. The engine in SRX 210 was, naturally, a Twin Cam and was carefully built by Jim Cox. The rear end featured a centre-fill fuel-tank cap as well, serving a 20gal (90ltr) petrol tank.

Testing ensued at MIRA, and the clutch failed: the solution was to fit a Hauseman unit as used in contemporary Porsches. For the initial outing to Le Mans, Colin Escott was due to share the driving exploits with Lund, but he suffered from back troubles and so it was decided to fit an interchangeable pair of alternative seat squabs: Lund's was green and Escott's red. Upon arrival at Le Mans in the week prior to the race, practice brought the first minor upset when Escott struck a sandbank at the Mulsanne corner, the consequence of which was a dent in the nose. Back at the team's base, the damage was knocked out again and repainted, admittedly not to the best bodywork quality, but sufficient for the immediate need. Gearbox pressure problems led to a change to another unit, and the same evening the final drive ratio was changed from 3.9:1 to 4.1:1.

The 1959 Le Mans Race

The race started as usual at four o'clock on the Saturday afternoon, and SRX 210 proceeded to run without drama until the following morning, when with Colin Escott driving, and running in eighth place after twenty-one hours, an Alsatian ran on to the Mulsanne Straight and was struck by the MG, which killed the dog and mangled the radiator grille – and more importantly, distorted the cooling ducts, a situation made worse by the damage to the undertray.

There then followed a dilemma for the team management: either to stop and remove the undertray and allow more air through the engine compartment, or to keep going for a few laps until the car was brought in for the coolant and oil to be topped up. They opted to have SRX 210 crawl round the circuit for a few laps until coming back into the pit, but sadly the engine failed catastrophically out on the circuit, and as well as the engine, the gearbox was found to be beyond simple repair.

Despite the failure of the first effort, Lund was undaunted and arranged to buy the car from MG just after Le Mans 1960, although the factory continued to prepare it. A change in the regulations for 1960 meant that the half-height windscreen was no longer viable, so it was decided to build a specially designed fastback coupé roof and marry it to the MGA Coupé windscreen, the design work done largely by Don Hayter under the official code EX 212. The new panelwork was undertaken by MG's good friends at Midland Sheet Metal near Nuneaton; the company had worked on EX 181, and SRX 210 was repainted in the same colour of light

SRX 210 (AND WHAT BECAME OF LBL 303 AND LBL 304...)

Unpicking the story of SRX 210, the Ted Lund car, requires similar forensic study to that needed earlier in this chapter for LBL 301. Some records have in the past wrongly ascribed chassis number suffix '623' to this car (as noted above, it was actually YD3-627/S). The build dates are given as 3 September 1958, build completion on 17 November 1958, and although formal despatch is not recorded, the register notes that the car was 'completed in Development Shop' with a date of 8 January 1959. The original colour and trim were listed there as Orient Red with black trim and hood, and competition seats. The 'YD3' prefix ought to relate to a 'left hand drive roadster'.

The 'Keller car' we saw earlier (LBL 304 – *see* pages 268 to 271) was red, and was right-hand drive from the outset; the precise reasons may never be known for certain, but are probably tied up in factory 'politics'. Looking at the cars either side of it in the register, it is evident that the dates for '627' were rather out of sequence: '626' was built by 23 September and despatched on 24 September 1958, whilst '628' was built by 16 September and despatched on 22 September. Was it coincidence that the low-nosed LBL 304 so-called Keller car, in effect a 'twin-cam EX 182', came back from its expedition to Switzerland and Austria at almost the same time that the new Ted Lund Le Mans car came into being 'under the radar'? Steve Dixon believes there is a convincing argument: 'Having created a Twin-Cam EX 182 in July 1958 for the August Swiss trip it seems most unlikely that the Works would have dismantled it and built the body on to another chassis just a month or so later. There must be a strong probability that the whole Keller car and SRX 210 are one and the same.'

Adding to the theory is evidence in the form of an entry in the Abingdon 'Development Department Works' register, dated 11 June 1959, in which Alec Hounslow states, against 'DDW 638 – MGA Twin Cam LBL 304', that 'this DDW is now cancelled, as the body has now been used for Mr T. Lund's Le Mans car'. Steve Dixon notes 'the body-tub panels, replaced at the time of a rebuild in 1990, survive; they show that in the correct order between the earlier and later layers of green paint, there is copious evidence of red paint too'. Also intriguing is 'DDW No. 460: MGA Twin Cam Special Version - cancelled on Mr Enever's instruction', maybe an oblique reference to EX 186...

Meanwhile the first registered owner of SRX 210 was the MG Car Company, on 3 June 1959. Notwithstanding the debate about the use of the 'LBL 304' number for the trip to Switzerland described earlier, the alloy body structure appears to have its roots in that originally used on LBL 303, Ted Lund's 1955 Le Mans car, which had at that time still been fitted to the chassis from EX 182/40; from there, as we have seen, it went to Dundrod, and it also formed part of the Fitzgerald Team efforts at the 1957 Mille Miglia (*see* earlier). However, by the time that SRX 210 was conceived, a Twin Cam chassis was involved, and much of the 'original' body had been replaced. Having said that, close study of photos of the nose of SRX 210 at Le Mans in 1959 show evidence of where the low-mounted indicators had been fitted in the front valance of the 'low nose' alloy-bodied EX 182.

Writing for the *MGA Register Yearbook* in 2005, Steve Dixon explained that:

> *As we see the body today, only the inner panels (the 'tub') are original. Wings, doors, front shroud, hard top/rear shroud are all later additions. The nearside sill is steel. Even the vertical and horizontal elements of the front firewall are not original (occasioned by installation on a twin-cam chassis). The expression 'EX 182 body' must be seen in this light.*

For 1960, the car received extensive modifications under code EX 212, with design of its coupé body by Don Hayter and built by Midland Sheet Metal. The two large driving lamps set into the nose were 'Lund lamps', for which Ted Lund's father held the patents. The engine was changed for a 1762cc unit. The car formally became Lund's property in July 1960.

In the third and final version the nose of the car was reworked, losing the familiar MGA grille (and those Lund lamps) in favour of an aerodynamically efficient aperture. After the 1961 race, a further engine (16GU-306S) was fitted. Tentative plans to enter the 1962 Le Mans event were abandoned; Lund raced the car until 1968, then sold it to Rob McElroy in 1972. The car retained some of the quaint adaptations that Lund had made, such as a Colron wood-dye tin adapted to form a hydraulic fluid feed via piping to keep the front shock absorbers topped up, and a plastic drinks tube intended to fit into a Thermos flask of iced lemonade.

Meanwhile, what had happened to the identity of LBL 304? In a DDW entry of 11 June 1960, which lists 'cars in shop', there is an entry for an LBL 304 with chassis number HDE13/10102 – which was originally the chassis number of LJB 370. LBL 304 was still listed in a later 'shop' list, as a factory run-around in 1963, but appears to have been scrapped later. Several former Abingdon works staff have openly testified over the years on the fluidity of chassis numbers and registration numbers; evidently there were some hooks on the wall in Development on which would be hung chassis plates and licence plates, ready to be affixed to a car for road use. This certainly seems a likely explanation of how LBL 303 begat LBL 304, which in turn begat SRX 210, whilst another LBL 304 was created...

metallic green that had been used on the record breaker in its contemporary guise. Hayter told the author:

> Syd wanted a fastback roof for the GT 2-litre class, so I did the car that Ted Lund drove. That was a quick six-week job...we used to do quite a lot of things like that under Syd's budget, but then enter them as private entries – so that one became the Ted Lund car. But it was all done in the factory – body, engine and so on – all prepared by Alec Hounslow, and our mechanics went with it.

Because the car was destined to run in the 2-litre class, it was decided to bore out the new engine to 1762cc, using special pistons and dropping the traditional twin SUs for 40-DCOE Webers.

In the light of the terminal engine and gearbox coding problems in 1959 (due to the collision with the dog), SRX 210 was fitted with an oil temperature gauge; at the front end, the traditional MGA grille remained for this year, and two Lund driving lamps were mounted in a very modified front valance. Lund's father had designed and produced Lund lamps for years, and Ted Lund still supplied them, while Steve Dixon still has the lamps as fitted to SRX 210, and an invoice for them.

In 1961, for their third foray to Le Mans, Ted Lund had arranged with the factory for a smoother nose for SRX 210, which arguably robbed the car of a little of its MG identity, even if the aerodynamic efficiency was obviously enhanced. His co-driver this year was Bob Olthoff; the car lasted for fifteen laps.

BOB WEST

The 1960 Le Mans Race

The race number for SRX 210 for 1960 was 32. The race itself was more successful for the team this year, despite some near misses and a moment of slight panic for Lund when he found the windscreen wipers could not cope with the deluge of a sudden thunderstorm. At the end, SRX 210 not only finished, but won the 2-litre class – a really impressive result for an engine still less than 1.8 litres in capacity. The car had managed a fastest lap of 99.46mph (160km/h) – so near the magic '100' but frustratingly not quite there, and also slower than in 1959 by a small fraction of one mph – and the average over the full twenty-four hours was an equally impressive 91mph (146km/h). SRX also had the full undertray and faired-in inside wheel-arch panels, so the car was by then somewhat akin to the streamlining of the land-speed record cars.

For 1960, Lund and Escott were back again, but now their car looked very different, having gained a smooth, fast-back coupé roof courtesy of MG's Don Hayter, the work recorded in the EX Register as EX 212. Here the troupe pause outside a brasserie en route to Le Mans.

BOB WEST

SRX 210 at the pits at Le Mans in June 1960. The bodywork had been made by Midland Sheet Metal (who worked on the MG record breakers) and the Twin Cam was in 1762cc guise. This year the car finished and won the 2-litre class.

BOB WEST

ABOVE: **The engine bay of SRX 210 in 2018. The twin cam has a capacity of 1762cc.**
AUTHOR

ABOVE RIGHT: **The tiny cockpit of SRX 210 in coupé guise must have seemed a little claustrophobic at Le Mans in 1961.**
AUTHOR

ABOVE RIGHT AND RIGHT: **SRX 210 photographed in 2018. A plan to return to Le Mans in 1962 was abandoned (although an entry was made) and the car remained essentially in the same basic form as it had raced in 1961. Nowadays it is perhaps too historically important in terms of its many constituent parts, so its serious racing days are behind it.**
AUTHOR

Not long after the event, the special 1762cc engine was removed and sold to recoup some money, although in later years it resurfaced and is with the car today, albeit with the cylinder head and carburettors from 1961. In the following spring, buoyed up by their success in 1960, Lund embarked on a third (and in the event final) entry for June 1961. Body modifications were primarily focused at the front end, where the MGA grille was discarded and the nose reshaped, with removable airflow reducing choke panel, and reshaped steel wings (the headlamps were set further back), which reduced the size of the intake aperture and improved the streamlining. Another so-called 'Le Mans specification' 1762cc engine was fitted, but this time with bigger 45DCOE Weber carburettors.

Sadly, the last Le Mans outing for SRX 210 did not prove to be the hoped-for glorious finale, lasting barely three hours, for, as Lund told Jonathan Wood: 'I blew up in a big way; I was doing 140mph down the straight when there was a terrific bang; fumes and bits of metal were flying everywhere, and everything

TED LUND, LE MANS AND SRX 210

Year	Days	Body Configuration	Colour(s)	Drivers	Car No.	Notes
1959	21–22 June	Roadster 'EX 182' body	Ash Green with British Racing Green sides	Ted Lund/Colin Escott	33	Collision with Alsatian dog in the twenty-first hour of the race (on the Mulsanne Straight) led to over-heating and retirement from the race.
1960	25–26 June	Coupé with conventional grille	Metallic green all over ('EX' Green)	Ted Lund/Colin Escott	32	1762cc and twin Weber 40DCOE carburettors. Finished twelfth on distance and won the 2-litre class.
1961	10–11 June	Coupé now with streamlined nose	Metallic green with BRG side flash	Ted Lund/Bob Olthoff	58	Another 1762cc engine; twin Weber 45DCOE carburettors. Car retired after fifteen laps with engine trouble.

Footnotes:
The chassis number of SRX 210 was YD3-627/S ('YD3' implies left-hand drive; the 'S' was added to the factory build records in blue crayon. After the engine failure in 1961, SRX 210 was fitted with a spare engine '16 GU 306S'.

ALSO WITH LE MANS AMBITIONS...

Although Ted Lund is the privateer most commonly associated with Le Mans in the context of the MGA, he was not the only person with ambitions to race at la Sarthe. David Grahame Dixon of Pickett's Field, Great Missenden in Buckinghamshire, had acquired YD1-851, an early Twin Cam, in the autumn of 1958. Despatched from Abingdon on 26 November 1958 and first registered two days later as VXT 280, the car was soon out on British circuits. Dixon raced under his own stable, 'Ecurie Chiltern' (named for the area where he lived), although he was not averse to racing as part of a wider group, such as the 'Octagon Stable' – whereupon its original engine, 16-GB-U-484, blew up at Silverstone on 15 August 1959. The present owner of the car (2018), Peter Reason, says that the replacement engine (AEH 37 RS 13803) has remained with the car ever since. Dixon's grandest plan for his MG was to race at Le Mans, and Reason has a copy of the original application papers, processed through the RAC, which record Dixon's payment of the essential £37 entry fee, on 2 February 1959 (50,000 French francs, roughly equivalent to £850 in 2018 terms). Sadly, however, the entry was ultimately rejected – the paperwork has the hand-written note '*concurrants non acceptés*' (literally 'competitors not accepted'). The precise reason for this is not known; it could have been that the class was over-subscribed, it could have been due to rule changes by the ACO Le Mans – or one imagines it could simply have been Gallic indifference.

David Dixon raced his MGA Twin Cam under the umbrella of Ecurie Chiltern; he tried to enter Le Mans for the 1959 event, but his entry was rejected. This photo dates from 16 May 1959; the event is an MGCC race meeting at Silverstone, comprising a 30-minute high speed reliability trial and a ten-lap scratch race (with Le-Mans start).
PETER REASON

locked up solid.' The cause was later established as a broken big end bolt precipitating catastrophic engine failure – although this happened after Lund had lapped the Le Mans circuit at 101.66mph (163.57km/h), becoming the first MG to exceed 100mph (160km/h) for a lap. It was a pyrrhic victory, clearly.

After return to England, the spare engine was fitted and the car remained largely unchanged from its final Le Mans specification.

EUROPEAN SWANSONG: THE MGA'S LAST SEASON

As we have seen, with 1962 the MGA was entering its seventh year, as well as heading for the MG history books, as the record-breaking production total headed for 100,000. However, even the MGA's most devoted fans must have known in their hearts that the production story of the aerodynamic MG sports car was approaching the end – and with it, of course, any factory-backed racing.

Behind the scenes at BMC's Motor-Sports Department there were other changes, too, as Stuart Turner took over and made plans that would soon lead to the monumental successes of the coming decade, headlined by the all-conquering Abingdon-run Mini Coopers and big Healeys. So just as an era was ending at Sebring, as we shall see in the next section of this chapter, so the curtains were coming down on the MGA's factory competition story back in Europe.

The 1962 Monte Carlo Rally

Comps was not quite done with the MGA, however, and so in the autumn of 1961 a gorgeous red MGA Mark II Deluxe Coupé (GHD2/104429) was prepared at Abingdon, and road registered on 26 October 1961 as 151 ABL; it was made ready for the Monte Carlo Rally of 20–25 January 1962,

Johnny Organ of 'Comps' preparing the last works MGA, 151 ABL at Abingdon.
JOHN HALFPENNY

Inside the famous BMC Competitions Department at Abingdon ('Comps' for short) we can see 151 ABL off to the right in a workshop with various Austin-Healeys, an Austin A40 and the Mini Cooper. The Mini Traveller in the background will have been a mechanic's own car, worked on in his spare time.
JOHN HALFPENNY

151 ABL was an MGA Mark II Deluxe Coupé built at Abingdon in autumn 1961, in time for the MGA's rallying swansong the following year. Here we see Erle (left) and Don Morley during the thirty-first Monte Carlo Rally in January 1962.
AUTHOR'S COLLECTION

where it was to be raced by Suffolk-based brothers and farmers Don and Erle Morley as car no. 314. The 1962 Monte had eight starting points, each providing a roughly 2,000-mile (3,200km) initial jaunt to Chambéry in Savoie, within the Auvergne-Rhône-Alpes region in south-eastern France, where all the competitors, irrespective of their original start point, would compete along a common route of some 570 miles (920km), a highlight of which would be four laps around Monaco's famous Monte Carlo race circuit.

The Morleys set off from Oslo in unusually mild weather, evidenced by the lack of much snow on the first leg of their journey, and they duly plugged on through Hälsingborg (Sweden), then into Germany (Hamburg, Hanover and Frankfurt) and on into Belgium, passing through Liège. Entering France, the brothers finally encountered some snow near Chambéry, as they joined the competitors who had come from the other seven points of origin; the mobile Comps crew were on hand to quickly fit the red MGA with studded winter

Wet conditions for YRX 986 (a reconnoitre MGA Deluxe, Chassis No. GHD2-104428 – see table on page 162).
JOHN HALFPENNY

... contrasting with a snowy scene at Monte Carlo, redolent of a Christmas card.
JOHN HALFPENNY

In the 1962 Monte Carlo Rally: Donald and Erle Morley in 151 ABL finished twenty-eighth overall, first in their 2-litre class, and second in the GT category.
JOHN HALFPENNY

tyres, giving its crew an advantage over some of their less well organized rivals.

When they reached the famous winding passes of the Alpes Maritimes, near the coast between Cannes and Nice, the competitors found some treacherous patches of ice and many cars fell by the wayside – though even so, some 180 survivors of the 313 starters reached the Monaco circuit stage. At the end of the event, David Siegle-Morris and Tony Ambrose secured an honourable eighteenth place overall. Ten places behind were the Morleys in 151 ABL, who not only came twenty-eighth overall, but also had the distinction of winning their 2-litre class, which was particularly impressive given the 1622cc capacity of the MGA's power-plant; they also came second overall in the GT class.

Overall winner of the 1962 Monte Carlo were Swedish heroes Eric Carlsson and Gunnar Häggbom in their SAAB 96, proving that you did not have to have a powerful car to win the event. However, at least salving British prestige, the Sunbeam Rapier team took honours by finishing in third, fourth, tenth and seventeenth places, featuring some distinguished drivers including Paddy Hopkirk (soon to become a Mini driver) and race driver Graham Hill. Showing some of the future potential of the Mini Coopers, Stirling Moss's sister Pat co-drove one with Ann Wisdom (soon to marry Peter Riley) to twenty-sixth overall, two places ahead of the MGA.

The 1962 Tulip Rally

The next major outing for 151 ABL was at the Tulip Rally of 7 to 11 May, where two emerging talented Swedish drivers were recruited to drive the MGA, racing as car no. 11. Rauno Aaltonen – who had suffered injuries during the Monte Carlo Rally – and fellow Swede Gunnar Palm were to drive the MGA, while the Morley brothers were given a big Healey to drive. As the MGA was clearly less of a priority, it was later said by Stuart Turner that more or less all that was done in preparing it for the Tulip was to change the oil and the rally plates; this may be slightly underplaying the hard work of the Comps team, but the change of focus for the BMC team in favour of Healeys and Minis was clear.

Aaltonen had his work cut out because amongst the opposition were deadly rivals from Standard-Triumph, including some very professionally prepared TR4s, with the benefit of much larger 1991cc engines that could take maximum advantage of the same 2-litre class as the poor MGA, which was making do with 1622cc. The event stretched all

Rauno Aaltonen's stunning drive in 151 ABL for the Tulip Rally of May 1962 marked the start of a new era of superb Swedish drivers at BMC. The car is an MGA 1600 Mk II Deluxe Coupé.
JOHN HALFPENNY

the way from Noordwijk, on the southern Dutch coast, to Monaco and back again, taking in such seminal stages as the Nürburgring, where Aaltonen impressed by bringing 151 ABL into fifth place. Next at the Vosges Mountains, Aaltonen came in ahead of the TR4s until the roles were reversed at Mont Salève – known as 'the balcony of Geneva'.

The real surprise was yet to come, however, because despite some excellent performances by the leading opposition, at the Col de Turini Aaltonen took the little red MGA over the stage in 10 minutes 21 seconds, beating not only the feared 2-litre Triumphs, but every other competitor, finishing a remarkable 13 seconds ahead of anybody else, and warranting a mention in many press write-ups after the event. This achievement certainly boosted Aaltonen's reputation, and strengthened the case for recruiting such talented Scandinavian drivers into the BMC works team for future events.

Meanwhile the penultimate part of the Tulip was the return leg across the Alps, which included seven mountain stages, a special stage at the Belgian Spa Francorchamps Circuit, and a final stage in Holland. Aaltonen continued to take his battle to the Triumph TR4s, and finished fastest in his class in seven out of eighteen stages.

In the final Tulip Rally placings, 151 ABL and its crew impressed royally by finishing first in class, and they were placed fifteenth overall, a position calculated using the complex points system of the Tulip Rally. In fact this did not do justice to the outstanding performance of the Swedish drivers overall, not to mention the impressive showing of a car that was obviously near the end of its career, and which, as

In the 1962 Tulip Rally, Rauno Aaltonen and Gunnar Palm drove 151 ABL (car no. 11) to fifteenth place overall, winning their class.

noted earlier, gave away much to some of its rivals, particularly in terms of engine capacity.

The 1962 Liège–Sofia–Liège Event

Rauno Aaltonen would go on to achieve many more great BMC drives, but for 151 ABL and the factory MGA, all that was left was an outing planned for the Liège–Sofia–Liège event of 29 August to 2 September.

John Gott and Bill Shepherd made a bold effort in this notably arduous event, racing 151 ABL as car no. 49, over some of the worst roads of any contemporary European rallies – but sadly luck was not with them, and the pounding and tough time schedules contributed to their retirement after no fewer than two fuel-tank ruptures. It was the end of the road for 151 ABL – even if, thankfully, the car itself survives – and equally importantly, the end of the factory's involvement in racing the MGA. But later the same month, the new MGB would enter the world stage, and a new chapter in MG's motor-sports history would open up.

RACING IN AMERICA: THE MGA AT SEBRING

The MGA was an unashamedly British sports car, and its motor-sports activities in the European theatre were, as we have seen, an exciting and action-packed story; but the fact remains that with the vast majority of the cars being sold in North America to owners who were no less enthusiastic than their great many British, French, Irish, Italian, Belgian, Dutch, Australian, African, Japanese or German counterparts – or indeed those from other nations – the story of how the MGA was raced in the United States during the same period is equally important.

ABOVE RIGHT: **151 ABL (car no. 49) had its final factory outing in the 1962 Liège–Sofia–Liège, here passing a border checkpoint that looks as if it is straight out of a contemporary Cold War film. Eventually, the car retired.**
JOHN HALFPENNY

At the end of August, 151 ABL raced as no. 49 in the 1962 Liège–Sofia–Liège with John Gott and Bill Shepherd.
JOHN HALFPENNY

Joe Herson in his MG TF 1500, at what was probably the Beverly National Sports Car 'National' Race of Independence Day, 1955, in which he finished in eighth place, the highest placed MG. The race was won by a Porsche 356 Speedster, and was dominated by Porsches, which took all top seven places. Gus Ehrman was in twentieth place, in an MG TD Midget. Clearly the MGA could not come soon enough!

HERSON FAMILY ARCHIVE

The Sports Car Club of America deserves much of the credit for nurturing the local sporting prowess of the MG marque, as must the savvy importer/distributors (BMC/Hambro in the USA, Morris Motors (Canada) north of the border) and the many motor sports-minded dealers. Last but not least must come the loyal drivers who, as we shall see, became members of a 'BMC racing family' that would endure until the late 1960s. Racing took place across the USA and Canada just about every weekend, with individual races, regional and national championships to contend with; sadly there are too many to do justice to in this book, but one story deserves coverage in full, and that is the MGA racing from 1956 to 1962 at Sebring.

The small, unexceptional town of Sebring, Florida, became internationally famous in the wake of the arrival of Alec Ulmann at the disused Hendricks Army Airfield, a wartime USAF training base for Boeing B-17 Flying Fortress pilots. Ulmann saw the potential for use of the large flat field for motor racing, and in 1950 the inaugural event was the 'Sam Collier Six-Hour Memorial race'. In March 1952 the first twelve-hour event, loosely modelled on the Le Mans 24-Hours, took place.

The atmosphere at the circuit has been described many times, but seldom better than in the words of David Ash, seasoned MG racer, who wrote of Sebring in 1957:

MGA *Activities*

The Hambro Automotive Corporation, B.M.C. Concessionaires in U.S.A., sent us this picture which shows the MGA in the line-up ready to start in the Fairchild National Sports Car Races, held on the runways of the Hagerstown Airport in Maryland. In the second race of the day the MGA driven by Joe Hersen was first in its class.

Extracts from the news in America, where the recently announced M.G. Series MGA has held a prominent place

Gough Industries Inc. of Los Angeles chose to introduce the MGA in their territory at the Santa Anita Race Track. Members of the Press, representatives from Banks, Finance Companies, and Dealers were able to try for themselves the capabilities of the MGA.

More than 400 people attended a cocktail party given by J. S. Inskip Inc., of New York, to present the MGA. All visitors were most impressed by the appearance of the little car and predicted a great demand for the model. In the picture Mr. J. S. Inskip is pointing out some features of the car.

The first motorsports competition appearance in the USA was celebrated in the in-house publication *Nuffield News Exchange*.

Joe Herson captioned this photo: 'The no. 67 MGA has Bill Kincheloe in the driver's seat on the starting line at Marlboro racecourse in 1955, probably late in the year. That MGA was the first raced in the US just after its introduction.' Joe Herson drove it first, possibly at Hagerstown airport. Herson added that: 'The MGA in the background with the dented rear fender is being driven by another Air Force major, Cappy Capiello. The partial rear to the left is an Arnolt Bristol.'

HERSON FAMILY ARCHIVE

Taken at Harewood Acres, Ontario on 4 August 1956. Jim Fergusson's white MGA, race no. 68, sits alongside his Austin-Healey 100M and Alan Millar's 100S, race no. 77. Alan Miller and Ed Leavens drove the Healeys, and F. Williams was entered to drive the MGA. (Fred Williams was BMC Ontario Sales Manager until 1 May 1958; on that day, Williams and Leavens joined forces to create 'Williams and Leavens Motors' in London Ontario, selling BMC products.) Commenting on the photo, Robin Barker adds: 'I think that is Jim Fergusson and his wife Alice along with a mechanic wearing coveralls and a cap standing beside the 100S with their backs to the camera'.
COURTESY ROBERT SMYTH

It's big citrus country around Sebring and the scent of oranges and grapefruit hangs in the warm, still air. From six in the morning until past midnight, wherever you are you can hear, sometimes near and sometimes far away, the ripping snarl of somebody's straight pipes. Those are the two things you always bring away from Sebring: the smell of oranges, the bark of tight-tuned engines.

The rise of Sebring came just as MG sports car sales and competition entries were on the rise; the marque has never won the event outright, but in its early days was a consistent entrant and class winner. By the spring of 1956 – the first race after the launch of the MGA – MGs were a firm feature of the annual pilgrimage to Sebring; whilst BMC at Longbridge had stipulated an end to MG racing in the wake of the tragic 1955 Le Mans and Dundrod events, US and Canadian MG importers Hambro and BMC Canada had no such qualms.

A precedent for quasi-corporate BMC participation at Sebring had been set in 1954, when Donald Healey had entered Austin-Healeys in that year's event, and so the US Hambro marketing section, possibly under the watchful gaze of Ted Birt and his son Tony, laid plans for a team of the new MGA models to participate in the 1956 event, just as dealers across the territory were receiving some of their first significant deliveries.

THE 1956 SEBRING

It has occasionally been suggested that the 1956 Sebring cars were prepared at Abingdon; however, subsequent investigations have shown this was not the case, even if the idea might, just possibly, have been a twinkle in Marcus Chambers' eye. Although relatively little is known more than sixty years later about the identity or ultimate fate of the cars, it is now known that they were drawn from dealer stock and prepared locally in New York, Washington and Pennsylvania.

As the MGA itself was still very new on the scene in North America, it seems likely that Hambro financed and organized the cars and parts off their own back, with little direct involvement from Abingdon. In a contemporary report in Rhode Island's *Providence Journal* of 16 March 1956,

Gus Ehrman waits for his turn at the AMOCO fuel tanker on the morning of Saturday 26 March 1956, prior to the Sebring 12 Hours.
GUS EHRMAN

Gus Ehrman in car no. 49 during the 1956 Sebring race.
GUS EHRMAN

BELOW: **The three 1956 Sebring MGAs lined up in echelon formation, waiting for the start of the race.**
HERSON FAMILY ARCHIVE

Gus Ehrman (a local resident at the time) was quoted as saying that 'his' MGA (no. 49) was 'not yet shipped to this country', implying that the work to prepare it for the rigours of Sebring were undertaken to a tight schedule.

In a further report, published the Friday before the race, the same paper quoted Ehrman as finding that his car 'ran nicely in practice, except for clutch trouble'. The report added that Ehrman had driven his car at 70.17mph (112.90km/h), which he said was 'good for the little MG, but far too slow to compete in top speed with the more expensive, all-out race machines'.

Because all three cars came from different workshops, with the likelihood of few corporate guidelines apart from the American racing colours (white with twin blue stripes) and competition windscreens, they differed a little in detail. For example, the Inskip car, no. 49, benefited from two extra driving lights, mounted on the bodywork outboard of the grille, and had the weight-saving benefit of ditching the bumpers, which also allowed the racing stripes to be wrapped around the valance.

THE 1956 SEBRING MGA 1500

Race No.	Drivers (all USA)	Overall Placing (speed)	1600 cc GT Class	Laps
49	David ('Dave') Ash/Gus O. Ehrman/John ('Johnny') Van Driel	20th (105.304 kmph)	5th	151
50	William ('Bill') Kincheloe/Stephen ('Steve') Spitler	19th (105.304 kmph)	4th	151
51	Fred Allen/Sidney ('Sid') W. Blackman	22nd (96.936 kmph)	6th	139

Footnotes:
Race date was Saturday 24 March 1956; the three left-hand-drive, all-white cars (with blue racing stripes, which gave them the official racing colours for the USA) were formally entered by Hambro Automotive Company. Team Captain was Dave Ash; involved with the team management to some extent was Jim Fergusson of Toronto, but the 'pit chief' was Grant Tolley. Neither chassis nor engine numbers are known.

Car no. 49: This car was prepared by Performance Motors Ltd of Haverstraw, New York, but entered by Inskip Motors also of New York, who were David Ash's employers at the time. Performance Motors had also prepared Ash's 1955 Sebring MG TF entry.

Car no. 50: Preparation was at Manhattan Auto in Washington DC, a popular MG dealership owned by David L. Herson (he died in 1959; his son Joe, who ran the dealership, died in 2014).

Car no. 51: Prepared at the Keystone Garage in Warren, Pennsylvania.

Although they are known to have raced in SCCA events after Sebring, relatively little is known about the subsequent fate of these cars; according to Michael Eaton: 'It is doubtful we will ever know chassis or engine numbers for the '56 cars as none are known to exist. I have seen several different names attributed as to who drove the No. 51 car, including Bob Cron and Hank Dahl, but have never been able to confirm as all had passed away or could not be found by the time I was researching.' It seems conceivable that Hank Dahl 'had a go' in car 51, because his business was responsible for building it, but official records suggest it was Fred Allen who shared the driving with Blackman.

1956 Sebring car no. 50 on the starting grid...
HERSON FAMILY ARCHIVE

BELOW: **...and in action during the race.**
HERSON FAMILY ARCHIVE

Writing in *Sports Cars Illustrated* magazine a year after the race, Ash said that the cars were kept close to factory specification:

> We were entered strictly stock and we held tight to it. We pulled all three engines, of course, and stripped the cars, but we did little to them mechanically beyond careful, precision reassembly. We installed belts and tonneau covers, extra rear-view mirrors – driving a small car at Sebring you want to know when somebody's coming up behind – and an extra oil pressure warning light. We fixed hood safety straps, bolted in fire extinguishers, and strapped first aid kits and spare parts kits to chassis members and floorboards. We washed and waxed them, and loaded them on the trucks for the long ride south.

Car no. 50, from David and Joe Herson's workshop, kept its bumpers but had extra lights set into the grille (only one, in the left side, appeared to be there after the race); and the Keystone Garage car, no. 51, also kept its bumpers, had extra lights on both sides, and its rear-view mirror was faired in. These aspects of the Manhattan car were simply explained, according to Lynn Herson: 'The fact that the cars still had bumpers and driving lights was because they were driven to Sebring, not transported. My father said that only the wealthiest (and showiest) teams trailered their cars to the races.'

Dave Ash was described in Hambro reports as being the 'team captain', but many MGA Sebring experts are of the view that much of the hands-on management of the team effort was probably undertaken – under Ash's watchful eye – by Jim Fergusson of Toronto (see box above). The other important man on the day was Grant Tolley, in charge of the MG pit. The cars were prepared in separate workshops by different teams, but coordination and pit management had to be overseen by somebody with the time and experience, and Fergusson seems the most likely candidate.

Formal practice began on 22 March 1956, the Thursday before the race; the team soon appreciated that whilst the MGA might have been slower than the premium exotica, it was nevertheless the fastest MG to date. Ash wrote that the team had decided on a 4:35 to 4:40 lap time, but Gus Ehrman achieved a single 4:28 lap. Friday 23 March was spent refining the engine tune and bedding in tyres, and Ash and Ehrman ended the day with their best laps to date of 4:24.1 and 4:24.2.

In 1956, just as every year, the twelve-hour race was due to start at ten in the morning; before that the day began with queuing at the Amoco fuel tanker from 08:30; an hour later the drivers' meeting was over and the cars were soon lined up alongside their pits in echelon formation, Le Mans style, ready for their drivers to dash across the track, jump in and start their engines. The first stints were Ash in no. 49, Steve Spitler in no. 50 and Fred Allen in no. 51.

During the race, the Manhattan Auto Car (no. 50) had to come into the pits to have its throttle linkage repaired, costing it a lap; at four in the afternoon, Dave Ash's car (car no.

GUS EHRMAN AND DAVE ASH

Gus Ehrman flew Hawker Hurricanes for the RAF in World War II, so driving sports cars was a comparatively easy thing for him to do afterwards. This is a PR photo of him seated in an Austin-Healey 100/6.
GUS EHRMAN

David Ash was a friend of Ehrman's, and like him, took a leading role in promoting the MG marque in the USA. He is seen here looking thoughtful during the 1956 Sebring race, where MGAs took the team prize.
DAVID ASH

Gustave O. 'Gus' Ehrman (25 October 1922 – 17 September 2016) was born in Leipzig, Germany, but emigrated with his parents to England in 1932. After the war, Gus moved to the USA to pursue a career.

Gus raced his own TC Midget and spent some time in England at the end of the 1940s, spending time at Abingdon working under George Tuck. By then he had become a rising star not only within J. S. Inskip, but also on the racetrack, piloting a variety of interesting cars in the SCCA arena including Sebring. In 1959, he had his turn at the Bonneville Salt Flats in EX 219, a re-badged and re-branded (as an Austin-Healey) version of EX 179. He would go on to have a career in BMC/Hambro, relocating at one stage from New York to Los Angeles, and would return to Inskip (becoming its President from 1964) before finally returning to British Leyland, eventually retiring in 1978.

David H. Ash (4 July 1922–24 January 2006) was a graduate of Stamford High, Connecticut, Class of 1940. After graduation he served as an officer and fighter pilot in the United States Air Force. As noted above, Ash and Ehrman became good friends as well as work colleagues. Between 1952 and 1957, David became known in North America as 'Mister MG', largely on account of being the only driver to start and finish five Sebring races in five attempts. After his exploits at Sebring in 1956 and 1957, he was part of the MG record-breaking team at the Bonneville Salt Flats, also in 1957.

In this photo at Bonneville, behind EX 179, the slightly nervous-looking figure at the left is US F1 driver Phil Hill, whilst to his right is David Ash, looking for all the world as if he has just stepped from flying a Bell X-1 jet plane.
ENEVER FAMILY

49) began suffering from brake fade – 'I found it look four shots at the pedal to get them ... at Sebring you have to brake hard five times to the lap, and you just better have them!' he wrote – and finally, car no. 51 spun off the circuit and collided with a sandbank at dusk. After thirty minutes or so the driver managed to dig himself free, and continued the race with no other problem.

Just after dark, the Portago-Kimberly Ferrari came into its pit and retired, making the MGAs the only team still in the race. 'Our no. 49 was stopping, if you could call it that, on the rivets, but we knew we could hold out,' Ash said. Less than half an hour before the end of the race the three cars were called in and instructed to take things easily, using a lap time of five minutes instead of the time of 4:37, which had been the earlier plan. They were also told to finish line abreast, which they did, coming in nineteenth, twentieth and twenty-second places and winning the team prize. 'We'd started three MGs and we'd finished three MGs, so we weren't mad at anybody!' Ash said.

After the race was over, Dave Ash drove 'his' car back from Florida to New York, 'bringing home its driver and pit manager', as the Hambro press release put it, without clarifying if this referred to one or two people, but adding that 'after a brief and well earned rest on display at the Hambro showroom at 29 West 57th Street, New York City, the car will be entered in competitions throughout the country, with driver David Ash expected to add to its laurels.' As far as can be determined, however, all three cars were disposed of, doubtless helping to defray the costs; their subsequent fate is sadly not known, and they have long been assumed to be lost – but of course, miracles may yet happen.

THE 1957 SEBRING

Flushed with the positive publicity of the team prize in 1956, Hambro Automotive decided to repeat the experiment the following year, once more drawing cars from North American dealer stock. Whilst the race numbers for 1957 were the same as those for 1956, there was a key change this time in that one of the cars, a right-hand-drive specimen (thought to have been originally owned by Jim Fergusson) was painted in the Canadian racing colours of British Racing Green with twin longitudinal white stripes.

The reason behind this change was the fact that car no. 49 was to be driven by a pair of Canadian drivers, Alan

The jubilant 1956 MGA race team and supporters after the race. Some of the key people are: (1) Grant Tolley (MGA Team Captain); (2) Gus Ehrman (Car 49); (3) David Ash (Car 49); (4) John Van Driel (Car 49); (5) John Murray; (6) Anese Ash; (7) Jim Fergusson; (8) Bill Kincheloe (Car 50); (9) David Herson (Manhattan Auto); (10) Joe Herson (Manhattan Auto); (11) Toby Royston; (12) Steve Spitler (Car 50); (13) Bernie Mills (Manhattan Auto); (14) Bob Cron; (15) Ann Blackman; (16) Luis Michelin (of BMC Canada); (17) Sid Blackman (Car 51).

GUS EHRMAN

BEHIND THE 1956 SEBRING CARS: INSKIP, MANHATTAN AUTOS AND KEYSTONE

Joe Herson with a new MGA photographed outside Manhattan Auto, when it was located at 7th and R Streets, NW, Washington DC.
HERSON FAMILY ARCHIVE

John Swanel Inskip (15 July 1885–8 September 1961) started out as a Rolls-Royce importer in New York, and after buying out the bankrupt stock of Brewster, a coachbuilder of some repute, he formed the business of J. S. Inskip in 1937, based in Queens, New York. Whilst Inskip made his name as a distinguished Rolls-Royce retailer, in the early 1950s he began to branch out into other specialized cars, with branches in Providence, Rhode Island and West Palm Beach, Florida. Marques retailed by Inskip in this period included MG, and Inskip even offered its own home-brewed four-seat MG TD. By the time the MGA came along, Inskip's MG offering was well established, and amongst its key personnel were Gus Ehrman and Dave Ash. However, what is seldom appreciated is that Inskip took little direct interest in the preparation of these race cars, the work being contracted out in 1956 to Performance Motors Ltd of Haverstraw, New York.

Manhattan Auto was a business in Washington DC that grew into an empire under the ownership and management of David Herson and, in due course, his son Joe (Joseph Lee Herson, 17 April 1929–8 August 2014). The latter's daughter, Lynn Herson, takes up the story:

Manhattan Auto was established by my grandfather, David L. Herson in 1914. Under his, and later my father's, direction, Manhattan became a leader in selling and servicing imported cars, became involved in the sports-car racing field, and sponsored championship MG, Austin-Healey, Porsche and Jaguar vehicles in national road and rally race events. My father, Joseph Herson, managed factory teams of vehicles at the 12 Hours of Sebring and at Lime Rock, Connecticut. Joseph was involved in the establishment of the Marlboro Raceway, and was a member of the famed Lavender Hill Mob Racing Association (LHMRA).

***From left to right* behind this car are Fred Roston, Steve Spitler, Joe Herson, David Herson and Bernie Mills; both David and Joe Herson and Bernie are sporting the 'Lavender Hill Mob Racing Association' patch on their jackets.**
HERSON FAMILY ARCHIVE

When it came to Sebring, the trip became something of a family affair, but in a very hands-on manner: 'My mother and father and the team used to *drive*, not transport, the cars to Sebring!' Lynn Herson explains. Both before and after the MGA, the Herson family maintained a special relationship with the marque:

My father maintained a love for the MG sports car throughout his life. He raced MGTFs in the 1950s, sold MGs until they were no longer available to the US market, and with the help of one of his buddies from the Lavender Hill Mob Racing Association (LHMRA), Ace Rosner, acquired a 1949 MGTC in the 1970s – a car that his wife, children, grandchildren and great-grandchildren continue to enjoy today.

My father was exceedingly modest, and greatly downplayed the significance of his involvement in racing. What was shared, however, was his enthusiasm for the cars and the sport. He spoke mostly about his involvement in the LHMRA and Marlboro Raceway, and his management of the 1958 Austin-Healey team at the request of Donald Healey.

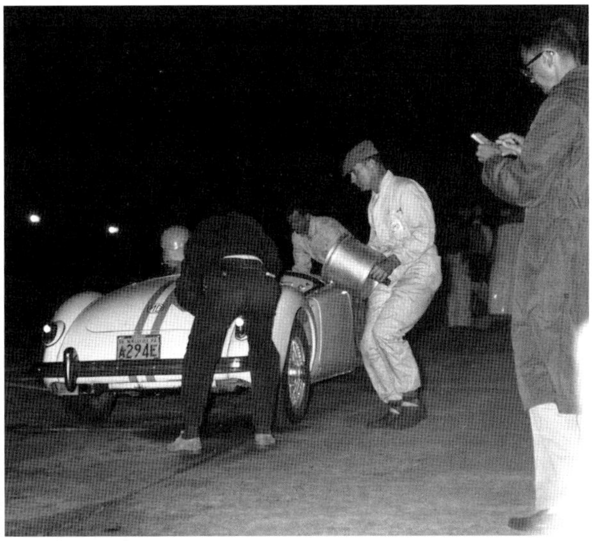

Manhattan Autos car no. 50 in the pit at an unspecified event. Notice that the car still has a licence plate on it, as it was driven to the track.
HERSON FAMILY ARCHIVE

That year the Hambro team of three Austin-Healey 100/6s finished third, fourth and fifth in their class at Sebring – though this would be the final full-on entry managed by the Hersons: 'Although the Manhattan cars were successful in racing, and my father and grandfather perceived a value in showcasing what their marques could achieve, racing was a financial drain on the business. As a result, Manhattan's involvement in racing was short lived, ending in 1958.' After his father passed away in 1959, Joe Herson would take over the business (aged thirty) and build it into a great success through the following decades. Joe Herson died in 2014.

The Keystone Garage in Warren Pennsylvania, which had been incorporated on 13 November 1945, made something of a splash about its involvement at Sebring in 1956, opening new premises in June, an event covered by the local newspaper, the *Warren Times*:

Both owners of the garage, Henry 'Hank' Dahl and Sidney Blackman, have sports cars as hobbies and bring to the business a unique inclination for doing an engine job as it should be done. Specializing in sports cars and imported perfections of all stylings and price ranges, the Keystone Garage can order for its patrons anything from the plush splendor (sic) of a $20,000 Rolls-Royce to the sturdy versatility of a Hillman 'Husky' station wagon for something under $1,600.

As well as MG, the garage handled Aston-Martin, Hillman, Jaguar, Lancia, Morris, Riley, Sunbeam and Triumph, as well as domestic Packard and Clipper lines (for 1956 only, Clipper was classified as a stand-alone marque but was made by Packard). Henry James 'Hank' Dahl died in 2016 aged 102, and Sidney W. Blackman died in 1997.

Millar and Ed Leavens, albeit together with American Rowland Keith. A contemporary Canadian newspaper reported that it was Toronto-based Jim Fergusson who managed the 1957 team effort, although his role has seldom been credited. Unquestionably Dave Ash was the man in overall charge of the 1956 and 1957 efforts – and deserves the credit as team mastermind – but he could not have done it without the hands-on support of Fergusson.

MGA no. 51, the driving of which was shared by David Ash, Gus Ehrman and Jack Van Driel.
BOB VITRIKAS

JIM FERGUSSON, TEAM MANAGER FOR THE 1956 AND 1957 SEBRING CARS

Jim Fergusson of Toronto is one of the lesser known faces of the 1956 and 1957 MGA entries at Sebring.
ROBIN BARKER

James 'Jim' William Fergusson (31 January 1910–13 January 1976) was born in Brandon, Manitoba; the family moved to Toronto when he was fourteen, and in 1928 his father opened a garage business there. The same year the British Empire Motor Club (BEMC) was formed by a group of Toronto-based motorcycle enthusiasts, some of them meeting at the Fergusson family garage.

Jim became the BEMC President in the late 1930s. He was the first BEMC member to own a British sports car, a 1928 MG 14/40, which he acquired in the late thirties, beginning a love affair with small, fast, foreign (mostly British) cars. In 1950, the BEMC began automobile racing at Edenvale, Ontario, on an abandoned World War II British Commonwealth Flight Training School airfield, and at the end of the same year he took part in the very first Sebring race where he finished in eleventh place in a Morris Minor.

In 1955 he acquired one of the first of the rare Austin-Healey 100S race cars, and participated at that year's Sebring event. With the launch of the MGA later that year, Fergusson acquired an early car from the UK and began racing it, with frequent Corvette driver Ed Leavens often behind the wheel.

By 1956 he was an MG dealer on Yonge Street, Toronto, Canada, and his interests were turning towards team management: he therefore took a leading role in the MG Sebring team entries in 1956 and 1957. Fergusson's connections to Alan Millar, BMC Canada's Sales Manager, undoubtedly helped cement his role at Sebring; it seems possible that the white, right-hand drive MGA which Fergusson had raced in 1956 formed the basis of the green car.

In 1959 Fergusson ran a two-car racing team of MGA Twin Cams.

Len Coates, in his book *Challenge: the Story of Canadian Road Racing*, wrote: 'If Jim Fergusson was managing your car in a long distance race, there was little else to do but listen carefully to everything he told you, do it, then show up to collect the awards at the trophy presentation...' Jim Fergusson and his wife later relocated to Pennsylvania when the Canadian market changed and they continued their adventures, including driving a Citroen in the 1972 Cannonball Run. Jim Fergusson died in 1976, nearly twenty years after his first MGA endeavours at Sebring. He surely deserves the credit that BMC failed to give him.

Car no. 50, which, like no. 49, appears to have been finished in 'Canadian Racing' livery (but with circular white roundels), had a half-height competition windscreen. Despite not being painted white, car no. 50 was piloted by Americans Steve Spitler and Bill Kincheloe, and is believed to have hailed from Manhattan Auto again.

Photographs of the 1957 Sebring MGA that raced with no. 50 are quite rare, so the author is grateful to the Herson family for this gem. Judging by the licence plate hanging under the grille, the car was being driven on the road when this photo was taken.
HERSON FAMILY ARCHIVE

BELOW: **1957 MGA no. 50 went on to finish fourth in class, helping to secure a team prize for MG for the second year running. Steve Spitler and Bill Kincheloe did the driving honours in the race.**
BOB VITRIKAS

ABOVE RIGHT: **BMC Canada management and guests at Sebring 1957, with car no. 49, are (*left to right*): Alan Millar, Jim Fergusson, Peter Millard, Major Gil Geitner (an ex-US Air Force man who drove BMC cars as well as Ferraris and Aston Martins at Sebring and Le Mans, and would drive one of the 1960 Sebring Austin-Healeys), Luis Michelin (BMC Canada President) and mechanic Eric Vale.**
COURTESY ROBERT SMYTH

MGA no. 51 would go on to finish second in its class, completing 150 laps.
BOB VITRIKAS

A great overhead shot of 1957 Sebring car no. 49, which was driven by the Canadians Alan Millar and Ed Leavens – hence the Canadian racing livery of green with twin white stripes.

DAVE NICHOLAS/BARCBOYS

The third member of the team, car no. 51 – in similar US Racing White livery – was driven by Dave Ash, Gus Ehrman and Jack Van Driel. With Ash and Ehrman's links to J. S. Inskip, that was understandably where their car was prepared; it had special features such as a cut-down windscreen, no bumpers, and a small wing-mounted lamp to illuminate the octagon-wrapped race number.

An effective self-publicist as well as an accomplished driver, Dave Ash starred in a professionally produced 'home movie' which covered the story of his car being prepared and driven to the race, ostensibly after persuading his wife of the attractions of a 'drive down to Florida' for the Sebring event. The film is a wonderful record of the 1957 race as a whole, but usefully for students of MGA racing history, the cars are also featured – even though car no. 50 often remained fairly elusive of the cameras.

Whilst the cars were prepared in North America, as in the previous year, the factory nevertheless had prepared a series of engines, recorded in the EX Register under Project EX 178 ('Austin 1500 Engine Tuning') as EX 178/46 to EX 178/52 inclusive, with the entry itself annotated for all seven units as '1955 Le Mans type but standard camshaft and ⅜ tubular push-rods'. A separate entry under EX 178/53 referred to a 'list of parts special to USA competition engines'. It seems that in 2018, only one of the two known survivors, car no. 51 owned by Michael Eaton, still carries its original unit, EX 178/49.

All three cars ran fairly uneventfully and were able to win the Team Prize. The Canadian car (car no. 49) eased ahead of his team-mates to win the GT 1600 class (twenty-third overall), while car no. 51 was second in class (twenty-seventh overall), and finally car no. 50 finished fourth in class (thirty-sixth overall); the class third position was taken by von Hanstein and Linge in their Porsche 356A Carrera (car no. 40; thirty-first overall).

THE 1957 SEBRING MGA 1500

Race No.	Chassis No.	Engine No.	Drivers (Home Nation)	Overall Placing	1600cc GT Class	Laps
49	HDR23/11279	Not known	Alan R. N. Millar (CAN)/Ed Leavens (CAN)/Rowland ('Rowley') Davenport Hazard Keith (USA)	23rd	1st	154
50	Not known	Not known	Stephen ('Steve') Spitler (USA)/William Kincheloe (USA)	36th	4th	137
51	HDR43/24460	EX 178/49	David Ash (USA)/Gus Ehrman (USA)/John (Jack) Van Driel (USA)	27th	2nd	150

Footnotes:

Race date was Saturday 23 March 1957. Team manager for the MGAs was Jim Fergusson of Toronto.

Car no. 49: This right-hand-drive car was finished in the traditional Canadian racing colours of British Racing Green with twin white stripes, in honour of its Canadian principal drivers Alan Millar and Ed Leavens. The facia was white, suggesting very strongly that the original build colour of the whole car was also white, as does the chassis plate colour code (although the car nowadays bears a replica of the original). At the rear end, even in the race, there was a licence plate – probably a 1957 Ontario Canada one – number unknown. It seems likely that Jim Fergusson was the original owner of this car; he had certainly bought and raced an early white right-hand-drive MGA throughout 1956. The race numbers for the 1957 Sebring event were set inside plain white octagons, and as an added nod to Canada, a maple leaf emblem was reversed out of a small white octagon on the left-hand side of the bootlid; the fuel filler was centrally mounted to aid rapid refuelling. After Sebring, the car was raced by one of the team mechanics for a while before he 'retired' it to, it is said, a front porch in Toronto, where it evidently sat for a number of years before being sold to a man who had plans (never realized) to restore it as a road-going car. As of 2018, it is owned by Lino Baggio of Ontario.

Car no. 50: At the race this car was British Racing Green with twin narrow white stripes, fairly similar to car no. 49, but with round white race roundels rather than octagons. The drivers, Steve Spitler and William Kincheloe, were both Americans. Lifelong MGA and Sebring fan Dave Nicholas believes that it was later driven by Don Urian, who raced it (at one point painted white) until 1959, when he went into the Army. Painted British Racing Green again, Urian's father-in-law Dan Donoghue took it on and later sold it to Dickson Werner, who raced it with some success, winning a regional SCCA race at Vineland (Cumberland County, New Jersey) in 1959. However, the subsequent history of this car is sadly not well documented and it is also not known (as of 2018) if it survives.

Car no. 51: This left-hand-drive car, driven to the event by Dave Ash, was in a similar white livery to the 1956 team cars, with dark racing stripes and octagonal race number surrounds. After Sebring, Gordon Morris of Morris Garage in Maryland, NY purchased the car from Inskip, and Ted Rounds bought it in 1959. The car was then raced briefly, but after the 1959 SCCA season it was sold and retired from racing. Dave Nicholas remembers: '*Ted Rounds later sold the car to David Zych of Binghamton, NY, who maintained and drove it for many years. He had it longer than anyone up until Mike Eaton; from 1960 until MG collector Jerry Goguen of Vermont* [who bought it in 1975] *it was pretty much a daily driver by Dave Zych*.' When Jerry Goguen's collection was broken up, the car was acquired by present owner Michael Eaton and his father.

As of 2018, Canadian enthusiast Lino Baggio is custodian of the former Ed Leavens/Rowland Keith/Alan Millar 1957 Sebring car, no. 49, which won its class.
LINO BAGGIO

Also in the mix was another Hambro entry, the long-nosed 4-cylinder Austin-Healey 100S Special (car no. 25) of Americans Gilbert Gietner and Ray Cuomo, which finished in twenty-sixth overall and second in its larger-engined GT class, although this was the only one of three similar cars that had been entered to actually finish. On the face of it, the results for MG at Sebring in 1957 would seem to have achieved more obvious marketing rewards than their in-house rivals from Warwick.

In his summary report on BMC motorsports activities over 1956 and 1957, Marcus Chambers made reference to these events, recording that 'the money spent in the USA has been put to good use. The MGAs won the team prize at Sebring for the second year running, though we understand there is room for improvement in race control.'

THE 1959 SEBRING

In 1958, the BMC hierarchy decided that there would be no MG entries at Sebring for that year, despite the impressive potential that the MGA demonstrated in the previous two years. The imminent but as yet unlaunched MGA Twin Cam was on the way, but when Sebring came round the new model was still four months from being unveiled, and so could not yet be subjected to such a highly public race outing. There were few European forays on the cards for the MGA, and so instead of MG, BMC decided to field a trio of the 6-cylinder Austin-Healey 100/6 models at the Florida circuit: the cars finished in fourteenth, seventeenth and twenty-third places overall (third, fourth and fifth in their GT 3.5 class).

Gus Ehrman reunited with his 1957 Sebring MGA at Amelia Island in 2012, courtesy of Michael Eaton, present-day owner of the car.
MICHAEL EATON

Michael Eaton owns 1957 Sebring car no. 51.
MICHAEL EATON

THE EARLY SEBRING MGA DRIVERS

Joe Herson captioned this Taz Rufty photo as follows: 'The no. 50 MGA is the Manhattan 1957 Sebring car. The XK-SS and MGA were getting last-minute checkovers before the start of the 1957 Marlboro Six-Hour Enduro. The XK-SS, driven by Duncan Black, won the race.' Joe remarked that he had forgotten that Manhattan also ran the MGA in that event. While he didn't remember who drove, he was certain that the car finished the race.

HERSON FAMILY ARCHIVE

The ex-Sebring car no. 50 at Marlboro. Joe Herson's mother, Gertrude Herson, is in the light-coloured dress behind the car, and his wife is standing to her left.

HERSON FAMILY ARCHIVE

BMC was always concerned to ensure that the company's entries at Sebring did not look like an entirely British invasion: they wanted to ensure that local drivers and support crews would be at the heart of the effort. This wasn't entirely altruistic, of course: it was clearly cheaper and simpler to lean upon local resources rather than bringing everything in from the UK.

In 1956, the three cars were each prepared by private dealerships so this naturally gave them a head start in terms of choosing the drivers. For example, Inskip man David Ash partnered his good friend Gus Ehrman, while Sid Blackman in car no. 51 was one of the principals of the Keystone Garage where that car was prepared. For the following year, whilst Toronto MG dealer Jim Fergusson still managed the team, BMC Canada became more involved, so along with the welcome influx of technical expertise, some Canadian drivers became involved, making the 1957 Sebring a true 'North American' effort.

British ex-patriot A.R.M. (Alan) Millar was Sales Manager at BMC Canada, and according to his colleague Peter Millard, it was Millar who picked the Canadian drivers for 1957 onwards: 'Alan picked drivers who were his racing buddies, who were well known in the Ontario, Canada sports-car racing scene, and who were connected to BMC. Ed Leavens and Bill Brack were MG dealers, while Al Pease was a part-time racer and a mechanic at a BMC dealership.' Millard says that in 1957, Millar identified himself to race, along with Leavens and Rowland ('Rowley') Keith. 'Keith was an old-time Sebring racer and a good friend of Jim Fergusson.'

Steve Spitler, a driver whose promising career was cut short, deserves an honourable mention too; he was employed by Joe Herson: 'Steve Spitler was a mechanic who worked on our racing programme. He was a good driver. I hired him after he consistently beat me in a similar MG TF to mine, and he continued to beat me thereafter. In 1957 at a National SCCA event at Marlboro, Steve borrowed somebody's D-Type Jag and crashed it, and died from his injuries'.

From 1959 onwards, Marcus Chambers and later Stuart Turner would pick British drivers (such as Colin Escott and Ted Lund in 1960, both also having their own Le Mans MGAs), and Kjell Qvale from the west coast USA always had an involvement with Sebring: Parkinson and Flaherty, who raced in 1959, worked in Qvale's organization.

Whilst the mandarins at BMC might have tried to argue that MG and Austin-Healey were members of the same happy family, the fact remained that sports-car marque enthusiasts are generally rather tribal in their loyalties, and although the still-secret new Sprite was on the way (it would be launched on 20 May 1958), in general the prevailing Austin-Healey models in March 1958 sat somewhere between MG and Jaguar in the pecking order, and it could fairly be argued that more attention needed to be given to the growing strength of Standard Triumph and Rootes (Sunbeam).

RIGHT, BELOW LEFT AND BELOW RIGHT: **The BMC/Hambro party wisely shelter under an aircraft wing at a very wet Sebring in March 1959.**
DAVE NICHOLAS/BARCBOYS

BOTTOM: **Two of the 1959 Sebring Twin Cam Coupés, with the Ehrman/ Saidel car (No. 28) in the foreground, in the MG Sebring team garage**

Writing a year later in the new magazine *Safety Fast!*, and with the clear benefit of hindsight, Marcus Chambers bemoaned the poor decision by his masters in 1958, noting that 'too late it was realized that far and away the largest number of any one marque of imported car in the car park at Sebring was of MG, and all these good folk had no one to shout for. Such a thing could not be allowed to happen again.' With these thoughts in mind, BMC Canada and Hambro Automotive jointly lobbied BMC for a return to MG entries in 1959.

From July 1958, MG had the new Twin Cam available, and so it was agreed that a fresh attack on the team awards would be mounted at Florida for 1959. Whilst MG at Abingdon had provided engines and advice for 1957, this time round it was decided that in order to field a uniform high-quality team effort

Car no. 28 at Sebring 1959.
DAVE NICHOLAS/BARCBOYS

The 1959 Sebring MGAs, all in a line.
DAVE NICHOLAS/BARCBOYS

with a professional aura, the cars would be built at Abingdon and shipped out after testing for final checks in Florida in the run-up to the race, and the support on the ground would be organized under the direction of BMC Canada.

As well as the MGA Twin Cam, the Austin-Healey Sprite also arrived in 1958, and so in order to satisfy both the MG and Healey camps, teams of both models were entered for the 1959 event. In November 1958, four MGA Twin Cam Roadsters, bearing chassis numbers YD2 931 to 934 inclusive, were wheeled out of production and into the Development Shop, where, under the tender care of Alec Hounslow and his men, they were stripped and rebuilt as Coupés.

This was no mean feat, and there has been much speculation over the years as to why MG took the somewhat curious approach of starting with roadsters only to switch over to coupé bodyshells part way through the build process. And as Abingdon was an outfit known never to waste anything, this has also led to some educated speculation about the eventual fate of the 'spare' roadster shells; Canadian MG Sebring expert Robin Barker has shown that all four roadster shells probably had a competition future of their own, and at least two of them were almost certainly the starting point for two of the four 1960 Sebring MGA Twin Cams, which, as we shall see later, used roadster bodies but with bolted-on alloy roofs.

All four of the MGAs, by now wearing their MGA Coupé bodies but still in Ash Green paint, were despatched on 9 February. It should be noted that even if, to casual inspection, the 1959 MGA entries might have looked almost 'stock', they were truly competition-prepared cars: they were quite

All four of the 1959 Sebring MGA Twin Cams can just be made out at the team pit (in particular race cars, Nos. 29, 28 and 30, lined up to the left of the photo), along with the three blue and white Austin-Healey Sprites.
DAVE NICHOLAS/BARCBOYS

THE 1959 MGA TWIN CAM CARS – FACTORY BUILD DETAILS

Chassis No. *(role in race)*	Start Build Date	Production End Date	Dispatch Date	Engine No.
YD2-931	26 November 1958	9 February 1959	9 February 1959	Not known
YD2-932 *(Car No. 28)*	27 November 1958	9 February 1959	9 February 1959	18131-2
YD2-933	28 November 1958	9 February 1959	9 February 1959	Not known
YD2-934	28 November 1958	9 February 1959	9 February 1959	Not known

Footnotes:
All four cars started out as Ash Green right-hand-drive export roadsters (hence the 'YD2' prefixes) with black trim and a blue hood. The factory records indicate that 'bodies changed to Green-Grey Coupé by Competition Department'. Speculation by Robin Barker suggests that the process of changing over to Coupé bodies resulted in four surplus MGA Twin Cam Roadster bodyshells, and he has identified possible subjects for the adoption of these competition-prepared shells as YD3-957, YD1-1626, YD2-2571 (1960 Sebring race car no. 40 – *see later*) and YD2-2572 (the 1960 Sebring practice car).

The EX Register contains thirteen specific entries related to the 1959 Sebring MGA Twin Cams under EX 187/288 (dated 12 November 1958) to EX 187/300 (dated 28 January 1959). The next entry, EX 187/301, was dated 21 May 1959, and refers to 'Piston – BC.16.GB to prevent detonation'.

heavily modified, with such special features as the large central fuel filler and large capacity tank, and a cold air intake from the hood scoop, while all the windows except the windscreen were plexi-glass, and the interior featured racing instruments, including a chronometric rev counter.

Meanwhile three Sprites – also in production at Abingdon – were shipped off to Warwick for separate preparation at the Healey works.

Testing of the race cars ensued – governed by the vagaries of the British winter weather – and having been despatched together, they were then made ready to be shipped to Florida in order to arrive a week before the race. At the last minute, Eddie Maher discovered a fault with the batch of pistons for the sequence of cars that happened to include the race cars, and he contacted Marcus Chambers just in time before the latter flew out to New York from London Airport on a Britannic night flight. As this was Chambers' first trip to Sebring with the BMC team, he was bound to hope this was not a portentous omen.

By the time that Chambers and Douggie Watts arrived in Florida, the MGA Twin Cams had already been brought from the docks and were sitting prone, their engines stripped out and ready to receive the new pistons, although according to Bill Price, writing in his seminal history of the BMC Competitions team, the two men from Abingdon were not especially happy with the conditions in the worshop, which was full of dust and sand.

The team of mechanics included no fewer than fifteen Canadians – under the management of Pete Millard, BMC's Service Chief from Ontario – and the fourteen drivers were a mixture of Americans and Canadians, although for 1959 the MG pilots would all be from the USA. The MG mechanic contingent was overseen by Abingdon's Douggie Watts, while Geoff Healey was in charge of the Austin-Healey side of the operation. John Thornley was able to combine a business trip with an opportunity to oversee the whole ensemble, assisted by Hambro's Service Manager Frank Harrison, whilst Marcus Chambers managed, amongst other things, the diplomacy.

Although the cars were soon in good fettle, and the mechanics in good spirits, the 'Sunshine State' of Florida failed to live up to its name in the period up to and including the 1959 event. The entourage made their base just down the road at Avon Park, where they were spread across two motels, but the weather was inhospitable, and at least one practice session at the circuit was completely washed out, whilst heavy rain persisted for about five days.

The four MGA Twin Cams were equipped with slightly dubious fake number plates, more or less resembling UK licence plates (despite the hyphens between the letters and the numbers), but they bore no real authority: the undoubted intention was to try to reduce the inquisitive attention of the local Sebring traffic police, who would be on the lookout for unregistered race cars driving up and down the roads to and from the circuit.

Practice saw a great deal of work not only to the cars themselves but also the pit techniques, and here Gus Ehrman and Hal Wallace came up with a special funnel device intended to speed up the refuelling process. However, Marcus Chambers became alarmed at the quantities of fuel that poured off the cars and on to the pit floor, and he made an ultimatum that either the leaks stopped or the Ehrman/Wallace contraption would be banned.

The two men worked hard on their creation and in the end it was made to work well enough that Chambers was satisfied with its merits: the fact that, with care, it could administer fuel at the remarkable rate of a gallon a second made it an indispensable tool to reduce the time of pit stops during the twelve-hour race. After the race, Chambers conceded that 'next time it will be considered essential... and with production modifications, perhaps it will be less frightening than the prototype.'

On the morning of Saturday 21 March, the BMC crew were safely ensconced in their pits by 08:30, and the team were visited by a selection of management including Lester Suffield (of BMC Canada), Babe Learoyd and Hambro's PR man in New York, British-born Tony Birt. The race started at 10:00, and all six BMC entries got off to a satisfactory start.

The only known survivor of the four cars taken to Sebring in 1959 (three raced, plus a practice car) is this one, no. 28, which is owned by Michael Eaton.

MICHAEL EATON

The wet weather in the race did not let up until near dusk, and severely hampered all the drivers in their efforts to achieve and maintain high average speeds; at least the hardtop roofs and reasonable headroom in the MGA Coupés helped to some extent. Even so, heat build-up in the tight cockpits had shown up during testing to be a significant problem; the makeshift solution was to drill holes in the toe board behind the pedals, which let in some air but also copious amounts of water – after the race Gus Ehrman ceremoniously took off his trousers and wrung them out, much to his wife's consternation.

During the race, car no. 28 managed to slide off the wet circuit into a straw bale, although the damage was only slight, while car no. 29 suffered from a faulty starter motor which drew it into the pits for an hour; both would go on to finish respectably, although a long way down the field. Dusk brought a cessation in the rain and one of those beautiful orange sunsets beloved of Hollywood movies, the bronze light shimmering on the lakes around the waterlogged circuit.

Sherm Decker had proved to be something of a wet-weather wizard in practice, and so, despite having been

THE 1959 SEBRING MGA TWIN CAMS

Race No.	Chassis No.	Engine No.	Reg. No. (all false)	Drivers (all USA)	Overall Placing	1600 cc GT Class	Laps
28	YD2 932	18131-2	MJB-167	Gus O. Ehrman/Ray Saidel	27th (11th Grand Touring)	2nd	155
29	YD2 93? (*1, 3 or 4*)	Not known	PRX-707	James H ('Jim') Parkinson/John ('Jack') Dalton	34th (17th Grand Touring)	3rd	145
30	YD2 93? (*1, 3 or 4*)	Not known	OMO-700	Ray Pickering/John ('Jack') Flaherty/Sherman ('Sherm') Decker	45th (25th Grand Touring)	4th	121
28P	YD2 93? (*1, 3 or 4*)	Not known	RMO-101	N/A	N/A	N/A	N/A

Footnotes:

Race date was Saturday 21 March 1959; there were three race cars entered and a single practice car.

The cars (YD2-931 to 934 inclusive) were entered by the Hambro Automotive Corporation of New York; they had started as export specification RHD MGA Twin Cam Roadsters (for which the chassis number had a YD2 prefix) and were converted to Coupés (normal prefix YM2). Paint colour was Ash Green. The licence plates seen at Sebring were fictitious as far as the cars themselves were concerned; the *real* 'MJB 167' started life on a 1956 MGA 1500, and the *real* 'PRX 707' and 'RMO 101' appear earlier in this chapter.

Car no. 28 (YD2 932): The only one of the four cars known to have survived. Although race entries list three drivers, the third man, Sherm Decker, did not drive no. 28 but instead drove no. 30. After the 1959 event, YD2 932 was sold to the famous American automotive writer, Leon Mandel (working at the time for Jack Flaherty), who, after supposedly little more than a change of spark plugs (if the contemporary BMC advert is to be believed) promptly drove it to California (in convoy with Sprite no. 55). After this he drove it and raced it (possibly just once) during the remainder of the year. Mandel later told Jonathan Stein that en route to California he was 'busted by the New Mexico state police for doing 125mph (200km/h)'. Present owner Michael Eaton of Virginia originally discovered the car lying derelict in a Californian field, but with sufficient original parts to support a thorough restoration to its present condition. The engine number is unusual, but believed to be authentic.

Car no. 29 went to Gough Industries in Los Angeles, where it was retained for a while for Jim Parkinson to drive, ostensibly without distinction, as the car was sold off and so seemingly the trail went cold.

Car no. 30 is believed to have also headed west to California, perhaps for Jack Flaherty and Ray Pickering to drive. Like car no. 29, its subsequent history is presently unknown.

Car no. 28P, the practice car, is understood to have gone to Minnesota where its new owner raced it until around 1965/66, according to research by Michael Eaton.

THE CANADIAN MGA CONNECTION FROM 1959 ONWARDS

Peter Millard of BMC Canada shows off the MGA Twin Cam engine in UMO 95 at the 1960 Sebring event.
BOB VITRIKAS

As we have seen, a critical component of the BMC efforts at Sebring was the support given from Canada. There were good reasons for this: unlike the USA, where BMC leaned heavily on Hambro Automotive for sales and distribution, the organization in Canada was a wholly owned BMC subsidiary, and included directly employed management and teams of mechanics.

BMC Canada's Service Manager was Peter Millard, who had started his career in the UK as a Rolls-Royce apprentice; he had first come to Canada after the war, and his involvement in the factory's team efforts at Sebring started with the 1959 event.

Millard picked most of the Sebring mechanics personally: 'I always chose fellows who knew their way around a car. They might not be all that familiar with a particular model and certainly had never seen the modified Sebring cars before, but they were all technical guys.' He avoided picking people from the Parts Department: 'I always had to have guys who knew how to pull wrenches. Sometimes we would take guys who worked for Canadian Morris, MG or Austin and Austin-Healey dealerships, and not just those who worked for BMC Canada. Occasionally a driver would ask for his own regular race mechanic to come.'

Part of this trip involved two mechanics driving the BMC Canada Austin A50 van down to Sebring. Millard recalled that Eric Vale was always one of the mechanics who drove; as he told Robin Barker: *'Eric was the Technical Service Manager for the Austin side of BMC Canada. The van was an Austin A50, painted red and white and had British Motor Corporation Competition Department on the side. We used it for all of the races in Canada too: it was a piece of shit. This van was one of the first vehicles where BMC tried a column mounted shift lever. It never worked and we had a small production line in Hamilton rebuilding them at one point. The van was loaded with tools, but no parts. Those came with the cars. The rest of the mechanics and myself always flew, then we had rental cars to get us to the track at Sebring.'*

It was Peter Millard who settled on the Avon Park team venue: 'We showed up as a team for the first time in 1959 and all of the good spots closer to the track were already taken. I simply drove around until I found this motel (Bennett's, later to be Reed's). But then we needed a place to work on the cars, and the lady in the motel told me to try next door (Murphy's Shell). That worked out well, too – we were out at the track during the day when he needed the service bays, and at night when we were back our cars drew quite a crowd and he pumped lots of gas...'

The motel also happened to be close to a restaurant, 'Chalet Susan', where the team ate regularly: 'It was just up the highway on the other side of the road. They treated us very well, and after a while knew what everyone wanted as soon as we walked in…' Millard was also responsible for all the expenses for the team personnel: 'Before we left for the race we got a cheque from the UK to cover the expenses at Sebring; I would go to the bank in Hamilton near the BMC Canada plant on Kenilworth Avenue and buy travellers' cheques.' Each year, Millard paid for just about everything with travellers' cheques. At the end of the event, there was usually some money left over when they got back to Canada: 'I simply turned it back over to the President, Lester Suffield. I didn't have to hand in any receipts or an expense report, I just handed back the balance. There was no accounting – nothing!'

intended as a reserve driver, was sent out during the race in car no. 30; he kept it going well after dark, until around two hours from the end of the race, when a fault with the engine forced him to push the car, unaided, for a mile and a half in the pouring rain until he was exhausted and unable to go further. A broken piston appeared to be the problem, and Decker tried driving the car in short spurts until the engine seized; eventually the car was pushed over the line, thereby qualifying and so salving MG's prestige. Meanwhile the Austin-Healey Sprites finished '1-2-3' in their 750-1000cc class.

Thus it was that at the end of the race, all six BMC cars finished, with the MGA Twin Cams finishing in twenty-seventh (car no. 28), thirty-fourth (car no. 29) and forty-fifth places (car no. 30). It was a worthy result, and testament to the staying power of the cars and their drivers in tough circumstances – but in a race dominated by Ferraris and Porsches, it was clear that MG was less of the Sebring force than it once had been.

Sebring 1960 – and cars 38 and 40 are checked over. This year, the cars were MGA Twin Cam Roadsters with bolted-on Vanden Plas alloy hardtops.

MICHAEL EATON COLLECTION

1960 SEBRING: MGA TWIN CAM

The start of the new decade also marked the demise of the MGA Twin Cam, problems in service and a growing reputation for poor reliability meaning that production would soon be terminated. For the time being, however, it was still in production, and so it formed the basis of MG's presence at Sebring in March 1960, at the 'Tenth Annual Sebring International Grand Prix of Endurance for the Amoco Trophy'. Hambro were once again avoiding the 'too many eggs in one basket' approach by sponsoring a trio of Austin-Healey 3000s and a pair of Sprites, one of the latter appearing in Friday's four-hour race.

Preparations for the MGs had begun the previous November, when the first two of a sequence of five Twin Cam Roadsters, with chassis numbers in the number series 2571 to 2575 inclusive, started down the line at Abingdon. All were finished in British Racing Green with black competition seats, and they were fitted with bolted-on alloy hardtops, which added to the overall structural strength and contributed better aerodynamics. Mindful of the sweltering heat at Sebring, a small air intake in front of the windscreen was designed to provide some relief for the driver during the race, with less likelihood of them being soaked if it rained.

Sylvia Belcher Beeks – Miss Sebring 1960 – risks denting the bonnet of UMO 95, while Californians Jim Parkinson and Jack Flaherty (drivers of UMO 93) admire the view.

BOB VITRIKAS

Miss Sebring 1960, Sylvia Belcher Beeks, photographed with UMO 95 at the Avon Park Motel, just down the road from Sebring, where the MG team were based. Ms Beeks is holding a copy of the 1960 official Sebring poster.

BOB VITRIKAS

The three 1960 Sebring cars – from the camera they are UMO 95 (race no. 38), UMO 96 (no. 39) and at the rear, UMO 93 (no. 40). Note the white mechanics' overalls with their BMC rosettes. The cars were painted Brooklands Green.
STEVE WOODYARD

Extraneous parts such as the bumpers were omitted, but oil coolers, additional driving lamps and marker lights were added. Similarly, the torrential rains at the 1959 event had prompted the fitment of two-speed windscreen wipers. One of the more unusual changes was a modification to the internal panelwork behind the driver to accommodate the mandatory FIA suitcase, a peculiar quirk of the rule book.

Mechanically, the engines were not too far from stock specification, with a 9.9:1 compression ratio, but were fitted with twin 2in SU carburettors, and drove to the 4.55:1 rear axles through close-ratio gearboxes. Somewhat curiously, the 4.55:1 axles also seem to have been fitted more or less as a *de facto* standard to at least two dozen batches of production Twin Cams shipped to Mexico from October 1959; for the 1960 Sebring cars, limited slip differentials were fitted.

Here the 1960 Practice Car UMO 94 (with a 'P' marked on the roundel) sits ahead of UMO 95 (no. 38) of Britons Ted Lund and Colin Escott. The practice car is believed to have eventually ended up on the ocean floor, as explained in the text.
DAVE NICHOLAS/BARCBOYS

The 'Canadian livery' 1960 Sebring MGA Twin Cam (no. 39) in British Racing Green with twin white stripes passes by during the race of 26 March 1960. Drivers were Fred Hayes and Ed Leavens, both Canadians.
DAVE NICHOLAS/BARCBOYS

The 1960 Sebring MGA Twin Cam (no. 40) of Californians Jim Parkinson and Jack Flaherty.
DAVE NICHOLAS/BARCBOYS

UMO 95 runs ahead of UMO 93 at a 2012 Sebring reunion parade.
STEVE WOODYARD

Pre-race testing in the UK was undertaken in the usual manner, prior to shipment: thus three cars were destined to race in the main event, while a fourth car fulfilled a role as a practice car in the run-up to the race, whilst the final car was sent to Canada to support marketing activities there prior to being sold on.

All three cars started the race, part of a field of sixty-five cars, but the Lund/Escott car only made it through to part of its third lap and was forced to retire with a broken valve spring. Regular pit-stop repairs were necessary for the surviving two cars, the brake lines proving especially fragile on the rough Sebring track surface.

ABOVE: **UMO 93 survives in remarkable condition, a testament to its careful ownership and sensitive care over the years by its handful of owners.**

LEFT: **UMO 93 was sold by Ship and Shore Motors of West Palm Beach. It was later acquired by Lyle York, one of the founding members of the North American MGA Twin Cam Register, who sold it in 2002 to John Wright, NAMGAR Founding Member. As of 2018, it was on sale through DK Engineering in the UK.**
DK ENGINEERING

THE 1960 SEBRING MGA TWIN CAMS

Race No.	Chassis No.	Engine No.	UK Reg. No.	Drivers (Home Nation)	Overall Placing (speed)	1600cc GT Class	Laps
38	YD2 2573	16GB DA 2011	UMO 95	E.W.K. ('Ted') Lund (UK)/Colin G. Escott (UK)	Retired	63rd	2½
39	YD2 2575	16GB DA 2233	UMO 96	Frederick John ('Fred') Hayes (CAN)/Edward ('Ed') Leavens (CAN)	24th (68.5mph)	3rd	160
40	YD2 2571	16GB DA 2231	UMO 93	Jim Parkinson (USA)/John ('Jack') Flaherty (USA)	29th	4th	148
P	YD2 2572	16GB DA 2039	UMO 94	Practice car	N/A	N/A	N/A
N/A	YD2 2574	Not known	N/A	N/A	N/A	N/A	N/A

Footnotes:

Race date was Saturday 26 March 1960; there were three race cars entered, in addition there was a practice car, and a further car that was not part of the formal entry. The cars were roadsters with bolted-on Vanden Plas alloy hardtops, and were completed in February 1960, being painted British Racing Green. They were registered UMO 93–96 inclusive on 17 February 1960. They had 2in SU carburettors, 4.55-ratio rear axles and close-ratio gearboxes and oil coolers. Steve Woodyard, who has owned YD2 2573, added: 'The cars apparently were fitted with limited slip 4:55 differentials, which no. 38 still has. There was some discussion that perhaps the original limited slip units were removed before the cars were subsequently auctioned off, but no. 38 has a Dana limited slip unit in place, as I believe no. 40 did, as well. I strongly suspect those were the original units as they were available in that time frame.' (*See also* the footnotes to the 1961 Sebring race later in this chapter.)

Car no. 38 (YD2 2573): Finished in British Racing Green. Retired after 2½ laps (broken valve spring). After the race, this car was sold off and its subsequent racing and owner history is well documented; the most recent restoration was started by Tony Simms of Marco Island, Florida; in 2017 it was owned by Steve Woodyard, who recounts: 'I owned the car twice, first purchasing it in 1977. It was very original at that time, but after sale to Tony Simms in 1984 it was converted to left-hand drive, also fuel cell, roll-bar and other pure racing modifications were added, and the car was successfully campaigned for a number of years, with increasingly more powerful engines, the last producing 178 HP. When I repurchased the car in 2007, no restoration had begun, but all original parts accompanied the car, including the unmolested original engine, making accurate restoration possible. It was returned to its original right-hand-drive configuration and subsequently shown in a number of Concours D'Elegance events, including Amelia Island in 2012.' Restoration was completed by Steve Woodyard in July 2007; as of 2018 it is owned by Pat Orino of Tacoma, Washington.

Car No. 39 (YD2 2575; body no. B1891): Finished in British Racing Green with twin white stripes (traditional Canadian racing colours). This car went through a series of New York owners and its history is well documented; it was sold in July 1960 to 'Ecurie Pip' of Buffalo, New York. The twin-cam engine was removed and the engine later fitted was AEH 37RS 14707. Between 1961 and 1964 the car was owned by Jim Weissenborn, whose friend Gordon Lipe took out the twin-cam engine and supposedly used it as a boat anchor in the lake at Skaneateles, NY. Dave Nicholas purchased UMO 96 in 1968: 'I kept that car until 1985 when I moved to Maryland from New York. I took the car from its storage and entrusted it to a body shop person but when I returned to get the car it was gone and the business was closed. Years later a friend from England sent me an article showing it was in England and totally restored.' The car is now (2018) owned by Stephan Pröpsting in Germany. There is a further plot twist too: when MGA Twin Cam enthusiast David Humphreys was looking for a twin cam engine for his car he acquired one from Jim Alcorn in the USA; when Humphreys looked more closely the engine number appeared to be the same as the ex-Sebring engine from the Leavens/Hayes car, 16GB DA 2233. Perhaps it was another engine that ended up as a boat anchor in 1961? Sometimes life is stranger than fiction.

Car No. 40 (YD2 2571): In British Racing Green with white stripe and white triangular accent on the rear wing. The body number of this car is 68625, which suggests it has its origins in the build for the 1959 race (see earlier). After the race, this car was sold off through 'Ship and Shore' (Florida dealers). Later raced in Florida and Georgia, but suffered when racing at Daytona and placed into storage; later bought by enthusiast Lyle York, founder of the North American MGA Twin Cam Register. From Lyle York it passed to John Wright, who owned it from 2002, undertook a thorough mechanical restoration, and eventually sold it in 2015 at Pebble Beach. It is now resident in the UK (2018) in the ownership of DK Engineering.

'P': (YD2 2572): After it was sold this car was strapped on to the deck of a boat that was sunk in the Caribbean during a hurricane. The remains, including the original race engine, are presumably still there.

YD2 2574: Car never raced at Sebring; it was instead shipped to Canada where it appeared in a series of minor races, before being acquired by MGA enthusiast Robin Barker.

THE 1960 MGA TWIN CAM CARS – FACTORY BUILD DETAILS

Chassis Number *(role in race)*	Start Build Date	Production End Date	Dispatch Date	Engine No.
YD2-2571 (car no. 40)	12 December 1959	16 February 1960	17 February 1960	2231
YD2-2572 (practice car)	12 December 1959	16 February 1960	17 February 1960	2039
YD2-2573 (car no. 38)	14 January 1960	16 February 1960	17 February 1960	2011
YD2-2574 (not raced)	14 January 1960	16 February 1960	17 February 1960	Unknown
YD2-2575 (car no. 39)	18 January 1960	16 February 1960	17 February 1960	2233

Footnotes:

The build start dates indicate that work on YD2-2571 and YD2-2572 started considerably earlier than on the other three cars. Investigations by Robin Barker indicate a high level of probability that YD2-2571 started life as one of the abandoned MGA Twin Cam Roadster bodies originally intended for the 1959 Sebring race (see earlier tables). For reasons which will become apparent below, although it seems likely that YD2-2572 had a similar basis, it also seems likely that the truth may never be known for certain.

ABOVE: **The cockpit of UMO 93, where in 1960 Jim Parkinson and Jack Flaherty had shared twelve hours of race driving at Sebring.**
DK ENGINEERING

BELOW: **1960 was the second and last time that twin-cam engines raced under the bonnet of a factory MG at Sebring. This is the engine bay of car no. 40, photographed in 2017.**
DK ENGINEERING

BOTTOM: **UMO 95 (1960 Sebring race no. 38) on display at LeMay Car Museum, in Tacoma, Washington in 2017.**
STEVE WOODYARD

UMO 96, race no. 39, is notable for its Canadian racing livery of British Racing Green with twin white stripes. It now lives in Germany where it is treasured by Stephan Pröpsting.
STEPHAN PRÖPSTING

The top eleven places at the 1960 event were almost inevitably taken by Ferraris and Porsches, and amongst the other marques that also finished ahead of the MGs were various AC, Alfa-Romeo, Arnolt-Bristol, Austin-Healey, Chevrolet, Lola and Osca race cars; the two finishing MGs ended up in twenty-fourth and twenty-ninth places. The MGA Twin Cams also ceded the top spots in their GT 1600 class to a pair of Porsches.

The workmanlike cockpit of UMO 96 as it is today.
STEPHAN PRÖPSTING

The Twin Cam engine in UMO 96; this was the swansong of this unit as far as Sebring was concerned.
STEPHAN PRÖPSTING

THE 1961 SEBRING

By the time the factory got round to planning the MGA entry for 1961, the race specification had evolved to make the cars slightly more specialized and, more significantly, lighter. Crucially under the bonnet, the twin-cam engine was nowhere to be seen; for 1961, MG reverted to the conventions of overhead valves. Despite the abandonment of the twin-cam engine, the owner of one of the cars, Ian Prior, has confirmed that the chassis was of the proper Twin Cam type; obviously this had the four-wheel disc brakes and Dunlop centre-lock wheels of the by now discontinued Twin Cam variant. The body type this year reverted to Coupés, although it is not thought that there was any of the curious body-swapping of the kind seen in 1959.

Some body panels had been replaced by alloy, glass was replaced with Plexiglas, within safe limits the chassis and suspension were drilled extensively to lighten them, and lightweight red-coloured Microcell racing seats, with black-and-white checked fabric on the seating surfaces, were fitted in the cockpit. The 1961 Sebring cars were built at Abingdon over a fourteen-day period in January, with a different mechanic having responsibility for each car, which partly explains some of the differences between the two of them.

An internal worksheet signed by Syd Enever on 9 January 1961 (DDW no. 1145; also reissued several times with revision dates) describes an order to 'build three MGA 1588cc uprated engines for Sebring', and sets out all the work involved. It lists the engine numbers for the three units as EX 178/42, 43 and 44, but there is some evident confusion, as someone has marked the copy as 'EX 176' and then crossed out the changes again; this confusion between EX 176 and EX 178 is also reflected in the EX Register itself. Although three engines were to be built, as noted there were two entries for 1961 rather than three; the third was logically enough a spare.

In the rear axles were ZF limited slip differentials; Frank Graham (owner of car no. 43) told the author:

> My brother, who worked for Jaguar USA, had regular dealings with a ZF representative, and using the numbers etched on the internals of my diff confirmed there had been a small run of these LSDs made for BMC in 1960. This was after the 1960 Sebring race, when the 1960 team cars used Dana LSDs, which were derived from Studebaker and Jeep. The diff housing on no. 43 is stamped ZF 9/41 (a 4.55:1), but no. 44 is stamped ZF 10/43 and 'new diff 2-2-61'.

For 1961, there were just two cars entered, both MGA 1600 Coupés. Both finished, in fourteenth and sixteenth places overall (first and second in their class).
BOB VITRIKAS

This overhead view of car no. 43 at Sebring in 1961 clearly shows the bogus PR-120 registration number. Note the SAAB official Sebring cars in the background.
FRANK GRAHAM

Set into the nose were two additional auxiliary air intakes on either side of the front grill, made of aluminium and used pieces of an early 'Frog-eye' Austin-Healey Sprite front grill. Frank Graham, who owns car no. 43, notes that on his car, these grill pieces are cut so that they are orientated horizontal and vertical, but on the other car the grills are set on the diagonal; as he notes, this detail makes it possible to distinguish the cars in the photos taken before the racing numbers were applied. The headlamps were fitted with transparent covers to protect against flying stones.

At the rear, four small round lamps – two a side – were fitted on the trailing edges, one of each pair fitted into the otherwise unused bumper bracket holes, with second holes drilled alongside to complete the array. Projecting into the boot were large 17gal (20 US gallon) competition fuel tanks, feeding the twin $1\frac{3}{4}$in HS6 SUs via twin fuel pumps – more for reliability through redundancy than a need to deliver more petrol.

After testing at Silverstone, both cars were dispatched to Southampton and loaded into the hold of the *Queen Elizabeth*, bound for New York. They were then trucked to Sebring. Bogus licence plates were fitted; SRX 149 was a genuine number on a 1959 MGA 1600, and Ian Prior (current owner of car no. 44) suggests that 'PR-120' might have been a nod to Peter Riley. As of 2018, the 'real' PR 120 resides on a 2006 Skoda Fabia!

Peter Riley, driving No. 43, told Jonathan Stein for *Automobile Quarterly* that 'part of the fun of driving the slower car in the great classic races of the time was that you could watch the great master drivers at work from the best pos-

Jim Parkinson and Jack Flaherty's car, no. 44, receives attention.
DAVE NICHOLAS VIA IAN PRIOR

The two factory MGA 1600 Coupés lined up at Sebring in March 1961.
JOHN WRIGHT COLLECTION

THE 1961 SEBRING MGA 1600 DELUXE-STYLE COUPÉS

Race No.	Chassis No.	Engine No.	Reg. No. (all false)	Drivers (Home Nation)	Overall Placing	1600cc GT Class	Laps
43	GHD/100149	EX 178/43	PR-120	Peter Riley UK)/Sir John Whitmore (UK)	16th	2nd	173
44	GHD/100148	EX 178/44	SRX-149	Jim Parkinson (USA)/Jack Flaherty (USA)	14th	1st	175

Footnotes:

Race date was Saturday 25 March 1961; there were two factory MGA 1600 Coupés entered, which were close to 'Deluxes' in format. These were built on Twin Cam-type chassis and used specially prepared pushrod engines. Although the colour may be referred to under the generic term 'British Racing Green', Ian Prior (owner of no. 44) believes the colour is more correctly 'Brooklands Green', which was the pre-war MG factory racing colour as used on the K3 Magnette; this also applies to the 1960 cars, in his view. MG Twin Cam expert Edward Vandyk told the author: 'I feel that the two 1961 Sebring cars are not Deluxes and should not be counted in the Deluxe numbers, because they are not delineated in the production records as Deluxes'. Ian Prior, who owns car no. 44 (*see* below) points out that the chassis is a genuine Twin Cam one: 'I have another Twin Cam (YD3-2028) and I have checked, comparing the two chassis, and the extended steering rack brackets and extended front brake hose brackets are the same length on both cars. The five extra holes in the front cross-member for the sump bolts are not all there, but there are many extra large holes drilled on the top, bottom and vertical surfaces on GHD 100148. The square right-hand-side engine mount is present on both chassis.'

Although some records have occasionally added South African Bob Olthoff to the driving rota, several people have shown that this was not so. For example Edward Vandyk told the author: 'I don't think Olthoff drove in the 1961 race, he was the mechanic and reserve driver, he drove in the 1962 race.' This was also shown in an interview from *Classic Car Africa* of August 1996 in which Olthoff confirmed his frustration, to the writer of the article, Ken Macleod, that '...despite all his hopes, nobody fell ill, so he was an interested spectator!' Finally, further corroboration comes from Frank Graham, who told the author that he met Olthoff in his then home in South Carolina in 2002: 'He told me that he had practised in both cars doing both day and night sessions in 1961, but never had the opportunity to take the wheel during the race.' As we shall see later, Olthoff was luckier the following year.

Car No. 43: This car is owned (2018) by Frank Graham who has a website dedicated to the car and its restoration. It was painted all over in Green. After its outing at Sebring, no. 43 (as well as no. 44) was passed from 'Ship and Shore' (MG dealers for the south-eastern USA) to 'Hooper Import Center' on Merritt Island, near Cape Canaveral, where it was advertised for sale. Present owner Frank Graham notes that it remained largely unaltered mechanically, implying it was never raced again, although this would not have precluded its participation in rallies.

Frank Graham has tracked down its history in detail: 'By 1967 No. 43 had had the roof and side lights removed, had been resprayed black, and the interior completely redone in white. I have a photo of it on a used car lot in Daytona. There was still a dealer sticker on the rear of the car when I acquired it from Feddon Motors of Daytona. I managed to contact the son of the proprietor years ago who told me that his father and uncle had the business for only three years from 1966-68 and they specialized in used sports and performance cars. Unfortunately his father had passed and his uncle though alive at the time suffered from dementia. The son had been serving in Vietnam at the time and had no knowledge of the car. A fellow from Louisiana named Don Fabre, whose business was the restoration and maintenance of Rolls-Royce and Bentley automobiles, bought the car from the lot in Daytona in 1967 having recognized it as a works entry and brought it to Baton Rouge, Louisiana. From that point on I have a very detailed history of the car. When I bought the car in 1989, Don Fabre presented me with the original driving lights, carbs, and the one-off chrome cap for the front valence and a few other original bits that he still had.'

Car No. 44: Although the body was British Racing Green, like no. 43, the front valance was painted white to help with recognition out on the circuit. This car is now with Ian Prior in Australia (2018) who has documented its history from its sale in January 1962 to Fred Ball, a DJ from local Titusville Radio Station WRHF. Prior eventually acquired the car in 1977 from former owner Robson, who had been storing it with Don Loftis of Titusville, Florida with the intention of a restoration. Prior told the author: 'No. 44 competed at Daytona in 1964 and 1965 in the 2,000km Continental Races, as these were important FIA races and had factory support from all the leading manufacturers.'

sible viewpoint.' Riley's co-driver Sir John Whitmore said of the 1961 Sebring cars that 'they were embarrassingly slow, and we were constantly trying to keep out of the way of the faster traffic...' – even though the MGAs 'ran flawlessly throughout, requiring only fuel and a little oil'.

While Riley and Whitmore were taking turns in no. 43 (with South African Bob Olthoff as reserve driver, sitting frustrated on the sidelines) the Californian duo of Flaherty and Parkinson drove car no. 44. Up against the MGAs were three Sunbeam Alpines, but in the end the two MGs secured the top places in their GT 1600 class.

Despite Riley and Whitmore's assertion that the little MGs were underpowered and outclassed, the only cars that finished ahead of them in the overall placings were various high-end Ferraris, Porsches, plus a Corvette and a Lola, while dovetailed between the two MGs, in fifteenth place overall, was a Donald Healey Motor Company Sprite. Meanwhile the Alpines finished in third, fourth and fifth in class, but other than the highest placed (at seventeenth overall, snapping at the heels of car no. 43), the remaining Rootes sports cars were some way down the field.

Peter Riley and John Whitmore drove MGA no. 43 in the 1961 race.

BOB VITRIKAS

1961 Sebring: MGA no. 44 is behind the S.H. Arnolt-entered Arnolt Bristol (no. 87) of Seaverns /Gary (which finished in twenty-first place), the Ferrari 250 TR 59 Fantuzzi Spyder (no. 10) of Sharp /Hissom (finished fourth), and nearest the camera, the Maserati Tipo 63 (no. 20) of Hansgen /McLaren (which did not finish). The MGA, driven by Jim Parkinson and Jack Flaherty, finished first in their class and an equally impressive fourteenth overall.

BOB VITRIKAS

The MGA 1600 Coupé no. 44 of Jim Parkinson and Jack Flaherty is lifted on to a jack during the 1961 Sebring race.

IAN PRIOR

ABOVE: **The two 1961 Sebring cars were both offered around in this advertisement by the Hooper Import Center (at the time based at Highway 520, Cocoa, Merritt Island, Florida).**

LEFT: **Ship and Shore Motors were based in West Palm Beach, Florida.**

IAN PRIOR

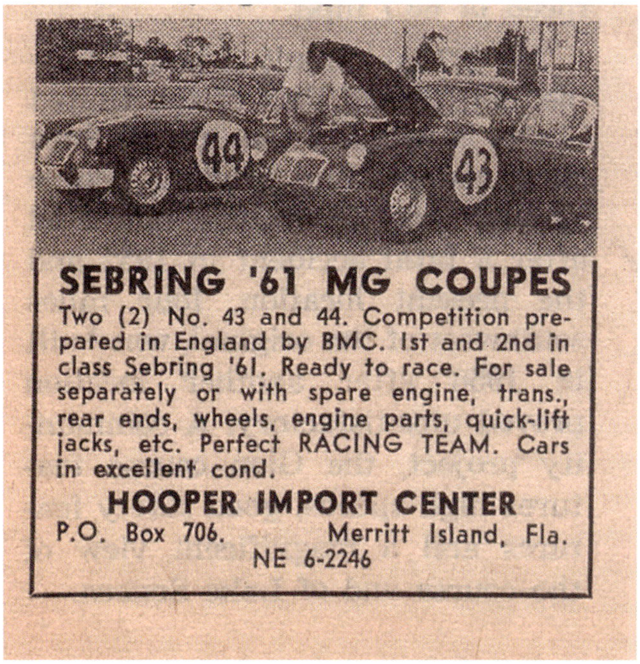
SEBRING '61 MG COUPES
Two (2) No. 43 and 44. Competition prepared in England by BMC. 1st and 2nd in class Sebring '61. Ready to race. For sale separately or with spare engine, trans., rear ends, wheels, engine parts, quick-lift jacks, etc. Perfect RACING TEAM. Cars in excellent cond.
HOOPER IMPORT CENTER
P.O. Box 706. Merritt Island, Fla.
NE 6-2246

A second advertisement, dating from 29 July 1961, for the two Sebring MGAs.
FRANK GRAHAM

Research by Frank Graham shows that after the race, both the MGA 1600 Deluxe-style Coupés were taken to Ship and Shore Motors in West Palm Beach. Ian Prior has a copy of a contemporary advertisement which indicates that the numbers were at least initially retained, along with the marker lights on the roof and wings. Both cars were eventually sold off. 'The no. 44 car was later raced in SCCA events and received a roll-bar and properly mounted seatbelts; no. 43 remained unchanged, indicating that it was never raced again, though it may have been used for rallies,' Graham says; while Ian Prior confirms that no. 44 continued to race, notably at Daytona in 1964 and 1965.

Thankfully both these beautiful cars survive, like several of the other Sebring MGAs, in the hands of dedicated enthusiasts.

THE 1962 SEBRING

By the spring of 1962, the production line planners at Abingdon were preparing to wind down the MGA line and get ready for the first series-build MGB roadsters. However, advertising remained geared to the MGA 1600 Mk II, and even if it was becoming a poorly guarded secret that there

The two 1961 Sebring MGAs united for probably the first time since they left the Hooper Import Center forecourt in early 1962.
IAN PRIOR

Note the distinctive inset circular tail-lamps in both 43 and 44.
IAN PRIOR

The morning of Saturday 24 March 1962, and the countdown to the race in which the MGA is about to run its last 1962 Sebring event.
BOB VITRIKAS

would be no new MGAs in 1963, BMC still had to shift stock, and racing was clearly still a good way to help keep MG at the forefront of sports-car sales. Thus BMC Comps prepared a team of three MGA 1600 Deluxe Coupés, using some of the last of the chassis originally intended for the MGA Twin Cams.

There was a challenge presented by the engine size of the latest production MGA, however: its 1622cc capacity would push it over the 1.6-litre class threshold and into the 2-litre category – throwing the MG into the lions' den against some serious sports-car opposition. Thus it was that although the

THE 1962 SEBRING MGA 1600 DELUXE COUPÉS

Race No.	Chassis No.	Engine No.	UK Reg. No.	Drivers (Home Nation)	Overall Placing	1600cc GT Class	Laps
51	GHN2/106075	Not known	None	Jim Parkinson (USA)/Jack Flaherty (USA)	17th	6th	171
52	GHN2/106073	Not known	None	Jack Sears (UK)/Andrew Hedges (UK)	16th	4th	172
53	GHN2/106074	XSP1860/3	None	Robert ('Bob') Olthoff (RSA)/Sir John Whitmore (UK)/Frank Morrill (USA)	20th	5th	169

Footnotes:
Race date was Saturday 24 March 1962; there were three factory MGA 1600 Deluxe Coupés entered under the name of 'Ecurie Safety Fast'. The front wings were lightweight glass-reinforced plastic, [1/8]in thick. John Wright notes that the 1962 British Racing Green colour was not the same as the 1961 Brooklands Green. Although by this stage the MGA 1600 Mk II was in production with its larger engine and trim changes, the Sebring cars were largely to Mark I specification, with 1588cc engines (9.6:1 compression ratio and 105 horsepower output), allowing them to compete in the under 1600cc class. All three cars actually bear 'GHN2' chassis number prefixes, where the 'N' would ordinarily signify roadsters, whereas Coupés (as these cars were) would be expected to have 'D' in their chassis number prefixes. The removal of alternate grille bars improved airflow into the engine compartment to benefit cooling. The engines were 1622 blocks (with '1622' cast into the side of the block, as would be normal). Note that they were not sleeved 1622 and re-bored to 1588: they were 1588 at first bore. Water passages to the head were never bored in block, only pushrod holes, stud holes and a single oil-feed hole to accept the 'O'-ring. Cylinder-head water holes were plugged with brass, not aluminium.

Car 51: This car uniquely had a white stripe over the centre bonnet, roof and tail. Current owner (2018) is Jim Plowden. As usual, the cars were all sold off after the race to help defray costs; in 1962 it is believed they were sold through 'Bill Ussery Motors' in Miami; the first owner of No. 51 was Bob Bush, who acquired it for $3,500, which included the car and an extra set of wheels and tyres. Plowden tracked down Bush who told him that he raced it in SCCA races *'but because of the fibreglass finders, SCCA forced him into the F Modified Class. He discarded the fibreglass fenders and installed metal fenders which allowed him to race in F Production. Bob raced* until he broke a crankshaft during a race at Osceola, Florida. After this, having a family and other priorities, Bush sold the car, probably to a Jack Howard, who in turn sold it to Emery Vass in 1968. Emery raced the car at Sebring, Daytona, Road Atlanta and other tracks under SCCA, and he would drive the car from West Palm Beach to the race tracks. Plowden recalled: 'My first encounter with no. 51 – or "Lucille", as she was to become known – was in 1979 at a West Palm International SCCA event, and it was love at first sight. I was pitted next to John Kelly, who had just purchased no. 51 from Emery Vass.' For more than thirty years Plowden stayed in touch with John Kelly, wanting to buy no. 51, and finally, just prior to Christmas 2012, Kelly agreed to part with her.

Car 52: This car survives in Virginia, where it is owned by Hugh and Liz Burruss. David Harrison has helped document the story and relates that after the 1962 race, car No. 52 was reputedly bought by a Miami drug dealer. who, as he puts it, *'presumably needed a fast getaway car'* after this person's untimely demise, It was then abandoned for many years before being brought to Virginia in derelict condition and purchased by Burruss. Finally in 2001 the car sat unrestored for years until Hugh was energised in 2001 by the upcoming 50th anniversary of the Sebring race. The car was restored by Bruce Woodson in record time from "British Racing Rust to British Racing Green, and returned to the Sebring track in March 2002 for the 50th Sebring MGA Reunion. Since then, car No. 52 has competed extensively in SVRA races at Watkins Glen and Sebring, and most recently at Laguna Seca, where all three Sebring cars were reunited on the track for the first time since 1962. Car No. 52 is currently on display at the Moss Motors Museum in Petersburg, alongside Michael Eaton's 1959 Twin Cam Sebring Coupé.

Car 53: Uniquely, No. 53 had a white painted nose. According to current owner John Wright, '106074 was a true barn find, having sat undisturbed for forty years in a New Jersey cinder block dirt-floor garage. In October 2004 Wright received a phone call from a friend who had located the car. Although in rough and neglected condition, the car clearly still had many of the original features, such as the distinctive four small round tail-lamps, roof lamp, air-scoop in front of the windscreen and elliptical vents either side of the radiator grille. Most importantly too, the original engine, transmission, brakes and most of its other unique parts were still in situ, making the subsequent restoration all the more rewarding.

Bob Olthoff and John Whitmore stand alongside MGA no. 53 during the 1962 Sebring event. They look calm, so this was probably during practice...
JOHN WRIGHT

MGA 1600 Deluxe Coupé no. 51 (Parkinson/Flaherty) gets attention at Sebring 1962. Note the longitudinal white stripe uniquely on this car.
BOB VITRIKAS

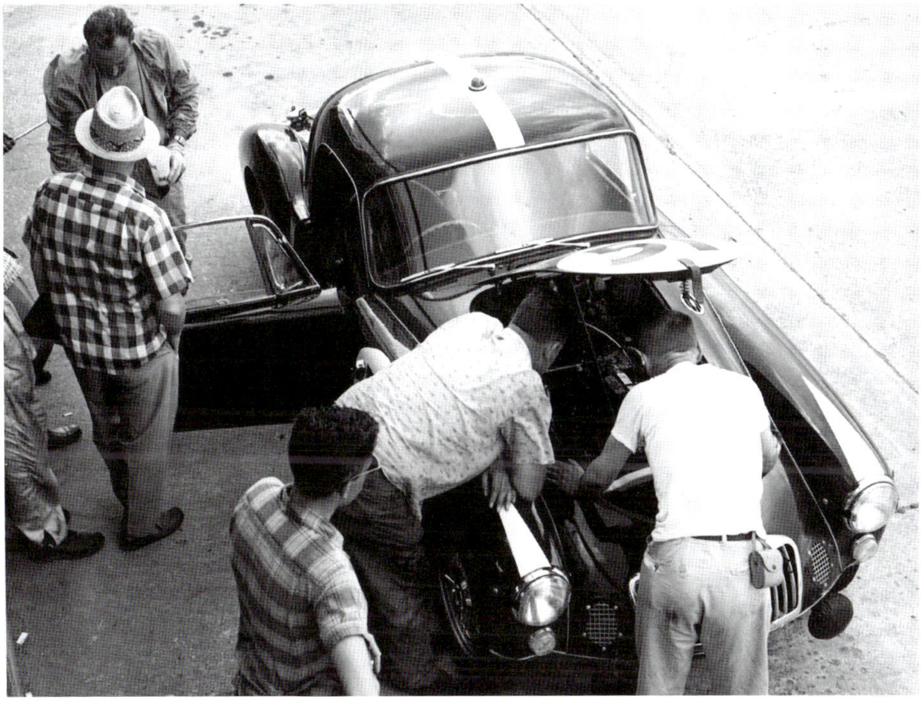

Sebring cars for 1962 were fitted with 1622 blocks (with the numbers '1622' cast into the side of the block as it would for production cars), the capacities were 1,588cc – basically, therefore, they were to the new engine design but to the old capacity, and with aluminium plugs to block the water passage holes.

The cars were built to a clean, bumper-free body specification, with slim front valances, pairs of driving lamps set neatly on fabricated pods on the valance, on the bumper line, whilst at the rear, four small round tail-lamps were set neatly into the trailing edge, rather like the 1961 tail-lights. In addition there was a quick-release fuel filler behind the rear window, and marker lamps in strategic places. The noses were also distinguished by Mark I-style radiator grilles with alternate grille bars removed to the benefit of cooling. Although all three cars were finished in British Racing Green, car no. 53 was uniquely picked out with a white nose, and no. 51 had a nose-to-tail white stripe. Testing in February was at Silverstone as usual, with a wrap-up in time for the cars to be shipped across to Florida.

Car no. 52 (Sears and Hedges) in the pits at Sebring 1962.
BOB VITRIKAS

The MGA team lined up at the pits in the Sebring race of 24 March 1962.

JOHN WRIGHT

Jim Parkinson started the first session in car no. 51, leading his class for the first ten laps, although he had to fall back to avoid overheating problems spoiling his chances of finishing. Even so, the MGAs did better than many in their class. Meanwhile this year Bob Olthoff finally had a stint behind the wheel in No. 53 (he had been a reserve driver in 1961), making up a fairly international Anglo-American-South African crew, whilst Americans piloted no. 51 and Britons Andrew Hedges and 'Gentleman Jack' Sears were in No. 52.

In the race itself, the three cars all ran well and finished fourth, fifth and sixth in their 1600 GT class, but overall they were some way down the field, the best showing (car no. 52, with Sears and Hedges) finishing in sixteenth place overall. Ahead of them in the same class were two factory Porsche 356B Carrera Abarth GTLs, and, gratingly for the BMC men, a Sunbeam Alpine which was third in class. Right at the top, winning the race, was a Ferrari 250 TRI/61, which achieved thirty-five more laps than the leading MG, thereby demonstrating with obvious clarity how it was getting ever harder for a car close to affordable showroom-stock specification to make a real showing at Sebring.

Car no. 52, driven by the British duo of Jack Sears and Andrew Hedges, finished fourth in class – and highest of the three factory MGA 1600 Deluxes, all of which finished.

BOB VITRIKAS

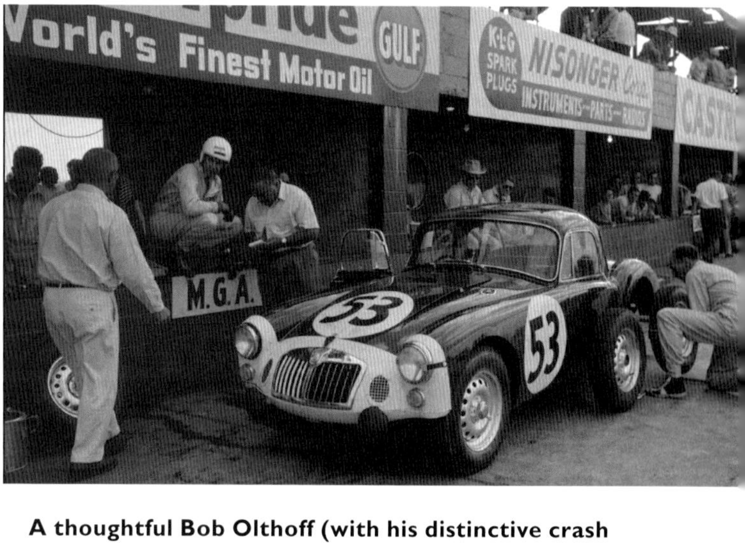

A thoughtful Bob Olthoff (with his distinctive crash helmet) crouches on the pit counter, discussing race times with officials, while Canadian mechanic Des Bradley changes a rear wheel (no. 53), during the 1962 Sebring race.

JOHN WRIGHT

The mechanics tend the Olthoff/Whitmore/Morrill car (no. 53) during the 1962 Sebring race. Note the distinctive (and unique) white-painted nose of this car.
JOHN WRIGHT

Des Bradley on the left and Denis Prophet, two of the BMC Canada mechanics, alongside 1962 Sebring no. 53 in the pits.
JOHN WRIGHT

THE HOMOLOGATION QUESTION

Jack Sears in MGA no. 52 passes underneath the famous Sebring 'Safety Fast' MG bridge during the 1962 race.
DAVE NICHOLAS/BARCBOYS

For cars to be eligible to race in certain classes, they need to be compliant with the specification rules, and in order to comply, they need to be homologated. The requirements generally include certain minimum build numbers – and these often proved tricky to meet and as a result, the precise details sometimes fall into what one might term 'grey areas'. Edward Vandyk has looked into the homologation story of the 1961 and 1962 Sebring MGAs, and believes there are some intriguing unanswered questions:

Some of the bespoke specifications evolved for the 1961 and 1962 Sebring entries may be explained by what appears to be the confused state of the FIA homologations for the MGA at that time. The 1600 Coupé was not homologated until days before the 1962 Sebring race, nine months after production of that model had ceased, which may explain why the three 1962 Deluxe Coupés were given Roadster VIN numbers and why these 1600 Mark II cars were modified to look exactly like the 1600 Coupés entered in 1961. Although MG were never going to be refused entry to Sebring on a scrutineering technicality, quite how the 1961 entries were deemed eligible as Coupés and not Roadsters, seems a challenge, as does the subsequent homologation of the Dunlop disc-brake-all-round option for the 1600 Coupé, as only eleven were built with this option fitted – notwithstanding a letter from the RAC to the FIA confirming a build figure in excess of the required 100...

And so, whilst, as we have seen, the MGA would race a few more times for the factory in Europe, 1962 finally saw the end of the road at Sebring for a car which had begun life on Syd Enever's dining-room table. For 1963, BMC would turn its attention to the MGB, in what would turn out to be a disappointing debut for the MGA's successor – but that is truly a story for another book…

RIGHT: **The engine compartment of John Wright's 1962 Sebring MGA, restored to perfection.**
JOHN WRIGHT

BELOW: **The three 1962 Sebring MGAs were reunited for the first time in fifty-four years at the Laguna Seca racetrack in California in 2016.**
HUGH BURRUSS

Hugh Burruss's 1962 Sebring MGA takes the corkscrew at Laguna Seca in 2016, as driven fifty-four years previously by Jack Sears and Andrew Hedges.
LARRY SMITH

APPENDICES

USEFUL REFERENCES

Press Releases and Magazine Articles

This is not intended to be a definitive list but includes material referenced by the author in the course of research for this book. Some of these documents may occasionally be found either through specialist dealers or via popular on-line auction sites.

In the modern age of the internet, Google and, dare I say it, Wikipedia, there are many resources on the world-wide web. Inevitably they vary greatly in quality, but have the advantages that they can constantly evolve, if well designed can have excellent searchability, and can, in theory, comprise many terabytes of information. Head and shoulders above most of the rest is the 'MGA Guru' web site, owned and maintained by Barney Gaylord. You can find the front page at http://mgaguru.com/and thereafter navigate your way to MGA Nirvana.

For the most avid MGA enthusiasts, once they have exhausted the attractions of the internet, there are many magazines and other books worthy of investigation. It is impossible to be completely comprehensive here, but the following tables are intended to give an overview of some of the more useful reference sources to look out for.

SOME OLDER RETROSPECTIVE ARTICLES

Date	Magazine	Details
4 February 1971	*Autocar*	Article by Geoffrey Howard and Lionel Burrell on the Le Mans MG EX 182 prototypes
May 1974	*Motorsport*	Article 'Looking back with Dick Jacobs'.
January 1975	*Thoroughbred & Classic Cars*	Le Mans MGA: Jonathan Wood recounts its entries at Sarthe in 1959, 1960 and 1961 (SRX 210).
February 1977	*Thoroughbred & Classic Cars*	'The man in charge looks back at the competition history of the prototype MGAs.' Article by Marcus Chambers on MGA competition history.
November 1979	*Collector's Car Magazine*	Two articles: 'Why Top Brass tried to drown the MGA', article on the MGA by Doug Nye; and 'Lust for Dust', article by John Sprinzel on the MGA Twin Cam.
March and April 1982	*Thoroughbred & Classic Cars*	Two-part article by Mike Reed about his Mille Miglia exploits in 1957.
March 1987	*Thoroughbred & Classic Cars*	An article by Wilson McComb about the factory racing MGA Twin Cam ORX 885.
October 1987	*Thoroughbred & Classic Cars*	'Ice Queen' – a profile of Nancy Mitchell by Wilson McComb.
July 1988	*Thoroughbred & Classic Cars*	Thirtieth anniversary report by Wilson McComb, which harks back to the launch of the MG MGA Twin Cam.
June 1989	*Thoroughbred & Classic Cars*	Article on the experimental MGA Coupé, 'KMO 326'.
August 1991	*Classic Cars*	'Works Winner': article by Clive White on Ted Lund's Le Mans MGA Twin Cam SRX 210.

BIBLIOGRAPHY

There are a great many books with varying degrees of relevance to the MGA story; the following list is inevitably incomplete but provides a guide to useful further reading.

Allison, Mike and Browning, Peter *The Works MGs* (Haynes, 2000)
Peter Browning covers the MGA racing exploits in the second half of this book, jointly written with Mike Allison (who covers the pre-war story).

Chambers, Marcus *Works Wonders* (Motor Racing Publications, 1995)
The motor-sports management career of the former BMC Competitions Department Manager; a very personal autobiography with useful vignettes of the people involved in the team.

Jacobs, Dick *An MG Experience* (Transport Bookman Publications, 1976)
Jacobs ran a garage and also a race team, and he also drove at Le Mans; this autobiography tells his story including his own team's efforts.

MG Car Club *Pay it Yourself*
The remarkable story of the Ted Lund MGA SRX 210.

Moylan, Brian *Works Rally Mechanic: Tales of the BMC/BL Works Rally Department 1955–1979* (Veloce, 1998)
A personal recollection of one of the key members of the BMC Competition Team from his own perspective as a Works Mechanic. Brian died in February 2017 and his books are a worthy legacy of his twenty-nine years at Abingdon.

Pressnell, Jon *Morris: The Complete History* (Haynes, 2013)
One of the foremost experts on Morris history, Jon Pressnell's book makes for often sobering reading to understand the atmosphere in which MG had to operate in the early post-war period.

Robson, Graham *The Mighty MGs* (Motor Racing Publications, 1983)
One of the first books to cover the MGA Twin Cam in detail; includes an analysis of production of both the Twin Cam and the Deluxe.

Robson, Graham *MGA, MGB and MGC: A Collector's Guide* (Motor Racing Publications, 1978, 2000)
An excellent enthusiasts' primer on the MGA, MGB and MGC families.

Stone, Henry W. *MG Mania – 'The Insomnia Crew'* – as told to Dick Knudson (New England MG T Register, 1983)
Hard to find yet worth the effort, this slim 120-page soft-back book records the memories of Henry Stone, who was a life-long stalwart of the MG factory's racing and development teams, right through the MGA era.
Thornley, John *Maintaining The Breed – The Saga of MG Racing Cars* (Motor Racing Publications, 1990)
The seminal history of MG's racing and record breaking, up to the MGA with hints at (but not coverage of) the Twin Cam.
Thornley, Peter J. H. *Mister MG* (Magna Press, 2003)
A wonderful biographical tribute to John Thornley by his son Peter.
Ullyett, Kenneth *The MG Companion* (Stanley Paul, 1960, revised 1965)
One of the first comprehensive histories of the MG marque, other than John Thornley's.
Various *MG Twin Cam: The First Fifty Years* (MGCC MGA Twin Cam Group, 2008)
A remarkably thorough 100-page biography of the MGA Twin Cam.
Vitrikas, Robert P. *MGA. A History & Restoration Guide* (Scarborough Faire, 1980 & 1989)
Without question one of the first and the best biographies of the MGA, first published in 1980. Bob Vitrikas contacted many of the players in the MGA saga and has been a great help to the author with this present book.
Whisler, Professor Timothy R. *At the End of the Road: Rise and Fall of Austin-Healey, MG and Triumph Sports Cars* (JAI Press, Elsevier Publications, 1995)
At first sight a dry academic book, which formed part of an academic series, this is nevertheless a fascinating fact-filled journey into the period of British sports-car history, including the MGA.
Wilson McComb, F. *MGA 1500, 1600, Twin Cam* (Osprey, 1983)
A compact book in the Osprey 'AutoHistory' series of the early 1980s; includes a personal viewpoint on the MGA from the doyen of MG historians who also worked as Press Officer at the factory.

In addition to the above, there are the obvious factory publications, driver's handbooks, parts manuals and service manuals. Collectors will also seek out the various contemporary sales brochures, accessory pamphlets and price lists.

Factory project codes – the Cowley 'DO' (Design Order) numbers, the Abingdon EX-Register, and finally the BMC 'ADO' (Austin or Amalgamated Drawing Office) numbers all have a bearing on the MGA story.

The Four Main Chassis Number Series

Car/Chassis Numbers

MGA 1500:	10101–68850
MGA 1600:	68851–100351
MGA 1600 Mark II:	100352–109070
MGA Twin Cam:	501–2611

EXTRACTS FROM THE COWLEY D.O. ('DESIGN ORDER') REGISTER D.O. NUMBERS LINKED TO REPLACEMENT OF THE MGA'S PREDECESSORS

D.O. Number	DESCRIPTION [author's notes in square brackets]	APPROXIMATE DATES
802	MG 1¼-litre Saloon, Midget Sports saloon [referred to in Minutes of Board meeting 11 April 1947]	1947
811	MG 1¼-litre Saloon, Midget Sports saloon	1943
914	1¼-litre MG saloon, 1945 [believed to be the 'MG Ten' which became the post-war YA].	?/1945
920	MG version of Morris Oxford [referred to in Minutes of Board meeting 11 April 1947]	1947
926	MG Midget Major [two-seater sports car based on the Morris Minor; both Coupé and open Tourer versions envisaged]	1946/7
928	MG 1¼-litre Saloon, Midget Sports Tourer [referred to in Minutes of Board meeting 11 April 1947]	1947
963	MG Midget two-seater [with full width body; both open and coupé versions considered. One of a family of three Riley-engined proposals]	6/1948
965	MG 1½-litre saloon [styling related to DO 963]	6/1948
967	MG 1½-litre convertible [styling related to DO 965]	10/1948
968	MG TD Midget seater [based upon YA chassis and suspension]	1949
986	1¼ litre MG YB saloon	1950
998	1¼-litre MG YB saloon	1950
999	2½-litre saloon [Riley Pathfinder]	1951
1008	1¼-litre racing programme [cross-refer EX Register, EX 173]	1951
1009	2-litre racing programme [cross-refer EX Register, EX 174]	1951
1010	New Magnette [ZA]	1951/2
1017	Aluminium panels for MG TD Midget	–
1035	New Midget (small) with AS.3 engine [AS.3 was the Austin A30 saloon, launched in October 1951. This shows that Cowley gave some thought to using this engine for a true small sports car, as did Austin and, later, BMC]	–
1041	MG TD Midget with Austin engine [probably the 50bhp twin-SU Austin A40 Sports engine, precursor to the B series which first appeared in the production ZA Magnette]	–
1042	MG Midget with 1½-litre Riley engine	–
1047	MG TF Midget modified front [*see also* EX Register, EX 177]	1953
1048	MG Magna – streamlined	–
1049	New MG Midget for 1954	1953
1060	MG TF Midget with larger capacity engine [i.e. TF 1500, involving change from 1266cc XPAG to 1466cc XPEG. Also in EX Register against EX 176]	1954
1062	New MG Midget [note annotated: 'MGA'. First MG factory entries dated 3 June 1954]	1954–66

EXTRACTS FROM THE MG 'EX' REGISTER

EX Number	DESCRIPTION [author's notes in square brackets]	APPROXIMATE DATES
171	TD Midget converted to road-racing specification (Dick Jacobs) [forty-four drawings]	25 September 1950
172	TD Midget for Le Mans with streamlined body. Chassis number TD/C.5336 [sixteen drawings; this is the famous UMG 400, with the Syd Enever-designed body which ultimately inspired the MGA. The body was very similar to the MGA, and the styling was adapted for a road-going prototype – EX 175 (*see* below)]	5 January 1951
173	TD engines for Record Car - Job No. ZM.13366; Cowley DO 1008	January 1951
174	DO 1009 2-litre converted Wolseley 6/80 engine for Record Car	February 1951
175	1500cc streamlined Midget two-seater [forty-four drawings; drawing EX 175/1 is car outline; this is the second stage in the evolutionary process, which led to the MGA. EX 175/1 – registered HMO 6 – was the car shown to Leonard Lord but rejected by him in favour of the Healey 100]	[February 1952]
177	TF Midget [twenty-seven drawings, not all dated in the register; EX 177/15 is dated as 7 May 1953]	May 1953
178	Austin 1500 engine tuning [sixty-eight drawings. This was clearly involvement of MG with the Austin-designed 'B' series, which appeared in the ZA Magnette and later in the MGA. Race car engine numbers also feature in the EX 178 sequence. Not all entries in the register are dated – but drawing EX 178/63 is dated 21/3/1957, and drawings EX 178/67 and 68 refer to 1622cc version of engine, and are dated 2 March 1961]	1953–1961
179	Record car for 1954 (job no. ZM.18757) [115 entries for this famous record breaker. Only drawings EX 179/70 onwards are dated; 13 April 1956 for EX 179/70 up to 9 January 1959 for EX 179/115]	1953–1959
181	Record car (special) [the famous record breaker driven by Phil Hill and Stirling Moss, and known to the media as the 'Roaring Raindrop'. Most of the 276 drawings date from 1957 to 1960, but there are later entries from no. EX 181/273 onwards].	1957–1978
182	Special parts for Series M.G.A. [note stops in MGA] for Le Mans 1955 [sixty-eight drawings detailing parts such as oil cooler, tanks and mountings, brakes etc. Nos EX 182/38, 39, 40 and 41 are listed as 'chassis numbers for Le Mans cars nos. 1, 2, 3 and 4' respectively. Engine numbers for the Le Mans cars were similarly given numbers EX 182/42–45 inclusive. The last two drawings are dated 15 March 1960]	1955–1960
183	Experimental 1956 Le Mans car (tubular chassis) [twenty-seven drawings]	–
186	Twin overhead-camshaft 'Le Mans' type 1956 with MGA-type chassis [202 drawings detailing 4½ J [x] 15-alloy disc wheels, suspension, chassis reinforcements etc. Last entry dated 3 September 1959]	? –1959
187	Twin overhead-camshaft version of MGA with disc brakes [318 drawings; 2 June 1955 to 26 November 1962]	1955–1962
188	New Midget with [Austin] A30 [A-series] engine – MGD [no previous mention of MGB or MGC in register! No drawings or anything else listed, but this may have been related to Cowley's DO 1035]	n/a
189	Four-seater version of MGA – MGE [like EX 188, nothing listed in register]	n/a
191	Development work on production MGA [450 drawings; dated from 19 May 1955 to 7 February 1961. Cross-refer ADO 31 in 'ADO' list]	1955–1961
194	MGA police modifications [C-type engine dynamo and larger batteries. Seventeen drawings]	–
195	MGA 'cheap version' [seventy-two drawings, dated from 11 October 1955 to 31 August 1959, detailing ideas for a lower cost MGA with Austin A30 steering box, 13in or 14in wheels, single 1¾in SU carburettor, Morris Minor propshaft etc.]	1955–1959
196	MGA hardtop [single entry EX 196/1 dated 7 February 1956 'MGA hardtop']	7 February 1956
197	Fixed-head coupé MGA: 'All prototype and production part numbers issued by Bodies Branch, Coventry, for new panels, glasses, trim and hardware' [no entries in register]	n/a
205	MG Two-Seater (ADO 23), eleven drawings [all described as having been 'transferred into ADO 23 book'; from June 1957 to February 1958. Includes drawing of Frua-bodied MGA]	1957–1958
212	Fixed-head coupé MGA Twin Cam [no entries in register, but this is the Don Hayter-schemed coupé built on the basis of Ted Lund's MGA twin-cam roadster SRX 210, for Ted to race at Le Mans]	[undated]
214	Replacement for MGA – body facelift, wings etc. [twelve drawings detailing the first thoughts for what became the ADO 23 MGB. Drawing EX 214/1 is for ¼-scale body lines, dated 9 June 1958; EX 214/12 is for ¼-scale body lines with wide radiator grille – i.e. the prototype MGB with coil-sprung rear suspension, dated 1 May 1959]	1958–1959
216	V4 power unit in MGA [thirteen drawings detailing modifications to front cross member and other installation requirements. The V4 engine was one of a proposed new family of Longbridge-designed BMC units which was eventually abandoned because of cost and balancing problems. Its demise was not a disappointment to Abingdon. Drawings dated 16 September 1958 to 3 December 1958]	late 1958

EXTRACTS FROM THE 'ADO' CODE NUMBERS

ADO Number	DESCRIPTION [author's notes in square brackets]	APPROXIMATE DATES
ADO 23	MG MGB [*see also* EX-Register. Launched 1962]	1958–78
ADO 31	MG MGA 1600	1959–61

GRAND TOTAL MGA PRODUCTION

Year	1500	1600	Twin Cam	1600 Mark II	Total by year
1955	1,003				1,003
1956	13,410				13,410
1957	20,571				20,571
1958	16,122	541			16,663
1959	7,644	1,519	14,156		23,319
1960		51	16,930		16,981
1961			415	5,670	6,085
1962				3,049	3,049
Total	*58,750*	*2,111*	*31,501*	*8,719*	***101,081***

INDEX

1 MTW 6, 276, 278
100 Octane petrol 156, 168
100,000th MG (of any kind) 90
100,000th MGA (GHNL2-107989) 7, 10, 12, 67, 90, 172, 173, 174, 291
10106 – see HDC43-10106
151 ABL 6, 162, 291, 292, 293, 294, 295
2 MTW 6, 276, 278
2.2-litre engine for MGA 205, 206
301 LBL (replica of LBL 301) 251
4 UML 166
50,000th sports car built in one year at Abingdon 158
596 KTB 205
777 ENK 131
899 CFC 154
908 AWL 107

A90 Austin engine 49
AA – see Automobile Association
AAA (American Automobile Association) 227
Aaltonen, Rauno 184, 293, 294, 295
Abingdon Angels 213
AC 253, 277, 318
Ace Mercury wheel-discs 167
ACO Le Mans 42, 216, 284, 290
Acropolis Rally (1959) 273, 274
Adams, Bruce 195
Adderley Park East Works 83
ADO 10R Riley saloon proposal 147
ADO 10W Wolseley 6/99 147
ADO 13 Austin-Healey Sprite 207
ADO 15 Mini 127, 166, 168
ADO 16 (BMC 1100/1300) 204
ADO 17 (BMC 1800) 168, 204
ADO 23 (MGB) 10, 202, 207, 211
ADO 31 MGA 1600 150, 160, 161, 204
ADO 41 Austin-Healey Sprite Mark II – see Austin-Healey Sprite Mark II
ADO 47 MG Midget – see MG Midget 1961–79
ADO 52 MG MGC 207
ADO 9 Farina Magnette 63, 147
Air France 155
Albemarle Aircraft – nose-cone contract 25
Alfa Romeo 1900 (of 1950) 114, 115
Alfa Romeo cars in general 50, 113, 114, 115, 118, 240, 241, 318
Allard 247, 256
Allen, Fred 9, 298, 299
Allison, Michael 6, 231
Alpine Rally 1955 (cancelled event) 227, 229, 230, 234, 248
Alpine Rally 1956 9, 103, 248, 249, 250
Alpine Rally 1957 (cancelled event) 267
Alpine Rally 1958 268
Alpine Rally 1959 273, 274
Alvis cars 27
Ambrose, Tony 293
American Motors (Rambler) 194
AMOCO Fuel 297, 299, 314
Anderson, Mick 6
Andrews, Bill 116, 118
Anglesey 231
Anglo-French Trade Agreement 74
Antill, Pat 237
Antrodoco Pass (Italy) 260, 261
Appendix J FIA Class 153
Appleby, Bill 116, 124, 127, 229, 233
Appleyards of Leeds 220
Ardegar hoists 84
Ards Circuit 231
Armstrong-Siddeley 68
Armstrong-Whitworth 37, 46, 120, 214
Arnage (Le Mans) 225, 226
Arnolt 32, 34, 35, 296, 318, 322
Arnolt, Stanley Harold II ('Wacky') 35
Arnott race car (at 1955 Le Mans) 221
A-Series engine – see BMC A-Series
Ash, Anese 301
Ash, David 9, 57, 131, 296, 298, 299, 300, 301, 302, 303, 306, 308
Aslett, Brian 6
Aston-Martin cars in general 124, 220, 222, 254, 303
Aston-Martin DB2 38, 256
Aston-Martin DB2/4 (as inspiration for MGA Coupé) 101
Aston-Martin DB3 256
Aston-Martin DB3S 277
Aston-Martin DB4 208
Attlee, Clement 28
Austin A30 124, 204, 207
Austin A40 Cambridge 53
Austin A40 Devon 29, 31, 49, 59
Austin A40 Dorset 49
Austin A40 Farina 200, 291
Austin A40 Sports 49
Austin A50 Cambridge 53, 227, 228
Austin A50 Van 313
Austin A55 Cambridge 53, 167
Austin A55 Utility (Australian pick-up) 186
Austin A60 Cambridge 167
Austin A70 (Hampshire and Hereford) 206, 262, 263
Austin A90 Atlantic 23, 49
Austin A90 Westminster 77, 116, 145, 147, 214, 227, 228
Austin A99 Westminster (ADO 10, Farina) 147
Austin and Nuffield merger – see Nuffield and Austin
Austin Apprentices 6
Austin Cambridge (in general) 65
Austin cars in general 181, 185, 186, 214, 215, 273, 313
Austin Commercial Vehicles 181
Austin Engines (Longbridge) 53, 116, 118, 119, 122, 124, 144, 206, 216, 231, 233
Austin exports 30
Austin four-litre engine 49
Austin Gipsy 206
Austin Maestro (LC10) 63
Austin Metro (LC8) 63
Austin Metropolitan – see Nash
Austin Mini Cooper – see Mini Cooper
Austin Motor Company 20, 21, 23, 28, 29, 30, 31, 32, 45, 48, 49, 52, 53, 59, 61, 119, 181, 184, 186, 204, 215
Austin Public Relations Officer 45
Austin Se7en (Mini ADO 15) 134, 164, 200, 215
Austin Seven (Austin 7) 22, 116, 204
Austin twin-cam engines 118, 119, 144, 233
Austin wind tunnel at Longbridge 64
Austin, Herbert (Lord) – see Lord Austin
Austin-Healey 100/4 47, 49, 55, 67, 74, 75, 94, 285
Austin-Healey 100/6 116, 146, 147, 258, 268, 272, 300, 303, 307
Austin-Healey 100M 297
Austin-Healey 100S 224, 297, 304, 307
Austin-Healey 30, 47, 48–9
Austin-Healey 3000 147, 155, 159, 160, 215, 223, 272, 314
Austin-Healey cars in general 47, 49, 84, 86, 90, 92, 94, 120, 124, 147, 155, 159, 181, 184, 214, 215, 224, 235, 236, 268, 273, 274, 276, 291, 293, 297, 300, 302, 305, 308, 311, 313, 318
Austin-Healey Sprite (ADO 13) 57, 62, 84, 85, 95, 159, 204, 207, 268, 310, 311, 313, 314, 320, 321
Austin-Healey Sprite Mark II (ADO 41) 167
Austin-Healey transfer to Abingdon in 1957 47, 49, 120
Australian CKD MGA assembly 186–193
Austrian Air Force 269
Austrian Grand Prix 269
Austrian Tyrol 270
Autocar Magazine 28, 58, 78, 79, 88, 110, 121, 131, 135, 137, 139, 140, 143, 149, 156, 168, 229, 230, 245, 251
Automobile Association (AA) 262
Automobile Club de France 77
Automobile Club de L'Ouest – see ACO
Automobile Quarterly 46, 320
Automotive News Magazine 32
Automóviles Ingleses SA 181, 184, 185
Autosport Magazine 42, 43, 78, 80, 99, 111, 128, 130, 155, 213, 235, 239, 241, 253, 254
Autosport Race Championship 241, 246, 247, 248, 252, 276, 278, 279
Auto-Union 74
Avenell, Reg 43
Avon Park (Sebring) 311, 313, 314

B. J. Henry Ltd 97
Babbitt (engine bearing alloy) 114
Baggio, Lino 6, 306, 307
Baily, Claude 115
Baird, Gil 278
Ball, Fred 321
BARC events 277
Barcelona, 1959 Motor Show 138
Bareham, Eric 53, 119
Barker, Robin 6, 85, 140, 297, 310, 311, 313, 317
Barker, Vernon 6
Barrett, John 6, 163, 164
Barron, Geoff 6
Barwell Engineering Ltd 276, 277
Bary, Cliff 56
Baxter, Fred 176
Beauman, Don 225
Bedford (commercial vehicles) 53
Beech, George 38
Belcher Beeks, Sylvia 314
Belfast Airport 233
Belgian roads 80, 135
Bell X1 Aircraft 300
BEMC (British Empire Motor Club) 304
Bensted-Smith, Richard 252, 273, 274
Bentley cars in general 15, 31, 43, 220, 321
Bertone 34, 35
Bertone, Giovanni 35
Bertone, Giuseppe 35
Bertone, Nuccio 35
Best, Ken 250
Bettles, Ron 218
Beverley National Sports Car National Race (4 July 1955) 296
Biennial Cup at Le Mans – see Le Mans
Big Healey – see Austin-Healey
Bignor Park 243, 267
Bill Ussery Motors 324
Binnington, Tim 278
Birmingham University 14
Birt family 6
Birt, Ted 297
Birt, Tony 94, 297, 311
Bishop, Reginald Arthur 45, 214
Black Forest 251
Black Mamba – MGA Twin Cam Coupé 131, 195, 197
Black, Duncan 308
Black, Sir John 55
Blackman, Ann 301
Blackman, Sidney 298, 301, 303, 308
Blaksley, John 6, 254, 255, 256, 258, 259, 261, 264, 265, 267
Blaksley, Mary 6, 254, 255, 256
Blaksley, Richard 6, 255
Bleustein-Blanchet, Marcel 75
BLMC ('British Leyland') 6, 30, 31, 59, 68, 117, 127, 181, 184, 300
Bloody Mary – hillclimb car 128
Bloxham, Jean 263, 265
Bloxham, Roy 213, 276, 278
BMC (British Motor Corporation) 6, 7, 9, 19, 20, 21, 28, 30, 31, 40, 45, 47, 50, 51, 53, 55, 59, 60, 64, 72, 73, 76, 83, 92, 94, 95, 105, 109, 111, 115, 116, 117, 118, 126, 127, 130, 140, 142, 147, 151, 152, 154, 155, 158, 159, 160, 169, 173, 181, 185, 197, 203, 204, 207, 210, 211, 213, 214, 225, 227, 233, 236, 240, 251, 258, 280, 283, 284, 285, 291, 297, 304, 307, 308
BMC (USA) Ltd 31
BMC A-Series engine 53, 57, 117, 119, 203
BMC Australia 186, 187
BMC B-Series engine 8, 9, 10, 49, 50, 53, 54, 55, 68, 113, 114, 115, 116, 118, 119, 122, 165, 166, 168, 188, 203, 216, 217, 232, 233, 280
BMC Canada 7, 32, 82, 153, 297, 301, 304, 305, 308, 309, 310, 311, 313, 327
BMC Central Publicity 214
BMC Chairman 47, 49
BMC Chief Designer, Engines and Gearboxes 116
BMC Competitions Committee 214, 236, 284
BMC Competitions Department Transporter ('Camion' LBL 405) 220, 249, 251, 254, 255, 292
BMC Competitions Department – see also 'Comps' and 'MG Competitions Department' 7, 213, 214, 215, 222, 223, 228, 236, 248, 263, 267, 268, 272, 273, 291, 293, 295, 307, 311, 313, 314, 324
BMC C-Series engine 77, 116, 147
BMC C-Series Twin Cam concept 147, 214
BMC Demonstration Day (14 July, 1958) 126, 128, 129–130, 132, 141
BMC Directorships 27, 32, 45, 51, 59, 60, 66, 99, 127
BMC Experimental Vehicle – see MG EX179
BMC Joint Board 50, 51, 53, 54, 99, 146, 258
BMC merger – see Nuffield and Austin merger
BMC Production Director 145
BMC Publicity Department 125
BMC Rosette (badge) 315
BMC Service Department 150, 167
BMC South Africa 198
BMC Strike of 1956 92, 93
BMC Sweden 265
BMC Tractor and Transmissions Branch 83
BMC/Hambro (see also Hambro Automotive) 31, 80, 81, 82, 88, 93, 95, 107, 157, 161, 174, 175, 181, 296, 300, 309, 311, 313, 314
BMCD – British Motor Car Distributors of San Francisco (see also Qvale) 58, 82, 157, 281
BMH – see British Motor Holdings
BMIHT 7, 50
BMW 5-Series 93
BOAC (Airline) 15
Boddy, Bill 128
Boden, Oliver 15
body numbers 84, 85, 154, 164
Boeing B-17 Flying Fortress 296
Bolster, John 111, 112, 128, 130
Bonhams 6
Bonneville Salt Flats 57, 108, 122, 140, 300
Boobier, Ernie 158
Booth Poole & Co Ltd 7, 141, 148, 181, 182, 183, 184
Booth, Lionel 181
Booy, Rutger 6, 198, 199
Bouwmeester, Ad 200, 273
Bownes, Tommy 126
BP (British Petroleum) 88
Brack, Bill 308
Bradley, Des 326, 327
Bradstock, Mike 126, 127
Bramley, J. F. (BMC Director of Export sales) 92
Brands Hatch 105, 247, 279
Bray, Cliff 128, 204, 217, 219, 220, 221, 222, 269, 270, 283
BRDC (British Racing Drivers' Club) 254
Brenner Pass (Italy) 251
Breslauer, Ken 6
Brewster (coachbuilders) 302
Briault, Paul 277
Bridger, Tommy 213, 272, 276, 278
Bristol Freighter (aircraft) 91
Britannic Airways 311
British Leyland Motor Corporation – see BL & BLMC
British media 236
British Motor Car Distributors – see BMCD
British Motor Corporation – see BMC
British Motor Corporation/Hambro Inc. – see BMC/Hambro
British Motor Heritage Ltd 184
British Motor Holdings (BMH) 59, 60
British Motor Industry Heritage Trust – see BMIHT
British Motor Museum (Gaydon) 46, 138, 150, 210
British Motors Building (San Francisco) 281
British Motors Limited 45
British Rail Western Region 21
Brittains Ltd (Brittains Group) 181, 182, 184
Broad, Phil 158
Brocklehurst, Roy 45, 46, 51, 61, 63, 68, 115, 120, 122, 203, 211
Brolén, Pehr 265
Bromsgrove 14
Brookes, Ray 249, 250, 251, 271, 272, 273, 274
Brooklands, race circuit 25, 114, 117
Brown, Alison 6
Browning, Peter 231, 240
B-Series engine – see BMC B-Series engine
Buckle, Phyllis 6, 7, 37
Bugatti Blue paint finish 152
build cards 84
Burgess, Gerry 252
Burrell, George 76
Burruss, Hugh and Liz 6, 324, 328
Burt, Patsy 263, 264, 265
Busch, Helmut 265
Bush, Bob 324
Butler, Donald 62–3, 65, 67, 68, 101, 102
Butler, Robert 236
buzz-box (small sports car) 204

Cadillac 52, 243
Cairn Terrier 105
Cannonball Run race 304
Capiello, Cappy 296
Carlisle, Christabel 162
Carlsson, Erik 215, 293
Carnegie, Jean Margaret 264
Carnegie, Robin 6, 235, 240, 241, 242, 243, 244, 245, 246, 247, 248, 252, 253, 254, 255, 256, 257, 258, 259, 260, 261, 262, 263, 264, 265, 266, 267, 274, 275, 276
Carrozzeria Pietro Frua – see Frua
Carter brothers (of MG factory) 167
Carter, Eric 46, 62, 66, 67, 68, 101, 102, 124
Carter, Len 176
Castagneto, Renzo 259
Castrol Oil 56, 88, 212, 214, 225
Chamberlain, Neville 59
Chambers, Marcus 17, 77, 145, 214, 215, 218, 219, 220, 221, 222, 225, 226, 227, 229, 233, 234, 239, 241, 249, 250, 254, 257, 267, 272, 273, 297, 307, 308, 309, 311
Chambers, Patricia (Mrs) 220, 221, 226
Champion spark plugs 141, 142, 143, 270
Championnat D'Europe de la Montagne 270
Chapman family 6
Chapman, Colin 278
Charles Hayward & Sons 220
Charles, H. N. (Hubert Noel) 25
Chassis frames – welding of 66, 83
Chassis Numbers 84, 85, 98, 148, 177, 183 (Irish MGA Twin Cams, table), 185 (MGA Twin cams in Mexico, table), 188–190 (Australia CKD), 195–8 (South African CKD), 199–200 (Dutch CKD)
Château Chêne de Cœur 220, 221
Chevrolet cars in general 318
Chevrolet Corvette 304, 321
Chief Designer, MG and Riley Cars – see Harry Rush and Gerald Palmer
Chief Engineer of Morris Motors 28
Chief Inspector, MG 100
Christian, Linda 260
Christy, John 79
Chrysler Corporation 32, 45, 186, 193
Churchill, Sir Winston 28
Citroën cars in general 304
Citroën DS19 9, 74
Citroën ID19 82
CKD MGA Assembly 7, 68, 85, 95, 98, 141, 168, Chapter Eight
Clarence Tally Auto Company 32
Clarendon Yard (Oxford) 16, 25
Clark, K. R. 107
Clarke, Jeff 282
Classic & Sportscar magazine 144
Classic Car Africa magazine 321
Clausager, Anders Ditlev 103
Clifton Hampden 97
Clipper cars 303
Coates, Len 304
Col d'Allos 251
Col de Avaris 250
Col de L'Iseran 228, 229
Col de la Croix-de-Fer 249, 250
Col de Lauteret 252
Col de Montgenèvre 249
Col de Turini 294
Col de Vars 251
Col du Galibier 228
Colden Common (Winchester) 16
Coleman, Trevor 195
Collectors' Car Magazine 43
Collier Brothers of New York (Motor Sport Inc.) 21
Colonial Development Corporation 15
Colron Wood dye tin 287
Commercial Motors (Manila) 181, 185, 186
Communist Eastern Europe 74
Competitions Committee of MG and Riley 214
Completely Knocked Down – see CKD
Comps (BMC Competitions Department) 7
Compton, Mike 195
Comtesse de Vautibault 220
Connaught racing cars 254
continental Europe – see Europe
Converting an MGA Twin Cam to a 1600 150
Cook, Richard 237
Cooper, Charles 40
Cooper, John 40
Cooper-Climax 264
Copse Corner (Silverstone) 106
Cordin, Mr. 47
Cortaulds 59
Cosmides, Pete 6
Cosmoline 95
Cottingham, James 6
Cotton, Billy 17
Coulthard, Tom 6
Coupes des Alpes 248, 250, 251
Coupes des Dames 248, 250
Cousins, Cecil 14, 15, 16, 20, 21, 24, 25, 26, 33, 47, 90, 100, 127, 143, 158
Coventry Climax 68, 221
Coventry Ordnance 59
Cowley Experimental Shop 46
Cowley factory (within Oxford suburb, home of Morris Motors) 8, 9, 13, 15, 17, 18, 19, 20, 21, 22, 23, 24, 25, 26, 27, 28, 29, 30, 32, 33, 36, 38, 40, 42, 45, 46, 48, 49, 50, 51, 52, 59, 60, 61, 62, 63, 66, 67, 68, 69, 71, 83, 85, 88, 92, 95, 99, 113, 116, 126, 127, 134, 165, 179, 180, 181, 184, 186, 187, 188, 190, 214
Cowley T-Block 180
Cox, Jim 6, 47, 53, 143, 145, 216, 217, 219, 220, 221, 222, 223, 224, 231, 233, 236, 286
Coyne, Pat 6
Cragg, Jacqueline 243
Cribbins, Bernard 178
Croft-Pearson, Sam 252
Cron, Bob 298, 301
Crooke, Jack 43, 222
Crossley, Fred 220, 225
Cuban MGA 7, 180
Cuff-Miller, Ellis 256, 264, 265
Cummings, Worthy 281
Cuomo, Ray 307
Customer Supply Order (CSO) Numbers 85

Dahl, Hank 298, 303
Daily Express newspaper 276
Daily Herald newspaper 252
Daily Telegraph newspaper 155

Daimler cars 68
Daimler-Benz (Mercedes) 74
Dale, Michael 6, 181
Dalton, Jack 131, 312
Damerell, Lady Mary Barbara (sister of Robin Carnegie) 6, 245, 246, 247
Dana (limited slip differentials) 317, 319
Dangerfield, Neil 236
Daniel Schmidt & Co. 6
Daniell, Roger 6, 276, 278
Dashwood, John 276
Dauphiné Alps 228
Davis, Pedr 6, 192
Davis, Sammy (racing driver) 214, 220, 223
Daytona race circuit 317, 321, 323, 324
De Dion rear axle and suspension 61, 211, 280, 281, 282, 284
De Goudse (Dutch insurers) 200
De Luxe MGA – see MG MGA Deluxe
De Selincourt, Bill 276
Début by Demonstration – see BMC Demonstration Day
Decker, Sherman 'Sherm' 312, 313
Deer's Leap (Dundrod) 232
DeMiere, Andreea
Denis Ferranti Ltd 102, 103
Dennis Commercial Vehicles 182
Deroy - Gerald Palmer's unique sports car prototype 27, 50
Design Order Numbers ('DO Numbers') 8, 23
DeSoto cars 193
Detroit Motor Show, 1958 138
Development Department at MG – see MG Car Company Development Department
Dickson, Bobbie 224
Dierkes, Stefan 6
Dixon, David 252, 290
Dixon, Steve 6, 244, 270, 287, 288
DK Engineering 6, 316, 317
DO 1010 (see *also* MG Z Magnette) 8, 38, 51, 54, 55, 62
DO 1017 'Aluminium panels for MG TD Midget' 38
DO 1041 'MG TD Midget with Austin engine' 54
DO 1042 'MG Midget with 1½ litre Riley engine' 54
DO 1047 MG Midget facelift, 1953 50
DO 1048 ('Magna' – 'modern-style' body – see *also* Palmer's MG Midget) 50, 51, 65
DO 1049 ('New Midget for 1954' - 'traditional style' body – see *also* Gerald Palmer and Palmer's MG Midget) 8, 50, 51, 65
DO 1060 (see *also* MG TF, MG TF 1500 and MG EX177) 52, 58
DO 1062 (see *also* MG MGA) 8, 46, 54, 62, 63, 64, 65, 67, 68, 118, 119, 203, 207, 214, 216
DO 1067 (twin-cam six-cylinder Riley project) 147
DO 802 22
DO 811 (MG 1¼ Litre) 18
DO 926 – see MG Midget Major
DO 928 MG YT Prototype 33
DO 963 MG Midget Roadster concept ca 1948 25, 26, 36
DO 965 MG 1½ litre saloon concept ca 1948 25, 26, 36
DO 967 MG 1½ litre convertible cabriolet concept ca 1948 25, 26, 36
DO 968 MG TD prototype 33
DO 999 Riley Pathfinder 44, 61
Dobson, Arthur 17
Dodge cars 193
Doherty Motor Components 15
Dolan, Patrick 31
Dolcini, Carlo 260
dollar – see US Dollar
Dominion Motors (New Zealand) 181, 201
Donald Healey Motor Company Ltd (see *also* under Healey and Austin-Healey) 214, 321
Donington Race Circuit 231
Dono, George 28, 51, 65
Donoghue, Dan 306
Douchet, Philippe 6
Dover (UK port) 219, 220, 245, 247
Dron, Tony 235
Drury, Dennis 46, 54
Dugdale, John 58
Dún Laoghaire Corporation 182
Dundrod Race Circuit and TT Races 6, 43, 119, 230, 231, 232, 233, 234, 236, 238, 262, 268, 284, 286, 287, 297
Dunlop Bridge (at Le Mans) 224
Dunlop disc brakes 123, 128, 130, 134, 137, 139, 140, 150, 153, 154, 155, 158, 160, 161, 162, 167, 204, 214, 257, 280, 283, 284, 327
Dunlop Roadspeed Tyres 160, 161, 162, 167
Dunlop Tyres 83, 160, 187
Dunlop Wheels 83, 114, 122, 180, 319
Dunlopillo 88
Durban Body Number 195
Durham, Thomas 6
Dutch MGA launch brochure 90
Dutch MGA Register 201
Dutch MGA sales & assembly 198–201
Dutton, George 6
Dvoretsky, Harold 130
Dzus fasteners 216, 284

Eagle Comic 63
Earls Court Motor Show 1948 26, 29, 34, 45, 75
Earls Court Motor Show 1949 33
Earls Court Motor Show 1951 8
Earls Court Motor Show 1952 48, 49
Earls Court Motor Show 1953 8, 55
Earls Court Motor Show 1954 116
Earls Court Motor Show 1955 9, 69, 70, 73, 75, 76, 88
Earls Court Motor Show 1956 9, 92, 104, 107, 147
Earls Court Motor Show 1958 137, 138
Earls Court Motor Show 1959 138
Earls Court Motor Show 1961 166, 168
Eastbourne Rally (1947) 236
Eaton, Michael 6, 298, 306, 307, 312, 324
Eber, Herr 72
Ebert, Mr. (of Missouri, USA) 21
economy, the 28
Ecurie Chiltern 290
Ecurie Oppidans 254, 255, 257, 267
Ecurie Pip 317
Ecurie Safety Fast 324
Edwards, Derek 6
Edwards, Derrick 254, 255, 258, 259, 262, 264, 267
Ehlers, Bob 109
Ehrlich, Joe 124
Ehrman, Gus 6, 9, 151, 169, 203, 296, 297, 298, 299, 300, 301, 302, 303, 306, 307, 308, 309, 311, 312
Eke, Graham and Jill 6, 53, 77
Elizabeth, H.M. Queen 243
Ellaway, Bert 83
Ellery, Joan 243
Elliott, Ian 6
Ellman-Brown, Michael 6, 9, 10, 146, 147, 148, 198
Elmhorn, Bo 264, 265
Elva cars 247, 276
EMC Motorcycles 124
empire markets (Australia & South Africa) 29
Enever sisters 16
Enever, Ivy 16
Enever, Jane 105
Enever, Maud 16
Enever, Roger 6, 11, 69, 105, 106, 107, 182, 281
Enever, Susan 41
Enever, Syd 11, 12, 15, 16, 18, 19, 20, 33, 36, 37, 38, 40, 41, 42, 43, 44, 46, 47, 49, 51, 52, 56, 58, 59, 60, 61, 62, 63, 64, 66, 67, 80, 101, 105, 106, 107, 114, 115, 118, 120, 122, 124, 125, 126, 128, 138, 158, 175, 182, 184, 202, 203, 205, 206, 207, 208, 209, 210, 216, 217, 219, 220, 222, 223, 227, 228, 233, 236, 280, 281, 283, 285, 287, 319, 328
Engine Numbers – MGA Twin Cam 149
engineering Coordinator, BMC 40
Enjoying MG Magazine (MG Owners' Club) 58
Ensign Motors of Toronto 82
Epstein, Jacob 166
Escott, Colin 285, 288, 290, 308, 315, 316, 317
Estaglass Ltd 102
Europe (and European markets) 42, 52, 73, 101, 110, 113, 142, 159, 199, 200, 212, 215, 328
European Hillclimb Championship (1958) 269, 270
European Union (EEC) 200
Everard, Tony 253, 255, 256
Evershed & Vignoles 124
Ewing, Norman 6
EX Codes – see MG EX
EXP 926 – see MG Midget Major DO 926
expansion at Abingdon 94
export drive (post-war) 13, 28, 59, 75
Export or Die 26, 28
Eyston, Captain George 17, 18, 56, 58, 88, 120, 214, 218, 219, 220
Eyston's Dancing Daughters 219

F.L.M. Panelcraft Ltd 149
Fabar 185
Fabre, Don 321
factory road-testing 86–7, 167
Faichney, Pat 237, 238, 239, 240, 248, 250, 251
Fairman, Jack 232
Fangio, Juan Manuel 223
Fattori & Montani 35, 90
Feddon Motors (Daytona) 321
Felco electric cranes 84
Felmingham, Tony 211
Fergusson, Alice 297, 304
Fergusson, Jim 297, 298, 299, 301, 303, 304, 305, 306, 308
Ferranti Laminations Ltd 7, 102
Ferrari 250TR59 Fantuzzi Spyder 322
Ferrari 275GTB 243
Ferrari cars in general 239, 259, 260, 301, 314, 318, 321
Ferrari TRI/61 326
Ferryfield (Lydd) Airport 76
FIA (Fédération Internationale de l'Automobile) 153, 227, 315, 327
FIA Suitcase 315
Fianna Fáil 182
Fiat 500 259
FIAT Cars 194, 238
Field, J. J. 139
Field, Tanya 6
Fighting Vehicles Research and Development Establishment – see Ministry of Supply, Fighting Vehicles Research and Development Establishment
First LHD Production MGA – see HDC43-10106
First World War 14, 47
Fisher & Ludlow Ltd 28, 49
Fishguard to Rosslaire ferry 182
Fishpool, Mr 210
Fitch, John 236
Fitz – see Richard W-Fitzwilliam
Fitzwilliam – see also W-Fitzwilliam
Fitzwilliam allowance 243
Fitzwilliam Racing Team 7, 232, 234, 241, 244, 253, 254, 256, 257, 258, 259, 262, 264, 265, 267, 274 (twin cams), 275, 276, 277, 287
Fitzwilliam, George Charles 242
Fitzwilliam, Sir John 242
Flaherty, Jack 308, 312, 314, 316, 317, 318, 320, 321, 322, 324, 325
Fletcher, Paul 275, 276, 277
Flockhart, Ron 76, 231, 232, 233, 236
Flüela Pass (Switzerland) 114
Flux, M. H. J. 277
Flynn, Errol 40
Flynn, Joe 9, 220, 221, 225, 226
Foden Commercial Vehicles 182
Follet, John 183
Ford Model T 27
Ford Motor Company 32, 45, 74, 203, 207
Ford Special 247
Ford Station Wagon 57
Ford Zephyr Mark II 96, 205, 244, 245
Formula Junior race cars 276
Forsyth, Jock 30
Foster, Alan 213, 245, 246, 247, 248, 252, 253, 264, 267, 272, 276, 277, 278
four-seater MGA 206
Foy, Roger Allan 6
Frankfurt Motor Show 1955 9, 30, 70, 73, 74, 75, 231, 233, 244
Frankfurt Motor Show 1957 94
Frazer-Nash 49, 273
French Alps 228, 249
French Grand Prix 43
French MGA launch brochure 90
French roads 80
French, Ron 60
Frère, Paul 128
Frisch, Terry 6, 131, 132
Frost, Derek 116, 118, 120
Frua (see *also* Pietro Frua) 6, 207
Frua body on MGA (EX205/2) 207–9
Frua Register 6
Frua, Carla 6
Frua, Pietro 6, 7, 207, 208, 209
Furlow, Edward 31
Futa Pass (Italy) 260
FVRDE – see Ministry of Supply, Fighting Vehicles Research and Development Establishment

Gaisberg Hillclimb (Austria) 268, 269
Galpern, Jennifer 6
Gardner Record Breaking cars (see *also* MG EX135) 115
Gardner, Lt Colonel A. T. 'Goldie' 16, 36, 41, 56, 100, 115, 214
Gary, Robert 322
Gavia Pass (Italy) 251
Gaylord, Barney 6
Geitner, Major Gilbert 'Gil' 305, 307
General Motors 32, 45
Geneva Salon (Motor Show) 1953 35, 55
Geneva Salon (Motor Show) 1956 90, 91
Geneva Salon (Motor Show) 1958 95, 138
German Grand Prix 1956 247
German MGA brochures 74, 174
German MGA launch brochure 90
GHD 109071 – Chassis Number for 'KMO 326' MGA Coupé 106
Ghia-Aigle MG TD Midget 34, 35
GHNL2-107989 – see 100,000th MGA
GHQ Mechanical Transport Inspection Dept. 20
Ghurkhas 30
Giambagli, Julien 6
Gibson, G. 227
Giersing, Bo 6, 194, 195, 196, 197, 198
Gilbert & Sullivan 128
Gillespie, Mervyn 6
Gillow, Victor 117
Ginger (nickname of racing mechanic) 254, 255, 258, 259, 262, 264, 267
Girling brakes 232
Girling master cylinders 284
Glamorganshire Constabulary 205
Glasgow 273, 274
glass-reinforced plastic (GRP) hardtops 102, 103, 104
GMB Union 92
Goguen, Jerry 234, 235, 206
Golden Jubilee TT Race, Dundrod (1955) 230, 231
Goldsworthy, Simon 6
Goodenough, Adrian 6, 83
Goodman, Paul 6
Goodwood race circuit 235, 241, 242, 243, 247, 248, 255, 257, 261, 266, 272, 275, 276, 277, 278
Goodwood Tourist Trophy Race (1958) 272
Goodwood Tourist Trophy Race (1960) 276, 278
Goodyear 187
Gott, John (MBE) 77, 78, 131, 227, 249, 250, 251, 252, 267, 271, 272, 273, 274, 295
Gough Industries (Southern California) 31, 80, 96, 157, 179, 312
Gough, Phillip 31
government policy 18, 23, 28, 29, 45
Graham, Douglas 276
Graham, Frank 6, 143, 144, 319, 320, 321, 323
Graham, W Gordon 47
Grant, Gregor 128, 130, 155, 239
Graubünden Pass (Switzerland) 114
Green, Malcolm 6
Green, Michael 6, 222
Green, Richard 'Dickie' 6, 218, 220, 221, 222–3, 226
Greig, Scotty 194
Grice, Bob 214
Griffin, Charles 40, 63
Grosser Bergpreis von Österreich – Salzburg–Gaisberg 269
Gunderson, Joe and Cathy 6, 281, 282
Guy Commercial Vehicles 182
GWK (car make) 100
GWR (Great Western Railway) 20, 21

H.M. Customs & Excise 209, 210
Hacquin, Georges 267
Häggbom, Gunnar 293
Haig Whisky 260, 262
Haig, Tom 122, 126, 128, 131, 142, 237, 238, 240, 281
Halfpenny, John and Sharen 6
Hall family 241
Hall, Anne 252
Hall, Leslie 60, 62, 63
Hall, Nobby 86
Hall-Jones, Derrick 195
Hamblin, Doug 262
Hambro (see *also* Hambro Bank, Hambro Automotive, Hambro Organization, Hambro Trading) 6, 21, 30, 31, 32, 88, 91, 92
Hambro Automotive Corporation (see *also* BMC/Hambro) 91, 92, 94, 97, 108, 109, 154, 165, 181, 297, 298, 299, 301, 312, 313, 314
Hambro Bank 21, 29, 30, 31
Hambro Trading Corporation of America 31
Hambro, Calmer 31
Hambro, Major Jocelyn 6, 29, 31, 32
Hambro, Rupert 6
Hambro, Silvia 31
Hamilton, Peter 6
Hands, Laurie 143
Hanks, Reginald 8, 20, 23, 24, 26, 27, 29, 30, 31, 32, 45, 48, 49, 60, 65, 99, 119, 127
Hansgen, Walt 322
Harper, Peter 240
Harriman, Sir George 9, 28, 45, 59–60, 118, 119, 144, 145, 208, 214, 236
Harris, George 267
Harrison, David 324
Harrison, Donald 20, 21, 30, 32, 36, 40, 65
Harrison, Frank 311
Harvey, Richard 205
Hastings, Harold 230
Hauseman racing clutch 286
Hawker Hurricane aircraft 300
Haworth, Bill 108
Hawthorn, Mike 224, 236
Hayes, Fred 315, 317
Hayles, David 274
Hayter, Don 6, 16, 105, 123, 124, 203, 210, 211, 286, 287, 288
Haywood, Jack 158
HDA13-13355 (MGA Coupé prototype) 102, 104
HDC43-100106 – first LHD Production MGA 7, 9, 69, 70
HDC43-10101 (first production MGA, 'LJB 439') 123
HDD43-10151 Geneva 1956 Motor Show MGA 90
HDK23-14652 Invercargill New Zealand 1956 Motor Show MGA 181, 201
Healey (see *also* Austin-Healey) 48
Healey Hundred (Healey 100) (see *also* Austin-Healey 100) 8, 47, 48, 49
Healey Motor Company (Warwick) (see *also* Donald Healey Motor Company) 311
Healey Silverstone 256
Healey, Brian 184
Healey, Donald 8, 47, 48, 49, 59, 184, 204, 297, 302
Healey, Geoffrey 184, 311
Heathrow – see London Airport
Hedges, Andrew 184, 324, 325, 326, 328
Hellenic Air Force 274
Hembroe – see Hambro
Henderson, Bruce 6
Henderson, Gordon 194
Herring, Harry 6, 7, 37, 38, 46, 120, 202, 203, 205, 206, 207, 208, 209, 210, 216, 283
Herring, John (Jack) 37
Herring, John (junior) 37, 176
Herring, Nigel 6
Herson Grad, Lynn 6, 299, 302
Herson, David 298, 299, 301, 302
Herson, Gertrude 308
Herson, Joe (see *also* Manhattan Autos) 6, 296, 298, 299, 301, 302, 303, 308
Hess, Alan 45
Hester, Mark 6, 123, 131, 133, 149, 159, 161, 164
Heuer, Pierre 6, 270
Heuer, Samuel 6, 270, 271
Higginbotham, Chris 6
Higgins, Rob 6
Hill, Graham 293
Hill, Phil (race driver) 20, 121, 300
Hillier, Brian 'Bunny' 280
Hillman cars in general 303
Hillman Husky 303
Himpson, Sid 172
Hissom, Robert 322
HMD13-53352 MGA Coupé 'PRX 14' 152
HMO 6 (MG EX175 Prototype) 44, 46, 47, 64, 67
HMR13-23387 MGA Coupé 'NJB 381' 110
HMR13-48248 MGA Coupé 'PBL 497' 109
Hobbs, Wilfred 65
Hogan, Jane 6
Hogg, Brian 6, 161, 194
Hogg, John 255, 256, 258, 259, 260, 261, 265, 267
Holbrook & Sons 59
Holland, Willie 195
Hollick & Pratt 68
Hollywood Sports Cars 161
Holmes, George 125
Hooper Import Center 321, 322, 323
Hopkirk, Paddy 184, 223, 293
Horner, James 152
Horsfield, Noel 195
Hotchkiss et Cie 59, 112
Hounslow, Alec 7, 17, 18, 33, 38, 39, 41, 42, 43, 56, 67, 76, 100, 114, 121, 122, 126, 143, 144, 145, 205, 215, 217, 219, 220, 221, 222, 226, 227, 239, 262, 263, 269, 270, 282, 287, 288, 310
Howard, Jack 324
Howard, Robin 7, 250
HRG (cars) 215, 236, 273
hub-caps – Magnette ones fitted to MGA in error 154
Hubbard, Piers 7
Hudman, Lisa 7
Huffaker, Joe Jnr 131
Hughes, John 7, 131
Humber Car Company 22
Humphreys, David 7, 317

Ibsley 247
Iley, Geoffrey 7, 25, 40, 90, 92, 95, 99, 118, 125, 126, 127, 128, 129, 141, 144
import taxes 29
independent rear suspension 210
Inskip, J. S. ('John Swanel Inskip') 6, 58, 81, 82, 298, 300, 302, 306, 308
Insomnia Crew (1930s) 68, 100
Institution of Automobile Engineers 27
Institution of Mechanical Engineers 117
Invercargill Motor Show (New Zealand, 1956) 181, 201
Issigonis, Alec 21, 22, 22, 23, 27, 28, 61, 203
Italian MGA launch brochure 90
Italian styling 35
ITN News 129

J. Arthur Rank Films 178
J. Heinz Keller AG 7, 92, 93, 162

J. J. Molenaar's Automobielbedrijf N.V. 198, 200, 201
Jabekke Highway (Belgium) 55
Jackson, Barrie and Maggie 7, 41
Jackson, Reginald 'Jacko' 16, 18, 87, 90, 100, 127
Jacobs Midget 62, 213
Jacobs, Dick 6, 7, 9, 17, 33, 36, 47, 123, 144, 145, 213, 217, 218, 220, 221, 223, 224, 225, 226, 231, 245, 264, 272, 276 (twin cams; table), 278
Jaguar Cars in general 6, 58, 60, 90, 113, 115, 131, 147, 159, 181, 225, 226, 280, 302, 303, 308
Jaguar Cars Inc. (USA) 319
Jaguar C-Type 247, 253, 256, 280
Jaguar D-Type 122, 224, 225, 226, 236, 280, 281, 308
Jaguar Mark I & Mark 2 147
Jaguar XF & XG engines 115
Jaguar XK engines 113, 115, 147
Jaguar XK100 (prototype only) 115
Jaguar XK120 34, 38, 55, 115, 241, 247
Jaguar XK140 74
Jaguar XK-SS 308
James Auto-Cycle Company 21, 31, 32
James, F. E. (of Nuffield Exports) 21
James, Sid 178
Jamieson, Tom Murray 116, 233
Japanese imports 200
Jeep cars 32, 319
Jenkins, Clive 217
Jenkins, John 237
Jenkinson, Denis 'Jenks' 260
Jennings, Tony 118
Jensen Interceptor 49
Jensen Motors 16, 48, 49, 67
Jeser, Josef 224
jig for CKD assembly 188
Johannesburg (South Africa) 170, 278
John Bryant & Sons 136
John Thompson Pressings Ltd 37, 66, 83, 84
John Tune Import Motors 172
Johns, Douglas 250
Johns, Joan 228, 267
Johnson, Michael 7
Jones, Bill 'Jonesie' 253, 258, 259, 260, 261
Jones, Denis 42
Jones, Mel 148
Joseph Lucas Ltd – see Lucas Industries
Josephson, Cuffari & Company 108
Jowett Javelin 27
Jowett Ltd 26, 27
Joyce, Carol 72, 73
Juda, Hans Peter 28

Keeling, Johnny 247, 253, 254, 255, 256, 258, 259, 267, 276
Keenan, Gregory 7
Keith, Rowland 7, 303, 306, 307, 308
Keller Car (so-called) – LBL 304 286, 287
Keller, Heinz (see also J. Heinz Keller AG) 7, 93, 122, 162, 227, 228, 229, 234, 268, 269, 270
Keller, Jürg 7, 93, 162, 270
Kelly, Grace 38
Kelly, John 324
Kelly, William 194
Kemm, Garry 7, 186, 187, 190, 191, 193
Kennedy, Alistair 7
Keystone Garage (Warren, Pennsylvania) 298, 299, 303, 308
Kimber, Cecil 13, 14, 15, 16, 18, 22, 24, 25, 26, 27, 56, 159, 284
Kimberly, James ('Jim') 301
Kimpsey, Wally 38, 42
Kincheloe, Bill 9, 296, 298, 301, 304, 306
King, Michael 221, 225
King, S. B. 161, 167
Kirksite tooling 67
Kirschner, Bill 7
Kithead Trust 235
KMO 326 6, 69, 70, 77, 105–7, 138, 175, 236
Knott, Stephanie 7
Kodak film 243
Krause, Ernesto 185
KRX 820 (Riley Pathfinder) 77
Kyalami 9-Hour race, 1961 196

L'autodrome de Linas- Montlhéry – see Montlhéry
La Sarthe (Circuit de la Sarthe Le Mans) 218
Labour government (post-war) 28
Lady Nuffield 59
Lago Talbot 240, 241, 247
Laguna Seca (California) 131, 324, 328
Lambert, Captain Gordon (TWA Pilot) 72
Lambury, Lord (see also Leonard Lord) 19, 59, 60
Lancia cars 194, 203, 303
Land Rover 29, 186, 206
Langford, Nick 131
Lapalisse 249
Larke Consolidated Industries 186
Larke, Neave and Carter 186
Lavender Hill Mob Racing Association 302
Law, John 56
Lawrence, Chris 247
LBL 301 7, 9, 219, 221, 227, 228, 230, 231, 232, 234–5, 247, 254, 255, 257, 258, 261, 262, 265, 267, 287
LBL 302 9, 219, 221, 234
LBL 303 9, 219, 221, 229, 230, 231, 232, 234, 243, 254, 255, 257, 258, 259, 261, 262, 264, 265, 266, 270
LBL 304 9, 70, 148, 218, 219, 221, 230, 232, 234, 268, 269, 270, 271, 286, 287
LBL 405 – see BMC Competitions Department Transporter
Le Mans Biennial Cup 219
Le Mans TD Midget Mark II Special – see MG EX172
Le Mans, 1927 race 220
Le Mans, 1930 race 219
Le Mans, 1933 race 219
Le Mans, 1934 race 219
Le Mans, 1949 race 42, 219
Le Mans, 1950 race 36, 42, 219
Le Mans, 1951 race 36, 42, 43, 44, 219
Le Mans, 1955 race 17, 70, 118, 119, 213, 214, 215, 218, 219, 221, 222, 223, 224, 226, 227, 231, 236, 238, 248, 278, 280, 281, 284, 286, 297
Le Mans, 1955 re-numbering changes on MG EX182 221
Le Mans, 1956 race 219, 241, 280
Le Mans, 1959 race 284, 286, 287, 290
Le Mans, 1960 race 284, 286, 287, 288
Le Mans, 1961 race 284, 287, 288, 289, 290, 291
Le Mans, 1962 race 287, 289
Le Mans, 1965 race (with MGB) 184
Le Mans, Quatre-Vingt Heures (see also by year) 6, 8, 9, 11, 17, 28, 36, 41, 53, 64, 124, 184, 212, 214, 215, 216, 217, 219, 255, 258, 263, 283, 284, 296
Lea Francis 48
Learoyd, Wing Cdr. Roderick 'Babe' 220, 311
Leavens, Ed 297, 303, 304, 306, 307, 308, 315, 317
Lee, David 7, 109
Lefton, Norman 131
LeMay Car Museum (Tacoma, Washington) 318
Les Coupés Emgee 248
Leston, Les 278
Levegh, Pierre 224
Levy, Calmer Joachim 31
Leyland Motor Corporation 31, 59, 60
Liège–Rome–Liège Rally (1956) 251, 252 (table)
Liège–Rome–Liège Rally (1957) 267
Liège–Rome–Liège Rally (1958) 271, 272, 273
Liège–Sofia–Liège Rally (1962) 295
Life Magazine 31
Light Car Magazine 14
Lime Rock race circuit (Connecticut) 131, 302
Linder, Charles 67
Lindley 122
Linge, Herbert 306
Lipe, Gordon 317
LJB 205 70, 232, 234, 255, 257, 258, 261, 262–3, 265, 267
LJB 370 70, 93, 211, 227, 228, 287
LJB 439 70, 79, 123
Lockett, Johnny 9, 122, 218, 220, 221, 223, 225, 231, 232, 233, 234
Lockheed disc brakes (MGA 1600) 153, 154, 155
Lockheed SpeedPak 72, 73
Lockheed Super Constellation 72, 73
Loftis, Don 321
Lola race cars 318, 321
London Airport (now Heathrow) 9, 72, 311
Longbridge (Birmingham) 28, 29, 45, 48, 49, 51, 53, 59, 60, 61, 63, 64, 67, 84, 85, 92, 99, 116, 118, 119, 122, 124, 125, 127, 134, 159, 203, 204, 214, 215, 216, 233, 281, 297
Longridge, Chris 105
Longshaw, Ernie 126
Lord Austin 45, 59, 119
Lord Nuffield 13, 14, 15, 19, 20, 21, 22, 23, 30, 49, 59, 76, 99, 114, 119, 186, 200, 222
Lord Thomas of Remenham – see Miles Thomas
Lord, Sir Leonard (see also Lord Hambury) 9, 17, 19, 26, 29, 40, 45, 47, 48, 49, 51, 55, 58, 59, 60, 65, 66, 76, 114, 118, 194, 203, 204, 214, 226, 240
Lotus cars in general 247, 278
Lotus Elite 276
Lotus-Ford Twin Cam engine 115
Lowndes, Frank 25
Lowndes, Jack 158
Lowry, Meg 220
Lowry, Russell 220, 221, 223, 225, 226
LRX 238 70
LRX 4 101
Lucas Industries 92, 161, 214, 216, 230, 284
Lucas, Tony 126, 128, 129
Luftwaffe 19
Lumsden, Peter 276
Lund lights 287, 288
Lund, Ted 6, 9, 17, 33, 36, 47, 124, 213, 220, 221, 223, 224, 225, 226, 231, 232, 234, 279, 281, 284, 285, 286, 287, 288, 289, 290, 291, 308, 315, 316, 317
Lydd Airport 76, 244, 269
Lydden Hill Circuit 273
Lynch, Silas 31
Lyons, Sir William 115
Lyster, Evelyn 242

Mackenzie, Ken 264, 267
Macklin, Lance 214, 224, 226
Macleod, Ken 321
Madgewick Corner (Goodwood) 278
Magnette – see also MG Z Magnette
Maher, Eddie 7, 114, 116, 117, 118, 120, 121, 124, 231, 233, 236, 311
Maher, Eddy (son of Eddie Maher) 7
Maher, Maud 117
Mainz, Harry 273
Maison Blanche ('White House' – corner at Le Mans) 9, 225
Mallory Park (race circuit) 246
Mallory, George 212
Malthouse, Adrian 7, 136, 170, 171
Manchester Motor Club 284
Manchester, Neil 7, 201
Mandel, Leon 312
Manhattan Autos (see also Joe Herson) 6, 298, 299, 301, 302, 303, 304
Manley, Colin 7
Mantis, Ian 195
Manx Cup 256
Marathon de la Route – see Liège-Rome-Liège Rally
Marchal headlamps 214
Margaret, H.M. Princess 243
Marlboro Raceway races & course 296, 302, 308
Marr, Leslie 254
Martin, Charles 158
Martin, Roger 247
Martyn, Chris 275, 276
Maserati 208, 238, 259
Maserati Tipo 63 322
Mason, George 48
Mathews, Jack 158
Mays, Raymond 245
MBL 867 ('MaBeL') 70, 236, 237, 238, 239, 249, 250, 252
McCarthy Rodway 195
McCarthy, Pam 7, 131
McCarthy, Roy 7, 131
McComb, Wilson 115, 118, 131, 148, 172, 240
McElroy, Rob 287
McKenzie, Bill 155, 156
McLaren, Bruce 322
McLellan, John 7, 12, 26
Mercedes-Benz 300SL 252, 285
Mercedes-Benz 300SLR 280, 281
Mercedes-Benz cars in general 9, 185, 223, 224, 225, 231, 236
Merging of MG and Riley franchises (short-lived idea in 1951) 36, 213
Merlin engine 117
Mertens, Roy 236
Messrs J. A. Woodhouse – see Woodhouse
Mexican-assembled CKD MGA 7, 181, 184, 185, 197, 315
Mexico 7, 181, 185, 197
MG (as a marque) 14, 18, 21, 32, 36
MG 1 (registration number) 148
MG 1¼ Litre (see also MG Y-Type) 18, 19, 32, 33
MG 1¼ Litre Tourer – see MG YT
MG 1100 (ADO 16 saloon, 1962–71) 184
MG 1100 (as proposed name for DO 926 'MG Midget Major' concept) 23, 29
MG 1300 (ADO 16 saloon, 1967–71) 184
MG 14/40 304
MG 18/100 Tigress 15, 17
MG 18/80 100
MG and Riley Drawing Office (Cowley) 61, 62, 117
MG and Wolseley 'commonising' of saloons (leading to MG Z Magnette and Wolseley 4/44) 36
MG Car Club – see also various entries under MGCC 42, 43, 84, 132, 159, 161, 215, 290
MG Car Club in California (1948) 31
MG Car Club in France 142
MG Car Company Development Department 7, 8, 40
MG Car Company Experimental Department 16
MG Car Company Ltd and Riley Motors Ltd (as an entity) 18, 24, 26, 27, 36, 39, 44, 47, 61, 117, 214
MG Car Company Ltd 7, 13, 18, 24, 70, 83, 86, 109, 126, 182, 213, 219, 223, 236, 253, 254, 255, 296
MG Cars – see also MG Car Company Ltd
MG cars in general 25, 26, 27, 30, 48, 126, 147, 159, 181, 182, 200, 215, 302, 303, 308, 309, 313
MG Chief Engineer (see also Syd Enever) 12
MG Competitions Department (see also BMC Competitions, and 'Comps') 8, 70, 184, 213, 214, 219, 222, 278
MG Design Drawing Office at Abingdon 8, 16, 60, 64
MG Development Department 38, 68, 121, 123, 124, 143, 183, 184, 205, 210, 211, 215, 216, 219, 222, 223, 269, 270, 280, 281, 284, 287, 310
MG Distributors 161, 167
MG Double-Twelve Race at Brooklands 25
MG Enthusiast Magazine 6
MG EX Register 123
MG EX135 16, 36, 37, 56, 57, 115
MG EX172 ('UMG 400') 7, 8, 25, 28, 36, 37, 38, 39, 40, 41, 42, 43, 44, 46, 47, 53, 58, 101, 219, 222
MG EX175 ('HMO 6') 8, 18, 25, 44, 45, 46, 47, 51, 52, 54, 55, 56, 57, 63, 64, 67, 68, 114, 216, 222
MG EX176 319
MG EX177 (MG TF Midget) 50, 52
MG EX178 'Austin 1500 engine tuning') 306, 319
MG EX179 Record Breaker 18, 46, 56, 57, 58, 60, 74, 120, 121, 206, 216, 281, 300, 306
MG EX180 Morris Minor tuning 216
MG EX181 Record Breaker 7, 37, 116, 120–1, 126, 128, 129, 130, 140, 206, 216, 281, 286
MG EX182 6, 9, 54, 55, 63, 67, 82, 70, 119, 207, 214, 216, 217, 218, 220, 221, 222, 224, 227, 230, 232, 234, 235, 254, 262, 268, 269, 280, 287
MG EX183 204, 280, 285
MG EX186 6, 62, 122, 124, 204, 280, 281, 282, 283–4, 285, 287
MG EX187 (MGA Twin Cam) 123, 207, 280, 283, 311
MG EX188 204
MG EX189 ('four-seater MGA') 206
MG EX191 ('development work' on MGA) 148, 204, 207
MG EX194 Police MGA
MG EX195 ('cheaper MGA') 204
MG EX196 9, 103
MG EX197 9, 101, 102, 105
MG EX202 MG Magnette Six-Cylinder 62
MG EX205 MGB concept 202, 210
MG EX205/1 210
MG EX205/2 (Frua MGA) 207, 208, 210
MG EX205/3 210
MG EX206 & MG EX207 – Riley large saloon projects 147
MG EX210 (larger sports car) 207
MG EX212 Lund Coupé 'SRX 210' 286, 287, 288
MG EX214 MGB 202, 207, 210, 211
MG EX216 203
MG EX219 record breaker 57, 300
MG EX233 (record breaker, model only) 11
MG Experimental Shop 33, 39
MG General Manager (see also John Thornley and Jack Tatlow) 12, 47, 114, 119
MG J2 Midget 17
MG J4 Midget 15
MG K3 Magnette 17, 55, 56, 93, 219, 231, 238, 321
MG Live event 159
MG Magna (1953–4) – see MG Midget Gerald Palmer
MG Magna name (in general) 65
MG Magnette Mark III 53, 63, 145
MG Magnette name (use of) 26, 55, 65
MG Magnette Twin Cam concept 145, 214
MG MGA – first use of the name 55, 65
MG MGA – larger engines considered (1.7 & 2.2 litres) 151, 167, 205
MG MGA 100,000th – see 100,000th MGA
MG MGA 1500 9, 54, Chapter Four, 129, 130, 142, last car 153, 184, 187, 188, 199, 201, 214
MG MGA 1600 9, 54, 95, 100, 102, 103, 105, 109, 112, 142, 145, 146, 149, Chapter Seven, 187, 188, 199, 201, 204, 319
MG MGA 1600 Deluxe 150, Chapter Seven
MG MGA 1600 Mark II 'Competition' 161, 164
MG MGA 1600 Mark II 10, 105, 109, 112, 146, Chapter Seven, 175 (last car), 187, 188, 191, 193, 198, 199, 201, 204, 292, 293, 294, 323, 327
MG MGA 1600 Spezial" 140
MG MGA Austin Twin Cam engine 144, 232, 233
MG MGA Cabriolet (concept only) 104
MG MGA Coupé 'PBL 497' 7, 109, 130
MG MGA Coupé 9, 62, 67, 68, 69, 85, 92, 93, Chapter Five, 126, 130, 138, 291, 292, 294
MG MGA Deluxe 9, 160–1, 291, 292, 294, 321, 326, 327
MG MGA Four-Seater (EX 189/'MGE') 206
MG MGA Hard Top (removable) 9, 167
MG MGA launch brochures – Dutch, French, German, Italian 90
MG MGA Morris Twin Cam engine 8, 28, 144, 232, 233
MG MGA Police Cars 205
MG MGA radiator grille 62
MG MGA replacement – Chapter Nine
MG MGA Twin Cam – first five production cars 131 (table)
MG MGA Twin Cam – last production cars 146 (table), 147, 148
MG MGA Twin Cam 'PMO 326' 7
MG MGA Twin Cam Coupé in South Africa 194, 195, 196
MG MGA Twin Cam Launch event – see BMC Demonstration Day
MG MGA Twin Cam, 6, 62, 64, 78, 84, 93, 95, 99, 107, 109, 110, 112, Chapter Six, 152, 153, 154, 155, 158, 159, 160, 161, 162, 181, 182, 183, 184, 185, 187, 194, 199, 200, 201, 202, 203, 205, 207, 213, 214, 222, 248, 268, 270, 271, 272, 273, 274, 275, 276, 277, 279, 285, 286, 287, 288, 289, 290, 304, 307, 309, 310, 311, 314, 315, 316, 317, 318, 319, 324
MG MGB – as proposed name for twin cam MGA 119, 202
MG MGB – first production car 10
MG MGB 12, 22, 28, 46, 53, 62, 65, 68, 105, 106, 123, 124, 151, 152, 159, 162, 164, 168, 169, 170, 175, 176, 182, 184, 188, 193, 202, 203, 204, 206, 207, 210, 211, 215, 295, 323, 328
MG MGB ADO23 – see ADO23
MG MGB GT 148, 184
MG MGB GT V8 16, 17, 87
MG MGC 16, 22, 65, 207
MG MGD (EX 188 – name only) 207
MG MGE (EX 189 – name only) 207
MG Midget (from 1961 to 1979) 16, 62, 63, 84, 148, 160, 167, 184, 215
MG Midget (see also relevant model, such as MG TC, MG TD, MG TF etc.) 11, 13, 15, 17, 18, 19, 21, 23, 25, 33, 34, 36, 50, 62, 65
MG Midget Gerald Palmer's sports car concepts 27, 28, 49, 50–1, 52, 53, 65, 113, 118, 202
MG Midget Major (concept only - DO 926) 22, 23, 32
MG model names 207
MG Mosquito (see also Morris Mosquito) 29
MG M-Type Midget 17, 18, 19, 219
MG M-Type Midget 'Double Twelve' (1930) 219
MG Old Number One 14, 25, 173
MG PA Midget 17, 219
MG PB Midget 17, 284
MG P-Type Midget 17
MG Racing (pre-war) 16, 17
MG Rectification Department 222
MG R-Type Midget 44
MG RV8 184
MG SA 104
MG Series MGA 8
MG Series UA – see MG UA
MG Service Manager 36
MG Show Shop 278
MG TA Midget 17, 20
MG TB Midget 17, 20
MG TC Midget 17, 20, 21, 23, 29, 30, 31, 32, 33, 34, 42, 52, 146, 213, 222, 223, 300, 302
MG TC Phillips Special 36, 42, 219
MG TD Inskip four-seater 302
MG TD Midget 8, 22, 25, 32, 33, 34, 35, 36, 37, 40, 41, 43, 44, 46, 47, 48, 49, 52, 54, 55, 58, 61, 179, 182, 184, 194, 200, 213, 222, 231, 284, 296
MG TD Midget Arnolt bodied 34, 35, 36, 38

MG TD Phillips Special – see MG EX172
MG TF 1250 Midget 8, 35, 37, 50, 52, 53, 55, 56, 58, 63, 64, 65, 66, 68, 69, 179, 182, 184, 223, 302
MG TF 1500 (Midget) 9, 54, 58, 70, 75, 81, 90, 94, 179, 182, 184, 214, 222, 236, 296, 308
MG Tigress – see MG 18/100
MG Transport Section 126
MG T-Type Midgets (in general – see *also* MG TA, TB, TC, TD, TF) 19, 23, 44, 48, 50, 63, 68, 70, 97, 100, 104, 113, 114, 213, 230
MG UA Series 53, 55, 65
MG Vintage Racers 7
MG XPower SV 66
MG YA Saloon 40
MG YB Saloon 55
MG YT Tourer 22, 26, 29, 40
MG Y-Type (see *also* MG YA, YB, YT) 18, 22, 25, 26, 29, 33, 51, 52, 113, 114, 116, 213
MG Z Magnette 8, 26, 27, 36, 38, 51, 53, 54, 55, 58, 60, 62, 75, 76, 78, 84, 88, 100, 108, 120, 130, 152, 204, 213, 216, 222, 227, 229, 236, 239, 241, 248, 249, 259, 269, 270
MG ZA Magnette – see MG Z Magnette
MG ZB Magnette 'Varitone' 55, 138, 207
MG ZB Magnette 9, 55, 95, 126, 138, 207
MGA – see MG MGA
MGA Register – see MGCC MGA Register
MGA Register (Holland) 7
MGA Register Yearbook (2005) 287
MGA Twin Cam 60th Anniversary event 125, 127, 278
MGA Twin Cam Group – see MGCC MGA Twin Cam Group
MGB – see MG MGB
MGC – see MG MGC
MGCC (MG Car Club)
MGCC Archives 7
MGCC Australia 7
MGCC Dutch Centre 200
MGCC MGA Register 6, 7, 70, 160, 241, 247
MGCC MGA Twin Cam Group 6, 7, 122, 125, 131, 145, 149, 164, 278
MGCC North Western Centre 6, 281, 284
MGCC Registers in general 84
MGCC *Safety Fast!* Magazine 7, 16, 121, 161, 213, 241, 309
MGCC South Africa 6
MGCC South Eastern Centre 6
MGCC US & Canadian Centres 125
Michelin Tyres 83
Michelin, Luis 301, 305
Michelotti, Giovanni 35
Microcell racing seats 319
Midland Sheet Metal Ltd 57, 120, 280, 281, 283, 284, 286, 287, 288
Midnight Sun Rally of the Sun (1958) 268
Miles, Ken 9, 58, 122, 220, 221, 225, 226, 234
Miles, Roy 61
Mill Garage 123, 213, 226, 248
Millar, Alan 297, 301, 304, 305, 307, 308
Millard, Peter 7, 305, 308, 311, 313
Mille Miglia (in general) 212, 237–8, 259
Mille Miglia 1933 race 17, 55, 238
Mille Miglia 1953 race 259
Mille Miglia 1956 race 237, 238, 239, 240 (table of results), 259
Mille Miglia 1957 race 247, 255, 256, 258–61, 262, 263, 267, 287
Mills, Bernie 301, 302
Milne, John 277, 249, 250, 252, 267, 273, 274
Mini Coopers (and Cooper 'S') in general 40, 117, 215, 223, 291, 293
Mini Traveller 291
Mini-Marcos 265
Ministry of Information 28
Ministry of Supply, Fighting Vehicles Research and Development Establishment (based at Chobham, Surrey) 9, 125, 126
Ministry of Supply 29
MIRA Test Circuit 78, 105, 122, 123, 143, 203, 211, 231, 233, 286
Mitchell Specials 61
Mitchell, Clive 194
Mitchell, Nancy 6, 104, 152, 236, 237, 238, 239, 240, 248, 249, 250, 251, 252, 267, 268
Mitchell, Terry 7, 56, 57, 60, 61, 62, 63, 120, 121, 124, 145, 280, 281
Mitchell, Theresa 7
Mitholz-Kandestes hillclimb (1958) 270
Mittenvald (Bavaria) 251
MJB 167 7, 237, 240, 250, 267, 312
MJB 191 7, 249, 250, 251, 252
MJB 778 277
MJB 994 93, 107
Modern Motor Magazine 130
Molenaar Automobielen 181, 198, 199, 200, 201
Molenaar, Jacob 200
Mont Salève ('Balcony of Geneva') 294
Monte Carlo Rally, 1955 222
Monte Carlo Rally, 1956 228, 236
Monte Carlo Rally, 1959 272, 273, 274
Monte Carlo Rally, 1962 162, 291, 292, 293
Montlhéry 69, 70, 76, 77, 105, 212, 227, 228, 229, 236
Morgan cars 48, 247
Morley, Don 292, 293
Morley, Erle 292, 293
Morrell, Peter 7
Morren, Donald 58, 90
Morrill, Frank 324, 327
Morris Bodies – see Morris Motors Ltd, Bodies Branch
Morris cars in general 14, 15, 21, 22, 23, 30, 32, 95, 126, 181, 184, 186, 200, 215, 303, 313
Morris Commercial Cars Ltd 30, 47, 59, 181, 182, 200
Morris Cowley 53, 68
Morris Eight (Morris 8) 21, 27
Morris Engines – see Morris Motors Engines Branch
Morris Engines Apprentice/Apprenticeships 7
Morris flat four engine concept 23, 28
Morris Garage (Maryland, USA) 306
Morris Garages Specials 14
Morris Garages 13, 14, 15, 16, 24, 83, 109
Morris Isis 78, 116, 147
Morris J-Type Van 186, 200
Morris Major (concept only) 22
Morris Mini Cooper – see Mini Cooper
Morris Mini Minor (see *also* Mini) 127, 134, 164
Morris Minor 1000 130, 204, 215
Morris Minor 15, 22, 23, 28, 29, 34, 45, 57, 60, 61, 92, 126, 200, 304
Morris Minor Series 'MM' 26
Morris Minor Traveller 66, 68, 84, 159
Morris Minor Van 66, 159
Morris Mosquito 21, 22, 23, 61
Morris Motors (Canada) Ltd 142, 181, 296, 313
Morris Motors Band 128, 129
Morris Motors Board 8, 9, 26, 33, 36, 40, 48, 50, 51, 55, 59, 64, 66, 93, 99, 101, 113, 116, 127, 147, 186, 213, 214
Morris Motors Drawing Office & Experimental Department, Cowley 18
Morris Motors Ltd Bodies Branch 19, 24, 28, 46, 62, 64, 65, 66, 67, 68, 83, 84, 85, 102, 104, 105, 123, 124, 159, 216, 229
Morris Motors Ltd Drawing Office 62
Morris Motors Ltd Engines Branch 7, 12, 26, 53, 56, 59, 114, 115, 116, 117, 118, 119, 120, 122, 124, 126, 145, 147, 159, 230, 233, 234
Morris Motors Ltd Experimental Pattern Shop 62
Morris Motors Ltd Pressings Branch 28
Morris Motors Ltd Radiators Branch 62
Morris Motors Ltd Service Technical Department 20
Morris Motors Ltd Specifications Department 62
Morris Motors Ltd 7, 8, 14, 15, 19, 20, 21, 22, 26, 27, 28, 30, 32, 33, 38, 52, 59, 61, 62, 69, 99, 113, 200
Morris Oxford 53, 65, 200
Morris Oxford Series V 167
Morris Oxford Series VI 167
Morris Oxford Traveller 239
Morris Radiators Branch 18
Morris Six 200
Morris Taxi 66
Morris Ten (Morris 10) 22
Morris, 'Buzzer' 83
Morris, Bob 87
Morris, Frederick & Emily 14
Morris, George 158, 222
Morris, Gordon 306
Morris, William Richard – see Lord Nuffield
MOSS Motors 174, 324
Moss, (Sir) Stirling 121, 140, 214, 236, 243, 250
Moss, Pat 215, 217, 228, 236, 240, 268, 272, 293
Motor Assemblies Ltd. (Durban) 181, 193, 194, 195, 196, 197
Motor Industry Research Association – see MIRA
Motor Life Magazine 81
Motor Magazine 14, 78, 79, 90, 111, 134, 135, 137, 139, 143, 155, 156
Motor Show – see Earls Court, Frankfurt, Geneva, New York, Paris Salon, Turin as appropriate
motor shows in general in 1955/56 70
Motor Sport Inc. – see Collier Brothers
Motor Trend Magazine 79, 156
Motoring (Nuffield magazine) 126, 132, 272
Motoring News magazine 215
Motorsport Magazine 74, 87, 110, 112, 155, 223, 225, 235, 236, 239, 260, 278
Moylan, Brian 218, 262, 263
MRX 42 6, 249, 250, 252, 267
MRX 43 249, 250, 252, 267
M-Series engine – see Rover M-Series
Mulsanne Straight (Le Mans) 8, 43, 219, 223, 224, 225, 286, 290
Muncie Import Auto 173
Munro, Janet 178
Murray, John 301
Murray, Neil 197
Muys, John 200

NAMGAR 6
NAMGATCR 316, 317
Nash Kelvinator Corporation 48, 49
Nash Metropolitan 49, 53, 96
Nash, Sam 87
Nash-Healey 48
Nässil, Bertil 264, 265
National Cats-Eyes' Rally (1956) 236
Nava, Pietro 259, 261
Neal, Peter 7, 102, 161, 203, 206, 207, 208, 211, 280
Necropolis Cristobel (Cuba) 180
NEMGTR (New England MG T Register) 143, 234
Nevada Grand Prix 131
New Midget for 1954 – see DO 1049
New York Coliseum 82, 138, 162
New York Motor Show 1948 29
New York Motor Show 1953 35
New York Motor Show 1956 80, 82, 90
New York Motor Show 1958 138
New York Motor Show 1962 10, 162, 172, 173
New York Museum of Modern Art 36
Nicholas, Dave 'Kahuna' 7, 306, 317
Nicholls, Stan 221
Nikas, John 7
Nissan 194
NJB 381 110, 112
NMP – see Nuffield Metal Products
North American MGA Register – see NAMGAR
North American MGA Twin Cam Register – see NAMGATCR
North Downs Engineering 222
Northesk, Earl of 247
Nürburgring 1,000km race, 1956 241, 244, 249, 264
Nürburgring 1,000km race, 1957 256, 262, 263, 264, 265 (table)
Nürburgring 1,000km race, 1958 274
Nürburgring 1,000km race, 1959 275, 276
Nürburgring 1,000km race, 1961 279
Nürburgring 1,000km race, 1962 279
Nürburgring race circuit 212, 227, 244, 245, 247, 256, 262, 264, 276
Nuffield (Lord) – see Lord Nuffield
Nuffield and Austin merger 8, 19, 20, 21, 28, 29, 30, 45, 48, 55, 58, 59, 113, 118, 119
Nuffield Australia - Nuffield (Australia) Pty Ltd 188
Nuffield Competitions Committee 214, 215
Nuffield Cowley KD Department 180, 190, 191
Nuffield Distributor 36
Nuffield engine family (see *also* XPAG & XPEG) 113, 114, 115, 116
Nuffield Exports Ltd 7, 20, 21, 29, 30, 31, 32, 40, 68, 73, 85, 88, 90, 95, 96, 97, 130, 141, 142, 161, 167, 179, 180, 181, 182, 183, 187, 209
Nuffield Exports Technical Service Dept. 109, 141, 142
Nuffield Group – see Nuffield Organisation
Nuffield Group Technical Director 38
Nuffield House (Piccadilly) 107
Nuffield Mechanization Ltd 20
Nuffield Metal Products Ltd 20, 28, 50, 51
Nuffield *News Exchange* Magazine 73, 296
Nuffield Organisation Central Publicity Department (and press releases) 45, 71, 89, 127, 139, 165, 167, 172
Nuffield Organisation 7, 8, 12, 15, 18, 19, 20, 21, 23, 24, 26, 28, 29, 30, 31, 32, 45, 48, 49, 51, 56, 70, 77, 114, 119, 127, 156, 167, 172, 186, 193, 214, 225, 228
Nuffield Press 88, 140, 272
Nuffield Teamwork Magazine 27, 77, 78, 86, 129, 156, 158, 217
Nuffield Trust for Special Areas 59
Nuneaton 280, 286
NUVB (National Union of Vehicle Builders) 92
Nuvolari, Tazio 17
Nuvon material 168
Nye, Doug 7, 43, 46, 66, 67

O'Neill, Jim 7, 33, 37, 46, 51, 60, 61–2, 63, 65, 67, 68, 101, 102, 103, 165, 204, 207, 210, 280
O'Neill, Sandi 7
O'Neill, Terry 7
Oak, A.V. (Victor) 18, 20, 27, 28, 33, 36, 39, 40, 50, 60, 113
OBL 311 237, 267, 268
Octagon Stable 290
Octane magazine 235
Odendahl, Herr 72
Oesterle, Bill 7, 138
O'Farril, Rómulo 185
Olivier, Gustave 224
Ollon-Villars Hillclimb (1958) 270
Olthoff, Bob 131, 133, 184, 197, 278, 279, 280, 288, 290, 321, 324, 325, 326, 327
Olympic Batteries (Australia) 187
Optional extras 167
Organ, Johnny 291
Orino, Pat 317
Orton-Villars race 6
Orwell, George 28
ORX 885 7, 114, 116, 122, 126, 129, 131, 133
Osbourn, Brian 7, 102
Osca race car 318
Oulton Park (Cheshire) 162, 242, 245, 248, 252, 253
Ouroussoff, Nicholas 235
Oxford, University of 235, 256
PA Images 7
PA/Reuters 97
Packard cars 303
paint colours – see tables e.g. pages 98, 112
Palm, Gunnar 293, 294
Palmer Midgets – see MG Midget Gerald Palmer
Palmer, Gerald 8, 21, 25, 26, 27–8, 28, 36, 44, 48, 49, 50, 51, 53, 55, 60, 65, 67, 113, 116, 117, 118, 145, 147, 202, 233
Panter, Colin 7
Parade Motors of Mitcham 148, 161
Paris Salon de l'Automobile 1955 9, 74, 75
Paris Salon de l'Automobile 1958 7, 137, 138
Paris Salon de l'Automobile 1959 138
Paris Salon de l'Automobile 1960 159, 162
Paris Salon (see *also* by year) 7
Parkinson, Jim 308, 312, 314, 316, 317, 318, 320, 321, 322, 324, 325, 326
Passo di Gardena 249
Pathé Film *'BMC - Ladies First'* 250
Pathé Film Crew 221
Pathé News 72, 78, 92, 218, 221
Patrick, John 109
Pavlova Leather Works 13, 23
Payton, Ernest 45
PBL 497 7, 109, 130
Pearcy, Colin 131
Pease, Al 308
Pebble Beach Concours 317
Peel Fabrications Ltd 277
Peel, Fred 277
Performance Motors Ltd (New York) 298, 302
Peterborough Motor Club 212
Peters, Mike 7, 152
Philco radios 31
Phillips, Barbara 42
Phillips, George 8, 17, 33, 36, 37, 38, 39, 41, 42, 43, 44, 47, 101, 213, 219, 231
Phoenix Park Grand Prix 117, 279
Phoenix Special 183, 184
Pickering, Ray 312
Pierce, Olly 86
PJB 147 123, 129, 132, 133, 268, 269
PKD (partially knocked down) – see SKD
Platt, Maurice 28
Plexiglas windows 103
Plowden, Jim 7, 324
Plymouth cars 193
PMO 325 129, 131, 133, 134
PMO 326 7, 125, 129, 131, 132, 139, 148
PMO 946 125, 129, 130, 133, 148
police 138, 205
Poole, Alec 7, 117, 182, 184
Poole, William ('Billy') 7, 181, 182
Porsche 356 Speedster 296
Porsche 356A 265, 306
Porsche 356B Carrera Abarth GTL 326
Porsche 550 RSK 269
Porsche 550 Spyder 224, 244
Porsche 718 RSK 269
Porsche Carrera 249
Porsche cars in general 90, 101, 119, 210, 232, 247, 252, 256, 269, 270, 278, 302, 314, 318
Portago, Marquis of 260, 261, 301
Porter, Bob 77
Porter, Mollie 77
post-war drive 30
Presley, Elvis 178
Pressed Metal Corporation (PMC) (Australia) 9, 186, 187, 188, 191, 192
Pressed Steel Ltd (Cowley) 28, 46, 60, 61, 62, 66, 67, 68, 83, 123, 124
Pressed Steel Ltd (Swindon) 105
Pressnell, Jon 7, 23, 58, 75, 90, 142, 144, 203
Price, Bill 218, 231, 311
Prior, Ian 7, 319, 320, 321, 323
Privett, Jack 172
Proctor, Jim 7
Project 41 (Morris Motors – for MG TF Midget)
Project 44 (Morris Motors – for DO 1049) 51
Project 45 (Morris Motors – for 'high-performance version of B-Series engine') 118
Project 56 (Morris Motors – for DO 1062 MGA) 64, 65
Project 60 (Morris Motors – for DO1067 Riley twin-cam six cylinder engine) 147
Project B11 (Morris Motors – for MGA Coupé) 101
Propert, George 14, 21, 24, 25, 26, 47
Prophet, Denis 273, 327
Pröpsting, Stephan 7, 317, 318
PRX 14 7, 109, 130, 152
PRX 707 272, 273, 312
Publicis (French press agency) 75
Purcell, Noell 178

Qin, Li 211
Quayle, Howard 7, 160, 161
Queen Elizabeth (liner) 320
Queen Mary (liner) 121, 172
Qvale, Bruce 7
Qvale, Kjell 7, 16, 31, 32, 58, 82, 131, 157, 281, 308

RAC (Royal Automobile Club) 153, 227, 236, 290, 327
RAC Rally (1956) 215, 236, 249
RAC Rally in general 273
RAF (Royal Air Force) 20, 30, 300
Rallye des Alpes (1948) 236
Rallye des Alpes (1956) – see Alpine Rally
Ramsay, Tom 33
RAOC (Royal Army Ordnance Corps) 18
rationalisation of car ranges 29
Raybould, Pablo 7
Reason, Peter 7, 290
recessions in USA – see US recession
Rectification Department (MG) 87, 88
red livery on MGA in lieu of green 238–9
Redford, Robert 6, 178
Redmill, Hubert 63
Regalia, Andy 58
Reid, Mike 7, 259, 260, 277
Reid, Tim 7
Reilly, Calcott 27
Reims 12 hours – 1956 245, 249
Reims 12 hours – 1957 256, 266, 267
Reims race circuit 227, 246, 262
Rennicks, Robin 181
Ribolla, Giuseppe 259, 261
Rich, Doreen 228
Richard, Jean-Pierre 30, 75, 142
Richards, Robin 241
Richardson, Clive 225
Richardson, Simon 277
Richardson, Tom (Planning Engineer, Morris Motors) 26
Richer, Phil 7, 145, 273
Riddell, Harry 56
Riley – relocation to Abingdon 26
Riley 2 ½ Litre 33
Riley 2.6 – see Riley Two-Point-Six
Riley 4/68 (ADO 9R) 53, 147, 167
Riley 4/72 167
Riley and MG – see 'MG Car Company Ltd and Riley Motors Ltd' and 'MG and Riley'
Riley Car Company Ltd (and Riley cars in general) 8, 18, 21, 22, 24, 26, 27, 30, 32, 36, 47, 66, 68, 84, 85, 95, 116, 117, 119, 126, 147, 181, 184, 215, 231, 303
Riley diamond badge 26
Riley DP25R engine 117, 147
Riley Engines 7, 26, 48, 49, 53, 119, 147
Riley four-seater version of MGA – concept 119
Riley Nine Brooklands 117
Riley One-Point-Five 53, 126, 130, 204, 236
Riley Pathfinder 27, 28, 44, 51, 61, 77, 84, 116, 117, 130, 147, 220, 221, 230, 231
Riley Register 6, 7, 117
Riley RM Series 25, 68
Riley Service 126
Riley Two-Point-Six 116, 126, 147
Riley, Percy 117

Riley, Peter 276, 293, 320, 321
Riley, Victor 23, 119
Riley-Healey 48
Riley-Smith, Hamish 7, 182, 183
Rippon Special 42
Rippon, Alan 8, 42, 44
Rivers-Fletcher, Alec & Penny 152
Rix, Johnny 53, 119
RMO 101 272, 273, 274, 312
Road & Track Magazine 58, 80, 81, 88, 125, 135, 137, 169, 193
Roaring Raindrop – see MG EX181
ROB 423 (Austin-Healey 100/4) 77
Robbins, Brian 27
Robertson, Bob 66
Robinson, Phil 7
Robson, Graham 7, 26, 145, 162, 203
Rogoli, Roberto 7
ROH 744 (Austin A90 Westminster) 77
Rolls-Royce cars in general 31, 117, 243, 302, 303, 313, 321
Rootes Group 61, 62, 124, 213, 215, 308, 321
Rosner, Ace 302
Roston, Fred 302
Rounds, Ted 306
Rover 213 62
Rover cars 47, 186
Rover Group 63
Rover M-Series engine 115
Rover T-Series engine 115
Roy Hesketh Six-Hour Race (1959) 194, 195
Royal Aeronautical Society 117
Royal Engineers 223
Royal Navy 30
Royston, Toby 301
Rudd, Ken 253
Ruf, Mandi 270
Rufty, Taz 308
Rush, Harry (Riley) 26, 47
Ryder, Harold (H.A.) 14, 15, 18, 20, 23, 33, 40

S. H. Arnolt – see Arnolt
S. H. Lynch of Dallas, Texas 31
SAAB 93 82
SAAB 96 293, 320
safety belts 165
Safety Fast Magazine – see MGCC 'Safety Fast!'
Safety Fast! – motto/slogan 52, 86, 135, 154, 156, 158, 174, 327
Saidel, Ray 309, 312
Saint-Jean-de-Maurienne 249
Salzburg Rallye Club 7, 269, 270
Salzkammergut Mountains 268
Sam Collier Six-Hour Memorial Race 296
San Gabriel Mountains 80
Sanderson, Ninian 224
Sandle, Derek 236
Saorstát Cup 117
Savage, Jon & Jeremy 7, 234
SBL 707 273, 274
Scaglioni, Franco 35
Scammell factory (Watford) 27
SCCA (Sports Car Club of America) 296, 298, 300, 306, 308, 323, 324
Schipol Airport 198, 199
Schlitz beer 31
Scholes, Paul 7
Schwartz, Hermann 7, 270
Scorror, Doreen Ann 243
Scott Russell, Peter 237, 238, 240
Seager, Stuart 7, 148, 172
Sears ('Gentleman Jack') Jack 152, 249, 250, 324, 325, 326, 327, 328
Seaverns, Bud 322
Seberg jukeboxes 31
Sebring 1956 12-Hours 9, 297, 298, 299, 300, 302, 304, 308
Sebring 1957 12-Hours 300, 304, 305, 306, 307, 308, 309
Sebring 1958 12-Hours 268, 302, 307
Sebring 1959 12-Hours 273, 307, 308, 309, 310, 311, 312 (race table), 313
Sebring 1960 12-Hours 145, 278, 305, 310, 311, 314, 315, 317, 318
Sebring 1961 12-Hours 279, 319, 320, 321, 322, 323, 327
Sebring 1962 12-Hours 323, 324, 325, 326, 327
Sebring Races, Town and Circuit (*see also* by year) 6, 7, 70, 93, 143, 145, 149, 184, 295, 296, 297, 300, 302, 304, 305, 308, 313 (Canadian drivers), 320, 324
Second World War (and aftermath) 11, 13, 14, 17, 178, 20, 21, 25, 26, 27, 28, 32, 47, 59, 73, 75, 90, 99, 115, 117, 124, 127, 182, 185, 200, 215, 222, 223, 300, 304
Seymour, Bob 7, 141, 142, 145, 146, 183
Seymour, Peter 7, 14, 15, 59, 109, 110, 130
Sharp 322
Sharp, John 105, 106, 130, 133
Sharpe, Roger 7
Sheffield 84
Sheffield-Simplex 14
Shelby, Carroll 20
Shell Oil 75, 88
Shepherd, Bill 227, 249, 250, 267, 295
Sherwood, Doreen 222
Ship and Shore of Florida 32, 316, 317, 322, 323
shipping – shortage of space 90
Shipside (business) – see T Shipside Ltd
Shipside (Schipol Airport) 199
Shipside, Bill 36
Siegle-Morris, David 293
Sikorsky profiles 120
Silver City Airways 76, 91, 244, 262, 269
Silverstone Race Circuit 47, 106, 212, 217, 218, 247, 250, 267, 276, 277, 290, 320, 325
Simmons, Steve 7
Simms, Tony 317
Simpson, June 7
Simpson, Peter 246, 247, 252, 253, 255, 256, 258, 259, 261, 264, 266, 267
Sinclair, Mr. 263
Singleton, Bill 158, 172
six-cylinder C-Series – see BMC C-Series Twin Cam
SKD - semi knocked down 179, 181, 186, 198
Sketch & Arrangement Drawing Register 160
Skinner, Roger 7, 275, 277
Škoda Fabia 320
Skomp, Christopher 7
Skomp, Fred & Cindy 7, 173
Skomp, Russell 172, 173
skuk – CKD assembly process 186
Smallbone, S.G.K. 20
Smith, Barry 'Sideways' 235
Smith, Donald 7, 131
Smith, George 46
Smith, John 148
Smith, Larry 7
Smith, S.V. (Sidney Victor) 18, 23, 32, 38, 39, 40, 49, 55, 65, 66, 99, 118, 119, 127, 147
Smiths Industries 139
SMO 907 156
Smyth, Robert 7
Snetterton 213, 241, 267, 278
Society of Motor Manufacturers and Traders (SMMT) 58, 90
soft tools for MGA (*see also* Kirksite) 66, 67, 68
Solex carburettors 231, 233
Solihull 99
Somerville, Bob 7
South African MGA CKD assembly 193–8
Southam, Wilson 235
Spa race circuit (Belgium) 251, 252, 294
Sparrow, Jack 85
Sparrowe, Jeff 259, 261
SpeedPak – see Lockheed SpeedPak
Spiers, Jacques and Annie 259, 261
Spitler, Steve 9, 298, 299, 301, 302, 304, 305, 306, 308
sports car – as defined by Syd Enever 12
Sports Car and Lotus Owner magazine 128
Sports Car Graphic magazine 79, 114, 161, 164
Sports Car Illustrated magazine 134, 299
Sports Car World magazine 192
Sprinzel, John 273, 274
Squire Cars 17
SRU 555 260
SRX 210 6, 270, 279, 281, 284, 285, 286, 287, 288, 289, 290 (table of results)
SS Cars (Jaguar) 115
St George, Andrew 31
St Gothard Tunnel 258, 262
St Lawrence Seaway 181
Standard Motor Company Ltd 21, 48, 55
Standard-Triumph 48, 186, 193, 213, 273, 293, 308
Stapleford Aerodrome 248
Steele, Tommy 178
Steering Wheel Club 212, 240
Stein, Jonathan 7, 137, 169, 320
Stellite-tipped valves 216
Stelvio Pass (Italy) 251
Stephenson, D. N. 149
Stevens, Dick 176
Stevens, Frank 25
Stimpson, Jim 61
Stokes, Donald (later Sir; Lord Stokes of Leyland) 117
Stone, Henry 17, 24, 33, 38, 42, 43, 56, 57, 62, 68, 76, 122, 124, 128, 219, 222, 223, 231, 281, 282, 286, 287
Stoop, Dickie 232
Strauss, George 29
Struijk, Kees 201
Struijk, Koen 7, 201
Stuart, Dr, Duncan 203
Studebaker cars 319
SU carburettors 83, 108, 143, 203, 204, 216, 233, 245, 288, 320
SU fuel pump 284
SU fuel-injection system (concept) 113, 116
Suez crisis 267
Suffield, Lester 311, 313
Sully, John 197
Sumner, Cliff 7, 131
Sunbeam Alpine 38, 321, 326
Sunbeam cars in general 159, 213, 303, 308
Sunbeam Rapier 240, 293
Sunbeam-Talbot 90 drop-head 38
Supermarine Spifire 117
Supershell Petrol 228
Suppi, Alessandro 239, 240
Swedish Grand Prix 265
Swinton, Viscount 59
Swiss Alps 114, 122, 155, 228, 234, 262, 269, 294

T Shipside Ltd (Nuffield Distributor) 36
Tandon Motorcycles 124
Targa Florio race 184
Tatlow, Jack 18, 25, 26, 38, 47, 214
tax-free sales 74
Taylor, Simon 223
TD Midget – see MG TD Midget
Technical Director of Morris Motors 40
Terragnoli, Emo 239, 240
Thames Estuary Auto Club 236
The Ambassador – British Export Magazine 28
The Commercial Motor Magazine 20, 27
The Morris Owner Magazine 14
The Rush of Green (statues) 166
Thomas, Barrie 194
Thomas, Sir Miles 14, 15, 18, 20, 21, 22, 23, 26, 29, 33, 34, 45
Thompson & Taylor Ltd 114
Thompson, James Rochester 114, 116, 119
Thompsons – see John Thompson Motor Pressings
Thornley OBE, John 7, 8, 9, 11, 12, 16, 18, 19, 21, 25, 33, 36, 39, 42, 44, 47, 49, 51, 52, 53, 54, 55, 60, 63, 64, 65, 67, 80, 82, 90, 92, 94, 99, 101, 102, 113, 114, 118, 119, 120, 121, 122, 125, 126, 127, 144, 145, 147, 148, 158, 162, 175, 202, 204, 207, 213, 214, 216, 217, 218, 219, 220, 225, 226, 227, 232, 236, 240, 254, 263, 267, 268, 278, 280, 281, 284, 285, 311
Thornley, Ann 125
Thornley, Joan 125, 126, 220
Thornley, Peter 7, 12, 30, 126, 162, 240
Thoroughbred & Classic Cars magazine 226, 229, 233
Tickford coachwork 104
Tiffanys (jewellers) 125, 126
Titanic 227
Titterington, Desmond 236
Tolley, Grant 298, 301
Tommy The Toreador – film 178
Tooley, Chris 251, 252, 267, 273, 274
Toronto, Canada 82, 180, 299, 304, 306, 308
Tourist Trophy race – see TT
Toyota 194
Trans World Airlines – see TWA
Transfermatic machinery 122
Transol Car Sales (The Hague) 199
Trasler, Richard 7
Tremulis, Alex 7
Tremulis, Steve 7
Triple M – collective term for pre-war MG sports cars (Midget, Magna, Magnette) 19
Triumph Acclaim 61, 62
Triumph cars in general 159, 303
Triumph Herald 121
Triumph TR2 8, 52, 55, 74, 221, 224, 226, 232
Triumph TR3 75, 213, 215, 252
Triumph TR3A 146
Triumph TR4 293, 294
Triumph TRX prototype 23
Trodd, Michael 30, 73
T-Series engine – see Rover T-Series
Tsinghua University (China) 211
TT Race (*see also* Dundrod) 17, 43, 119, 140, 231, 233
Tuck, George 197, 273, 300
Tugwell, Ken 131
Tulip Rally, 1958 200, 268
Tulip Rally, 1959 273, 274
Tulip Rally, 1962 162, 293, 294
Turin Motor Show 1952 35
Turin Motor Show 1958 138
Turner, Margaret 215
Turner, Stuart 7, 215, 223, 273, 274, 291, 293, 308
TWA 7, 9, 72
twin cam engines – *see also* MG MGA Twin Cam engine 28, 50, 51, 101, 113, 115, 117, 119, 214
twin Cam Six-cylinder C-Series – see BMC C-Series Twin Cam
Twite, Michael 155
TWN 900 275, 276

UK Government 159
ULJ 426 102, 104, 107
Ullyett, Kenneth 144, 202
Ulmann, Alec 296
UMG 400 (MG EX 172) 8, 38, 41, 42, 43
UMO 93 314, 315, 316, 317, 318
UMO 94 315, 317
UMO 95 313, 315, 316, 317, 318
UMO 96 7, 315, 317, 318, 319
Universal Laminations 102, 103
University Motors Ltd (London) 70, 71, 107, 126, 129, 131, 133, 161, 166
University of London 18
UPO 929 6, 241, 242, 244, 245, 246, 247, 248, 252, 253, 255, 257, 258, 259, 261, 262, 264, 265, 266, 267, 274
Urian, Don 306
US Dollar revenue earned for Nuffield and later BMC 9, 29, 45, 95, 156, 172, 181
US Dollar–sterling exchange rate 29, 33
US market 21, 23, 29, 33, 49, 50, 52, 54, 56, 58, 60, 63, 74, 90, 95, 97, 112, 122, 125, 156, 159, 172, 181, 208, 213, 297
US recession of 1957–58 93
US recession of 1960 146, 158, 159
US Servicemen based in Europe 74, 117
US trips by Nuffield staff from 1946 onwards 20, 40
USA News (BMC/Hambro publication) 82
USAC (United States Automobile Club) 227
USAF (United States Air Force) 296, 300
Utah Salt Flats (*see also* Bonneville) 58, 120, 121, 140
V4 engine 27, 203
V6 engine 203
Vaca Valley Road Race 131
Vale, Eric 305, 313
Valencia Motor Show, 1959 138
van Damm, Sheila 240
van der Veer, Pim 7, 83, 200
van der Veer, Willem 7
van Driel, John 9, 298, 301, 303, 306
van Kalleveen, Jerry 7
van Zoest, Marc 7, 184, 185
Vanden Plas 9, 102, 103, 104, 250, 259, 271, 314, 317
Vandervell Ltd 114
Vandyk, Edward 7, 160, 161, 197, 279, 280, 320, 327
Vass, Emery 324
Vauxhall 28, 207
Vetter, Han 200
Vicat-Cole, Rex 273
Victoria, H.M. Queen 31
VIN (Vehicle Identification Numbers) 84, 85
Viner, Tom 87
Viscount Swinton 59
Vitrikas, Bob 7, 44
Vivione 251
VJB 112 161, 162
VLP 500 129, 130, 131, 133
Vogue magazine 236
Volkswagen 21, 74, 203
Volkswagen de México SA de CV 185
Volkswagen VR6 engine 203
Volvo cars 193
von Hanstein, Fritz Huschke 306
von Reiswitz, Dieter 264, 265
von Suppé, Franz 128
von Tripps, Wolfgang 269
Vosges Mountains (France) 294
VUF 541 274, 275, 276
VW (Volkswagen) in general 185
VW Beetle 74
VXT 280 7, 290

Waco 32
Wade Engineering 222
Waeffler, Hans 9, 220, 221, 224, 225, 226, 234, 284
Wake, Fred 90, 158
Wales, Basil 7, 116, 118, 120, 121, 122, 145, 233
Wallace, Hal 311
Warner, Graham 213
Watson, Craig 7, 186
Watson, Percy 127
Watson, William 277
Watts, Douglas ('Douggie') 7, 68, 76, 78, 216, 217, 218, 219, 220, 221, 222, 223, 227, 239, 249, 311
Watts, Hilary 7
Watts, Isla 7, 223
Watts, Mike 7
Weber carburettors 144, 231, 284, 288, 290
Weber, Herr 72
Weissenborn, Jim 317
Wellman, Tommy 76, 78, 216, 217, 219, 222, 231, 233
Wentworth-Fitzwilliam – see W-Fitzwilliam
Wentworth-Fitzwilliam family 242, 247, 254
Wentworth-Woodhouse, Rotherham 242
Werner, Dickson 306
Weslake, Harry 53, 115, 118, 216
West, Bob 7, 70, 107, 131, 234, 235, 237, 247, 257, 265, 275
W-Fitzwilliam, Amanda 6, 243
W-Fitzwilliam, Doreen (née Scorror) 241, 243, 246, 253, 255, 258, 259, 262, 263, 265
W-Fitzwilliam, Richard ('Fitz') 6, 138, 234, 240, 241, 242–3, 244, 245, 248, 249, 252, 253, 254, 255, 256, 259, 261, 262, 264, 266, 274, 275, 278
W-Fitzwilliam, Robin 6, 240, 242, 243, 262
W-Fitzwilliam, Sallianne 243
W-Fitzwilliam, Toby 242, 243
W-Fitzwilliam, Tom 243
WGN 734 7, 275, 276, 277
Wharton, Ken 76, 77, 78, 217, 218
White House (Le Mans) – *see* Maison Blanche
White, Harry 61, 62, 124
White, Peter 195
White, Richard 7
Whiteway, Parker 7, 180
Whitmore, Sir John 279, 321, 324, 325, 327
Wiffen, Gerald 220, 222, 223
Wiggan, A.W. 136
Wiggins, Harold 56, 57, 68, 216, 222, 223, 280
Wiggo The Wonder Welder 223
Wilkins, Billy 33
Wilkins, Gordon 114
Willcutts, Bob 7
Williams and Leavens Motors 297
Williams F1 126
Williams, Denis 7, 48, 50, 54, 60, 61, 62, 63, 122, 214, 280, 281
Williams, Kenneth 178
Williams, Maynard Mark 7, 69
Williamson, John 227, 250
Willis, Steve 281, 282
Wilson, Peter 232
Wilson, Tom 7
Wilton-Clarke, Gillian 268
Winterbottom, Eric 36, 42, 43
Wirdnam, Bert 90, 159, 222
Wisdom, Ann 215, 236, 268, 272, 293
WJB 405 162
Wolseley 15/50 53
Wolseley 15/60 53, 167
Wolseley 1500 53
Wolseley 16/60 167
Wolseley 4/44 27, 36, 49, 52, 62, 75
Wolseley 6/80 26
Wolseley 6/90 27, 28, 51, 116, 147
Wolseley 6/99 (ADO 10) 147
Wolseley apprenticeship 99, 127
Wolseley cars in general 15, 21, 22, 23, 26, 27, 30, 32, 55, 59, 83, 95, 127, 181, 182, 186, 215
Wolseley engines 147
Wolseley Ten (10) concept , 7736
Wolseley Wasp concept 23
Wood, Jonathan 226, 285, 290
Wood, Peter 136, 277
Woodcock, James R. 9, 99, 127
Woodcote (corner at Goodwood) 235
Woodfield, A. (Vice President of Hambro Auto. Corp.) 92
Woodhouse, J. A. (Jack) 72, 73, 140, 244
Woodland Green (paint colour) 10, 146, 148
Woodson, Bruce 324
Woodward, Steven 7, 317
World War I – see First World War
World War II – see Second World War
Wright, Dickie 7, 124, 280, 281
Wright, John 7, 317, 324, 328
Wright, Mrs Susan 7
Wright, Tim 7

XFC 213 (Wolseley 6/90) 77
XPAG engine (MG TD type) 36, 42, 44, 47, 49, 53, 55, 58, 67, 100, 114, 115, 216
XPAW engine (Wolseley) 55
XPEG 1.5-litre engine 8, 52, 53, 58, 68, 100, 114, 122, 216
XWU 825 273

Y Type – see MG Y Type
YA – see MG Y Type
YD1-2611 (last MGA Twin Cam) 10
YD1-501 (first production MGA Twin Cam) 9
YD1-501 to YD3-505 131, 132
YM1-551, YM1-552, YM1-553, YM2-554 131
York, Lyle 316, 317
YRX 310 279, 280
YRX 986 162, 292
YWL 15 101

Z Magnette – see MG Z Magnette
Zagato 240
ZC11G possible new MG engine ca 1946 23
Zeltweg Airfield 268, 269, 270
ZF limited slip differential 319
Zimmerman, K.H. 265
Zwart, Jacques 273
Zweifel, Hans (Harry) 227, 268, 269
Zych, David 306